A Publication of The National Underwriter Company

Field Guide to
FINANCIAL PLANNING

Donald F. Cady,
J.D., LL.M.

The
NATIONAL
UNDERWRITER
Company
PROFESSIONAL PUBLISHING GROUP

P.O. Box 14367 • Cincinnati, Ohio 45250-0367
1-800-543-0874 • www.nationalunderwriter.com

Page Layout Design: Donald R. Heyl

This publication is designed to provide accurate and authoritative information in regard to the subject matter covered. It is sold with the understanding that the publisher is not engaged in rendering legal, accounting or other professional service. If legal advice or other expert assistance is required, the services of a competent professional should be sought. **– From a Declaration of Principles jointly adopted by a Committee of the American Bar Association and a Committee of Publishers and Associations.**

ISBN: 0-87218-617-2

Library of Congress Control Number: 2003107219

Printed in U. S. A.

ACKNOWLEDGMENTS

I am most grateful to the many individuals – financial services professionals, clients, students, and allied professionals – who over the years have both knowingly and unknowingly contributed to this book. It is the product of their many insights, tough questions, and planning ideas.

I also wish to express my sincere appreciation to the staff of The National Underwriter Company, particularly April K. Caudill, J.D., CLU, ChFC, John H. Fenton, J.D., M.S.B.A., Sonya E. King, J.D., LL.M., Deborah A. Miner, J.D., CLU, ChFC, Joseph F. Stenken, J.D., CLU, ChFC, and William J. Wagner, J.D., LL.M., CLU, for their shared tax expertise, to Connie L. Jump and Mary P. O'Leary for their able and cheerful assistance in preparing and proofing the manuscript.

And finally, a special word of thanks to my wife, Joan, for her love and understanding in providing me the time and environment for writing.

D.F.C. 2003
Fort Myers Beach, Florida

ABOUT THE AUTHOR

Donald F. Cady is a graduate of St. Lawrence University with a B.A. in Economics. He holds a J.D. degree from Columbia University School of Law, an LL.M. in Taxation from Emory University School of Law, and is a member of the New York Bar. He also holds the Chartered Life Underwriter designation from The American College.

Don is an independent consultant providing support materials and services to the financial planning industry. In addition to *Field Guide To Financial Planning*, he is the author of *Field Guide To Estate Planning, Business Planning, & Employee Benefits*, published annually since 1989 by The National Underwriter Company. He is the author of *Field Guide Online[1]*, the web version of this book updated monthly throughout the year.

For twenty years Don was with the Aetna Life Insurance & Annuity Company in various advanced planning positions. Prior to this, Don was a member of the U.S. Army Judge Advocate Generals Corps, with tours of duty in both Vietnam and Europe. He and his wife live in Fort Myers Beach, Florida.

Don is a frequent speaker on the subjects of financial planning, estate and business planning before business and professional organizations, financial planning associations, life underwriter's meetings and various civic groups. Through these appearances, together with his work with planners, their clients and advisers, Don has shared the frustrations of trying to effectively explain and communicate planning concepts and techniques to both student and laymen. Both of his books represent his response to that challenge. Don can be reached by e-mail at DonCady@efieldguide.com.

---

[1] *Field Guide Online* is a trademark of The National Underwriter Company.

TABLE OF CONTENTS

Page

Chapter 9: Mutual Funds

Chapter 10: Tangible Assets

Chapter 11: Property & Liability Insurance

Page

Page

Chapter 16: Planning For Death

Page

Tables

Index

INTRODUCTION

The concept of financial planning cuts a wide swath across what has been traditionally viewed as investment planning, retirement planning, tax planning, estate planning, business planning, and risk management. While it might generally be agreed that financial planning is about money and financial security, there is no universally recognized definition of financial planning. Despite this, there is no lack of books available on the subject. (Go to amazon.com, search for books on "financial planning," and you will get in excess of 1,500 hits.) The vast majority of these books are self-help books intended for the consumer. Surprisingly, there are a limited number of books that attempt to comprehensively cover the subject of financial planning.

This book is intended to provide you with a unique and comprehensive resource that will allow you to readily identify and understand the basic concepts and techniques associated with financial planning. While comprehensive in scope, by definition a "field guide" is limited as to the depth of treatment that can be given to any one subject. The author has found this to be painfully true with a subject so vast in scope as "financial planning."

Every attempt has been made to provide you with concise and readable descriptions of the tools and techniques used in financial planning. As with The National Underwriter Company's companion book, *Field Guide To Estate Planning, Business Planning, & Employee Benefits*, the format of this book recognizes that we live in a world of visual communication. Thus, a large number of relevant tables, charts, and graphs have been included in order to aid your understanding of the materials covered. To assist you in delving deeper into the subjects covered, numerous references are provided to other books and online resources.

Jobs and Growth Tax Relief Act of 2003

The Jobs and Growth Tax Relief Act of 2003 (JGTRRA 2003) was signed into law on May 28, 2003. The fortuitous timing of this act has made it possible for this book to reflect the changes made by that legislation (e.g., the income tax tables on page 451 incorporate the new and lower tax rates).

Cross References To Tax Facts

No attempt is made to provide either an exhaustive technical analysis or extensive citations to legal authority. For these purposes, you are encouraged to refer to the appropriate questions in the 2003 editions of *Tax Facts 1* (covering life & health insurance, annuities, employee plans, estates & trusts, and business continuation) and *Tax Facts 2* (covering stocks, bonds, mutual funds, real estate, oil & gas, puts, calls, futures, gold, and savings deposits). Footnotes may direct you to key questions in these publications by The National Underwriter Company.

Callouts & Links

The keeping current callout provides you with references to the print edition of *The Wall Street Journal* and to other relevant print and online resources. For example, this callout from page 51 tells you where the latest federal funds rates can be found.

> **Keeping Current**
>
> The federal funds rate is given daily under the **Money Rates** table of *The Wall Street Journal.*

The Internet has become a rich resource of information on financial planning. The digging deeper callout provides references and links to materials that will assist you in better understanding the subject. This callout, from page 171, takes you to the website of the Investment Company Institute where you will find a substantial amount of information on mutual funds. Although all Internet links (URLs) in this book were current as of June 2003, the fact remains that these links are constantly changing and you may find some that are no longer current or available.

> **Digging Deeper**
>
> The federal funds rate is given daily under the **Money Rates** table of *The Wall Street Journal.*

The Internet links provide you with the web address of the organization or subject being discussed. This callout, from page 63, takes you to Standard & Poor's main web page, where you will find a wealth of information about their indexes and the equity markets.

www.spglobal.com

Your Feedback

The first edition of this book has proven to be an ambitious undertaking. Future additions will undoubtedly include new and expanded materials. As you use this book, sooner or later you will likely discover subjects that you feel should be added, covered in more depth, or treated differently. Please share your suggestions with the author at *DonCady@efieldguide.com.* Your thoughts and suggestions will be much appreciated by the author and will enhance the value of future editions.

THE SCOPE OF FINANCIAL PLANNING

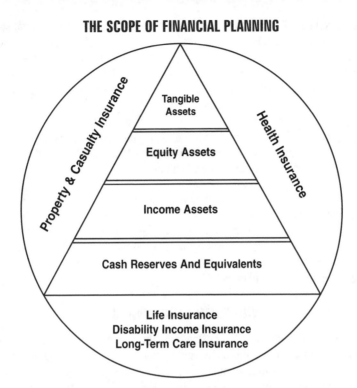

There is no universally recognized definition of financial planning. However, before discussing the financial planning process it may be helpful to identify some of the activities and individuals that are commonly understood to be a part of the process. For instance, each of the following might reasonably stake claim to falling within the realm of "financial planning."

Single Transaction. From the perspective of the individual client, financial planning could mean nothing more than locating the least expensive credit card, or finding the best way to save for a child's college education. From the perspective of the "financial planner," it could be the advice given by an investment adviser or stockbroker on what stocks the client should purchase, or the ledgers provided by a life insurance agent comparing the relative advantages and disadvantages of purchasing term or permanent life insurance. The difficulty here is that the process tends to be focused on doing, but short on planning.

Source And Depth Of Advice. It could also be argued that financial planning does not begin until the individual client consults with his investment adviser, insurance agent, tax attorney, CPA, or other such advisor, on *more in-depth* matters relating to either investment, insurance, or tax planning. Again, the difficulty here is that the process may be appropriately in-depth, but is narrow in scope and fails to consider all aspects of the client's financial situation.

Comprehensive Planning. And finally, there is the comprehensive must-do-it-all approach to financial planning. Clearly, this approach takes the high ground in maintaining that true financial planning involves a coordinated process of gathering facts relating to all areas of the client's financial affairs, determining the client's overall financial goals and objectives, and designing and implementing plans and strategies for attaining these goals. Although individuals involved in the financial planning process come from diverse backgrounds, the focus should not be so much on who is working with the client, but rather on assuring that the client receives comprehensive and in-depth advice that is implemented in coordination with the client's overall financial situation.

Another approach to defining "financial planning" might be to ask what the client should reasonably expect of persons holding themselves out as financial planners. If the process involves a fee for services, then clearly "comprehensive" financial planning is indicated. But for many persons, the need for sound advice regarding specific investment, insurance, or tax planning issues clearly falls within the scope of financial planning.

WHY FINANCIAL PLANNING?

During our lifetime we are constantly in the process of making, managing, banking, investing, protecting, and spending money. More often than not, we carry on intuitively from day to day, without taking the time to either plan or coordinate our financial affairs. Financial issues, problems, and decisions are compartmentalized. Many people, who would not dream of beginning a cross country road trip without a good road atlas, never even consider the importance of having a "financial road map" during the many years they will engage in earning and spending money. Without an adequate map, they are unlikely to reach a destination of financial security. The financial planning process should produce just such a financial road map.

Today's decision to spend an extra $500 to upgrade to the promenade deck on a Caribbean cruise, or to spend an extra $6.95 per month for cable TV's super upgrade package, are typically made with little regard for the long-term impact on our financial future. In fact, each and every one of our day-to-day "spend or save" decisions will have a direct and calculable impact upon our financial well being in the years to come. Over a lifetime of making and spending money, the cumulative effect of these seemingly small decisions can be enormous. However, the degree of impact depends upon our individual time horizon, as demonstrated in the following table.

Small Decisions – Big Consequences				
	If Invested – Value Of Funds			
	10 years	20 years	30 years	40 years
$500 cruise upgrade	$1,041	$3,456	$8,670	$19,927
$6.95/month super TV package	$1,208	$3,816	$9,447	$21,605
Assumptions: Funds are invested at 8% net after taxes, compounded annually.				

Of course, this is a very simplified example, but it makes the point. The financial planning process is important, not only in creating a "financial road map," but also in creating a better awareness of the short and long-term consequences of every-day financial and consumption decisions. Once armed with this knowledge, financial planning will become a day-to-day exercise, not just a once every few years or a once in a lifetime event.

THE FINANCIAL PLANNING PROCESS

The process of comprehensive financial planning is generally recognized to include the following seven steps:

Preliminary Meeting & Evaluation. During the initial interview, the financial planner and the prospective client get to know one another. This generally involves a first meeting during which the planner explains the nature of services to be provided and the way in which he or she is paid for these services. In turn, the prospective client has an opportunity to determine whether the planner has the ability to offer the types of services that are needed. The planner should take this opportunity to get some general idea of the prospective client's current financial position and long-term goals. It is important for both parties that the relationship begins on a basis of mutual trust and confidence. If it is deter-

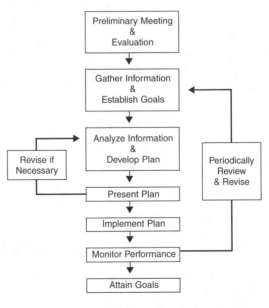

mined to proceed, then the planner should provide the prospective client with an *engagement letter* that serves as a contract setting forth the services to be provided, the charges for these services, and the client's responsibilities during the financial planning process. If the planner is a registered investment advisor with the Securities and Exchange Commission, the planner will provide the prospective client with a "disclosure brochure" describing the services offered and the method by which the financial planner is compensated. SEC Rule 204-3 requires this disclosure.

Gather Information & Establish Goals. Effective planning cannot be done without gathering a substantial amount of information about the client. The information gathered can be either *quantitative* (e.g., financial information about the client's income, expenditures, and assets) or *qualitative* (e.g., non-financial information about the client's risk tolerance, expectations as to future standards of living, and health of the client and family members). Both the short-term and long-term *goals* of the client must be identified. Such a goal might be to have "adequate income in retirement," or to "provide for a child's education." In contrast to goals, at least one commentator uses the term *objectives* to indicate the shorter intermediate steps that must be accomplished in order to meet a goal.[1] For example, in order to meet the goal of having adequate income in retirement an individual might establish the objective of setting aside 5% of net income in a retirement plan. Goals must be both *realistic* and *well defined*. While "information gathering" and "goal setting" could be viewed as separate and distinct steps within the financial planning process, in truth they are probably more effectively accomplished during the give and take of an interactive discussion between financial planner and client. Once goals have been determined, it is essential to *prioritize* or rank them in order of importance. Some of the key financial and legal documents that must be secured during the data-gathering phase include:

(1) Wills, trusts, and powers of attorney.

(2) Personal financial statements.

(3) Budgets.

(4) Retirement plan statements, brokerage account statements, and mutual fund statements.

(5) Insurance policies (life, disability, health, and property and casualty).

(6) Divorce settlements.

(7) Federal and state income tax returns.

(8) Buy-sell agreements.

Analyze Information & Develop Plan. It is here that the planner takes the information obtained and agreed-upon client goals and translates them into a specific financial plan intended to achieve these goals using selected financial strategies and instruments. In effect, the plan translates client goals into specific action steps. To assist in the process, the planner will often use computer programs to supplement a written analysis and recommendations. At a minimum, a comprehensive analysis generally includes a review of assets, liabilities, current and projected income, and insurance coverages, and investments. Legal documents will also be examined and, if authorized by the client, the planner may seek the assistance of other professionals.

Present Plan. In presenting the plan, the financial planner meets with the client, explains the recommendations and provides the client with a copy of the written plan. However, before the formal plan presentation, the financial planner is well advised to informally discuss *tentative* observations and *preliminary* recommendations. Such a discussion gives the planner an opportunity to address additional questions and items that arose during the design process, such as unrealistic client expectations and incomplete data. It is also an excellent means of allowing the client to participate in the design process and get client acceptance of key recommendations. Without such client "buy-in," it is unlikely that the final plan will be implemented. If necessary, the plan can then be revised prior to final presentation. The key elements of a written financial plan are likely to include the following:

(1) Review of the client's stated goals.

(2) Analysis of the client's current situation, including both quantitative and qualitative data.

(3) Specific recommendations to include actions, strategies and recommended financial products.

(4) Action plan designed to implement the financial plan, to include time frames and assignment of responsibilities to named individuals.

Implement Plan. This stage is probably the most important of all. Plan implementation involves motivating the client to take those steps as set forth in the *action plan* in paragraph (4) above. Typically, this may involve a variety of tasks, including the purchase and sale of investments, modification of insurance coverages, adoption of legal instruments, and changes in spending and savings habits. It may also include working with other professionals (e.g., check with the attorney that the new will and trust have not only been drafted and presented to the client, but that the client has actually signed them). Without implementation, the best of recommendations will fail and the client's objectives will not be reached.

Monitor Performance. Few, if any, financial plans are perfect and all clients are subject to changing circumstances. This stage involves evaluating the effectiveness of the plan in achieving the client's objectives. Unsatisfactory progress or performance requires that corrective action be taken (e.g., the market is down, the client becomes less risk tolerant, and the client is willing to accept lower returns and a reduced retirement lifestyle).

Periodically Review & Revise Plan. Financial planning is not a goal, but rather an ongoing process. The client's personal circumstances will change and the financial plan must be adjusted accordingly. The client may have gotten married, gotten divorced, had a new child, experienced a change in health, changed jobs, suffered a financial setback, or experienced a financial windfall. Outside factors, such as changes in the tax laws or investment climate, must also be considered. Assumptions underlying the original plan are evaluated. An annual periodic review will identify these changes by gathering and updating client information and determining new or revised client goals. From here, the process and steps repeat themselves.

Attain Goals. This is the "come and get it day." The client has sufficient funds to send his child to college, to buy that second home, or to retire in the desired lifestyle at the intended time. Financial planning has played a very important part in achieving each of these goals.

TYPICAL GOALS OF FINANCIAL PLANNING

It has been said that financial planning involves risk management; the risks of dying too soon, becoming disabled, and living too long. While this is certainly true, some of the following goals clearly fall outside of the concept of risk management, yet are important elements in many financial plans.

(1) Improve current standard of living.

(2) Protect property from loss and damage.

(3) Protect family from large medical expenses.

(4) Reduce or eliminate debt, particularly high-interest credit card debt.

(5) Provide for ongoing income in case of disability.

(6) Create an emergency fund.

(7) Increase net worth through savings and investments.

(8) Minimize income taxes.

(9) Accumulate funds for specific large investments, such as weddings, vacation homes, and extensive travels.

(10) Provide funds for child's education.

(11) Provide for a comfortable retirement.

(12) Protect family in case of premature death.

(13) Create an estate plan for disposition of assets at death.

(14) Pass business interest to surviving family members.

THE FINANCIAL PLANNING DATA SHEET

A variety of forms are available to the financial planner, from the 10-minute drill to the 100-page compendium. Although it is generally agreed that it is better to have more rather than less information, the planner must be careful not to intimidate his client, particularly in the early stages of the financial planning process. On the other hand, an abbreviated form will likely yield insufficient information to develop a relevant and effective financial plan.

The following sample data sheet contains the very minimum of required information broken down into: (1) personal data; (2) assets and liabilities; (3) income and expenses; (4) property and casualty; (5) legal documents; (6) advisors; and (7) planning considerations. Note that these categories are the same as the classification of assets set forth in the chart on page 14.

---

[1] Jeffrey H. Rattiner, *Getting Started As A Financial Planner* (Princeton: Bloomberg Press, 2000), p. 63.

FINANCIAL PLANNING DATA SHEET

Date:

Client's Name:		Spouse's Name:	
Date Of Birth:	Age:	Date Of Birth:	Age:
Employer:		Employer:	
Occupation:		Occupation:	
Business Phone:		Business Phone:	
Address:			
		Zip:	
Home Phone:			

RESOURCES & ASSETS

CASH RESERVES

Checking Accounts	Name of Institution	Rate	Current Value	Owner
Savings Accounts				
Money Market Accounts				
Certificates Of Deposit				
Other				

Life Insurance	Type	Insured	Premium	Death Benefit	Cash Values
(Company)					

Ownership of policies if other than insured:

Notes:

RESOURCES & ASSETS (cont'd)

INCOME ASSETS

Income Funds	Name of Institution	Rate	Amount	Owner
Name				

Corporate Bonds	Cost	Maturity Date	Coupon Rate	Current Value	Owner
Name					
Federal Bonds					
Name					
State & Municipal Bonds					
Name					

Fixed Dollar Annuities	Type	Income Received	or	Cash Value	Owner
Company					

Mortgages Held	Income Received	Maturity Date	Type	Current Value	Owner
Debtor					
Loans Receivable					
Debtor					

EQUITY ASSETS

Stocks	Number Shares	Date Of Purchase	Cost	Market Value
Company				

RESOURCES & ASSETS (cont'd)

EQUITY ASSETS (cont'd)

Mutual Funds	Number Shares	Date Of Purchase	Cost	Market Value
Company				

Variable Annuities	Type	Income Received	or	Cash Value	Owner
Company					

TANGIBLE ASSETS

Personal Property	Value

Real Estate	Market Value -	Mortgage =	Equity Value
Description			

Other Tax Shelters	Tax Advantages	Cost	Market Value
Description			

Notes:

CASH EXPENDITURES

INCOME			EXPENSES	
Client	Salary		Mortgage, Rent	
	Bonuses		Household Expenses	
	Commissions		Food	
			Utilities	
Spouse	Salary		Clothing	
	Bonuses		Medical	
	Commissions		Car - payment	
			- operating	
Dividends			Insurance	
Interest				
Real Estate Income			Loan Payments	
Other			Education	
			Charitable	
			Taxes	
			Miscellaneous	
	Total Income		Total Expenses	
	Less Total Expenses			
	Available For Investment			
Tax Bracket (state & federal)	%			
	Annual Income Increase	%		

PLANNING CONSIDERATIONS

Is there a current will?

Is the client covered by a pension plan?

Number of years before retirement?

Desired monthly income at retirement? $

Years payable on home mortgage?

Disability income: Monthly income required $

Salary continuation $ Length of time?

Present coverage $ Days wait   To age

Educational costs for children

Name of Child	Age	Years Before College	Estimated Yearly Cost	Estimated Total Cost

Notes:

BALANCED FINANCIAL GROWTH

A sound plan for achieving financial security requires balanced financial growth. In seeking balanced financial growth, the investor must continually evaluate risk and return. It is said that risk and reward go hand in hand. An investment providing the opportunity for higher returns will generally involve higher risk. Conversely, an investment offering lower returns will generally involve lower risk. In seeking higher returns, only the individual investor can determine exactly how much risk to take. The higher on the investment pyramid, the greater the risk . . . the lower on the investment pyramid, the lower the risk.

Cash reserves and equivalents provide a financial cushion for emergencies, repairs, and other unexpected cash needs. Typically, this base will include money market accounts, life insurance cash values, regular savings, and certificates of deposit. Adequate health, property and casualty insurance is also essential to provide protection from financial disaster.

Equity assets can be purchased if the investor's primary objective is to achieve capital appreciation. However, it is important to understand that the market value of these investments can go *down* as well as *up*, and rates of return can vary, even after they are purchased. Stocks, mutual funds, and variable annuities are all examples of equity assets found in many investment portfolios. Some equity assets may provide current income, while others will accrue income or reinvest earnings with the expectation of realizing greater appreciation.

Income assets should be considered if the investor's objective is to obtain income as opposed to growth. Some investments will provide immediate dividends or interest income; others will accrue earnings until maturity. A variety of debt assets are available with many different characteristics.

Income funds offer investment management with the objective of providing maximum income consistent with security of principal. Fixed dollar annuities pay a guaranteed and stable income no matter how long a person lives. Corporate, municipal, state and federal bonds are issued in a variety of forms and maturity dates.

Tangible assets are tax-advantaged investments that involve the greatest risk. Because of this, they are for the sophisticated investor who has already established a firm financial foundation and is interested in tax deductions providing the opportunity for speculative profit. They include real estate ventures, research and development partnerships, oil and gas partnerships, farming, cattle and coal operations, and leasing arrangements.

Risk and Return By Asset Class

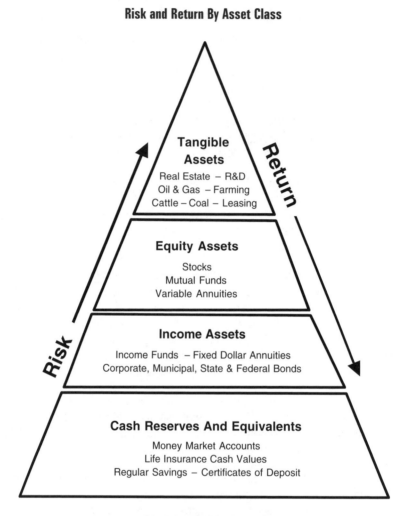

Tangible Assets
Real Estate – R&D
Oil & Gas – Farming
Cattle – Coal – Leasing

Equity Assets
Stocks
Mutual Funds
Variable Annuities

Income Assets
Income Funds – Fixed Dollar Annuities
Corporate, Municipal, State & Federal Bonds

Cash Reserves And Equivalents
Money Market Accounts
Life Insurance Cash Values
Regular Savings – Certificates of Deposit

ASSET CLASSIFICATIONS

An asset class can be defined as a grouping of investments with similar risk and return characteristics or profiles. The value of assets within the same class will tend to move in tandem as their markets rise and fall. The grouping of assets into classes is extremely important when discussing modern portfolio theory, diversification, reallocation, and other such concepts. The context within which the term "asset class" is used will influence how assets are classified. For example, the major mutual fund asset classes are either debt instruments or equity instruments, or some combination of both debt and equity instruments. In contrast, in assembling a diversified portfolio, asset classes might be broken down into U.S. Treasury bills, long-term corporate bonds, international bonds, large company stocks, small company stocks, international stocks, and equity REITS (see Cross-Correlation Matrix, page 25).

But there appears to be no general consensus regarding asset classes and their appropriate rankings. Some commentators believe that "natural resources" are deserving of a class onto themselves.[1] Other commentators break down assets into the two major classes of debt and equity.[2] Finally, others just list them, with no attempt at sorting them out according to relative risks.[3] When grouping assets by class, it may be difficult to accurately determine their risk correlations (see page 24). For example, bonds come in many shades of risk; from government bonds with no risk of default, to utility and corporate bonds that may well have a substantial degree of risk.

The Risk and Return By Asset Class chart (page 14) refers to assets in the following four major classes: (1) *cash equivalents* such as money market accounts, life insurance cash values, savings accounts, certificates of deposit, Treasury bills, and Series EE and HH bonds; (2) *income (debt) assets* such as income funds, fixed-dollar annuities, corporate bonds, munic-

By Class Of Investment

ipal bonds and treasury notes; (3) *equity assets* such as stocks (in turn broken down into large cap stocks, medium cap stocks, small cap stocks, and international stocks), mutual funds, and variable annuities; and (4) *tangible assets* such as real estate, raw land, farming, cattle, lumber, coal, oil and gas, leasing, research and development, art, metals, coins, collectibles, and commodities. Other classifications might justifiably consider domestic common stocks a separate class from foreign common stocks, domestic bonds a separate class from foreign bonds, and high-yield (junk) bonds a separate class from domestic bonds. As can be seen from this chart, the higher the risk the higher the return, and the lower the risk the lower the return.

GENERAL CONCEPTS OF RISK

Although there are many definitions of risk, the single common denominator is the uncertainty of loss. Risk can be minimized, but it cannot be eliminated. Sometimes it can be *reduced* through proper planning techniques and strategies, other times it can be *insured* against. There are many categories and types of risks, from physical risks to social risks, and ethical risks to monetary risks. The following risks are those most often associated with risk management in financial planning.

Active Risk vs. Passive Risk. Some risks are considered active risks, whereas other risks are considered passive risks. An active risk is investing in the stock market, where the investment will be subject to a market risk. A passive risk is putting your money under your bed, where it will be subject to an inflation risk.

Liability Risk. This is a pure risk involving only the possibility of loss. When a person injures someone else or his or her property, the person is subject to a liability risk. Automobile accidents, dog bites, and household accidents are all examples of situations involving liability risk. It is considered a major risk since our legal system rarely, if ever, places limits on the amount of damages that an individual may be sued for when another person is injured through negligence or tort. Financial planning must anticipate and plan for liability risks.

Personal Risk. Premature death, disability, unemployment, poor health, and insufficient retirement income are all examples of *personal* risks. Financial planning must anticipate and plan for personal risks.

Property Risk. Homes, cars, business, and personal property are all subject to property risk from theft, fire, accident and natural causes. The losses can be both direct and indirect. A *direct* loss is the damage to a house when it burns down, whereas an *indirect* loss would be the cost of renting an apartment while the house is being rebuilt. Financial planning must anticipate and plan for property risks.

Pure Risk vs. Speculative Risk. Pure risk involves only the possibility of either *loss* or *no loss*, whereas speculative risk involves the possibility of either *loss* or *gain*. The risk of a house burning down is a pure risk that is insurable, but investing in the commodities market, or betting on a horse race, is a speculative risk that is generally not insurable.

RISKS ASSOCIATED WITH INVESTING

The following risks have an unequal impact on specific investments, both as to severity and frequency. Some will more specifically impact fixed-income securities, whereas others will have a greater impact upon equity (stock) investments. Although they are listed alphabetically, the risks most affecting investors are inflation risk, interest rate risk, investment risk, and market risk.

Additional Commitment Risk. The risk that an investor will be forced to commit additional funds to an investment, should certain conditions occur that are beyond the investor's control. If the additional investment is not made, the investment may be subject to losses. For example, some limited partnerships may require additional contributions, and real estate, in general, often requires substantial outlays to both repair and improve properties. Additional commitment risk is also faced by the investor who gets a margin call (page 148). In order to restore the account to its original margin requirements, the investor is required to deposit additional funds in his account.

Call Risk. The risk that the issuers of callable bonds and preferred stock will redeem them when comparable market rates fall significantly below the rates paid by the securities. Whereas the interest rate risk can actually result in a *loss* of value, the call risk results in *lower* returns when funds are subsequently reinvested. This risk is also referred to as "redemption risk."

Concentration Risk. The risk that concentration of investments in a particular stock, bond, or market segment could result in a large loss of portfolio value (e.g., investing 75% of a portfolio in a particular stock). Acquiring a combination of fixed and equity investments, including mutual funds, can reduce this risk.

Currency Risk. The risk that a decrease in the underlying value of a nation's currency will reduce the purchasing power of income or investments paid in that currency.

Default Risk. The risk that a business enterprise will fail from a variety of causes, including deteriorating market position and poor management. Most often applied to investments in bonds that fail to pay interest as scheduled, or default in the repayment of principal. This risk is also variously referred to as "business risk," "credit risk," "financial risk," or "fundamental risk."

Economic Risk. The risk that the economic environment will decrease the value of an investment or other source of income. For example, the increasing costs of the Social Security system might require a change in the amount or timing of benefits.

Event Risk. The risk that an individual event, more limited in scope than a market risk, will affect the risk of a particular investment. For example, takeover moves involving leveraged buyouts can increase the debt to equity ratio of the target company, thereby causing a fall in the price of previously issued bonds.

Inflation Risk. The risk that goods and services will cost more in future years and that inflation will erode the purchasing power of fixed income or investments. Inflation risk is also referred to as "purchasing-power risk."

Interest Rate Risk. The risk that interest rates will rise, decreasing the value of bonds or other fixed interest rate investments.

Investment Risk. Investment risk refers to the *uncertainty of an investment outcome*. It can be distinguished from many other risks, in that it involves the potential for *gain* as well as loss.

Liquidity Risk. The risk that there may be a loss of value if an asset must be converted into cash within a very short period of time (e.g., the loss of interest if a certificate of deposit is redeemed prior to its redemption date). Some commentators maintain that this is not really a risk, but rather a condition inherent in the underlying investment.

Longevity Risk. The risk that a person's longevity will result in outliving his income or suffering a loss of purchasing power. This risk can be reduced through the purchase of life annuities and equity investments.

Market Risk. The risk that unrelated external factors will decrease the value of an investment (i.e., budget deficit, unemployment, world events, or legislation). Market risk can be lessened by diversification of investments and dollar cost averaging (see pages 23 and 28). This risk is also referred to as "technical risk."

Marketability Risk. The risk that an asset cannot be sold quickly at current market prices without depressing the market and accepting a lesser price (e.g., the distressed sale of real estate in order to generate funds for emergency purposes).

Political Risk. The risk that the political climate will result in changes in regulations and laws that impact the economy, tax laws, and Social Security benefits.

Security Risk. The risk that there could be a failure of a financial institution (e.g., bank or insurance company).

Short-Maturity Risk. The risk that an investment will mature at a time of lower interest rates and that the funds must be reinvested at lower yields. This is similar to the call risk.

Systematic Risk. The inherent risk of being invested in the securities market. As such, it is said to be a *nondiversifiable* risk.

Tax Risk. The risk that changes in the tax laws will result in greater taxes. For example, prior to 1984, Social Security benefits were free of income taxes, but under present law up to 85% of Social Security benefits could be subject to income taxes.

Unsystematic Risk. The risk associated with a particular economic sector, industry, company, or an individual security. It is considered a *diversifiable* risk.

Time And Risk. The element of time is an essential consideration in investment planning, and can have a direct impact upon the risks assumed with individual investments. For example, a short time frame may cause the "late start" investor to accept greater degrees of risk in attempting to meet desired retirement goals (see page 41). In contrast, the disciplined "early start" investor will typically assume far less risk in reaching the same retirement goals. See also the Early Saver vs. Late Saver table (page 398).

INVESTMENT STRATEGIES

The following investment strategies, or styles, are not mutually exclusive. More often than not, the individual investor, or mutual fund manager, will employ one or more strategies, depending upon the investment objectives.

Market Timing. The strategy of market timing focuses on market trends in an attempt to generate quick profits from short-term changes in security prices. With the objective of buying low and selling high, individuals who employ market timing use a variety of indicators and models that they believe will signal a time to either buy or sell. Although widely practiced by professionals and day traders, there appears to be no long-term track record documenting the validity of any particular system.

In contrast to a buy-and-hold strategy, the *disadvantages* of market timing include: (1) transaction costs are high; (2) much time must be devoted to trading and portfolio maintenance; and (3) taxation is potentially triggered each time a security is sold. Because the largest market gains tend to be concentrated in short time periods, the biggest disadvantage of market timing is that the investor may be out of the market when stocks experience their largest gains.

Annual Rate Of Return
S&P 500 - 1983 to 2002

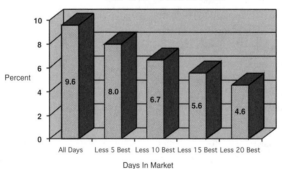

The above chart shows the penalty for missing out on the best days of the S&P 500 Index during the period 1983-2002 (5,049 total trading days).[4]

Buy-And-Hold. Buy-and-hold is a fairly passive investment strategy under which the investor takes a long-term view of the market. The investor who employs a buy-and-hold strategy uses fundamental analysis to select strong stocks that offer good value (see page 29). Little attention is paid to the market or economic trends. Once purchased, bonds are typically held to their maturity date, and stocks are held through both bull and bear markets. Given time, the strategy can be very effective, provided the investor is successful in initially selecting fundamentally strong stocks. The advantages of a buy-and-hold strategy include: (1) transaction costs are kept to a minimum; (2) time devoted to portfolio maintenance is comparatively low; and (3) taxation is delayed until the investment is sold. The buy-and-hold strategy is the opposite of market timing.

Contrarian Investing. As the term indicates, the contrarian investor sells when others are buying, and buys when others are selling. By going against the crowd, the contrarian buys low and hopes to sell high. Contrarians recognize that stock prices are driven up when the demand for stocks is greater than supply (i.e., there are more buyers than sellers). Once prices increase, most investors who intended to purchase have already done so and there is no one left to buy (i.e., the demand for stock evaporates). Without buyers, stocks lose momentum, and this causes a chain reaction of more selling and less buying. The market then peaks and a decline follows. The same phenomenon occurs when the market bottoms, only in reverse. Once a contrarian investor has purchased a stock, he is most likely to patiently follow a buy-and-hold strategy, waiting for the market to reverse itself in order to sell for long-term capital gain.

Value Investing. The best indicator of a stock's value is not necessarily the price in the market on any particular day. Stocks fall in and out of favor with investors and, over the short term, the market frequently overreacts to bad news, thus depressing

> As a falling tide lowers all boats, so does a falling market depress both bad and good stocks.

the prices of both good stocks and bad stocks. Likewise, whole industries fall out of favor with investors, often without regard to their future earnings potential. Value investors look for both stocks and industries that are out of favor in the market, yet represent good growth potential. The value investor looks at factors such as sales, earnings history and outlook, assets, and stockholder equity, and compares them to the stock's current market price. If the stock is judged to be undervalued, it is purchased. Value can flow from low price-earnings ratios, low price-to-book ratios, and high dividend yields. Value investors look for companies where book value may exceed market value, new companies not yet "discovered" by other investors, and hidden value that other investors have failed to find (e.g., a restructuring that will turn the company around or a new product about to be launched). Value investing involves elements of both the fundamentalist (focusing on the financials), and the contrarian (buying what others are not), both combined with a buy-and-hold strategy (patiently waiting for the stock to raise in price). Although the value investor feels that he can cull out the good from the bad, value investing is not without risk. A failing industry or company with a low price earnings ratio may never recover.

Growth Investing. The growth investor employs a strategy of finding and investing in growth stocks of companies within industries that are expected to experience substantial growth. The investor is typically looking for that well managed small to medium size company that is well positioned to generate revenues or earnings greater than the market as a whole. Returns from growth investing are expected to come from increases in stock values, not from dividends paid to stockholders.

MODERN PORTFOLIO THEORY

Under modern portfolio theory it is assumed that investors are inherently risk adverse and that financial markets are basically efficient, with all participants having equal access to information about the market and the securities within the market. Focus is placed on the entire portfolio, rather than on the individual investments within the portfolio, with the objective of optimizing portfolio returns relative to portfolio risk. Mathematical models are used to analyze expected returns, volatility, and correlations of individual asset classes in order to quantitatively express the relationship between risk and return. The following are some of the key concepts, tools, and measurements used in modern portfolio theory.

Portfolio. A portfolio is the blend of investment assets held by an investor. Building a portfolio is the process of adding additional stocks, bonds, and other investments to the mix, with the goal of accumulating a diverse selection of investment assets.

Beta. This is the measure of what is called "systematic risk," that part of a stock's (or mutual fund's) volatility coming from sensitivity to changes in the overall market (see page 18). To track beta, the stock is compared to a benchmark such as the S&P 500 Index. A stock having a beta of 1 is expected to be as volatile as the S&P 500 Index, a stock having a beta greater than 1 is expected to be more volatile than the S&P 500 Index, and a stock having a beta less than 1 is expected to be less volatile than the S&P 500 Index. A stock with a low beta (e.g., 0.76) is likely to be stable, but it also is likely to under perform the S&P 500 Index in a rising market. On the other hand, a stock with a high beta (e.g., 1.54) is likely to be somewhat unstable and more volatile than the S&P 500 Index, but it is expected to outperform the S&P 500 Index in a rising market. Stocks that are considered *growth* stocks will have high beta values. *Income* stocks will generally have low beta values. See also, page 187.

Alpha. This is the measure of what is called "unsystematic risk," that part of a stock's (or mutual fund's) volatility that is unique to the particular company (i.e., *not* coming from sensitivity to changes in the overall market). For example, when an analyst assigns an alpha of 1.09 to a stock, this means that it is estimated that the stock's price will rise 9% in a year when the overall market is flat. Stocks with high alphas are generally considered undervalued in light of current financial performance and expected earnings growth.

Efficient Frontier. Under modern portfolio theory, a portfolio that achieves the highest return commensurate with the risk assumed is considered to be efficient. Portfolio risk is measured by what is called the standard deviation (see page 36). The higher the standard deviation, the more volatile the portfolio (i.e., the returns are likely to be more variable). For any given value of standard deviation, or risk, the ideal is to achieve the greatest possible rate of return. For example, in the chart below the upward-sloping curve represents the efficient frontier. Typically, portfolios lying on the efficient frontier are the ones that are the most highly diversified, with less diversified portfolios tending to be closer to the middle of the achievable area.

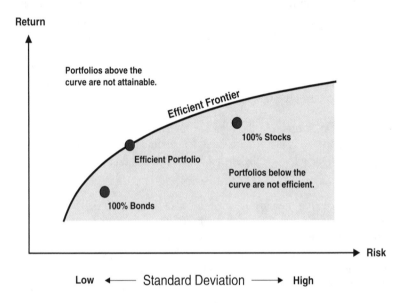

Achievable portfolios fall within the gray region. For every point within this region, there is at least one portfolio that could be constructed from all the investments in the universe that would have a risk and return profile corresponding to that point. The area above the gray region is unachievable and no portfolio could be constructed corresponding to a point in this area.

Note that a curved line represents the efficient frontier, it is not a straight line. This fact is the key to understanding how diversification can improve a portfolio's reward-to-risk ratio (i.e., risk can be reduced without a corresponding reduction in return). However, to accomplish this diversification, the portfolio must be comprised of assets having a negative correlation (see page 24).

Allocation. Consistent with modern portfolio theory, asset allocation involves the allocation of investments between different asset classes. Research has well demonstrated that a portfolio's asset allocation policy is the overwhelming determinant of investment performance.[5] Successful investing depends more upon selecting the right mix of asset classes, rather then selecting specific stocks, bonds, mutual funds, or other assets within a class. Since every portfolio has an inherent risk and reward profile, it is often possible to use asset modeling to reduce risk without sacrificing return, increase returns without increasing risk, or even reduce risk while increasing returns.

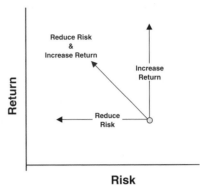

The process of asset allocation involves: (1) defining investment objectives or goals by considering factors such as age, time horizon, family situation, risk tolerances, income level, liquidity needs, and tax status; (2) selecting asset classes consistent with these investment objectives; (3) determining the weight to be given each asset class within the portfolio (see page 14); and (4) rebalancing as required. In selecting asset classes, and assigning a weight to each class, it is important to choose classes that are dissimilar (i.e., not covariant, see page 24). Asset allocation models prepared by brokerage houses and other financial institutions are typically focused upon securities and cash equivalents (see Asset Allocation Pie Charts, page 47). For example, an investor might allocate 60% of his portfolio to common stocks, 30% to corporate bonds, and the remaining 10% to cash equivalents. However, it is entirely appropriate to include other investments, such as real estate and tangibles.

Diversification. This is a defensive investment strategy that involves spreading investment dollars *within* a particular asset class. Such diversification can be accomplished in a number of ways, including securities of different industries, or bonds with different maturity dates. Although diversification cannot eliminate the risk of investment losses, in theory a totally diversified portfolio will eliminate all risk except market risk. The term diversification is more loosely used when referring to a "diversified portfolio" (i.e., to the idea of not putting all of your eggs in one basket).

One commentator has suggested that diversification is a matter of degree, and can be viewed: (1) narrowly, as in the diversification of securities within a portfolio (modern portfolio theory); (2) more broadly, to include assets other than securities (e.g., a home, collectibles, and real estate); and (3) most broadly, to include the investor's occupation, nature and stability of the investor's employer, and the investments used in employment-related retirement plans.[6]

The most effective way of reducing risk in a portfolio is by diversifying among various types of assets because diversification lowers a portfolio's volatility and can even increase returns. However, when it comes to diversifying a portfolio, merely holding a broad array of stocks will not reduce the overall risk profile. The portfolio must be comprised of noncorrelated assets.

Cross-Correlation Matrix							
	U.S. Treasury bills	Long-term corporate bonds	International bonds	Large company stocks	Large company stocks	International stocks	Equity REITS
U.S. Treasury bills	1.00						
Long-term corporate bonds	.05	1.00					
International bonds	-.09	.35	1.00				
Large company stocks	-.06	.39	.12	1.00			
Small company stocks	-.08	.24	.02	.79	1.00		
International stocks	-.09	.24	.64	.48	.38	1.00	
Equity REITS	-.09	.27	.13	.65	.75	.41	1.00

The values shown for the seven asset classes listed are based upon the 22-year time period from 1973 through 1994.

Source: Adapted from Roger C. Gibson, *Asset Allocation: Balancing Financial Risk*, 3rd ed. (New York: McGraw-Hill, 1996), p. 183. Used with permission.

Correlation. If a portfolio is to be well diversified, it is extremely important to consider the correlation of assets within the portfolio. Two assets are said to be correlated if they tend to move together. Analysts use **correlation coefficients** to measure the strength of such relationships by means of a single number varying between +1.0 and -1.0. The

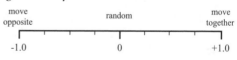

higher the number, the more the assets move in tandem or similarly (+1.0 is considered a perfect match). Conversely, the lower the number, the more the assets move opposite each other (-1.0 is a perfect negative, or inverse correlation). When there is no relationship between the predicted asset values and the actual values the correlation coefficient is 0 or very low (i.e., the predicted values are no better than random numbers).

When there is a *negative* correlation between assets, this generally means that the portfolio will be more diversified and therefore subject to less risk. In contrast, a *positive* correlation between assets generally means that the portfolio will be less diversified and subject to more risk. However, a positive correlation does not necessarily indicate a causal relationship. The term **covariance** is also used to describe the concept of correlation. As the term indicates, covariance means varying together.[7]

It takes considerable statistical effort to create and maintain a useful table of asset correlations. Tables are typically constructed in the form of a matrix with asset names listed on both the X and Y-axis. The numerical correlation coefficients are then placed at the points of intersection. The following Cross-Correlation Matrix is a simplified example of how a correlation table is constructed.[8] Descriptive terms are also used to indicate the general degree of correlation.

Rebalancing. Portfolio rebalancing, also known as reallocation, is the periodic transfer of funds between various asset classes in order to maintain or achieve a desired mix of assets. There are many reasons to consider rebalancing a portfolio. Most often, rebalancing is designed to counter what is called "risk creep" (i.e., the disproportionate increase in value of equity assets that increases the overall risk profile of the portfolio). Other reasons for rebalancing include the need to modify asset allocations in response to changed investment objectives, age, or investment horizons (see page 41).

The rebalancing technique is particularly useful in a tax-deferred retirement plan, where the sale of individual securities does not trigger the current payment of income taxes (i.e., taxation on the gain is deferred until funds are distributed from the plan, but then taxed as ordinary income, not capital gains).

Rebalancing may actually improve the investment performance of a portfolio by disciplining the investor to systematically "buy low and sell high." For example, rebalancing a portfolio after a run up of the stock market will force the investor to sell high performing stocks and purchase low performing bonds or money market securities. Alternatively, when stocks fall, rebalancing triggers the sale of the better performing bonds and money market securities in order to purchase depressed stocks. The discipline of rebalancing helps to overcome two of the biggest challenges to every investor, greed and fear.

Rebalancing Worksheet					
Investments	Target Allocation	Current Value	Current Allocation	Required Purchase (Sale)	Resulting Value
Aggressive Growth	16.00%		21.72%		
Asset A	6.00%	$101,690	8.69%	($31,475)	$70,215
Asset B	5.00%	$56,844	4.86%	$1,668	$58,512
Asset C	5.00%	$95,678	8.18%	($37,166)	$58,512
Growth	40.00%		38.03%		
Asset D	12.00%	$128,900	11.01%	$11,530	$140,430
Asset E	10.00%	$101,343	8.66%	$15,682	$117,025
Asset F	10.00%	$125,966	10.76%	($8,941)	$117,025
Asset G	8.00%	$88,789	7.59%	$4,831	$93,620
Income	30.00%		28.27%		
Asset H	12.50%	$146,733	12.54%	($452)	$146,281
Asset I	12.50%	$141,943	12.13%	$4,338	$146,281
Asset J	5.00%	$42,189	3.61%	$16,323	$58,512
Cash Equivalents	14.00%		11.98%		
Asset K	9.00%	$84,500	7.22%	$20,822	$105,322
Asset L	5.00%	$55,672	4.76%	$2,840	$58,512
Totals	100.00%	$1,170,247	100.00%		$1,170,247

LADDERING

This is a strategy that is used to stagger the maturities on fixed-income investments such as certificates of deposit and bonds. The many advantages of laddering include:

(1) Reduces reinvestment risk caused when interest rates *fall* – the investor does not have to reinvest a large amount of funds at lower rates.

(2) Reduces interest rate risk caused when interest rates *rise* – as investments mature, the investor can take advantage of new investment opportunities paying a higher rate of interest.

(3) Provides funds for known future expenses, such as a child's college education, by the timing of maturity dates.

(4) Maturing CDs or bond investments can be used for current income, thereby avoiding the sale of stocks at depressed prices in a down stock market (i.e., the ladder would not be continued).

(5) Maturing CDs or bond investments can be used for unanticipated emergencies.

(6) Liquidity can be maintained while enjoying the higher rates of return or yields offered by longer-term investments.

(7) Gain greater stability and reduce volatility by purchasing shorter-term bonds that are less sensitive to changes in interest rates, thereby reducing market risk (page 18).

Establishing A 3-Year Ladder

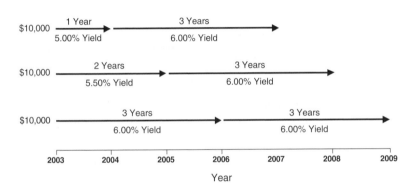

Ladders can be established for various lengths of time. For example, to establish a "3-year ladder" in 2003, the investor who has $30,000 to invest would purchase three CDs, one $10,000 CD paying 5.0% maturing in 1 year, another $10,000 CD paying 5.5% maturing in 2 years, and another $10,000 CD paying 6.0% maturing in 3 years.[9] Assuming interest rates remain constant, when the 1-year CD matures in 2004, it is replaced with a CD paying 6.0% maturing in 3 years. When the 2-year CD matures in 2005, it also is replaced with a CD paying 6.0% maturing in 3 years. At this point the ladder has been established and can thereafter be continued by replacing CDs as they come due each year with a 3-year CD at the prevailing interest rate. The rolling maturity dates and periodic reinvesting opportunities of a laddered portfolio provide a consistent pattern of investment similar to dollar-cost-averaging (see page 28).

Ladders of 5 and 10 years are often used when investing in corporate, municipal, and federal bonds. In the following 5-year ladder, beginning in year 2 the
maturing 5.00% bond is replaced with a 5-year bond yielding 6.00%. Notice that
the average maturity remains the same each and every year, but the yield of the
portfolio is increased each year during the first 5 years. (Assuming 6.00% 5-year
bonds continue to be available). For example, in year 2 the 5.00% bond is
replaced by a 6.00% bond yielding 1% more interest, and $200 of additional
interest earnings. This $200 represents an increase of 20 basis points in the port-
folio (6.00 - 5.00 = 1.00 ÷ 5 = .2).

Year 1					Year 2			
Amount	Yield	Maturity	Interest		Amount	Yield	Maturity	Interest
$20,000	5.00%	1 year	$1,000		$20,000	5.25%	1 year	$1,050
20,000	5.25%	2 year	1,050		20,000	5.50%	2 year	1,100
20,000	5.50%	3 year	1,100		20,000	5.75%	3 year	1,150
20,000	5.75%	4 year	1,150		20,000	6.00%	4 year	1,200
20,000	6.00%	5 year	1,200		20,000	6.00%	5 year	1,200
			$5,500					$5,700

Year 3					Year 4			
Amount	Yield	Maturity	Interest		Amount	Yield	Maturity	Interest
$20,000	5.50%	1 year	$1,100		$20,000	5.75%	1 year	$1,150
20,000	5.75%	2 year	1,150		20,000	6.00%	2 year	1,200
20,000	6.00%	3 year	1,200		20,000	6.00%	3 year	1,200
20,000	6.00%	4 year	1,200		20,000	6.00%	4 year	1,200
20,000	6.00%	5 year	1,200		20,000	6.00%	5 year	1,200
			$5,850					$5,950

Year 5			
Amount	Yield	Maturity	Interest
$20,000	6.00%	1 year	$1,200
20,000	6.00%	2 year	1,200
20,000	6.00%	3 year	1,200
20,000	6.00%	4 year	1,200
20,000	6.00%	5 year	1,200
			$6,000

DOLLAR COST AVERAGING

With dollar cost averaging, the investor engages in systematic investing, meaning that he invests the same amount of money at regular intervals. Investing a fixed
sum at regular intervals means that more shares are bought at low prices than
high prices and average cost is lower than average share price. It is a buy-and-
hold approach to building an investment portfolio that provides diversification
over time. Although the strategy of dollar cost averaging is the opposite of market
timing, it is tempting to suggest that for the non-sophisticated investor using dollar cost averaging to invest in the market time and time again offers the best of
"market timing." The investor who uses dollar cost averaging in a falling market

acquires more shares for his money then would be purchased in a raising market. However, dollar-cost-averaging does not assure a profit or protect against a loss in a declining market.

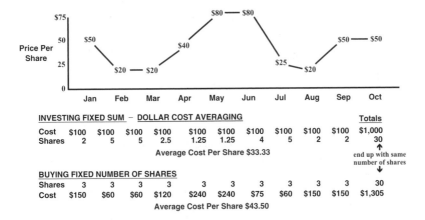

INVESTING FIXED SUM – DOLLAR COST AVERAGING										Totals
Cost	$100	$100	$100	$100	$100	$100	$100	$100	$100	$1,000
Shares	2	5	5	2.5	1.25	1.25	4	5	2	2	30

Average Cost Per Share $33.33

end up with same number of shares

BUYING FIXED NUMBER OF SHARES										
Shares	3	3	3	3	3	3	3	3	3	30
Cost	$150	$60	$60	$120	$240	$240	$75	$60	$150	$150	$1,305

Average Cost Per Share $43.50

For example, the above chart demonstrates the effects of dollar cost averaging. Assume investor #1 commits to purchasing $100 of stock each month for a period of ten months. At the end of ten months, he has invested $1,000 and purchased thirty shares of stock for an average cost of $33.33 per share. Compare these results with investor #2, who commits to purchasing three shares of stock each month, no matter the cost. Buying a fixed number of shares requires investor #2 to pay $1,305 to purchased thirty shares of stock, for an average cost of $43.50 per share.

A variation of dollar cost averaging, known as a **constant ratio plan,** disciplines the investor to continually buy low and sell high. Under this system, the market value of all stocks in an investor's portfolio is kept at a predetermined percentage, with other investments, such as money market funds or bonds, making up the remainder of the portfolio. Stocks must be sold if they rise in value more rapidly than the other investments, and purchased if they fall in value more rapidly than the other investments in the portfolio. The ratio can be 50/50, or some other ratio, as determined by the investor.

FUNDAMENTAL ANALYSIS

Fundamental analysis attempts to measure the intrinsic value of a particular stock based upon factors such as the overall economy, industry conditions, the financial condition and management of the company, and many other related factors. Focus is placed on analyzing the fundamentals of the company behind the stock rather than the market in which the stock is traded. As with most analysis, the goal is to derive a forecast for the future, thereby identifying currently undervalued stocks. If the present value of a stock is more than the current market price, then the stock is considered an attractive investment opportunity. Annual reports, talking to company management, evaluation of economic factors, and the analysis of a company's balance sheet are all used to determine the value of the company. The ultimate objective is to buy the stock at a price that is lower than liquidation value, at a price that is low when compared to the valuation of company net assets, or at a price that is low when compared to future projected earnings. Whereas technical analysis seeks to identify stocks that are either "overbought" or "oversold," fundamental analysis focuses on identifying stocks that are either "overvalued" or "undervalued." The following are some of the financial ratios used in fundamental analysis.

Book Value. Also known as shareholder equity or a company's net asset value (NAV). Book value is calculated   Assets - Liabilities
by subtracting all liabilities, including debt and the par value
of preferred stock, from total assets. A company's market value may be quite different from its book value. Book value is sometimes used as a means of determining if a company's assets are sufficient to cover its outstanding obligations and equity issues.

Book Value Per Common Share. This is a variation of the book value calculation and is a

$$\frac{\text{Book Value}}{\text{Number Of Common Shares Outstanding}}$$

measure of book value per share of outstanding common stock. The question addressed by this ratio: "Is a premium being paid by the investor for the future earnings and the goodwill of the company?" Uncertainty regarding operations of the company, or doubts regarding asset valuations, can result in companies being traded for less than book value. Alternatively, some investors may view a stock that is selling below book value as an indication that the stock is undervalued.

Current Ratio. Also called the "working capital" ratio. The question addressed by this ratio: "Does the business have enough current assets to meet the

$$\frac{\text{Total Current Assets}}{\text{Total Current Liabilities}}$$

payment schedule of its current debts with a margin of safety for possible losses in current assets?" A 2 to 1 ratio is generally acceptable.

Debt Equity Ratio. This is an indication of the extent to which a company is reliant on debt financing. A high ratio may be an indication the company is fast

$$\frac{\text{Long Term Debts}}{\text{Shareholder's Equity}}$$

growing, or that the company has overextended itself. Average ratios differ considerably from one industry to another.

Earnings Per Share. This is a measure of the net earnings of the company that are available

$$\frac{\text{Net Income}}{\text{Number Of Common Shares Outstanding}}$$

to common stockholders after paying taxes, bond holders, and owners of pre-ferred stock. It is considered a measure of how well the company is doing by its common stockholders.

Price Earning Ratio (P/E Ratio). Also known as a stock's multiple, this provides an estimate of the numbers of years it will take the company to generate the price paid for the stock (assuming income does not fluctuate). Companies with high P/E ratios are typically expected to experience rapid future growth. A low P/E ratio may be an indication of a company not yet discovered by the market, or of a company considered a poor investment risk. A trailing P/E ratio uses earnings for the last four quarters, whereas a forward P/E ratio uses earnings for the last two quarters plus an analyst's projections for the next two quarters.

$$\frac{\text{Stock Price}}{\text{Earnings Per Share}}$$

Quick Ratio. Also called the "acid-test" ratio and "quick current" test. The question addressed by this ratio: "If all sales revenues disappeared, could the business meet its current obligations with the readily convertible 'quick' funds at hand?" An acid test of 1 to 1 is typical. Quick funds are current assets minus inventory.

$$\frac{\text{Cash + Gov't Securities + Receivables}}{\text{Total Current Liabilities}}$$

Working Capital. This is a measure of cash flow and is considered an indication of the ability to withstand financial crises.

$$\text{Total Current Assets - Total Current Liabilities}$$

Debt/Worth Ratio. Indicates the extent to which the business is reliant on debt financing.

$$\frac{\text{Total Liabilities}}{\text{Total Current Liabilities}}$$

Gross Margin Ratio. Gross profit equals net sales minus cost of goods sold. This ratio measures the percentage of sales dollars remaining to pay overhead expenses.

$$\frac{\text{Gross Profit}}{\text{Net Sales}}$$

Net Profit Margin Ratio. This ratio measures "return on sales" and can be used to evaluate performance in comparison with similar businesses.

$$\frac{\text{Net Profit Before Tax}}{\text{Net Sales}}$$

Inventory Turnover. Measures how well inventory is managed. The more inventory is turned in a given operating cycle, the greater the profit.

$$\frac{\text{Net Sales}}{\text{Average Inventory At Cost}}$$

Return On Assets Ratio. Measures how efficiently profits are being generated from the assets employed in the business when compared with ratios of similar firms. A comparatively low ratio indicates an inefficient use of business assets.

$$\frac{\text{Net Profit Before Tax}}{\text{Total Assets}}$$

Return On Investment. A measure of the percentage of return on funds invested in the business. This is considered a very important ratio. If the ROI is

$$\frac{\text{Net Profit Before Tax}}{\text{Net Worth}}$$

less than the rate of return on an alternative, risk-free investment, the owner may wish to sell and invest elsewhere.

Current Ratio, Quick Ratio, and Working Capital are liquidity ratios that indicate the ease of turning assets into cash. Debt/Worth Ratio is a leverage ratio that measures how dependent the business is on debt financing. Gross Margin Ratio and Net Profit Margin Ratio are profitability ratios. Inventory Turnover, Return On Assets Ratio, and Return On Investment are management ratios.

TECHNICAL ANALYSIS

In contrast to fundamental analysis, technical analysis involves the evaluation of trading movements and trends, without regard to the underlying fundamentals of individual stocks. Technical analysis is the examination of past long-term and short-term price movements to forecast short-term trading patterns and future price

> "A technical analyst knows the price of everything, but the value of nothing."
>
> *The Psychology of Technical Analysis* by Tony Plummer

movements. Such analysis looks only for repetitive price patterns and is unconcerned about the financial data used in fundamental analysis (page 29) or the emotions of the market as used in sentiment analysis (page 39). Technical analysts are often referred to as chartists because they rely heavily on charts for their analysis.

Dow Theory. The Dow theory recognizes three movements in the securities markets: major trends, intermediate trends, and short-term trends. *Major trends* are broad-market movements, typically lasting several years (e.g., a major decline occurs when successive rallies fail to penetrate previous highs, but previous lows are penetrated). An upward major trend is called a "bull market," whereas a downward major trend is called a "bear market." Bull markets occur when upward rallies exceed prior highs and declines stay above previous lows. *Intermediate trends*, occurring within the major trend, are influenced by current events and can last for several weeks or even months. Intermediate trends can give rise to *technical corrections*, a term used to describe the adjustments that occur when markets are either overbought or oversold. *Short-term trends* are daily ripples that are considered to have no particular significance.

In order to predict what direction the market will take, the Dow theory employs both the Dow Jones Industrial Average and the Dow Jones Transportation Average. Movement of both averages upward signals a strong bull market, whereas movement of both averages downward signals a bear market. Movement of both averages in opposite directions signals uncertainty. A trend continues so long as the averages confirm each other.

The following charts and analytic concepts are employed in technical analysis:

Bar Charts. A simple vertical bar chart is shown. Bar charts, or graphs, are often used to display single events as Y-values (vertical axis) and the differences between them using a bar for each X-value (horizontal axis). They can be used to compare data sets against some variable data such as time or frequency. Other variations of bar charts include vertical stacked bar charts, vertical stacked floating bar charts, horizontal bar charts, horizontal stacked bar charts, and horizontal stacked floating bar charts.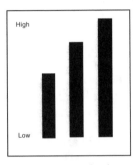

Bar charts can also be used to group data series together by category, displaying multiple bars within each category. The bars are often color-coded according to the series represented. For examples of many of these see: www.corda.com/examples/graph_styles.

Bar Chart (high-low).[10] High low charts display a Y-value for each X-value, and a range of Y-values for a given X-Value. Hi Lo charts are typically used to display a confidence range or the trading range of a stock. The range of Y-values represent the low and the high values for the given X value.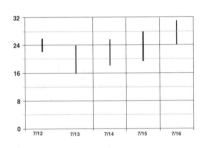

Bar Chart (high-low, open-close). Bar charts that incorporate the open-close feature display a Y-value for each X-value, a range of Y-values for a given X-value, and include a opening and closing point for the values. High-low open-close charts are typically used to display a confidence range or the trading range of a stock with opening and closing values

included in the range. These charts are typically used for showing daily stock prices over time, and showing statistical data with a confidence range over time.

Candlestick Charts. Candlestick charts utilize a series of boxes with lines projecting vertically up and down from the ends of the box, and drawn on an X-Y grid. The top and bottom of each box indicates the open and close values and allow the user to compare the relationship between the open and close as well as the high and low. If the close price is higher, the box is not filled (buying pressure). If the open price is higher, the box is filled (selling pressure). The vertical lines indicate the high and low values. The relationship between the open and close is considered vital information and forms the essence of candlesticks. The candlestick graph requires four data sets (open, high, low, and close values). Candlestick charts are primarily used for stock price activity.

Line Charts.[11] Line graphs are used to determine trends and cyclic variation based on interaction of data elements. The data points are plotted on the graph and connected with lines. Line graphs can display large amounts of data that varies along some accepted sequence such as price, time, volume, etc. Line graphs with multiple lines can be used to display several variables to conserve space and to facilitate comparison of more than one dependent variable on a single independent scale. Line graphs can be used for determining trends or cyclical variations, illustrating money distribution over time, depicting production over time, and showing price variations over time.

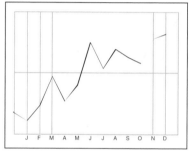

Point-And-Figure Charts.[12] Point-and-figure charts consist of columns of X's (uptrends) and O's (downtrends) that represent filtered price movements over time. When compared to the more traditional bar and candlestick charts, the proponents of point-and-figure charts maintain that they offer the following advantages: (1) remove the potential misleading effects of time from the analysis process; (2) eliminate the insignificant price movements that often make bar charts appear "cluttered"; (3) make recognizing support and resistance levels much easier; (4) facilitate the recognition of trend lines; and (5) keep the user focused on important long-term price trends and developments.

Moving Averages.
Moving averages are used in an attempt to filter out "noise" and to uncover trends. The averages are calculated by adding sets of data, then dividing the sum by the periods. The results display a smoothed out version of the trend. When the

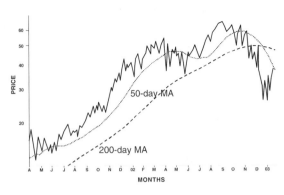

price crosses the moving average line (considered a crossover point) this indicates a reversal in trend. The longer the time span used in calculating the moving average, the more significant the crossover signal. For example, a price line that crosses, or penetrates, a 50-day moving average is not considered as significant as one that crosses a 200-day moving average. Before confirming a crossover, traders typically wait for the penetration to reach a predetermined number of days, or percentage of price. Different time periods are commonly used depending upon the type of trading (e.g., 20-day moving averages for short-term trading, 50-day moving averages for intermediate-term trading, and 200-day moving averages for long-term trading).

Resistance Level. This is the opposite of the support level and indicates the price *above* which it is difficult for a market or stock to *rise*. It is the upper level for trading, or the price at which sellers typically outnumber buyers. A "breakout" occurs when the price rises above the resistance level and a new level of resistance is formed that then becomes the new *support* level. Such a rise above the support level is considered bullish. Horizontal lines on stock price charts indicate resistance levels.

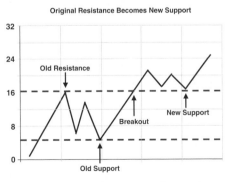

Support Level. This is the opposite of the resistance level and indicates the price *below* which it is difficult for a market or stock to *fall*. At this level there is more demand for the stock than supply and any decline in price is likely to stop. Support levels are formed over a period of time, typically months or even a year or more, and represent the accepted lower "trading range" for the stock. A "breakout" occurs when the price falls below the support level and a new level of resistance is formed that then becomes the new *resistance* level. Such a drop below the support level is considered bearish. Horizontal lines on stock price charts indicate support levels.

Standard Deviation. Standard deviation is a statistical measurement of how far a variable quantity, such as the price of a stock or the return on an investment, moves above or below its average (mean) value. As such, it is considered a good measure of volatility. An investment with high volatility is considered riskier than an investment with low volatility. Therefore, the lower the standard deviation, the lower the risk; and the higher the standard deviation, the higher the risk (i.e., the more spread apart the data is, the higher the "deviation").

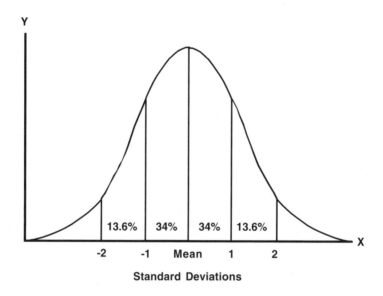

Standard Deviations

The bell curve above will help explain the concept. Assuming normally distributed data, approximately 68% (roughly two-thirds) of the time total returns are expected to differ from the average (mean) total return by not more than plus or minus *one* standard deviation. And approximately 95% of the time total returns are expected to differ from the average (mean) total return by not more than plus or minus *two* standard deviations. If the bell curve is steep and the returns are tightly bunched together, the standard deviation is small, indicating low volatility and less risk. Alternatively, if the bell curve is relatively flat and the returns are spread out, the standard deviation is large, signaling high volatility and more risk (i.e., the more spread apart the data, the higher the "deviation"). Note that the x-axis is the value that is being measured, such as annual, or monthly, returns from a stock mutual fund.

Calculation of the actual standard deviation is a bit complicated and consists of the following six distinct steps: (1) calculate the average return; (2) for each period subtract the average from the annual return (this is the deviation for that period); (3) square the deviation for each period; (4) sum the squared deviations; (5) divide the sum by the number of periods (this is known as the variance); and (6) calculate the square root of the sum of the squared deviations (this is the standard deviation). The following table calculates the standard deviation for the indicated returns over a period of 10 years. The steps in the process are labeled #1 through #6. Note that the average [mean] return is 6.2% and the standard deviation is 11.9. The results are plotted in graph **A**.

Calculation Of Standard Deviation			
Period	annual return	#2 deviation for each period	#3 deviation squared	
1	-3.4	-9.6	92.0	
2	9.9	3.7	13.8	
3	-2.0	-8.2	67.1	
4	21.7	15.5	240.6	
5	-6.2	-12.4	153.5	
6	11.0	4.8	23.1	
7	-9.1	-15.3	233.8	
8	13.1	6.9	47.7	
9	-1.5	-7.7	59.1	
10	28.4	22.2	493.3	
sum	61.9		1,424.0	#4 – sum of squared deviations
#1 average	6.2		142.4	#5 – divided by number of periods (variance)
			11.9	#6 – standard deviation (square root of variance)

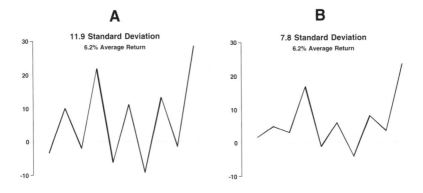

A

11.9 Standard Deviation
6.2% Average Return

B

7.8 Standard Deviation
6.2% Average Return

These swings in annual returns can be dampened while retaining the same average return by adding 5% to each negative return in years 1, 3, 5, 7 and 9, and subtracting 5% from each positive return in years 2, 4, 6, 8, and 10. As expected, average returns remain at 6.2%, but the volatility of returns are lowered as the standard deviation falls from 11.9 to 7.8 (the results are plotted in graph **B**). The smaller standard deviation indicates a more consistent investment with less risk to the investor. Armed with this information an investor would likely chose the less volatile investment (7.8 standard deviation), particularly if it is expected to produce the same 6.2% rate of return.

Standard deviation is often used in comparing the volatility and risk of various mutual funds. The Morningstar mutual fund ratings provide the standard deviation as an annualized statistic based on 36 monthly returns over a three-year period (see page 196). Assuming a fund's returns fall within the typical bell-shaped distribution, 68% of the time the fund's total returns are expected to differ from its average (mean) return by no more than plus or minus one standard deviation, and 95% of the time by no more than plus or minus two standard deviations. Thus, a fund with a mean of 26.53 and a standard deviation of 20.20 can be expected to return between 6.33% (26.53 − 20.20) and 46.73% (26.53 + 20.20) roughly two-thirds of the time. In general, a wider range of returns can be expected from the fund with the higher standard deviation and a lower range of returns can be expected from the fund with a lower standard deviation. However, it is important to recognize that by itself a low standard deviation means only that returns have been fairly stable; it does not indicate anything about the absolute amount of expected returns.

Bollinger Bands. This indicator allows users to compare volatility and relative price levels over a period of time.

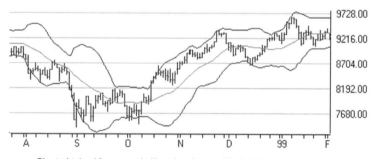

Chart obtained from www.bollingerbands.com. Used with permission

The indicator consists of three bands designed to encompass the majority of a security's price action: (1) a simple moving average in the middle; (2) an upper band reflecting the simple moving average plus 2 standard deviations; (3) a lower band reflecting the simple moving average minus 2 standard deviations.

Standard deviation is considered a good indication of volatility and ensures that the bands respond quickly to price movements, thereby reflecting periods of both high and low volatility (see page 36).

In periods of greater volatility, when there are sharp price increases or decreases, the bands widen. When the market becomes less volatile, the bands narrow. As indicators of *previous* market volatility the bands are used to augment other analysis techniques and indicators, but are not designed to predict the future direction of a security. The two primary uses of Bollinger Bands are to identify periods of high and low volatility, and periods when prices are at possibly unsustainable levels.

SENTIMENT ANALYSIS[13]

Unlike fundamental and technical analysis, each of which attempt to evaluate the market in terms of the *facts* relating to a particular stock's performance, or of the market as a whole, sentiment analysis attempts to measure the market environ-

> "Be fearful when others are greedy and greedy when others are fearful."
>
> Warren Buffett

ment in terms of the *attitudes* of investors and the "mass psychology" of the investment community as a whole. Interpretations of these indicators are often dependent upon the highly subjective evaluations of individual analysts.

A key element of sentiment analysis is the contrarian's belief that the average investor can often be wrong, particularly as the market approaches its highs and lows. Thus the investor using sentiment analysis will look to trade against the majority's view of the market.

Many qualitative and quantitative methods have been developed in order to evaluate sentiment. Most of these relate to the overall market, but many are relative to market segments and even individual stocks. The following are examples of some of these psychological market indicators.

Volatility Index. The CBOE Volatility Index (ticker VIX) computes the implied volatility of eight S&P 100 (OEX) put and call options.[14] A composite hypothetical option is developed by weighting the options according to the time remaining and the degree to which they are either in or out of the money (see pages 153-154). When the market is expected to move higher, excessive call contract buying will produce a low VIX. When the market is expected to move lower, disproportionate put buying will produce a high VIX. The investor using sentiment analysis views the volatility index from a contrarian's perspective, buying when the index is high and selling when the index is low.

Options Trading Volume. As with the CBOE Volatility Index, put buying is considered bearish and call buying is considered bullish. Therefore the ratio between put volume and call volume is considered a good indication of market mood. From a contrarian's perspective, a high volume of buyers or sellers is an indication that the small options investor is again wrong (a very high percentage of option contracts expire worthless). The investor using sentiment analysis will buy when there are a disproportionate number of put buyers and sell when there are a disproportionate number of call buyers.

Option Open Interest. Open interest is a measure of the number of outstanding option contracts that are available in a specific option series at the end of a trading day. Monitoring open interest provides a means of judging whether the market is bullish or bearish. A rise or fall in an option's open interest is a signal to the contrarian investor to trade against the market.

Put And Call Premiums. This is another indicator that is viewed from a contrarian's perspective. When put premiums are higher than call premiums, the market is bearish (i.e., the put premiums are higher because more investors are trying to sell than buy). When call premiums are higher than put premiums, the market is bullish (i.e., the call premiums are higher because more investors are trying to buy than sell). In either case, the contrarian investor interprets the indicator in order to trade against the market.

Professional Advisors. Apparently, professional advisors on a whole are no better or worse than everyone else at forecasting the market. A comparison of the number of bullish investment advisors to bearish investment advisors is interpreted as a contrarian indicator.

Mutual Funds. A large influx of cash and subsequent buying by mutual fund managers is seen as a bullish indicator, whereas a large number of mutual fund redemptions is viewed as bearish. As usual, the indicator is acted upon in a contrarian fashion in an attempt to buy low and sell high.

Odd-Lot Sellers. Odd-lots are typically bought by small investors with limited investment savvy and even less capital (see page 141). An increase in odd-lot short sales is viewed as a bullish indicator and a decrease as a bearish indicator. The contrarian interpretation is to sell when odd-lot short sales increase and buy when odd-lot short sales decrease.

RISK TOLERANCE AND ASSESSMENT

Understanding and measuring risk tolerance is essential to the process of investment planning. Some people are risk seekers, some are risk neutral, but most people are risk adverse. Being essentially risk adverse, an investor who accepts a degree of risk expects to be rewarded with a higher return on his investment than if no risk had been assumed (i.e., risk and return go hand in hand). Individual risk tolerance is not a constant; it changes over time, based upon factors such as age, changes in personal circumstances, and market conditions.

Time Horizon. Also known as a planning or investment horizon, this is a critical element to be considered when determining an investor's risk tolerance and the appropriate mix of stocks, bonds, and other assets in a portfolio. In determining the impact of an investor's time horizon, it is important to consider factors such as age, health, income potential, and near term objectives. An investor's life cycle can typically be broken down into three phases. During the accumulation phase, he is purchasing a home, setting funds aside for emergency purposes, and saving for a college education. These relatively near term objectives cause him to accept limited amounts of risk. For example, assume the purpose of the funds is to pay for a child's college education and the child is

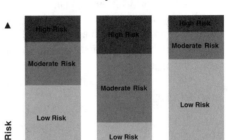

Life Cycle Phases

expected to graduate from high school within a couple of years. Such a near term objective would likely cause the investor to only accept low risk investments for these college education funds. However, once the child is educated, this same investor (being in the high-income years of his career) may well accept a moderate or even high-risk investment strategy in order to aggressively save for his retirement during the acceleration phase. As he approaches retirement, he then reaches the preservation and once again adapts to a more conservative and low risk investment profile.

Measurements Of Risk Tolerance. In measuring risk tolerance, the planner attempts to determine the investor's "comfort level" with risk. If the assessment process is *subjective*, or qualitative, the process is typically limited to information obtained in discussions with the investor. Based upon the information gleamed during these discussions, the planner then subjectively assesses the investor's tolerance for risk. In order to effectively evaluate the investor, it is important for the planner to possess good interviewing skills. If the assessment process is *objective*, or quantitative, the planner uses a questionnaire designed to provide a basis for applying a numerical score, or rating, to the individual investor's level of risk tolerance. The questions in the typical risk tolerance questionnaire are intended to provide a systematic and standardized measure of the investor's tolerance for risk. To be credible, the test must be both valid and reliable (i.e., it must accurately measure what it purports to measure, and it must render these results on a consistent basis). Unfortunately, most questionnaires used by financial planners have *not* been subject to rigorous testing based upon known standards. Recognizing this limitation, most financial planners use questionnaires in order to "begin the discussion," but then supplement the numerical scores produced by the questionnaire with a subjective analysis based upon discussions with the investor. A good example of such a questionnaire is contained on pages 43-45.

The Investment Profile. The development of an appropriate investment strategy requires obtaining an estimate of the investor's risk tolerance. The sample personal investor profile on page 46 places the investor in one of five investor categories, conservative, moderately conservative, moderate, moderately aggressive, and aggressive. Assigning a classification to an investor is an important part of developing an appropriate investment strategy. However, it must be remembered that measurements of risk tolerance are not uniform and the results are not subject to the rigors of scientific verification. In many ways, the process is as much art as science.

Matching Risk Tolerance To Investments. It was not that many years ago that planners would tend to avoid recommending equity investments to anyone over 50-55 years of age. But times have changed. For the investor facing retirement, the process often boils down to balancing the fear of loss of principal against the fear of loss of income. The investor must select assets appropriate to his tolerance for risk and further determine the mix of these assets in his portfolio. The pie charts on page 47 provide a useful example of matching risk tolerance and assets in assembling a portfolio.

The Retirement Challenge

loss of principal   loss of income

It must be remembered that effective portfolio selection requires much more than merely matching a risk tolerance score to a particular mix of potential investments. The process involves a careful evaluation of factors such as age, time horizon, family situation, income level, liquidity needs, and tax status. In this regard, see the asset allocation discussion on page 22.

SAMPLE INVESTOR PROFILE QUESTIONNAIRE

The following sample questionnaire addresses both life stage and attitude toward risk. The scores are then plotted on the graph on page 46 in order to place the investor in one of five investor categories. The questionnaire has the distinct advantage of simplicity and brevity.

Time Horizon

---

1. In approximately how many years do you plan to begin withdrawing money from your investments?

A.	Less than 3 years	0 points
B.	3-4 years	2 points
C.	5-7 years	5 points
D.	8-10 years	7 points
E.	11 years or more	10 points

Points: _____

2. Once you begin withdrawing funds from your investments, how many years do you need them to last?

A.	Less than 3 years	0 points
B.	3-4 years	2 points
C.	5-7 years	5 points
D.	8-10 years	7 points
E.	11 years or more	10 points

Points: _____

Time Horizon Subtotal - Add your points for questions 1 and 2: _____

(continued on next page)

Risk Tolerance

---

3. How would you describe your knowledge of investments?

A.	Non-existent	0 points
B.	Minimal	1 points
C.	Moderate	3 points
D.	Good	4 points
E.	Extensive	6 points

Points: _____

4. Which influences you when deciding how to invest your money, the potential for gain or the potential for loss?

A.	I am primarily influenced by the potential of my investment losing value.	0 points
B.	I am more influenced by the potential of my investment losing value, but I do care about its potential for gain.	2 points
C.	I am equally influenced by the potential of my investment to lose or gain value.	4 points
D.	I am more influenced by the potential of my investment gaining value, but I do care about its potential for loss.	6 points
E.	I am primarily influenced by the potential of my investment gaining value.	8 points

Points: _____

5. Over the past 3 months, an individual stock investment in your portfolio declined from $10,000 in value to $7,500. The overall stock market suffered a similar drop. What would you do with your stock investment?

A.	I'd sell all of the shares. It's a loser.	0 points
B.	I'd sell some of the shares.	2 points
C.	I'd hold on to what I have. It's still a good investment.	5 points
D.	I'd buy more shares. It's a bargain now.	8 points

Points: _____

(continued on next page)

Risk Tolerance (cont'd)

6. Assume you could choose between the five hypothetical portfolios described in the chart below. Each potential portfolio has a range of possible outcomes. Which portfolio appeals most to you?

Portfolios	Most Likely Annual Return (1 year)	Best-case Scenario (1 year)	Worst-case Scenario (1 year)	
A	6.0%	12.0%	-4.0%	0 points
B	8.0%	18.0%	-12.0%	3 points
C	9.0%	30.0%	-18.0%	6 points
D	10.5%	40.0%	-25.0%	9 points
E	12.0%	50.0%	-40.0%	12 points

Points: _____

7. Which of the following statements best describes your likely reaction to short-term fluctuations in your investment portfolio?

A.	I would be extremely concerned about short-term fluctuations.	0 points
B.	I would be somewhat concerned about short-term fluctuations.	2 points
C.	I would have some concerns about short-term fluctuations, but I would not lose any sleep at night.	5 points
D.	I would have few concerns about short-term fluctuations.	8 points

Points: _____

Risk Tolerance Subtotal - Add your points for questions 3 through 7:   _____

Enter Your Time Horizon Subtotal here: _____

Enter Your Risk Tolerance Subtotal here: _____

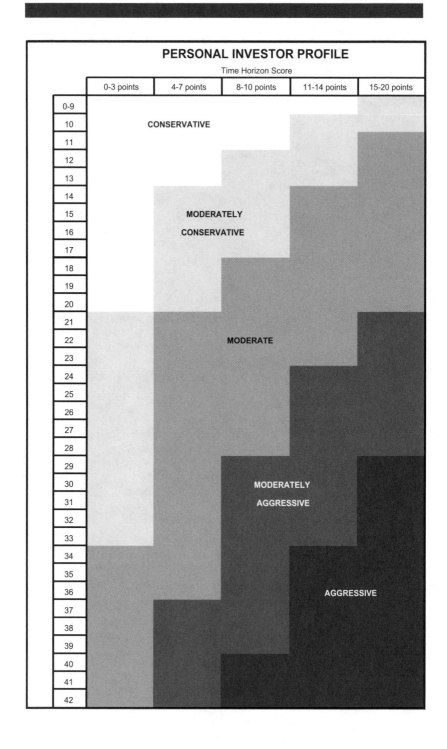

Asset Allocation Pie Charts

Aggressive Portfolio

5% in U.S. Bonds or Mutual Funds

95% in Stocks or Mutual Funds

- 40% in large-company stocks or mutual funds
- 30% in small-company stocks or mutual funds
- 25% in international stocks or mutual funds

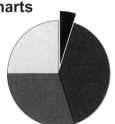

Moderately Aggressive Portfolio

5% in Cash or Cash Equivalents

15% in U.S. Bonds or Mutual Funds

80% in Stocks or Mutual Funds

- 35% in large-company stocks or mutual funds
- 25% in small-company stocks or mutual funds
- 20% in international stocks or mutual funds

Moderate Portfolio

10% in Cash or Cash Equivalents

30% in U.S. Bonds or Mutual Funds

60% in Stocks or Mutual Funds

- 30% in large-company stocks or mutual funds
- 15% in small-company stocks or mutual funds
- 15% in international stocks or mutual funds

Moderately Conservative Portfolio

15% in Cash or Cash Equivalents

40% in U.S. Bonds or Mutual Funds

45% in Stocks or Mutual Funds

- 25% in large-company stocks or mutual funds
- 10% in small-company stocks or mutual funds
- 10% in international stocks or mutual funds

Conservative Portfolio

25% in Cash or Cash Equivalents

50% in U.S. Bonds or Mutual Funds

25% in Stocks or Mutual Funds

- 15% in large-company stocks or mutual funds
- 5% in small-company stocks or mutual funds
- 5% in international stocks or mutual funds

[1] Stephan R. Leimberg et al., *The Tools and Techniques Of Financial Planning*, 6th ed. (Cincinnati: The National Underwriter Company, 2002), p. 36.

[2] Sid Mittra and Jeffrey H. Rattiner, *Practicing Financial Planning* (Rochester Hills, Michigan: Mittra & Associates, 1998), p. 13-6.

[3] G. Victor Hallman and Jerry S. Rosenbloom, *Personal Financial Planning*, 6th ed. (New York: McGraw-Hill, 2000), p. 255.

[4] Source of chart data is author calculations based upon S&P 500 index (daily opening and closing data) provided by economagic.com.

[5] For example, see Harry M. Markowitz, *Portfolio Selection*, 2nd ed. (Malden, Massachusetts: Blackwell Publishers, 2002); Gary Brinson, Randolph Hood and Gilbert Beebower, "Determinants of Portfolio Performance," Gary Brinson, Randolph Hood, and Gilbert Beebower, *Financial Analysis Journal* (July/August, 1986) and *Financial Analysis Journal* (May/Jun, 1991).

[6] William J. Ruckstuhl, "Investments and Investment Planning," *Fundamentals Of Financial Planning*, 4th ed. (Bryn Mawr, Pennsylvania: The American College, 1999), p. 533.

[7] For an expanded discussion of the correlation/covariance concept, see Stephan R. Leimberg et al., p. 27.

[8] A good example of an expanded correlation matrix can be found at Stephan R. Leimberg et al., pp. 50-51.

[9] Interest rates are hypothetical.

[10] This description was obtained from www.corda.com. Used with permission.

[11] Ibid.

[12] Parts of this description were obtained from www.stockcharts.com. Used with permission.

[13] For an excellent survey of the many and varied indicators used in sentiment analysis, see George A. Fontanills and Tom Gentile, *The Stock Market Course,* (New York: John Wiley & Sons, 2001), p. 290.

[14] CBOE stands for Chicago Board Options Exchange.

THE FEDERAL RESERVE SYSTEM

The Federal Reserve System is made up of twelve regional Reserve Banks together with the Board of Governors in Washington, D.C. The "Fed," as the system is commonly called, is an independent governmental entity created by Congress in 1913 to serve as the central bank of the United States. The Fed's primary role is to foster a sound monetary and financial system and a healthy economy. To advance this goal, the Fed helps formulate monetary policy; supervises banks and financial holding companies; helps maintain the stability of the financial system; and provides financial services to banks and other depository institutions and the federal government. In addition, it has important roles in operating the nation's payments systems and protecting consumers' rights in their dealings with banks.

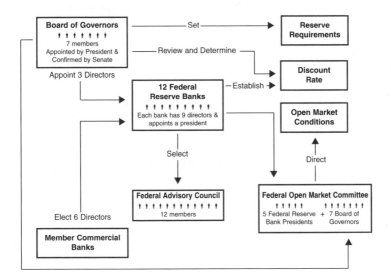

Federal Reserve Board of Governors. The chairman and the six other members of the Board of Governors are appointed by the President of the United States, confirmed by the Senate, and serve staggered 14-year terms. The Board has regulatory and supervisory responsibilities over member banks and other banking organizations that are subject to its jurisdiction; plays a key role in assuring the functioning and development of the nation's payments system; and issues a variety of banking and consumer-credit regulations (e.g., development and administration of regulations implementing the Truth in Lending Act and the Equal Credit Opportunity Act).

The Board approves the *discount rate* (the interest rate at which Federal Reserve Banks extend short-term loans to depository institutions) that is recommended by the board of directors of each of the twelve Federal Reserve Banks. Its power to *set margin requirements*, which limit the use of credit for purchasing or carrying securities, provides the Board with a limited role in regulating operations of the stock market. The Board can control the money supply by changing the *required reserve ratio*, which is the percentage of deposits that banks must maintain on reserve at the Federal Reserve banks. Reserve requirements currently are assessed on the depository institution's net transaction accounts (mostly checking accounts). (In 2003, the reserve requirement for *transaction deposits* is 3% on amounts over $6.0 million and 10% on amounts in excess of $42.1 million. There are no reserves required for *time deposits*.) Raising the reserve ratio requires banks to place more money in reserve thereby reducing the funds available and raising interest rates. However, the Open Market Committee's open-market operation is considered more flexible, and therefore is used more frequently as an instrument of monetary policy. The Board has a majority (7 out of 12) of the votes on the Federal Open Market Committee (FOMC) and plays a key role in the decisions of this committee.

Federal Open Market Committee (FOMC). The Open Market Committee is the most important monetary policymaking body of the Federal Reserve System. It determines the nation's monetary policy with the objective of promoting economic growth, full employment, stable prices, and a sustainable pattern of international trade and payments. It also makes key decisions regarding the conduct of open market operations (i.e., the purchase and sale of U.S. government and federal agency securities) which affect the provision of reserves to depository institutions and, in turn, the cost and availability of money and credit. The twelve members of the Open Market Committee consist of the seven members of the Board of Governors, the president of the Federal Reserve Bank of New York (the monetary policy of the Open Market Committee is implemented by the New York Fed), and four other Reserve Bank presidents, each of whom serve one-year terms as voting members on a rotating basis. The Chairman of the Board of Governors also serves as Chairman of the Open Market Committee. The Open Market Committee holds regularly scheduled meetings every six weeks.

If the Open Market Committee determines that the supply of money is critical in keeping the economy either expanding or contracting, it will direct the New York Fed to purchase U.S. government securities from banks and brokerage houses, thereby injecting cash into the financial system and expanding the monetary supply. This in turn enables the banks and brokerage houses to lend the money to clients. More money in the economy means money will be less expensive, interest rates will fall, and businesses will borrow the money and use it to create new jobs, goods, and services. Conversely, if the money supply grows too rapidly and inflation becomes a problem, the Open Market Committee will direct that federal securities be sold on the open market. These sales reduce bank reserves and therefore the ability of the banking system to create deposits. This tends to drive up the costs of money, businesses put off borrowing, and the economy cools down. At least, this is the theory. But there can be no doubt that the actions of the Fed have a very direct effect on the stock markets, and much attention is paid to any changes in money policy, particular impending changes in interest rates.

Federal Reserve Banks. Each of the twelve Federal Reserve Banks is headed by a president appointed by the bank's nine-member board of directors. Three of the board of directors represent the commercial banks in the bank's region that are members of the Federal Reserve System. The other six directors are selected to represent the public with due consideration to the interest of agriculture, commerce, industry, services, labor, and consumers. Three of these six directors are elected by member banks and the other three are chosen by the Board of Governors. Each Federal Reserve Bank supervises and regulates both bank holding companies and state chartered banks that are members of the Federal Reserve System; provides services to depository institutions; and functions as a fiscal agent of the U.S. government.

Federal Advisory Council. The Federal Advisory Council, composed of a representative from each of the twelve Federal Reserve Districts, confers periodically with the Board of Governors of the Federal Reserve System on business conditions and issues related to the banking industry. It also makes recommendations regarding system policies. Representatives are selected annually by the board of directors of each reserve bank.

Federal Funds Rate. When banks have more funds then needed to meet their reserve requirements they can make overnight deposits of these funds in a Federal Reserve Bank. Other banks can then borrow these funds in order to meet their own short-term reserve requirements. The rate charged between banks on this overnight borrowing is known as

Keeping Current

The federal funds rate is given daily under the **Money Rates** table of *The Wall Street Journal.*

the federal funds rate. This practice has benefits for the both the lending bank, which earns interest on otherwise idle funds, and the borrowing bank, which is able to increase its reserves in order to make more loans. A rise in the federal funds rate typically signals a withdrawal of reserves through the Fed's open market operations that will cause interest rates to increase (see page 50). In contrast, a lowering of the federal funds rate signals an easing of the Feds monetary policy and a lowering of interest rates. Investors closely watch the federal funds rate as an indicator of Federal Reserve monetary policy and movements in the rate can have a strong effect on stock prices. However, these rates tend to experience sharp daily fluctuations that can compromise their significance. (The daily movements are smoothed out in the Bonds & Interest chart found in the Markets Diary section of *The Wall Street Journal*.)

The Money Supply. The term money supply refers to the amount of money freely circulating in the economy that is available for individuals to spend. Control of the money supply by the Federal Reserve Bank is accomplished in one of three ways: buying and selling government securities; increasing or decreasing the required reserve ratios that banks must maintain with a Federal Reserve bank; and raising or lowering the discount rate (i.e., the interest rate banks pay on money borrowed from the Federal Reserve). See discussion of the discount rate on page 53. The following designations, also called money aggregates, are used to keep track of the money supply according to the degree of liquidity, with M1 being the most liquid:

> ### Keeping Current
>
> The latest M1, M2, and M3 figures can be obtained at: www.federalreserve.gov/ releases/h6/hist/h6hist1.txt.

M1 includes cash, traveler's checks, NOW accounts, and other demand deposit or checking accounts from which money can be withdrawn on demand (i.e., it is money that can be spent immediately). M1 is sometimes referred to as "narrow money."

M2 includes M1 *plus* savings and time deposits of $100,000 and under such as CDs, money market accounts, and money market mutual funds (i.e., assets that are invested for the short term). M2 is sometimes referred to as "broad money." For many years the M2 monetary aggregate maintained a stable, predictable relationship with output and inflation, allowing it to serve as a primary indicator of monetary policy. Although this relationship appeared to break down during the early 1990s, caused in part by a blurring of the distinctions between M1 and M2, M2 may have begun to regain its value as a policy indicator. It remains one of the ten components of the *leading economic indicators*, an index that is regarded as a barometer of economic activity.

M3 includes M2 *plus* savings deposits of more than $100,000, institutional money-market funds, and agreements among banks (i.e., big deposits). M3 is sometimes referred to as "broadest money."

L includes M3 *plus* commercial paper and private holdings of government securities, such as savings bonds and treasury notes. Economists do not agree on the actual effects changes in the money supply have on the economy. Keynesians maintain that increases in the money supply will lead to increased employment and output, whereas monetarists maintain that an increase in the money supply only results in price increases and inflation, without an increase in output.

Discount Rate. This is the rate charged by the twelve Federal Reserve banks for short-term loans made to member banks. Typically this acts as a benchmark for the rate used for consumer borrowing from banks. The stock market views a rise in the discount rate as bearish since rising interest rates tend to indicate a fall in stock prices. Conversely, a fall in interest rates is viewed as bullish, but this view appears to have gotten quite clouded by the 2001-2002 markets.

> **Keeping Current**
>
> Both the discount rate and the prime rate are given daily under the **Money Rates** table of *The Wall Street Journal*.

Prime Rate. This is the rate that large commercial banks charge their best corporate customers. Again, a rising prime rate is considered bearish, whereas a falling prime rate is considered bullish.

OTHER REGULATORS & AGENCIES

Federal Deposit Insurance Corporation (FDIC). The FDIC *insures* bank depositors against loss if a bank experiences financial difficulties. The insurance provided extends to deposits of up to $100,000 in virtually all United States banks and savings associations (also called savings and loan associations or S&Ls). It does not *regulate* banks, that is the job of the Federal Reserve and state agencies. The FDIC also is the primary federal regulator of about 6,000 state-chartered "nonmember" banks (commercial and savings banks that are not members of the Federal Reserve System).

www.fdic.gov

Securities Investor Protection Corporation (SIPC). When a brokerage firm is closed due to bankruptcy or other financial difficulties, the SIPC, *within limits*, steps in and works to return an investor's cash, stock and other securities. However, insurance for investment fraud does not exist in the U.S. The risk-based investment marketplace is quite different from the world of banking and it is important to understand that in the world of securities the SIPC is not the equivalent of the Federal Deposit Insurance Corporation (FDIC). Protection only extends to customers of SIPC members and, even then, it is not the purpose of the SIPC to compensate all victims in the event of loss due to investment fraud. That said, the SPIC's track record is quite impressive, with no fewer than 99% of eligible investors getting their investments back through the efforts of the SIPC.

www.sipc.org

Securities And Exchange Commissions (SEC). The SEC is the primary overseer and regulator of the U.S. securities markets. Critical to its mission is to protect investors and maintain the integrity of the securities markets by assuring a steady flow of timely, comprehensive and accurate information. So that people can make sound investment decisions the SEC requires public companies to disclose meaningful financial and other information to the public. The SEC also oversees other key participants in the securities world, including stock exchanges, broker-dealers, investment advisors, mutual funds, and public utility holding companies. In exercising its enforcement authority, the SEC brings civil enforcement actions against individuals and companies that break the securities laws. Typical infractions include insider trading, accounting fraud, and providing false or misleading information about securities and the companies that issue them.

www.sec.gov

National Association Of Securities Dealers (NASD). Overseeing the activities of over 5,500 member securities firms, together with over one half million registered securities professionals, makes the NASD the largest securities-industry self-regulatory organization in the world. Together with its subsidiaries it develops rules and regulations, conducts regulatory reviews of members' business activities, disciplines violators, provides arbitration and mediation services, and regulates securities markets for the benefit and protection of the investing public.

www.nasd.com

FINANCIAL INSTITUTIONS & MARKETS

Commercial Banks. Of all deposit-type financial institutions commercial banks are the largest and most visible. They offer a full range of financial products and services, including checking accounts, savings accounts, credit cards, consumer and business loans, trust services, safe deposit boxes, traveler's checks, ATM services, check cashing privileges, overdraft protection, savings accounts with check writing privileges, foreign exchange services, and financial counseling. Until the mid-1970s, the full-service nature of commercial banks afforded them a substantial competitive edge over other financial institutions. (Interestingly, the term "Full Service Bank" is a registered trademark of the American Bankers Association.) However, the deregulation of the financial market in the 1980s has in many ways blurred the differences between commercial banks and other deposit-type institutions. In 1999, the playing field was further leveled by legislative changes that enabled commercial banks to act as broker/dealers, meaning they can now sell securities, mutual funds, and variable annuities. Deposits up to $100,000 are federally insured through the Federal Deposit Insurance Corporation (FDIC). See page 53.

Credit Unions. Credit unions are essentially cooperatives providing financial products and services to a group of individuals who share the same employer or some other common interest or characteristic. Only members may save at or borrow from a credit union. They offer many different forms of savings accounts, including interest paying checking accounts, called share draft accounts. As mutual associations, they pay dividends, rather than interest, on savings accounts. Because they are nonprofit, the savings rates tend to be somewhat higher than those offered by commercial banks. Likewise, their loans rates tend to be lower. A variety of loans are typically offered, including auto loans, home equity loans, secured and unsecured loans, and both single payment and installment loans. Deposits up to $100,000 are insured by the National Credit Union Share Insurance Fund (NCUSIF), which is administered by the National Credit Union Administration and backed by the "full faith and credit" of _____ *www.ncua.gov* the U.S. Government.

Savings And Loan Associations (S&Ls). Second only to commercial banks in the size of their savings deposits and assets, savings and loan associations are organized as either mutual associations owned by their depositors, or as corporations owned by their stockholders. Since deregulation, except for demand deposits (i.e., checking accounts), they tend to offer the same products and services as commercial banks. However, their savings accounts generally pay somewhat higher rates than those available at commercial banks. Most savings and loan associations are federally insured through the Federal Deposit Insurance Corporation (FDIC) for deposits up to $100,000. (In 1989 the Federal Savings and Loan Insurance Corporation (FSLIC) was abolished and its functions were transferred to the FDIC.) In New England, S&Ls are often known as cooperative banks.

Mutual Savings Banks. Mutual savings banks are found primarily on the east coast. They are mutual associations owned by their depositors, and are very similar to savings and loan associations. The deposits in most mutual savings banks are federally insured through the Federal Deposit Insurance Corporation (FDIC).

Brokerage Services. Both "full-service brokers" and "discount brokers" offer these services. Discount brokers generally execute trades for substantially less than the amount charged by full-service brokers. However, the full-service broker often provides clients with a wide variety of services such as research reports, newsletters, advice on security selection, and financial planning. Both full-service and discount brokers now offer extensive online services.

NASDAQ. This is the acronym for the National Association of Securities Dealers Automatic Quotation System. It is a computerized system linking brokers and dealers in providing price quotations for both over-the-counter and some New York Stock Exchange listed securities. Traditionally the home of emerging companies, telecommunications, and high-tech stocks, securities traded on the NASDAQ must meet specific listing criteria regarding both market capitalization and trading activity. The NASDAQ is considered a very active and highly volatile market. In the United States it is owned *www.nasdaq.com* and operated by the NASD.

Over-The-Counter Market. Also referred to as the OTC market, this is a decentralized market comprised of geographically dispersed dealers who are linked via electronic communications and telephones. Securities are bought and sold by dealers, who in turn sell them to and buy them from investors. In contrast to the organized exchanges where prices are set by *auction*, the OTC market sets prices by *negotiation*. Securities purchased OTC are often referred to as **OTC instruments**, whereas securities purchased on organized exchanges are referred to as **exchange-traded contracts**. In addition to bonds and other fixed income securities, derivatives and small capitalization stocks are traded OTC.

Digging Deeper

To learn more about the over-the-counter market go to: www.pinksheets.com.

Exchanges. This is the place where securities, commodities, options, and futures are traded, generally using an auction or open outcry system. The principal United States exchanges are the New York Stock Exchange (NYSE), the American Stock Exchange (AMEX), and the National Association of Securities Dealers Automatic Quotation System (NASDAQ). The NYSE is often *www.amex.com* referred to as "The Exchange," or the *www.nyse.com* "Big Board."

ECONOMIC INDICATORS

As the economic cycle goes through alternating waves of expansion and contraction, it experiences five phases; peak, trough, recovery, expansion, and new peak. Economic indicators provide a means of measuring this cycle based upon the direction of current and future economic activity. As such, they are considered very important gauges of the economy and where it is headed. Being able to identify and quantify the future direction of economic activity is important to the individual investor, as well as

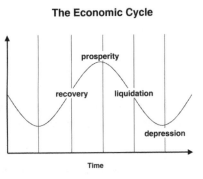

The Economic Cycle

the business community. In 1995, The Conference Board, an independent research organization, assumed from the U.S. Department of Commerce the responsibility for computing the composite indexes. The Conference Board's leading, coincident, and lagging indexes are essentially composite averages of between four and ten individual indicators. Together they are often referred to as the three "composite indexes."

Leading Index. Of all indexes the U.S. Leading Index is the most widely watched business cycle indicator. It is also described as the "composite index of leading economic indicators" and "the Conference Board's index of leading economic indicators." However, use of the term "leading" is not intended to describe the importance of this indicator, but rather to describe its usefulness as a *predictor* of future economic activity (i.e., leading versus trailing). A rising index signals that in the near future eco-

> ### Keeping Current
>
> The latest leading index can be found at: www.conference-board.org.

nomic activity can generally be expected to increase, whereas a falling index signals that economic activity can be expected to decrease. As a *composite* index, it is expected that the volatility of the individual components will be smoothed out, thereby revealing more clearly and more accurately the patterns of cyclical turning points in the business cycle. This index includes the following ten components:

(1) Average weekly hours, manufacturing.
(2) Average weekly initial claims for unemployment insurance.
(3) Manufacturers' new orders, consumer goods and materials.
(4) Vendor performance, slower deliveries diffusion index.

(5) Manufacturers' new orders, nondefense capital goods.
(6) Building permits, new private housing units.
(7) Common stock prices (S&P 500).
(8) Money supply (M2). See page 52.
(9) Interest rate spread, 10-year Treasury bonds less federal funds.
(10) Index of consumer expectations (University of Michigan).

Coincident Index. In contrast to the leading index, the cyclical turning points in the coincident index generally occur at about *the same time* as those reflecting total economic activity. It is also described as the "Conference Board's coincident index." This index includes the following four components:

(1) Employees on nonagricultural payrolls.
(2) Personal income less transfer payments.
(3) Industrial production.
(4) Manufacturing and trade sales.

Lagging Index. The cyclical turning points in the lagging index generally occur *after* those reflecting total economic activity. Thus, the indicator is expected to reach a peak after the economic has peaked and to hit bottom after the economy has bottomed out. It is also described as the "Conference Board's lagging index." This index includes the following seven components:

(1) Average duration of unemployment.
(2) Inventories to sales ratio, manufacturing and trade.
(3) Labor cost per unit of output, manufacturing.
(4) Average prime rate.
(5) Commercial and industrial loans.
(6) Consumer installment credit to personal income ratio.
(7) Consumer price index for services.

Consumer Price Index. The CPI represents changes in prices of all goods and services purchased for consumption by urban households. User fees (such as water and sewer service) and sales and excise taxes paid by the consumer are also included, but income taxes and investment items (like stocks, bonds, and life insurance) are not included. Prices for the goods and services that are used to calculate the CPI are collected in 87 urban areas throughout the United States and from about 23,000 retail and service establishments (see table on page 402). The CPI is used for a variety of purposes, to include:

Keeping Current

The latest CPI figure can be found at: http://stats.bls.gov.

(1) As an economic indicator. As the most widely used measure of inflation, the CPI is an indicator of the effectiveness of government policy. In addition, business executives, labor leaders and other private citizens use the index as a guide in making economic decisions.

(2) As a deflator of other economic series. The CPI and its components are used to adjust other economic series for price changes and to translate these series into inflation-free dollars.

(3) As a means for adjusting income payments. Workers are frequently covered by collective bargaining agreements tied to the CPI. The index also affects the income of 47.8 million Social Security beneficiaries, 4.1 million military and federal civil service retirees and survivors, and 22.4 million food stamp recipients. Some private firms and individuals use the CPI to keep rents, royalties, alimony payments, and child support payments in line with changing prices. The CPI is also used to adjust the federal income tax structure to prevent inflation-induced increases in taxes.

Consumer Confidence Index. The Consumer Confidence Index is a monthly measure of the public's confidence in the health of the United States economy. Also described as the "Conference Board's Index of Consumer Confidence" and the "Consumer Confidence Survey," it measures how 5,000 United States households feel about the *current* state of the econo-

> ### Keeping Current
>
> The latest consumer confidence index figure can be found at: www.conference-board.org.

my, as well as their *expectations* for the economy over the next six months. Questions are asked relating to both employment and income. If consumer attitudes and sentiment are high, then it is expected that their continued spending and borrowing will contribute to a healthy economy. The University of Michigan Institute conducts a similar survey monthly for Social Research (this survey includes consumer expectations regarding household income and willingness to purchase homes and vehicles).

Gross Domestic Product (GDP). The GDP represents the total value of all goods and services produced by labor and property located in the United States. It is released quarterly by the U.S. Department of Commerce. In order to more accurately compare the levels of output over different periods of time it is

> ### Keeping Current
>
> The latest estimates of the GDP can be found at: www.bea.doc.gov.

adjusted for inflation. The adjusted figure is referred to as the *real* gross domestic product or *constant-dollar* gross domestic product. Note that there is a difference between the Gross Domestic Product (GDP) and the Gross National Product (GNP). GDP measures output and earnings *within* the United States without regard to the earner's nationality, whereas GNP is a measurement of output and earnings of American citizens, no matter where they live and work.

Industrial Production. Also referred to as "Factory Output", this is an index designed to measure changes in the level of output in the industrial sector of the economy. The index is grouped by both products (consumer goods, business equipment, intermediate goods, and materials) and industry (manufacturing, mining, and utilities). The Board of

Keeping Current

The latest industrial production figures can be found at: www.federalreserve.gov/releases/G17/Current/default.htm.

Governors of the Federal Reserve System releases it monthly. While the industrial sector of the economy represents only about 20% of GDP, because changes in GDP are heavily concentrated in the industrial sector, changes in this index provide useful information on the current growth of GDP. The level of capacity utilization in the industrial sector provides information on the overall level of resource utilization in the economy that may, in turn, provide information on the likely future course of inflation.

Business Inventories. This monthly report by the U.S. Department of Commerce, Bureau of the Census, gives the total current-dollar sales and inventories for the manufacturing, wholesale, and retail sectors of the economy. This release is the primary source of data on inventories. The rate of inventory accumulation plays a key role in determining

Keeping Current

The latest business inventory figures can be found at: www.census.gov/mtis/www/current.html.

the current pace of economic growth and often provides useful clues about the future pace of growth as well. For example, if inventories are accumulating at a rapid pace, such that inventory sales ratios are rising, it may portend a slowing of growth in the near future as firms cut production to bring inventories back into line with sales. Vice versa, if inventories are growing slowly or actually falling, it may signal a future pickup in production.

Keeping Current

The latest retail sales figures can be found at: www.census.gov/mtis/www/current.html.

Retail Sales. This is a report of the results of a survey of about 12,000 retail businesses throughout the country and is released monthly by the U.S. Department of Commerce. One of the most closely watched economic indicators, the data is widely used throughout government, academic, and business communities. For example, the Bureau of Labor Statistics uses the estimates to develop consumer price indexes and productivity measurements, the Federal Reserve Board uses the estimates to assess recent trends in consumer purchases, the media use the estimates to report news of recent consumer activity, and financial and investment companies use the estimates to measure recent economic trends.

Other Economic Indicators. Government agencies, the Conference Board, and other organizations regularly report many other indicators. For example, there are indexes dealing with construction spending, housing starts, sales of new and existing homes, capacity utilization, personal income, and factory orders.

Digging Deeper

An excellent source of free and comprehensive data can be found at: www.economagic.com.

STOCK MARKET INDEXES

Indexes contain a group of stocks from within a particular financial market, from within a number of related markets, or from the economy as a whole. Indexes that measure major or senior averages are board-based and designed to reflect the movements of an entire market. Other indexes are intended to track the performance of companies based upon their market capitalization. Still other indexes are tailored to represent a particular group of companies in the same economic sector or industry (e.g., transportation or utilities). Indexes that are weighted place more significance on some elements than on other elements (e.g., market capitalization versus stock price). Price changes, sales volume, and volatility are reported and tracked over different periods of time (e.g., hourly, daily, weekly, or yearly). Each stock index is different.

Dow Jones Industrial Average (DJIA). Of all the stock indexes, "the Dow" is clearly the oldest, best-known, and most widely followed market index in the world. It is a price-weighted average of 30 very large and significant stocks traded on the New York Stock Exchange and the NASDAQ.[1] The component stocks of the Dow Industrials changes periodically. The editors of *The Wall Street Journal* select companies that comprise the three Dow Jones Averages and it is

Keeping Current

The Dow averages for Industrials, Transportation, Utilities, and Composite are published daily under **Markets Lineup** in *The Wall Street Journal*.

solely at their discretion that companies are either added or deleted. While there are no rules for component selection, a stock typically is added only if it has an excellent reputation, demonstrates sustained growth, is of interest to a large number of investors and accurately represents the sector(s) covered by the average. The Dow Jones averages are unique in that they are price weighted rather than market capitalization weighted. Their component weightings are therefore affected only by changes in the stocks' prices, in contrast with other indexes' weightings that are affected by both price changes and changes in the number of shares outstanding. Each stock in the Dow Jones Industrial Average represents 1/30th of the overall average. In order to better compare the stock index values across time, the Dow is calculated by totalling the prices of the 30 individual stocks and then dividing the total by a divisor that adjusts for stock splits, spin offs, and other changes (as of March 19, 2003, the "divisor" stood at 0.14279922). The advantages of the Dow are seen as its longevity and stability of its companies. However, with its narrow focus on only 30 companies it does not serve all *www.fdjindexes.com/jsp/index.jsp* that well as a benchmark for the market as a whole.

Dow Jones Transportation Average. This index is comprised of 20 airlines, railroads, and trucking companies.[2] Each stock in the Dow Jones Transportation Average represents 1/20th of the overall average.

Dow Jones Utilities Average. This index is comprised of 15 gas, electric, and power companies.[3] Each stock in the Dow Jones Utilities Average represents 1/15th of the overall average.

Dow Jones Composite Average. This is a composition of all of the companies in the Industrial, Transportation, and Utilities averages.

Dow Jones Global-US. Also referred to as the "Dow Total Market Index," this index is comprised of 1,575 (as of March 19, 2003) United States companies representing more than 100 industries that are traded on the New York Stock Exchange, the American Stock Exchange, and the NASDAQ Stock Market (it is intended to represent 95% of the U.S. market capitalization). The index is capitalization weighted, meaning that a stock's effect on the index is in proportion to its current price multiplied by the total of shares outstanding.

Standard & Poors 500 (S&P 500). In contrast to the Dow's 30 companies, the 500 large-cap companies in the S&P 500 provide great diversification. As a leading benchmark of the United States

> **Keeping Current**
>
> The Standard & Poor's Indexes are published daily under **Markets Lineup** in *The Wall Street Journal.*

stock markets, it is frequently used as a measure of a mutual fund's performance (e.g., "the XYZ fund has outperformed the S&P 500 in three of the last four years"). The S&P 500 attempts to cover all major areas of the United States economy and contains widely held companies that are chosen for their market size, liquidity, and industry representation (industrial, transportation, utility, and financial sectors are all represented). As a market-value weighted index, each stock's weight in the overall index is proportionate to its market value (i.e., market value equals price times outstanding shares). However, this results in the top 45 companies representing more than 50% of the index's value. Many mutual funds are offered that reflect the S&P 500. Other S&P indexes include:

www.spglobal.com

(1) **S&P Mid-Cap 400 Index.** This index consists of 400 domestic stocks chosen for market size, liquidity, and industry group representation. It is also a market-value weighted index and was the first benchmark of mid-cap stock price movement.

(2) **S&P Small-Cap 600 Index.** This index consists of 600 domestic stocks chosen for market size, liquidity, (bid-asked spread, ownership, share turnover and number of no trade days) and industry group representation. It is a market-value weighted index, with each stock's weight in the index proportionate to its market value.

(3) **S&P 500 Barra Value Index.** This is a value subset of the S&P 500 Index. The index is constructed by dividing the stocks in the S&P 500 index according to a single attribute: book-to-price ratio (i.e., book value divided by the market capitalization). Each company in the index is then assigned to either the value or growth index so that the two style indexes "add up" to the full index. The value index contains companies with the higher book-to-price ratios. It is felt that the book-to-price ratio has the advantage of being simple and easy to understand, is mutually exclusive, and captures one of the fundamental differences between companies generally classified as value companies or growth companies. As with the full S&P indexes, the value and growth indexes are capitalization-weighted, meaning that each stock is weighted in proportion to its market value.

(4) **S&P 500 Barra Growth Index.** This is a growth subset of the S&P 500 Index. In contrast to the S&P 500 Barra Value Index, the growth index contains companies with lower book-to-price ratios.

NASDAQ Composite Index. This index contains over 4,000 large-cap, mid-cap, and small-cap stocks that are traded on the NASDAQ Stock Market (acronym for National Association of Securities Dealers' Automatic Quotation system). Although it contains a wide range of financial, consumer, and industrial stocks, it is most heavily weighted in tech-

> **Keeping Current**
>
> The NASDAQ Indexes are published daily under **Markets Lineup** in The *Wall Street Journal.*

nology and Internet stocks that tend to heavily influence the index. It is market value weighted, with each company weighting being proportionate to its market value. Because these companies are generally more speculative and risky, the NASDAQ Composite Index is much more volatile than other indices. However, the high growth potential of the NASDAQ listed companies make it one of the most widely followed indexes.

www.nasdaq.com

NASDAQ-100 Index. The NASDAQ-100 Index includes 100 of the largest domestic and international non-financial companies listed on the NASDAQ Stock Market based on market capitalization. The index reflects companies across major industry groups including computer hardware and software, telecommunications, retail/wholesale trade, and biotechnology. It does not contain financial companies, including investment companies. The NASDAQ-100 Index is calculated under a modified capitalization-weighted methodology.

Wilshire 5000 Index. Also known as the Wilshire Total Market Index, this index contains nearly 6,000 stocks that trade in the United States. It includes all New York Stock Exchange and American Stock Exchange stocks, plus the most actively traded stocks on the NASDAQ. The index is capitalization weighted, meaning that a stock's effect on the index is in proportion to its current price mul-

> **Keeping Current**
>
> The Wilshire 5000 Index is published daily under **Markets Lineup** in *The Wall Street Journal.*

tiplied by the total of shares outstanding. Although it is the broadest and most diversified index in the world, it only contains companies that are headquartered in the United States. Because it is capitalization weighted it suffers from the same "top heavy" effect as the S&P 500.

www.wilshire.com

Russell 3000 Index. The Russell 3000 Index measures the performance of the 3,000 largest United States companies based on total market capitalization, which represents approximately 98% of the investable U.S. equity market.

www.russell.com

Russell 2000 Index. The Russell 2000 is a small-cap index that consists of the *smallest* 2,000 companies in the Russell 3000 Index, representing approximately 8% of the total market capitalization of the Russell 3000. It is often used as a performance measure of small-cap stocks. It measures the performance of smaller stocks from various industries that are typically left out of the larger indices. Excluded are stocks under $1 and those listed on the pink sheets (see Over-The-Counter, page 56). Although it is a well diversified index for smaller companies that have high growth potential, the performance of the Russell 2000 Index tends to be very uneven.

> **Keeping Current**
>
> The Russell 2000 Index is published daily under **Markets Lineup** in *The Wall Street Journal.*

Russell 1000 Index. The Russell 1000 is a large-cap index that consists of the *largest* 1,000 companies in the Russell 3000 Index, representing approximately 92% of the total market capitalization of the Russell 3000. It is often used as a performance measure of large-cap stocks.

Value Line Composite Index (VLG). Contains approximately 1,700 stocks that are traded on the New York Stock Exchange, the American Stock Exchange, and the NASDAQ Stock Market. This index assumes equally weighted positions in every stock covered in The Value Line Investment Survey; that is, it is presupposed that an equal amount of dollars is invested in each and every stock. The VLG is averaged geometrically every day across all the stocks in the index, and consequently, is frequently referred to as the Value Line Geometric Index. It is intended to provide a rough approximation of how the median stock in the Value Line Universe performed.

> **Keeping Current**
>
> The Value Line Composite Index is published daily under **Markets Lineup** in *The Wall Street Journal.*

www.valueline.com

Keeping Current

The Amex Composite Index is published daily under **Markets Lineup** in *The Wall Street Journal.*

Amex Composite Index. The Amex Composite Index is a market capitalization-weighted index of the stocks listed on the American Stock Exchange. Components of the index include the common stocks or American Depositary Receipts of all Amex-listed companies, REITs, master limited partner-

www.amex.com

ships, and closed end investment vehicles.

Morgan Stanley Capital International (MSCI). MSCI publishes a family of international equity and fixed income indexes and calculates daily more than 11,000 standard "end-of-day" indexes. Covered are 51 national stock markets, plus regional, sector, industry group, and industry aggregations. Over 90% of international institutional equity assets in the United States are benchmarked to MSCI indexes.

www.msci.com/equity

---

[1] The 30 stocks of the Dow Jones Industrial Average are (as of April 2003):

Company	Stock Symbol
3M Co.	MMM
Alcoa Inc.	AA
Altria Group Inc.	MO
American Express Co.	AXP
AT&T Corp.	T
Boeing Co.	BA
Caterpillar Inc.	CAT
Citigroup Inc.	C
Coca-Cola Co.	KO
E.I. Du Pont de Nemours & Co.	DD
Eastman Kodak Co.	EK
Exxon Mobil Corp.	XOM
General Electric Co.	GE
General Motors Corp.	GM
Hewlett-Packard Co.	HPQ
Home Depot Inc	HD
Honeywell International Inc.	HON
Intel Corp.	INTC
International Business Machines Corp.	IBM
International Paper Co.	IP
J. P. Morgan Chase & Co.	JPM
Johnson & Johnson	JNJ
McDonald's Corp.	MCD
Merck & Co. Inc.	MRK
Microsoft Corp.	MSFT
Procter & Gamble Co.	PG
SBC Communications Inc.	SBC

United Technologies Corp.   UTX
Wal-Mart Stores Inc.   WMT
Walt Disney Co.   DIS

[2] The 20 stocks of the Dow Jones Transportation Average are (as of April 2003):

Company	Stock Symbol
Airborne Inc.	ABF
Alexander & Baldwin, Inc.	ALEX
AMR Corp.	AMR
Burlington Northern Santa Fe Corp.	BNI
CNF Inc.	CNF
Continental Airlines Inc. Cl B	CAL
CSX Corp.	CSX
Delta Air Lines Inc.	DAL
FedEx Corp.	FDX
GATX Corp.	GMT
J.B. Hunt Transport Services Inc.	JBHT
Norfolk Southern Corp.	NSC
Northwest Airlines Corp.	NWAC
Roadway Corp.	ROAD
Ryder System Inc.	R
Southwest Airlines Co.	LUV
Union Pacific Corp.	UNP
United Parcel Service Inc. Cl B	UPS
USFreightways Corp.	USFC
Yellow Corp.	YELL

[3] The 15 stocks of the Dow Jones Utility Average are (as of April 2003):

Company	Stock Symbol
AES Corp.	AES
American Electric Power Co. Inc.	AEP
CenterPoint Energy Inc.	CNP
Consolidated Edison Inc.	ED
Dominion Resources Inc. (Virginia)	D
Duke Energy Corp.	DUK
Edison International	EIX
Exelon Corp.	EXC
FirstEnergy Corp.	FE
NiSource Inc.	NI
PG&E Corp.	PCG
Public Service Enterprise Group Inc.	PEG
Southern Co.	SO
TXU Corp.	TXU
Williams Cos.	WMB

THE IMPORTANCE OF TIME VALUE CALCULATIONS

Understanding the time value of money is essential in financial planning. It has often been said that time is money. When we postpone the use of our money by lending or investing it, we expect to be compensated by some form of return on our money. Spending and investing decisions involve tradeoffs. If we defer receiving a payment there is an *opportunity cost*, measured as the highest-valued investment alternative that is given up (i.e., we have lost an opportunity to currently investment or otherwise use the funds). Interest is used to quantify opportunity cost. For example, given the choice of being paid $1.00 today, or $1.50 four years from now you would need to quantify the opportunity cost of not being paid $1.00 today. The minimum opportunity cost is that amount that you could earn by investing the $1.00 in a virtually risk-free 3-month U.S. Treasury bill. Were you to invest in a vehicle that involved any risk of loss you would demand a higher rate of return. The difference between this higher rate or return and the risk-free rate of return is known as a **risk premium**.

Time value of money calculations also help us to make a variety of daily decisions, from how much needs to be saved each month in order to have money for a down payment for a home purchase in 5 years; to deciding which purchase and payment plan is best when buying a new automobile (e.g., zero percent financing for 3 years or taking a $500 discount from purchase price). Interest and annuity calculations are essential in making less frequent, but even more critical, cash flow decisions such as deciding between various payout options offered by a retirement plan (lump sum or annuity payout) or how much can be safely withdrawn from retirement savings.

THE MAGIC OF COMPOUND INTEREST

American history tells us that, in the year 1626 a Mr. Peter Minuit purchased the island of Manhattan from the Indians for approximately $24 worth of trinkets and beads. Based upon the obvious value of Manhattan today, we might conclude that this was a very savvy investment. However, what if Mr. Minuit could have converted his trinkets and beads into $24 and deposited it in a bank account paying 7% compound interest net after taxes? With the magic of compound interest, and more than just a little bit of time, in 2003 the value of this deposit would be $2,870,089,428,515. That is to say, after three hundred and seventy seven years, his twenty-four dollars has grown to two trillion, eight hundred and seventy billion, eighty nine million, four hundred and twenty eight thousand, five hundred and fifteen dollars. It has been said that examples like this will make you want to live forever. Needless to say this is a rather fanciful example of the magic of compounding interest.

Now let's apply the magic of compound interest to the real world. Assume an individual, age 25, receives an inheritance of $10,000 and puts it aside for retirement in an account accruing at 7% compound interest net after taxes. In twenty years the account will grow to $38,597. Although his money has almost quadrupled in just 20 years, it will hardly secure him in his retirement years. Notice the rather flat upwards curve in the diagram; it is the interest being credited to his account.

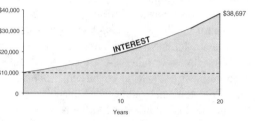

Since this individual does not intend to retire at age 45, he is now able to leave the $38,697 on deposit, and it continues to grow at 7% compound interest. By age 65 he will have $149,745 in his account. During the first 20 years his original $10,000 grew by only $28,697, but during the next 20 years his money grew by an additional $111,048 (149,745 - 38,697 = 111,048). This escalation in the *amount* of growth of the original $10,000 is represented by the increasingly steep curve in the following chart.

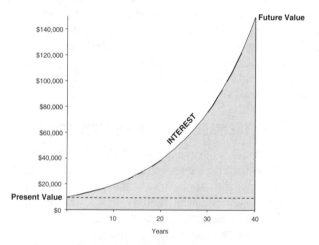

COMPOUNDING VERSUS DISCOUNTING

In the above example **it is compound interest that serves as a link between the present value of money and the future value of money.** As we used interest to determine the *future* value of a present sum of money, in the same way we can use interest to calculate the *present* value of a future sum of money. When we know the present value we can use interest and *compounding* to move up the curve in order to determine future value. On the other hand, when we know the future value, we can use interest and *discounting* to move down the curve to determine present value.

COMPOUND INTEREST & FUTURE VALUE OF MONEY

The future value of money is a very important concept in financial planning. For instance, given the choice of being paid $1.00 today, or $1.00 four years from now, you would obviously choose to be paid $1.00 today (i.e., the earlier the better). Likewise, given the choice of being paid $1.00 today, or $4.00 four years from now, you would probably choose to be paid $4.00 four years from now (i.e., a four-fold increase in only four years). However, given the choice of being paid $1.00 today, or $1.50 four years from now, your decision would likely require a careful consideration of the future value of money.

☑ $1.00 Today   or   ☐ $1.00 In 4 Years

☐ $1.00 Today   or   ☑ $4.00 In 4 Years

☐ $1.00 Today   **?**   ☐ $1.50 In 4 Years

The future value of money can be best understood by referring to the Future Value Table on pages 456-457. If you took the $1.00 today and could invest it at 8%, you would have $1.36 in four years (read down the 8% rate column until year 4). By waiting four years, you could receive $1.50, which is 14 cents more than you would get by taking the money and investing it at 8%. However, if you believed that you could invest your funds at 15%, you would expect to have $1.75 in four years ($1.00 × 1.7490 = $1.75). In this case you would probably take the $1.00 today rather than the $1.50 in four years.

But what if your choice was as follows: being paid $1.00 each year for the next 4 years, or being paid $5.50 4 years from now. The Future Value Table on pages 458-459 will help you make the decision, since it shows the sum to which one dollar per year will grow if placed in accounts at varying rates of interest. If you took the $1.00 each year and were able to invest it at 8%, you would have $4.87 in four years ($1.00 × 4.8666 = $4.87). By waiting four years, you could receive $5.50, which is 63 cents more than you would have by taking the money and investing it at 8%. However, if you believed that you could invest your funds at 15%, you would expect to have $5.74 in four years ($1.00 × 5.7424 = $5.74). In this case you would probably take the $1.00 each year for the next four years.

COMPOUND INTEREST & PRESENT VALUE OF MONEY

Present value concepts are also very important in financial planning. For instance, given the choice of being paid $1.00 three years from now, or $1.00 four years from now, you would obviously choose to be paid $1.00 three years from now (i.e., the earlier the better). Likewise, given the choice of being paid $1.00 three years from now, or $2.00 four years from now, you would probably choose to be paid $2.00 four years from now (i.e., double your money in only one year).

However, given the choice of being paid $1.00 three years from now, or $1.15 four years from now, again your decision would likely require a careful consideration of the present value of money.

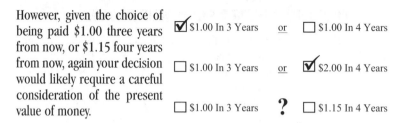

The present value of money can be calculated by referring to the Present Value Table on pages 462-463. If you viewed money as having a time value of 8%, the present value of that $1.00 payment due in *three years* from now is 79 cents ($1.00 × .7938 = $.7938). The present value of a $1.15 payment *four years* from now is 84 cents ($1.15 × .7350 = $.8453). You would accept payment of $1.15 four years from now.

However, if you viewed money as having a time value of 18%, the present value of that $1.00 payment due in *three years* from now is 61 cents ($1.00 × .6086 = $.6086). The present value of a $1.15 payment *four years* from now is only 59 cents ($1.15 × .5158 = $.5932). You would not accept the offer to pay $1.15 four years from now, but would rather demand payment of $1.00 three years from now.

But what if your choice was as follows: being paid $1.25 at the end of each year for the next 3 years, or being paid $1.00 at the end of each year for the next 4 years. The Present Value Table on pages 466-467 will help you make the decision. If you viewed money as having a time value of 8%, the present value of that $1.25 payment at the end of each year for the next *three years* is $3.22 ($1.25 × 2.5771 = $3.2214). The present value of a $1.00 payment each year for *four years* is $3.31 ($1.00 × 3.3121 = $3.3121). You would accept payment of $1.00 per year for the next four years. However, if you viewed money as having a time value of 18%, the present value of that $1.25 payment at the end of each year for the next three years is $2.72 ($1.25 × 2.1743 = $2.7179). The present value of a $1.00 payment each year for four years is $2.69 ($1.00 × 2.6901 = $2.6901). You would not accept payment of $1.00 per year for four years, but would rather demand payment of $1.25 per year for the next three years.

Compounding Periods Can Make A Difference. Simple interest is the payment of interest on the initial principal sum. In contrast, compound interest is the payment of interest on the initial principal sum plus payment of interest on interest accrued in prior periods. As can be seen from the following table, as between simple and compound interest there is a substantial difference in the interest paid. More frequent compounding will result a higher effective interest rate. While the difference is not as dramatic between the various frequencies of compounding, the amount of additional interest becomes more meaningful with higher rates of interest and longer periods of compounding.

Total Interest Paid On $1,000 Deposit
7% Rate Of Interest

	5 Years	10 Years	20 Years
Simple Interest	350.00	700.00	1,400.00
Compounded Annually	402.55	967.15	2,869.68
Compounded Quarterly	414.78	1,001.60	3,006.39
Compounded Monthly	417.63	1,009.66	3,038.74

Rule Of 72. The rule of 72 offers a handy method of determining the approximate number of years it will take an asset to double in value (the *known rate of interest* is divided into 72). Thus, at 8% interest an investment of $10,000 will double in value to $20,000 in 9 years (72 ÷ 8 = 9). At only 6% interest it will take 12 years for the investment to double in value (72 ÷ 6 = 12). Conversely, given the period of an investment the rule of 72 can also be used to determine the interest rate that would have to be obtained in order for the investment to double in value (the *known number of years* is divided into 72). For example, over 9 years an investment of $10,000 will double in value to $20,000 provided in pays 8% interest (72 ÷ 9 = 8). However, over 12 years it will require only 6% interest for the investment to double in value (72 ÷ 12 = 6).

FUTURE VALUE OF A SINGLE SUM

Example 1: Calculate the value after one year of a single deposit of $5,000 made in a savings account yielding 6% interest compounded annually.

Solution using table: $5,000 \times 1.0600 = 5,300$

Formula behind the table:
$$FV_{ss} = PV_{ss} (1 + i)^n$$
$$FV_{ss} = \text{future value of a single sum}$$
$$PV_{ss} = \text{present value of a single sum}$$
$$i = \text{interest rate (annual)}$$
$$n = \text{number of years}$$

Application of formula:
$$FV_{ss} = 5,000 (1 + .06)^1$$
$$= 5,000 (1.06)$$
$$= 5,300$$

Example 2: Calculate the value after three years of a single deposit of $7,500 made in a savings account yielding 8% interest compounded annually.

Solution using table: $7,500 \times 1.2597 = 9,447.75$

Application of formula:
$$FV_{ss} = 7,500 (1 + .08)^3$$
$$= 7,500 ((1.08)(1.08)(1.08))$$
$$= 9,447.84$$

Because the values in the table are rounded off, the answers are slightly different, in this example by nine cents (i.e., $9,447.84 – $9,447.75 = $.09).

FUTURE VALUE TABLE
The Sum To Which One Dollar Principal Will Increase
(complete table is located on pages 456-457)

				Rate				
	3%	4%	5%	6%	7%	8%	9%	10%
Years								
1	1.0300	1.0400	1.0500	1.0600	1.0700	1.0800	1.0900	1.1000
2	1.0609	1.0816	1.1025	1.1236	1.1449	1.1664	1.1881	1.2100
3	1.0927	1.1249	1.1576	1.1910	1.2250	1.2597	1.2950	1.3310
4	1.1255	1.1699	1.2155	1.2625	1.3108	1.3605	1.4116	1.4641
5	1.1593	1.2167	1.2763	1.3382	1.4026	1.4693	1.5386	1.6105

Example 3: Calculate the value after three years of a single deposit of $7,500 made in a savings account yielding 8% interest compounded *semi*annually (i.e., two times each year).

$$\text{Formula:} \quad FV_{ss} = PV_{ss} (1 + i/m)^{mn}$$

FV_{ss} = future value of a single sum

PV_{ss} = present value of a single sum

i = interest rate (annual)

m = number of compounding periods

n = number of years

$$\text{Application of formula:} \quad FV_{ss} = 7,500 (1 + .08/2)^{2 \times 3}$$
$$= 7,500 ((1.04)(1.04)(1.04)(1.04)(1.04)(1.04))$$
$$= 9,489.89$$

Compared to example 2, semiannual compounding has produced an additional $42.05 of savings ($9,489.89 − $9,447.84 = $42.05).

PRESENT VALUE OF A SINGLE SUM

Example: Calculate the amount necessary to deposit in a savings account yielding 5% interest, compounded annually, so that four years from now there will be $10,000 in the account.

Solution using table: $10,000 \times .82270 = 8,227.00$

Formula behind the table: $PV_{SS} = \dfrac{FV_{SS}}{(1 + i)^n}$

PV_{SS} = present value of a single sum

FV_{SS} = future value of a single sum

i = interest rate (annual)

n = number of years

Application of formula: $PV_{SS} = \dfrac{10,000}{(1 + .05)^4}$

$$= \dfrac{10,000}{((1.05)\,(1.05)\,(1.05)\,(1.05))}$$

$$= 8,227.02$$

Because the values in the table are rounded off, the answers are slightly different, in this example by two cents (i.e., $8,227.02 - $8,227.00 = $.02).

PRESENT VALUE TABLE
The Worth Today of One Dollar Due In The Future
(complete table is located on pages 462-463)

	Rate							
	3%	4%	5%	6%	7%	8%	9%	10%
Years								
1	.9709	.9615	.9524	.9434	.9346	.9259	.9174	.9091
2	.9426	.9246	.9070	.8900	.8734	.8573	.8417	.8264
3	.9151	.8890	.8638	.8396	.8163	.7938	.7722	.7513
4	.8885	.8548	.8227	.7921	.7629	.7350	.7084	.6830
5	.8626	.8219	.7835	.7473	.7130	.6806	.6499	.6209

FUTURE VALUE OF AN ORDINARY ANNUITY

Example: Calculate the value at the end of four years of a series of $500 annual deposits made at the end of each year to an account paying 7% interest, compounded annually (an ordinary *annuity* is a series of equal payments made at the *end* of each period).

Solution using table: $500 \times 4.4399 = 2,219.95$

Formula behind the table: $\quad FV_A = \left[\dfrac{(1+i)^n - 1}{i} \right] A$

$$
\begin{aligned}
FV_A &= \text{future value of an annuity} \\
i &= \text{interest rate (annual)} \\
n &= \text{number of years} \\
A &= \text{amount of annual payment}
\end{aligned}
$$

Application of formula: $\quad FV_A = \left[\dfrac{(1 + .07)^4 - 1}{.07} \right] 500$

$$= \left[\dfrac{(1.07)\,(1.07)\,(1.07)\,(1.07) - 1}{.07} \right] 500$$

$$= 2,219.97$$

Because the values in the table are rounded off, the answers are slightly different, in this example by two cents (i.e., $2,219.97 - $2,219.95 = $.02).

FUTURE VALUE TABLE
The Sum To Which One Dollar Per Annum,
Paid At The End Of Each Year, Will Increase
(complete table is located on pages 460-461)

				Rate				
Years	3%	4%	5%	6%	7%	8%	9%	10%
1	1.0000	1.0000	1.0000	1.0000	1.0000	1.0000	1.0000	1.0000
2	2.0300	2.0400	2.0500	2.0600	2.0700	2.0800	2.0900	2.1000
3	3.0909	3.1216	3.1525	3.1836	3.2149	3.2464	3.2781	3.3100
4	4.1836	4.2465	4.3101	4.3746	4.4399	4.5061	4.5731	4.6410
5	5.3091	5.4163	5.5256	5.6371	5.7507	5.8666	5.9847	6.1051

FUTURE VALUE OF AN ANNUITY DUE

Example: Calculate the value at the end of three years of a series of $1,000 annual deposits made at the beginning of each year to an account paying 8% interest, compounded annually (an *annuity due* is a series of equal payments made at the *beginning* of each period).

Solution using table: $1,000 \times 3.5061 = 3,506.10$

Formula behind the table: $\quad FV_{AD} = (1 + i) \left[\dfrac{(1 + i)^n - 1}{i} \right] \quad A$

FV_{AD} = future value of an annuity due

i = interest rate (annual)

n = number of years

A = amount of annual payment

Application of formula: $\quad FV_{AD} = (1 + .08) \left[\dfrac{(1 + .08)^3 - 1}{.08} \right] 1,000$

$$= 1.08 \left[\dfrac{((1.08)\,(1.08)\,(1.08)) - 1}{.08} \right] 1,000$$

$$= 3,506.11$$

Because the values in the table are rounded off, the answers are slightly different, in this example by one cent (i.e., $3,506.11 - $3,506.10 = $.01).

FUTURE VALUE TABLE
The Sum To Which One Dollar Per Annum,
Paid At The Beginning Of Each Year, Will Increase
(complete table is located on pages 458-459)

				Rate				
	3%	4%	5%	6%	7%	8%	9%	10%
Years								
1	1.0300	1.0400	1.0500	1.0600	1.0700	1.0800	1.0900	1.1000
2	2.0909	2.1216	2.1525	2.1836	2.2149	2.2464	2.2781	2.3100
3	3.1836	3.2465	3.3101	3.3746	3.4399	3.5061	3.5731	3.6410
4	4.3091	4.4163	4.5256	4.6371	4.7507	4.8666	4.9847	5.1051
5	5.4684	5.6330	5.8019	5.9753	6.1533	6.3359	6.5233	6.7156

PRESENT VALUE OF AN ORDINARY ANNUITY

Example: Calculate the present value of a series of $2,000 annual payments to be made at the end of each year for the next four years, assuming a discount rate of 5% (an ordinary *annuity* is a series of equal payments made at the *end* of each period).

Solution using table: $2,000 \times 3.5460 = 7,092.00$

Formula behind the table: $PV_A = \left[\dfrac{1 - \left[\dfrac{1}{(1 + i)^n} \right]}{i} \right] A$

PV_A = present value of an annuity
i = interest rate (annual)
n = number of years
A = amount of annual payment

Application of formula: $PV_A = \left[\dfrac{1 - \left[\dfrac{1}{(1 + .05)^4} \right]}{.05} \right] 2,000$

$= \left[\dfrac{1 - \left[\dfrac{1}{((1.05)(1.05)(1.05)(1.05))} \right]}{.05} \right] 2,000$

$= 7,091.90$

Because the values in the table are rounded off, the answers are slightly different, in this example by 10 cents (i.e., $7,092.00 - $7,091.90 = $.10).

PRESENT VALUE TABLE
The Worth Today of One Dollar Per Annum, Paid At The End Of Each Year
(complete table is located on pages 466-467)

				Rate				
	3%	4%	5%	6%	7%	8%	9%	10%
Years								
1	.9709	.9615	.9524	.9434	.9346	.9259	.9174	.9091
2	1.9135	1.8861	1.8594	1.8334	1.8080	1.7833	1.7591	1.7355
3	2.8286	2.7751	2.7232	2.6730	2.6243	2.5771	2.5313	2.4869
4	3.7171	3.6299	3.5460	3.4651	3.3872	3.3121	3.2397	3.1699
5	4.5797	4.4518	4.3295	4.2124	4.1002	3.9927	3.8897	3.7908

PRESENT VALUE OF AN ANNUITY DUE

Example: Calculate the present value of a series of $10,000 annual payments to be made at the beginning of each year for the next three years, assuming a discount rate of 9% (an *annuity due* is a series of equal payments made at the *beginning* of each period).

Solution using table: $10,000 \times 2.7591 = 27,591.00$

Formula behind the table: $PV_{AD} = (1 + i) \left[\dfrac{1 - \left[\dfrac{1}{(1 + i)^n} \right]}{i} \right] A$

PV_{AD} = present value of an annuity due
i = interest rate (annual)
n = number of years
A = amount of annual payment

Application of formula: $PV_{AD} = (1 + .09) \left[\dfrac{1 - \left[\dfrac{1}{(1 + .09)^3} \right]}{.09} \right] 10,000$

$$= 1.09 \left[\dfrac{1 - \left[\dfrac{1}{((1.09)(1.09)(1.09))} \right]}{.09} \right] 10,000$$

$$= 27,591.11$$

Because the values in the table are rounded off, the answers are slightly different, in this example by 11 cents (i.e., $27,591.11 - $27,591.00 = $.11).

PRESENT VALUE TABLE
The Worth Today of One Dollar Per Annum, Paid At The Beginning Of Each Year
(complete table is located on pages 464-465)

Years	3%	4%	5%	6%	7%	8%	9%	10%
1	1.0000	1.0000	1.0000	1.0000	1.0000	1.0000	1.0000	1.0000
2	1.9709	1.9615	1.9524	1.9434	1.9346	1.9259	1.9174	1.9091
3	2.9135	2.8861	2.8594	2.8334	2.8080	2.7833	2.7591	2.7355
4	3.8286	3.7751	3.7232	3.6730	3.6243	3.5771	3.5313	3.4869
5	4.7171	4.6299	4.5460	4.4651	4.3872	4.3121	4.2397	4.1699

A SHORT HISTORY OF MONEY

Much of financial planning involves money: earning it, spending it, and saving it. But before money there was barter. In the old world, Roman soldiers were often paid with sacks of salt, giving us the word "salary." In the new world, perhaps the best-known example of barter was when Peter Minuit exchanged $24 of trinkets and beads for the island of Manhattan (see page 69). Although a great deal of barter continues throughout the world, barter is inefficient when it comes to paying for goods and services. As early as 2,500 BC, precious metals began to be used throughout Egypt and Asia Minor. This naturally led to the minting of the metals into coins that facilitated the process of exchange, with the value of the coin being determined by the value of the underlying metal (e.g., pound sterling).

The American dollar owes its name to a silver coin called the Joachimsthaler that was first minted in Bohemia in 1519. Widely circulated throughout Europe, in England it became known as the dollar. In the United States paper money first appeared when it was issued in varying denominations by the colonies. To finance the American Revolution, the Continental Congress issued notes that were declared to be redeemable in either gold or silver coins, but these notes eventually became virtually worthless due to the lack of sufficient gold and silver reserves. Although the federal government first minted silver "dollars" in 1794, it was not until 1863 that a uniform currency was established that replaced the paper money that had previously been issued by local banks. Today, circulating currency, both paper and coin, is no longer backed by either gold or silver reserves, but rather by the full faith and credit of the United States.

Traditionally, there have been three basic forms of money: currency, coins, and checks drawn on banks and other financial firms. To these should be added credit cards, debit cards, and electronic payments (both preauthorized and remote). The following table of consumer payment systems by method of payment suggests that credit cards, debit cards, and electronic payments will be increasingly used as a substitute for payment by check.[1]

	Amount (bil. dol.)		Percent Distribution	
	2001	2005 proj.	1990	2005 proj.
Cash	1,058	1,246	25.0	19.3
Direct Check Payments	2,250	2,056	51.1	41.1
Credit Cards	1,341	1,727	18.6	24.5
Debit Cards	384	726	0.4	7.0
Electronic Payments	275	745	0.9	5.0

SAVINGS VEHICLES

Savings generally involves shorter-term goals with an emphasis upon liquidity and safety of principal. In contrast, *investing* involves longer-term goals with lower liquidity and less safety of principal. For example, funds are *saved* in short-term interest-bearing debt instruments such as certificates of deposit or United States Treasury bills (created and transferred in the money market), whereas funds are *invested* in longer-term debt or equity such as corporate bonds or common stocks (created and traded in the capital markets).[2] Unfortunately, in practice the terms are often used interchangeably.[3]

Checking Accounts. Also known as regular checking, these are demand accounts that allow the depositor to issue checks directing the financial institution to pay the party listed on the check a specific sum of money. The credit union version of a checking account is known as a *share draft account*. Provided there are sufficient funds in the account, there are no limitations on the withdrawal. A *regular* checking account pays no interest on the account balance. Service charges may be applied, but are often waived if a minimum account balance is maintained or the account holder is over a certain age (the so-called "senior" account). Both automated teller machines (ATMs) and debit cards have become very popular ways of accessing funds in checking accounts (see page 86).

NOW Accounts. In contrast to regular checking accounts, the NOW (negotiated order of withdrawal) account pays interest on account balances. Many other institution-specific names are used to describe these accounts (e.g., "Checkplus Account"). Although all savings account interest rate ceilings and minimum balance requirements at commercial banks and savings institutions were removed in 1986, most financial institutions impose their own minimum balance limits for interest to be credited, often between $500 and $1,000. Interest is credited at whatever rate is set by the institution and is typically increased (tiered) if larger balances are maintained (e.g., amounts over $2,500). Since fees will offset interest earned, evaluation of a particular account should include determining exactly what, if any, monthly or other fees are charged. Provided a minimum balance is maintained monthly fees are often waived. The *dividend bearing share draft account* is the credit union version of a NOW account.

Super NOW Accounts. These are NOW accounts that are generally less restrictive than Money Market Deposit Accounts (MMDAs). Interest rates are usually higher than NOW accounts, but less than MMDAs. Tiered interest rates are usually offered. Some accounts charge per item processing fees for checks or deposits, some accounts do not impose these fees, and still other accounts waive these fees provided a minimum balance is maintained.

Savings Accounts. These accounts, also referred to as *passbook accounts*, are considered the most basic of bank savings vehicles. The term *statement account* is often used in reference to savings accounts that record transactions by computer and provide either monthly or quarterly statements in lieu of passbook entries. In contrast to demand deposits, or checking accounts, savings accounts are also referred to as *time deposits*, since the funds are expected to remain on deposit for longer periods. In fact, many accounts stipulate that depositors may be required to wait a stated number of days before receiving payment. However, this requirement is often waived. While funds in a savings account are both safe and liquid, the rates paid on savings accounts are typically the lowest rates offered. Higher, or tiered, rates of interest are usually paid on larger account balances or for time deposits.

Money Market Mutual Funds (MMMF). Also referred to as *Money Market Funds*, these funds, issued by investment companies and insurance companies, are handled by mutual fund managers. Shares are purchased at a fixed price of $1 each and form a pool of money that is used to purchase short-term and high-quality debt obligations of government entities, commercial banks, and corporations (e.g., in Treasury bills, bank certificate of deposits, and corporate commercial paper). MMMFs are sold as no load funds (i.e., no sales commission), but management fees are charged. Although earnings are technically dividends, they are taxed as interest income. Because the securities purchased are of very high denominations, MMMFs are able to obtain the highest rates available on the market. The interest rates change daily due to the fluctuating nature of the funds portfolio of debts instruments. The minimum initial investment and check writing privileges vary from one account to another. Typically, checks must be for a minimum amount varying from $250 to $500. Although not insured by the FDIC, if purchased from a brokerage firm MMMFs are considered securities and are insured against the bankruptcy of the firm by the Securities Investor Protection Corporation (SIPC); but they are not insured against a loss stemming from the underlying investments. However, because of their short-term nature and high quality, most experts regard them about as safe as commercial paper (commercial paper is unsecured, short-term debt instruments issued by banks and corporations in order to meet immediate cash needs). See also, page 177.

Money Market Deposit Accounts (MMDA). These accounts, also referred to as *Money Market Accounts*, were developed by financial institutions in order to compete against the Money Market Mutual Funds (MMMF) offered by investment and insurance companies. Interest is market-based, meaning that the rate will vary from week to week. Although the interest rates are generally lower than those available with a MMMF, they offer two advantages not enjoyed by the MMMF; the convenience of a local bank or savings association, and the safety of being federally insured (up to $100,000). A minimum balance is required, and withdrawals by check or electronic transfer are usually very limited in number, with fees changed for any excess number of withdrawals (e.g., more than 3 per month). Because of these fees, MMDAs are more in the nature of savings accounts than checking accounts.

Certificates Of Deposit (CD). Certificates of deposit are issued by commercial banks, savings and loan associations, savings banks, and credit unions. The most common maturity periods range from three months to five years. Because funds are being committed for a longer period of time, the rate of return earned on CDs is typically higher than those offered on savings accounts and money market instruments. However, if the funds are withdrawn prior to maturity, a *penalty* in the form of forfeited interest is

> ### Keeping Current
>
> Current CD rates by locale, maturity, and size are available at: www.banx.com.

assessed (e.g., three months interest). Tiered rates are typically offered, with higher rates for longer terms and larger amounts. Because rates can differ substantially from one region of the country to another, it is wise to shop around for the best rate (see WSJ). Higher yields can also be obtained from *brokered CDs.* These are larger denomination bank CDs ($1,000 and up) that are purchased through brokers who shop nationally for the highest available rates. The bank pays commissions for brokered CDs. Unlike the typical CD; the funds in brokered CDs can often be accessed early and without a bank-imposed penalty by having a broker sell them in secondary markets. However, *rising* interest rates will depress the value of a fixed-rate CD. Laddering can be an effective way of providing some protection against *falling* interest rates (see page 26). Although the rates are typically fixed, there are hybrid CDs that offer variable rates tied to a specific market index (e.g., the S&P 500). Because the frequency with which interest is compounded is an important determinant of a CD's return, it is important to determine the yield, not just the interest rate (see page 85). While the vast majority of CDs are issued by institutions insured by the FDIC, it is always important to verify that a CD is federally insured.

Asset Management Accounts (AMA). These accounts might be better named "central asset accounts," in that the financial institution is not actual managing the depositor's assets, but rather acting as a central depository and agent who acts upon the directions of the depositor. They were begun as bank-like services offered by large brokerage firms and mutual funds, but are now also offered by insurance companies and larger banks. They are intended to foster a consolidation of both banking and investing services into one relationship. AMAs are opened with a minimum deposit of cash or securities, offer different levels of service, and charge varying annual and transaction fees. They typically offer unlimited free checking, purchase and safekeeping of securities, debit and credit cards, access to automatic teller machines (ATM), direct deposit, automatic "borrowing" and overdraft coverage, online access to account information, bill-payment services, and advice from financial advisors. A distinguishing feature of AMAs is the automatic daily, or weekly, "sweep" of excess balances into a savings account paying interest at higher money market rates. Another very attractive feature is the monthly and year-end statement that summarizes all account transactions, often in a format that facilitates the accounting necessary for filing of income tax returns. The extension of credit in AMAs is often in the form of a margin account, with the underlying securities serving as collateral for any credit extended. Unlike a bank loan, a substantial decline in the market price of these securities could trigger a margin call (see page 148).

Treasury Bills. See page 109.

Zero-Coupon Treasuries. Also known as STRIPS, see page 111.

ANNUAL PERCENTAGE YIELD (APY)

This is the effective, or true, annual rate of return earned in an interest-bearing account or instrument, expressed as a percentage. It takes into consideration the effect of compounding. When the APY is higher than the declared interest rate, the interest is compounded (i.e., interest is being paid on interest). For example, if $1,000 placed in a CD paying 5% interest (*compounded monthly*) earns $51.16 during the period April 1 to the following March 31, the APY is 5.116%. If interest were *compounded quarterly*, the APY would be 5.095% and the interest earned would be $50.95. If the interest were not compounded, the interest earned would be only $50.00 (i.e., simple versus compounded interest). See also, The Magic Of Compound Interest, page 69.

www.bankrate.com/brm/ calc/cdc/CertDeposit.asp

PAYMENT CARDS (AKA PLASTIC)

Credit Cards. Credit cards generally include any card that is repeatedly used to borrow money or buy goods and services on credit. They are issued by banks, savings and loans, retail stores, and other businesses. Included are *bank cards* issued by banks and other financial institutions, *prestige cards* providing a high limit of credit and other benefits, *affinity cards* issued to groups of individuals with a common bond or tie, *retail credit cards* accepted only by the issuing retail establishment, and *travel and entertainment cards* that typically require payment of the entire balance when billed. Provided balances are paid in full as billed, they offer an attractive way of making purchases (and taking advantage of the float between time of purchase and time of payment). When balances are not paid in full, high rates of interest are charged. In 2001, the annual average finance rate charged by credit card plans was 14.89%.[4] In 1998, over 44% of all United States families carried a balance on their credit card with a median debt of $1,700.[5] In contrast, a *charge card* is also used for making payments, but charges must be paid in full when the statement is received.

Debit Cards. The debit card may resemble a credit card in appearance, but functions more like a checking account. When a purchase is made, the transaction is immediately deducted from the cardholder's checking account. Because the debit card is machine-readable, funds can generally be withdrawn using automated teller machines (ATMs). Unlike the credit card, a debit card does not have any float.

ELECTRONIC FUNDS TRANSFER (EFT)

Also referred to as the *electronic funds transfer system (EFTS)*, this is the transfer of funds electronically rather than by check or cash. Application of this technology to consumer transactions includes Automated Teller Machines (ATMs) found in banks and other convenient locations, Point of Sale Terminals (POS) used in retail establishments, preauthorized payments of mortgages and other recurring bills, automatic deposits of employee paychecks, telephone transfer systems, and internet banking services using personal computers. The Federal Reserve's Fedwire system and automated clearinghouses (ACHs) are both part of the EFT system.

JOINT ACCOUNTS

The method of ownership of property, including savings and investment vehicles, can have substantial consequences for the account holders.

Joint Ownership With Rights Of Survivorship. When an account is established in joint ownership with rights of survivorship, upon the death of one owner the surviving joint owner immediately takes full ownership of the account without the need for probate of the deceased's will or resort to state intestacy statues. Although joint ownership is typically established between husband and wife, two or more related and unrelated persons can also effectively use it. Each joint tenant has an equal and undivided interest in the entire property. Any co-owner of jointly held property may use, withdraw, sell, or give away the property interest without the consent of the other owner(s). The entire property interest is exposed to creditor claims of any co-owner.

Tenancy In Common. Under this form of joint tenancy each co-owner has a fractional, divisible interest in the property (i.e., it is the opposite of joint tenancy with rights of survivorship). Upon the death of a co-owner, his fractional interest is probate property and passes by will or by state intestacy laws. Each surviving co-tenant retains his proportionate interest in the property.

Tenancy By The Entirety. This is a form of joint tenancy that can only exist between husband and wife. While some states do not recognize tenancy by the entirety, others may place restrictions as to the type of property that can be so titled (e.g., limited real property). Unlike joint ownership with rights of survivorship, both tenants in a tenancy by the entirety must agree to a transfer of the property interest.

---

[1] Source of consumer payment projections is *Statistical Abstracts of the United States*, 2002, Table 1162, p. 727. See www.census.gov/prod/www/statistical-abstract-02.html.

[2] See George E. Rejda and Michael J. McNamara, *Personal Financial Planning*, (Reading, Massachusetts: Addison-Wesley, 1998), p. 76.

[3] See Robert J. Garner et al., *Ernst & Young's Personal Financial Planning Guide*, (New York: John Wiley & Sons, 2002), p. 63.

[4] Source of credit card rates is *Statistical Abstracts of the United States*, 2002, Table 1164, p. 728. See www.census.gov/prod/www/statistical-abstract-02.html.

[5] Source of debt information is *Statistical Abstracts of the United States*, 2001, Table 1169, p. 727. See www.census.gov/prod/www/statistical-abstract-02.html.

OVERVIEW & BOND CLASSIFICATIONS

Bonds are negotiable long-term debt obligations issued for periods of more than one year that represent a promise by the issuer to pay periodic interest at a fixed rate (i.e., the coupon) and to repay loan principal at a specific maturity date. (Zero coupon bonds are an exception to the periodic interest payment characteristic included in this definition.) Payment of both interest and principal to corporate bondholders takes precedence over payment of dividends to preferred and common stockholders. Unlike stocks, bonds do not give the investor an ownership interest in the entity that issues the bond. Because they provide for payments at specific rates and upon determined dates, bonds are referred to as **fixed-income securities**. In contrast, stocks are referred to as **equity securities**.

Notes. Except for their maturity dates, there appears to be no generally accepted distinction between corporate bonds and corporate notes. For example, the term "note" was used to describe zero coupon senior securities of the Pharmaceuticals Corporation due in 2032.[1] When a distinction is made, notes are of a shorter duration than bonds (see the discussion of a bond's "term" on page 94).

Securities. Securities are financial instruments that establish ownership of either debt or property. This debt or property can take the form of *bonds* (debentures) that demonstrate loans to a company, municipality, or government; *stocks* that demonstrate current ownership of a corporation; or *options*, *rights*, and *warrants* that demonstrate the right to a future ownership interest. Although these instruments have traditionally been physical documents, the introduction of electronic record keeping has resulted in their being increasingly replaced by electronic documentation (this is referred to as "book-entry" – see page 91).

Bond Classifications. It is helpful to categorize bonds according to the entities that issue them. Marketable bonds can generally be classified as: corporate bonds; municipal bonds; Treasury bonds, notes, and bills; and agency bonds. In contrast, U.S. Savings Bonds are not considered marketable bonds. See the Bond Matrix on page 90.

Bond Matrix			
	Referred To As	**Characteristics**	**See Pages**
Corporate Bonds/Notes	Corporates	Taxable – par value $1,000 – maturity periods vary from 1 to 20 years and up – varying amounts of risk, but highly rated bonds are generally considered low risk.*	103-108
Municipal Bonds	Munis	Exempt from federal taxes, sometimes exempt from state and local taxes – par value $5,000 and up – maturity periods vary from 1 to 20 years and up – some risk.	118-121
Treasury Bonds	T-Bonds	Exempt from state and local taxes – par value $1,000 and higher – maturity period is over 10 years up to 30 years – no credit risk.	109-110 113
Treasury Notes	T-Notes	Exempt from state and local taxes – par value $1,000 and higher – maturity periods vary from 2 to 10 years – no credit risk	109-110 115
Treasury Bills	T-Bills	Exempt from state and local taxes – par value $1,000 and higher – maturity periods 4, 13, and 26 weeks – no credit risk.	109-110 114
Agency Securities	Ginnie Maes (GNMA) Fannie Maes (FNMA) Freddie Macs (FHLM) Many Others[2]	Ginnie Maes, Fannie Maes, and Freddie Macs are subject to federal taxes, other federal agencies are exempt from state and local taxes – par value $1,000 to $25,000 and up – maturity periods from 1 month to 20 years – slight credit risk.	121-122
U.S. Savings Bonds	Series EE/E Series HH/H Series I	Are not marketable. Federal taxation varies, but subject to state and local taxes – issued in amounts of $50 to $10,0000 – maturity periods vary from 17 to 30 years – no credit risk.	116-118

* Risk refers to *default risk*. All bonds are subject to varying amounts of other risks, including call risk and interest rate risk (see page 17).

BUYING AND TRADING BONDS

Bonds are purchased and sold in a variety of ways, depending upon the type of issuer and whether the bond is a new or outstanding issue. New bond issues are sold or auctioned on the **initial-issue market** and can be subsequently resold on very active (and dynamic) secondary markets. In fact, bond trading in the **secondary markets** tends to have a very direct impact on the coupon rates for newly issued bonds (see page 92). The following table provides a general summary of these markets.

Where Bonds Are Traded		
	New Issues	**Outstanding Issues**
Corporate Bonds/Notes	From brokers or underwriters, on an exchange or OTC*	Through brokers, on an exchange or OTC.*
Municipal Bonds	From brokers.	Through brokers.
Treasury Bonds/Notes	From brokers. Can also be purchased through TreasuryDirect (see below).	Through brokers. Can also be sold through the Treasury *SellDirect®* program.
Treasury Bills	Sold by auction; individual investors submit noncompetitive bids (see page 92). Can also be purchased through TreasuryDirect.	Through brokers, on an exchange or OTC.*
Agency Bonds	From brokers, OTC or banks.	Through brokers, OTC or banks.
U.S. Savings Bonds	From commercial banks, brokers, and by payroll deduction. Can also be purchased through Treasury Direct.	Not resold (i.e., savings bonds are not marketable).

*Major exchanges that trade bonds include the New York Stock Exchange and the American Stock Exchange. See discussion of OTC (over-the-counter) on page 56.

Commercial Book-Entry System. In the commercial book-entry system, the investor maintains a relationship with a financial institution, broker, or dealer and typically pays a fee for their services. Unlike TreasuryDirect, the commercial book-entry system allows investors to use their securities for collateral and to hold zero-coupon Treasuries (see STRIPs, page 111). Securities can be easily transferred between TreasuryDirect and the commercial book-entry system.

TreasuryDirect. TreasuryDirect is a program that allows investors to purchase Treasury securities directly from the U.S. government, rather than through a bank or broker. The program is intended for investors who buy securities at original issue and hold them until maturity. TreasuryDirect makes payments by direct deposit to the investor's bank account and sends statements directly to the investor. No fees are charged for opening an account or buying securities, but a modest maintenance fee is charged if an account has a total par amount of more than $100,000. TreasuryDirect also allows the investor to automatically reinvest the proceeds from most maturing securities. Financial institutions, government securities brokers, or dealers can submit a bid for a security to be delivered to TreasuryDirect for the investor.

www.treasurydirect.gov

Noncompetitive Bidding. There are the two types of bidding for a Treasury security. When bidding for a Treasury bill, note, or bond, the bidder must choose whether to bid competitively or noncompetitively. If a *noncompetitive* bid is placed, the Treasury guarantees the bidder will receive the desired security. By bidding noncompetitively the bidder agrees to accept whatever rate or yield is determined at the auction. Investors who don't consider themselves expert securities traders usually bid noncompetitively. A *competitive* bid is one where the bidder specifies the rate or yield he will accept, and the Treasury may reject the bid or grant it in less than the full amount

BOND TERMINOLOGY

Call Provision. Also referred to as a "call feature," this provision allows the issuer to redeem, or "call," the bond before the bond's redemption date. Bonds are most often called when the prevailing interest rates have dropped significantly since the bonds were issued. See also, "Yield To First Call" on page 101, and "Callable Bond" on page 103.

Coupon Rate. This is the stated rate of interest that is to be paid during the term of the bond. For example, a $1,000 bond that has a coupon rate of 7% pays annual interest of $70, usually at a frequency of $35 every six months. The term is derived from the coupons that were once attached to bonds, which were then clipped and submitted to the issuer (or the issuer's agent) in order to receive interest payments. Such bonds were also referred to as **bearer bonds** because the bearer of the bond had physical possession of the attached coupons and was, therefore, entitled to the interest payments. Today, bearer bonds, or coupon bonds, are no longer issued. As with stock certificates, bond certificates have given way to the computer age, with virtually all new bond issues, called **book-entry bonds**, being electronically registered. However, the term "coupon rate" continues to be widely used in describing a bond's interest rate.

"Fallen Angel." This term is generally applied to an existing bond issue whose investment rating has been downgraded because of deterioration in the issuer's financial condition (see Bond Risk & Ratings, page 101). Typically, the reduction in market price, or value, of a fallen angel reflects the downgrade by a rating service from investment grade to speculative grade (see also Junk Bond, page 104). In contrast, a **rising star** is a bond whose rating has been increased as a result of improvement in the issuer's credit quality.

Floating An Issue. This is the process of initially offering a bond issue to investors for a specific period of time and at a specific rate of interest. Not all initial offerings float — some sink, as did the issue by Trump Hotels & Casinos in May of 2002.[3]

Indenture. Also called the bond agreement, bond covenant, or deed of trust, this is the written agreement setting forth the bond terms, such as maturity date, interest rate, and callability. A failure of the issuer to meet the contractual terms of the bond indenture results in a default of the bond issue.

Issuer. This is the entity, such as a corporation or municipality, that borrows funds from investors by selling bonds, and that has the legal obligation to make timely payments of both interest and principal as set forth in the bond indenture.

Original Issue Discount (OID). This is a bond that is originally sold at a discount from its face amount. For bonds issued after May 27, 1969, this discount is taxable over the life of the bond, even though there has been no cash payment.[4] Although bonds issued with original issue discount can also pay interest, zero-coupon bonds are the ultimate example of original issue discounting — they pay no interest until maturity (see page 105).

Par Value. Also referred to as the **nominal**, **face**, or **maturity value**, bonds are usually issued with a par value of $1,000, representing the principal, or the amount of money borrowed. If a bond is selling at **par** it is worth the same as its original issue value. In contrast, a bond selling at a **premium** is selling for more than par, and a bond selling at a **discount** is selling for less than par (see page 96). (A bond priced at 105 means $1,050.)

Sinking Fund. Not all bond issues have sinking funds, but when they are established it is for the purpose of annually paying off portions of the bond issue prior to maturity. The specific bonds to be retired are typically selected by lottery. Use of a sinking fund to retire debt over time can benefit the bondholder by reducing the risk of default. However, sinking fund redemptions can work to the bondholder's disadvantage by enabling the corporation to retire at par bonds whose market price is in excess of par.

Spread. Although used in many different ways, with respect to bonds this term is most often used as follows. **Spread-to-Treasury** compares the yield on the bond with the yield on a Treasury security of comparable maturity. For example, the spread between a 10-year Treasury bond yielding 4.80% and a 10-year corporate bond yielding 5.25% is 45 basis points. Referred to as a **yield spread**, it is expressed in terms of **basis points**, with 100 basis points being equal to 1%. The term is also used to describe a **dealer's spread**, or profit, on a bond transaction (e.g., the difference between the price paid to the issuer and the price obtained from the first holder of the bond). Lastly, the **bid-ask spread** is used as a measure of the liquidity of a bond. A small spread, or "gap," with more actively traded bonds provides greater liquidity and indicates a lower liquidity risk. As the spread rises on less actively traded bonds, so does liquidity risk. A large spread between what buyers are bidding and sellers are asking indicates a higher liquidity risk (see page 17).

Term. A bond's "term" is the number of years that must pass before the issuer redeems the bond; it is a function of the bond's **maturity date**. For example, a bond issued in 2002 with a maturity date in 2032 has a 30-year term. Again, there appears to be no general agreement as to the specific lengths of short-term, medium-term, and long-term notes or bonds. The following definitions of corporate notes and bonds are used by the Bond Market Association, an association that represents securities firms and banks that underwrite, trade and sell debt securities:[5]

(1) Short-term notes - maturities of 1-4 years.

(2) Medium-term notes/bonds - maturities of 5-12 years.

(3) Long-term bonds - maturities greater than 12 years.

PRICES & YIELDS

The market price, or value, of a bond is a function of three factors: (1) the annual payment (**coupon rate**); (2) the number of years to maturity; and (3) prevailing market interest rates. The essential consideration is, "What is an investor willing to pay *today* for a *future* stream of income (i.e., the interest payments), plus eventual repayment of the bond principal?"

Yield Curve. This is a graph that illustrates the relationship between interest rates and maturity dates for securities of equal risk. For example, the yield curve will often compare the return on short-term Treasury bills with the return on 30-year Treasury bonds.

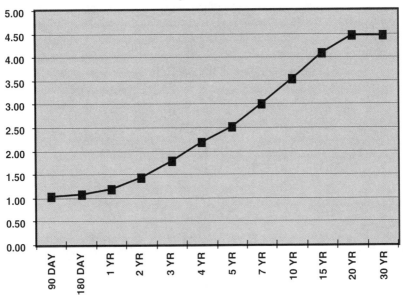

The sample yield curves, above, compare the relative yields of different Treasury issues. The vertical axis is percent, and the durations illustrated are 90-day, 180-day, and 1, 2, 3, 4, 5, 7, 10, 15, 20, and 30-years.

Yield curves are also used to compare the relationship between interest rates paid on short-term and long-term bonds, using bonds of the same investment quality. It is generally expected that long-term interest rates will be higher than short-term interest rates (i.e., a greater risk is associated with investing funds for a longer term and a higher return is required). Thus, a yield curve depicting long-term rates that are *higher* than short-term rates is said to be a **normal yield curve** (also known as a "positive yield curve"); whereas a yield curve depicting long-term rates that are *lower* than short-term rates is said to be an **inverted yield curve** (also known as a "negative yield curve"). It is believed that changes in the yield curve indicate turning points in the business cycle (e.g., an inversion of the yield curve is a precursor of a recession).

Yields on debt instruments of lower quality are expressed in terms of a spread relative to the default-free yield curve. The **spread-to-Treasury** is the difference between the yield on a lower quality debt instrument to the yield on a Treasury security of a similar maturity. For example, if a 10-year Treasury note yields 4.25% and a 10-year corporate note yields 5.00%, the spread is 75 basis points. Knowing the spread enables the investor to judge whether the lower quality security is paying an "adequate" risk premium (see page 69).

Market Interest Rates. Bond prices move counter to changes in market interest rates. When market interest rates go up, bond prices go down; and when market interest rates go down, bond prices go up. The longer the period to maturity, the greater the magnitude of the rise and fall of bond prices.

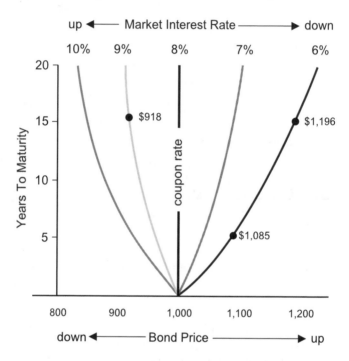

For example, assume a $1,000 par value bond is purchased with a coupon rate of 8%. If market interest rates stay at 8%, the market price, or value, of the bond will remain at $1,000. However, if there are 15 years to maturity, and market interest rates fall to 6%, the value of the bond will increase to $1,196. Because a purchaser will realize 2% more interest income than currently available in the market, the *seller* will demand a $196 **premium** for the bond (1,196 − 1,000 = 196). But if market interest rates increase to 9%, the market price of the bond will fall to $918. Because a purchaser will realize 1% less than current market interest rates, the *purchaser* will demand to purchase the bond at a $82 **discount** (1,000 − 918 = 82). But what if market interest rates fall again to 6%, but there are only 5 years to maturity? Now the price of the bond is $1,085 and the premium is only $85. Clearly, the present value of the extra 2% earnings for only 5 years is substantially less than the extra 2% earnings for 15 years. See the following page for a table containing the values used in the above graph.

Value Of A $1,000 Bond With 8% Coupon

Years To Maturity	Market Interest Rates				
	10%	9%	8%	7%	6%
1	981	991	1,000	1,009	1,019
2	965	982	1,000	1,018	1,037
3	949	974	1,000	1,027	1,054
4	935	967	1,000	1,034	1,070
5	923	960	1,000	1,042	1,085
6	911	954	1,000	1,048	1,100
7	901	949	1,000	1,055	1,113
8	892	944	1,000	1,060	1,126
9	883	939	1,000	1,066	1,138
10	875	935	1,000	1,071	1,149
11	868	931	1,000	1,076	1,159
12	862	928	1,000	1,080	1,169
13	856	924	1,000	1,084	1,179
14	851	921	1,000	1,088	1,188
15	846	919	1,000	1,092	1,196
16	842	916	1,000	1,095	1,204
17	838	914	1,000	1,099	1,211
18	835	912	1,000	1,101	1,218
19	831	910	1,000	1,104	1,225
20	828	908	1,000	1,107	1,231

Percent Loss/Gain Of A $1,000 Bond With 8% Coupon

Years To Maturity	Market Interest Rates				
	10%	9%	8%	7%	6%
1	1.9% loss	0.9% loss	0	0.9% gain	1.9% gain
5	7.7% loss	4.0% loss	0	4.2% gain	8.5% gain
10	12.5% loss	6.5% loss	0	7.1% gain	14.9% gain
15	15.4 loss	8.1% loss	0	9.2% gain	19.6% gain
20	17.2% loss	9.2% loss	0	10.7% gain	23.1% gain

Calculating Bond Prices. The price of a bond can be calculated by determining the present value of the stream of interest payments plus the present value of the bond's redemption (par) value. This is expressed in the following formula, where the Present Value Of Annuity represents the present value of the interest payments, and the Present Value Of A Single Sum represents the present value of the amount that will be received when the bond is redeemed. Note that in order to reflect the fact that bonds pay interest every six months, the market interest rate (i) is divided by 2 and the years to maturity (n) is multiplied by 2 (i.e., the interest rate is one-half the annual rate and the number of periods is equal to the number of 6-month periods). For example, a 15-year 9% bond pays 4.5% interest every 6 months for 15 years (i.e., thirty 6-month periods). (See also the discussions of the present value of a single sum on page 76, and the present value of an ordinary annuity on page 79.)

$$PP = \text{Present Value} + \text{Present Value}$$
$$\text{Of An Annuity} \qquad \text{Of A Single Sum}$$

$$PP = A\left(\frac{1 - \left(\frac{1}{(1+i)^n}\right)}{i}\right) + \frac{par}{(1+i^n)}$$

PP	=	purchase price
A	=	semiannual interest payment (coupon)
i	=	market interest rate ÷ 2
n	=	years to maturity × 2
par	=	face value of bond (par value)

Assume that we have a $1,000 bond that will mature in 15 years that has an 8% coupon (i.e., it pays $80 per year in interest). Assume also that we want to pay a price that will result in the bond yielding 9% to maturity. We can use the above formula to determine the purchase price.

$$PP = 40\left(\frac{1 - \left(\frac{1}{(1+.045)^{30}}\right)}{.045}\right) + \frac{1,000}{(1+.045)^{30}}$$

$$PP = 40\left(\frac{1 - \left(\frac{1}{3.745318}\right)}{.045}\right) + \frac{1,000}{3.745318}$$

$$PP = 40\left(\frac{1 - .267000}{.045}\right) + 267$$

$$PP = 919$$

Nominal Yield. This is also referred to as the "stated yield," "coupon yield," or "coupon rate." See the discussion of "coupon rate" on page 92.

Current Yield. This is the annual (coupon) interest payment divided by the *current* (market) price of the bond. The formula is:

$$\text{Current Yield} \quad = \quad \frac{\text{Annual Interest Payment}}{\text{Current Price}}$$

When purchasing an outstanding bond issue on the secondary market, the current yield is not necessarily an accurate measure of the investment value of a bond, since it *ignores any difference between the bond's face value and the current price*. In effect, it fails to account for the bond's maturity date and the premium paid or the discount received when the bond is purchased at the current market price. The following table summarizes the three possible scenarios involving current yield calculations.

Limitation Of Current Yield			
Face Value	Current Price	Current Yield	Analysis
$1,000	$930	$\dfrac{70}{930}$ = 7.53	Current yield fails to recognize that the investor pays $70 *less* than par, and will receive a $70 gain when the bond is redeemed for $1,000.
$1,000	$1,000	$\dfrac{70}{1,000}$ = 7.00	Current yield accurately reflects the investment value of bond; the investor will have no gain or loss when the bond is redeemed for $1,000.
$1,000	$1,040	$\dfrac{70}{1,040}$ = 6.73	Current yield fails to recognize investor pays $40 *more* than par and will suffer a $40 loss when the bond is redeemed for $1,000.
The above assumes a par $1,000 bond with 7.00% coupon paying $70 interest per year.			

Yield To Maturity. Because it calculates the total return, yield to maturity is a more meaningful measure of a bond's investment value than current yield (see above). Use of yield to maturity also allows for comparison of bonds with different maturities and coupons, since it accounts for both interest income and any gain or loss when the bond is redeemed.

The variable "i" in the following formula, as used on page 98 to calculate a bond's purchase price, represents the yield to maturity figure that investors most often want to determine:

$$PP \ = \ A\left(\frac{1 - \left(\frac{1}{(1 + i)^n}\right)}{i}\right) + \frac{par}{(1 + i)^n}$$

With a computer program the value for i can be solved using a process of trial and error, but it is very difficult to use the above formula, or any other mathematical methods, to directly solve for "i" (i.e., the interest rate representing the yield to maturity). Absent application of a computer driven program, the following formula can be used to solve for the *approximate* yield to maturity.[6]

$$\text{Approximate Yield To Maturity} \ = \ \frac{A + \left(\frac{par - PP}{n}\right)}{\left(\frac{PP + par}{2}\right)}$$

$$
\begin{aligned}
A &= \text{annual interest payment (coupon)} \\
par &= \text{face value of bond (par value)} \\
PP &= \text{purchase price} \\
n &= \text{years to maturity}
\end{aligned}
$$

Assume that we have a $1,000 bond that will mature in 9 years and has a 7% coupon (i.e., it pays $70 per year in interest). Assume also that we have paid $937 for the bond. The *approximate* yield to maturity is calculated as follows:

$$\text{Approximate Yield To Maturity} \ = \ \frac{70 + \left(\frac{1,000 - 937}{9}\right)}{\left(\frac{937 + 1,000}{2}\right)}$$

$$\text{Approximate Yield To Maturity} \ = \ \frac{77}{968.50}$$

$$\text{Approximate Yield To Maturity} \ = \ .0795 \text{ or } 7.95\%$$

Note that this represents a deviation from the true yield to maturity of .05 of 1% (.0800 − .0795 = .0005). In dollar terms .0005 × $1,000 = 50 cents. (Not all that bad for an approximate calculation.)

Yield To First Call. This is the annual yield considering both the yearly interest payments and any gain or loss upon redemption of the bond, but it is assumed that the issuer will call the bond at the earliest date allowed under the bond indenture. Yield to call is calculated the same way as yield to maturity, only the "number of years" figure is reduced to reflect the years remaining to the first call date. This is an important consideration if an investor is considering purchasing a bond at a premium (i.e., for more than the bond's par value). For example, assume an investor paid $1,040 for a $1,000 par value bond with a 7% coupon. Over the next year the investor receives $70 of interest. If the bond were then called by the issuer at par value the investor would receive only $1,000 for a bond that had been purchased one year earlier for $1,040. This loss of $40 will substantially reduce the investor's yield on the bond. Yield to first call considers both the interest payments received and the loss suffered upon early redemption of the bond.

Annual Rate Of Return. This is the amount that a bondholder receives from a bond divided by the amount invested, considering yearly interest payments and any gain or loss upon sale. It is the same as "yield to maturity" if the bond is held to maturity, and the same as "yield to first call" if the bond is called by the issuer at the earliest date allowed under the bond indenture. However, calculation of the annual rate of return is useful if the bondholder sells the bond prior to maturity. For example, assume an investor pays $1,040 for a $1,000 par value bond with a 7% coupon. Over the next four years the investor receives $280 of interest (4 × 70 = 280). If the investor then sells the bond for $1,025 the investor receives $15 less than paid for the bond (1,040 − 1,025 = 15). Annual rate of return reflects the $280 of interest payments and the $15 loss on sale of the bond.

BOND RISK & RATINGS

Bonds can vary substantially in their degree of risk, from United States Treasury securities that are considered without risk, to junk bonds that are considered highly speculative. In particular, credit quality is an important factor in valuing *long-term* bonds whose issuers are expected to meet payments over many years in the future.

Rating services such as Standard & Poor's, Moody's, and Fitch assign credit ratings to individual bond issues based upon their research into the issuer's management, financial soundness, creditworthiness, debt characteristics, and the specific revenue sources securing the bond (see the table of Bond Credit Ratings on page 102). The highest ratings are AAA (S&P and Fitch) and Aaa (Moody's), whereas the lowest ratings are DD (S&P and Fitch) and C (Moody's). Bonds rated BBB and higher are considered investment grade, whereas bonds rated BB and below are considered below investment grade (see Junk Bonds, page 104). The key question being addressed in the rating process is whether the issuer will be able to meet its regularly scheduled interest payments and the payment of bond principal upon maturity.

Credit ratings that are given to individual bond issues directly impact the amount of the coupon (i.e., rate of interest). Rating agencies not only assign ratings when a bond is issued, but also monitor developments during the bond's lifetime and will (occasionally) downgrade or upgrade a bond before maturity. Rating agencies will typically signal that they are considering a rating change by placing the bond on CreditWatch (S&P), Under Review (Moody's), or on Rating Watch (Fitch). Any changes will impact the market price of the affected bond.

Bond Credit Ratings			
	Standard & Poor's	Moody's	Fitch
Investment Grade			
Highest quality	AAA	Aaa	AAA
High quality (very strong)	AA	Aa	AA
Upper medium grade (strong)	A	A	A
Medium grade	BBB	Baa	BBB
Below Investment Grade			
Somewhat speculative	BB	Ba	BB
Speculative	B	B	B
Highly speculative	CCC	Caa	CCC
Most speculative	CC	Ca	CC
Imminent default	C	C	C
Default	D	C	D

Some ratings may be modified by a plus (+) or minus (-) sign or numerical designators in order to show further relative standings within a major rating category.

Each of these services maintains a web site that provides useful additional information. Although access to specific ratings is typically restricted to paying clients with usernames and passwords, current rating actions, watchlists, and other information are generally available.

Standard & Poor's – www.standardandpoors.com

Moody's – www.moodys.com

Fitch – www.fitchratings.com

Bond Insurance. The credit quality of a bond issue can be enhanced by bond insurance issued by specialized insurance firms that guarantee the timely payments of interest and principal. These insurance firms are rated by one or more nationally recognized rating agencies and the insured bonds receive the same rating as the insurance firms. In the past, bond insurance was most often used with municipal bonds, mortgage bonds, and other asset-backed securities, but it is now being expanded to other securities.

CORPORATE BONDS

Types Of Corporate Bonds. Unlike government bonds, corporate bonds contain an element of default risk, which varies according to the issuer (see page 17). Some bonds are secured, while others are unsecured and the ability to make timely payments of interest and principal depends upon the creditworthiness of the company issuing the bonds. In general, **senior bonds** are backed by some type of collateral, whereas **junior bonds** are backed by only the good faith and credit of the issuer. A large variety of corporate bonds are sold or auctioned on the initial issue market and traded on the secondary markets.

(1) **Callable bonds** can be "retired" by the issuer *before* their scheduled maturity date. The specific call provisions are set forth in the **bond indenture** (see page 93). These provisions may stipulate a required time delay after the original issue date during which the bond is not vulnerable to being called. Furthermore, if a bond is called the issuer may be required to pay the bondholder a **call premium** above the par value of the bond (see Par Value, page 93). The process of recalling a bond is referred to as a **redemption**. It is then said that the bond has been **called away**. Bonds are typically called when interest rates have fallen to a point that the issuer will save money by issuing new bonds with lower coupons (interest rates). In fact, the process is similar to when a homeowner refinances his home mortgage at a lower interest rate. Callable bonds involve an **interest rate risk**, because the bondholder whose bonds have been called away is faced with having to reinvest the proceeds at lower rates of interest than those paid on the original issue. This feature is an important consideration in selecting bonds, and it is clearly indicated in bond listings (see page 107).

(2) **Collateral trust bonds** are similar to mortgage bonds but are secured by collateral such as other bonds, notes, or stocks.

(3) **Convertible bonds** offer bondholders the opportunity to exchange their bonds for a specific number of shares of the issuer's common stock.[7] In exchange for this conversion feature, the bonds generally carry a lower coupon (interest rate). The terms of conversion, such as the price of the stock, are established when the bonds are issued. Although conversion is at the discretion of the bondholder, the decision can be forced (e.g., a bond containing a call option is called in a low-interest market). Investors purchase convertible bonds because of their added flexibility. For example, if the issuer's stock increases in price, the bond will increase in value.

The bondholder can then chose to either convert the bond to stock or sell the bond at the higher price. Zero coupon convertible bonds are also issued (see page 105).

(4) **Debentures** are the most common form of bond. These bonds are unsecured and give the bondholder the status of a general creditor who is subordinate to the claims of secured creditors. Despite this subordinate status, debentures are generally considered high quality investments provided the issuer enjoys a high credit rating from the rating agencies (see page 101).

(5) **Equipment trust certificates** are issued by a trust (the lessor) that is formed to purchase specific assets and lease them to a lessee (e.g., purchase of a freight car that is leased to a railroad). Once the certificates have been repaid the lessee takes title to the equipment.

(6) **Guaranteed bonds** are guaranteed by someone other than the issuer. Typically the guarantee extends to interest and principal payments. With corporate bonds, the guarantor is often an affiliate or parent company; with government bonds the guarantor can be another government agency.

(7) **Income bonds** provide for interest payments that are contingent upon the issuer's earnings, but typically guarantee repayment of principal. In this sense income bonds are similar to preferred stock. These bonds are generally not investment grade, and are often used after a business has been reorganized due to financial difficulties.

(8) **Junk bonds**, also referred to as **high yield bonds**, these bonds carry ratings *below* BBB from Standard & Poor's or Baa from Moody's (see page 101). They are considered speculative and, therefore, entail a relatively high default risk (see page 17). Junk bonds are often less liquid then investment grade bonds. Junk bonds may be originally issued with below investment grade ratings, or junk status can result from a decline from an original investment grade rating (see "Fallen Angel," page 92). In order to attract investors, junk

> ### Keeping Current
>
> Trading in junk bonds is reported daily under **High-Yield Bonds** in the Bond Market Data Bank section of *The Wall Street Journal.*

bonds will typically offer interest rates that are from three to four percentage points higher than safer government issues (i.e., 300 to 400 basis points). This difference is known as the "yield spread" (see page 94).

(9) **Mortgage bonds** are secured by a mortgage lien against the issuer's real property (e.g., a mortgage against property interests of a utility company). The mortgage lien can be a senior or a junior lien.

(10) **Original Issue Discount (OID).** This is a bond that is issued at a price that is less than its par, or maturity value (the principal amount). OID is considered to be a form of interest that must be reported as income over the life of the bond. Both corporate and Treasury bonds are available as OID securities. A debt instrument that pays no interest prior to maturity, such as a zero coupon bond, is presumed to be issued at a discount. When a bond is purchased at a market price that is lower than par *and* lower than its issue price, the discount is referred to as a "market discount."[8]

(11) **Participation bonds** provide for a minimum coupon (interest rate), but then make additional interest payments based upon the issuer's earnings. In contrast, convertible bonds allow the bondholder to participate in the issuer's earnings growth by purchasing stock.

(12) **Zero Coupon Bonds.** Unlike bonds that pay interest every six months, these bonds pay no interest until maturity. (In bondspeak, they are said to have no "periodic coupon.") When issued, zero coupon bonds are sold at a deep discount from face (par) value, and upon maturity the amount redeemed is equal to face value, typically $1,000. For example, a 10-year zero coupon bond might be issued at a purchase price of $725. No interest would be paid until maturity, at which time the $1,000 redemption payment would represent a return of principal of $725, plus accrued interest of $275, compounded semiannually. Another variation of zero coupon bonds is created from bonds that are originally issued as interest paying bonds, but are then subsequently stripped of their coupons and resold as zero coupon bonds.

The semiannual reinvestment of interest works to the bondholder's advantage when interest rates fall (because accrued interest is reinvested at a *higher* rate then currently available), but can also work to the bondholder's disadvantage when interest rates rise (because accrued interest is invested at a *lower* rate then currently available). This feature causes zero coupon bonds to be far more volatile in the secondary markets then coupon (interest paying) bonds. The bondholder is required to pay income taxes annually on the accrued interest, even though no interest is received during the life of the bond. However, federal income taxes can be *deferred* by purchasing zero coupon bonds within a qualified retirement plan, or *avoided* by purchasing zero coupon municipal bonds (see page 118). As with coupon bonds, zero coupon bonds are issued with call and conversion features (see pages 92 and 103). Zero coupon bonds are issued by corporations, municipalities, and the United States Treasury.

Taxation Of Corporate Bonds. From a *corporation's* perspective, the interest payments made to bondholders have the advantage of being deductible for federal income tax purposes, whereas dividends paid to stockholders are nondeductible. From the *investor's* perspective, interest payments are included in income at ordinary income tax rates, but any gain on the sale of a bond held for more than one year offers the advantage of being taxed at lower long-term capital gains rates.[9] Also, if a bond is purchased for less than its maturity (par) value, the excess of the amount received at maturity over the purchase price is treated as long-term capital gain (provided the bond has been held for over one year).

Tracking Availability & Performance. Corporate bond prices are printed daily in newspapers throughout the country (see page 108 for an example from *The Wall Street Journal*). Typically these consist of tables of representative bond prices from recent bond trading. However, it is important to recognize that the bond market is primarily a dynamic, over-the-counter market in which bond prices are negotiated continually throughout the day. Going online offers a very easy way to appreciate the dynamic nature of this market. The bond quotation below contains the essential information needed by an investor who is contemplating purchase of corporate bonds, except for the specific **markup** or sales charge. The markup is included in the quoted price and varies according to the dealer.

Digging Deeper

The Bond Market Association offers an excellent online resource for information about bonds at: www.investing inbonds.com.

Corporate *Bond Detail*

MAY DEPT STORES CO   **Coupon: 8.300**   Maturity: 07-15-2026
Callable

Description
CUSIP	577778BA0
Listed?	No
Ratings	A2/A+
Industry	Industrial
Delivery	Book Entry
Dated Date	07-15-1996
First Coupon	01-15-1997
Pay Frequency	Semi-Annual
Settlement Date	06-19-2002

Offering
Quantity Available	1000
Order Quantity	20
Minimum	
Price	109.000
Yld to Mat	7.487
Yld to Call	6.643
	to **07-15-2006**
Current Yld	7.615

Call Schedule
Date	Price	Yield
07-15-2006	104.150	6.643
07-15-2007	103.735	6.799
07-15-2008	103.320	6.908
07-15-2009	102.905	6.988
07-15-2010	102.490	7.052

Net Money
Principal	$21,800.00
Acc'd Int	$710.11
Misc. Fee	$50.00
Total	$22,560.11

The quotation above was obtained on June 14, 2002. The bond was issued by May Department Stores Company with a maturity of July 15, 2026, and a coupon of 8.3%. It is rated A2 by Moody's and A+ by Standard & Poor's. Purchasing the bond at the current price of 109.000% of face (i.e., $1,090 each) would produce a yield to maturity of 7.487%. However, this bond is callable, with the first call date being July 15, 2006. If it were called on that date at a redemption price of 104.150 percent of face (i.e., $1,041.50 for a $1,000 par bond), the yield to call would be 6.643%. If it were not called on July 15, 2006, the next call date would be July 15, 2007. If then called at $1,037.35 per $1,000 par bond, the yield to call would be 6.799%. The total price for 20 bonds is $22,560.11, consisting of: a principal payment of $21,800.00; accrued interest of $710.11; and a miscellaneous fee of $50.00 charged on orders of less than 100 bonds. The first coupon payment was on January 15, 1997; therefore, interest is payable on January 15 and July 15. If 20 bonds were purchased, the semiannual interest payment would be $830 ($1,000 \times .083 = 83 \div 2 = 41.50 \times 20 = 830$).

The following is a typical listing of representative corporate bond sales as reported daily in *The Wall Street Journal*.

U.S. Exchange Bonds

4 p.m. ET Friday, May 17, 2002

NEW YORK BONDS
Corporation Bonds

BONDS	CUR YLD	VOL	CLOSE	NET CHG
JPMChse 6⅛08	6.1	163	101	-0.38
KCS En 8⅞06	11.2	75	79.50	...
K&B Hm 7¾04	7.5	8	103	0.13
K&B Hm 9⅝06	9.2	10	104.25	...
Leucadia 7¾13	7.6	10	101.25	0.75
Lucent 7¼06	8.8	257	82.13	-0.25
Lucent 5½08	7.9	15	69.75	-0.63
Lucent 6½28	10.2	82	64	-0.25
Lucent 6.45s29	10.1	36	63.88	0.88
MBNA 8.28s26	8.5	50	97	-1.25
Malan 9½04	cv	150	88.50	0.50
McDnl 6⅝05	6.6	50	101	-0.50
McDnl 7⅜33	7.4	5	100	0.25
MD... 9¼05	4.5	5	95.38	0.13

BONDS	CUR YLD	VOL	CLOSE	NET CHG
Lucent 7¼ 06	8.8	257	82.13	-0.25

The current yield is 8.8%, which is the interest return as a percentage of the current selling price of $821.30 (note the deep discount of $178.70 from the $1,000 face). The dollar volume of sales was $257,000 (257 × 1,000).

Lucent Technologies issued this bond paying 7¼ rate of interest (i.e., $36.25 every 6 months, or $72.50 total interest per year). It matures in 06, or the year 2006.

On May 17, 2002, the bond closed at 82.13, or $821.30 (82.13% of the face amount of $1,000). The net change from the prior closing price (on May 16th) was down .25 percent. This fraction is based on the par value of the bond, or $1,000. Therefore, it was down $2.50 (.0025 × 1,000 = 2.50). The prior close on May 16th was 84.63 (82.13 + 2.50 = 84.63).

TREASURY ISSUES

United States Treasury securities, also referred to as "Treasuries," include Treasury bills, notes, and bonds. These are debt instruments issued by the United States Treasury to raise the money needed to operate the federal government and to pay off maturing obligations. They are considered a safe and secure investment option because the full faith and credit of the United States government guarantees that interest and principal payments will be made on time. Treasury bills, notes, and bonds (but not U.S. *savings* bonds) are classified as "marketable securities" because after they are issued they can be sold prior to maturity in the secondary market at prevailing market prices.

Treasury Bills.[10] Also referred to as "T-bills," these are short-term securities that mature in one year or less from their issue date. T-bills are purchased at a discount (i.e., for a price less than their par (face) value). When they mature, the par value is paid to the investor (see page 93). For example, if a 26-week $10,000 T-bill is bought for $9,750 and held it until maturity, the investor would receive interest of $250. Instead of receiving interest payments the T-bill purchaser pays less than the par (face) value and

Keeping Current

Representative over-the-counter quotations for T-bills are reported daily under **Treasury Bills** in the Treasury Bonds, Notes and Bills section of *The Wall Street Journal.*

receives the full face amount upon maturity (i.e., T-bills are purchased at a discount). There are two ways of calculating the interest rate – the discount rate and the coupon-equivalent yield (see page 111).

Treasury Notes And Bonds.[11] These securities pay a fixed rate of interest every six months until the maturity date, when the fixed, or inflation-adjusted, principal is paid. The Treasury issues two kinds of notes and bonds – fixed-principal and inflation-indexed (see page 110). The only difference between notes and bonds is their length until maturity. Treasury notes mature in more than a year, but not more than 10 years from their issue date. Bonds, on the other hand, mature in more than 10 years. Notes and bonds are typi-

Keeping Current

Representative over-the-counter quotations for government bonds and notes are reported daily under **Government Bonds & Notes** in the Treasury Bonds, Notes and Bills section of *The Wall Street Journal.*

cally purchased for a price close to their par value. Treasury bonds have not been offered since the Treasury's decision in October of 2001 to suspend issuance of the 30-year bond.

Matrix - Treasury Bills, Notes & Bonds			
	Interest Rate & How Paid	Maturities	Taxation
Treasury Bills (T-bills)	Sold at a discount with the rate determined at weekly auctions.	1 year and under, but currently most auctions offer maturities of 4-weeks, 13-weeks and 26-weeks.	1. Not subject to state or local income taxes. 2. Included in federal income taxes upon maturity, or earlier if sold on secondary market.
Treasury Notes	Interest is paid every 6 months.	Current maturities offered are 2-years, 5-years, and 10-years. Other maturities are available on secondary market.	1. Not subject to state or local income taxes. 2. Included in federal income taxes as interest is paid.
Treasury Bonds	Interest is paid every 6 months.	Over 10 years, but currently new bond issues have been suspended. Existing bonds are available on secondary market.	1. Not subject to state or local income taxes. 2. Included in federal income taxes as interest is paid.

The minimum issue amount of any Treasury bill, note, or bond is $1,000. Additional amounts must be in multiples of $1,000. The price is set at the average of competitive bids accepted. Treasury bills, notes, and bonds can be purchased in a number of different ways. **New issues** can be purchased by bid (noncompetitive "tender" offer) placed directly with the government in a program called TreasuryDirect (see page 91), or placed through brokers, dealers, or financial institutions, in what is called the Commercial Book-Entry System (see page 91). **Previously issued securities** can be *bought and sold* on the secondary market through brokers, dealers, or financial institutions. Provided the bondholder is a TreasuryDirect customer, previously issued securities can also be *sold* thought a government program known as SellDirect.

For additional information see: www.publicdebt.treas.gov/sec/sec.htm. Although poorly organized, this cite contains a great deal of information.

Treasury Inflation-Protection Securities (TIPS).[12] Also called "Treasury Inflation-Indexed Securities," TIPS are a special type of Treasury notes and bonds intended to avoid loss of value due to inflation. As with other Treasury notes and bonds, TIPS make semi-annual interest payments and pay principal when the security matures. However, unlike other Treasury notes and bonds, the interest and redemption payments for TIPS are tied to inflation. The principal value of a TIP is adjusted based on the Consumer Price Index. At maturity the security is redeemed at the greater of its inflation-adjusted principal amount or its par value. Therefore, in the unlikely event of deflation, the redemption amount cannot be less than the amount paid for the security. TIPS pay a fixed rate of interest, but this rate is applied not to the par amount of the security, but to the inflation-adjusted principal. If inflation occurs throughout the life of the security, interest payments will increase. However, in the event of deflation, interest payments could decrease. Specifically, each interest payment is calculated by multiplying the inflation-indexed principal (regardless of whether it's greater or less than the par value) by one-half the fixed interest rate as determined at auction.

For example, assume a TIP was issued with a par value of $1,000 and an annual interest rate of 4.6%. Also assume that during the first year the CPI increased by 3.4%. Without inflation-indexing, the semi-annual interest payment would be $23.00 (1,000 × .046 = 46.00 ÷ 2 = 23.00). However, with inflation indexing the inflation-indexed principal would be $1,034 (1,000 × 1.034 = 1,034). Applying the annual interest rate of 4.6% to this inflation-indexed principal produces a semi-annual interest payment of $23.78 (1,034 × .046 = 47.56 ÷ 2 = 23.78). Currently, 10-year Inflation-Indexed notes are auctioned in July, October and January. They may be purchased through TreasuryDirect or the Commercial Book-Entry System (see page 91). Like other Treasury notes and bonds, TIPS are exempt from state and local taxes. However, both interest income and any inflation-adjusted increase in principal are subject to federal income taxes.

STRIPs. Also known as "zero-coupon securities," these are Treasury securities that do not make periodic interest payments. Market participants create STRIPs by separating the interest and principal parts of a Treasury note or bond. For example, a 10-year Treasury note consists of 20 interest payments, one every six months for 10 years, and a principal payment payable at maturity. When this security is "stripped," each of the 20 interest payments and the principal payment become separate securities and can be held and transferred separately. STRIPS can only be bought and sold through a financial institution, broker, or dealer and are held in the commercial book-entry system (see page 91).

Measuring Returns. Generally one of two methods is used to measure the returns on Treasury bonds and notes.

(1) **Discount Rate.** Also known as the "discount yield," this method of calculating the interest rate divides the annual interest received by the face value. For example, if the interest was $500 and the face was $10,000 then the discount rate would be 5% (500 ÷ 10,000 = .05). Typically used in newspaper reports, this method understates the actual yield.

(2) **Coupon-Equivalent Yield.** This is a more accurate method of calculating the interest rate; it is determined by dividing the annual interest received by the amount actually paid. For example, if the interest was $500 and the amount paid was $9,500, then the coupon equivalent yield would be 5.26% (500 ÷ 9,500 = .0526). To calculate the coupon equivalent yield for 13-week and 26-week T-bills an appropriate time multiplier must be used.

Treasury Auctions. All Treasury issues, except savings bonds, are sold at public auction. At Treasury auctions, all successful bidders are awarded securities at the same price, which is the price equal to the highest rate or yield of the competitive bids accepted. Approximately one week before each auction, a press release is issued announcing the type of security being sold, the amount being sold, the auction date, and other perti- *www.treasurydirect.gov* nent information. Many newspapers also report Treasury auction schedules in their financial sections. To participate in an auction, a bid may be submitted either "noncompetitively" or "competitively." An investor who bids *noncompetitively* receives the full amount of the security requested at the return as determined at that auction, but noncompetitive bids are limited to $1 million in Treasury bill auctions and $5 million in Treasury note or bond auctions. Most individual investors bid noncompetitively.

Bid And Ask Prices. The bid and ask prices of Treasury bonds and notes are

Decimal Equivalents Of 32nds							
# 32nds	Decimal	# 32nds	decimal	# 32nds	decimal	# 32nds	decimal
1	0.03125	9	0.28125	17	0.53125	25	0.78125
2	0.06250	10	0.31250	18	0.56250	26	0.81250
3	0.09375	11	0.34375	19	0.59375	27	0.84375
4	0.12500	12	0.37500	20	0.62500	28	0.87500
5	0.15625	13	0.40625	21	0.65625	29	0.90625
6	0.18750	14	0.43750	22	0.68750	30	0.93750
7	0.21875	15	0.46875	23	0.71875	31	0.96875
8	0.25000	16	0.50000	24	0.75000	32	1.00000

often referred to in 32nds. The following table provides the decimal equivalents.

Tracking Availability & Performance. Prices of Treasury issues are given daily in newspapers throughout the country. Typically these consist of representative tables of bond prices from recent bond trading. However, it is important to recognize that the bond market is primarily a dynamic over-the-counter market in which bond prices are negotiated continually throughout the day. As with corporate bonds, going online offers a very easy way to appreciate the dynamic nature of this market. The following bond quotation contains the essential information needed by an investor contemplating a purchase of bonds.

Treasury *Bond Detail*

T-BOND Non Callable		**Coupon:** 5.250	**Maturity:** 11-15-2028

Description

CUSIP	912810FF0
Dated Date	11-15-1998
First Coupon	05-15-1999
Pay Frequency	Semi-Annual
Settlement Date	06-24-2002

Offering

Quantity Available	2000
Order Quantity	50

Minimum	
Price	96.526
Yld to Mat	5.501
Yld to Call	
Current Yld	5.439

Call Schedule

Date Price Yield

Non Callable

Net Money

Principal	$48,263.00
Acc'd Int	$285.33
Total	$48,598.33

The above quotation was obtained on June 21, 2002. This 30-year Treasury bond was issued on November 15, 1998, with a maturity of November 15, 2028, and a coupon of 5.25%. Purchasing the bond at the current price of 96.526% of face (i.e., $965.26 each) would produce a yield to maturity of 5.501%. The bond is not callable. For 50 bonds the total price of $48,598.33 consists of a principal payment of $48,263.00 and accrued interest of $285.33. According to the dealer, the markup is included in the quoted price, except for a miscellaneous fee of $50.00, which is charged on orders of less than 100 bonds. The first coupon payment was on May 15, 1999; therefore interest is payable on May 15 and November 15. If 50 bonds were purchased, the semiannual interest payment would be $1,312.50 ($1,000 \times .0525 = 52.50 \div 2 = 26.25 \times 50 = 1,312.50$). The current yield of 5.439% is determined by dividing the annual interest payment by the purchase price ($52.50 \div 965.26 = .05439$). Because the bond can be purchased at a **discount** from face, the yield to maturity of 5.501% is higher than the coupon of 5.25%. See Yield To Maturity on page 100.

Treasury Bills. The following is a listing of representative over-the-counter T-bill sales of $1,000,000 or more as reported daily in *The Wall Street Journal*. Notes and bond sales are listed separately (see page 115).

Treasury Bonds, Notes and Bills

Treasury Bills

MATURITY	DAYS TO MAT	BID	ASKED	CHG	ASK YLD
Jun 06 02	1	1.69	1.68	0.01	1.70
Jun 13 02	8	1.71	1.70	0.02	1.72
Jun 20 02	15	1.69	1.68	...	1.70
Jun 27 02	22	1.70	1.69	0.01	1.72
Jul 05 02	30	1.71	1.70	0.02	1.73
Jul 11 02	36	1.70	1.69	0.03	1.72
Jul 18 02	43	1.68	1.67	0.02	1.70
Jul 25 02	50	1.67	1.66	...	1.69
Aug 01 02	57	1.69	1.68	0.02	1.71
Aug 08 02	64	1.68	1.67	...	1.70
Aug 15 02	71	1.70	1.69	0.01	1.72
Aug 22 02	78	1.71	1.70	...	1.73
Au~ ~~ ~~	85	~~~~	1.70	-0.0~	~73

MATURITY	DAYS TO MAT	BID	ASK	CHG	ASK YLD
Jul 18 02	43	1.68	1.67	0.02	-0.25

This is a Treasury bill that matures on July 18, 2002, or 43 days from the settlement date.

CHG refers to the change in the bid price from the previous trading day. The **bid** price has increased by .02 of one percent, or $.20 per $1,000 of face amount (.0002 × 1,000 = .20). A bid price that has fallen is preceded by a minus sign ("-"). **ASK YLD** refers to the rate of return an investor would receive if the bill were purchased at the **ask** price of $983.20. It is the yield to maturity. See page 100.

Bills are quoted at a discount from the par, or face, value. The bid and asked figures represent a rate of discount. The **bid** of 1.68 means that the price offered to sellers was a 1.68% discount from face. Assuming a $1,000 face, the bid price would have been $983.20 (1,000 – (.0168 × 1,000) = 1,000 – 16.80 = 983.20). The **ask** of 1.67 means that the lowest price a seller would accept was a 1.67% discount from face. Again, assuming a $1,000 face, the ask price would have been $983.30 (1,000 – (.0167 × 1,000) = 1,000 – 16.70 = 983.30). These quotes are as of mid-afternoon of the previous trading day.

Treasury Bonds And Notes. The following is a listing of representative over-the-counter government bond and note sales of $1,000,000 or more as reported daily in *The Wall Street Journal*. Bill sales are listed separately (see page 114).

Treasury Bonds, Notes and Bills

RATE	MATURITY MO/YR	BID	ASKED	CHG	ASK YLD
Government Bonds & Notes					
9.125	May 09	111:04	111:05	-3	3.14
6.000	Aug 09n	107:06	107:07	-9	4.80
10.375	Nov 09	115:25	115:26	-4	3.55
4.250	Jan 10i	108:15	108:16	-4	2.99
6.500	Feb 10n	110:09	110:10	-9	4.87
11.750	Feb 10	120:13	120:14	-3	3.70
10.000	May 10	116:30	116:31	-4	3.84
5.750	Aug 10n	105:12	105:13	-10	4.94
12.750	Nov 10	127:28	127:29	-5	3.98
3.500	Jan 11i	103:12	103:13	-5	3.04
5.000	Feb 11n	100:01	100:02	-11	4.99
13.875	May 11	135:03	135:04	-6	4.12
5.000	Aug 11n	99:24	99:25	-11	5.03
14.000	Nov 11	139:01	139:02	-7	4.25

RATE	MATURITY MO/YR	BID	ASKED	CHG	ASK YLD
6.500	Feb 10n	110:09	110:10	-9	4.87

This is a Treasury note paying its holders 6.5% interest and that is due to mature in February 2010 ("n" indicates a Treasury note, "i" indicates an inflation-indexed issue, and no letter indicates a Treasury bond).

CHG refers to the change in the bid price from the previous trading day. The **bid** price has fallen 9/32nds of a percent (.28125%), or $2.81 per $1,000 face amount (.0028125 × 1,000). ASK YLD refers to the rate of return an investor would receive if the note were purchased at the **ask** price of $1,103.12. It is the yield to maturity. See page 100.

These quotes are a percentage of the note's face value ($1,000) as of mid-afternoon on the previous trading day. Figures after the colons represent 32nds. Therefore, the number 09 in the bid quote represents 9/32nds of one percent, or .2812%; and the number 10 in the ask quote represents 10/32nds of one percent, or .3125%. The **bid** of 110:09 or $1,102.81 (1.102812 × 1,000), was the highest price being offered by buyers. The **ask** of 110:10, or $1,103.12 (1.103125 × 1,000), was the lowest price sellers would accept. The difference (spread) was 31 cents per $1,000 face amount. See page 112 for a table of decimal equivalents.

Treasury Bonds vs. Savings Bonds. Both of these bonds are issued by the Department of the Treasury, but they are not the same. One of the primary differences is that Treasury bonds are *marketable* and savings bonds are not; that is, the owner of a Treasury bond can sell his bond prior to maturity, but the owner of a savings bond cannot transfer his security. Reference to a "Treasury bond" means a marketable security, not a savings bond. Also, reference to "Treasury securities" means only marketable Treasury securities. Treasury securities can be purchased on the secondary market; savings bonds cannot. Since 1986, all securities issued by the Treasury Department have been *book*-entry, meaning they exist only as electronic records in computers. Savings bonds are currently available in paper and electronic format. (But on May 5, 2003, the Treasury Department announced that it intends to transform the savings bond program from paper certificates to accounts accessed over the Internet.)

Savings Bonds. Savings bonds are Treasury issues that are payable to only the person to whom they are registered. They are not negotiable. Savings bonds can be purchased for as little as $25 and can earn interest for up to 30 years; but they can be cashed 12 months after purchase (6 months for bonds purchased before February 1, 2003). Series EE bonds and Series I bonds can be purchased for cash, but Series HH bonds can be acquired only in exchange for Series EE/E bonds and savings notes, or when the bondholder reinvests the proceeds of matured Series H bonds.

(1) **Series E/EE Bonds.**[13] These bonds and savings notes are accrual securities. As the investor holds these bonds, interest is periodically added to the amount that was originally paid, to establish the current redemption value. As this interest accrues, the value of the bond increases. When the investor cashes an E/EE bond or savings note, he receives the redemption value, which represents the return of his original investment, plus the interest earned while he held the bond.

(2) **I Bonds.**[14] I Bonds are a type of bond designed for investors seeking to protect the purchasing power of their investments and earn a guaranteed real rate of return. I Bonds are an accrual-type security, meaning interest is added to the bond monthly and paid when the bond is cashed. I Bonds are sold at face value and grow in value with inflation-indexed earnings for up to 30 years. The chart below provides an overview of the major differences between EE Bonds and I Bonds.

(3) **Series H/HH Bonds.**[15] These bonds cannot be purchased for cash; they can only be acquired in exchange for Series EE/E bonds, or upon reinvestment of the proceeds of matured Series H bonds. Series HH bonds are current-income securities and unlike EE bonds, the bond itself does not increase in value. A fixed rate of interest is paid every six months. Series H

bonds were issued from June 1952 through December 1979, whereas Series HH bonds have been issued from January 1980 to the present.

Comparison – EE Bond vs. I Bond		
	EE Bond	**I Bond**
Features	Paper: Issued at 50% of face value. (A $100 paper EE Bond costs $50.) Electronic: Issued for any amount of $25 or more to the penny.	Issued at face value. (A $100 I Bond costs $100.)
	Paper: Offered in 8 denominations ($50, $75, $100, $200, $500, $1,000, $5,000, and $10,000). Electronic: Issued for any amount above $25, regardless of denomination.	Offered in 8 denominations ($50, $75, $100, $200, $500, $1,000, $5,000, and $10,000).
	Paper: $15,000 annual purchase limit ($30,000 face value, per person). Electronic: $30,000 per person, per year.	$30,000 annual purchase limit per Social Security Number.
Interest	Calculated as 90% of 6-month averages of 5-year Treasury Security yields.	Calculated **as an earning of a** fixed rate of return and a semiannual inflation rate based on CPI-U.
	Rates announced every May 1 and November 1.	Rate Announcement: Same as EE.
	Guaranteed to reach face value in 17 years.	No guaranteed level of earnings.
	Increases in value monthly and compound semiannually. Interest is paid when the bond is redeemed.	Generally increases in value monthly and interest compounds semiannually (except in periods of deflation when the bond value could remain unchanged). Interest is paid when the bond is redeemed.
	Earns interest for up to 30 years.	Life span: Same as EE.
Exchange	Can be exchanged for Series HH savings bonds.	Cannot be exchanged for any other series of savings bonds.
Cashing	Can be redeemed after first 12 months.	Same as EE.
	A 3-month interest penalty applies to bonds redeemed during the first 5 years.	Same as EE.

Comparison – EE Bond vs. I Bond (cont'd)		
	EE Bond	**I Bond**
Cashing (cont'd)	Financial institution reports interest earnings (i.e., difference between redemption value and purchase price) on IRS form 1099-INT. Savings bonds are exempt from state and local income taxes.	Same as EE.
	Eligible for tax benefits upon redemption when used for qualified education expenses.	Same as EE.

Source: www.publicdebt.treas.gov/sav/sbieevsi.htm

MUNICIPAL BONDS

Municipal bonds, also referred to as "tax-exempt bonds," are issued by states, counties, cities, and other political units in order to fund a variety of projects. The main attraction for the investor of "munis" has been the exemption from federal, and sometimes, state income taxes. Because munis typically pay lower coupon rates, they are most attractive to high-income investors whose after-tax return will be higher despite lower rates of interest (see table of Equivalent Taxable Yields on page 120). As with corporate bonds, municipal bonds often have call provisions, meaning that bonds with coupon rates exceeding market rates are likely to be redeemed by their issuer.

> **Keeping Current**
>
> A survey of current national municipal bond yields can be found at: www.bloomberg.com/markets/rates.

Types Of Municipal Bonds. The two basic categories of municipal bonds are general-obligation bonds and revenue bonds. The *general-obligation bond,* also referred to as a "full faith and credit bond," is backed by the taxing authority of the issuer. If the taxing power of the issuer is subject to a legal limit, then the general obligation bond is known as a *limited tax bond.* When there is no such limit, the general obligation bond is referred to as an *unlimited tax bond.* In contrast to the general obligation bond, the *revenue bond* relies upon income produced by the underlying project to pay bond principal and interest. The *industrial development bond* is a variation of the revenue bond issued by development agencies as established by local authorities. This bond is secured only by the lease payments made under by a corporation for use of the underlying facility. Industrial development bonds issued after 1987 may be subject to federal income taxes, unless they are used to fund civic services, such as pollution control facilities and airports.

Municipal Bond Ratings & Insurance. Many municipal bonds are rated by the same rating services that rate corporate bonds (see page 101). As with corporate ratings, a bond rating of BB and below is considered below investment grade, whereas a bond rating of BBB, Baa, or better, is considered "investment grade." Investment grade municipal bonds are generally viewed as falling between highly rated corporate bonds and government agency bonds (see table of Bond Credit Ratings on page 102). To enhance their ratings, private municipal bond insurance companies frequently insure municipal bonds. Typically these bond insurers will themselves have very high ratings of AAA or AA from the ratings services. Insurance guarantees that the bond investor will receive timely payments of both interest and principal, but it does not insure against the risk of a bond's market value falling due to increased interest rates. The investor assessing an insured municipal bond's credit worthiness would be better advised to ignore the *issuer's* ratings, relying instead on the *insurer's* rating.

Federal Taxation.[16] Depending upon their purpose and date of issue, the interest paid on municipal bonds may or may not be tax-exempt, or subject to the alternative minimum tax. The following chart provides an overview of how interest payments are treated for federal income tax purposes. The funding examples are not all inclusive.

Taxation Of Interest Payments On Municipal Bonds

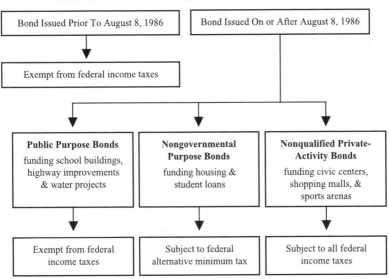

Profit from the purchase and sale of municipal bonds may be subject to federal taxation. For example, if a bond is purchased at a premium the premium amount must be amortized over the remaining life of the bond and this affects the bondholder's basis. The holder's basis in the bond includes the amount originally paid for the bond plus any additions to basis, such as original issue discount (OID). When the bond is sold or redeemed prior to maturity any amounts received in excess of basis are generally taxed as capital gains. These calculations can be quite complicated and the advice of tax counsel should be sought.[17]

State Taxation. Most states and municipalities do not tax interest income received from tax-exempt bonds issued by that state, its agencies, or its political subdivisions. In contrast, virtually every state imposing an income tax also taxes interest income received from bonds issued by other states, out-of-state agencies and political subdivisions. The state exemptions for interest on in-state bonds may not extend to: (1) capital gains resulting from a sale or other disposition of the bonds; and (2) ordinary income resulting from application of the market discount rules. Again, the advice of tax counsel should be sought.

Tax-Free vs. Taxable Yield Comparisons. Due to their tax-free nature, municipal bonds typically offer lower interest rates than comparable corporate and Treasury bonds. Depending upon the investor's individual marginal income tax bracket, a higher interest paying taxable bond may provide more after-tax earnings than a lower interest tax-free municipal bond. The following table provides equivalent taxable yields based upon assumed tax-exempt yields in one-quarter percent increments from 2.00% to 6.00%.

Equivalent Taxable Yields					
2003 Federal Income Tax Brackets (updated for JGTRRA 2003)					
Tax Exempt Yield	15%	25%	28%	33%	35%
2.00	2.35	2.67	2.78	2.99	3.08
2.25	2.65	3.00	3.13	3.36	3.46
2.50	2.94	3.33	3.47	3.73	3.85
2.75	3.24	3.67	3.82	4.10	4.23
3.00	3.53	4.00	4.17	4.48	4.62
3.25	3.82	4.33	4.51	4.85	5.00
3.50	4.12	4.67	4.86	5.22	5.38
3.75	4.41	5.00	5.21	5.60	5.77
4.00	4.71	5.33	5.56	5.97	6.15
4.25	5.00	5.67	5.90	6.34	6.54
4.50	5.29	6.00	6.25	6.72	6.92
4.75	5.59	6.33	6.60	7.09	7.31
5.00	5.88	6.67	6.94	7.46	7.69
5.25	6.18	7.00	7.29	7.84	8.08
5.50	6.47	7.33	7.64	8.21	8.46
5.75	6.76	7.67	7.99	8.58	8.85
6.00	7.06	8.00	8.33	8.96	9.23
This table assumes the investor is subject to federal income taxes only.					

For example, assume John, an investor in a 28% tax bracket had the choice of investing in a 4.25% tax-free municipal bond or a 6.15% Treasury bond. For John, a 4.25% tax-free yield is the same as a 5.90% taxable yield, meaning that any taxable return over 5.90% will provide greater after-tax earnings than the 4.25% tax-free return. Therefore, John would choose to invest in the taxable 6.15% Treasury bond. On the other hand, if the choice was between investing in a 4.25% tax-free municipal bond or a 5.75% Treasury bond, John would chose the 4.25% tax-free municipal bond.

When a municipal bond is also exempt from state and local income taxes it is important to consider the investor's maximum effective tax bracket including these state and local taxes. Assume Jane, an investor, is in a 28% federal tax bracket, but is also subject to an additional 6% of state income taxes, for a total maximum tax rate of 34%. The following formula can be used to determine the equivalent taxable yield for Jane, who is considering investing in a 4.25% tax-free municipal bond.

$$\text{Equivalent Taxable Yield} = \frac{\text{Tax-Free Yield}}{100 - \text{Tax Bracket}}$$

$$\text{Equivalent Taxable Yield} = \frac{4.25}{100 - 34}$$

$$\text{Equivalent Taxable Yield} = \frac{4.25}{66}$$

$$\text{Equivalent Taxable Yield} = .0644 \text{ or } 6.44\%$$

AGENCY SECURITIES

A wide array of agency securities is available on the market. Some are issued by **federally related institutions** such as the Government National Mortgage Association (GNMA), while others are issued by **government-sponsored entities** such as the Federal National Mortgage Association (Fannie Mae) and the Federal Home Loan Mortgage Corporation (Freddie Mac).[18] Funds are raised in one of two ways – either the agency directly issues its own securities, or the agency guarantees the timely payment of principal and interest on the indebtedness of its constituents (e.g., mortgages placed on private homes – see Mortgage-Backed Securities on page 122).

Investment Considerations. Although agency securities are generally not obligations of the federal government, some have direct government guarantees, and all are backed by various state and federal agencies. Because of this, most investors view them as having very low default risk. However, as with other securities, if purchased at a premium agency securities are subject to interest rate risk (see page 17). Often these securities are also subject to **prepayment risk**, meaning that in the event of prepayment the investor is likely to be faced with having to reinvest proceeds at prevailing lower interest rates (similar to the bond call risk, see page 17). When compared to Treasury securities, other limitations of agency securities include high minimum purchase requirements and a more restricted resale market that can make them more difficult and expensive to trade. Short-term agency securities, similar to Treasury bills, are issued at a discount from face value and pay no interest until maturity. Long-term agency securities, similar to Treasury notes and bonds, are issued at face value and pay interest every six months. Mortgage-backed agency securities can be complicated to understand and often involve more demanding record keeping. Although interest payments are subject to federal income taxes, they may be exempt from state and local income taxes; but this should be confirmed before making an investment decision. Despite these limitations, the variety of available securities and the somewhat higher interest rates can make agency securities attractive to investors. As with other investment vehicles, mutual funds consisting of agency securities can also be purchased. Regarding the use of unit trusts and mutual funds, see Bond Funds vs. Individual Bonds on page 126.

Mortgage-Backed Securities.[19] These are securities that are secured by a pool of mortgage loans. (See table on page 125.) For example, issues of the Government National Mortgage Association (GNMA), commonly known as **Ginnie Maes**, are collections of mortgages with the same interest rate and maturity date that are secured by similar properties with similar values (e.g., single-family homes).[20] Each mortgage pool forms the basis of a security that is purchased by investors. Mortgage-backed securities are in turn classified as either of the following:

> ### Keeping Current
>
> Every day in *The Wall Street Journal* under the **Bond Market Data Bank** there is a report containing prices, yields, and spreads of mortgage-backed securities.

1. **Pass-throughs** pass interest and principal payments to investors *in direct proportion* to their pro-rata interests in the pool of mortgages.

2. **Collateralized Mortgage Obligations (CMOs)**, also known as **pay-throughs**, pass payments to investors according to a *pre-determined schedule* that can accommodate a variety of investment objectives. For example, Investor Class A might receive principal payments before Investor Class B, and Investor Class B would also receive a higher rate of interest as compensation for the delayed payments of principal (i.e., investments with longer maturities typically receive higher rates of interest). These various classes of ownership are known as **tranches**. While the wide diversity of CMOs makes them attractive to many investors, they can be complicated and difficult to evaluate.

Probably the biggest disadvantage of investing in mortgage-backed securities is the difficulty of accurately predicting the life span of a new security. Unlike corporate and government bonds, periodic payments include both interest and principal. In a market of falling interest rates, individuals prepay and refinance their mortgages. These prepayments force holders of mortgage-backed securities to reinvest these proceeds at lower prevailing rates of interest. Unlike the investor who purchases bonds with known callable dates, the investor in mortgage-backed securities cannot predict when, if ever, mortgages will be prepaid. Prepayment rate assumptions based on average experience are used to predict cash flows. The importance of predicting prepayment rates is important, as demonstrated by the following graph.

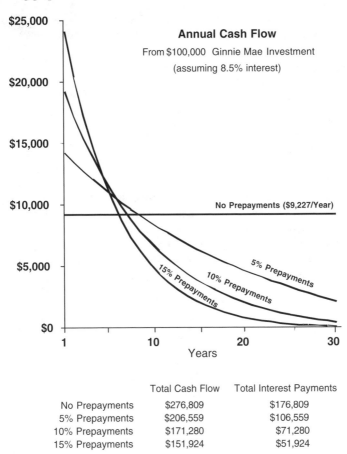

Annual Cash Flow
From $100,000 Ginnie Mae Investment
(assuming 8.5% interest)

No Prepayments ($9,227/Year)

5% Prepayments

10% Prepayments

15% Prepayments

Years

	Total Cash Flow	Total Interest Payments
No Prepayments	$276,809	$176,809
5% Prepayments	$206,559	$106,559
10% Prepayments	$171,280	$71,280
15% Prepayments	$151,924	$51,924

Assuming no prepayments, the investor would receive a level annual cash flow of $9,227 per year. (Of course, as with any amortization schedule, these annual payments would consist of interest and principal, with the interest payments decreasing each year and the principal payments increasing each year.) But if 5%

of the outstanding mortgages were prepaid each year, the investor would receive $14,189 in year 1, decreasing to $2,085 in year 30. Assuming 10% repayment, the investor would receive $19,151 in year 1, decreasing to $435 in year 30. Assuming 15% repayment, the investor would receive $24,114 in year 1, decreasing to $83 in year 30. Total interest payments would drop from $176,809 to just $51,924.

Real Estate Mortgage Investment Conduit (REMIC).[21] REMICs are pass-through, or flow-through, tax entities that hold mortgages secured by various types of real property, including residential and commercial properties. Many residential mortgage-backed securities guaranteed by government agencies are available as REMICs (see page 121). Most transactions in "commercial mortgage backed securities" (CMBS) are also now structured as REMICs. They offer investment flexibility because each REMIC is designed according to specific investor needs. Cash flows from the underlying collateral are allocated to individual bonds, called **tranches**, of varying maturities, coupons and payment priorities. A REMIC may include any number of classes of *regular* interests and must include a single *residual* interest class. These classes are assigned a coupon (fixed, floating, or zero interest rate), and the terms and conditions for payments to the investor. The income from a "regular" interest in a REMIC is treated as interest (i.e., reporting of original issue discount or market discount is made under the rules that apply to bonds). REMICs are complex investments that require careful consideration before investing, including consideration of various tax issues.[22]

Digging Deeper

For information about REMICs available from Freddie Mac, see:
www.freddiemac.com/mbs

Types Of Mortgage-Backed Securities					
	Ginnie Mae	**Freddie Mac PC**	**Freddie Mac GMC**	**FNMA CMBS**	**Mortgage-Backed Bond**
Payment Stream	Monthly; guaranteed 15-day delay; periodic prepayments	Monthly; guaranteed 44-day delay; periodic prepayments	Semi-annually; annual principal payments	Monthly; guaranteed 25-day delay; periodic prepayments	Semi-annually; principal at maturity or sale
Underlying Asset	FHA/VA mortgages	Conventional mortgages	Conventional mortgages	Conventional mortgages	General assets
Guarantee	Full faith and credit of U.S. Treasury	Freddie Mac's net worth; private mortgage insurance on mortgages with LTV over 80%	Freddie Mac's net worth; private mortgage insurance on mortgages with LTV over 80%	Freddie Mac's net worth; private mortgage insurance on mortgages with LTV over 80%	Overcollateralized by 150-200% with mortgage portfolio
Liquidity/ Secondary Market	Active market due to high volume of issue; risk-free status	Active market due to high volume of issue; low-risk status	Less active due to high volume of issue; lower issue volume	Unknown at this time	Same as Institutional PC
Rating/ Risk Equivalent	Government security; no rating required	Considered nearly equivalent to a government security; no rating	Same as Freddie Mac PC	Same as Freddie Mac PC	AAA due to continuous maintenance of position; overcollateralized position

Source: Stephen R. Leimberg et al., *The Tools and Techniques of Financial Planning*, 6th ed. (Cincinnati: The National Underwriter Company, 2002), p.422.

Bond Funds vs. Individual Bonds

	Bond Mutual Funds	Bond Unit Investment Trusts	Individual Bonds
Pros	Diversification; professional management; liquidity	Diversification; fixed maturity; fixed interest income	Higher yields; fixed maturity dates
Cons	More expensive: higher costs mean lower yields; no fixed maturity date	Not as liquid as mutual funds; higher sales charges than individual bonds	Not as liquid as funds; investor must manage
Brief Description	Managed portfolio of bonds	Fixed portfolio of bonds held in a trust	Individual securities
Maturity Date	No maturity date - bonds are constantly bought and sold	Trust buys a set of bonds with fixed maturities	Set maturity date, choice of 10+ years
Income Payments	Fluctuating monthly payments	Investor's choice: fixed monthly, quarterly, or semiannual payments	Semiannual, except zero coupon bonds
Liquidity	Sell anytime at current fund value	Sell anytime at current market price; less liquid than funds	Sell anytime at current market price; some bonds less liquid
Diversification	Constantly changing portfolio	Fixed diversity of investments	Individual chooses from multiple issues
Management	Professional	Monitored; not managed	Investor managed
Costs	Annual management; may have a load	Sales charge at purchase; annual fee	One-time charge at purchase or sale
Minimum Investment	Varies among funds	Often $1,000	Usually $5,000, and increments of $5,000
Reinvestment	Dividends can be reinvested	Some trusts allow reinvestment	Investor is required to reinvest
Availability	Always available	Can be limited by trust	Limited by issue

Source: www.bondsonline.com. Used with permission.

[1] Announcement in *The Wall Street Journal*, May 16, 2002, page C5.

[2] These include the Federal Home Loan Bank, the Federal Farm Credit Bank, and the Federal National Mortgage Association.

[3] See *The Wall Street Journal*, May 20, 2002, page C13.

[4] The taxation of original issue discount bonds varies according to the issue date and can be complicated. See *Tax Facts 2* (Cincinnati: The National Underwriter Company, 2003, revised annually), **Question 116** – How is original issue discount on corporate and Treasury obligations issued after July 1, 1982 included in income?

[5] See www.bondmarkets.com and *An Investor's Guide to Corporate Bonds* at www.investingin-bonds.com.

[6] See also Lawrence J. Gitman and Michael D. Joehnk, *Personal Financial Planning*, 7th ed. (Fort Worth: The Dryden Press, 1996), p. 472.

[7] See *Tax Facts 2*, **Question 105** – How is a convertible bond taxed on conversion?

[8] See *Tax Facts 2*, **Question 111** – How is gain or loss treated when a market discount bond is sold?

[9] See *Tax Facts 2*, **Question 103** – How are proceeds on the sale or retirement of a corporate bond taxed?

[10] See *Tax Facts 2*, **Question 93** – Is an investor who holds a T-bill required to include interest in income prior to sale or maturity of the bill? and **Question 94** – How is an investor taxed on the gain or loss on the sale or maturity of a Treasury bill?

[11] See *Tax Facts 2*, **Question 99** – What does the holder of a Treasury note or bond include in annual income? and **Question 100** – How are the proceeds taxed on sale or redemption of Treasury notes and bonds?

[12] See *Tax Facts 2*, **Question 108** – How are inflation-indexed bonds treated for tax purposes?

[13] See *Tax Facts 2*, **Question 139** – When is the interest on United States Savings Bonds Series E or EE taxed?

[14] See *Tax Facts 2*, **Question 144** – How is the owner of Series I bonds taxed?

[15] See *Tax Facts 2*, **Question 143** – How is the owner of Series H or HH bonds taxed?

[16] See *Tax Facts 2*, **Question 123** – Is interest on obligations issued by state and local governments taxable? and **Question 124** – Is tax-exempt interest treated as an item of tax preference for purposes of the alternative minimum tax?

[17] See *Tax Facts 2*, **Question 125** – How is gain or loss taxed on sale or redemption of tax-exempt bonds issued by a state or local government? and **Question 126** – Is premium paid for a tax-exempt bond deductible? Must basis in a tax-exempt bond be reduced by bond premium?

[18] Other government-sponsored entities include the Federal Farm Credit Bank System, the Farm Credit Financial Assistance Corporation, the Federal Home Loan Bank, the Student Loan Marketing Association (Sallie Mae), and the Resolution Trust Company. For an excellent discussion of agency securities and mortgage-backed securities see Robert Zipf, *How the Bond Market Works*, 2nd ed. (Paramus, New Jersey: New York Institute Of Finance, 1997), p. 57.

[19] An excellent source of information about mortgage-backed securities is Stephen R. Leimberg et al., *Tools & Techniques Of Financial Planning*, 6th ed. (Cincinnati: The National Underwriter Company, 2002), p. 417.

[20] See *Tax Facts 2*, **Question 146** – How is the monthly payment on Ginnie Mae mortgage backed pass-through certificates taxed?

[21] See *Tax Facts 2*, **Question 148** – How is the owner of a REMIC interest taxed?

[22] See Leimberg, et al., p. 503.

TYPES OF STOCK

Stocks, also referred to as shares, securities or equities, represent ownership interests in a company (see Securities on page 89). Although these ownership interests can take many different forms, generally a public corporation has two types of stock, preferred stock and common stock.

Preferred Stocks. The characteristics of preferred stocks make them a hybrid between common stocks and bonds. These characteristics can vary substantially from one preferred stock to another and it is important to carefully review the specifics of each issue. Although they typically provide for *fixed dividends* that cannot be changed by the board of directors, and must be paid before common stock dividends, preferred stock dividends are nevertheless dependent upon company earnings. The dividends are stated as either a specific dollar amount

> ### Keeping Current
>
> Each day a listing of preferred stocks traded on the AMEX, NASDAQ and NYSE are published under Preferred Stock Listings in *The Wall Street Journal.*

or as a "coupon" (i.e., 6% of face value). If the preferred stock is *cumulative* then no common stock dividends can be paid until all preferred dividends in arrears have been paid. Unlike common stockholders, the holders of preferred stock do not have a right to vote (except under limited circumstances, such as dividends being in arrears). In liquidation, the claims of preferred stockholders are senior to those of common stockholders, but subordinate to those of the corporation's general creditors and bondholders. However, preference with respect to assets and dividends comes at a cost. Unlike common stockholders, preferred stockholders will not receive increased dividends if a company prospers, and the price of preferred stocks will typically experience only limited appreciation (i.e., in this sense preferred stocks are more akin to bonds than common stocks). Although preferred stocks do not have maturity dates, they are often *callable* at the discretion of company management. Preferred stock with a *convertible* feature can be converted to a specific number of common shares at a set price. *Participating* preferred stocks give the stockholder, under certain conditions, a right to receive additional earnings payouts over and above the specified dividend rate (e.g., when common stock dividends exceed a specific amount).

Common Stocks. These are securities that represent the fundamental equity ownership of a corporation. Holders of common stock have the right to elect the company's board of directors and vote on corporate policy. When a company is successful, the common stockholders benefit

> ### Keeping Current
>
> Each day a listing of common stocks traded on the NYSE, AMEX, and NASDAQ are published in *The Wall Street Journal.*

through dividend payments and increases in stock value (i.e., capital appreciation). However, unlike preferred stockholders, dividend payments to common stockholders are discretionary, they are not guaranteed. In liquidation, the claims of common stockholders are subordinate to those of the corporation's general creditors, bondholders, and preferred stockholders (i.e., virtually the whole world). Although it is possible for stockholders to lose the entire value of their investment, they are not responsible for corporate debt or liabilities.

CLASSIFICATIONS OF COMMON STOCK

The following are some of the traditional broad classifications used by investors when categorizing common stocks. In general, these classifications tend to be made according to size, dividend policy, rate of growth, and stability. Note that income stocks, growth stocks, cyclical stocks, and defensive stocks are all classified according to the *nature of their objectives*; whereas large-cap, mid-cap, small-cap, and micro-cap stocks are primarily determined with regard to their *market value*. These categories are not mutually exclusive, there can be more than a bit of overlapping (e.g., a large-cap blue-chip stock that is also considered to be an income stock).

Income Stocks. These are stocks of more mature companies that have a history of making regular and higher-than-average dividend payments to common stockholders. They are purchased by investors for their current high dividend yield (see Dividend Yield, page 133). Unlike growth stocks, income stocks are not expected to experience the rapid expansion that produces substantial increases in stock values (i.e., corporate after-tax income is paid out as dividends, it is not reinvested for growth). However, unlike bonds and preferred stock, the income from dividends is likely to increase over time. Utility and auto stocks are a good examples of income stocks.

Growth Stocks. These are stocks of well-managed companies involved in aggressive innovation or research that are expected to continually produce expanding sales and earnings. Although they sell at relatively high P/E ratios, investors purchase growth stocks because of their potential for substantial price appreciation. However, with betas in excess of 1.0 they tend to be more volatile than income stocks (see Beta, page 21). Because earnings are retained for growth they pay no or relatively small dividends. These stocks are often traded over-the-counter. Technology stocks are a good example of growth stocks.

Cyclical Stocks. The performance of cyclical stocks is very closely tied to the business cycle and their values raise and fall with the ebb and flow of the economy. When there is an upturn in the economy, both consumers and businesses increase their demands for goods and services. This in turn increases the revenues and profits of companies engaged in cyclical businesses (e.g., automobile manufacturers, airlines, and hotel chains). These increased profits produce higher stock values. However, when there is a downturn in the economy revenues and profits suffer and the value of cyclical stocks fall. Cyclical stocks have betas higher than 1.

Defensive Stocks. Also referred to as non-cyclical stocks or countercyclicals, defensive stocks are less susceptible to the business cycle and tend to be more stable in price as the economy expands and contracts. They are recession-resistant because their products and services are in demand in both good times and bad times. Conservative investors are attracted to their continuous earnings, stable dividends, and relatively low betas. Defensive stocks are found in industries that provide necessities such as health care, food, and electricity.

Blue-Chip Stocks. These are the common stocks of large well-regarded and financially-sound companies with a stable history of growth and dividend payments in both bad economic times and good times. However, they typically are mature companies that will experience slower growth than either mid-cap or small-cap stocks. They offer solid value, entail low risk, and hold leading or important positions within their industries with a reputation for quality products and services. Most stocks that comprise the DJIA are considered blue-chip (see page 61). They fall within the large-cap classification. The name "blue chip" comes from the poker chip which has the highest value. At least one commentator feels that the term "blue-chip" is rather vague and not very helpful in investment analysis.[1]

Value Stocks. These are stocks that appear to be undervalued considered their earnings outlook or financial situation. Although they have low price/book ratios or price/earnings ratios, they are considered value stocks because of their high turn-around potential or "hidden value" that is not yet discovered by the market (e.g., company restructurings, undervalued balance sheet assets, or innovative new products). Value investors buy value stocks with the expectation that their prices will increase substantially once their value becomes apparent in the market (see Value Investing, page 20).

Speculative Stocks. These are the stocks of new and unproven companies with no track records, or companies that have fallen out of favor with investors. The purchaser of speculative stocks is assuming an unusually large amount of risk in hopes that his gamble will pay off with the discovery of a new resource, the development of a new technology, the filing of a particularly valuable patent, or other such event that will cause a short-term increase in the stock's market price. Initial public offerings of these stocks are often accompanied with a great deal of hype and their betas are well in excess of 1.0 (see Beta, page 21). Because they are often thinly traded, it can be difficult to sell speculative stocks in a falling market. Speculative stocks are found in industries such as oil and gas, electronics, and biotech.

Turnaround Stocks. These are stocks that have suffered severe losses, often being on the edge of bankruptcy, but are now considered good candidates for explosive growth. They are high-risk investments with no guarantees. The trick for the investor is to select those companies with sound fundamentals who have good turnaround potential from those that will continue their downward slide.

Large-Cap. These are stocks of companies with high levels of market capitalization, probably at least $5 billion market value.[2] When it comes to large-cap companies the only thing that can be known for sure about their dollar size is that they are big, but there appears to be little agreement as to exactly how big is BIG.[3] The exact definition can also vary between brokerage houses. They are typically characterized by reliable dividends, less risk, and slower growth than small-caps. Stocks included within the DJIA mostly fall here (see page 61). Blue-chips are commonly considered to be large-cap stocks, and the S&P 500 is largely made up of large-caps. Large-caps are generally less volatile than either mid-cap or small-cap stocks. However, the fact that they are big does not mean that they can't get into trouble. It would be well to remember that both Enron and Kmart were once considered large-cap companies.

Mid-Cap. Mid-cap stocks offer investors relatively modest prices and good growth potential. They are less volatile than small-caps. As with large-caps, the exact definition of a mid-cap stock can vary. These are stocks of companies with mid levels of market capitalization, probably between $500 million and $5 billion. These figures are approximations that can change over time and between brokerage houses. For example, various sources have defined mid-caps as companies with market values of: (1) $500 million to $2 billion; (2) $500 million to $5 billion; (3) $1 billion to $5 billion; and (4) $2 billion to $10 billion.

Small-Cap. Again, the exact definition of a small-cap stock can vary. These are stocks of companies with relatively small levels of market capitalization, typically between $150 million and $500 million. As with both large-caps and mid-caps, these figures are approximations that can change over time and between brokerage houses. For example, typical ranges found have been: (1) less than $250 million; (2) less than $500 million; and (3) between $300 million to $2 billion. Although small-caps offer the potential for increased growth and higher returns, they are more volatile than large-caps and mid-caps. Large institutional investors are often limited in the amount of small-caps they can acquire, giving individual investors an opportunity to acquire early positions in small cap stocks at attractive prices. However, small-cap stocks have a high failure rate. Small-caps are tracked by the Russell 2000 Index (see page 65).

Micro-Cap. Microcap stocks are issued by companies with very small or "micro" capitalizations, usually less than $150 million, although this figure can vary widely between brokerage houses. For example, typical ranges found are:

(1) $50 to $300 million; and (2) $50 to $150 million. These are the smallest and most volatile of the publicly traded corporations. There are typically fewer shares of a micro-cap company in the market, and because they are thinly traded single large transactions can impact their price. They can be difficult to sell in a down market. Some commentators see no difference between micro-caps and penny stocks.[4]

Penny Stocks. These are stocks that generally sell for less than one dollar, although with heavy promotion their price can range to as much as ten dollars per share. Penny stocks are traded over-the-counter (OTC) in many regional exchanges (see page 56). They are considered to be extremely volatile high-risk investments. Although these high risks can produce big returns over time, it is far more likely they will result in worthless stocks.[5]

MEASURES OF VALUE

Earnings Per Share. This is a measure of the net earnings of the company that are available to common stockholders (see page 129).

$$\frac{\text{Net Income}}{\text{Number Of Common Shares Outstanding}}$$

When reported as *trailing earnings* this implies that the earnings are for the previous year (e.g., the last four quarters) as opposed to present earnings or estimated future earnings. *Diluted earnings per share* assume that all convertible securities are exercised (i.e., all employee stock options, warrants, and convertible bonds are converted into common stock).

Price Earnings Ratio (P/E Ratio). This is the market price of stock divided by the current earnings per share.

$$\frac{\text{Stock Price}}{\text{Earnings Per Share}}$$

The measure is given great weight by investors because it gives an indication of a stock's price measured against its earnings power. See also, page 31.

Dividend Yield. This is the annual cash dividend per share divided by the price per share. It is an indication of the potential income to be generated by the stock.

$$\frac{\text{Annual Cash Dividend}}{\text{Price Per Share}}$$

For example, if the stock were trading at $100 and the dividends equaled $3.25, then the yield would be 3.25%. An investor looking for returns in the form of capital appreciation would probably not be concerned about a low or nonexistent dividend yield.

Payout Ratio. This is calculated by dividing the dividend per share by the earnings per share (or total dividends paid on common shares divided by the net income).

$$\frac{\text{Dividend Per Share}}{\text{Earnings Per Share}}$$

The ratio provides an idea of how well earnings support the dividend payments. For example, a ratio of 45% means that a company is distributing forty-five percent of its profits to stockholders.

STOCK OWNERSHIP – GAINS & LOSSES

When an investor purchases stock he accepts the risk of owning an equity interest in a corporation. This risk is not insignificant.[6] In return, the investor expects, but does not always receive, a return from his investment composed of periodic stock dividends and appreciation in the value of the underlying stock. Before proceeding, it will be helpful to fully understand the following graph, since similar risk/return graphs will subsequently be used to illustrate more advanced concepts.

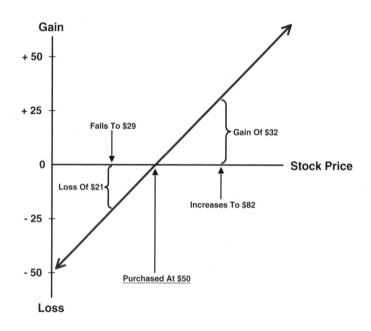

For example, assume an investor purchased stock at $50 per share. If the stock thereafter *increases* to $82 per share he has enjoyed a gain of $32 per share.[7] However, what if the stock *falls* in price to $29 per share? He would then have a loss of $21 per share. Of course, if the company failed and the stock became worthless, the maximum loss he could suffer would be the $50 per share invested in the stock (i.e., the downside). Compared to his exposure to risk, in theory his maximum gain is limitless (i.e., the upside).

Now assume that instead of purchasing just one share of stock, the investor purchases 100 shares of ABC company stock at $50 per share. This is known as being "long 100 shares ABC @ 50.00" (see Go Long, page 141).

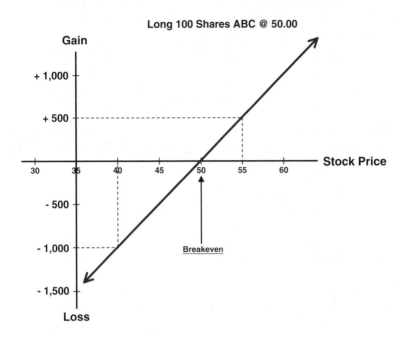

The risk/return graph would look as above. If the stock increased by $5 per share the investor would have a gain of $500. But if the stock price decreased by $10 the investor would suffer a loss of $1,000. The breakeven point is the price that the investor originally paid for the stock.

COMPANY REPORTS

Annual Report. The annual report to shareholders is the principal document used by most public companies to disclose corporate information to shareholders. It is usually a state-of-the-company report including an opening letter from the Chief Executive Officer, financial data, results of continuing operations, market segment information, new product plans, subsidiary activities, and research and development activities on future programs.

Earnings Reports. Publicly traded companies in the United States are required to report financial results every quarter. Although they are generally referred to as "earnings reports," companies report both earnings and losses (i.e., negative earnings). As a company's "report card," it is closely followed by the markets, since *good earnings* indicate

Keeping Current

Each day reported earnings are listed under **Digest Of Corporate Earnings Reports** in *The Wall Street Journal.*

high profits, high profits lead to substantial returns on investments, substantial returns drive up stock prices, and this leads to satisfied investors. Conversely, *bad earnings* (lower than expected earnings, or even losses) result in lower stock prices and unsatisfied investors. Earnings reports that fall within "analyst's estimates" generally do not impact stock prices, but those that are "disappointing poor," or "surprisingly above," can have a major impact upon prices.

Dividend Reports. Dividends are declared by a company's board of directors and paid to stockholders out of corporate earnings. Although generally in the form of cash, dividends can be paid out in the form of additional shares or scrip. High growth companies often do not pay dividends, preferring instead to reinvest earnings in order to generate growth.

> **Keeping Current**
>
> Each day reported dividends are listed under **Corporate Dividend News** in *The Wall Street Journal.*

Prospectus. The prospectus contains the basic business and financial information on an issuer with respect to a particular securities offering. Investors use the prospectus to help appraise the merits of the offering and make educated investment decisions. A prospectus in its preliminary form is frequently called a "red herring" prospectus and is subject to completion or amendment before the registration statement becomes effective, after which a final prospectus is issued and sales can be consummated.

Form 10-K. All public corporations having at least 500 shareholders and assets of over $10 million must, within 90 days of the end of the company's fiscal year, file this form with the Securities and Exchange Commission (see page 53). It provides a comprehensive overview of the company's business and is popular with investors wanting to learn more about company finances (it contains the raw data of the annual report, but without the glitz). Items contained in the form 10-K include the balance sheet, income statement, statement of cash flows, and an analysis of financial results. A form 10-Q is similar to a 10-K, but it is filed quarterly and does not require audited figures.

STOCK TABLES

The daily trading activity for the major exchanges is reported in major newspapers throughout the country. The following is a brief explanation of the information reported in *The Wall Street Journal* regarding the trading of IBM stock on May 29, 2002.

NEW YORK STOCK EXCHANGE COMPOSITE TRANSACTIONS

YTD %CHG	52-WEEK HI	52-WEEK LO	STOCK (SYM)	DIV	YLD %	PE	VOL 100s	CLOSE	NET CHG
43.9	40	26.83	Innogy ADS IOG	.42e	1.1	...	1	40	0.15
12.7	14.25	7.10	InptOutpt IO		...	dd	1135	9.25	0.35
-10.2	12.98	8.97	InsigniaFnl IFS	...	...		85	9.70	-0.30
12.8	33	24	IntgtDef IDE n	...	...		298	28.20	-0.31
3.9	9.95	3.07	IntgtElec IES	...		15	3083	5.32	0.02
-14.2	26.68	15.50▲	IntAlum IAL	1.20	5.8	69	40	20.60	0.55
-32.5	126.39	75.92	IBM IBM	.60f	.7	20	44900	81.60	-0.48
12.0	37.45	24.10	IntFlavor IFF	.60	1.8	23	7207	33.27	-0.47
-9.7	71.95	35.70▲	IntGameTch IGT	.12	.2	21	4043	61.66	0.89
10.3	28.92	15.89	IntMultfood IMK		...	53	187	26.37	0.12
6.8	46.20	30.70	IntPaper IP	1.00	2.3	dd	24873	43.08	-0.47
-5.4	46.74	24.95	IntPwr ADS IPR		...	...	26	27.74	-0.86

YTD %CHG	52-WEEK HI	LO	STOCK(SYM)	DIV	YLD %	PE	VOL 100s	CLOSE	NET CHG
-32.5	126.39	75.92	IBM IBM	.60f	.7	20	44900	81.60	-0.48

Since the first of the year IBM common stock has fallen 32.5%.

Over the past year IBM stock has traded as high as $126.39, and as low as $75.92 per share.

Total annual cash dividends have been 60 cents. The yield of .7% is an expression of these dividends as a percentage of the closing price (.60 ÷ 81.60 = .7). The f means that this is the annual rate and it was increased at the latest declaration.

The closing (last) price on May 29 was $81.60. This price was down 48 cents from the previous closing price.

Total sales on May 29 were 4,490,000 (44,900 × 100 = 4,490,000).

The total price of the stock divided by earnings (not dividends) per share. The closing price of $81.60 is 20 times its earnings per share over the past year. Thus, earnings per share were $4.08 (81.60 ÷ 20 = 4.08).

STOCK ORDERS

Day Order. This is an order to buy or sell that, if not cancelled or executed, automatically expires at the end of the trading day for which it was entered. All orders are day orders unless otherwise specified. In contrast, a good-till-cancelled (GTC) order remains on the broker's books until it is either filled or the firm's time limit expires.

Fill-Or-Kill Order (FOK). This is a market or limit order that must be *immediately* executed in its *entirety* or it is cancelled. Partial fills are not acceptable. In comparison, an **immediate or cancel order** can be executed either in whole or in part, and an **all or none order (AON)** can only be executed in its entirety, but the AON order is not treated as cancelled if not immediately executed.

Good-Till-Cancelled Order (GTC). Also referred to as an "open order," this is order to buy or sell that remains in effect until it is either executed or cancelled. Brokerage firms usually set a limit of 30-60 days, at which time the GTC expires if not restated. A GTC order is the opposite of a day order.

Limit Order. This is an order to *buy* a predetermined number of shares at or *below* a specified price, or to *sell* a predetermined number of shares at or *above* a specified price. For example, a limit order might read, "buy 100 shares of ABD Corporation at $16 or less" or "sell 100 shares of ABC Corporation at $18 or better." These orders will not be executed until the stock reaches the specified price. This is a conditional trading order that is particularly useful when the stock is highly volatile or when the trading volume is low.

Market Order. Also referred to as an "unrestricted order," this is order to buy or sell a predetermined number of shares at the best price currently available. Unlike limit orders, no restrictions can be set with a market order. It is the only order that guarantees execution. Although market orders account for the majority of trades, with low volume stocks market orders can result in unexpected higher or lower prices (i.e., ask price higher or bid price lower than current market price).

Market-On-Close Order (MOC). This is an order to buy or sell at the markets *closing* price for the day. It can include a limit order. The period during which the closing price is set varies from market-to-market and exchange-to-exchange (e.g., the last five minutes of trading). Because of this large orders placed at the very end of the day can impact the closing price. If the MOC order is not executed it is considered cancelled.

Market-On-Open Order. This is similar to a market-on-close order, but it is an order to buy or sell at the *opening* of the market. Again, the opening period during which the price is established varies from market-to-market and exchange-to-exchange.

Stop Order (STP). Also referred to as a "stop-loss order," this is an order to buy or sell at the market price once the stock has reached a specified price called the stop price. Stop orders are designed to limit an investor's loss or lock in an investor's profit. A **sell stop order** is placed below the prevailing market price and becomes a market order when the market *declines* to the stop price or lower.

A **buy stop order** is placed above the market and becomes a market order when the market *advances* to the stop price or higher. The buy stop is used when an investor has sold a security short in an attempt to reduce loss or protect a profit should the price rise unexpectedly. A stop order may be a day-limit order, a good-till-cancelled (GTC) order, or any other form of time-limit order.

Stop-Limit Order (STP LMT). It is a combination of a stop order and a limit order. In contrast to the stop order, which becomes a market order once the stop is reached, the stop-limit order becomes a limit order once the stop is reached. This type of order can only be executed at a particular price or within a rather narrow price range, thus protecting the investor from a major price move beyond the limit. In the case of a *sell* stop-limit, a stop price is given and the same or lower limit price is also given. The market must decline down to this price or range to become executable. In the case of a *buy* stop-limit, a stop price is given and the same or higher limit price is also given. For example, an order to buy at "55 stop 58 limit," is an order to buy a stock once the price raises to $55, but not at more than $58. A stop-limit order may never be executed if the specified limit price never occurs because the stock's price leapfrogs the limit.

TERMS & CONCEPTS

There appears to be no end to the number of terms used in securities trading and investing. The following are some that are frequently encountered (see page 142 for a listing of online glossaries).

Ask Price. This is the price at which an investor can *buy* from a broker-dealer (i.e., the price paid by an off-floor trader). The difference between the asked price and the bid price is called the **bid-asked spread**. Ask prices are typically reported to the media for over-the-counter (OTC) transactions and commodities.

Bear Market. A market characterized by falling prices for a prolonged period (six months or more). The downturn in prices is typically in the range of 15-20% or more from previous highs. A *stock* bear market occurs when investors sell stocks in anticipation of deteriorating economic conditions and declining profits. See page 143. A *bond* bear market is typically caused by rising interest rates.

Bid Price. This is the price at which an investor can *sell* to a broker-dealer (i.e., the price obtained by an off-floor trader). Bid prices are typically reported to the media for over-the-counter (OTC) transactions and commodities.

Bull Market. A market characterized by raising prices for a prolonged period (six months or more). Both the rate of price increases and the length of a bull market can vary. Although prices generally trend upwards, prices do fluctuate, and some may decline.

Capitalization. In general terms, this is the mix of equity and debt that funds a company's assets (e.g., the sum of preferred and common stock, bonds, debentures, and surplus). More specifically, the term "market capitalization" is used in reference to the current value of a corporation's outstanding shares and is calculated by multiplying the total number of outstanding shares by the price of the stock. For example, if a corporation has 100,000,000 shares and they are currently trading at $30 a share, the market capitalization is $3,000,000,000 (considered a "large-cap" stock, see page 132).

Cash Account. The cash account represents the "cash and carry" approach to buying stocks. With a cash account the investor is required by the Federal Reserve Board's Regulation T to pay in full not later than two days after the standard payment period set by the NASD.[8] See also, Buying On Margin on page 147.

Cover The Short. This is the purchase of a security in order to offset an existing short position. For example, an individual who previously sold short now offsets that position by purchasing a contract to acquire the underlying security (see Selling Short, page 146). With respect to options, a short call is covered if the writer of the option actually owns the stock (i.e., in "option speak," a short call option collateralized by a long position). See Options, page 151.

Dividend Reinvestment Plan (DRIP). Also known as a Dividend Reinvestment Program, a DRIP provides existing stockholders with the opportunity to acquire additional shares of stock by receiving dividends in the form of additional shares of stock. The stock is typically purchased without commissions and at a discount from market value, but the dividend is treated as a cash dividend for tax purposes.[9] These plans allow stockholders to accumulate stock over an extended period of time using dollar cost averaging (see page 28).

Dogs Of The Dow. This is an investment strategy that involves buying the 10 highest-yielding stocks in the Dow Jones Industrial Average (DJIA) at the beginning of the year and holding them for a year (i.e., these "dog stocks" represent depressed prices and consequently higher yields). (See the listing of DJIA stocks on page 66.) The following year these 10 stocks are sold and a new batch of the 10 highest-yielding DJIA stocks are purchased and held for a year. The premise of this theory is that these stocks will produce a total return that is higher than the return on the DJIA taken as a whole. The strategy assumes that investors buy stocks for their high yield, demand for these stocks will increase, prices will tend to rise, because of rising prices current yields are reduced (i.e., they are no longer dogs), the stocks are then sold at the higher price, and the cycle is then repeated by purchasing a new batch of 10 dogs.

www.dogsofthedow.com

Ex-Dividend. This literally means "without dividend." During the interval between the **record date** and the **payment date** stocks are sold ex-dividend. When sold "ex-dividend" the seller is entitled to any recently declared but unpaid dividends (i.e., the new purchaser did not own the stock on the record date). The ex-dividend period may run from a week to a month or more. Stock prices tend to increase as the ex-dividend date approaches, but drop back down on the first day of the ex-dividend period. When stocks go "ex-dividend," the stock tables include the symbol "x" following the name.

Go Long. When an investor says that "I am long 100 IBM," he means that he owns 100 shares of IBM stock. It is also used as in "going long." The investor expects the price of the stock to increase. This is the antithesis of going short. With regard to options, the owner of an option (whether it is a put or a call) is referred to as holding a **long position**. Thus, it is always the holder of the long position who may choose to exercise the contract or permit it to lapse. See pages 158-159.

Go Short. When an investor says that "I am short 100 IBM," he means that he has either sold 100 shares of IBM stock or sold the right to someone else to purchase 100 shares of IBM stock. It is also used as in "going short." The investor expects the price of the stock to decrease. This is the antithesis of going long. With regard to options, the writer (i.e., grantor or seller) of an option is referred to as holding a **short position**. Thus, it is always the holder of the short position who is obligated to perform on the contract. See Option Matrix on page 152.

Initial Public Offering (IPO). Also known as "going public," this is a company's first sale of stock to the public. Usually intended to raise cash for growing young companies, IPOs present the possibility for large gains, but they can be risky for investors. A company planning an IPO must first register with the Securities and Exchange Commission (SEC). New shares are sold to investment banks, who in turn sell them to the public. After the initial offering, securities are said to trade in the **secondary market**.

Round & Odd Lots. Stocks are sold in either round lots of 100 or odd lots of fewer than 100 shares. Because of the additional processing required for odd lots, a higher brokerage commission, called an **odd-lot differential**, is charged for odd lots. A purchase of 450 shares would represent a purchase of 4 round lots and one odd lot. Under the theory that small investors typically lag the market, at one time it was thought that

Keeping Current

Odd-lot transactions are given daily under **Odd-Lot Trading** located at the end of the stock listings in the New York Stock Exchange Composite Transactions in *The Wall Street Journal.*

a high ratio of odd-lot buying to selling was indicative of a market peak, and thus a good time to sell (and a low ratio was a good time to buy). However, as the small investor has turned from direct stock ownership to mutual funds this indicator has lost much of its significance.

Short Position. This term is generally used to describe a position that *appreciates* in value when the underlying market price *decreases*. For example, selling a stock short (page 146), selling a call (page 160), or buying a put (page 159) are all considered short positions. In contrast, a short put (page 161) benefits from an *increase* in the price of the underlying stock.

Stock Rights. Also known as "subscription rights" or "subscription warrants," these are issued by a company to current stockholders giving them the opportunity to purchase, within a short period of time, additional shares in proportion to the number of shares currently owned. Because they are usually offered at a discount from current market price, rights have a market value of their own and are often actively traded (i.e., they are transferable). In "option speak," because they give the owner the right to purchase shares at below market rights, they are said to be "in-the-money" at issue (see page 153). Thus, if they are not exercised or sold within a relatively short period the holder is likely to suffer a loss.

Stock Splits. The purpose of a stock split is to cause a company's shares to be more attractive and affordable to a larger number of potential investors. This creates more shares at a lower price, but it does not increase the current stockholder's equity in the company. For example, after a 2-for-1 stock split a stockholder owning 10 shares worth $10.00 per share now owns 20 worth $5.00 per share (the total value of $100 remains the same). Stock splits are often interpreted as an indication that the company is doing well and that it's share price has increased to the point that a split will make the stock more attractive and available to investors. However, the split does not in and of itself make the stock more valuable. A **reverse stock split** occurs when a company reduces the number of outstanding shares (e.g., with a 1-for-5 split by exchanging one new share for every five shares outstanding). These splits are often undertaken in an attempt to make a low-priced stock look more attractive to investors.

Online Glossaries. The following is a sample of helpful online glossaries:

(1) www.oasismanagement.com/glossary – Barkley's Comprehensive Financial Glossary.

(2) www.amex.com – American Stock Exchange (click on Word of the Day).

(3) www.nyse.com – New York Stock Exchange (click on Glossary).

(4) www.investorwords.com – WebFinance Inc. (browse by letter or by subject).

(5) www.morganstanleyindividual.com/customerservice/dictionary/ – Glossary licensed by Morgan Stanley from Lightbulb Press.[10]

(6) www.investopedia.com and www.taxopedia.com – Equade Internet Ltd. (for glossary go to bottom of screen).

(7) www.duke.edu/~charvey/Classes/wpg/glossary.htm – Glossary by Campbell R. Harvey, professor at the Fuqua School of Business, Duke University.

(8) www.smartmoneyuniversity.com – Dow Jones & Company and Hearst Communications (glossary link at bottom of screen).

(9) www.optionetics.com – Global Investment Research Corp. (glossary located under Trading Education tab).

SURVIVING A BEAR MARKET

There is no precise definition of a bear market. As with many other aspects of the stock market, the concept is susceptible to a whole host of definitions and interpretations. One approach is to recognize that a bear market may begin where a market correction ends, with a *market correction* occurring when the market is down by 10%, and a *bear market* occurring when the market it is down by 20% (i.e., market corrections are sharper and more sudden, whereas bears are slower, longer, and deeper). Many analysts use the Dow Jones Industrial Average (DJIA) as a benchmark in determining market cycles. Others use broader market measures such as Standard & Poors 500 or the Russell 1000 (see pages 61, 62, and 65). No matter what benchmark is used and definition applied, what is important is how investors react to market downturns.

It is well to remember that bear markets are an expected part of the market cycle, and investors who capitulate at the bottom of the market are left out when recovery returns (e.g., it makes sense to adjust an investment plan as circumstances warrant, but don't abandon it). *Long-term investors* who have developed sound plans to reach their personal and financial goals should resist the temptation to become *short-term traders* (e.g., those who dollar cost average have historically profited from their continuing investment in the stock markets, see page 28). Just as investor and media response to bull markets can lead to *irrational exuberance*, so too can investor and media response to bear markets lead to *irrational pessimism* (i.e., it is never as good as it seems, nor as bad). It may also be instructive to recall the strategy of the contrarian investor, who behaves in opposition to the prevailing wisdom, by buying when others are pessimistic and selling, and selling when others are optimistic and buying (see page 20).

In dealing with a bear market, Ernie Ankrim, Ph.D., Director of Portfolio Research at the Russell Investment Group, suggests the following:[11]

1. It's easier to predict a market bounce-back than a market bottom. From top to bottom, bear markets have lasted as long as three and a half years or as short as two months. By definition, prices can always go lower in a bear market. It's only with hindsight that investors can identify the bottom.
2. In most bear markets, some price losses occur when some investors panic and sell out irrationally. During the bounce-back, some of these same investors move back into the market (usually at higher prices).
3. Bear markets include a degree of pessimism about the future of economic growth and corporate profits. It's important to remember that there are major long-term economic drivers present in the U.S. economy, ranging from immigration to tech-driven productivity. When confidence in the economy begins to return, bounce-backs can happen quickly.
4. Historically, bear markets have occurred about once every five or six years. The last period without a bear (1990-2000) was unusually long. A smart investor expects a difficult market every few years and "prepares for the bear."
5. The best way to prepare is to develop a realistic plan for achieving strategic long-term goals, based on historic market returns, and then diversify across asset classes.
6. When the bear hits, hunker down and wait it out. If you are investing systematically (i.e., dollar cost averaging), try to maintain your program. If and when the bounce-back occurs, shares you purchased at the bottom will look like bargains.

These tables should be useful in addressing the following questions that come up during bear markets:

- "Why can't I time the market?" – **Bear Table A** demonstrates the impact of getting it wrong.

- "Are we there yet?" – **Bear Table B** provides a historical perspective on how previous bear markets have progressed.

- "Why did I lose money?" – **Bear Table C** addresses the common misconception that if the market goes down by 30% the investor will recoup all of his paper losses if the market then goes back up by 30%.

Bear Table A – The Risk Of Market Timing			
	Market Value of $100 Investment	Annualized Return	Dollar Loss
Fully Invested For 20 Years	$625.54	9.6%	n/a
Missed 5 best days	$465.36	8.0%	$160.18
Missed 10 best days	$366.34	6.7%	$259.20
Missed 15 best days	$299.73	5.6%	$325.81
Missed 20 best days	$248.04	4.6%	$377.50

Explanation of table: The column entitled "Market Value of $100 Investment" are the results of a $100 investment in a portfolio reflecting the results of the S&P 500 index over the 20-year period 1983 to 2002 (from the opening of market on January 3, 1983 to the close of market on December 31, 2002). The S&P 500 index is used for illustration only, it cannot be invested in directly.

Source: Author calculations based upon S&P 500 index (daily opening and closing data) provided by economagic.com.

Bear Table B – Tracking The S&P 500 Index[A]					
From	**To**	**Over**[B]	**The S&P 500 Fell**	**Breakeven**[C] **Occurred On**	**This Took An Additional**
August 2, 1956	October 21, 1957	306 Trading Days	-21.47%	September 23, 1958	233 Trading Days
December 11, 1961	June 26, 1962	136 Trading Days	-27.97%	June 14, 1963	244 Trading Days
February 9, 1966	October 7, 1966	167 Trading Days	-22.18%	May 4, 1967	143 Trading Days
November 29, 1968	May 26, 1970	369 Trading Days	-35.99%	March 6, 1972	451 Trading Days
January 11, 1973	October 3, 1974	436 Trading Days	-48.20%	July 17, 1980	1,462 Trading Days
January 5, 1981	August 12, 1982	406 Trading Days	-25.77%	October 20, 1982	48 Trading Days
August 25, 1987	December 4, 1987	71 Trading Days	-33.49%	July 26, 1989	414 Trading Days
July 16, 1990	October 11, 1990	62 Trading Days	-19.92%	February 13, 1991	86 Trading Days
March 24, 2000	October 9, 2002	637 Trading Days	-49.15%	As of April 16, 2003, was still down -42.39%	130 Trading Days and Counting

[A] See page 62 for an explanation of the S&P 500 index.

[B] During the years 1956-2002 there were an average of 252 trading days per year and 21 trading days per month.

[C] Breakeven is determined by that date on which the index, after falling to a low on the date indicated (column headed "To"), then recovers and first reaches or exceeds the prior high (column headed "From"). (During some recoveries the index subsequently dropped below the breakeven point for relatively brief periods.) For example, on August 2, 1956, the S&P 500 index closed at 49.64. Thereafter, it did not close at or above that level until September 23, 1958, when it closed at 49.78. In the meantime, it fell to a low of 38.98 as of closing on October 21, 1957. Gains during the one-year period after breakeven ranged from +4.60% (May 3, 1968 – no trading on May 4th) to +19.92% (October 20, 1983).

Source: Author calculations based upon S&P 500 index (daily closing data) provided by economagic.com.

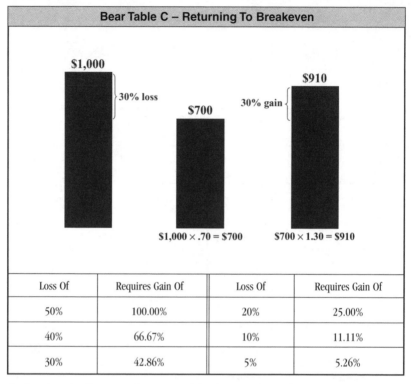

Bear Table C – Returning To Breakeven

$1,000

30% loss

$700

$910

30% gain

$1,000 × .70 = $700

$700 × 1.30 = $910

Loss Of	Requires Gain Of	Loss Of	Requires Gain Of
50%	100.00%	20%	25.00%
40%	66.67%	10%	11.11%
30%	42.86%	5%	5.26%

Explanation of table: Assume that an investor has $1,000 in the stock and the value of this stock decreases by 30%. The loss of $300 will result in the investor's stock worth $700. If the stock then increases by 30% it will gain $210 in value ($700 × .30 = $210). The investor's stock is now worth $910 ($700 + $210 = $910). Referring to the table, it can be seen that the stock will have to increase by 42.86% in order to return to breakeven ($700 × .4286 = $300 + $700 = $1,000).

SELLING SHORT

The objective of trading in the market is to buy low, then sell high. Selling short reverses the order, the investor first sells high, then attempts to buy low. Selling short involves selling a stock that the investor does not own in anticipation that the price of the stock will fall. To do this the investor sells shares that are *borrowed* from his broker. The investor who has sold short is said to then have a **short position**. Purchasing and returning the shares to the broker is referred to as **covering the short position**. In contrast, a short sale against the box occurs when the investor actually owns the stock, but does not want to close out his position.

The conditions under which short sales may be made on the national exchanges is governed by both the individual exchanges and by federal regulations. For instance, in order to sell short the investor must have established a margin account with his broker, and deposited the required margin that can equal 150% of the total credit received from the sale (see below). Typically, most brokers require that short sales involve a minimum of 100 shares selling at specific minimum prices. Stock can be sold short only after an upward movement in the market price of the stock. Once sold, all proceeds from the short sale must be held by the broker.[12]

Short interest is the total number of shares of a stock that have been sold short and not yet repurchased. The **short-interest ratio** is calculated by dividing short interest by average daily volume over some period, often 30 days (i.e., it indicates the number of days it would take short sellers to cover their positions, assuming the stock's average trading volume). A high ratio is viewed as a bullish indicator, whereas a low ratio is seen as a bearish indicator.

These borrowed shares must be returned to the broker, and if the stock's price increase the investor will suffer a loss when replacement shares are purchased. The short seller assumes the *unlimited* risk of having to purchase the stock at higher market prices. Commissions on the transactions and interest on the borrowed shares must also be paid.

Short selling is considered a legitimate but more aggressive investment strategy that should only be used by more sophisticated investors. In contrast, a defensive strategy called **selling short against the box** is sometimes used by investors who actually currently own the stock but desire to protect paper profits.[13] A similarly hedged position can be attained by *purchasing a put* option (page 159).

BUYING ON MARGIN

Also referred to as "margin trading," this is the purchase of securities with a portion of the purchase price borrowed from a brokerage firm. In order to buy on margin the investor must first establish a **margin account** by signing a margin agreement and meeting certain other margin requirements. A margin account can be used to buy on margin, sell short, or day trade.

The amount of the equity (cash) that an investor must put up is known as the **margin requirement**. The *initial* margin requirement is set by the Federal Reserve Board Of Governors (see page 49). As of April of 2003, this requirement was $2,000, or 50% of the securities to be purchased on margin. For example, assume that an investor purchases on margin 200 shares of stock at $10 per share, for a total purchase of $2,000. To meet the 50% margin requirement he must pay cash equal to at least 50% of the stock purchased. Assume that he makes the purchase using $1,000 of his own money (the "amount investment") and borrows the balance of $1,000 from his broker-dealer at an annual rate of 6%. This **margin loan** is collateralized by the stock that is held in the margin account.

A margin loan allows the investor to **leverage** his purchase by buying twice as many shares of stock. If the 200 shares of stock *appreciates* from $10 to $16 per share the total gain will be $1,170 (($6 × 200) − $30 = $1,170, assuming he pays $30 interest, see table on page 150). This is almost twice the gain with a cash purchase of only 100 shares of stock. In the following chart $1,000 represents the amount invested in February, exclusive of the margin loan.

In addition to the initial margin requirement there is also a minimum *maintenance* margin requirement of 25% that is set by the New York Stock Exchange (NYSE) and the National Association of Securities Dealers (NASD. (Some brokerage firms may set higher amounts, such as 30%.)

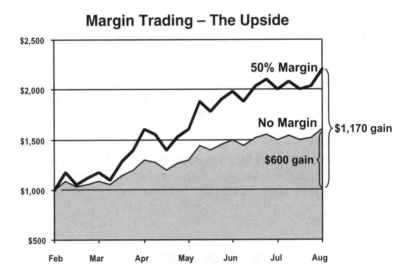

The leverage provided by margin trading can work against the investor when the stock falls in price and reduces the investor's equity below a certain threshold of the account's total value. If the value of the stock drops sufficiently, the investor will get a **margin call**. This is a demand for more funds to restore an account to its margin requirement level. The investor will then be forced to either deposit more money in the account or sell off some of the account assets (delicately described as "recovering a safe position"). For example, assume that rather than appreciating, the 200 shares of stock purchased on margin *decrease* from $10 to $6 per share.

Account value falls to	$1,200	(200 shares at $6 per share)
Less: loan amount	(1,000)	
Equity value	$200	(must be => 25% of account value)
Percentage	16.7	(200 ÷ 1,200 = .167)

Since the equity value has fallen to less than 25% of the account value (i.e., it is only 16.7%), this fall in value to $6 per share will trigger a margin call of $100 ($1,200 × .25 = $300 - $200 = $100)).

Now assume that the market price of the shares falls all the way to $4 per share. If the shares are then sold to **meet the call** the investor will receive gross proceeds of only $800 ($4 × 200 = $800). The original amount invested, the amount borrowed, and the interest due must be subtracted from these gross proceeds in order to determine the *net loss* of $1,230 (see table on page 150).[14] Under these circumstances, the leverage provided by margin trading has worked very much to the investor's *disadvantage*; he has actually lost $230 more than his original cash investment ($1,230 - $1,000 = $230).

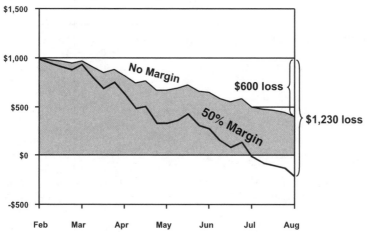

Margin Trading – The Downside

The table below compares in detail the results obtained when the market price appreciates to $16 per share, as in the graph "Margin Trading – The Upside" (page 148), or falls to $4 per share, as in the graph "Margin Trading – The Downside" (page 149).

Cash Purchase Compared To Margin Purchase		
	Cash	**50% Margin**
Amount invested	$1,000	$1,000
Amount borrowed	+ 0	+1,000
Total purchased	$1,000	$2,000
Shares purchased @ $10 each	100 shares	200 shares
If shares *increase* to $16 each:		
Shares owned	100	200
Gain per share ($16 - $10)	× $6	× $6
Gross proceeds	$600	$1,200
Less: Interest[A]	0	30
Total Gain	$600	$1,170
If shares *decrease* to $4 each:		
Shares owned	100	200
Loss per share ($10 - $4)	× $6	× $6
Total loss	($600)	($1,200)
If this decrease forces a sale:		
Shares owned	100	200
Price per share	× $4	× $4
Gross proceeds	$400	$800
Less: Amount invested	1,000	1,000
Amount borrowed	0	1,000
Interest[A]	0	30
Net Loss[B]	($600)	($1,230)

[A] Brokerage firms typically set the interest rate at 1% to 3% above prime, but this may be less for larger accounts. In this example the margin loan is outstanding for only 6 months, therefore interest is $30.00, not $60.00 (($1,000 × .06) ÷ 2 = $30.00).

[B] Does not include commissions paid for purchase and sale of shares.

OPTIONS

Equity options provide for the *purchase* (call) or the *sale* (put), within a pre-determined period, of a fixed number of shares of an underlying stock at a specified price. Since its value is set by the underlying stock, an option is a form of derivative (a futures contract is another form of derivative). Typically each option contract is worth 100 shares of stock. There are currently five exchanges in the United States that list and trade standardized options: The American Stock Exchange (AMEX), the Chicago Board Options Exchange (CBOE), the Philadelphia Stock Exchange (PHLX), the Pacific Exchange (PCX), and the International Securities Exchange. (Options are not available for every stock.) The options traded on these exchanges are referred to as **exchanged-listed options**. In addition to individual stocks, other options that can be purchased and sold include commodities, bonds, currencies, United States Treasury bills and bonds, and the S&P 500 index (as well as other stock and bond indexes).

The average investor who lacks years of investment experience is often advised not to get involved in pure options trading. It has been said that, "time is on your side when you own shares of superior companies . . . [but] . . . against you when you own options."[15] However, it is important to understand options, because they can be prudently used by the average investor as a way of protecting gains and reducing losses. Before proceeding it is essential to understand the terminology used in option trading.

Digging Deeper

The learning center of the Chicago Board Options Exchange offers online tutorials and courses at: www.cboe.com/LearnCenter.

In "option speak" an option position results from an opening purchase transaction, either a long call or long put. The Option Matrix on page 152 summarizes the basic four basic relationships created in options trading: (1) buyer acquires a right to buy stock; (2) buyer acquires a right to sell stock; (3) seller assumes an obligation to sell stock; and (4) seller assumes an obligation to buy stock.

Option Matrix		
	Buyer ("holder" - goes long)	**Seller** ("writer" - goes short)
Call Option	Has a right to *buy*, but no obligation to buy – it is known as a **long call**. Risk is limited to the cost of the premium paid. When used: buyer is bullish and believes the market will rise.[16] See page 158.	Has an obligation to *sell* – the seller has "written a call" and it is known as a **short call** (see page 160). Risk is very high and not known if the seller does not already own the stock (referred to as a **naked call**). If seller already owns the stock it is known as a **covered call** (see page 162). When used: seller is bearish and believes the market will fall.[17] See page 160.
Put Option	Has a right to *sell*, but no obligation to sell – it is known as a **long put**. Risk is limited to the cost of the premium paid. When used: buyer is bearish and believes the market will fall.[18] See page 159.	Has an obligation to *buy* – the seller has "written a put" and it is known as a **short put**. Risk is high but known since it is limited to the strike price (i.e., stock goes to zero value and must be purchased at strike price). When used: seller is bullish and believes the market will rise.[19] See page 161.

Option Premium. Although the price of the underlying stock fluctuates with the market, factors that influence the option premium include the current price of the underlying

> Intrinsic Value
> +
> Time Value

stock, the strike price, the time remaining until the option expires, and the volatility of the stock. The option premium has the following two components:

(1) **Intrinsic Value.** This is the value of the option in relation to the current value of the stock. Expressed another way, it is the amount by which either a put or call option is in-the-money (see below). For example, a call option on a stock with a $50 strike price when the stock is currently selling for $62 per share has an intrinsic value of $12 (i.e., it is $12 "in-the-money"). Options that are either at-the-money or out-of-the-money have no intrinsic value (see below). An option gains intrinsic value, and loses time value, as it becomes more in-the-money.

(2) **Time Value.** Also referred to as the "time premium" or "extrinsic value," this is the amount of the current market price of an option that exceeds its intrinsic value. Stocks with higher degrees of volatility have higher time values (i.e., there is more chance that the strike price will be reached).

Strike Price. Also referred to as the "exercise price," this is the price at which an option can be exercised. In the case of a *call* it is the price paid for the stock, whereas in the case of a *put* it is the price received for the stock. It is set at 2½ point (or dollar) intervals for stocks priced at $25 and less, at 5-point intervals for stocks priced over $25 to $200, and at 10-point intervals for stocks over $200. For example, a call contract may allow the buyer to purchase 500 shares of ABC Corporation at any time in the next three months at an exercise of $55.00.

Expiration Date. This is the last day on which the option can be exercised. Listed options are available for the current month and the next month as well as specific future months. A stock option expires at close of business on the 3rd Friday of the expiration month.[20] Regular options have expiration dates up to nine months after they are issued. Long-term options, known as LEAPS, have expirations up to three years after issue. If the option is not exercised by this date it is said to **expire worthless**. Each stock has a corresponding cycle of months that they offer options in. There are three fixed expiration cycles available. Each cycle has a four-month interval: (1) January, April, July and October; (2) February, May, August and November; and (3) March, June, September and December.

At-The-Money (ATM). Both call options and put options are said to be at-the-money when the current market price is equal to the strike price (market price = strike price). Once an option has reached the strike price (at-the-money) the owner can: (1) do nothing and wait for it to move further; (2) exercise the option and either buy (call) or sell (put) the stock; (3) sell the option to another investor for a profit; or (4) neutralize the option with an offsetting order. In order to more clearly illustrate the concepts of puts and calls, the graphs on pages 158-163 are all illustrations of "at-the-money" options.

In-The-Money (ITM). On option is in-the-money when it can be exercised with a profit. If it is a *call* option the current market price is above the strike price (market price > strike price). If it is a *put* option the current market price is below the strike price (market price < strike price). For example, a call option on a stock that is currently selling in the market for $62 per share is in-the-money if the strike price is $50. A person exercising the option could buy the stock for $50 and sell it for $62, thereby realizing a gross profit of $12 per share (net profit would require subtracting the cost of the option premium). See page 158 for an example of an in-the-money call option.

Out-Of-The-Money (OTM). On option is out-of-the-money when it cannot be exercised with a profit. If it is a *call* option the current market price is below the strike price (market price < strike price). If it is a *put* option the current market price is above the strike price (market price > strike price). For example, a put option on a stock that is currently selling in the market for $62 per share is out-of-the-money if the strike price is $58. When he could sell stock in the market at $62 per share, a person would not exercise the option and sell the stock at $58 per share.

Naming Conventions. Stock Options names are written in the following manner: SYMBOL MP, where SYMBOL denotes the company, M the expiration month, and P the strike price. For example:

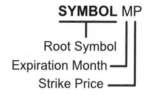

SYMBOL MP

Root Symbol
Expiration Month
Strike Price

Quotations. The following represents a typical on-line quotation. It is for Home Depot stock for call options purchase on June 3, 2002. Since Home Depot closed at $40.52 the July strike prices of $35 and $40 were both out-of-the-money, whereas the July strike prices of $45 and $50 were both in-the-money. For option expiration month codes and strike price codes see page 156.

HOME DEPOT INC (HD)							40.52		-1.17 ▼
Symbol	Last	Time	Net	Bid	Ask	Open	High	Low	Close	Vol
HD	40.52	16:02	-1.17	0.00	0.00	41.15	42.05	40.30	41.69	8727300

			Calls				Jun 2002
Ticker	Last	Net	Bid	Ask	Vol	Open Interest	Strike
HD FG	6.10	-0.90	5.40	5.90	9	136	35
HD FH	1.70	-0.80	1.60	1.70	3187	16049	40
HD FI	0.20	-0.10	0.10	0.20	957	15377	45
HD FJ	0.05	0.00	0.00	0.05	98	10489	50

			Calls				Jul 2002
Ticker	Last	Net	Bid	Ask	Vol	Open Interest	Strike
HD GG	6.90	0.00	5.70	6.20		22	35
HD GH	2.70	-0.50	2.15	2.45	251	608	40
HD GI	0.55	-0.20	0.50	0.55	189	2408	45
HD GJ	0.1000	0.0000	0.0500	0.1500		2417	50

			Calls				Aug 2002
Ticker	Last	Net	Bid	Ask	Vol	Open Interest	Strike
HD HG	6.80	-1.10	6.10	6.60	3	325	35
HD HH	2.75	-0.95	2.70	3.00	71	882	40
HD HI	0.90	-0.35	0.75	0.95	640	3370	45
HD HJ	0.30	-0.05	0.15	0.30	107	9572	50

HD GH

Home Depot
Expires In July
Strike Price is $40

Source of on-line quotation: pcquote.com. Reprinted by permission.

Option Expiration Month Codes					
Month	**Call**	**Put**	**Month**	**Call**	**Put**
January	A	M	July	G	S
February	B	N	August	H	T
March	C	O	September	I	U
April	D	P	October	J	V
May	E	Q	November	K	W
June	F	R	December	L	X

Strike Price Codes					
Code	**Price**				
A	5	105	205	305	405
B	10	110	210	310	410
C	15	115	215	315	415
D	20	120	220	320	420
E	25	125	225	325	425
F	30	130	230	330	430
G	35	135	235	335	435
H	40	140	240	340	440
I	45	145	245	345	445
J	50	150	250	350	450
K	55	155	255	355	455
L	60	160	260	360	460
M	65	165	265	365	465
N	70	170	270	370	470
O	75	175	275	375	475
P	80	180	280	380	480
Q	85	185	285	385	485
R	90	190	290	390	490
S	95	195	295	395	495
T	100	200	300	400	500

LISTED OPTIONS QUOTATIONS

Wednesday, May 29, 2002

Composite volume and close for actively traded equity and LEAPS, or long-term options, with results for the corresponding put or call contract. Volume figures are unofficial. Open interest is total outstanding for all exchanges and reflects previous trading day. Close when possible is shown for the underlying stock or primary market. XC-Composite. p-Put. o-Strike price adjusted for split.

Most Active Contracts

OPTION/STRIKE			VOL	EXCH	LAST	NET CHG	CLOSE	OPEN INT	OPTION/STRIKE			VOL	EXCH	LAST	NET CHG	CLOSE	OPEN INT
LSI	Jul	10	p	55,012	XC	0.50	0.05	11.41	1,884	AOL TW	Jul	17.50	p	8,659	XC	0.80	0.05	18.56	15,646
Nasd100Tr	Jun	30		27,985	XC	1.05	0.25	30.28	152,695	Tycolntl	Jun	20	p	7,683	XC	1.15	0.35	21.13	31,695
Cisco	Jun	15	p	24,140	XC	0.50	0.15	15.65	32,114	VerizonCm	Oct	50		6,936	XC	1	-0.05	43.89	9,779
Nasd100Tr	Jun	31		20,490	XC	0.85	-0.45	30.28	47,455	SunMicro	Jun	7.50		6,927	XC	0.15	-0.10	6.76	72,407
Comcst sp	Oct	27.50	p	15,200	XC	2.65	0.45	28.15	724	DellCptr	Jun	25	p	6,714	XC	0.50	0.10	26.58	20,093
Comcst sp	Jul	27.50	p	13,730	XC	1.35	0.10	28.15	6,190	Nasd100Tr	Jun	34		6,703	XC	0.15	-0.15	30.28	91,528
Nasd100Tr	Jun	32		12,993	XC	0.55	-0.30	30.28	102,281	Ph Mor	Jun	55	p	6,666	XC	0.55	-0.30	56.01	43,429
Nasd100Tr	Jun	30		12,914	XC	1.40	-0.55	30.28	55,741	Nasd100Tr	Jul	32		6,531	XC	1.05	-0.35	30.28	23,189
Tycolntl	Jul	25		12,442	XC	1	-0.25	21.13	54,051	AMCC	Nov	5	p	6,504	XC	0.70	0.05	6.26	1,807
Nasd100Tr	Jun	32	p	12,311	XC	2.25	0.50	30.28	133,294	BrMySq	Sep	35		6,466	XC	0.80	-0.05	30.03	19,107
EKodak	Jun	30		11,827	XC	4.80	-0.10	34.89	1,560	Nasd100Tr	Jul	36		6,288	XC	0.25	-0.10	30.28	42,562
Nasd100Tr	Jun	29	p	11,599	XC	0.65	0.10	30.28	27,546	Nasd100Tr	Jun	33		6,169	XC	0.30	-0.20	30.28	90,408

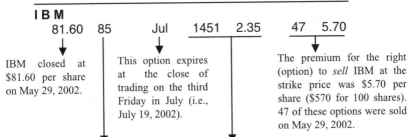

OPTION/STRIKE	EXP	-CALL- VOL	LAST	-PUT- VOL	LAST	OPTION/STRIKE	EXP	VOL	LAST	VOL	LAST	OPTION/STRIKE	EXP	VOL	LAST	VOL	LAST
AOL TW	17.50	Jul	184	1.80	8659	0.80	FHLB	65	Jan	8	4.80	1003	4.40		43.40	45	Jun	1754	2	812	3.50
18.56	17.50	Oct	5	2.95	1176	1.65	65.00	7f	Jan	1037	2.35	10	6.90		43.40	55	Jun	1052	0.20	20	11
18.56	20	Jun	2341	0.30	179	1.65	Gap		Jun	818	0.45	205	1.40	NvidiaCp	30	Jun	398	5.80	1259	0.90
...bath	30	Jul	...	...	...	0.50	27.27	27.50	Oct	1002	3.20	104	3		...	...	...	603	2.89	...
BestBuy	50	Jun	129	0.55	2959	4.80	27.27	30	Jun	3255	0.35	2859	2.90	SBC Cm	35	Jul	1092	1.50	137	1.70
Biogen	40	Oct	...	...	1820	1.60	27.27	30	Jun	2042	0.95	567	3.40	35.05	35	Oct	3072	2.55	60	2.65
50.37	55	Oct	1392	3.20	...	...	27.27	30	Jan	2054	3	583	5.20	SLM Corp	95	Jul	1000	4.20	...	...
BrMySq	30	Jun	2191	1.65	119	1.70	27.27	32.50	Jun	2351	0.10	76	5.30	SciAtlanta	20	Jun	2540	0.75	70	1.65
30.03	35	Jun	1493	0.15	1	5	27.27	32.50	Jul	1759	0.40	...	...	SealdAir o	40	Oct	...	...	1000	2.35
30.03	35	Sep	6466	0.80	...	...	I B M	80	Jun	1107	3.80	961	1.70	44.96	45	Jan	...	...	2000	4.80
Broadcom	22.50	Jun	511	2	818	1.90	81.60	80	Jul	165	4.90	1170	3	SemiHTr	12.50	Jun	3300	0.70	992	4.20
22.41	25	Jun	714	1	2963	3.50	81.60	85	Jul	1451	2.35	47	5.70	38.85	37.50	Jun	1166	2.80	2588	1.25
22.41	30	Jun	581	0.20	1622	7.50	81.60	115	Jul	5	0.05	1503	33	38.85	40	Jul	1202	2.45	85	3.40
Brocade	20	Jun	2009	1.15	221	2.75	81.60	120	Jun	120	0.05	1500	38	38.85	45	Jun	813	0.25	23	6.10
18.33	22.50	Jul	865	1.20	12	5.20	81.60	125	Jan	...	...	950	43	SiebelSys	17.50	Jun	236	2.10	1526	1.10
CV Thera	20	Jun	877	1.45	1790	2.25	81.60	130	Jan	...	...	1086	48	18.40	20	Jun	1640	0.90	592	2.35
19.25	25	Jun	1225	0.35	17	5.50	In Pap	40	Jul	64	3.80	1400	0.60	18.40	22.50	Jun	1606	0.30	317	4.20
Calpine	10	Jun	888	0.80	1163	0.90	43.08	40	Jun	5225	5.90	...	2.50	18.40	25	Jun	1242	0.10	230	6.50
													SmrtForce	5	Jun	...	...	2400	0.20

OPTION/STRIKE	EXP	-CALL- VOL	LAST	-PUT- VOL	LAST
I B M					
81.60	85	Jul	1451	2.35	47	5.70

IBM closed at $81.60 per share on May 29, 2002.

This option expires at the close of trading on the third Friday in July (i.e., July 19, 2002).

The premium for the right (option) to *sell* IBM at the strike price was $5.70 per share ($570 for 100 shares). 47 of these options were sold on May 29, 2002.

The price at which the holder of this option may buy (with a call) or sell (with a put) this stock. Note that IBM strike prices range from $80.00 to $130.00.

The premium for the right (option) to *buy* IBM at the strike price was $2.35 per share ($235 for 100 shares). 1,451 of these options were sold on May 29, 2002.

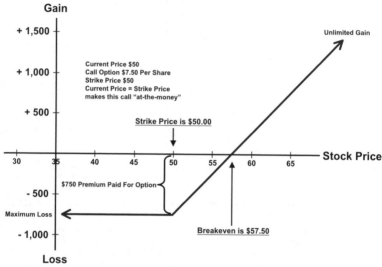

The investor has acquired an option to purchase stock. One of four things will happen: **(1)** The stock either remains at $50.00, or falls to less than $50.00 – the investor losses $750 and the option expires worthless; **(2)** The stock increases to over $50.00 but less than $57.50 – the investor exercises the option, purchases the stock for $50.00, and recoups a *portion* of the $750 premium; **(3)** The stock increases to $57.50 – the investor purchases the stock for $50.00 and recoups *all* of the $750 premium paid for the option (breakeven); **(4)** The stock increases to over $57.50 – the investor has a gain. For example, if it went to $62.50 the investor would purchase the stock for $50.00, receiving $1,250, or a net gain of $500 after subtracting the $750 premium paid ($1,250 - $750 = $500). The following graph illustrates these four possibilities.

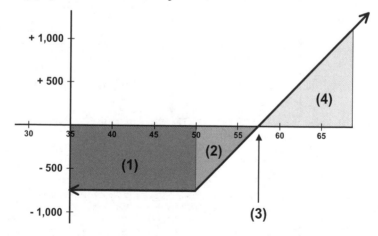

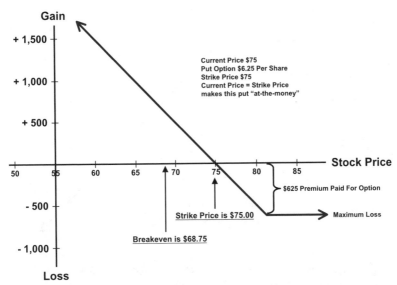

Option Acquired To Sell Stock
Short 1 ABC September 75 Put @ 6.25

Current Price $75
Put Option $6.25 Per Share
Strike Price $75
Current Price = Strike Price
makes this put "at-the-money"

$625 Premium Paid For Option

Maximum Loss

Strike Price is $75.00

Breakeven is $68.75

The investor has acquired an option to sell stock. One of four things will happen: **(1)** The stock either remains at $75.00 or higher – the investor losses $625 and allows the option to expire worthless; **(2)** The stock falls to under $75.00 but more than $68.75 – the investor purchases the stock, sells it for the $75.00 strike price, and recoups a *portion* of the $625 premium; **(3)** The stock falls to $68.75 – the investor purchases the stock for $68.75, sells it for $75.00, and recoups *all* of the $625 premium he paid for the option (breakeven); **(4)** The stock falls to less than $68.75 – the investor has a gain. For example, if the price falls to $60.00, the investor purchases the stock for $60.00, exercises the option for the $75.00 strike price, and realizes $1,500; or a net gain of $875 after subtracting the $625 premium paid ($1,500 - $625 = $875). The following graph illustrates these four possibilities.

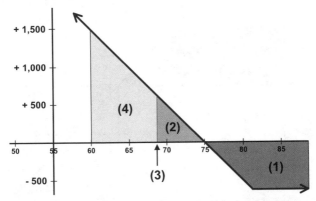

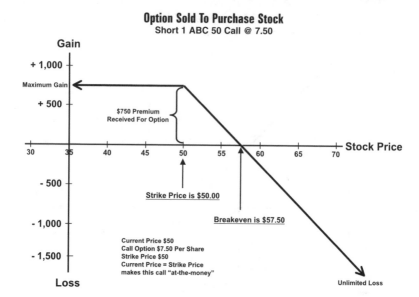

Option Sold To Purchase Stock
Short 1 ABC 50 Call @ 7.50

The investor has sold an option to purchase stock (i.e., "written a call"). One of four things will happen: **(1)** The stock either remains at $50.00, or falls below $50.00 – the option expires worthless and the investor has a gain of $750; **(2)** The stock increases to over $50.00 but less than $57.50 – the option is exercised, the investor must purchase the stock at market price and losses a *portion* of the $750 premium; **(3)** The stock increases to $57.50 – the investor must purchase 100 shares for $5,750 and loses *all* of the $750 premium received for the option (breakeven); **(4)** The stock increases to over $57.50 – the investor has a potentially very large and unlimited loss. For example, if the stock increases to $70.00 the investor must purchase 100 shares for $7,000. After subtracting the premium received he would have a net loss of $1,250 (($7,000 - $5,000) - $750 = $1,250). The following graph illustrates these four possibilities.

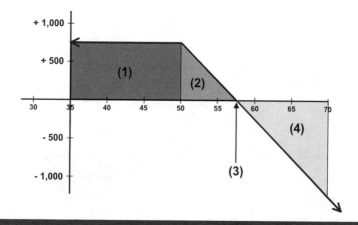

Option Sold To Sell Stock
Short 1 ABC 50 Call @ 6.25

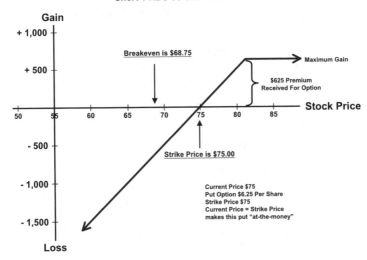

The investor has sold an option to sell stock (i.e., "written a put"). One of four things will happen: (**1**) The stock either remains at $75.00 or higher – the option expires worthless and the investor has a gain of $625; (**2**) The stock falls to under $75.00 but more than $68.50 – the option is exercised, the investor must purchase the stock and losses a *portion* of the $625 premium; (**3**) The stock falls to $68.50 – the investor must purchase 100 shares for $6,850 and loses *all* of the $625 premium received for the option (breakeven); (**4**) The stock falls to under $68.75 – the investor has a potentially very large loss. For example, if the stock falls to $60.00 the investor must purchase 100 shares for $7,500. After subtracting the premium received there is a net loss of $1,250 (($7,500 - $6,000) - $625 = $875). The following graph illustrates these four possibilities.

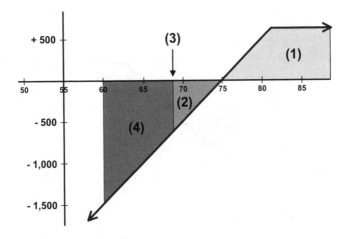

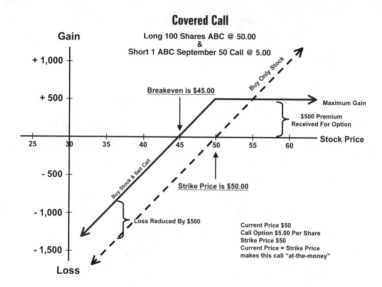

Covered Call

The investor has sold an option to purchase stock that is currently owned (i.e., "written a covered call"). One of five things will happen: **(1)** The stock increases to over $50.00 – the option is exercised, the investor sells stock and has a gain equal to the $500 premium received for the option; **(2)** The stock remains at $50.00 – the option expires worthless and the investor has a gain equal to the $500 premium received for the option; **(3)** The stock falls to above $45.00 – the option expires worthless and the $500 gain from the premium received is partially offset by the fall in the stock's value; **(4)** The stock falls to $45.00 – the option expires worthless and the fall in stock's value is offset by the premium received (breakeven); **(5)** The stock falls to under $45.00 – the option expires worthless and the investor's loss is reduced by the $500 premium received. The following graph illustrates these five possibilities.

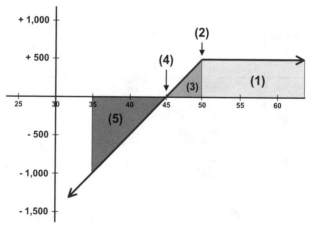

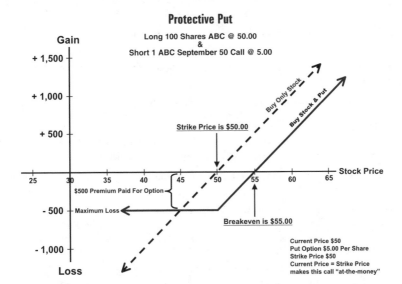

Protective Put

Long 100 Shares ABC @ 50.00
&
Short 1 ABC September 50 Call @ 5.00

The investor has acquired an option to sell stock that is currently owned (i.e., "purchased a protective put"). One of five things will happen: **(1)** The stock falls to under $50.00 – the investor sells stock for $50.00 and any loss is limited to the $500 premium; **(2)** The stock remains at $50.00 – the option expires worthless and the loss is the $500 premium; **(3)** The stock increases over $50.00 but under $55.00 – the option expires worthless and the $500 premium paid is partially offset by the increase in the value of the stock; **(4)** The stock increases to $55.00 – the option expires worthless and the $500 premium paid is fully offset by the increase in the value of the stock (breakeven); **(5)** The stock increases to over $55.00 – the option expires worthless and the gain in value of the stock is reduced by the $500 premium paid. The following graph illustrates these five possibilities.

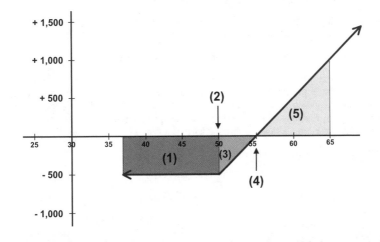

[1] See G. Victor Hallman and Jerry S. Rosenbloom, *Personal Financial Planning*, 6th ed. (New York: McGraw-Hill, 2000), p. 178.

[2] Market capitalization is calculated by multiplying the number of outstanding shares by the current share price.

[3] The estimates run all the way from "$2-$3 billion" (Lawrence J. Gitman and Michael D. Joehnk, Personal Financial Planning, 7th ed. (Fort Worth: The Dryden Press, 1996), p. 457), to "over $5 billion" (David and Tom Gardner, The Motley Fool Investment Guide (New York: Simon & Schuster, 2001), p. 92), and then to "between $10 billion and $200 billion . . . [t]hese are the big kahunas of the financial world" (www.investopedia.com/terms/l/large-cap.asp).

[4] Harvey states that micro-caps and penny stocks are the same. See www.duke.edu/~charvey/ Classes/wpg/bfglosm.htm.

[5] Penny stocks are not held in high regard by most financial advisors. For example, Jane Bryant Quinn observes, "Shares trading at around $5 or less are called penny stocks. They'll reduce your $5 to pennies – count on it." Jane Bryant Quinn, *Making The Most Of Your Money* (New York: Simon & Schuster, 1997), p. 710.

[6] In the stock market crash of October 29, 1929, the DJIA lost $14 billion of its value (12.8%), and in the crash of October 19, 1987, the DJIA lost $500 billion (22.6%). On September 17, 2001, in the aftermath of September 11, the DJIA lost $183 billion (5.7%).

[7] See *Tax Facts 2* (Cincinnati: The National Underwriter Company, 2003, revised annually), **Question 17** – How is a shareholder taxed on the sale or exchange of his stock?

[8] Regulation T is the Federal Reserve Board regulation that governs cash accounts and the amount of credit that brokerage firms and dealers may extend to customers for the purchase of securities in margin accounts. Regulation T currently sets the loan value of marginable securities at 50% and the payment deadline at two days after regular way settlement.

[9] See *Tax Facts 2*, **Question 15** – How is a shareholder taxed if he participates in a dividend reinvestment plan?

[10] Lightbulb Press offers a series of easy-to-understand and easy-to-use primers on an assortment of financial planning topics. Their solid content make them good reading for both the investing public and the professional planner. Also, their extensive and effective use of colorful graphics make them great stocking stuffers. See www.lightbulbpress.com.

[11] Ernie Ankrim, Ph.D., *A Historical Look at Bear Market Recovery* (Frank Russell Company, 2001), at http://ei.russelllink.com.

[12] See *Tax Facts 2*, **Question 22** – When and how is a short sale taxed?

[13] At one time, an investor was able to defer gain on the sale of a stock by selling short the same number of shares owned (i.e., by "selling short against the box," the box being his safe deposit box where the unsold shares remained). The 1997 Tax Reform Act revised the tax treatment of this strategy by requiring investors to recognize gain upon entering into a constructive sale of an appreciated financial position (i.e., selling short stock that had appreciated in value).

[14] The chart does not include commissions paid, if any.

[15] Peter Lynch, *Beating The Street* (New York: Simon & Schuster, 1994), p. 307.

[16] See *Tax Facts 2*, **Question 49** – How is an investor taxed when he purchases a put or call? and **Question 53** – How is an owner taxed if he exercises a call?

[17] See *Tax Facts 2*, **Question 63** – How is the writer of a call taxed when the option is exercised by the owner?

[18] See *Tax Facts 2*, **Question 49** – How is an investor taxed when he purchases a put or call? and **Question 58** – How is the owner of a put taxed if he exercises it?

[19] See *Tax Facts 2*, **Question 64** – How is the writer of a put taxed when the option is exercised by the owner?

[20] This is known as an "American-style" option.

INVESTMENT COMPANIES

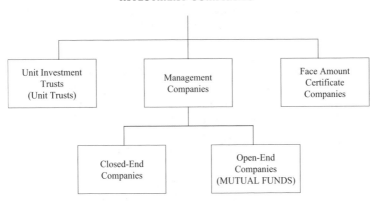

There are three basic types of investment companies: (1) unit investment trusts; (2) management companies; and (3) face amount certificate companies. Management companies are either "closed-end" or "open-end" companies, also known as mutual funds. Mutual funds are by far the most predominate form of investment company and are regulated under the Investment Company Act of 1940.

(1) **Unit Investment Trusts (UITs).**[1] Also referred to as "unit trusts," UITs are registered investment companies that buy and hold a fixed portfolio of income-producing stocks, bonds, or other securities. For example, municipal bond unit trusts are an alternative to municipal bond mutual funds. They are attractive to the investor who wants diversification, relatively low costs, and initial portfolio selection, but not ongoing portfolio management. Unlike a managed company, a UIT does not have an actively managed investment portfolio. UITs are often structured as "contractual" or "periodic payment" plans. "Units" in the trust are sold to investors or "unit holders." Investment interest, principal repayments and accelerated payments are not retained and reinvested by the fund, but instead are paid out to the investors who receive their proportionate share of distributions. Unlike other investment companies, a UIT has a stated date for termination that varies according to the investments held in its portfolio. Prior to termination, investors may either redeem units from the trust for their net asset value (NAV) or resell units on the secondary market. At termination, investors receive their proportionate share of the net assets of UIT, and the trust ends.

(2) **Face Amount Certificate Companies.** These investment companies issue face amount certificates that have a fixed maturity value and a schedule of redemption values – much like a United States savings bond. The

purchaser typically makes periodic payments through a program of installment purchases. However, they are not equity investments and are, therefore, sometimes used in funding annuities used in tax deferred annuity
plans.

(3) **Management Companies.** Management companies are formed as corporations or trusts for the purpose of managing a portfolio of securities in
accordance with specific investment objectives. They can function as
"closed-end" or "open-end" companies.

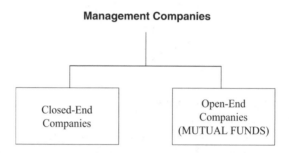

Management Companies

(a) **Closed-End Companies.** Closed-end investment companies are not
mutual funds. Rather, they are investment companies that issue a
fixed number of shares in closed-end funds, which are actively traded on a stock exchange or in the over-the-counter market. Assets of a
closed-end fund are professionally managed in accordance with the
fund's investment objectives and policies, and may be invested in
stocks, bonds, or a combination of both. Like other publicly traded
securities, the market price of closed-end fund shares fluctuates and
is determined by supply and demand in the marketplace.[2]

(b) **Open-End Companies.** Better known as mutual funds, these companies are considered "open-end" investment companies under federal law for two reasons. First, they are required to redeem (or buy
back) outstanding shares at any time upon a shareholder's request,
and at a price based on the current value of the fund's net assets (see
Net Asset Value on page 185). Second, although not required, virtually all mutual funds continuously offer new fund shares to the public.

Exchange-Traded Funds (ETFs).[3] While exchange-traded funds are registered with the Securities and Exchange Commission as investment companies – as unit investment trusts or open-end funds – they differ from traditional mutual funds both in how their shares are issued and redeemed, and in how their shares or units are traded. Unlike traditional mutual funds, or unit investment trusts, ETF shares are created by an institutional investor depositing a specified block of securities with the ETF. In return for this deposit, the institutional investor receives a fixed amount of ETF shares, some or all of which may then be sold on a stock exchange. The institutional investor may obtain its deposited securities by redeeming the same number of ETF shares it received from the ETF. Retail investors can buy and sell the ETF shares only when they are listed on an exchange, much as they can buy or sell any listed equity security. Unlike an institutional investor, a retail investor cannot purchase or redeem shares directly from the ETF, as with a traditional mutual fund or unit investment trust. Shares are traded intraday (i.e., throughout the day) on national stock exchanges at market-determined prices. Because exchange-traded fund shares can be sold short and bought on margin, they are often promoted as offering the benefits of index investing at a lower cost, and with greater trading flexibility in comparison to mutual funds. There were 114 ETFs in the United States in March of 2003, of which 66 were domestic equity index funds, 40 were global equity index funds, and 8 were bond index funds.[4]

STRUCTURE OF A MUTUAL FUND

Mutual funds are typically externally managed. Instead of functioning as an operating company with employees in the traditional sense, mutual funds rely upon third parties, either affiliated organizations or independent contractors, to carry out their business activities.

Like shareholders of other companies, mutual fund shareholders have specific voting rights, including the right to elect directors. Shareholders must also approve material changes in the terms of a fund's contract with its investment adviser, the entity that manages the fund's assets. When mutual funds desire to change investment objectives, or policies that are deemed fundamental, they must seek shareholder approval.

These relationships are summarized in the following diagram, showing the principal service providers to a mutual fund and its shareholders.

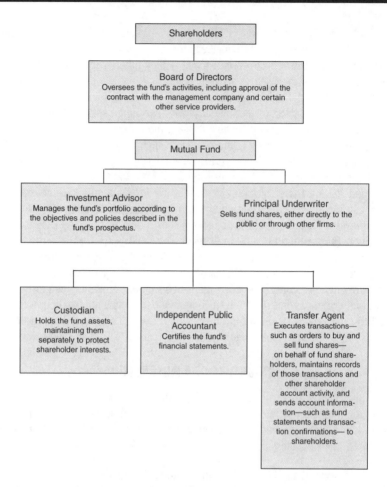

Source: *2003 Mutual Fund Fact Book*, Copyright© 2003 by the Investment Company Institute (www.ici.org). Reprinted with permission.

POPULARITY & ADVANTAGES OF MUTUAL FUNDS

The Investment Company Institute has reported that as of the end of 2002 there were 250,981,045 shareholder accounts, and in May of 2002 49.6% of U.S. households owned mutual funds.[5] In the United States, as of January 2003, there were 8,260 funds holding assets worth $6,333,500,000,000 (that's 6⅓ trillion dollars). Of these 8,260 funds, 4,752 were stock funds, 478 were hybrid funds, 2,041 were bond funds, and 989 were money market funds.[6] Interestingly, the number of mutual funds exceeded the total of 8,137 securities listed on the New York, American, and NASDAQ exchanges.[7]

Mutual funds pool investors' funds to purchase a diversified portfolio of investments according to specified goals. Their investments can include stocks, bonds, and money market instruments. Through these collective investments, each investor shares in the returns from the fund's portfolio while benefiting from professional investment management, diversification, liquidity, and other services. The key advantages of mutual fund investing include:[8]

Digging Deeper

The Investment Company Institute offers an array of data and information about mutual funds, including investor awareness & educational resources, at: www.ici.org.

(1) **Professional Management.** Investors benefit from the knowledge and experience of professional investment managers who are dedicated to security analysis, evaluation and selection.

(2) **Diversification.** Because mutual funds invest in a variety of securities, they provide shareholders with investment diversification in stocks, bonds, or money market instruments. A diversified portfolio helps reduce risk by offsetting losses from some securities with gains from others.

(3) **Liquidity.** Since mutual funds are required by law to redeem shares on a daily basis, fund shares are very liquid investments. Most mutual funds also continually offer new shares to investors. Many fund companies allow shareholders to transfer money – or make "exchanges" – from one fund to another within the same fund family. Mutual funds process sales, redemptions, and exchanges as a normal part of daily business activity.

(4) **Cost Efficiency.** By investing in a mutual fund, the average small investor is able to purchase shares in an economical way and obtain the same kind of professional money management and diversification that is available to large institutions and wealthy investors.

(5) **Service.** Custody of assets, tax reporting and record keeping are among the many services mutual fund companies provide. Many mutual funds also provide investors with a wide array of other shareholder services, including quarterly reports, duplicate statements, fund performance updates and extended hours during tax season.

INVESTMENT OBJECTIVES

Key to understanding a mutual fund is knowing the fund's stated investment objective. Mutual funds offer investors a variety of goals, depending on the particular fund and its investment charter. For example, some funds seek to generate income on a regular basis. Others strive to achieve modest gains as they preserve the investor's capital, while others seek large gains by investing in companies that are expected to grow at a rapid pace. When a fund fails to invest according to its stated objectives, this is referred to as "style slippage" (see page 178).

CATEGORIES OF MUTUAL FUNDS

Categories By Risk. The type of fund and investment objectives are often classified according to the risk an investor assumes in relation to the potential for returns.

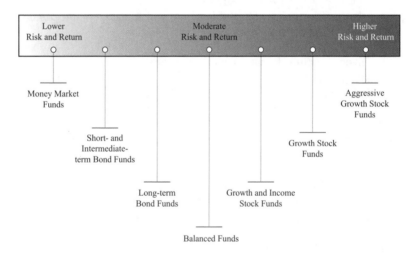

Source: *A Guide to Understanding Mutual Funds*, Copyright© 2000 by the Investment Company Institute (www.ici.org). Reprinted with permission.

General Categories By Investment. Although there are many categories of mutual funds, the three *main* categories of mutual funds include:

(1) **Stock Funds.** Also called "equity funds," these funds invest primarily in stocks. Over time, stocks historically have performed better than other investments, such as bonds and money market instruments. Over the 30-year period 1973-2002, stocks (as measured by the S&P 500) have produced a 10.68% average annual rate of return. In contrast, corporate bonds have returned 9.71%, government bonds 9.13%, and Treasury bills 6.70% (see table below, Historical Rates Of Return). However, since there

is no guarantee that this historical trend will be true in the future, stock funds are best used as long-term investments. When an investor purchases stock he accepts any number of risks (see Risks Associated With Investing, page 16).

(2) **Bond Funds.** These funds invest primarily in bonds and other fixed-income securities. Although there have been exceptions in the past, bond funds tend to be less volatile than stock funds and often produce regular income. For these reasons, investors often use bond funds to diversify, provide a stream of income, or invest for intermediate-term goals. Like stock funds, bond funds have risks (e.g., default risk and market risk, see pages 17-18) and can make or lose money (as was most vividly demonstrated by the WorldCom and Enron bond losses in 2002).

(3) **Money Market Funds.** These funds invest in pools of short-term, interest-bearing securities. A money market instrument is a short-term IOU issued by the United States government, a U.S. corporation, or a state and local government. Money market instruments have maturity dates of less than 13 months, and are relatively stable because of their short maturities and high quality.

Historical Rates Of Return[9]

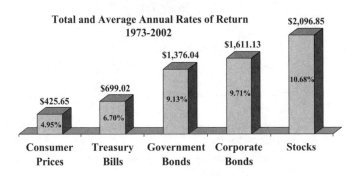

Total and Average Annual Rates of Return 1973-2002

$425.65 — 4.95% — Consumer Prices
$699.02 — 6.70% — Treasury Bills
$1,376.04 — 9.13% — Government Bonds
$1,611.13 — 9.71% — Corporate Bonds
$2,096.85 — 10.68% — Stocks

Past performance is no guarantee of future results.

Specific Categories By Objective. When it comes to specific classifications according to investment objective, the combinations and permutations of available mutual funds are many and varied. For example, in its monthly review of mutual funds, *The Wall Street Journal* currently uses 45 categories of mutual funds (based on classifications by Lipper, Inc.), but in its online "Daily Mutual Fund Scorecards," *The Wall Street Journal* uses more than 100 categories of mutual funds. The Investment Company Institute classifies United States mutual funds into the following 33 investment objective categories:[10]

EQUITY FUNDS

Capital Appreciation Funds seek capital appreciation; dividends are not a primary consideration.
- *Aggressive growth funds* invest primarily in common stocks of small, growth companies.
- *Growth funds* invest primarily in common stocks of well-established companies.
- *Sector funds* invest primarily in companies in related fields.

Total Return Funds seek a combination of current income and capital appreciation.
- *Growth-and-income funds* invest primarily in common stocks of established companies with the potential for growth and a consistent record of dividend payments.
- *Income-equity funds* invest primarily in equity securities of companies with a consistent record of dividend payments. They seek income more than capital appreciation.

World Equity Funds invest primarily in stocks of foreign companies.
- *Emerging market funds* invest primarily in companies based in developing regions of the world.
- *Global equity funds* invest primarily in equity securities traded worldwide, including those of U.S. companies.
- *International equity funds* invest primarily in equity securities of companies located outside the United States.
- *Regional equity funds* invest in companies based in a specific part of the world.

HYBRID FUNDS

Hybrid Funds may invest in a mix of equities, fixed-income securities, and derivative instruments.
- *Asset allocation funds* invest in various asset classes including, but not limited to, equities, fixed-income securities, and money market instruments. They seek high total return by maintaining precise weightings in asset classes. Global asset allocation funds invest in a mix of equity and debt securities issued worldwide.

HYBRID FUNDS (cont'd)

- *Balanced funds* invest in a mix of equity securities and bonds with the three-part objective of conserving principal, providing income, and achieving long-term growth of both principal and income. These funds maintain target percentages in asset classes.

- *Flexible portfolio funds* invest in common stocks, bonds, other debt securities, and money market securities to provide high total return. These funds may invest up to 100 percent in any one type of security and may easily change weightings depending upon market conditions.

- *Income-mixed funds* invest in a variety of income-producing securities, including equities and fixed-income instruments. These funds seek a high level of current income without regard to capital appreciation.

TAXABLE BOND FUNDS

Corporate Bond Funds seek current income by investing in high-quality debt securities issued by U.S. corporations.

- *Corporate bond funds (general)* invest two-thirds or more of their portfolios in U.S. corporate bonds with no explicit restrictions on average maturity.

- *Corporate bond funds (intermediate-term)* invest two-thirds or more of their portfolios in U.S. corporate bonds with an average maturity of five to 10 years. These funds seek a high level of income with less price volatility than longer-term bond funds.

- *Corporate bond funds(short-term)* invest two-thirds or more of their portfolios in U.S. corporate bonds with an average maturity of one to five years. These funds seek a high level of income with less price volatility than intermediate-term bond funds.

High-Yield Funds invest two-thirds or more of their portfolios in lower-rated U.S. corporate bonds (Baa or lower by Moody's and BBB or lower by Standard and Poor's rating services).

World Bond Funds invest in debt securities offered by foreign companies and governments. They seek the highest level of current income available worldwide.

- *Global bond funds–general* invest in worldwide debt securities with no stated average maturity or an average maturity of five years or more. These funds may invest up to 25 percent of assets in companies located in the United States.

- *Global bond funds–short-term* invest in debt securities worldwide with an average maturity of one to five years. These funds may invest up to 25 percent of assets in companies located in the United States.

- *Other world bond funds*, such as international bond and emerging market debt funds, invest in foreign government and corporate debt instruments. Two thirds of an international bond fund's portfolio must be invested outside the United States. Emerging market debt funds invest primarily in debt from underdeveloped regions of the world.

TAXABLE BOND FUNDS (cont'd)

Government Bond Funds invest in U.S. government bonds of varying maturities. They seek high current income.

- *Government bond funds–general* invest two-thirds or more of their portfolios in U.S. government securities of no stated average maturity. Securities utilized by investment managers may change with market conditions.

- *Government bond funds–intermediate-term* invest two-thirds or more of their portfolios in U.S. government securities with an average maturity of five to 10 years. Securities utilized by investment managers may change with market conditions.

- *Government bond funds–short-term* invest two-thirds or more of their portfolios in U.S. government securities with an average maturity of one to five years. Securities utilized by investment managers may change with market conditions.

- *Mortgage-backed funds* invest two-thirds or more of their portfolios in pooled mortgage-backed securities.

Strategic Income Funds invest in a combination of U.S. fixed-income securities to provide a high level of current income.

TAX-FREE BOND FUNDS

State Municipal Bond Funds invest primarily in municipal bonds issued by a particular state. These funds seek high after-tax income for residents of individual states.

- *State municipal bond funds–general* invest primarily in single-state municipal bonds with an average maturity of greater than five years, or no specific stated maturity. The income from these funds is largely exempt from federal and state income tax for residents of that state.

- *State municipal bond funds–short-term* invest primarily in single-state municipal bonds with an average maturity of one to five years. The income of these funds is largely exempt from federal and state income tax for residents of that state.

National Municipal Bond Funds invest primarily in the bonds of various municipal issuers throughout the United States. These funds seek high current income free from federal tax.

- *National municipal bond funds–general* invest primarily in municipal bonds with an average maturity of more than five years or no specific stated maturity.

- *National municipal bond funds–short-term* invest primarily in municipal bonds with an average maturity of one to five years.

MONEY MARKET FUNDS

Taxable Money Market Funds invest in short-term, high-grade money market securities and must have average maturities of 90 days or less. These funds seek the highest level of income consistent with preservation of capital (i.e., maintaining a stable share price).

- *Taxable money market funds–government* invest primarily in U.S. Treasury obligations and other financial instruments issued or guaranteed by the U.S. government, its agencies, or its instrumentalities.

- *Taxable money market funds–nongovernment* invest primarily in a variety of money market instruments, including certificates of deposit from large banks, commercial paper, and bankers acceptances.

Tax-Exempt Money Market Funds invest in short-term municipal securities and must have average maturities of 90 days or less. These funds seek the highest level of income – free from federal and, in some cases, state and local taxes – consistent with preservation of capital.

- *National tax-exempt money market funds* invest in short-term securities of various U.S. municipal issuers.

- *State tax-exempt money market funds* invest primarily in short-term securities of municipal issuers in a single state to achieve the highest level of tax-free income for residents of that state.

Source: 2003 Mutual Fund Fact Book, Copyright © 2003 by the Investment Company Institute (www.ici.org).

SELECTION OF MUTUAL FUNDS

Passively Managed vs. Actively Managed Funds. Investment managers who oversee "passively managed" funds, generally try to track a market index – such as the S&P 500 – by buying and holding all, or a large representative sample, of the securities in the index. Investment advisers who oversee "actively managed" fund portfolios base their investment decisions on extensive knowledge and research of market conditions and the financial performance of individual companies and specific securities in the effort to meet or beat average market returns. As economic conditions change, the fund

> **Digging Deeper**
>
> An excellent resource providing investment education programs and information about index funds is made available by Index Fund Advisors at: www.ifa.tv/index.html.

investment adviser may adjust the mix of the fund's investments to adopt a more aggressive or a more defensive posture in meeting its investment objectives.

Typically, the fees charged by actively managed funds exceed those charged by passively managed funds.

Style Slippage. Also referred to as "style drift," this occurs when the active management of a fund portfolio changes from its stated investment purpose by investing in a different asset class or different ratios of assets within the same class. For example, an investor may invest in a fund that is expected to produce long-term gain through growth investing. If the fund manager invests a large portion of assets in large money market funds and bonds there is style slippage that reduces the investor's risk and potential for gain. Alternatively, an investment manager may drift from mid-cap growth value to small-cap growth, thereby increasing the investor's risk exposure. Style slippage is often difficult for the investor to detect without diligently monitoring the holdings of the fund in relation to the stated objectives of the fund. See the discussion of Morningstar's Style Box on page 199.

Portfolio Turnover Rate. Also known merely as the "turnover rate," or a fund's "turnover ratio," this is a measure of the frequency with which securities are bought and sold during a year. For example, if a fund's assets totalled $100,000,000 and the fund bought and sold $100,000,000 worth of securities during the year, its turnover rate would be 100%. The lower the turnover rate, the better the opportunity for tax deferral. A higher turnover rate will generally add to the fund's expenses, and in strong markets can increase the likelihood that a fund will realize gains that will be distributed to shareholders (see Tax Issues on page 189). The turnover rate is an indication not only of the fund's trading activity, but also of the fund manager's investment philosophy. Aggressively managed funds generally have higher portfolio turnover rates than do conservative funds that invest for the long term. The turnover rate is provided in the fund's prospectus.

Share Classes. Funds that charge a front-end load typically offer shares with different sales charges, or "loads," and different fee structures. In effect, the investor who desires to purchase a particular mutual fund has a choice of how he will pay the sales charge. ("No-load" funds do not have share classes and are offered for sale without brokerage fees or sales loads.) Although there is currently no standardized method of classification, the following basic definitions of share classes appear to have gained some industry acceptance:[11]

> **A Shares** – typically called "load funds," these are offered through brokers and sold with an initial, or "front-end," sales charge (usually 3%-6%) that is deducted from the initial investment. In addition, these funds usually charge a 12b-1 marketing fee (averaging around 0.25%), which is deducted from the fund's assets each year.
>
> **B Shares** – have no front-end sales charge, but carry a redemption fee, or "back-end" load that is paid when shares are redeemed within a cer-

tain number of years. This load (called a "CDSC" or "contingent deferred sales charge") declines every year until it disappears – usually after six years. B share funds also carry a 12b-1 marketing fee that is typically higher than the 12b-1 fee of A shares. After the time period ends, some funds will convert B shares to A shares so these fees are reduced.

C Shares – known as a "level-load" shares, C shares have no front-end sales charge and no redemption fee, but they carry a 12b-1 marketing fee that is paid each and every year. This load is similar to no-load funds that charge 12b-1 fees.

D Shares – are offered by some funds, most of which are variations of A, B and C Shares.

PURCHASE OF MUTUAL FUNDS

Prospectus. A mutual fund's prospectus describes the fund's goals, fees and expenses, investment strategies and risks, and provides information on how to buy and sell shares. The Securities and Exchange Commission (SEC) requires a fund to provide a full prospectus either before an investment is made, or with the confirmation statement for the initial investment. In addition, periodic shareholder reports, prepared at least every six months by funds, discuss the fund's recent performance and include other important information, such as the fund's financial statements. By examining these reports, an investor can learn if a fund has been effective in meeting the goals and investment strategies described in the fund's prospectus.

Statement Of Additional Information (SAI). The SAI provides detailed information that expands upon the information provided in the fund's prospectus. Although most SAIs are lengthy and fairly technical, they do include many additional details about the fund that should be of interest to investors. For example, the SAI will give more information about the fund's: management; securities, risks, and policies; past investment performance; audited financial statements; portfolio securities as of the date of the SAI; and information about anyone who owns 5% or more of the fund's shares. Generally the SAI must be specifically requested, but once requested will be provided by the fund without charge.

Letter Of Intent. This is an assurance by a mutual fund shareholder that in exchange for lower sales charges, a certain amount of money (the target amount) will be invested over a specific period of time (not to exceed 13 months). The letter of intent is binding only on the mutual fund. Although not binding on the investor, if the target amount is not purchased by the end of the specified period, the sales charge on prior purchases is adjusted upward to reflect the amount that would have been paid absent the letter of intent program.

Fees, Costs & Expenses. The fees must be listed in the fund's prospectus and are typically categorized according to whether they are paid directly by the investor or paid from fund assets.

(1) **No-Load.** Mutual funds that do not charge any sales or transaction fees are known as "no-load" funds. With a no-load fund, the purchase price of the fund's shares is equal to its "net asset value," or NAV (see page 185). Likewise, redemption of shares is also done at the NAV. Like all mutual funds, however, no-load funds charge for annual operating expenses.

(2) **Front-End Load.** This is the fee (or commission) charged by some funds at the time of the initial purchase (i.e., a sales charge). Funds that impose these fees are known as "load" funds. This fee may also be charged on reinvested distributions and is sometimes referred to as a "re-load." As the size of the purchase increases, these fees are typically reduced at set "breakpoints." Sales charges can also be reduced by "letters of intent" and "rights of accumulation" (see pages 179 and 184). The amount of the load is equal to the difference between the "offering price" and the "net asset value" (see page 185). If a load is charged upon the initial purchase, normally upon the subsequent redemption or sale there is no charge (i.e., there is no back-end load). See A Shares on page 178.

(3) **Back-End Load.** Also referred to as a "contingent deferred sales charge (CDSC)," a "back-end" load is the commission charged for redeeming mutual fund shares. These fees typically range from 4% to 6% and are levied in order to discourage an investor from frequent buying and selling of fund shares (i.e., "in-and-out trading"). Generally, back-end fees decrease over time, with the time period varying from 90 days to 5 years. See B Shares on page 178.

(4) **12b-1 Fee.** Also referred to as a "distribution and service fee," "marketing fee," or "trailer," this fee is intended to cover marketing and advertising costs, and sometimes sales commissions and employee bonuses. Under SEC Rule 12b-1, this annual fee cannot exceed a maximum of 1.25% of the fund's "net asset value" (see NAV on page 185). Both "load" and "no-load" funds can impose 12b-1 fees, but if a fund charges an annual 12b-1 fee of more than 0.25%, it cannot advertise itself as a no-load fund (i.e., a true "no-load" fund cannot charge more than 0.25%). Funds that impose these fees are sometimes known as "12b-1 funds."

(5) **Level Load.** This is an annual fee that is charged, typically in lieu of front-end and back-end loads (e.g., the mutual fund does not charge an up-front or back-end commission, but instead deducts up to 1.25% of average daily fund assets).

(6) **Management Fee.** This fee is assessed annually and represents the cost of the professional money managers who manage and invest the fund's portfolio. Typically this fee is graduated. Both load and no-load funds impose management fees.

(7) **Operating Fees & Expenses.** These fees pay the operating costs and expenses of running the fund and include items such as employees' salaries, phone lines, marketing expenses, printing, and mailing costs. Both load and no-load funds impose operating fees.

(8) **Exchange Fee.** Also referred to as a "transfer fee," this is the fee that is charged when money is shifted between funds within the same mutual fund company.

(9) **Overall Maximums Allowed.** Total sales charges and fees cannot exceed 8.5% of the net asset value. Note that this 8.5% limitation *does not* include annual management and operating fees.

The actual percentage sales charge is higher then the load percentage when determined with respect to the net amount actually invested. For example, assume an investor purchased fund shares that imposed the maximum 8.5% load. Investing $10,000 would result in a load of $850 (10,000 × .085 = 850). Therefore the net amount actually invested is $9,150 (10,000 - 850 = 9,150). The shares of the fund owned by the investor have a NAV of $9,150. Taken as percentage of the NAV the sales charge is 9.3% (850 ÷ 9,150 = 9.3%).

Expense Ratios. The "expense ratio" is the ratio of total fund expenses to net assets of the fund. If a fund has $890,000 of expenses and $100,000,000 of net assets, then its expense ratio is 0.89 of one percent (890,000 ÷ 100,000,000 = .0089). This ratio includes management fees, 12b-1 fees if any, transaction costs, the cost of shareholder mailings and other administrative expenses. A fund with an active management style and high turnover rate will generally have a higher expense ratio than a fund with a passive management style and low turnover rate (see page 195). The ratio is often a function of the fund's size, rather than the operating efficiency of the fund management, but can also depend on the nature of the investments in the fund. Although 12b-1 fees are included in the expense ratio calculation, sales and commission expenses are not included.

Mutual Fund Expense Disclosure Tables. The SEC requires that a summary of fees and costs appear in the prospectus. The following is an example of such a table from a **no-load** fund. Note that the shareholder fees are *transaction* costs, whereas the annual fees are *operating* costs.

The following table describes the fees and expenses that are incurred when you buy, hold, or sell shares of the fund.

A. Shareholder fees (paid by the investor directly)

Sales charge (load) on purchases	None
Sales charge (load) on reinvested distributions	None
Deferred sales charge (load) on redemptions	None

B. Annual fund operating expenses (paid from fund assets)

Management fee	0.66%
Distribution and Service (12b-1) fees	None
Other expenses	0.23%
Total annual fund operating expenses	0.89%

C. Example of fund expenses over time. The following example helps you compare the cost of investing in the fund with the cost of investing in other mutual funds. It assumes a hypothetical annual return of 5% and that shareholder fees and annual fund operating expenses are exactly as described above. For every $10,000 you invested, here's how much you would pay in total expenses if you sell all of your shares at the end of each time period indicated:

1-year	3-years	5-years	10-years
$91	$284	$493	$1,096

The following tables provide examples of the expenses for a **load fund**:

Annual Fund Operating Expenses (deducted from fund assets)

	Class A	Class B	Class C
Management Fees	.29%	.29%	.29%
Distribution and/or Service (12b-1) Fees[1]	.25%	1.00%	1.00%
Other Expenses	.11%	.12%	.22
Total Annual Fund Operating Expenses	.65%	1.41%	1.51%

[1] Class A and 12b-1 fees may not exceed .025% and .50%, respectively, of the class' average net assets annually.

Fees Paid Directly from Shareholder's Investment

	Class A	Class B	Class C
Maximum sales charge imposed on purchases (expressed as a percentage of the offering price)	5.75%[1]	None	None
Maximum sales charge imposed on reinvested dividends	None	None	None
Maximum deferred sales charge	None[2]	5.00%[3]	1.00%[4]
Redemption or exchange fees	None	None	None

[1] Sales charges are reduced or eliminated for purchases of $25,000 or more.
[2] A contingent deferred sales charge of 1% applies on certain redemptions made within 12 months following purchases of $1.
[3] Deferred sales charge is reduced after 12 months and eliminated after six years.
[4] Deferred sales charge is eliminated after 12 months.

Example Of Fund Expenses Over Time: The following examples are intended to help the shareholder compare the cost of investing in the fund with the cost of investing in other mutual funds. The examples assume that: the shareholder invests $10,000 in the fund for the indicated time periods; the shareholder's investment has a 5% return each year; all dividend and capital gain distributions are reinvested; and the fund's operating expenses remain the same as above. The examples assume redemption, and do not reflect the effect of any taxable gain or loss at the time of the redemption.

	One Year	Three Years	Five Years	Ten Years
Class A[1]	$638	$771	$916	$1,339
Class B[2]	$644	$846	$971	$1,483
Class C[3]	$254	$477	$824	$1,802

[1] Assuming redemption. Reflects the maximum initial sales charges in the first year.

[2] Assuming redemption. Reflects the applicable contingent deferred sales charges through year six, and Class A expenses for years nine and ten (because Class B shares automatically convert to Class A shares after eight years.

[3] Assuming redemption. Reflects contingent deferred sales charge during the first year.

Rights Of Accumulation. These rights use *breakpoints* to reduce sales charges. Rights of accumulation differ from a "letter of intent" (see page 179) in that they do not require any stated amount to be invested over any particular period of time, and such rights only apply to cumulative purchases *above* the break points. For example, assume the following breakpoints applied:

Cumulative Purchase	Sales Charge
Under 10,000	3.0%
10,000 to 25,000	2.5%
25,000 to 50,000	2.0%
50,000 to 75,000	1.5%
75,000 to 100,000	1.0%
100,000 to 250,000	0.5%
Over 250,000	NAV

Based upon these breakpoints, an investor who made purchases under rights of accumulation would pay the following sales charges:

Date	Purchase Amount	Calculation of Sales Charge		Cumulative Purchases	Sales Charges
1/20/03	$8,000	$8,000 × .03 =	$240	$8,000	$240
3/3/03	$8,000	$2,000 × .03 =	60		
		$6,000 × .025 =	150		
		Total	$210	$16,000	$450
4/14/03	$44,000	$9,000 × .025 =	$225		
		$25,000 × .020 =	500		
		$10,000 × .015 =	150		
		Total =	$875	$60,000	$1,325

This result can be compared with an investor who received a reduced sales charge of 1.5% based upon a letter of intent to purchase $60,000 of mutual funds over a 90-day period:

Date	Purchase Amount	Calculation of Sales charge	Cumulative Purchases	Sales Charges
1/20/03	$8,000	$8,000 × .015 = $120	$8,000	$120
3/3/03	$8,000	$8,000 × .015 = $120	$16,000	$240
4/14/03	$44,000	$44,000 × .015 = $660	$60,000	$900

VALUATION & MEASURING RETURN

Net Asset Value (NAV). "NAV" is the current market value of all the fund's assets, minus liabilities, divided by the total number of outstanding shares (see formula below). The price at which a fund's shares may be purchased is its NAV per share, *plus* any applicable front-end sales charge (thus, the offering price of a fund *without* a sales charge would be the same as its NAV per share). For example, assume Mutual Fund X owns a portfolio of stocks worth $600,000,000; its liabilities are $60,000; and its shareholders own 500,000 shares. The NAV of $11.88 is calculated as follows:

$$NAV = \frac{Market\ Value\ Of\ Fund's\ Securities -}{Number\ of\ Investor\ Shares\ Outstanding}$$

$$NAV = \frac{\$6,000,000 - \$60,000}{500,000} = \$11.88$$

The NAV must reflect the *current market value* of the fund's securities, as long as market quotations for those securities are readily available. Other assets are priced at *fair value*, determined in good faith by the fund's board of directors. The Investment Company Act of 1940 requires "forward pricing," meaning that shareholders who purchase or redeem shares receive the next computed share price following the fund's receipt of the transaction order (typically computed at the end of each trading day). Income and expenses (including fees, if any) must be accrued through the date the share price is calculated. Fund share prices appear in the financial pages of most major newspapers. A fund's share price can also be found in its semiannual and annual reports. Funds typically value exchange-traded securities using the closing prices from the exchange on which the securities are principally traded, even if the exchange closes before the fund's daily pricing time (which occurs with many foreign securities).

Yield. "Yield" is the measure of net income (dividends and interest less the fund's expenses) earned by the securities in a mutual fund's portfolio during a specified period. Yield is expressed as a percentage of the fund's NAV at the beginning of the period (including the highest applicable sales charge, if any). For example, assume a fund's purchase price (NAV) was $50 at the beginning of the year and ended the year at $53. Also assume that the blended fund of stocks and bonds paid out $1.50 in dividend income, $2.75 in interest earnings, and had

$.50 in expenses during the year. The yield of 7.5% would be calculated as follows (note that the yield calculation does *not* take into consideration the appreciation in NAV from $50 at the beginning of the year to $53 at the end of the year):

$$\text{Yield} = \frac{\text{Dividends} + \text{Interest} - \text{Expenses}}{\text{NAV At Beginning Of Year}}$$

$$\text{Yield} = \frac{\$1.50 + \$2.75 - \$.50}{\$.50}$$

$$\text{Yield} = 7.5\%$$

Total Return. This is the percentage of gain or loss a fund has provided, assuming that all distributions have been reinvested. It is generally regarded as the best and most comprehensive measure of fund performance. Total return includes dividend and capital gain distributions along with any changes in the fund's share price. A *dividend distribution* comes from the interest and dividends earned by the securities held by a fund; a *capital gain distribution* represents any net gains resulting from the sale of the securities held by a fund. For example, assume a fund's purchase price (NAV) was $50 at the beginning of the year and $53 at the end of the year (an increase of $3.00 per share). Also assume that during the year the fund paid out $1.25 in dividend distributions and $2.00 in *realized* capital gain distributions (both long-term and short-term).[12] The total return of 12.5% would be calculated as follows:

$$\text{Total Return} = \frac{\substack{\text{Dividend} \\ \text{Distributions}} + \substack{\text{Capital Gains} \\ \text{Distributions}} + \substack{\text{Increase In} \\ \text{NAV}}}{\text{NAV At Beginning Of Year}}$$

$$\text{Total Return} = \frac{\$1.25 + \$2.00 + \$3.00}{\$50}$$

$$\text{Total Return} = 12.5\%$$

Risk Adjusted Rates Of Return. These measures of performance are potentially useful because they may give investors a tool for balancing the potential returns of a fund against the risks of the fund. For instance, if a fund has historical annual returns which are 2% above a market index, historical risk measures may provide some indication of the risks that were taken to produce the increased returns. However, use of these measures is not without controversy.[13]

(1) **Beta.** "Beta" is generally used in connection with equity securities, but is also used with respect to equity funds (see also, the discussion of Beta on page 21). Beta measures the sensitivity of a security's, or portfolio's, return to the market's return. The market's beta is, by definition, equal to "1." Portfolios with betas greater than 1 are more volatile than the market, and

portfolios with betas less than 1 are less volatile than the market. For example, if a portfolio has a beta of 2, a 10% market return would result in a 20% portfolio return, and a 10% market loss would result in a 20% portfolio loss (excluding the effects of any firm-specific risk that has not been eliminated through diversification). The calculation of a fund's historical beta requires the selection of a benchmark market index, such as the S&P 500 (see the discussion of "Other Measures" in the Morningstar report on page 196). With many funds it may be difficult to find an appropriate index. For example, since a gold fund has very little correlation with an index such as the S&P 500, a gold fund might compute its beta with respect to a gold index, but this would be useless when making a comparison to other types of funds.

(2) **Standard Deviation.** This is a statistical measure of the range of a fund's performance. A high rating means that there is greater potential for volatility. See page 36.

(3) **Sharpe Ratio.** Also known as the "Sharpe index," or the "reward-to-variability ratio," this ratio is computed by dividing the fund's return minus a risk-fee return (such as that obtainable with a T-bill) by the fund's standard deviation (i.e., it is the ratio of a fund's average return in *excess* of the risk-free rate of return, or average excess return). A higher ratio means that the fund offers a better trade-off between risk and reward. A Sharpe Ratio over "1.0" is generally considered "pretty good," but anything over "2.0" is likely to be considered "outstanding."

(4) **Treynor Ratio.** Also known as the "Treynor Index," or "reward-to-volatility ratio," this is the ratio of a fund's average *excess* return to the fund's beta. It measures the returns earned in excess of those that could have been earned on a riskless investment per unit of market risk assumed. Unlike the Sharpe Ratio, the Treynor Ratio uses market risk (beta), rather than total risk (standard deviation), as the measure of risk. It is an attempt to remove from the fund's return that portion due to market risk, leaving only the portion of the return attributable to other factors, such as the skill of the portfolio manager.

(5) **Jensen's Alpha.** Also known as "Jensen's measure," this is the difference between a fund's actual returns and those that could have been earned on a benchmark portfolio with the same amount of market risk (i.e., the same beta as the portfolio). Jensen's Alpha measures the ability of active management to increase returns above those that are purely a reward for accepting market risk. A portfolio having consistently positive excess returns (adjusted for risk) will have a positive Jensen's Alpha, whereas a portfolio with consistently negative excess returns (adjusted for risk) will have a negative Jensen's Alpha.

MUTUAL FUND LISTINGS

The daily performance of many mutual funds is reported in major newspapers throughout the country. The following is a brief explanation of the information reported in *The Wall Street Journal* regarding the Fidelity Contrafund on March 20, 2003.

MUTUAL FUNDS

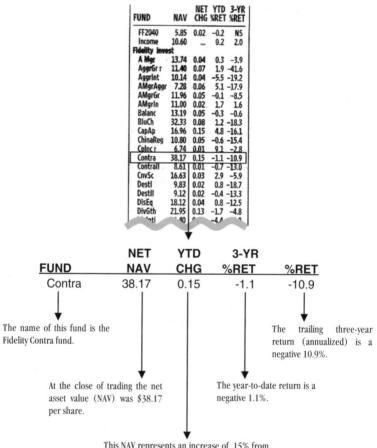

FUND	NAV	NET CHG	YTD %RET	3-YR %RET
FF2040	5.85	0.02	-0.2	NS
Income	10.60	...	0.2	2.0
Fidelity Invest				
A Mgr	13.74	0.04	0.3	-3.9
AggrGr r	11.40	0.07	1.9	-41.6
Aggrint	10.14	0.04	-5.5	-19.2
AMgrAggr	7.28	0.06	5.1	-17.9
AMgrGr	11.96	0.05	-0.1	-8.5
AMgrIn	11.00	0.02	1.7	1.6
Balanc	13.19	0.05	-0.3	-0.6
BluCh	32.33	0.08	1.2	-18.3
CapAp	16.96	0.15	4.8	-16.1
ChinaReg	10.80	0.05	-0.6	-15.4
CpInc r	6.74	0.01	9.1	-2.8
Contra	38.17	0.15	-1.1	-10.9
Contrall	8.61	0.01	-0.7	-13.0
CnvSc	16.63	0.03	2.9	-5.9
DestI	9.83	0.02	0.8	-18.7
DestII	9.12	0.02	-0.4	-13.3
DisEq	18.12	0.04	0.8	-12.5
DivGth	21.95	0.13	-1.7	-4.8
Inti	40	0	-4.4	

FUND	NET NAV	YTD CHG	3-YR %RET	%RET
Contra	38.17	0.15	-1.1	-10.9

The name of this fund is the Fidelity Contra fund.

The trailing three-year return (annualized) is a negative 10.9%.

At the close of trading the net asset value (NAV) was $38.17 per share.

The year-to-date return is a negative 1.1%.

This NAV represents an increase of .15% from the previous day's trading.

TAX ISSUES[14]

Unlike most corporations, a mutual fund generally distributes all of its earnings each year. Because of the specialized "pass-through" tax treatment of mutual fund income and capital gains, fund investors are ultimately responsible for paying tax on a fund's earnings, whether or not they receive the distributions in cash, or reinvest them in additional fund shares.

Taxable Distributions. Mutual funds make two types of taxable distributions to shareholders every year: dividends and capital gains.[15]

(1) **Dividend Distributions.** Dividend distributions come primarily from the interest and dividends earned by the securities in a fund's portfolio, after expenses are paid by the fund. These distributions must generally be reported as dividends on an investor's tax return. *Under JGTRRA 2003, dividends paid by a mutual fund may be taxable at the 15% tax rate if the income being passed from the fund to the investors is "qualified dividend income" (i.e., corporate stock dividends) in the hands of the fund, and not short-term capital gains or interest from bonds (which continues to be taxed at ordinary income tax rates).*

(2) **Capital Gain Distributions.** Capital gain distributions represent a fund's net gains, if any, from the sale of securities held in its portfolio for more than one year. When gains from these sales exceed losses, they are distributed to shareholders. *Under JGTRRA 2003, distributions of capital gains on assets held by a mutual fund for more than one year are generally taxable at the 15% rate.*

Share Sales & Exchanges.[16] An investor who sells mutual fund shares usually incurs a capital gain or loss in the year the shares are sold. (For the method of determining gain or loss upon the sale or exchange of shares, see page 190). The exchange of shares between funds in the same fund family also results in either a capital gain or loss (see Tax-Deferred Retirement Accounts on page 191 for exceptions to these rules). Investors are liable for tax on any capital gain arising from the sale of fund shares, just as they would be if they sold a stock, bond, or any other security. Capital losses from mutual fund share sales and exchanges (just as capital losses from other investments) may be used to offset other gains in the current year, and thereafter.

Tax-Managed Funds. When a mutual fund is owned outside of a tax-deferred retirement account, it is important to consider how a fund's investment activity will result in taxation of the fund investor. Tax-managed funds attempt to minimize dividends, interest, and realized capital gains. *Dividends* are minimized by emphasizing investments in long-term growth stocks rather than dividend-paying stocks.

Interest is avoided by investing in equities in preference to fixed-income securities. *Capital gains* are minimized by taking a buy-and-hold approach to investing. If capital gains are realized, the fund is likely to sell other stocks that may generate offsetting capital losses. When stocks must be sold in order to meet redemptions, or for investment purposes, the fund sells stocks with the highest cost basis. To discourage investors from forcing sales, redemption fees are often assessed for funds that have been held for less than two years.

DETERMINING GAIN OR LOSS UPON SALE

The amount of a shareholder's gain or loss on fund shares is determined by the difference between the cost basis of the shares (generally, the purchase price for shares, including those acquired with reinvested dividends) and the sale price.[17]

Cost Basis In Shares. Many funds provide cost basis information to shareholders or compute gains and losses for shares sold. When funds are acquired over a period of time, and for different prices, the investor has some flexibility in determining his income tax basis according to one of the following methods:

(1) **Specific Identification Method.** If the shareholder can adequately identify the group from which the shares came, that basis and holding period can be used.

(2) **First-In, First-Out Method (FIFO).** Under the FIFO method, it is assumed that the first shares purchased are sold. If the shareholder is unable to adequately identify when the shares were purchased, he will usually be deemed to have sold or transferred the shares in the order in which they were acquired using the FIFO method. Assuming an appreciating market, this may result in a low cost basis, high realized gain, and increased taxes.

(3) **Average Basis Methods.** The shareholder may elect to use either one of two average basis methods if the shares are held in a custodial account maintained for the acquisition or redemption of fund shares and the shareholder purchased or acquired the shares for different bases.

(a) **Single Category.** Under the single category method, all shares in the mutual fund account are added together. The basis of each share in the account is the total cost (or other basis) of all the shares in the account, divided by the total number of shares.

(b) **Double Category.** Under the double category method, all shares in the mutual fund account are divided into two categories – those with a holding period of more than one year, and those with a holding period of one year or less. The basis for each share in either category is the total cost (or other basis) of all the shares in that category, divided by the number of shares in that category. The shareholder can then elect to have the shares being sold to come from either one of the categories.

Tax-Exempt Funds. Tax-exempt bond funds pay dividends earned from municipal bond interest. This income is exempt from federal income tax and, in some cases, state and local taxes as well. Tax-exempt money market funds invest in short term municipal securities and also pay exempt-interest dividends. Even though income from these two types of funds is generally tax-exempt, investors must report it on their federal income tax returns. Tax-exempt mutual funds provide investors with this information in a year-end statement. They typically explain how to handle tax-exempt dividends on a state-by-state basis. For some taxpayers, portions of income earned by tax-exempt funds may also be subject to the federal alternative minimum tax. Even though municipal bond dividends and interest may be tax-free, an investor who redeems tax-exempt fund shares may realize a taxable capital gain. An investor may also realize a taxable gain from a tax-exempt fund if the fund manager sells securities during the year for a net gain.[18]

Tax-Deferred Retirement Accounts. No tax is incurred as a result of the sale of mutual fund shares within retirement accounts. Generally, any mutual fund capital gains in retirement accounts accrue tax-deferred until they are distributed to the account holder (i.e., taxation is delayed until the funds are distributed). Distributions from tax-deferred accounts are treated as income subject to the individual's federal income tax rate at the time of distribution, except for nondeductible (after-tax) contributions that are not subject to taxation upon distribution, and most distributions from Roth IRAs. For most individuals, distributions from tax-deferred accounts begin at or near retirement age, at which time the individual may be in a lower income tax bracket. Individuals who receive proceeds from tax-deferred accounts prior to age 59½ may incur a tax penalty in addition to federal, state, and local income taxes.

> **Digging Deeper**
>
> An excellent resource for information about the use of mutual funds in retirement accounts is made available by the Mutual Fund Investor's Center™ at: www.mfea.com.

FUND COMPARISONS & SELECTION

Sorting through the more than eight thousand mutual funds can be a daunting task. Making "apples to apples" comparisons of mutual funds, their past performance and future potential, requires use of a rating service offering comprehensive, independent, and accurate mutual fund information. The primary print services include *Value Line Mutual Fund Survey* (www.valueline.com), *Lipper Analytical Services* (www.lipperweb.com), *Morningstar Mutual Funds,* and an abridged version available as *Morningstar FundInvestor* (www.morningstar.com).[19]

Morningstar Mutual Funds.[20] The comprehensive report produced by this service is generally recognized as the leader in its field. Key features of this product include full-page reports on more than 1,600 mutual funds, twice-a-month analysis sections with updated reports for 160 funds, twice-a-month summary sections with updates on key data points, editorial analysis, Morningstar's proprietary style boxes and star ratings, commentary on the fund industry, tax analysis, and aggregate performance data for 49 investment categories. The following examination of the specific information presented in the single-page stock-fund report provides

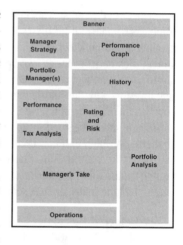

an overview of the essential information that is required in comparing and selecting mutual funds.[21]

Manager Strategy. This section explains what criteria a manager uses in selecting stocks, and how risky a given approach may be. It may often focus on what size and type of company a manger prefers, together with a discussion regarding how growth and value factors are balanced.

> ### Fidelity Contrafund
> **Manager Strategy**
> Call it forced evolution. As this fund has grown into a behemoth, with nearly $30 billion in assets, manager Will Danoff has had to move away from mid-caps and small caps and adopt a growth-at-a-reasonable-price philosophy. He still continues to keep a big part of the fund in mid-caps, but the fund is now dominated by larger fare. The fund tends to be more conservative than most of its large-blend rivals, with a big underweighting in racy sectors such as technology.

Portfolio Manager(s). This section provides a profile of the portfolio manager, including a listing of any other funds the manager runs. To determine how much of the fund's record is attributable to the manager, check the start date (e.g., since September 1990).

> **Portfolio Manager(s)**
> William Danoff. Since 09-90. BA'82 Harvard U., MBA'86 U. of Pennsylvania; MA'86 University of Pennsylvania, Wharton School.

Performance. This section gives the quarterly returns over the past five years. Morningstar suggests that this is a good place for the investor to quickly test his risk tolerance.

Performance 01-31-03					
	1st Qtr	2nd Qtr	3rd Qtr	4th Qtr	Total
1998	12.28	4.48	-9.36	23.73	31.57
1999	5.79	5.51	-4.66	17.50	25.03
2000	5.56	-6.58	1.13	-6.54	-6.80
2001	-13.18	3.47	-8.80	6.70	-12.59
2002	2.88	-3.68	-9.86	1.18	-9.63

Trailing	Total Return%	+/- S&P 500	+/- Russ 1000	%Rank All Cat	Growth of $10,000
3 Mo	-4.17	-1.23	-1.61	85 80	9,583
6 Mo	-5.09	0.16	0.21	61 27	9,491
1 Yr	-11.90	11.11	10.66	43 3	8,810
3 Yr Avg	-9.57	4.26	4.09	62 16	7,394
5 Yr Avg	3.32	4.64	4.53	43 5	11,773
10 Yr Avg	10.82	1.86	1.98	5 5	27,926
15 Yr Avg	15.56	4.59	4.57	2 1	87,509

Quarterly returns are compounded to obtain the year-end total shown on the right.

Trailing returns provide performance over short and long periods with comparisons against appropriate benchmarks and peers. **Total Return%** is calculated by taking the change in net asset value, reinvesting all income and capital gain distributions during the period, and dividing by the starting net asset value. The measure of the difference between the stock fund's total return and the total return of the S&P 500 Index is **+/- S&P 500** (see page 62). The measure of the difference between the fund's total return and the total return of the Russell 1000 Index is **+/-Russ 1000** (see page 65). With both of these measures, the minus sign ("-") means that the fund underperformed the index, and the plus sign ("+") means that the fund outperformed the index. For example, a listing of −1.23 means that the fund underperformed the S&P 500 Index by 1.23 percentage points. Another performance measure, **%Rank All/Cat**, provides two total return percentile rankings for each fund for the periods indicated. The first compares a fund with all funds in the Morningstar database (**% Rank All**), while the second compares the fund's total return for that period against the funds in the same Morningstar Category (**% Rank Cat**). With both rankings "1" is the highest or best percentile and "100" is the lowest, or worst.

Tax Analysis. This section lists the fund's tax-adjusted returns (**Tax-Adj Rtn%**) and the percentage point reduction in annualized returns that results from taxes (**Tax-Cost Rat**). Each figure is then given a percentile rank (**%Rank Cat**) in the fund's category

Tax Analysis	Tax-Adj Rtn%	%Rank Cat	Tax-Cost Rat	%Rank Cat
3 Yr Avg	-11.37	18	0.99	41
5 Yr Avg	0.96	7	1.68	66
10 Yr Avg	8.16	7	2.09	67
Potential Capital Gain Exposure: -10% of assets				

("1" is the best, "100" is the worst). Morningstar warns that high tax-adjusted returns do not necessarily mean that a fund is tax-efficient; a very tax-efficient fund with poor returns may result in low after-tax results. This section is probably best used in determining whether a fund should be held in a tax-deferred or taxable account.

Morningstar's Take. This section reflects the interpretation by Morningstar's analysts and is based upon the data displayed and an interview of the fund's manager, that is designed to uncover those strategies guiding investment decisions. The "how and why" of a fund's success or failure is provided and recommendations are made regarding inclusion in the investor's portfolio.

Morningstar's Take by Christopher Traulsen 02-03-03

Fidelity Contrafund's manager still hasn't found much to like in the technology sector.

Will Danoff has been skeptical of the technology sector since early 2001, when he sold down most of the fund's holdings in the area. Put simply, he didn't think the sell-off made tech stocks much more attractive from a valuation perspective, as their earnings had shrunk along with their share prices. As of late 2002, he remained skeptical of their earnings power, and that apparently hadn't changed by year-end. As of Dec. 31, 2002, Contrafund had just 3.1% of its assets in the technology sector, according to Fidelity's numbers. In contrast, tech stocks were 14.3% of the S&P 500 index on the same date.

Instead of tech, Danoff continued to favor steadier financials, consumer staples, and health-care names at year-end. In addition, he maintained a significant overweight in materials issues relative to the S&P 500 Index, and had also stashed a large percentage of the fund's assets in mid-caps and overseas stocks.

With the exception of a notable blowup at Tenet Healthcare, Danoff's positioning and stock-picking was spot-on for most of 2002. Strong showings from top holdings such as Lockheed Martin, Avon Products, and Newmont Mining helped limit the fund's 2002 loss to 9.2%. No one likes to lose money, but the fund beat the S&P 500 Index and the average large-blend offering by 12.5 percentage points on the year--a huge margin.

Danoff's bets carry risk: The fund isn't likely to participate much in a rally driven by the tech sector. Indeed, it badly lagged its peer group and the S&P 500 in 2002's buoyant fourth quarter. That said, we think the true measure of a fund's worth is its strength over time. On that score, Contrafund excels: Its three-, five-, and 10-year returns all best the category average and the S&P 500 by sizable margins, and it has been less volatile than both benchmarks. Investors seeking a core holding should find much to like here.

Operations. This section lists the mailing address, phone number and web address of the fund. Also listed are the inception date, advisor,

Address:	82 Devonshire Street	Minimum Purchase:	$2500	Add: $250 IRA: $500
	Boston, MA 02109	Min Auto Inv Plan:	$2500	Add: $250
	800-544-8888	Sales Fees:	3.00%L	
Web Address:	www.fidelity.com	Management Fee:	0.30%, 0.20%P	
Inception:	05-17-67	Actual Fees:	Mgt:0.45%	Dist: ---
Advisor:	Fidelity Management & Research	Expense Projections:	3Yr:$502	5Yr:$851 10Yr:$1086
Subadvisor:	FMR (Far East), FMR (U.K.)	Income Distrib:	Annually	
NTF Plans:	CommonWealth NTF, Fidelity Instl-NTF	Total Cost (relative to category):		Below Avg

minimum initial purchase, and breakdown of the fund's expenses into its components, including projections of the funds total costs, such as load, and annual expense ratio, based on a $10,000 investment over different periods of time. Lastly, the fund's total costs are given relative to its category.

Morningstar Category. This is the first stage in understanding a fund's portfolio. Morningstar sorts funds into 50 peer groups based on the types of securities held by the funds. Each category is assigned using a fundamental analysis of a fund's portfolio over a 3-year period. This portfolio analysis and the fund's category tells a great deal about a fund's performance and future volatil-

Mstar Category
Large Blend

ity. These categories are also helpful in selecting funds with a view toward diversifying a portfolio.

Investment Style.[22] These boxes indicate whether the fund manager sticks with a consistent style from year to year, or whether there is "style slippage" (see page 178). Purchase of a fund to fill a particular investment need in a balanced portfolio requires that the fund maintain that position if the investor is to achieve his goal. See the expanded illustration of this unique Morningstar feature on page 199. The figure below the boxes is the percentage of stock holdings. If there has been a change of manager, that occurrence is indicated by a "∇" placed over the quarter of change.

Fund Performance vs. Category Average. This graph compares a fund's quarterly returns with its category average. It indicates the volatility of a fund compared with others in the same category.

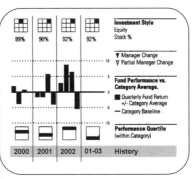

Performance Quartile. This graph shows in which quartile a fund's calendar-year returns finished relative to its category. Again, this is an indication of how consistent the fund has been from year to year.

History.[23] This table can be used to spot trends over the years. **NAV** is the fund's "net asset value" and represents its per-share price (see page 185). **Total Return** % includes income (in the form of dividends or interest payments) and capital gains or losses (the increases or decreases in the value of a security). Total return is calculated as a percentage by taking the change in a fund's NAV,

2000	2001	2002	01-03	History
49.18	42.77	38.60	37.42	NAV
-6.80	-12.59	-9.63	-3.06	Total Return %
2.30	-0.71	12.46	-0.44	+/-S&P 500
0.99	-0.14	12.02	-0.64	+/-Russ 1000
0.41	0.45	0.12	0.00	Income Return %
-7.21	-13.04	-9.75	-3.06	Capital Return %
46	56	3	81	Total Rtn % Rank Cat
0.24	0.22	0.05	0.00	Income $
6.62	0.00	0.00	0.00	Capital Gains $
0.84	0.91	—	—	Expense Ratio %
0.45	0.49	—	—	Income Ratio %
166	141	—	—	Turnover Rate %
40,285	32,321	27,695	26,729	Net Assets $mil

assuming the reinvestment of all income and capital gain distributions during the period, and then dividing by the initial NAV. The measure of the difference between the fund's total return and the total return of the S&P 500 Index is **+/-S&P 500** (see page 62). The measure of the difference between the fund's total return and the total return of the Russell 1000 Index is +/-**Russ 1000** (see page 65). With both measures, the minus sign ("-") means the fund underperformed the index, and the plus sign ("+") means the fund outperformed the index. For example, a listing of 12.26 means that the fund outperformed the S&P 500 Index by 12.26 percentage points. **Total Rtn %** **Rank Cat** measures the fund's total return compared to funds in the same Morningstar Category ("1" is the highest or best percentile, and "100" is the lowest, or worst). **Income $** is the fund's yearly income distribution expressed in per-share dollar amounts (dividends and interest). **Capital Gain $** is the fund's yearly capital gain distributions expressed in per-share dollar amounts (i.e., the profits received and distributed from the sale of securities within the portfolio). **Expense Ratio %** is the percentage of assets deducted each fiscal year for the fund's expenses, including 12b-1 fees, management fees, administrative fees, operating costs, and all other asset-based costs. **Income Ratio %** is the percentage of current income earned per share, and is calculated by dividing the fund's net investment income by its average net assets (net investment income is the total income of the fund, less expenses). **Turnover Rate %** is then determined by dividing the lesser of purchases or sales (expressed in dollars and excluding all securities with maturities of less than one year) by the fund's average monthly assets. This provides a rough estimate of the fund's level of trading activity (i.e., the percentage of the portfolio that has changed over the past year). **Net Assets $mil** is the fund's asset base in millions of dollars, net of fees and expenses.

Rating and Risk. This section provides the funds' risk, returns, and overall star rating over the 3-, 5-, and 10-year time periods. **Load-Adj Return %** provides the percentage returns by adjusting downward to account for sales charges (the calculation is adjusted for deferred and back-end loads that decline or disappear). **Morningstar Rtn vs Cat** indicates how the fund's returns compare with those of its peer group (*High* = top 10%; *Above*

Rating and Risk				
Time Period	Load-Adj Return %	Morningstar Rtn vs Cat	Morningstar Risk vs Cat	Morningstar Risk-Adj Rating
1 Yr	-14.54			
3 Yr	-10.49	+Avg	Low	★★★★
5 Yr	2.69	High	-Avg	★★★★★
10 Yr	10.48	High	-Avg	★★★★★
Incept	12.63			

Average = next 22.5%; *Average* = middle 35%; *Below Average* = next 22.5%; *Low* = bottom 10%). **Morningstar Return** is an assessment of a fund's excess return over a risk-free rate (the return of the 90-day Treasury bill) in comparison to similar funds, after adjusting for all applicable loans and sales charges. **Morningstar Risk vs Cat** ranks a fund's historical volatility versus that of its peer group (*Low Risk* = 10% of funds with lowest measured risk; *Below Average* = next 22.5%; *Average* = middle 35%; *Above Average* = next 22.5%; *High* = top 10%). **Morningstar Risk** is an assessment of the variations in a fund's monthly returns in comparison to similar funds (the greater the variation, the larger the risk score). **Morningstar Risk-Adj Rating** is derived by weighting and averaging the separate measures, and provides some idea of the consistency of the fund's historical risk-adjusted performance (*Highest* = 5 stars; *Above Average* = 4 stars; *Neutral* = 3 stars; *Below Average* = 2 stars; *Lowest* = 1 star).

Other Measures. These all provide additional views of risk. **Alpha** measures the difference between a fund's actual returns and its expected performance, given its level of risk as measured by "beta" (see page 21). A positive alpha figure indicates the fund has performed better than its beta would have predicted, and a negative alpha indicates that the fund has underperformed in light of the expectations established by the fund's beta. **Beta** is a measure of a fund's sensitivity to market move-

Other Measures	Standard Index S&P 500	Best Fit Index S&P Mid 400
Alpha	-4.3	-11.4
Beta	0.51	0.54
R-Squared	57	77
Standard Deviation	11.42	
Mean	-9.57	
Sharpe Ratio	-1.20	

ments (see page 187). Morningstar calculates beta using excess fund returns against excess index returns (some other methodologies use regression against raw returns). **R-Squared** is a measure of the performance patterns of the fund compared to the index. For beta and alpha to be reliable measures of risk, a fund must have a high correlation with its index. A high R-Squared (from 85 to 100) indicates that the fund's movements are in line with the benchmark index. A fund with a low R-Squared (70 or less) does not move with the index (e.g., an R-Square measure of 30 indicates that only 30% of the fund's movements can be explained by movements in the benchmark index). **Standard Deviation** is a statistical measure of the range of a fund's performance (see page 36). A high standard deviation indicates that the fund has a greater potential for volatility. The **Mean** is the annualized average monthly return from which the standard deviation is calculated (i.e., since the standard deviation is based upon 36 monthly returns, the mean is the same as the annualized trailing 3-year return figure; -9.57 in this example). The **Sharpe Ratio** is a risk-adjusted measure that is calculated using standard deviation and excess return to determine reward per unit of risk (see page 187). The higher the Sharpe Ratio, the better the fund's historical risk-adjusted performance. The **Best Fix Index** is the index that has the highest correlation with the fund; in this case the **S&P Mid 400 Index** (Standard and Poor's Mid-Cap 400 Index, see page 63).

Portfolio Analysis. This section provides information regarding the fund's holdings that help in understanding performance and potential volatility. Included are the fund's total holdings (**Total Stocks**), each stock's sector, price earnings ratio (**PE**), year-to-date returns (**YTD Ret%**), and percentage of fund assets devoted to the stock (**% Assets**). An increase in stock holdings is indicated by a plus sign (⊕) and a decrease is indicated by a minus (θ) sign. New additions are indicate by a star burst (❂).

Portfolio Analysis 10-31-02				
Share change since 12-01 Total Stocks:446	Sector	PE	YTD Ret%	% Assets
⊕ Lockheed Martin	Ind Mtrls	—	-13.16	3.39
⊖ PepsiCo	Goods	23.0	-4.74	2.68
⊕ Colgate-Palmolive	Goods	24.4	-1.57	2.68
⊕ Berkshire Hathaway Cl B	Financial	32.0	-10.69	2.40
⊖ 3M Company	Ind Mtrls	26.7	-0.23	2.26
⊕ Avon Products	Goods	27.5	-4.14	2.10
❂ Encana	—	—	—	1.89
⊖ BP PLC ADR	Energy	18.3	-7.33	1.87
⊕ Johnson & Johnson	Health	26.0	-2.96	1.77
⊕ Tenet Healthcare	Health	7.5	6.40	1.77
⊕ UnitedHealth Grp	Health	23.1	0.62	1.65
⊕ Fifth Third Bancorp	Financial	19.8	-9.89	1.43
⊖ Pfizer	Health	23.4	-2.10	1.23
⊖ American Intl Grp	Financial	20.4	-16.68	1.21
⊕ HCA - The Healthcare Com	Health	24.1	-2.07	1.15
⊕ First Data	Business	22.8	-4.66	1.14
⊕ Newmont Mng	Ind Mtrls	78.2	-1.48	1.12
⊖ ExxonMobil	Energy	23.2	-3.15	1.04
⊕ Gillette	Goods	29.6	-4.99	0.96
⊖ Fannie Mae	Financial	12.1	-1.47	0.92

Current Investment Style. This is the Morningstar style box for the current period (see page 199). Also shown is the **Market Cap** % giving a view of the different size companies in the fund's portfolio based upon percentiles (*Giant* = 1% of U.S. largest companies; *Large* = next 4%; *Mid* = 15%; *Small* = next 30%;

Current Investment Style		
Value Blnd Growth	Market Cap %	
	Giant	25.1
	Large	40.1
	Mid	29.9
	Small	4.5
	Micro	0.3
	Median $mil:	
	15,620	

Micro = bottom 50%). **Median $mil** gives the median market capitalization of the portfolio in millions of dollars.

Value Measures. This section provides key indicators of value (see Value Investing on page 20 and Value Stocks on page 131). **Price/Earnings** is the weighted average of the price/projected earnings ratio of all stocks in the fund's portfolio (see page 31). **Price/Book** is the weighted average of the price/book ratios of all the stocks in the fund's portfolio. **Price/Sales** is the weighted average of the price/sales ratios of all the stocks in the fund's portfolio. **Price/Cash Flow** is the weighted average of the price/cash-flow ratios of all the stocks in the

Value Measures		Rel S&P 500
Price/Earnings	25.4	1.5
Price/Book	3.7	1.7
Price/Sales	1.6	1.5
Price/Cash Flow	10.3	1.8
Dividend Yield %	0.8	0.4

fund's portfolio. **Dividend Yield %** is the weighted average of the dividend yield for each stock in the fund's portfolio (see page 133). To provide perspective the column entitled **Rel S&P 500** compares these measures with the figures for the broad-based S&P 500 Index.

Growth Measures. This section provides key indicators of the potential for growth. **Long-Term Erngs** is the weighted average of the projected growth in earnings for each stock in the fund's portfolio, as derived from polled analysts' estimates. **Book Value** is the weighted average of growth rates in book value for each stock in the fund's portfolio. **Sales** is the weighted average of the sales-growth rates for each stock in the fund's portfolio. **Cash Flow** is the

Growth Measures	%	Rel S&P 500
Long-Term Erngs	17.4	1.1
Book Value	9.0	1.1
Sales	8.5	1.0
Cash Flow	13.3	1.6
Historical Erngs	12.9	2.1

weighted average of the growth in cash flow for each stock in the fund's portfolio. **Historical Erngs** is the weighted average of the growth in earnings for each stock in the fund's portfolio. **Rel S&P 500** column compares these measures with the figures for the broad-based S&P 500 Index.

Profitability. This section provides key indicators of the potential for increased profitability. **Return on Equity** (ROE) is the weighted average of the fund's individual holdings' ROE. **Return on Assets** (ROA) is

Profitability	%	Rel S&P 500
Return on Equity	17.8	1.1
Return on Assets	9.3	1.1
Net Margin	7.2	0.8

equal to the weighted average ROA of the fund's individual holdings. **Net Margin** represents the weighted average of the individual stocks' net margins.

Sector Weightings. Morningstar divides the stock market into three broad "economic spheres": **Info** (information); **Service**; and **Mfg** (manufacturing). Each of these spheres is in turn divided into four specific industry sectors. The column headed **% of Stocks** gives the percentage of the fund's assets in each sphere and sector. The column headed **Rel S&P 500** gives the weightings relative to the S&P 500 Index. The last two columns give the fund's historical (3-year) range of the percentage of assets held in each sphere and sector.

Sector Weightings	% of Stocks	Rel S&P 500	3 Year High	Low
☁ Info	4.8	0.2	15	5
🔲 Software	1.6	0.3	6	2
🖥 Hardware	1.1	0.1	5	1
📱 Media	2.0	0.5	3	2
📶 Telecom	0.1	0.0	2	0
☎ Service	56.0	1.1	71	43
⚕ Health	19.2	1.3	21	16
🛒 Consumer	11.5	1.3	11	7
🏢 Business	8.7	2.2	11	5
$ Financial	16.7	0.8	28	15
🏭 Mfg	39.1	1.3	46	20
🏬 Goods	20.2	2.2	20	9
⚙ Ind Mtrls	13.8	1.3	14	5
◔ Energy	5.0	0.8	10	5
⬒ Utilities	0.1	0.0	3	0

Composition

● Cash	7.3
● Stocks	92.1
● Bonds	0.4
▨ Other	0.2
Foreign	22.3

(% of Stock)

Composition. This section shows the percentage of assets devoted to cash, stocks, bonds, and other, along with the percentage of stock assets invested in foreign securities.

Morningstar Style Box. The investment style box has been designed by Morningstar to provide a visual tool for better understanding a fund's true investment strategy. The following is the style box for funds falling within the Morningstar Category for domestic-stock funds, defined as those with at least 70% of their assets in domestic stocks (there is also an international-stock style box and a bond style box). Within the stock style box grid, nine possible combinations exist, ranging from large-cap value for the safest funds to small-cap growth for the riskiest. For stocks and stock funds, it classifies securities according to market capitalization (the vertical axis) and growth and value factors (the horizontal axis).

Stock Style Box

Average Weighted Market Capitalization

Risk	Investment Style			
	Value	Blend	Growth	
Low ○	Large-cap Value	Large-cap Blend	Large-cap Growth	Large
Moderate ◐	Mid-cap Value	Mid-cap Blend	Mid-cap Growth	Mid
High ●	Small-cap Value	Small-cap Blend	Small-cap Growth	Small

Large-cap stocks are defined as the group that accounts for the top 70% of the capitalization of the Morningstar domestic-stock universe (representing about

99% of the United States market for actively traded stocks); mid-cap stocks represent the next 20%; and small-cap stocks represent the balance. A fund's horizontal placement – value, growth, or blend – is determined by an asset-weighted average of the stocks' net value/growth scores (the scores include *value* measures such as price-to-projected earnings and dividend yield, and *growth* measures such as long-term projected earnings growth and book value growth).

---

[1] See *Tax Facts 2* (Cincinnati: The National Underwriter Company, 2003, revised annually), **Question 177** – What is a unit trust? How are unit holders taxed?

[2] See *Tax Facts 2*, **Question 174** – What is a closed-end fund? How are shareholders in a closed-end fund taxed?

[3] See *Tax Facts 2*, **Question 175** – What is an exchange-traded fund? How are shareholders in an exchange-traded fund taxed?

[4] As reported in a monthly statistical release by the Investment Company Institute, *Exchange-Traded Fund Assets March 2003,* at www.ici.org.

[5] See *2003 Mutual Fund Fact Book*, p. 61, and *Fundamentals*, Vol. 11, No. 5, October 2002, Investment Company Institute, p. 1 (www.ici.org/pdf/fm-v11n5.pdf).

[6] See *Trends In Mutual Fund Investing* (Investment Company Institute, January 2003) at www.ici.org.

[7] As of April 14, 2003, there were 3,600 securities listed on the NYSE, 802 on the American Stock Exchange and 3,735 on the NASDAQ.

[8] The advantages of mutual fund ownership were obtained from the *Mutual Fund Fact Book*, a very useful publication of the Investment Company Institute. The *Mutual Fund Fact Book* is an annual compilation of facts and figures on the United States mutual fund industry, to include information about the industry's history, regulation, taxation, and shareholders. The full text of this publication can be accessed at www.ici.org.

[9] This table uses data obtained from Global Financial Data, Los Angeles, CA, www.globalfindata.com (accessed: February 20, 2003). The base for all calculations is December 31, 1972 = 100. Consumer Prices are based upon the Bureau of Labor's Consumer Price Index. Returns on Treasury bills uses the yield on 3-month Treasury bills as found in Board of Governors of the Federal Reserve System, *Federal Reserve Bulletin* (1935-). Returns on government bonds uses the Federal Reserve Board's 10-year Treasury Bond index. Returns on corporate bonds uses data from Moody's index of yields on AAA corporate bonds. The source for returns on stocks is Standard and Poor's, *Security Price Index Record*, New York (S&P 500 composite).

[10] As listed in the *2003 Mutual Fund Fact Book*, Copyright © 2003 by the Investment Company Institute (www.ici.org). Reprinted with permission.

[11] The following definitions of share classes are based upon materials made available by the Mutual Fund Education Alliance™ in its online Mutual Fund Investor's Center (www.mfea.com). This web site is an excellent resource offering a largest collection of mutual fund companies, website links, fund listings and exclusive planning, tracking and monitoring tools. The Mutual Fund Education Alliance is the not-for-profit trade association of the no-load mutual fund industry.

[12] Note that only *realized* capital gain distributions are considered. Any appreciation in price is derived from *unrealized* capital gains.

[13] See Paul Schott Stevens and Amy Lancellotta, *Improving Mutual Fund Risk Disclosure*, 2nd (Investment Company Institute Perspective, Vol. 1, No. 2, November 1995).

[14] For an excellent discussion of the tax aspects of mutual funds, see Spring Bixby Leonard and April K. Caudill, *The Mutual Fund Handbook*, 2nd ed. (Cincinnati: The National Underwriter Company, 1999), pp. 171-196.

[15] See *Tax Facts 2*, **Question 161** – How are dividends received from a mutual fund taxed?

[16] See *Tax Facts 2*, **Question 170** – How is a shareholder taxed when he sells, exchanges, or redeems his mutual fund shares?

[17] Ibid.

[18] See also, Leonard and Caudill, pp. 54-56 and 179.

[19] Morningstar also offers a software product entitled *Morningstar Principia Mutual Funds*, providing the ability to analyze and construct portfolios by sorting and selecting funds using a variety of parameters.

[20] The information on pp. 192-199 was reprinted with permission of Morningstar, Inc.

[21] *Morningstar Mutual Funds* consists of a stock-fund report and a separate, but similar, bond-fund report. The following material is based upon information set forth in the *Morningstar Mutual Funds Resource Guide*, (Morningstar, Inc., 2003), provided as a supplement to subscribers to the *Morningstar Mutual Funds* service. This publication (#MFBRG030121) can be purchased by calling 312-696-6000.

[22] Morningstar provides style boxes for the current year plus the prior *eight* years, if available. To conserve space, only the prior three years are shown.

[23] Morningstar provides data for the current year plus the prior *eleven* years, if available. To conserve space, only the prior three years are shown.

CHARACTERISTICS OF TANGIBLE ASSETS

Tangible assets, also referred to as real assets, include such diverse property interests as primary residences, second homes, commercial buildings, raw land, works of art, precious metals, diamonds, art, and collectibles. An investment in tangible assets can be acquired by purchasing the asset itself, or by making an indirect investment by purchasing an interest in an entity such as a real estate investment trust (REIT) or real estate limited partnership (RELP) that owns the asset (see pages 218-219). Investments that provide legal methods for deferring or reducing current and future tax liabilities are variously referred to as "tax sheltered," "tax oriented," "tax benefited," or "tax favored." Characteristics common to these investments are the *leveraging* of borrowed funds to increase the size of investments, *deferral* of taxes by claiming depreciation and other deductions, and *conversion* of what would otherwise be ordinary income into favorable capital gains. In addition, real estate investments in low-income housing and rehabilitation of old and historic structures can provide *absolute* savings.[1]

FINANCIAL LEVERAGE

The attractiveness of many tax favored investments depends upon the availability of debt financing, the ability to use someone else's money to acquire investment property that will provide an acceptable return. For example, assume an investor has an opportunity to acquire a piece of property costing $100,000. Assume also, that the investor has $10,000 for a down payment and

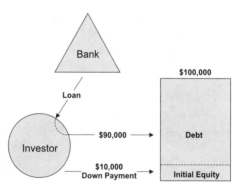

is able to borrow the remaining $90,000 from a bank at a favorable rate of interest. The $100,000 investment consists of $10,000 of initial equity and $90,000 of debt. If the property subsequently increases in value to $120,000, this appreciation represents 20% growth (120,000 - 100,000 = 20,000 ÷ 100,000 = .20). However, this represents a 200% return on the investor's $10,000 down payment. This return on equity is *ten times* the rate of growth of the property. Although using the financial leverage afforded by debt financing may look very attractive, it is important to consider other factors, such as risk, available

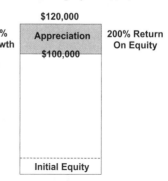

depreciation, after-tax cost of interest to carry the loan, property taxes, fees, maintenance, utilities, commissions, and positive or negative cash flow. Whether this would be considered a satisfactory return will also depend upon the investor's evaluation of alternative investments, as well as the time and effort required to buy, maintain, and sell the investment. Each of these factors should be carefully considered.

ESTIMATING INVESTMENT RETURNS

Before investing in real estate, it is important to estimate its potential for producing an acceptable rate of return. To do this requires projections of estimated rental income and fees, taxes, insurance, maintenance, interest, and depreciation. For example, assume an investor has the opportunity to purchase, maintain, and lease a single-family home as follows:

Purchase Information
    Purchase price – $175,000
    Value of house for depreciation purposes – $145,000
    Closing costs – $2,625.00 (1½% of purchase price)
    Down payment – $17,500 (10% of purchase price)
    Mortgage loan amount - $157,500 ($175,000 – $17,500)
    Term of mortgage – 15 years
    Interest rate – 7½%

Income and Expenses (annual)
    Rental income   – $15,000 ($1,250 per month)
        – projected to increase by 10% every two years
    Agent management fees at 7½% – $1,125 ($93.75 per month)
        – will increase with rental income
    Real estate taxes – $3,500
        – projected to increase by 7% per year
    Insurance   – $350
        – projected to increase by 5% per year
    Maintenance   – $750
        – projected to increase by 6% per year
    Payment on mortgage – $1,460.04 per month ($17,520.48 per year)
        – fixed rate 15-year mortgage
    Depreciation   – $5,273 (MACRS over 27.5 years; 145,000 ÷ 27.5)

Equity Projection
    Appreciation – 9% per year
    Sales commission – 6% of sales price
    Effective income tax rate – 41%
    Capital gains tax rate – 15%

Income And Expenses. This analysis is undertaken in order to project income and expenses while accounting for the effect of both depreciation (a non-cash expense that reduces current income taxes) and tax savings that are produced by deductible operating losses. Note that each year there are both before-tax and after-tax operating losses.

	Year				
	1	2	3	4	5
Income					
Gross Rental Income	$15,000	$15,000	$16,500	$16,500	$18,150
Less: Agent Fees	1,125	1,125	1,238	1,238	1,361
Net Rental Income	13,875	13,875	15,262	15,262	16,789
Expenses					
Taxes	3,500	3,745	4,007	4,287	4,587
Insurance	350	368	386	405	425
Maintenance	750	795	843	894	948
Interest	11,612	11,153	10,659	10,126	9,552
Depreciation	5,273	5,273	5,273	5,273	5,273
Total	21,485	21,334	21,168	20,985	20,785
Less: Net Rental Income	13,875	13,875	15,262	15,262	16,789
Before-Tax Operating Loss	7,610	7,459	5,906	5,723	3,996
Less: Tax Savings	3,120	3,058	2,422	2,347	1,639
After-Tax Operating Loss	4,490	4,401	3,484	3,376	2,357

Cash Flow Analysis. This analysis recaps the actual cash effect of income and expenses. Note that each year the negative cash flow is offset to some extent by the tax savings calculated in the above Income And Expense analysis (e.g., in year 1 negative cash flow of $8,246 is reduced by tax savings of $3,120, resulting a net cash loss of $5,126).

	Year				
	1	2	3	4	5
Taxes	$3,500	$3,745	$4,007	$4,287	$4,587
Insurance	350	368	386	405	425
Maintenance	750	795	843	894	948
Mortgage Payment	17,521	17,521	17,521	17,521	17,521
Total Cash Expenses	22,121	22,429	22,757	23,107	23,481
Less: Net Rental Income	13,875	13,875	15,262	15,262	16,789
Negative Cash Flow	8,246	8,554	7,495	7,845	6,692
Less: Tax Savings	3,120	3,058	2,422	2,347	1,639
Annual Net Cash Loss	5,126	5,496	5,073	5,498	5,053

Net Equity. This analysis projects the property's appreciation at the assumed rate of growth (9% per year) and subtracts from this amount the outstanding mortgage balance.

	Year				
	1	2	3	4	5
Property Value (year end)	$190,750	$207,918	$226,631	$247,028	$269,261
Less: Mortgage Remaining	151,592	145,225	138,363	130,969	123,001
Before-Tax Net Equity	39,158	62,693	88,268	116,059	146,260

Realized Upon Sale. Assuming the property is sold at the end of the 5th year for $269,261, this analysis determines the amount realized after taxes, taking into consideration depreciation, sales commission, and capital gains taxes.

Paid For Property	$175,000
Less: Depreciation Taken	26,365
Adjusted Basis	148,635
House Sales Price	269,261
Less: Sales Commission	16,156
Net From Sale	253,105
Less: Adjusted Basis	148,635
Gain On Sale	104,470
Less: Capital Gains Tax (15%)	15,670
Realized From Sale (After-Tax)	88,800

Return On Investment. The return on investment is estimated by discounting disbursements (amounts invested) and receipts (amounts realized from investments). The rate of return is obtained when the discounted present value of the disbursements (initial investment plus subsequent losses) is equal to discounted present value of the receipts (the amount realized after-taxes from the sale at the end of year 5). The present value of the $19,049 initial investment is equal to the down payment ($17,500), plus the after-tax closing costs of $1,549 ($2,625 less tax savings of $1,076). Note also, that the present value of this $19,049 initial investment is $19,049 (i.e., it occurs at the beginning of year 1). Calculation of the approximate return on investment can be done using the table on pages 462-463, but this can be very time consuming (it requires multiple calculations to determine the interest rate at which the present values of disbursements and receipts are approximately equal). A better way of determining the return on investment is to use a spreadsheet's present value (PV) function for each amount. By far the easiest method is to use a calculator such as the HP-12C.[2]

Upon Purchase

Closing Costs	$2,625
Less: Tax Savings	1,076
After-Tax Closing Costs	1,549
Down Payment	17,500
Initial Investment	19,049

Disbursements		Present Value At 20.8%
Initial Investment	$19,049	$19,049
Year 1 Net Loss	5,126	4,243
Year 2 Net Loss	5,496	3,766
Year 3 Net Loss	5,073	2,878
Year 4 Net Loss	5,498	2,582
Year 5 Net Loss	5,053	1,964
Total		34,482
Receipt		
Realized From Sale		
(After-Tax)	88,800	34,520

$38 difference results from calculating present value to one-tenth of one percent.

REAL ESTATE – FACTORS TO CONSIDER

Investment Considerations. Real estate has historically been viewed as a hedge against inflation, meaning that its value has more than kept pace with inflation. However, as with many other investments, real estate values can fall due to a deterioration in overall economic conditions, or changes in specific geographic areas. The investor who desires to invest in real estate must first determine the degree of direct involvement he is willing to assume. Purchasing a property with the intention of managing and maintaining it demands a substantial amount of ongoing time and energy, whereas purchasing an interest in a real estate investment trust (REIT), or real estate limited partnership (RELP), involves virtually no management effort (see pages 218-219).

Selection Considerations. As a minimum, the following factors should be carefully investigated and evaluated with respect to any anticipated purchase of either residential or commercial property:

(1) Location and neighborhood trends.

(2) Accessibility and right of ways.

(3) Association fees and deed restrictions.

(4) Clear titles and possible liens.

(5) Age and condition of property (amount of repairs needed).

(6) Amount of property taxes.

(7) Rental history.

(8) Local ordinances and zoning laws (e.g., restrictions on short-term rentals).

(9) Availability of competent management and cost of management fees (if the investor will not directly manage the property).

(10) Availability and cost of property insurance.

(11) Qualification for financing (debt servicing).

(12) Monthly cash flow requirements.

Tax Considerations. An investor in rental real estate can deduct the reasonable and necessary expenses paid or incurred, even if it produces a loss. This is because the rental and management of real property is generally considered a trade or business, even if the owner owns only one property, is actively engaged in another business, and carries on all management activities through an agent. Deductions typically fall within one of the following areas:

(1) **Repairs And Maintenance.** Amounts paid for routine repair and maintenance expenses are deductible in the year paid (as either business expenses or expenses incurred in connection with property held for the production of income), but the cost of capital improvements must be added to the owner's basis in the property and recovered through depreciation.

(2) **Mortgage Interest.** Amounts paid for mortgage interest are generally deductible, but subject to the passive loss rule (see below). However, there are additional limitations with respect to primary and vacation homes (see Deduction Of Interest, page 210).

(3) **Property Taxes.** Amounts paid for real property taxes are deductible, but local assessments for improvements that enhance the value of the property must be added to the investor's basis and depreciated.

(4) **Depreciation.** Buildings may be depreciated (either residential or non-residential improved real property), but not the land itself. This deduction does not require that the investor make any cash expenditure, and is not limited to his equity in the property (e.g., to his actual cash outlay for the property). Residential rental property and nonresidential property that is placed in service after 1986 is depreciated using straight-line depreciation under the Modified Cost Recovery System (MACRS). For example, residential rental property is depreciated over 27.5 years, and nonresidential real property is depreciated over 39 years. Upon eventual sale of this property the prior depreciation is not subject to recapture if the property was placed in service after 1986 (i.e., no depreciation is taken in excess of straight-line depreciation).

(5) **Limitations.** The above deductions may be affected by certain limitations under either the "passive loss" rule or the "at risk" rule.

(a) **Passive Loss Rule.** Under this rule losses from "passive" activities may generally be deducted only to the extent they do not exceed aggregate income from passive activities, and credits from passive activities may be taken against tax liability allocated only to passive activities. A passive activity is one that involves the conduct of a trade or business in which the taxpayer does not "*materially* participate." However, in the case of losses from rental real estate, special rules apply that allow a taxpayer who "*actively* participates" to deduct up to $25,000 of losses against nonpassive income (e.g., income from dividends or wages). This deduction is phased out at the rate of 50 cents for every dollar of adjusted gross income exceeding $100,000 (i.e., it is fully phased out when adjusted gross income reaches $150,000). Active participation is a less stringent standard than material participation.[3]

(b) **At Risk Rule.** Under this rule the current deductibility of "losses" generated by certain tax shelters and other activities are limited to the amount the taxpayer has "at risk" in the economic sense (e.g., he must be personally liable for repayment). However, the primary focus of the at risk rule is the limited partner and the nonrecourse financing of a limited partner's investment; and the rule does not prohibit an investor from offsetting his share of the deductions generated by the activity against the income he receives from the activity. Further, there is a special exception with respect to "qualified nonrecourse financing" of real property. Under this exception, provided they are secured by real property, loans provided by entities such as banks and mortgage companies are considered qualified nonrecourse financing.[4]

(6) **Taxation Of Gain Upon Sale.** Upon the sale of rental real estate held for more than one year the net gain is treated as a long-term capital gain and therefore subject to favorable capital gains rates, generally 15%.[5]

PRIMARY RESIDENCE

Clearly, for the large majority of individuals home ownership is one of the primary means of acquiring and increasing their financial assets. For example, it has been reported that in the United States 68% of families own the house they live in, on average owner-occupied housing accounts for 27% of families' wealth, and comprises 45% of non-Social Security net worth for households aged 65 and over.[6]

Advantages Of Home Ownership. The many advantages of home ownership include:

(1) **Personal Enjoyment.** It has been said that, "a man's home is his castle." Whether a home is "his castle," or "her castle," clearly it reflects the personal tastes and lifestyle desires of its owners. The contentment of owning a home is part of the American dream, and is often the single largest purchase most individuals will make during their lifetime.

(2) **Forced Savings.** Regular payment of a mortgage loan acts as a very effective form of forced savings. Unfortunately, use of second mortgages in recent years has eroded the equity being created by these savings. This could have

serious consequences for those individuals who will enter their retirement years with lessened home equity and ongoing mortgage payments.

(3) **Opportunity For Appreciation.** The purchase of a home has proven not only to be a good lifestyle decision, but has also historically provided the opportunity for appreciation over the long haul. However, as with most other investments, there is no guarantee that housing values will appreciate over any given period of time. Appreciation, or even depreciation, can vary substantially from one area of the county to another.

(4) **Deduction Of Interest.** Generally interest paid on a home mortgage (i.e., acquisition indebtedness) or home equity indebtedness with respect to the investor's residence is deductible, but within limits. Interest is deductible on up to $1,000,000 of mortgage "acquisition indebtedness," which is defined as debt incurred to finance the *purchase or improvement* of no more than two qualified residences (i.e., a primary residence and one other residence). A homeowner who wishes to *borrow against home equity* can deduct the interest only on $100,000 of such debt, or on the amount that is equal to his equity, whichever is less.[7] For this deduction to be of benefit, the homeowner must itemize deductions.

(5) **Deduction Of Real Estate Taxes.** State and local real property taxes may be taken as itemized deductions.[8]

(6) **Exclusion Of Gain Upon Sale.** Subject to ownership and use requirements, up to $250,000 of gain on the sale of a "principal residence" can be excluded from income (a married couple filing a joint tax return can exclude up to $500,000 of gain). To claim the full exclusion, during the 5-year period ending on the date of the sale, the taxpayer must have *owned* the home for at least 2 years (the ownership test), and *lived in* the home as his main home for at least 2 years (the use test). Any gain not excluded is taxable.[9]

Rent vs. Buy. Home ownership offers a predictable way of providing for shelter and protects against the "rent risk" (i.e., the risk associated with the uncertainty of future rent increases versus the certainty of a long-term fixed-rate mortgage and owner-determined maintenance costs).[10] Compared to the advantages, the disadvantages of home ownership are limited, but nevertheless must be considered. The following table sets forth some of the numerous factors that should be considered when deciding between renting and buying.

Digging Deeper

A rent versus buy calculator is available at: www.texasbesthomes.com/mortgageinfo.html.

Rent vs. Buy Comparison		
	Advantages	**Disadvantages**
Buy	Property builds equity	Responsible for maintenance
	Sense of community, stability, and security	Responsible for property taxes
	Free to change decor and landscaping	Possibility of foreclosure and loss of equity
	Not dependent on landlord to maintain property	Less mobility than renting
Rent	Little or no responsibility for maintenance	No tax benefits
	Easier to move	No equity is built up
		No control over rent increases
		Possibility of eviction
Source: www.ginniemae.gov		

Financing. Very few people purchase their homes outright. In fact, many of the investment advantages of home ownership stem from the leverage obtained by financing the purchase with a mortgage.

(1) **Sources.** The primary sources for financing include mortgage banks such as Countrywide Home Loans (www.countrywide.com) and Chase Manhattan Mortgage (www.chase.com); credit unions, which are non-profit financial cooperatives operated for the benefit of their members (www.creditunion.coop); savings banks; savings and loan associations; many life insurance companies; and government agencies such as the U.S. Department of Housing and Urban Development (HUD) (www.hud.gov).

(2) **Preapproval letter.** Although this is not a final loan commitment, it is an important part of the process in that it demonstrates the buyer's financial strength and shows that he has the ability to complete a purchase (i.e., the buyer's "borrowing power"). It is issued by a lender after a review of the applicant's financial situation, including a credit report and any other per-

tinent information. Typically, first-time buyers opt for the traditional 30-year loan, with either a floating interest rate or a fixed rate of interest over the life of the loan.

(3) **Qualification Guidelines.** Lending decisions depend on the applicant's employment history, credit scores, and other such factors. The following guidelines are examples of those used by lending institutions in qualifying an individual for a mortgage:[11]

   (a) **Housing-To-Income Ratio.** This ratio compares the sum of monthly housing expenses to monthly gross income. The mortgage industry's conservative guideline is that housing expenses should be *28% or less of income*. Monthly housing expenses include payments for principal, interest, property taxes, hazard insurance, private mortgage insurance (if required), and condo or homeowner's fees (if required). However, a lower ratio may be required if there is a low down payment (e.g., when the down payment represents 5% of the home price, a 25% housing expense-to-income ratio might be required). Alternatively, if other factors are thought to compensate for the higher risk of a loan made that exceeds the standard 28% ratio a lender can use a more aggressive ratio, such as 34% (e.g., when a larger down payment is made).

   (b) **Debt-To-Income Ratio.** This ratio compares the sum of monthly long term debt obligations (including the prospective mortgage) to monthly gross income. The mortgage industry's conservative guideline is that these debt payments should be 36% or less of income. However, as with the housing expense-to-income ratio, this is a flexible guideline.

(4) **Minimum Down Payment.** In the past, a down payment of at least 5% was required, but that has changed in recent years, with some mortgage programs allowing for a zero-down payment.

(5) **Points.** These are fees paid to induce lenders to make a mortgage loan. One point is equal to 1% of the amount of the mortgage loan (i.e., if a loan is made for $50,000, one point equals $500). It is a one-time charge that effectively reduces the amount of money borrowed and increases the rate of interest (see following paragraph, Annual Percentage Rate). When points are paid in connection with the *acquisition* of a principal residence they are generally deductible in the year paid, provided certain requirements are satisfied.[12] In contrast, when points are paid on *refinancing* a principal residence they must generally be amortized over the life of the mortgage.

(6) **Annual Percentage Rate (APR).** This is expressed as a percentage rate per year and is the rate of interest that a borrower actually pays, taking into consideration interest, points and loan origination fees. With an adjustable rate mortgage the APR assumes that the loan's index remains the same as its initial value. The APR helps borrowers compare various loan options, keeping in mind that loans with lower stated interest rates and high points or origination fees may be a bad value, or loans with higher stated interest rates and low or no points or origination fees may be a good value. The following table provides examples of how the APR affects the monthly payment, total payments, and total interest by comparing loans of 6% and 8% charging 0, 1, 2 and 3 points (assuming no other origination or loan fees are charged).

Digging Deeper

See the mortgage APR calculator at:
www.dinkytown.net/java/MortgageApr.html.

30-Year $100,000 Net Loan					
Interest Rate	Points	APR	Monthly Payment	Total Payments	Total Interest
6%	0	6.000	599.55	215,838	115,838
	1	6.093	605.55	217,998	117,998
	2	6.186	611.54	220,154	120,154
	3	6.278	617.54	222,314	122,314
8%	0	8.000	733.76	264,154	164,154
	1	8.105	741.10	266,796	166,796
	2	8.210	748.44	269,438	169,438
	3	8.314	755.78	272,081	172,081

Note: It is assumed that the loan is increased to pay points charged (i.e., the borrower requires a *net* amount of $100,000). For example, assuming 0 points a 6% loan for $100,000 will require monthly payments of $599.55, total payment of $215,838, and total interest of $115,838 over the 30-year life of the loan; whereas with 2 points a loan for $102,000 will require monthly payments of $611.54, total payments of $220,154, and total interest of $120,154 (total interest includes points of $2,000).

(7) **Types Of Mortgages.**[13] Most mortgages are generally for periods of either 15 or 30 years. If there is any doubt about being able to meet the higher monthly payments required by a 15-year mortgage, many individuals will take out a 30-year mortgage and then begin making early payments in order to pay off the mortgage earlier (assuming the mortgage does not have a prepayment penalty).

    (a) **Loan Term.** Choice of a loan term can dramatically affect the total interest paid over the loan term. The following table will give an idea of the savings involved by comparing shorter term loans to a 30-year loan.

Interest Savings – $200,000 Loan At 6% Rate			
Loan Term	Monthly Payment	Total Interest	Savings
30 years	$1,199.10	$231,676	n/a
25 years	$1,288.60	$186,580	$45,096
20 years	$1,432.86	$143,886	$87,790
15 years	$1,687.71	$103,788	$127,888

    (b) **Fixed Rate.** A fixed rate mortgage is known and does not change over the life of the loan. Given the historically low interest rates in 2002 and 2003 (rates averaged 6.54% in 2002), it makes sense to consider a fixed rate loan rather than an adjustable rate loan.[14]

    (c) **Adjustable Rate Mortgage (ARM).** After an initial period, the interest rate on an ARM loan is re-set periodically in order to reflect current market interest rates. For example, a 3/1 ARM loan provides a fixed rate for the first three years, thereafter adjusting once each year; and a 5/1 ARM loan provides a fixed rate for the first five years, thereafter adjusting yearly. To shield the borrower from very large rate increases, most ARMs have some form of "rate cap" that limits how far the interest rate can move (e.g., two percentage points from period to period, and a total of six percentage points over the life of the loan). The interest rate is set by adding a margin to an index rate. Common indexes include the One-Year U.S. Treasury Constant Maturity index, as calculated by the Treasury Department, and the Fannie Mae LIBOR.[15]

(d) **Conventional Loans.** Also know as "conforming loans," these are loans that are not guaranteed or insured by an agency of the federal government, but rather based on the credit of the borrower and on the collateral for the mortgage (i.e., they are subject to conditions established by the lending institution and state statutes). The conventional loan limit is subject to change, and in 2003 it was increased in Fannie Mae guidelines to $322,700.[16]

(e) **JUMBO Loans.** Also called nonconforming loans, these are loans that exceed mortgage amount limits (i.e., $322,700 in 2003).

(f) **FHA Loans.** The Federal Housing Administration (FHA) is a division of the Department of Housing and Urban Development (HUD) that serves as an insurer of loans made by private mortgage lenders. This enables individuals who might not otherwise qualify for conventional loans to qualify thru less strict debt to income ratios and lower down payments. FHA insured loans are also assumable loans. The FHA accommodates a variety of loan programs, including 30 or 15-year fixed rate loans and one-year ARMs. VA loans are similar to FHA loans, but they are available only to qualified service veterans and are guaranteed by the U.S. Department of Veteran's Affairs.

> **Digging Deeper**
>
> Information about FHA loans is available at: www.hud.gov.
> Information about VA loans is available at: http://homeloans.va.gov.

(g) **Convertible Mortgage Loans.** These are ARM loans that provide for converting to a fixed-rate loan at or before a specified time. This allows the borrower to start off with a low variable rate, and then subsequently lock in a fixed rate using the conversion feature.

(h) **Balloon Mortgage Loans.** These loans typically allow for minimized monthly payment by providing for interest-only payments for the loan term, with the entire loan amount coming due at the end of the loan term. The danger of balloon loans is that the borrower must then refinance with a new loan at prevailing interest rates.

(i) **Reverse Mortgages.** A reverse mortgage is a loan against a home that requires no repayment so long as the homeowner lives in the house. With a traditional mortgage, payments *made by* the homeowner increase home equity (rising equity, falling debt); whereas, with a reverse mortgage, payments *received by* the homeowner reduce home equity (falling equity, rising debt). The qualifications to obtain a reverse mortgage generally include: (1) all of the homeowners must be at least 62 years old; (2) the home cannot be subject to a mortgage (or the mortgage must either be paid off prior to the loan or paid from loan proceeds); and (3) the home must be the homeowner's principal residence (single family house, 2-4 housing unit, federally-approved condominium or planned unit development). Note that there are no income qualifications.

> ## Digging Deeper
>
> The following website is an outstanding resource for information about reverse mortgages: www.reverse.org.

Closing. The meeting at which all arrangements for the sale are finalized, documents are signed, payments are made, and title is transferred. At closing the borrower receives a "closing statement" summarizing the costs associated with the loan. The following list includes the principal charges encountered at closing:

(1) **Tile insurance** is required by virtually all commercial lenders and guarantees that the title is clear and unencumbered.

(2) **Appraisals** are generally required to assure that the amount of the mortgage is appropriate to the value of the property. It was reported in 2002 that 80.6% of lenders surveyed charged an average appraisal fee of $310.[17]

(3) **Application fees** are typically charged by lenders at the time of application for a loan, and may include charges for a credit report, property appraisal, etc.

(4) **Points**, also know as "origination fees," cover the cost of arranging a loan (see page 212).

(5) **Document preparation fees** are charged to defray the costs of preparing the deeds, which are required for closing. In 2002, 59.7% of lenders surveyed charged an average document preparation fee of $182.[18]

(6) **Escrow accounts** are often required to be established with the lender. The borrower makes monthly deposits into these accounts to cover recurring costs such as insurance and real estate taxes. At closing it is common to require an initial deposit into this account.

(7) **Insurance.** See generally, pages 229-240.

VACATION HOMES

In the 1990's vacation home ownership rose by 13% to 3.5 million homes, with one out of every seven homeowners over age 65 owning a "second home."[19] For some individuals the purchase of a second home may be more akin to a consumption expenditure rather than an investment decision (i.e., it is mostly for personal enjoyment).[20] However, for many investor's a vacation home represents a source of income and investment appreciation.

(1) Purchase of a second home in a resort area requires a careful consideration of the area location, the available management, tax implications, and cash flow requirements (see Estimating Investment Returns, page 204).

(2) Provided the investor's personal use of the property does not exceed the longer of 14 days per year, or 10% of the number of days the unit is rented at fair rental, he may deduct all ordinary and necessary expenses *allocable to rental use* even if they show a loss (provided the activity is engaged in for profit and subject to the passive loss rule, see page 208). "Personal use" includes not only use by the owner, but also use by a brother, sister, spouse, ancestor or lineal descendent of the owner.[21] If the investor's personal use exceeds either of the above limits, then the owner's deductions allocable to rental use are generally limited to gross rental income.

(3) If an individual rents his vacation home for fewer than 15 days during the year, and he has used it as a residence during the taxable year, the income received from such a rental is excluded from gross income and no deductions for rental are allowed.

CONDOMINIUMS

With a condominium the owners hold title by deeds that constitute a fee interest to the underlying real property, the common areas, and particularly to their specific units. Common elements such as recreational facilities, hallways, and land, are jointly owned, with monthly fees assessed to cover the costs of maintenance and property taxes on common areas. Generally, owners are totally free to sell their units without restriction. Oversight is typically conducted by a board of directors, or management council, consisting of elected owners who hire fulltime managers to oversee day-to-day operations. In contrast, a cooperative (co-op) is similar to a condominium, except that the units are owned by a corporation and operated for the benefit of the shareholders. The shareholders purchase shares in the corporation equivalent to the value of their specific housing unit. Stock ownership in a cooperative is often treated and equated to an interest in real property, with the stockholders holding title to their units indirectly as shareholders in the cooperative corporation together with proprietary leases.

INTERVAL OWNERSHIP

Also knows as "time shares," compared to other available real estate investments interval ownerships have rarely proven to be a good investment. In return for payment of the purchase price and the ongoing share of maintenance costs, insurance, and taxes, they offer the purchaser guaranteed use of the property for a particular period of time (e.g., the third week of July). *Advantages* include low investment requirements, and the flexibility of being able to exchange time periods for the particular development or participate in exchange programs involving units in other locations. *Disadvantages* include the difficulty of determining a reasonable price for a share in a condominium residence, higher management fees, and difficulty in selling at a gain. Time shares are generally held in low esteem by investment advisers. For example, in his book, *Investing For Dummies*, Eric Tyson uses a "Beware" shark's fin icon to label them as "shark invested waters."[22]

RAW LAND

Raw land is the least liquid and most speculative of all real estate investments. In general, investment in raw land will entail more risk than investment in a building that has a rental value. Subject to the "passive loss" rule, and the "investment interest" limitation, an investor in land may generally deduct real estate taxes, interest charges on indebtedness incurred to buy the land, and other expenses paid or incurred in connection with holding the land. Although the land is not depreciable, expenses incurred in managing, conserving, or maintaining the property may be deductible. For the investor intent on making an investment in raw land, a real estate investment trust or limited partnership may offer the experience and large capital outlays that are needed for such investments (see below).

REAL ESTATE INVESTMENT TRUSTS (REITS)

REITs (pronounced *reets*) are closed-end investment companies that invest primarily in real estate. Their workings are similar to closed-end mutual funds, in that they sell a limited number of share to investors and are traded over-the-count-

er and on the major exchanges just like stocks.
Some of the main advantages of REITs include:
(1) stockholder limited liability; (2) professional management; (3) continuity of interest; (4)
relatively high yields; and (5) ready marketability of shares. In order to meet the tax law
requirements, REITs must distribute each year
to their shareholders at least 90% of their taxable income.[23] Failure to meet this requirement
would subject them to the corporate income tax.
Stockholder distributions are taxed as either
ordinary income or capital gains (i.e., taxation
is similar to that of mutual fund shareholders).

Digging Deeper

An excellent source of
information about REITs is
maintained by the National
Association Of Real Estate
Investment Trusts at:
www.nareit.com.

In contrast to real estate partnerships, tax losses cannot be passed through to
REIT stockholders. The three major types of REITs include:

- **Equity REITs** own real estate and derive their revenue primarily from rental
  income and capital gains.

- **Mortgage REITs** derive their revenue from interest income by investing in
  real estate loans including construction loans, permanent mortgages, and
  sometimes mortgage-backed securities.

- **Hybrid REITs** own a combination of property and mortgages.

REITs vary widely as to investment philosophy, management performance, capital structure, employment of debt (leverage), and diversification. Given the difficulty of analyzing and evaluating individual REITs, many investors purchase REIT
mutual funds.

REAL ESTATE LIMITED PARTNERSHIPS (RELPS)

Also knows as "private limited partnerships," these are limited partnerships
made up of limited partners and a general partner. The limited partners do not
participate in the management and operation of the real estate, and their liability
is limited to their contribution to the partnership. The limited partnership "passes through" income, gain, losses, deductions and credits of its real estate operations directly to the limited partners, thereby providing virtually the same tax benefits offered by direct individual ownership. RELPs vary in their tax sheltering goals
and methods, with some emphasizing tax free cash flow, some losses that offset
other income, and some appreciation and equity build up. The arrangement can
be public, meaning that partnership interests can be purchased through a brokerage firm; or it can be private, meaning that it is formed by a group of individuals with a common investment objective. Unlike REITs, interests in RELPs are not

easily tradable, and investors must typically wait for the partnership to sell real estate and distribute the proceeds in order to liquidate their investment. Limited partnerships similar to RELPs are also used in equipment leasing, oil and gas, movie financing, and research & development.

OIL AND GAS

The four basic types of oil and gas drilling programs are: (1) exploratory programs; (2) development programs; (3) income programs; and (4) combination programs. The most commonly used method available to individual investors for investing capital in an oil and gas venture has been the purchase of an interest in an **oil and gas limited partnership**. However, C corporations, S corporations, and trusts are also used. Deductions for interest, taxes, depreciation, and operating expenses are passed through to limited partners, subject to certain limitations. For example, a limited partner's partnership losses are restricted by: (1) his adjusted tax basis in his partnership interest; (2) the extent he is "at risk" with respect to his partnership interest; and (3) the passive loss rules.[24] The two deductions that provide the major incentives for investing in an oil or gas limited partnership are the deductions for **intangible costs** for drilling and development and **depletion**.[25] Those partnerships that are traded on established securities markets, or are readily tradeable on a secondary market are referred to as **publicly traded partnerships**.

PRECIOUS METALS

Investing in precious metals has been considered as both a hedge against inflation and a protection against chaos in the stock market. In reality, this has not always proven to be true. Gold and silver can be purchased in the form of gold coins, jewelry or bullion. Investors are generally well advised to take physical possession of any such investments. Gain from the sale of metal is not subject to special rules relating to "collectibles gain," and will generally be taxed at a top capital gain rate of 20%.[26] Purchase of mining shares, or mutual funds investing in mining operations, offers an alternative to the direct purchase of metals.

COLLECTIBLES

When it comes to art and collectibles, it is important to distinguish between investing and collecting. Most individuals who purchase art and collectibles do so as a hobby, not for their investment value. Both art and collectibles are generally considered nice to own, but as investments they are both risky and illiquid, and generally not an important part of most investor's financial plan. That said, it still remains that investing in collectibles can produce a good return. Probably the only art that has consistently proved to be worthy of serious investment consideration is "museum-quality" art. Unfortunately, these pieces are well beyond the price range of most investors. Serious collectors pay close attention to such details such as a history, condition, composition, aesthetic qualities, and rarity. However, the ultimate value of a collectible is entirely dependant upon its popularity as a collectible. Gain from the sale of art or collectibles held for more than one year is treated as "collectibles gain," meaning that it generally results in being subject to a capital gains rate of 28% (not affected by JGTRRA 2003).[27]

COMMODITIES

Also referred to as "futures," a futures contract is a legally binding agreement between two parties to buy or sell in the future, on a designated exchange, a specific quantity of a commodity at a specific price.[28] The buyer and seller of a futures contract agree on a price for a product to be delivered or paid for at a set time in the future, known as the "settlement date." Although actual delivery of the commodity can take place in fulfillment of the contract, most futures contracts are actually closed out or offset prior to delivery. Futures contracts, and options on futures contracts, must be executed on, and are subject to the rules of, a commodity exchange. The individual investor cannot trade directly on an exchange, that is generally done for the investor by a commodities trader who must be registered with the Commodity Futures Trading Commission. As stated by this commission, "trading commodity futures and options is not for everyone. It is a volatile, complex, and risky business."[29]

> ### Keeping Current
>
> Each day, in a section entitled **Futures,** *The Wall Street Journal* carries a listing of commodity and other futures.

www.cftc.gov

Although most of the participants in the futures and options markets are commercial and institutional users of the commodities they trade, other individuals participate in the market as speculators who attempt to profit from changes in the prices of futures contracts. Trading in the commodities market is not an investment.

Hedging. This occurs when a company or individual holds an asset such as coffee, corn, soybeans, United States Treasury bonds, or a portfolio of stocks, with the expectation that the asset's value will increase. In order to minimize the risk of financial loss from holding those assets the company or individual may use the commodity markets to take an opposite position (i.e., a "put option" to sell the commodity at a specific price).

Speculating. Unlike a hedger, the speculator does not own the underlying commodity or product that forms the components of the underlying index. A speculator will either: (1) buy a futures contract or call option, or sell a put option, expecting to profit from *rising* prices; or (2) sell a futures contract or call option, or buy a put option, expecting to profit from *declining* prices (see generally, pages 151-163). The low margin requirements of about 10% lead to high risk when trading options, whereas the higher margin requirements for stocks present less risk (see Buying On Margin, page 147).

The current price of a commodity is know as the "spot price." In addition to commodity futures there are also financial futures that deal in contracts relating to currencies (e.g., the British Pound, the Eurodollar, and the American dollar), and to financial indexes (e.g., Standard and Poor's 500 stock index). See page 62.

---

[1] See *Tax Facts 2* (Cincinnati: The National Underwriter Company, 2003, revised annually), **Question 218** – How does real estate shelter income? See also, Stephen R. Leimberg et al., *The Tools & Techniques Of Financial Planning*, 6th ed., (Cincinnati: The National Underwriter Company, 2002), pp. 551-554.

[2] See Robert M. Crowe, "Time Value Analysis: Basic Concepts and Applications" as contained in David M. Cordell (editor), *Fundamentals Of Financial Planning*, 4th ed. (Bryn Mawr, Pennsylvania: The American College, 1999), p. 333.

[3] See *Tax Facts 2*, **Question 298** – What amount of passive losses (and the deduction-equivalent of credits) from rental real estate activities may an individual deduct against nonpassive income? See also, Leimberg et al., pp. 187-89.

[4] See *Tax Facts 2*, **Question 286** – How is an individual's "amount at risk" determined? See also, Leimberg et al., pp. 179-80.

[5] See *Tax Facts 2*, **Question 232** – How is gain or loss on sale of rental real estate treated?

[6] See Sinai and Souleles, "Owner Occupied Housing as Insurance Against Rent Risk," The Warton School, University of Pennsylvania, draft dated May 15, 2001, p. 1.

[7] See *Tax Facts 2*, **Question 302** – Is interest on debt secured by a taxpayer's residence deductible?

[8] See *Tax Facts 2*, **Question 425** – What itemized deductions may be taken by an individual taxpayer?

[9] See *Tax Facts 2*, **Question 238** – What exclusion is available for gain on the sale of a principal residence?

[10] See Sinai and Souleles, p. 3.

[11] These guidelines, typical of those used in the mortgage industry, were obtained from http://finance.realtor.com/HomeFinance/.

[12] See *Tax Facts 2*, **Question 302** – Is interest on debt secured by a taxpayer's residence deductible?

[13] www.interest.com/firsttime/whichmtge.shtml offers an informative table of various types of mortgages.

[14] www.freddiemac.com/pmms/pmms30.htm contains a 30-year history of fixed-rate mortgages.

[15] www.hsh.com/1ytvsliborgraph.html provides additional information about LIBOR (it stands for "London Interbank Offered Rate").

[16] www.hsh.com/maxhst.html gives the most recent conventional loan limit.

[17] For average fees and charges see www.hsh.com/cfee-sample.html.

[18] Ibid.

[19] Statistics obtained from Jeffrey Zaslow, "Mom Always Liked You Best; Who Gets The Beach House?," *The Wall Street Journal*, August 15, 2002.

[20] See Eric Tyson, *Investing For Dummies*, 2nd ed. (Forest City, California: IDG Books Worldwide, 1999), p. 231. See also Janet Bamford et al., *The Consumer Reports Money Book*, 3rd ed. (Yonkers, New York: Consumers Union, 1999), p. 401.

[21] See *Tax Facts 2*, **Question 224** – Are the expenses of a vacation rental home deductible?

[22] See Eric Tyson, p. 232.

[23] See *Tax Facts 2*, **Question 178** – How is a shareholder (or beneficiary) in a real estate investment trust taxed?

[24] See *Tax Facts 2*, **Question 244** – What limits apply to the deductibility of a limited partner's share of partnership losses?

[25] See *Tax Facts 2*, **Question 240** – Why are oil and gas limited partnerships attractive to individual investors?

[26] See *Tax Facts 2*, **Question 419** – How is an individual taxed on capital gains and losses?

[27] See *Tax Facts 2*, **Question 185** – When a collectible is sold, how is the transaction taxed?

[28] This and the following paragraph are based upon information provided in *Futures And Options – What You Should Know Before You Trade*, by The Commodity Futures Trading Commission, an independent agency of the United States government. Published on May 16, 2001.

[29] See also, www.cftc.gov/opa/brochures/opafutures.htm.

BASIC CONCEPTS

Property Insurance. Property insurance provides coverage for the loss of the insured's personal and real property by (i.e., it is intended to indemnify the insured for a loss).

(1) **Real Property** – real property covers dwellings, to include a home and outbuildings, but does not include land. The insurance policy will specifically define the property being covered. For example, the policy declarations page will state: "the insured's residence premise is 3400 Apple Street, Anytown, USA." Coverage may be for "named perils" (specified causes of loss) or "open perils" (any cause of loss not specifically excluded).

> ### Keeping Current
>
> The National Underwriter Company maintains an online property & casualty community that includes a Q&A of the week, articles and case interpretations, assessment tools, industry events, links, products, a message board, and a glossary. It can be accessed at (requires registration): www.national underwriter.com/FCSfx.

(2) **Personal Property** – personal property generally includes all forms of property other than real property. In contrast to real property, personal property is covered on a *comprehensive basis*, meaning that within *stated limits* the policy will cover all household and personal property that is incidental or usual to the occupancy of the dwelling and owned or used by the insured. There are stated limits for jewelry, guns, etc. (see Internal Limits, page 235). *Exclusions* may apply to certain types of personal property such as animals, birds, and fish (see Exclusions, page 234).

Liability Insurance. Liability insurance provides third-party coverage for injury to another because of the insured's negligence or other legal liability (the first and second parties are the insured and the insurer). Personal liability exposures include those flowing from personal negligence, as well as from the ownership and use of property such as homes, autos, and boats. Under homeowner's insurance an insured is protected from a broad range of personal injury and property damage exposures (see discussion of Comprehensive Personal Liability (CPL) coverage on page 233). Unlike property insurance, the insurer pays the injured party, not the insured (i.e., it is *third-party* coverage).

Perils Covered. A "peril" is the cause of a loss, such as fire, lightning, windstorm, hail, explosion, to name just a few.[1] There are two basic approaches to insuring property:

(1) **Named perils** – a policy covering only those perils that are specifically named or listed. HO-2 is a named perils policy (see chart, page 231).

(2) **Open perils** – a policy covering all perils except those specifically excluded.[2] Open perils coverage, also referred to as "risk of direct loss" coverage, is typically broader in scope than named perils coverage, but it costs somewhat more. HO-3 provides open perils coverage for dwellings, but named perils coverage for personal property (see chart, page 230). The term "comprehensive coverage" is often used to describe open perils coverage.

Principle Of Indemnity. Property and liability insurance contracts are said to be indemnity contracts, in that they are generally based upon the principal of indemnity. This principal limits compensation to the insured to an amount equal to his economic loss (i.e., he should be restored to essentially the same financial position as existed before the loss, but should not be able to gain from his loss). This concept distinguishes insurance from gambling or wagering. However, the principal of indemnity is relaxed when insurance contracts provide for replacing older used property with new property (see discussions on pages 235-237 of replacement cost, extended replacement cost, and guaranteed replacement cost). The concepts of **insurable interest, subrogation**, and **contributing insurance** arise out of and are related to the principal of indemnity.

In contrast, life insurance contracts are not indemnity contracts; they pay the contract's face amount upon the insured's death without regard to the specific loss suffered. It is expected that issues with respect to the appropriate amount life insurance will have been dealt with during the process of *financial* underwriting prior to contract issue.

Insurable Interest. Property insurance will not be issued unless an individual has an insurable interest in the property. Without an insurable interest requirement, insurance contracts could become wagering devices, and insureds might be tempted to deliberately destroy property in which they had no interest. An individual has an insurable interest if he is exposed to financial loss if the property is lost, damaged, or destroyed. Ownership of a home, automobile, or personal property such as furniture and clothing, gives an individual an insurable interest in that property. However, an insurable interest can also occur even when an individual does not own the property, as occurs when property is borrowed from another (e.g., the insured has an insurable interest in a lawn mower he borrows from his neighbor). Another example of such an insurable interest is where a purchaser has entered into a contract to buy a home. The purchaser has an insurable interest in the home even though he has yet to close and take title to the property.

Subrogation. This is the right of an insurance company to recover from another person who caused a loss any amount paid under the policy. Typically an insurance contract will specifically require that the insured assign all rights of recovery to the extent he is paid for his loss. This right of subrogation implements the principal of indemnity by preventing the injured insured from collecting twice for the very same loss. For example, assume $5,000 of damage is done to an insured's automobile that is covered by collision insurance with a $500 deductible. After paying the insured $4,500 for his loss, the right of subrogation allows the insurance company to collect the $4,500 from the negligent party. However, the injured insured retains any rights to collect from the negligent party damages over $4,500 (i.e., the $500 deductible). Without the right of subrogation the insured could potentially collect $5,000 from the negligent party and $4,500 from his insurance company under the collision coverage.

Broad Form. This is typically used to describe a package of insurance providing homeowners with a broad range of property and liability coverages extending beyond the basic coverage offered by HO-1. For example, HO-2 offers "broad form" coverage by adding additional named perils beyond those offered by HO-1 (e.g., it covers losses resulting from breakage of glass, falling objects, weight of snow, ice or sleet and water damage). However, HO-2 does not offer the better open perils coverage that is available under HO-3, which is known as the special coverage form. Therefore, "broad form" coverage is *not* the "broadest form" of coverage (see chart, page 230).

Occurrence-Based. Non-commercial liability insurance under homeowners or automobile insurance is written on an occurrence basis, meaning that the insurer will be responsible for all claims resulting from events that occur during the policy period, regardless of when a claim is filed. In contrast, when liability insurance is written on a **claims-made** basis under a commercial policy, the insurer is responsible only for claims that are actually filed during the policy period. (Claims-made coverage is typically written with respect to professional liability and products liability insurance.) Occurrence coverage provides far greater protection to the insured than claims-made coverage. For example, assume that Jack is invited over to a barbeque at Bob's. While crossing Bob's driveway Jack slips on an oil spot left on the driveway by Bob's son who had just finished changing oil in the family car. The next month Bob changes his homeowner's policy from Insurer A to Insurer B. Insurer A remains liable for any injury to Jack.

Contributing Insurance. The concept of contributing insurance is applied in order to prevent the insured from collecting for the very same loss from more than one insurer. Virtually every insurance policy contains an **other-insurance clause** that apportions losses between all applicable insurers. These apportionments can be done in one of two ways:

(1) **Pro rata liability** allocates the loss between carriers based upon each insurer's coverage in proportion to the *total* coverage issued by all insur-

ers. For example, assume a building is insured for $200,000 with Insurer A, $400,000 with Insurer B, and the loss is for $300,000. A's liability is $100,000 ((200,000 ÷ (200,000 + 400,000)) × 300,000). B's liability is $200,000 ((400,000 ÷ (400,000 + 200,000)) × 300,000).

(2) **Limit of liability** allocates the loss between carriers based upon the *maximum amount each insurer would have paid* had there been no other insurance. For example, again assume a building is insured for $200,000 with Insurer A, $400,000 with Insurer B, and the loss is for $300,000. A's liability is $120,000 ((200,000 ÷ (200,000 + 300,000)) × 300,000 = 120,000). B's liability is $180,000 ((300,000 ÷ (300,000 + 200,000)) × 300,000 = 180,000).

Taking An Inventory. Having adequate insurance on personal property is only as good as the insured's ability to collect should a loss be suffered. Under a paragraph entitled "Your Duties After Loss," Section I (property coverages) of homeowner's policy HO-3 contains the following specific language:

"In case of a loss to covered property, you must see that the following are done . . . *prepare an inventory* of damaged personal property showing the quantity, description, actual cash value and amount of loss. *Attach all bills, receipts and related documents* that justify the figures in the inventory [Emphasis added.]."[3]

Although most insurers will accept reasonable reconstructions from memory, the average insured would have a very difficult time itemizing from memory all of his covered personal property. Likewise, insureds are often surprised at how expensive it is to replace lost or damaged items. Every insured should consider taking the following steps *before* a loss:

(1) Prepare an itemized list of all personal and household items and maintain it annually (many insurers provide personal property inventory forms).

(2) Take photos, or use a video camera, to record personal property throughout the house. If using a video camera, discuss details concerning the property as it is filmed. Annotate on the back of pictures the date of purchase and cost.

(3) Keep copies of all receipts for major purchases.

(4) Maintain separate file containing property appraisals.

(5) Place all records and photos in a safe-deposit box or other safe location (*not* in the house).

(6) Review the listed items to ascertain whether there is sufficient insurance to cover potential losses. If additional coverage is indicated consider increasing limits under the basic homeowner's policy, obtaining a personal property floater, or purchasing separate supplemental coverage (see Endorsements & Extended Coverages, page 238).

Homeowner's Insurance. The modern homeowners policies are *package policies* in that they cover dwelling, contents, personal liability, and medical payments exposures. Previously, coverage for each of these exposures had to be provided through separate contracts, notably fire and comprehensive personal liability policies. The **Insurance Services Office (ISO)** and the **American Association Of Insurance Services (AAIS)** have developed standard multi-line package policies. (The AAIS standard homeowners program includes seven forms, as opposed to ISO's six.)

Although homeowner policies are fairly standard throughout the country, there are some differences between states and companies (e.g., similar policies may be given a variety of names, such as "standard" or "deluxe," or may contain various exclusions not in the standard form, or may drop other exclusions). Larger insurers often file their own HO forms and endorsements. Policies in the state of Texas vary substantially from policies in other states. The Texas Insurance Department provides information on its various homeowner's policies. *www.tdi.state.tx.us*

The chart below lists the basic ISO forms of coverage. Note that some of the terms used are "terms of art," and may be confusing to the uninformed. For example, "HO-2 Broad" may be broad as compared to "HO-1 Basic," but not as compared to "HO-3 Special," and HO-3 Special may have once been special, but is now the most widely used of all homeowner's policies (page 233).

Six Standard Types of Homeowner's Insurance

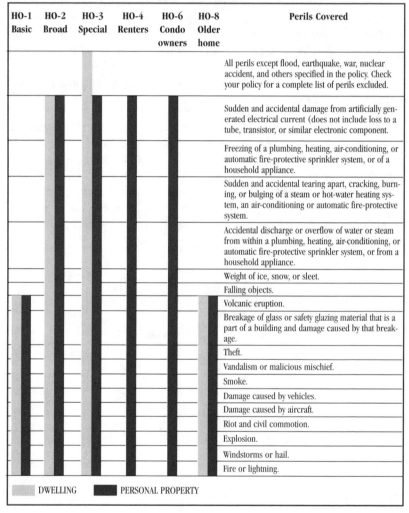

HO-1 Basic	HO-2 Broad	HO-3 Special	HO-4 Renters	HO-6 Condo owners	HO-8 Older home	Perils Covered
						All perils except flood, earthquake, war, nuclear accident, and others specified in the policy. Check your policy for a complete list of perils excluded.
						Sudden and accidental damage from artificially generated electrical current (does not include loss to a tube, transistor, or similar electronic component.
						Freezing of a plumbing, heating, air-conditioning, or automatic fire-protective sprinkler system, or of a household appliance.
						Sudden and accidental tearing apart, cracking, burning, or bulging of a steam or hot-water heating system, an air-conditioning or automatic fire-protective system.
						Accidental discharge or overflow of water or steam from within a plumbing, heating, air-conditioning, or automatic fire-protective sprinkler system, or from a household appliance.
						Weight of ice, snow, or sleet.
						Falling objects.
						Volcanic eruption.
						Breakage of glass or safety glazing material that is a part of a building and damage caused by that breakage.
						Theft.
						Vandalism or malicious mischief.
						Smoke.
						Damage caused by vehicles.
						Damage caused by aircraft.
						Riot and civil commotion.
						Explosion.
						Windstorms or hail.
						Fire or lightning.

DWELLING   PERSONAL PROPERTY

Source: *The Consumer Reports Money Book*, 3rd ed. (Yonkers, New York: Consumer Reports, A Division of Consumers Union) p.232. Reprinted with permission.

DESCRIPTIONS OF THE STANDARD POLICIES

HO-1: Basic Form – With its limited "bare bones" coverage this policy is no longer available in most states and has been withdrawn by ISO. It covers from 11 or 12 specified perils (risks) and generally limits reimbursement to actual cash value.

HO-2: Broad Form – By "broad" it is meant that HO-2 provides broader specified perils coverage than was available under HO-1. Protection is provided against 16 to 18 named perils. Reimbursement is generally limited to actual cash value (but is often upgradeable to replacement cost). A version of HO-2 is generally available for mobile homes.

HO-3: Special Form – Once considered "special," this is now the most widely used policy for the homeowner. All direct physical losses to the dwelling and other structures are covered, except certain losses that are specifically excluded (i.e., it is comprehensive open perils coverage). Coverage of personal property is generally in the broad form (see Personal Property, page 233), meaning that coverage is for 16 to 18 named perils (i.e., it *is not* comprehensive open perils coverage). However, some insurers will provide open perils coverage for personal property. Also includes payment for personal liability and medical payments to others. A modified version of HO-3 is generally available for mobile homes.

HO-4: Renters – Also referred to as "tenants insurance," this policy provides personal property protection for the same 16 to 18 named perils as in HO-2 (i.e., it is *not* comprehensive open perils coverage). This also covers the insured's improvements and betterments (i.e., any parts of the dwelling that the insured owns, such as new kitchen cabinets that have been installed).

HO-6: Condo Owners – For owners of condominiums this policy provides personal property protection for the same 16 to 18 named perils as in HO-2. Limited coverage is provided for damage to additions and alterations made by the unit owner inside the unit. (This additions-and-alterations coverage is considered to be excess insurance over and above insurance maintained by the condominium association.) In addition, coverage is also provided for personal liability and medical payments to others.

HO-8: Older Home – Intended for older or unique homes, this policy usually provides reimbursement based upon the home's market value (see Actual Cash Value, page 236). Full replacement cost policies may not be available for some older homes. As with HO-2, protection is provided against 16 to 18 named perils. In addition, coverage is also provided for personal liability and medical payments to others.

Homeowner's Standard Coverages. All homeowner's policies are divided into two sections: **Section I** covers property exposures; **Section II** covers liability and medical claims. Specific amounts of coverage are set forth under each section. For example, at the beginning of the popular HO-3 policy standard coverages and limits are typically as follows (assuming a home insured for $200,000):

SECTION I - property		
Coverage A	Dwelling	$200,000
Coverage B	Other Structures	$20,000 (10% of dwelling coverage)
Coverage C	Personal Property	
	Anywhere in the world	$100,000 (50% of dwelling coverage)
	Usually located at another residence (second home)	$20,000 (10% of dwelling coverage, but not less than $1,000)
Coverage D	Loss Of Use	$40,000 (20% of dwelling coverage)
SECTION II – liability		
Coverage E	Personal Liability	$100,000 each occurrence
Coverage F	Medical Payments To Others	$1,000 each person

The above amounts are frequently modified and increased by endorsements to the policy. For example, by endorsement the limits of liability on the policy can be amended to equal the current replacement cost of the dwelling, in which case Coverages B, C, and D are increased by the same percentage applied to coverage A. Also, since under the basic policy there is no coverage for loss resulting from "earth movement," by endorsement the insured can add earthquake as an insured peril for coverages A, B, and C.

HO-3 COVERAGES

Dwelling. Coverage A – this provides coverage to the insured's residence including attached structures (e.g., an attached garage). Coverage is provided on an *open perils basis* (page 226).

Other Structures. Coverage B – this covers nonbusiness detached structures that are located at the insured's residence, such as a detached garage, fence, driveway, swimming pool, shed, or guesthouse. Structures used for business purposes as not covered unless the use is purely incidental. Coverage is provided on an *open perils basis* (page 226).

Personal Property. Coverage C – this includes personal property such as clothes and furniture wherever it may be located. Named perils include fire, lightning, explosion, and theft, among others (see perils covered under HO-3 in chart on page 230). Certain types of personal property are excluded from coverage. For example, animals, birds, and fish are not covered. Nor are motorized vehicles, except for those used in the maintenance of the property (e.g., a lawnmower). This means that there is no coverage for motorcycles, automobiles, golf carts, or snowmobiles (but an exception covers small boats). Business inventory is not covered, but business property such as books typewriters, working materials, and computers are covered up to a maximum of $2,500. Coverage to personal property is provided on a *named perils basis* unless modified by endorsement. Some types of property have maximum dollar limits on the amount that will be paid for any one loss (see Internal Limits, page 235). Also, if the property is usually situated in a residence of the insured other than the "residence premises" (e.g., a vacation home) coverage is limited to the larger of 10% of the full coverage C limit or $1,000.

Loss Of Use. Coverage D – this provides for temporary additional living expenses if the insured and his family cannot continue to use the property while it is being repaired or rebuild. The covered living expenses are those required to maintain the household's normal standard of living.

Comprehensive Personal Liability (CPL). Coverage E – this protects the insured from a claim or suit for *bodily injury* or *property damage* caused by the insured's negligence. (This coverage can also be issued under a separate policy.) The "insured" includes not only the named insured, but also includes his spouse, his relatives provided they are residents of his household, and persons under age 21 who are in the care of the insured.[4] *Excluded* from coverage is injury or damage that is intentional caused by the insured, for libel or slander, or from business pursuits, automobiles, and large watercraft, among others. Some of these exclusions can be covered by separate liability insurance or by limited endorsements on the homeowner's policy. For example, one endorsement commonly used provides both business property and liability coverage for a variety of home businesses.

Medical Payments To Others. Coverage F – this provides $1,000 of medical payments for *accidents* causing bodily injury to anyone other than the named insured and regular residents of the premises (but resident employees are covered). The medical expenses must be incurred or ascertained within three years of the date of the accident. Bodily injury includes bodily harm, sickness, disease, and death. Interestingly, because the purpose of this coverage is to help deter lawsuits, medical payments to others will be made irrespective of the insured's negligence or fault.

EXCLUSIONS

Exclusions reduce the broad coverage provided in an insurance contract. For example, some of the exclusions contained in HO-3 are:

(1) Coverage A (dwelling) and Coverage B (other structures) in Section I do not include losses from freezing of plumbing, theft from a building that has been vacant more than 30 consecutive days immediately before the loss, and wear and tear, among others.

(2) Coverages A (dwelling), B (other structures), C (personal property), and D (loss of use) in Section I do not include losses caused by earth movement (earthquake), water damage (flood), neglect, war, or nuclear hazard, among others.

(3) Coverage E (personal liability) in Section II does not cover injury or damage that is intentionally caused by the insured, or from large watercraft, among others (page 233).

Proper planning requires that each policy be carefully reviewed to ascertain uncovered exposures and, where appropriate, to provide for them by endorsement or other coverage if available. For example, earthquake coverage can be obtained by endorsement to many policies, separate flood insurance can obtained in some flood-prone areas, and separate policies providing boat insurance is generally available (page 239).

PAYMENT LIMITATIONS

Policy Limits. The general policy limits are set forth at the beginning of the policy in the declaration section. The amount of coverage on the dwelling under Section A establishes the amounts applicable to other structures under Section B, the personal property limits under Section C, and the temporary living expenses under Section D. For example, the coverage for other structures is 20% of that for the dwelling (see Homeowner's Standard Coverages, page 232). However, subject to additional premiums these limits can often be increased by policy endorsement.

Internal Limits. Also referred to as "sublimits" or "special limits," these are specific limits applied to certain types of personal property under coverage C. They differ depending upon the cause of the loss. Note that the limit specified for each category is the total amount recoverable for one loss involving any or all of the kinds of property included in the category. Also, all of the property subject to these special internal limits is also subject to the total coverage C limit. These limits are not affected by increases or decreases of the basic policy limits.

If the loss is from *any covered peril*:

(1) $200 for money, bank notes, bullion, gold other than goldware, silver other than silverware, platinum, coins, and medals.

(2) $1,000 for securities, accounts, deeds, evidences of debt, letters of credit, notes other than bank notes, manuscripts, passports, tickets, and stamps.

(3) $1,000 for watercraft, including their trailers, furnishings, equipment, and outboard motors.

(4) $1,000 for trailers not used with watercraft.

(5) $1,000 for grave markers.

(6) $2,500 for property on the residence premises used for any business purpose.

(7) $250 on property away from the residence premises used for any business purpose

If the loss is from *theft*:

(1) $1,000 for jewelry, watches, furs, precious and semiprecious stones.

(2) $2,500 for silverware, silver-plated ware, goldware, gold-plated ware, and pewterware.

(3) $2,000 for firearms.

Because of these limits it is often advisable to provide additional coverage by adding scheduled endorsements providing increased limits of liability (see Endorsements & Extended Coverages, page 238).

Deductibles. Deductibles are used to reduce the cost of insurance by eliminating small claims that are relatively expensive to process. Although they are thought to decrease the moral hazard associated with frequent small claims, they can have just the opposite effect of encouraging insureds to exaggerate claims in order to fully collect on their losses. Under the "straight deductible" used in homeowner's and automobile insurance, the insured absorbs the loss equal to the amount of the deductible; after that, the insurer pays within the policy limits. Deductibles are usually applied to every loss, meaning that an insured that suffers two different losses on two separate occasions will be subject to two different deductibles (unlike medical insurance the deductible is not cumulative). Significant premiums savings are often possible for the insured that is willing to accept higher deductibles. Because insurers want to encourage reporting of potential third-party liabilities, deductibles are not applied to liability and medical payments under coverages E and F (pages 233-234).

Actual Cash Value. Up to the policy limits this coverage pays to replace or repair a building or personal property *minus a deduction for depreciation* (depreciation could be caused by normal physical wear, but it could also be caused by obsolescence). The actual cash value amount is based upon the *current* replacement value at the time of the loss. For example, assume a policy provides for $200,000 of coverage, the current replacement of value of the house is determined as $180,000, and there was $60,000 of depreciation. The policy will pay the actual cash value of $120,000 (180,000 − 60,000 = 120,000). Depreciation can be difficult to determine and is often the subject of claims disagreements. For the insured this is the *least desirable of coverages*.

Replacement Cost. Up to the policy limits this coverage pays to replace or repair a building or personal property *without any deduction for depreciation*. (Although originally restricted to real property, replacement cost insurance has now been extended to personal property by policy endorsement.) To be eligible for replacement cost coverage the insured must maintain an amount of insurance equal to at least 80% of current replacement cost. Failure to maintain 80% will result in a reduction of coverage under the co-insurance clause (see discussion on page 237). However, maintenance of this required level of coverage can be assured with an inflation-guard endorsement (page 239). Determination of replacement cost is influenced by the type of property insured, the information available to an appraiser, and the status of the owner (i.e., replacement cost of a refrigerator under a consumer's homeowners policy would be higher than the refrigerator's replacement cost under a retailer's commercial policy). For example:

(1) Assume a total loss, a policy provides for $200,000 of coverage, and the current replacement cost of the house is determined as $180,000. The policy will pay the replacement cost of $180,000 (i.e., there is no deduction for depreciation).

(2) Assume a total loss, policy provides for $200,000 of coverage, and the current replacement cost of the house is determined as $220,000. The policy will pay the maximum coverage under the policy of $200,000, a

loss of $20,000 to the homeowner since his loss has exceeded the replacement cost.

Replacement cost is better than *actual cash value*, but not as good as *guaranteed replacement cost*.

Guaranteed Replacement Cost. Even if it *exceeds the policy limits* this coverage pays whatever it costs to replace or repair a building or personal property without any deduction for depreciation. This provides protection against sudden increases in construction costs due to a shortage of building materials after a widespread disaster or other unexpected situations.[5] For example, assume a total loss, policy provides for $200,000 of coverage, and the current replacement of value of the house is determined as $280,000. The policy will pay $280,000 without regard for the maximum coverage under the policy of $200,000. Although this policy offers the highest level of protection, it may not be available for older homes, in all states, or from all companies.

Extended Replacement Cost. Even if it exceeds the policy limits this coverage pays a certain *percentage over the limit* to replace or repair a building or personal property without any deduction for depreciation. Generally, the additional coverage is from 20% to 25% more than the limit of the policy. For example, assume a total loss, policy provides for $200,000 of coverage, 20% extended replacement cost, and the current replacement of value of the house is determined as $280,000. The policy will pay $240,000, or 20% more than the policy limits $(200,000 + (200,000 \times .20) = 240,000)$. Some insurance companies offer extended rather than guaranteed replacement cost coverage. Extended replacement cost is better than *replacement cost*, but not as good as *guaranteed replacement cost*.

Coinsurance. This is a clause that restricts recovery for losses if the insured does not insure the property for a given percentage of the replacement cost of the insured property. Under the coinsurance clause, the insured must maintain an amount of insurance equal to at least 80% of current replacement cost (i.e., no reduction for depreciation) to be eligible for *replacement cost* coverage. If the insured fails to maintain this 80% required insurance, he will be treated as a "coinsurer," and the coverage will be reduced. For example:

(1) Assume a fire causes damages of $60,000, the full replacement cost of a dwelling is $200,000 and the insured has maintained $160,000 of insurance. The policy will pay the replacement cost of $60,000 (i.e., there is no deduction for depreciation).

(2) Again, assume a fire causes damages of $60,000, and the full replacement cost of a dwelling is $200,000; but the insured has maintained only

$100,000 of insurance. Recovery is limited to the ratio that the amount of insurance maintained bears to 80% of the full replacement cost. The policy will now only pay $37,500.

$$\text{Maximum Recovery} = \frac{\text{Insurance Maintained}}{.80 \times \text{Replacement Cost}} \times \text{Loss}$$

$$\text{Maximum Recovery} = \frac{\$100,000}{.80 \times \$200,000} \times \$60,000$$

$$\text{Maximum Recovery} = \quad \$37,500$$

ENDORSEMENTS & EXTENDED COVERAGES

Every policy should be carefully review as to exact coverages, limitations, and requirements. This is especially true since: (1) not all policies are the same, individual companies often have their own forms and each state can impose its own requirements for policy forms filed and approved by the state; and (2) even standard coverages are often changed by endorsements that increase the amount of insurance, broaden the coverage, or modify certain conditions or restrictions.

Personal Property Replacement-Cost Endorsement. Under the HO-3 policy, and other basic homeowner's policies, *personal property* is covered on the basis of actual cash value, which includes a deduction for depreciation (page 236). For an additional premium, the personal property replacement-cost endorsement provides replacement cost coverage for personal property covered in the policy.

Personal Property Floater (PPF). Also referred to as a "personal articles floater" (PAF), this provides extended coverage under a *separate policy* for personal property beyond the limits of the standard coverage available to the homeowner, renter and condo owner (i.e., that provided under the Schedule C limits, see Internal Limits, page 235). Typically this is *open perils coverage* that includes all direct physical losses except for those specifically excluded (page 226). Depending upon the contract, reimbursement may be based on either actual cash value or replacement cost (page 236). It is referred to as a **personal property endorsement** if this extended coverage is added by *endorsement* to the basic policy. Whether by separate policy, or by endorsement, the coverage can be either:

(1) **Blanket** (unscheduled) coverage providing for an overall increase of limits without specifically listing the individual items.

(2) **Scheduled** (itemized) coverage providing for specific amounts of coverage on individual items, such as expensive jewelry, furs, fine art, antiques, and other such items. In order to issue this coverage an insurer will usually require that each item be separately listed and appraised. When prop-

erty is itemized coverage is extended to include situations where the property is merely lost or misplaced (i.e., there is no requirement to show that it was either stolen or destroyed). Also, items are covered for damage resulting from accidental injury to the property (e.g., the insured spilling paint on a valued Persian rug).

Inflation Guard. Also referred to as "inflation protection," "home protector," "adjusted building cost endorsement," and other such names, this endorsement provides for automatic increases in the limits of property coverages under section I in order to avoid underinsurance due to inflation (see Consumer Price Index, page 402). This increase in coverage is done either annually or on a prorata basis throughout the year. An index of area construction costs is used as a measure of the annual percentage increase in construction costs. Often the insured is provided an opportunity to reject the increase in coverage, but rejection may result in the endorsement being deleted from the policy. This endorsement assures that the insured will maintain replacement coverage and is not subject to the coinsurance clause (see Coinsurance, page 237).

OTHER COVERAGES

Earthquake Coverage. Homeowner's policies exclude coverage for damages from earthquakes (i.e., earth movement). Despite the fact that earthquakes can cause catastrophic losses, a very large percentage of homeowner's in earthquake-prone areas do not carry this coverage. Unlike homeowner's property insurance, mortgage lenders do not always require it. Although available as a separate policy, earthquake coverage is more often issued by endorsement to the homeowner's policy as a additional insured peril for coverages A (dwelling), B (other structures), and C (contents). Deductibles are expressed as a percentage of the home's insured value (e.g., from 2% to 20%). Although somewhat expensive, and subject to rather large deductibles, earthquake insurance should be considered by those insureds living in the many areas throughout the country that are subject to earthquakes. Contrary to popular belief, earthquakes can, and do, strike outside of California.

Flood. Homeowner's policies also exclude coverage for damages from flood. However, flood insurance is available in those communities that have been designated as eligible by the Federal Emergency Management Agency (FEMA). While not generally written by private insurers, flood insurance is widely available through the National Flood Insurance Program (NFIP) in local communities that have implemented measures to reduce future flood risks. As with homeowner's property insurance, it is virtually always required by mortgage lenders. The coverage can generally be obtained from the same companies who issue homeowner's insurance. These insurers sell flood policies under their own names, collect premiums, keep a stipulated percentage of the premium to cover operating expenses and commissions, and invest the remainder. The insurers are then responsible for servicing the policies and adjusting losses and paying claims. The Federal government retains responsibility for any underwriting losses. Currently the maximum amount of coverage available for a single-family home is $250,000, with an additional $100,000 for contents. A separate deductible of $500 applies to both building and contents. (Property located in an emergency program community or certain flood hazard zones may be subject to a higher minimum deductible of $750.) Acceptance of a higher deductible will result in lower premiums.

Windstorm. Homeowner's policies generally provide coverage for the windstorm peril, except in those areas of the country that are particularly vulnerable to hurricane damages (e.g., the Atlantic and Gulf coasts). In these areas the insured should consider obtaining separate beach or windstorm coverage that may be available through state-sponsored programs. Again, although somewhat expensive, and subject to rather large deductibles, windstorm coverage should be considered by those insureds living in hurricane-prone areas; and will most likely be required by mortgage lenders.

Personal Umbrella Policy. This policy provides higher liability limits for personal injury and property damages than that contained in homeowner's and auto policies. (Some policies may actually provide broader coverage, but most simply give excess limits.) Because the umbrella policy is intended to be *excess* coverage over and above existing insurance, the insured must maintain a minimum amount of coverage in these underlying policies. For example, assume that Bob is involved in an at-fault auto accident that causes Jack to be seriously injured, and Bob is found to be legally liable to Jack for $750,000. Assume also that under the liability coverage in Bob's automobile policy he has $300,000 of coverage, plus an additional $1,000,000 of excess personal liability protection under an umbrella policy. In settlement of the claim against Bob the auto policy would pay the first $300,000 and the umbrella policy the remaining $450,000 (750,000 – 300,000 = 400,000).

Umbrella policies also may offer the following important *extensions of coverage* not found in all homeowner's and auto policies:

(1) Invasion of privacy.

(2) False arrest.

(3) Wrongful entry.

(4) Malicious prosecution.

(5) Libel and slander.

(6) Worldwide coverage without territorial restrictions.

(7) Property of others within the insured's care, custody, and control.

(8) Rental of residence.

Claims satisfied by these extensions of coverage are subject to a deductible called a **self-insured retention** that typically amounts to $250 or more (i.e., because there are no deductibles in the underlying policies they are imposed by the umbrella policy). Although the Insurance Services Office (ISO) has developed a prototype personal umbrella contract, many insurers have developed and issue their own forms. Because coverage is written on an open perils basis, umbrella policies typically contain extensive exclusions. These factors make it important for the insured to carefully review the exact coverages offered ———————————— under any particular contract.

www.iso.com

Professional Liability. Homeowner's and personal umbrella policies specifically exclude any coverage for professional liability. Professional liability insurance is issued as a separate or group policy covering errors and omissions of professionals in the practice of their professions. When it comes to professional liability medical malpractice immediately comes to mind. However, given our litigious society, other professionals such as lawyers, accountants, engineers, architects, and financial planners should consider obtaining this coverage. Unfortunately, professional liability coverage can be very expensive and is typically only available on a claims-made basis (see Occurrence-Based, page 227). In addition to obtaining insurance, in order to provide a degree of protection for their assets and their families, many professionals practice as either professional corporations or professional limited liability companies.[6]

Workers' Compensation. This coverage is required under state law in order to compensate workers who suffer on-the-job injuries and occupational diseases. (There are some *federal* laws that affect workers employed in areas beyond the authority of individual states, such as longshoremen, federal employees, coal miners, and seamen.) Because some states bring domestic, agricultural, and casual employees under their worker's compensation laws, it would be prudent for homeowners hiring such individuals to ascertain whether this insurance is required.

Director's And Officer's Liability. Every individual serving on the board of directors of a for-profit or nonprofit corporation (or other organization) should give serious consideration to the potential liability they are exposed to from suits for "wrongful acts" such as breach of duty, neglect, error, misstatement, misleading acts, or omissions. Directors and officers liability insurance actually consists of two distinct coverages; one for the personal liability of the directors and officers themselves, and one for the corporation's obligation, if any, to indemnify its directors and officers for certain actions against them. Both coverages can be purchased through separate insuring agreements in one policy, or either coverage can be purchased alone. Unfortunately, given our increasingly litigious atmosphere and the promulgation of class-action lawsuits, this coverage has become difficult to find and very expensive. Recent allegations of fraudulent corporate reporting of financial information will only make this coverage more difficult to obtain.

AT CLAIM TIME – HOMEOWNER'S INSURANCE

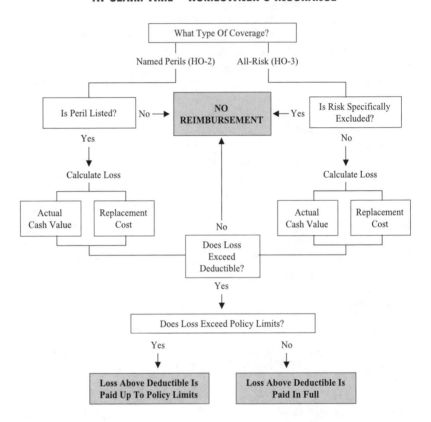

How To Use This Chart. This chart is intended to serve as a "quick-guide" to determining whether payment will be made under a homeowner's policy. For example, first determine whether the policy is the form of HO-2 or HO-3. If HO-3, then determine whether the risk specifically excluded from coverage under the policy. If "yes,' there is no coverage. If "no," then calculate the amount of the loss using either actual cash value or replacement cost, as provided for under the policy (page 236). Once the loss has been calculated, determine whether the amount of the loss exceeds the policy deductible. If "no," then the loss is too small and there is no reimbursement. If "yes," then determine whether the loss exceeds the policy limits (both general limits and internal limits, see pages 232 and 235). If "yes" then any loss above the deductible will be paid up to the policy limits. If "no" the loss above the deductible will be paid in full.

AUTOMOBILE INSURANCE

Automobile insurance is generally provided under the provisions of the personal automobile policy (PAP), as offered by the Insurance Services Office (ISO). The policy consists of a declarations page, a definitions section, and six lettered parts. Although this is the standard form for insuring private passenger autos in most jurisdictions, as with homeowner's insurance, some insurers have their own policies that may differ to some degree from this standard policy. Also, there are differences between individual state requirements, particularly as regards uninsured motorists coverage (page 244) and no-fault insurance (page 246). It is always advisable to carefully review each policy regarding coverages and their limits, and ask for clarification when appropriate. As with homeowner's insurance, individual policy endorsements frequently substantially modify provisions of the basic policy.

The six parts of standard policy are:

Part A – Liability Coverage.

Part B – Medical Payments Coverage.

Part C – Uninsured Motorists Coverage.

Part D – Damages To Covered Auto.[7]

Part E – Duties After An Accident Or Loss.

Part F – General Provisions.

Liability Coverage. Part A – Under this provision the insurer agrees to pay any damages for *bodily injury* and *property damages* for which the insured is legally responsible due to an auto accident. In addition, the insurer agrees to pay all defense costs. The insurer has both a duty to indemnify and a duty to defend, therefore defense costs are considered to be in addition to the limit of liability (i.e., defense costs are paid in addition to policy limits). The duty to defend includes defending against *civil* cases; it does not include defending against *criminal* charges (e.g., a drunken driving charge). Liability coverages can be written as either:

(1) **Single limits** – apply to the entire accident and include both bodily injury and property damages. For example, a combined single limit of $100,000 means that the insurer will pay up to $100,000 for all bodily injury and property damage arising out of each accident.

(2) **Split limits** – separately state the amount for bodily injury and property damages. The limits are often expressed in thousands of coverage. For example, if the policy provides for split limits of 10/20/50 this means that

for each accident there is a maximum of $100,000 of bodily injury coverage for each person, $200,000 for all bodily injury, and $50,000 for property damage. These limits may be expressed as follows:

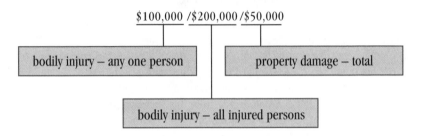

$100,000 /$200,000 /$50,000

| bodily injury – any one person | | property damage – total |

| bodily injury – all injured persons |

Under the financial responsibility and compulsory insurance laws (page 247), state minimum single limit requirements range from a low of $30,000 in Florida to a high of $125,000 in Alaska.[8] Split limit requirements run from a low of 10/20/5 in Mississippi to a high of 50/100/25 in Alaska. Given the number of very large personal injury lawsuits, most individuals who have acquired property interests would be well advised to obtain substantial amounts of personal injury coverage well in excess of state minimum requirements.

Medical Payments Coverage. Part B – This is an *optional* benefit that provides payment for reasonable expenses incurred for necessary medical and funeral services because of bodily injury caused by accident and sustained *by an insured*. Typically, the per-person limits under part B range from $1,000 to $10,000. For example, if the policy limit was $5,000, and six people were injured while riding in the insured's auto, medical payments could total $30,000 (5,000 × 6 = 30,000). Coverage applies to all passengers in the insured's auto, and to the insured and his family members when they are injured in an auto accident, whether or not the accident involves the insured's auto. For example, benefits would be payable under part B when a traffic accident results in injuries to an insured that is a pedestrian or bicyclist (but not a motorcyclist). Unlike the liability coverage under part A, payments under part B do not require that the insured be legally liable. To be covered the services must be "rendered" within three years of the accident. This "for services rendered" phrase would appear to require that services must actually be rendered within three years from the date of the accident (i.e., the insured can't prepay for deferred medical services).

Uninsured Motorists Coverage. Part C – Described as *reverse* liability insurance, under this provision the insured is provided compensatory damages for *bodily injury* from a negligent driver who is either uninsured, insured by a insolvent insurer, or is a hit-and-run driver. In a few states property damage is also included. The coverage generally provides a minimum amount of $10,000 to $20,000, but substantial additional amounts are often available. In order to receive benefits the insured must show that the uninsured driver was legally liable for the accident and there is no other available insurance (i.e., that the other vehicle truly was "uninsured"). Punitive damages are not covered. Coverage applies to the insured and his family members and to all passengers in the insured's auto. Contract provisions provide for arbitration if the insured and his insurer cannot agree as to liability or damages.

A variation of uninsured motorists coverage called **underinsured motorist coverage** is available by state-specific endorsement in many states. This insurance covers the gap that can exist when a negligent driver's insurance satisfies the state's financial responsibility law, but this is not sufficient to fully compensate the insured for his injuries. For example, assume Bob is an insured under a personal auto policy with an uninsured motorist limit of $100,000, and a negligent driver, Jack, whose $15,000/ $30,000 bodily injury limits satisfy the state's financial responsibility law, injures him. Under Bob's policy Jack's car is not consider an uninsured motor vehicle. Therefore, even if Bob's expenses exceed Jack's $15,000 liability limits, Bob cannot collect *uninsured* motorists insurance; but Bob could collect from his own insurer if he had *underinsured* motorists' coverage.

Damages To Covered Auto. Part D – Also called "physical damage," this provides coverage for the insured's own auto and other "nonowned" vehicles driven by the insured and his family. The coverage may also extend to rental cars that are used for nonbusiness purposes (and may even cover rental cars used for business purposes). The insurer should be consulted to determine the exact coverage.

Unlike liability coverage, which is third-party coverage, this is first-party coverage with damages paid directly to the insured. Although optional, when a vehicle is financed the financing company will require this coverage. Under this section two basic types of coverage are provided for "direct and accidental" damage:

(1) **Collision** insurance provides protection from upset of the auto or impact with another vehicle or object *regardless of who is at fault*. A deductible will apply, generally from $50 to $500 or higher. The agreement covers both the auto and its equipment.

(2) **Comprehensive** insurance (referred to as "other than collision" in the policy) protects the auto from losses such as fire, theft, windstorm, hail, flood, and vandalism, among others. This is very broad coverage that is subject to a limited number of exceptions (e.g., one exception is mechanical or electrical breakdown). A deductible will apply, but it is not necessarily the same amount as applies to collision coverage.

Under both collision and comprehensive the coverage is for *actual cash value*, meaning that the car will be depreciated in the course of settling the claim (page 236). Because of this, after considering premium costs in relation to potential benefits, insureds with older autos will often drop their collision and comprehensive coverages. For example, although replacing a seven-year-old auto with a new vehicle might cost $15,000-$20,000, its actual cash value may be only $2,000-$3,000. If the vehicle is damaged or destroyed this actual cash value is the most the insurer will pay.

Covered Insureds. The personal auto policy outlines four categories of insureds, which vary as to persons and vehicles. These include:

(1) The named insured and his family members. This means the named insured, his spouse living in the same household, family members who are related by blood, marriage, or adoption who are residing in the same household. An unmarried college student living away from home would usually be covered, but this should be verified with the insurer. For example, Bob and Karen have a son Jack, age 19, who is dependent upon his parents but going to college in another state. Jack is insured under the family auto policy.

(2) Any person using the named insured's covered auto, provided this person has "a reasonable belief" that he is entitled to borrow the auto. For example, Bob loans his auto to Ken who is his next-door neighbor. Ken is covered by the policy on Bob's auto.

(3) Any person or organization for liability arising out of any insured's *use of the covered auto* on behalf of that person or organization. For example, if Bob is employed by XYZ Company and drives his auto on business, XYZ Company is covered to the extent of its liability for a resulting accident.

(4) Any person or organization for liability arising out of any insured's *use of another auto* on behalf of that person or organization; but this auto cannot be owned by this "person or organization"(i.e., Bob is not covered while driving an auto owned by XYZ Company). For example, if Bob borrows Ken's auto and drives it on business, XYZ Company is covered to the extent of its liability for a resulting accident.

No-Fault Insurance. The basic objective of no-fault insurance is to eliminate or reduce costly lawsuits by having each party to an accident *recover from his own insurer* regardless of fault. No-fault insurance is meant to principally cover loss connected with bodily injury. There are actually three types of no-fault laws:

(1) **Pure no-fault** – the injured person cannot sue for damages at all and can collect damages only from his or her own insurer. No state has enacted such a statute.

(2) **Add-on plans** – pay certain benefits to the injured person without regard to fault. Some so-called no-fault states do not impose restrictions on the right to sue, but instead require the insured to purchase first-party coverage. This benefit is payable regardless of fault, yet the insured retains the right to sue the negligent party.

(3) **Modified no-fault plans** – provide many and varied alternatives depending upon state law. For example, the injured person might choose to sue for damages if the claim exceeds a certain threshold; the threshold may be monetary or verbal. A *verbal threshold* gives the right to sue for certain "serious" injuries (without consideration of cost), such as loss of life or limb, loss of sight, etc. A *monetary threshold* allows suit once expenses from an accident exceed a certain amount. Another example allows an insured to choose between a threshold and no threshold.

Despite the lofty objectives of no-fault insurance, all states now allow lawsuits if there are severe injuries, prolonged disabilities, or high expenses. Benefits under no-fault laws tend to be restricted to *economic* losses such as medical bills, lost wages, rehabilitation expenses, and funeral expenses. Claims for *noneconomic* losses exceeding these established thresholds, such as pain and suffering, are still settled in the tort system. If nothing else, the no-fault laws have allowed injured parties to be quickly paid for some losses without having to resort to the legal system.

Assuring Compensation For Victims. All states have laws that assure compensation for victims of automobile accidents. In addition to the no-fault laws (page 246) and uninsured motorists coverage (page 244), there are three additional methods of providing compensation:

(1) **Financial responsibility laws** – are statutes that do not require insurance or other proof of financial responsibility until *after* a driver is involved in his first accident or serious violation, such as driving under the influence. The nine states falling within this category are Alabama, Iowa, Mississippi, Nebraska, New Hampshire, Tennessee, Virginia, Washington, and Wisconsin.

(2) **Compulsory insurance laws** – require that every person who registers a motor vehicle in a given state prove or certify that he carries liability insurance equal to at least the state minimum requirements. However, enforcement of these laws are handled in a variety of ways, ranging from require proof of insurance when registering a car, to verification by the police at the time of an accident or ticket, to self-certification by sworn statement when applying for new or renewal license plates.

(3) **Unsatisfied judgment fund laws** – of several states provide for payments to victims who have been injured by an unknown driver or who have

obtained judgments against an uninsured driver and have exhausted all other means of recovery. These funds not considered the insurer of the driver responsible for the accident. Any recovery may be limited by the amount required under the individual state's financial responsibility limits.

---

[1] As with other areas of insurance, the lexicon of property and casualty insurance often uses different terms to describe the same concept. For example, perils are also referred to as either "disasters" or "risks." Named perils policies are also referred to as "specified perils contracts," and open perils contracts are also referred to as "comprehensive contracts."

[2] Open perils coverage has also been referred to as "all-risks coverage." However, use of the term "all-risks" is avoided in light of court decisions adversely effecting the insurer's attempts to exclude certain risks.

[3] "Damage" includes any loss of use, such as total destruction or theft.

[4] Although homeowners and renters insurance policies typically cover dog bite liability, some insurers will charge more for certain breeds of dogs.

[5] Replacement cost coverage generally won't cover the additional cost of upgrading a house to comply with current building codes. However, this coverage is generally available by policy endorsement.

[6] See Donald F. Cady, *Field Guide To Estate Planning, Business Planning, & Employee Benefits* (Cincinnati: The National Underwriter Company, 2003, revised annually), p. 454, and Thomas F. Commito, *Working With LLCs & FLPs*, 2nd ed. (Cincinnati: The National Underwriter Company, 2000).

[7] In the ISO form, this section is entitled "Coverage For Damage To Your Auto."

[8] These limits were obtained from a table of state requirements contained in the personal auto policy section of the personal lines chapter of The National Underwriter Company's *FC&S* reference service (FC&S stands for Fire, Casualty & Surety Bulletins). This excellent resource is a comprehensive industry standard reference service providing interpretation of both commercial and personal lines coverages. Additional information can be obtained at: www.nationalunderwriter.com/nucatalog/riskandinsurance.asp.

TYPES OF MEDICAL EXPENSE PLANS

There are essentially two basic types of medical expense insurance plans: the traditional indemnity (fee-for-service) plans and the managed care plans. A variety of managed care plans can be found, to include health maintenance organizations (HMOs), individual practice associations (IPAs), point-of-service (POS) plans, preferred provider organizations (PPOs), and exclusive provider organizations (EPOs). Although indemnity and managed care plans differ in how they pay for and provide health care, they typically cover an array of medical, surgical, and hospital expenses. Most cover prescription drugs, and some also offer dental coverage.

> **Digging Deeper**
>
> The website of the National Committee for Quality Assurance (NCQA) offers a useful listing of links to other websites providing health care information: www.ncqa.org/Main/links.htm.

Indemnity Plans. Also referred to as "fee-for-service" plans, under traditional indemnity plans participants can use any medical provider of their choice (e.g., doctor or hospital). The provider is paid on a fee-for-service basis and either the participant or the medical provider files the claims. Typically there are deductibles that must be met, after which reimbursement is based upon a percentage of the "usual and customary" charge for covered services. See the discussion of "coinsurance" on page 264. Policies generally have a yearly out-of-pocket maximum (good for the participant) and may be subject to maximum lifetime limits (bad for the participant). See the discussions of "stop-loss" and "maximum coverage limits" (page 265). If the provider charges more than what is considered usual and customary, the participant is responsible for the excess charges.

For example, assume that Jack is covered by a plan providing an annual deductible of $300 and coinsurance of 20% (referred to as 80/20 reimbursement). He has no prior medical claims in the year and incurs $1,900 for outpatient surgery. Unfortunately, according to his provider, the "usual and customary" charge for this particular procedure is $1,500. Jack is responsible for $940, consisting of the following amounts:

- $300 – the yearly deductible.

- $240 – the coinsurance amount ($(1,500 - 300) \times .20 = 240$).

- $400 – the amount in excess of the usual and customary charge.

In general, indemnity plans provide greater freedom and flexibility than managed care plans. However, they also cost the participant more out-of-pocket for health care.

Managed Care Plans. Managed care is a comprehensive approach to health care with the intent of lowering costs by arranging for care at predetermined or discounted rates, by specifying which doctors and hospitals the patient can use, and by overseeing physicians' treatments and referrals. These plans provide comprehensive health services to their members while offering financial incentives to members who use designated plan providers. It is reported that more than 90% of insured Americans have some kind of managed care plan.[1] The basic variations of managed care plans include:

(1) **Health Maintenance Organizations (HMOs).** For a prepaid premium these health plans provide a combination of coverages, to include payment of health-care costs and delivery of health care. Members receive services from individuals employed by or under contract to the HMO. HMOs generally require patients to select a primary-care physician (PCP) who coordinates the patient's care. Patients usually need referrals from the PCP before going to a specialist or a hospital. The PCP is often referred to as a "gatekeeper." In return for accepting these restrictions, patients are relieved of deductible or coinsurance payments and copayments are typically only $5 to $10 per doctor visit. This is in contrast to the traditional major medical plan or fee-for-service plan under which patients can choose both their doctors and hospitals, but must pay 20% of the costs (subject to caps).

(2) **Individual Practice Associations (IPAs).** Also referred to as a "open panel" or "open access" plan, this is a variation of the HMO under which the individual physicians maintain and practice out of their own offices and local community hospitals. Physicians who are part of an IPA typically treat both private patients and HMO members. IPAs generally provide HMO members with a wider range of choice than is available under the standard HMO. Members have the freedom to go to any physician who is part of the IPA.

(3) **Point-Of-Service (POS) Plans.** These plans offer a managed care option that allows members to seek care outside the HMO network, but at a higher cost (usually in the form of higher premiums, co-payments and deductibles).

(4) **Preferred Provider Organizations (PPOs).** Also referred to as "managed indemnity" plans, these are networks of independent physicians, hospitals, and other healthcare providers who contract with insurance companies to provide care at discounted rates. Members are given incentives to use the PPO physicians, but for a higher cost are allowed to use doctors and hospitals outside the network. The **exclusive provider organization (EPO)** is a variation of the PPO that only provides reimbursement

when the member goes to an affiliated provider (i.e., a member using another provider must pay the entire cost without reimbursement).

Managed care has been the target of much public criticism. In HMOs the direct relationship between the financing and delivery of health care has generated criticism of: (1) the existence of "gag rules" that prohibit physicians from discussing all possible treatment options with patients; (2) the denial of access to specialists; (3) the denial of reimbursements for emergency room charges in hospitals outside the plan; (4) limits placed on hospital stays for certain procedures; and (5) treatment decisions designed to save money that may be adverse to the patient's health. A number of states have passed consumer rights bills, and it is likely that the U.S. Congress will pass some form of federal legislation. The challenge faced by legislators will be to address these issues of choice and access, yet avoid substantial increases in health care costs or forcing health care providers out of the marketplace.

PROVIDERS OF HEALTH CARE INSURANCE

Commercial Insurance Companies. Both individual and group health care insurance is offered by large publicly held commercial insurance companies, such as Aetna, CIGNA, and Prudential. Although individual coverage is available, most individuals participate as members of a group plan. They offer a large variety of both indemnity and managed care plans, including HMOs, PPOs, and EPOs (see paragraphs (1) and (4), page 250).

Blue Cross and Blue Shield. These are regionally-operated health care providers affiliated with a large national health care organization. Through contracts with hospitals and individual service providers, they offer hospital, surgical, physician, and related medical expense coverages on a "service-type" basis (i.e., payments are made directly to the participating hospital or physician). Although individual coverage is readily available in most areas, most subscribers are covered by group plans. Both basic medical expense coverage and major medical insurance is provided. As with commercial insurance companies, both Blue Cross and Blue Shield offer a number of managed care plans, including HMOs and PPOs.

Digging Deeper

Additional information can be obtained at: www.bluecares.com.

Self-Funded Employee Health Benefits. Also referred to as "self-insured" plans, large employers will often "self-insure" their own employee health benefits. These programs are usually established using both third-party administrators and stop-loss insurance. Third-party administrators are separate organizations that conduct enrollments, pay claims, and maintain records. With stop-loss insurance the employer pays (i.e., self-insures) claims up to a maximum dollar amount, with a commercial insurer paying excess claims.

GOVERNMENT PROGRAMS

Medicare.[2] Medicare is a federal health insurance program for persons 65 or older, persons of any age with permanent kidney failure, and certain disabled persons. The program is administered by the Centers for Medicare & Medicaid Services (CMS), a federal agency in the Department of Health and Human Services. Various commercial insurance companies are under contract with CMS to process and pay Medicare claims. Medicare consists of three parts: Hospital Insurance protection, Medical Insurance protection, and Medicare+Choice.

> ### Digging Deeper
>
> A great deal of information and various publications on Medicare are available at: www.cms.hhs.gov.

(1) **Part A – Hospital Insurance** protection provides institutional care, including inpatient hospital care, skilled nursing home care, post-hospital home health care, and, under certain circumstances, hospice care.

    (a) **Enrollment.** Any person eligible for Social Security monthly benefits is automatically eligible for Hospital Insurance protection beginning with the first day of the month in which the person turns age 65. An individual who is *already receiving* Social Security monthly benefits need not file again to receive Medicare Part A benefits. A person *eligible for, but not yet receiving*, Social Security monthly benefits may apply separately for Medicare Part A benefits.

    (b) **Dependents.** A dependent or survivor of a person entitled to Hospital Insurance benefits is also eligible for benefits if the dependent or survivor is at least 65 years old.

    (c) **Coverage.** For the first 60 days, all covered hospital expenses are paid in full except for an initial inpatient deductible ($840 in 2003). For the next 30 days, the patient must pay a daily coinsurance charge ($210 per day in 2003). Thereafter, the patient has available an additional lifetime reserve of 60 hospital days during which the patient must pay a daily coinsurance charge ($420 per day in 2003). Beyond 150 days there is no coverage. See table on page 255. Skilled nursing facility care, home health care, and hospice care are also covered, but intermediate and *custodial care* are not covered (see paragraph (2)(d) below).

(2) **Part B – Medical Insurance** protection is a voluntary program of health insurance which covers physician services, outpatient hospital care, physical therapy, ambulance trips, medical equipment, prosthetics, and a number of other services not covered under Part A. This is also known as "Supplementary Medical Insurance (SMI)."

(a) **Enrollment.** Those who are receiving Social Security benefits are enrolled automatically at the time they become entitled to Hospital Insurance unless they elect not to be covered for Medical Insurance. In order to obtain coverage at the earliest possible date, a person must enroll before the beginning of the month in which age 65 is reached. For those individuals born after 1938 normal retirement age is not age 65 (see page 394). Unless they have elected to take early retirement, they would have to apply during the initial seven-month enrollment period. This period begins on the first day of the third month before a person turns age 65 and ends on the last day of the third month after a person turns age 65. For example, if a person's 65th birthday is May 10, 2003, the initial enrollment period begins February 1, 2003 and ends August 31, 2003.

(b) **Dependents.** A dependent or survivor who is entitled to Hospital Insurance (Part A) may enroll in Medical Insurance (Part B).

(c) **Coverage.** Medicare usually pays 80% of the approved charges for doctors' services and the cost of other services that are covered under Medical Insurance after the patient pays the first $100 of covered services in each calendar year. Medical Insurance helps pay for covered services received from the doctor in the doctor's office, in a hospital, in a skilled nursing facility, in the patient's home, or any other location. See table on page 255.

(d) **What is not covered.** Medical Insurance under Medicare *does not cover*: (1) most routine physical examinations and tests directly related to such examination; (2) most routine foot care and dental care; (3) examinations for prescribing or fitting eyeglasses or hearing aids, and most eyeglasses and hearing aids; (4) immunizations (except annual flu shots and limited vaccinations for certain persons at risk); (5) most cosmetic surgery; (6) most prescription drugs; and (7) custodial care at home or in a nursing home.

(3) **Part C – Medicare+Choice** permits contracts between CMS and a variety of different managed care and fee-for-service organizations.[3] These Medicare+Choice plans must provide all current Medicare-covered items and services and they may incorporate extra benefits in a basic package or

they may offer supplemental benefits priced separately from the basic package. Most Medicare beneficiaries can choose to receive benefits through the original Medicare fee-for-service program or through one of the following Medicare+Choice plans:

(a) **Coordinated care plans**, including Health Maintenance Organizations (HMOs), Preferred Provider Organizations (PPOs), and Provider-Sponsored Organizations (PSOs).

(b) **Private fee-for-service plans** that reimburse providers on a fee-for-service basis, and are authorized to charge enrolled beneficiaries up to 115% of the plan's payment schedule (which may be different from the Medicare fee schedule).

(c) **MSA/High Deductible Plans** (MSA stands for Medical Savings Accounts) were created by Congress as an another choice, but were never embraced by the insurance industry. The intention was to give beneficiaries the option of obtaining high deductible health policies that paid for at least all Medicare-covered items and services once the enrollee met an annual deductible of up to $6,000 (as indexed). The difference between the premiums for the high deductible policies and the applicable Medicare+Choice premium would then be placed by the Centers for Medicare & Medicaid Services into an account for the beneficiary to use in meeting deductible expenses. No high deductible plans were ever approved before the program expired on January 1, 2003.

Medicare – Table Of Benefits For 2003[4]

Benefit		Individual Pays	Medicare Pays
HOSPITAL (Part A)			
Hospitalization	first 60 days	$840	balance
	61st to 90th day	$210 a day	balance
	91st to 150th day	$420 a day	balance
	beyond 150 days	all costs	nothing
Skilled Nursing Facility Care	first 20 days	nothing	all (as approved)
	next 80 days	$105.00 a day	balance
	beyond 100 days	all costs	nothing
Home Health Care	first 100 days in spell of illness	nothing for services	all
		20% for durable medical equipment	balance
Hospice Care	unlimited (doctor must certify)	outpatient drugs and inpatient respite care	balance
MEDICAL (Part B)			
Medical Expenses	unlimited	$100 deductible plus 20% of remaining	balance
Clinical Laboratory Services	unlimited	nothing	all
Home Health Care	unlimited (but covers only what is not covered under Part A)	nothing for services	all
		20% for equipment	balance
Outpatient Hospital Treatment	unlimited	$100 deductible plus 20% of remaining	balance

Benefits must be medically necessary. Under Part A hospitalization benefits from 91st to 150th day are the 60 "reserve" days that may be used only once in a lifetime.

Medigap Insurance. Also known as "Medicare Supplement insurance," this coverage is intended to pay for many of the medical expenses not covered by Medicare. The federal government does not sell or service Medigap insurance, but rather regulates coverage offered by private companies.

(1) **What It Does.** Medigap insurance is designed to help pay deductibles or coinsurance incurred by beneficiaries who are in the original Medicare plan (also called fee-for-service Medicare). A Medigap policy may also pay for certain items or services not covered at all by Medicare, such as prescription drugs. Medigap is only available with the original fee-for-service Medicare plan. It does not cover out-of-pocket expenses, such as copayments, in a managed care plan.

(2) **Standardized Plans.** Congress has established federal standards for Medigap policies, and most states have now adopted regulations limiting the sale of Medigap insurance to no more than ten standard policies. These plans are identified by the letters A through J, with plan A being the core package.[5] The other nine plans have different combinations of benefits, but each includes the **core package** containing the following benefits:

(a) Hospital Insurance (Part A) coinsurance for the 61st through 90th day of hospitalization in any Medicare benefit period.

(b) Hospital Insurance coinsurance for the 91st through 150th day.

(c) Hospital Insurance expenses for an extra 365 days in the hospital.

(d) Hospital Insurance (Part A) and Medical Insurance (Part B) deductible for the cost of the first three pints of blood.

(e) Medical Insurance (Part B) coinsurance (20% of allowable charges).

(3) **Open Enrollment.** For six months immediately following the effective date of enrolling in Medicare Part B, a person age 65 or older cannot be denied Medigap insurance or charged higher premiums because of health problems. However, during the first six months the policy is in effect, it may exclude coverage for "pre-existing conditions." Pre-existing conditions are conditions that were either diagnosed or treated during the six-month period before the Medigap policy became effective.

(4) **Selection Process.** The Centers for Medicare & Medicaid Services offers the following suggestions when shopping for Medigap insurance:[6]

www.cms.hhs.gov

Review the plans. The benefits in each of the standardized Medigap policies are the same no matter which insurance company sells it. Review the plans and choose the benefits that you need most.

Shop carefully before you buy. Although each of the standardized Medigap policies is the same no matter which insurance company sells it, the costs may be very different. Companies use different ways to price Medigap policies. Companies also differ in customer service. Call different insurance companies and compare cost and service before you buy.

Don't buy more than one Medigap policy at a time. It is illegal for an insurance company to sell you a second Medigap policy unless you tell them in writing that you are going to cancel the first Medigap policy when the second Medigap policy goes into effect. You should report anyone who tries to sell you a Medigap policy when you already have one.

Check for pre-existing conditions exclusions. Before you buy a Medigap policy, you should find out whether it has a waiting period before it fully covers your pre-existing conditions. If you have a health problem that was diagnosed or treated during the six months immediately before the Medigap policy starts, the policy might not cover your costs right away for care related to that health problem. Medigap policies must cover pre-existing conditions after the policy has been in effect for six months. Some insurance companies may have shorter waiting periods before covering a pre-existing condition. Other insurance companies may not have any waiting period. If you buy a policy during your Medigap open enrollment period, the insurance company must shorten the waiting period for pre-existing conditions by the amount of previous health coverage you have.

Be careful of switching from one Medigap policy to another. You should only switch policies to get different benefits, better service, or a better price. However, do not keep a policy that does not meet your needs because you have had it for a long time. If you decide to buy a new Medigap policy, the company must count the time you had the same benefits under the first policy towards the pre-existing conditions waiting period. However, you may have a waiting period for pre-existing conditions for new benefits that you did not have under your first policy. You must also sign a statement that you plan to cancel the first policy. Do not cancel the first policy until you are sure that you want to keep the new policy. You have 30 days to decide if you want to keep the new policy. This is called your free look period.

Make sure you get your policy within 30 days. You should get your policy within 30 days. If you do not, call the company and ask them to put in writing why the policy was delayed. If 60 days go by without an answer, call your State Insurance Department.

Watch out for illegal marketing practices. It is illegal for an insurance company or agent to pressure you into buying a Medigap policy, or lie to you or mislead you to get you to switch from one company or policy to another. False advertising is also illegal. Another type of illegal advertising involves mailing cards to people who may want to buy insurance. If you fill out and return the card enclosed in the mailing, the card may be sold to an insurance agent who will try to sell you a policy.

Neither the state nor federal government sells or services Medigap policies. State Insurance Departments approve Medigap policies sold by private insurance companies. This means that the company and Medigap policy meet requirements of state law. Do not believe statements that Medigap insurance is a government-sponsored program. It is illegal for anyone to tell you that they are from the government and try to sell you a Medigap policy. If this happens to you, report that person to your State Insurance Department. It is also illegal for a company or agent to claim that a Medigap policy has been approved for sale in any state in which it has not been.

Find out if the insurance company is licensed. An insurance company must meet certain standards in order to sell policies in your state. You should check with your State Insurance Department to make sure that the insurance company you are doing business with is licensed in your state. This is for your protection. Insurance agents must also be licensed by your state and the state may require them to carry proof that they are licensed. The proof will show their name and the name of the companies they represent. Do not buy a policy from any insurance agent that cannot prove that he or she is licensed. A business card is not a license.

Start looking early so you won't be rushed. Do not be pressured into buying a Medigap policy. Good sales people will not rush you. Keep in mind, that if you are within your 6-month Medigap open enrollment period or in a situation where you have a guaranteed right to buy a Medigap policy, there are time limits you must follow. Buying the Medigap policy of your choice may be harder after the Medigap open enrollment or special protection period ends. This will be especially true if you have a pre-existing health condition. If you are not sure whether a Medigap policy is what you need, ask the salesperson to explain it to you with a friend or family member present.

Keep agents' and/or companies' names, addresses, and telephone numbers. Write down the agents' and/or companies' names, addresses, and telephone numbers or ask for a business card with this information.

If you decide to buy, fill out the application carefully. Do not believe an insurance agent who says your medical history on an application is not important. Some companies ask for detailed medical information. You must answer the medical questions even if you are applying during your Medigap open enrollment period or are in a situation where you have the right to buy a Medigap policy. During these two times, the company cannot use your answers to turn you down or use this information to decide how much to charge you for a Medigap policy. However, if you leave out any of the medical information they ask for, the company could refuse to cover you for a period of time for any medical condition you did not report. The company also could deny a claim or cancel your Medigap policy if you send in a bill for care of a health problem you did not report.

Beware of non-standardized plans. It is illegal for anyone to sell you a policy and call it a Medigap policy if it does not match the standardized Medigap policies sold in your state. A doctor may offer you a "retainer agreement" that says he/she can provide certain non-Medicare-covered services and not charge you the Medicare coinsurance and deductible amounts. This type of agreement may be illegal. If a doctor refuses to see you as a Medicare patient unless you pay him or her a yearly fee and sign a "retainer agreement," you should call 1-800-MEDICARE.

Look for an outline of coverage. You must be given a clearly worded summary of a Medigap policy. Read it carefully.

Do not pay cash. Pay by check, money order, or bank draft payable to the insurance company, not the agent or anyone else. Get a receipt with the insurance company's name, address, and telephone number for your records.

Medicare SELECT. This coverage is more restrictive than that provided by the regular Medigap insurance. A Medicare SELECT policy may (except in emergencies) limit Medigap benefits to items and services provided by certain selected health care professionals, or may pay only partial benefits if the patient gets health care from other health care professionals. The policies are required to meet certain federal standards and are regulated by the states in which they are approved. A person is able to choose from among the 10 Medigap policies, but the premiums charged for Medicare SELECT policies are generally lower than premiums for comparable Medigap policies that do not have the selected-provider feature.

Medicare HMOs.[7] These are HMOs that have contractual arrangements under which Medicare pays a set amount, and the HMO provides the patient's medical care. Some HMOs may charge an additional premium for supplementary benefits beyond those required under Medicare. Medicare HMOs generally offer plans without any deductibles (or a very low deductible) and modest copayments. Each plan has its own network of hospitals, skilled nursing facilities, home health agencies, doctors, and other professionals. Depending on how the plan is organized, services are usually provided either at one or more centrally located health facilities, or in the private practice offices of the doctors and other health care professionals that are part of the plan. A beneficiary generally must receive all covered care through the plan or from health care professionals referred to by the plan.

Medicaid.[8] This state-run public assistance program is intended for low-income individuals who can satisfy a stringent means test. In contrast to the Medicare system, which is funded and administered by the federal government, the Medicaid system is funded by both federal and state contributions, and the states have a great deal of discretion in setting up and administering their specific programs. Despite federal minimum requirements and standards, Medicaid planning can be made difficult by frequent changes in these rules; by administrative inconsistencies between the states; and by enforcement of income, resource, and transfer limitations that are intended to carry out the original objective of limiting Medicaid to the "indigent" individual in need of long-term custodial care.

(1) **Qualifying For Medicaid.** Basic to qualifying for Medicaid assistance is the requirement that the applicant not have sufficient *income* to provide for his own care. Most states permit an individual with excess income to qualify for Medicaid, provided he "spends down" this income by incurring medical expenses (but some "income cap" states deny benefits whenever there is excess income). Medicaid qualification also requires that the applicant have very limited amounts of personal *resources* (spousal impoverishment rules allow a non-institutionalized spouse to maintain separate property, see paragraph (2) below).

(2) **Medicaid Trusts.** In attempting to preserve family assets, individuals in the past have transferred assets outright to children, or to an irrevocable trust, often called a "Medicaid trust." However, the effectiveness of these techniques has been reduced by major changes in the rules governing transfers of assets, the periods of ineligibility, and the state's rights of recovery. For example, to discourage institutionalized applicants from making transfers for inadequate consideration, transfers during the 36 months before application for Medicaid benefits (the "look-back" period) can delay eligibility for a period equal to the amount of the transfers divided by the average cost to a private patient of nursing facilities in the state (e.g., a delay of 80 months assuming transfer of a $280,000 home and an average cost of $3,500 per month for nursing home care, $280,000 ÷ $3,500 = 80). The look-back period for certain transfers involving trusts is 60 months. These changes have substantially reduced the effectiveness of newly established or funded Medicaid trusts.

Workers' Compensation. State or federal law requires workers compensation benefits for nearly all employees who suffer job-related accidents or diseases. Employers are considered absolutely liable for such injuries or diseases (no matter who was at fault) and benefits are generally provided with no deductible or coinsurance requirements. The major benefits provided under workers' compensation include:

(1) **Medical care expenses** for hospital, surgical, and other related services are covered in full.

(2) **Disability income** is paid after a short waiting period of 3 to 7 days. The weekly benefit generally amounts to a specific percentage of workers' wages, subject to minimum and maximum limits in most states. The duration of payments vary widely between states.

(3) **Lump-sum payments** are made to workers who suffer dismemberments.

(4) **Rehabilitation services** to rehabilitate and retrain workers in order to assist them in returning to work.

(5) **Survivor payments** in the form of lump-sum death benefits, burial allowances, and weekly income benefits.

COVERAGES OFFERED BY PRIVATE CARRIERS

Distinctions between the various types of medical expense coverages have become blurred as insurers continue to introduce new features and plans. For example, a "basic plan" might be offered providing health care services associated with hospitalization, to include both traditional hospital insurance and surgical expense insurance.[9] Likewise, as managed care has become a major means of delivering health care, many of the traditional distinctions have become even further blurred. When considering and evaluating medical expense coverages, it is important to look beyond the labels and carefully examine the coverages provided. The generally recognized types of medical expense coverages include:

Hospital Insurance. This covers the costs incurred during a period of hospitalization. Typical expenses include room-and-board charges (semi-private room), operating room charges, nursing services, and miscellaneous charges such as x-rays, drugs, laboratory fees, supplies, and other such charges. Room-and-board coverage is often offered under either:

(1) **Indemnity plans** – providing for a flat per-day rate up to a maximum number of days (e.g., $450 per day for 90 days). These are also referred to as "expense reimbursement" contracts.

(2) **Service benefits** – providing for all room charges (reasonable and customary) for a maximum number of days, but subject to deductibles, coinsurance, and maximum limits.

Reimbursement limits for ancillary expenses (those expenses other than room-and-board) include daily maximums, overall per stay maximums, deductibles and coinsurance.

Surgical Expense Insurance. This covers the cost of both in-hospital and out-patient surgery. In addition to a surgeon's fees, other services may be included, such as costs and administration of anesthetics and x-ray procedures. If the surgery is considered elective, cosmetic, or experimental, it is usually excluded from coverage. Payment amounts are typically based on either a *scheduled* (fixed amount) or *service basis* (reasonable and customary). Although surgical expense coverage is available as a stand-alone policy, it is often included as an integral part of hospital insurance, or as a rider to a hospital insurance policy.

Physicians' Expense Insurance. This insurance generally covers physicians' charges for in-hospital nonsurgical care, although some plans may also cover office and home visits. Payment amounts are typically based on either a *scheduled* (fixed amount) or *service basis* (reasonable and customary). Reimbursement limits include deductibles, coinsurance, and maximum limits. This is also referred to as "medical expense" or "regular medical expense" insurance.

Major Medical Insurance. This type of coverage is intended to protect against the expenses of a catastrophic illness or injury. It provides broader coverage for all reasonable and necessary expenses than that provided by hospital, surgical, and physicians' expense coverages. Coverage typically *does not include* elective and cosmetic surgery, routine physical examinations, eyeglasses, hearing aids, and dental care. Compared to the basic coverages, major medical insurance offers high lifetime limits ranging from $250,000 to $1,000,000 and higher. Some plans have no maximum limits. Reimbursement limits include both deductibles and coinsurance, but coinsurance requirements are usually subject to specific stop-loss limits (see page 265). Internal limits often provide maximum amounts of coverage for specific services (e.g., a maximum of $600 per day for hospital coverage). Treatments for mental illness, alcoholism, and drug addition may be limited to maximum days of treatment.

Comprehensive Major Medical Insurance. This coverage combines the features and benefits of hospital-surgical and major medical expense policies. The term is often used to describe coverages offered by a wide range of health care providers, such as preferred provider organizations and other forms of managed health care (see page 250).

Dental Insurance. This coverage is most often available as group insurance, but can also be found in individual policies. Most routine dental expenses are covered, such as oral examinations, x-rays, cleanings, fillings, extractions, dentures, bridgework, and orthodontics. As with other health insurance policies, in order to control costs coverage is subject to annual deductibles, coinsurance requirements, and maximum limits. However, in order to encourage preventative dental care, many plans do not impose coinsurance requirements on one or two routine annual dental examinations. Coinsurance requirements are often set higher for orthodontics (e.g., rather than the normal 20% coinsurance, the participant pays 40% of charges above the deductible). Most plans exclude charges for cosmetic dental work.

Critical Illness Insurance. Critical illness insurance typically pays a benefit upon the diagnosis of the first occurrence of a named critical illness or condition. Some products provide for payments for a limited number of conditions, such as heart attack, stroke, or cancer. Other products pay upon such wide ranging conditions as Alzheimer's Disease, multiple sclerosis, major organ transplant, kidney failure, loss of sight, loss of use of two or more limbs, any terminal illness, or death.

Although often resembling the more common "dreaded disease" products, critical illness insurance typically offers substantially greater coverages and benefits. For example, proceeds might be used to provide for home health care needs, replace lost wages of the insured or a care-giver, provide for housekeeping or child care services, pay for "experimental" treatment or drugs, pay medical copayments and deductibles, or make modifications to automobiles and homes for a disabled survivor. Benefits can vary widely. The amount can be either a fixed sum or a percentage of a life insurance death benefit. Payments can be made as a lump sum or over a number of years.

It is currently offered in the form of a stand-alone product, as a rider to a life insurance policy, as group insurance, or as part of another health insurance policy. There is debate as to whether critical illness insurance can give the purchaser a false sense of security (i.e., when there is a need for comprehensive health insurance but the product covers only specific illnesses). Critical illness insurance is not available in many states.

Limited Coverage – Not Recommended. The following policies offer very narrow coverage that generally fails to provide the broad-based coverage needed in a well-designed insurance program.

(1) **Accident insurance** pays a specified sum for injury or death resulting from an accident (e.g., travel accident insurance purchased at airports). Unfortunately, coverage does not cover illnesses and the amount of insurance tends to bear little relationship to the loss.

(2) **Sickness policies,** including "dread disease" insurance, typically pay a specified sum for a very limited number of specified illnesses or diseases. Many states prohibit the sale of this coverage if coverage is limited to a single disease (e.g., cancer insurance).

(3) **Hospital income** insurance pays a fixed amount per day, per week, or per month, while the insured is hospitalized. Preexisting conditions and illnesses requiring long-term hospitalization are generally excluded (e.g., mental illness).

POLICY PROVISIONS

Payment Provisions. These provisions can differ widely between policies.

(1) **Deductibles.** The deductible is the initial amount that the insured is required to pay before benefits are paid under a health plan.

   (a) **Calendar-year** deductibles are generally applied each year to each individual covered under the plan. For example, if the plan has a $250 deductible, the plan participant must pay the first $250 of covered expenses. Once this amount has been paid the deductible has been "satisfied," and the plan covers any remaining expenses (but subject to other limitations such as the coinsurance provision). Calendar-year deductibles are applied to each participating family member or to an entire family (i.e., as a "per-family" deductible).

   (b) **Per-family** deductibles are used by many plans, in addition to individual deductibles, in order to minimize the payment burden for plan participants (i.e., per-family deductibles work to the advantage of participants). Once the per-family deductible is reached this generally satisfies further individual deductibles. For example, assume a family is covered by a policy providing for $250 individual deductibles and a $500 family deductible. At the beginning of the year father and mother each have over $250 of covered medical expenses. They have both met their individual $250 deductibles, and the $500 family deductible has also been satisfied. This means that other family members *do not* have to meet their $250 individual deductibles.

   (c) **Per-occurrence** deductibles apply to specific illnesses or accidents (e.g., three accidents during the calendar year would each be subject to a $500 deductible).

   (d) **Carry-over provisions** allow for carrying over expenses from the end of one year to the next (e.g., expenses during the last 3 months of the year are credited toward the next year's deductible requirements).

(2) **Co-insurance.** Also referred to as a "participation provision" or a "co-payment," this provision requires the insured to pay a percentage of costs that exceed the deductible amount. Co-insurance is considered both a cost-sharing and cost-containment technique (i.e., a device for controlling over-utilization of insurance benefits). Typically, the insured will bear between 10% and 30% of any costs above the deductible amount. For example, assume that, after a calendar-year deductible of $250, under a co-insurance provision plan participants are responsible for 20% of covered expenses. If Mary has covered medical expenses of $1,000, she pays

the first $250 to satisfy the deductible, after which she pays 20% of the balance, or a total of $400 ($250 + (.20 × ($1,000 - $250)) = $400). The insurer pays the remaining $600 (.80 × ($1,000 - $250) = $600). However, a **stop-loss provision** will generally place a cap on the amount of required participation. For example, assume that there is a $3,000 stop-loss provision and Mary's covered medical expenses are $20,000. Without a stop-loss Mary would pay $4,200; the first $250 to satisfy the deductible, plus $3,950 under the coinsurance provision ($250 + (.20 × ($20,000 - $250)) = $4,200). With the stop-loss provision she would pay $3,250 ($250 + $3,000 = $3,250). The insurer pays the remaining $16,750 ($20,000 - $3,250 = $16,750). Alternatively, stop-loss provisions may also count deductibles toward coinsurance limits.

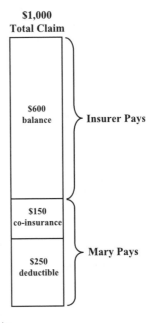

(3) **Maximum Coverage Limits.** Plans often use per individual upper life-time limits to control their ultimate liability. These limits have typically ranged from $250,000 to $1,000,000, although plans are now offering unlimited lifetime benefits.

(4) **Internal Limits.** In contrast to the overall policy limits, specific internal limits may restrict the amount paid for particular services such as room-and-board charges, surgical fees, and hospitalization for mental illnesses and drug rehabilitation. For example, room-and-board charges might be limited to a maximum of $250 per day for a maximum of 90 days.

(5) **Coordination Of Benefits.** Unlike most property and casualty insurance, health care policies are not contracts of indemnity. Without a coordina-tion-of-benefits provision insurers would be required to pay no matter what benefits were available from other sources. This provision is used to prevent individuals from collecting benefits from two different insurers for the same medical expenses. Interestingly, some insurers advertise that benefits are paid regardless of other coverage (i.e., the contract has no coordination-of-benefits provision). Most coordination-of-benefit provi-sions apply between group policies, not between group and individual policies. The following are two examples of the guidelines provided under the coordination-of-benefits provisions developed by the National Association of Insurance Commissioners (NAIC):

(a) *Active employee's plan pays first*: Both husband and wife work and are covered as dependents under each other's policies. If the husband gets sick, his plan pays first, his wife's plan pays second.

(b) *First birthday pays first*: Both husband and wife work and their children are covered as dependents under both of their plans. If a child gets sick, the plan of parent whose birthday occurs first in the year pays first.

Coverage Limitations & Provisions. It is important to understand not only the payment limitations, but also any limitations as to individuals covered under the plan, geographic areas of coverage, coverage of preexisting conditions, and specific procedures that are excluded from coverage.

(1) **Individuals Covered.** Although most plans provide family coverage, some plans cover only the named insured. Plans can also provide varying benefits for children as they grow older. Some plans terminate benefits at age 18, while others continue benefits to an older age, provided the child is a full-time student (e.g., to age 24). Plans may differ and the specific contract provisions should be carefully checked.

(2) **Divorce.** Group plans covered under COBRA provide specific continuation benefits in case of divorce (see page 269). However, individual policies generally provide no such ongoing coverage, nor do they give a divorced spouse the right to purchase coverage. Children living with another parent are likely to be covered under both group and individual plans. However, plans may differ, and contract provisions should be carefully checked.

(3) **Places Covered.** Plans differ widely, with some plans offering worldwide coverage, some offering coverage only in the United States, and still others offering limited coverage in other countries. Again, contract provisions should be carefully checked.

(4) **Cancellation.** Some insurers reserve the right to cancel coverage at any time. These plans should be avoided.

(5) **Continuation Of Group Insurance.** See COBRA, page 269.

(6) **Rehabilitation.** This coverage is similar to that often found in disability income contracts. The objective is to rehabilitate as well as medicate, thereby helping the disabled individual to return to a normal and productive life.

(7) **Preexisting Conditions.** These provisions vary depending upon whether coverage is provided under a group or individual policy:

    (a) **Individual policies** issued to individuals who were not previously covered under a group plan can generally completely exclude coverage for pre-existing conditions, restrict coverage for a specific period of time, or impose higher premiums. Some state laws may impose limits on an insurer's denial of coverage or rating of premiums. Individual state laws should be checked.

    (b) **Group plans** can impose waiting periods before benefits start. Preexisting conditions are considered to be those for which medical treatment or advice was recommended or received within the six-month period prior to enrollment. However, exclusions for preexisting conditions cannot extend for more than 12 months. These limitations on exclusions for preexisting conditions are imposed by the tax laws relating to group insurance (i.e., an employer wanting the tax benefits must comply with the requirements for group health plan coverages).[10] See also, the discussions of portability and COBRA on page 269. Likewise, under group health plans individuals may not be excluded, or required to pay extra premiums, on account of:

        i.   Health status.

        ii. Medical condition – both physical and mental.

        iii. Claims experience.

        iv. Receipt of health care.

        v. Medical history.

        vi. Genetic information.

        vii. Evidence of insurability.

        viii. Disability.

(8) **Pregnancy And Abortion.** Again, these provisions can vary depending upon whether coverage is provided under a group or individual policy:

    (a) **Individual policies** will likely excluded expenditures for pregnancy and abortion unless provided under a special rider, but a few states require these benefits. However, complications of pregnancy and Caesarean sections are normally covered.

(b) **Group plans** generally cover pregnancy and abortion as any other medical procedures. Pre-existing condition clauses may be used to deny coverage for pregnancy and related conditions, but only if such clauses are enforced uniformly for all pre-existing conditions.

(9) **Mental Illness.** While many plans provide for some coverage, it is more likely that the coverage will be limited as to both duration and amount of covered expenses (e.g., hospitalized treatment limited to 30 days, and payment limited to 50% of covered expenses).

(10) **Drug And Alcohol Abuse.** As with treatments for mental illness, those plans providing coverage will most likely limit both the duration and amount of coverage.

(11) **Exclusions.** Most plans generally excluded coverage for elective cosmetic surgery, eyeglasses, hearing aids, and experimental surgery. Routine medical examinations may be covered by some plans, particularly those offered by HMOs. Most plans will also exclude any benefits that are already covered under state workers' compensation laws.

TAX CONSIDERATIONS

Employer-Provided Health Insurance. Health insurance receives very favorable tax treatment both as to the premiums paid and benefits received.

(1) **Employer.** The employer may generally deduct as a business expense all insurance premiums paid for an insured plan or benefits paid under an uninsured plan.[11]

(2) **Employee.** The value of coverage under an employer-provided accident and health plan, including premiums paid by an employer, are excludable from the employee's gross income. Benefits paid or reimbursed for hospital, surgical, and other medical expenses incurred for the employee, his spouse, and dependents are tax-exempt without limit.[12]

Self-Employed Persons. Self-employed individuals may generally deduct as a business expense 100% of amounts paid for medical insurance for themselves and their dependents. However, this deduction cannot exceed the individual's earned income from self-employment.[13]

Personally Purchased Health Insurance. A taxpayer who itemizes deductions may deduct unreimbursed *medical expenses* for medical care of himself, his spouse, and dependents to the extent that such expenses exceed 7.5% of adjusted gross income (i.e., only those medical expenses that exceed 7.5% of adjusted gross income are deductible). *Premiums paid* for medical expense insurance (hospital, surgical and medical expense reimbursement coverage) are included with other medical expenses. As a general rule, benefits from personal health insurance are wholly exempt from income tax. This includes dismemberment and loss of sight benefits, hospital, surgical, and other medical expense reimbursement.[14]

PORTABILITY

The Health Insurance Portability and Accountability Act of 1996 (HIPAA) regulates the application of any preexisting conditions exclusions when a participant moves from one group plan to another (under group health plans exclusions for preexisting conditions cannot extend for more than 12 months, see page 267). In general, the exclusion period must be reduced by the length of prior coverage under another group health plan. However, an individual will not receive credit for prior coverage if there was a break in coverage of 63 or more days. HIPAA also prohibits group health plans from imposing a preexisting conditions exclusion on a newborn, or adopted child under the age of 18, for a 30-day period beginning with the date of birth or the date of adoption.

COBRA

COBRA stands for Consolidated Omnibus Budget Reconciliation Act. Under its provisions, each qualified beneficiary who would lose coverage under a group health plan as a result of a "qualifying event" must be permitted to elect, within a given period, continued coverage under the plan (excepted are employers who have fewer than 20 employees). Government and church plans are exempt from COBRA. Typical qualifying events include death, voluntary or involuntary termination, divorce, separation, and ceasing to be a dependent of an employee. Continuation coverage must be identical to that provided under the plan.

Premiums Required. Premiums may be required of the former employee or beneficiary, but they may not exceed 102% of the cost of the coverage (a disabled beneficiary may, under some circumstances, be required to pay as much as 150% during an extended period of coverage).

Period Of Continuation. The period of continuation depends upon the circumstances surrounding the employee's termination (i.e., the "qualifying event").

(1) **Continuation for 36 months** is required upon:

    (a) Employee's death – surviving spouse and dependents receive coverage.

    (b) Employee's divorce or legal separation – former spouse and dependents receive coverage.

(c) Employee's entitlement to Medicare benefits.

(d) Employee's child ceasing to be a dependent – child receives coverage.

(e) Employer's bankruptcy after employee's retirement.

(2) **Continuation for 29 months** is required if a qualified beneficiary is determined to be disabled within the first 60 days of coverage;

(3) **Continuation for 18 months** is required upon the employee's reduction in hours of employment or termination (other than for gross misconduct).

Termination Of Continued Coverage. The required coverage can be terminated early if:

(1) The employer terminates the health plan for all employees;

(2) The required premium is not paid;

(3) The employee or beneficiary becomes covered under another medical care plan, providing this plan does not exclude a pre-existing condition.

MEDICAL SAVINGS ACCOUNTS

A medical savings account, renamed Archer medical savings account (Archer MSA), may be established, in conjunction with a "high deductible health plan," by self-employed individuals or "small employers" (generally those employing 50 or fewer employees). This is a pilot program, scheduled to terminate at the end of 2003, that limits participation to a maximum of 750,000 individuals over a period of up to four years.

High Deductible Health Plan. In 2003, a high deductible health plan is one that has an annual deductible for individuals of $1,700 to $2,500 and for families of $3,350 to $5,050. Further, annual out-of-pocket expenses (other than premiums) that are required to be paid must not exceed $3,350 for individual coverage and $6,150 for family coverage.

Contributions. Maximum annual contributions to an Archer MSA are 65% of the annual deductible amount under the high deductible plan for single coverage and 75% of the annual deductible amount for family coverage (i.e., if Mr. Smith had a $4,000 annual deductible for his family coverage under a high deductible health plan, then that year he could contribute up to $3,000 to his Archer MSA). Either the employer or the account holder can make contributions, but not both in the same year.

Taxation Of Contributions. Employee contributions to an Archer MSA are fully deductible from income. Employer contributions are excludable from the employee's income and are not subject to Social Security taxes. Employer contributions must be "comparable" (i.e., same dollar amount or percentage of the annual deductible limit). Earnings within the Archer MSA are exempt from income tax.[15]

Taxation Of Distributions. Distributions from an Archer MSA for qualified medical expenses are not taxable to the individual, provided the expenses are not covered by insurance. The payment of health insurance premiums is not considered a qualified medical expense, with limited exceptions. Any distributions that are included in income are subject to an additional 15-percent-penalty tax, except for distributions received after the Archer MSA holder becomes disabled, dies, or reaches the age of Medicare eligibility. Unlike flexible spending accounts, funds unused at the end of each year are *not* forfeited by the account holder, meaning that very substantial amounts might be accumulated over the years. Generally, transfers of an Archer MSA to a spouse pursuant to a divorce are not taxable. If a spouse is named beneficiary of the account, then, upon the account holder's death, the Archer MSA becomes the surviving spouse's Archer MSA without taxation. With a beneficiary other than the spouse, the value of the account is included in the beneficiary's gross income.[16]

LONG-TERM CARE

Planning for long-term care should be an integral part any financial plan. Long-term care consists of a continuum of services including nursing home care, assisted living, home health care, and adult day care. The need can arise from an accident, illness, or advanced age.

The Risk. Statistics make a very good case for long-term care planning when considering retirement. For example, a 65-year-old woman can expect to live another 19.2 years, and a 65-year-old man can expect to live another 15.5 years.[17] During these years it is estimated that the risk of entering a nursing home ranges anywhere from 20% to 49%.

The Cost. Long-term care is expensive and varies widely from one region of the country to another.

(1) **Nursing Home Costs.** In 2002, MetLife's Mature Market Institute reported the average cost of a nursing home stay was $168 per day for a private room, or $61,320 per year. The average nursing home stay was two and a half years. Based on these numbers, the average nursing home stay was $153,300. According to the U.S. Department of Labor, the national average cost of for nursing home care averages $56,000/year. These costs are different across the country.

(2) **Assisted Living Costs.** In 2002, the average base cost of an assisted living facility was $2,159 per month, or $25,908 per year.[18] Of course, these costs vary in different parts of the country and can be higher for residents who need greater care.

(3) **Home Care Costs.** The costs for home care differs substantially according to both the care needed and the provider:

(a) **Licensed practical nurse.** In 2002, MetLife's Mature Market Institute reported that the cost of a licensed practical nurse averaged $37 per hour nationally. Based upon this rate, two hours of skilled nursing care three times per week would cost $11,544 per year ($37 × 2 × 3 × 52 = $11,544).

(b) **Health care aide.** In 2002, MetLife's Mature Market Institute also reported that the cost of a home health care aide averaged $18 per hour nationally. Based upon this rate, two hours of personal care three times per week would cost $5,616 per year ($18 × 2 × 3 × 52 = $5,616).

(c) **Basic home care.** According to the U.S. Department of Labor, the national average cost of part-time basic home care ranges from $12,000 to $16,000 per year. These costs are different across the country.

Managing The Risk. In planning for long-term care there are essentially only three alternatives: self-insurance, government programs, or private insurance.

(1) **Self-insurance** may be a realistic option for an individual with substantial retirement income and assets. As can be seen from the How Money Goes table on page 401, assuming an after-tax rate of return of 5%, $103,187 of capital will produce $678 per month for 20 years or $430 per month forever; and $592,947 of capital will produce $3,897 per month for 20 years or $2,471 per month forever. In the right circumstances, an annuity might produce even larger returns for any given capital sum (see page 374).

(2) **Government programs** are available within strict limitations, but the coverage may not be satisfactory to many individuals.

(a) **Medicare.** In 2003, after a minimum three-day hospital stay Medicare will only pay for the first 20 days of skilled nursing care. From days 21 through 100, the patient must pay the first $105.00 per day, and must pay all costs after 100 days. Medicare will pay for medically necessary home health visits that are restorative in nature (i.e., the patient must be improving). However, *Medicare will not pay for intermediate care or custodial care.* It should also be noted that Medigap coverage only pays Medicare deductibles or coinsurance, it does not extend the basic coverage (see page 256).

(b) **Medicaid.** Although Medicaid will pay for custodial care, the patient must first "spend down" assets in order to qualify. Simply put, "spend down" means liquidating assets to pay for long-term care until a level of financial indigence is reached and it is possible to qualify for Medicaid. When does such a "financial meltdown" become significant? The answer depends upon marital status. In most states a single individual cannot have more than $2,000 in countable assets. However, the "indigent spouse rules" provide better treatment to a married couple with an at-home spouse. In 2003, most states allowed them to retain up to $90,660, plus the home, automobile, household goods, and personal belongings (and a minimum monthly income of $1,492.50 for the at-home spouse).

If an individual needs 24-hour-a-day custodial care, under Medicaid there is little or no provision for "community based care" (i.e., home care, assisted living, or adult day care). It is understood that, on average, Medicaid pays about two-thirds as much as the private pay patient. Although a nursing home cannot, by law, treat patients differently depending on who is paying the bills, quality of care remains an issue. Medicaid patients do not get private rooms. If the quality of care deteriorates, the family of a private pay patient can move him to a different facility.

(3) **Private insurance** provides asset protection from the Medicaid spend down requirements, and is often considered by those desiring independence and choice of care and benefits. Private insurance provides flexibility by allowing individuals to obtain care in various settings and at different levels (skilled nursing, intermediate, and custodial care). Contracts generally do not require prior hospitalization, are guaranteed renewable, and offer level premiums. (Long-term care insurance is also available on a group basis or as permanent life insurance that advances the death benefit.)

(a) **Benefit amounts and periods.** Daily benefits run from $50 to $300 or more. The benefit periods are typically from 2 to 5 years, or lifetime.

(b) **Deductibles.** A deductible, in the form of a waiting or elimination period, will generally last from 0 to 180 days or more. Accepting a longer waiting period can often substantially reduce premiums. Alternatively, there might be a favorable tradeoff between accepting an increased waiting period, in exchange for obtaining a longer benefit period.

(c) **Benefit triggers.** A benefit is paid when the insured has a cognitive impairment, or is unable to perform certain activities called "benefit triggers" (referred to as "gatekeeper provisions"). Typically, benefit payments are triggered by the loss of two or more activities of daily living (ADLs). These activities commonly include eating, toileting, transferring, bathing, dressing, and continence. There has been considerable debate regarding tax-qualified versus nontax-qualified products (i.e., the use by nontax-qualified products of the more liberal "medical necessity" standard to determine payment of benefits). See page 276.

(d) **Guaranteed renewable.** Most contracts are guaranteed renewable. This means that the contract cannot be cancelled, provided the premiums are paid. However, *premiums may be increased* on a class basis if the insurer's claims experience is poor. Those policies that are "optionally renewable" allow the policy to be non-renewed at the insurer's discretion.

(e) **Covered services.** Although the range of coverage can differ widely, most policies cover skilled nursing, intermediate, and custodial care. The range of coverages include:

1. **Skilled nursing care** provided 24-hours per day by skilled medical personal under the supervision of a physician.

2. **Intermediate nursing care** includes similar skilled nursing care, but on a more periodic basis (i.e., intermittent care as opposed to 24-hour nursing care).

3. **Custodial care** provides assistance with the activities of daily living (ADLs), such as bathing, eating, dressing, walking, and using the toilet.

(f) **Home health care.** Many policies allow the above covered services to be provided at the insured's home rather than in a nursing home. However, where home health care is provided, the benefits are often limited to a reduced percentage of the nursing home benefit. Most policies do not cover such homemaking duties as meal preparation and housecleaning.

(g) **Adult day care.** Provisions for home health care and adult day care allow the beneficiary to remain in the community.

(h) **Waiver of premium.** Various waiver benefits are offered. The best contracts waive premiums once benefits have commenced under the policy (i.e., after the elimination period). However, some policies may not waive premiums until some specific period has elapsed after the commencement of benefits (e.g., 30 days), and other waiver provisions may not apply if the insured is receiving home health care.

(i) **Inflation protection**. The General Accounting Office has projected that long-term care costs would increase at an annual compound rate of 5.8%.[19] For younger insureds inflation protection is particularly important (e.g., a 50-year-old will not likely claim benefits as soon as a 70-year-old, thus the 50-year-old's care will cost more). Assuming only 5% inflation per year, care that costs $3,750 a month today will cost $6,108 in 10 years and $9,948 in 20 years. In order to ensure an adequate daily benefit in the future, optional protection against inflation is generally provided in a number of very different ways:

1. Option to purchase specific amounts of additional coverage at given future dates without evidence of insurability (i.e., guaranteed insurability). When purchased, an additional premium is required.

2. Automatic benefit increase of a specific percentage of the basic daily benefit for a given number of years (e.g., 5% increase per year for 20 years). The initial premium typically includes the cost of these increases, and it can be quite expensive. The increases are generally calculated in one of two ways:

   a. **Simple interest calculation** involves increasing the benefit by some fixed percentage of the *initial* benefit. For example, a $100 daily benefit increased at a simple rate of 5% would increase by a level $5.00 each year. By year 20 the daily benefit would equal $195.00 ($100 + ($5.00 × 19) = $195).

   b. **Compound interest calculation** involves increasing the benefit by some fixed percentage of the *increased* benefit. For example, a $100 daily benefit increased at a compound rate of 5% would increase by $5.00 at the end of the first year, $5.25 at the end of the second year, $5.51 at the end of the third year, etc. By year 20 the daily benefit would equal $252.70 (almost 30% more than with a simple rate of increase).

(j) **Other benefits.** In addition to these basic components, other benefits are often available. These features include spousal discounts, respite care, hospice care, caregiver training, bed reservation, medical equipment, cognitive reinstatement, non-forfeiture benefits, case management, and referral services. Choosing from such a range of contract options requires a balancing of benefits and flexibility against premium costs.

(k) **When To Purchase.** The "cost of waiting" to buy long-term care insurance can be considerable. Not only are premiums substantially more at older ages but additional coverage must be purchased to cover inflation. See paragraph (i) on page 275.

Nonqualified Long-Term Care Insurance. The Internal Revenue Code does not directly address the income taxation of premiums paid for or benefits received from *nonqualified* policies and there is uncertainty regarding the tax treatment of nonqualified long-term care contracts issued after January 1, 1997.[20] It is maintained by many commentators that some nonqualified contracts actually provide better protection to the insured than qualified contracts. The following table contrasts the triggers under a typical "triple-trigger" nonqualified contract with the triggers required of a qualified contract under Code section 213. Note that under Code section 213: (1) the ADL triggers were expanded from 5 to 6 (good for the insured), but then a 90-day requirement was added (bad for the insured); (2) the word "severe" was added to the cognitive impairment trigger (bad for the insured); and (3) there is no medical necessity trigger, and no to-be-defined trigger as been established (bad for the insured). Clearly, a case can be made that qualified contracts are not as favorable to the insured as the nonqualified "triple-trigger" contracts. Nevertheless, the tax consequences of a qualified contact are known and are very favorable to the insured.[21]

Benefit Triggers		
Trigger*	Nonqualified "Triple-Trigger" Contracts	Qualified Contracts
Activities Of Daily Living (ADLs).	Inability to perform 2 of 5 ADLs.	Inability to perform 2 of 5 or 6 ADLs - but subject to an additional requirement that the loss of functional activity is expected to last at least 90-days.
Cognitive impairment.	Suffers a cognitive impairment.	Suffers a *severe* cognitive impairment.
Medical necessity.	Doctor prescribed due to medical necessity.	n/a
To-be-defined.	n/a	Drawn up in collaboration with Treasury and HHS departments (not yet done).
*Only one benefit trigger must be met in order to qualify for benefits.		

Qualified Long-Term Care Insurance.[22] A "qualified" long-term care insurance contract is any contract that:

(1) Was issued before January 1, 1997, which met the long-term care insurance requirements of the state in which the contract was sitused at the time it was issued (the grandfather provision in HIPAA).

(2) Meets all of the following requirements:

(a) Must provide only coverage for "qualified long-term care services;"

(b) Cannot pay or reimburse for services covered under Medicare;

(c) Must be guaranteed renewable;

(d) Cannot provide a cash surrender value;

(e) Must apply premium refunds or dividends to either reduce future premiums or increase future benefits;

(f) Must satisfy consumer protection provisions, disclosure, and nonforfeitability requirements as set forth by the National Association of Insurance Commissioners (NAIC).

Qualified long-term care services are defined as necessary diagnostic, preventive, therapeutic, curing, treating, mitigating, and rehabilitative services, and maintenance or personal care services, which are required by a chronically ill individual, and which are provided under a plan of care set forth by a licensed health care practitioner. A person is considered "chronically ill," if certified by a health care professional as unable to perform, for a period of at least 90 days, without substantial assistance, at least two activities of daily living (i.e., eating, toileting, transferring, bathing, dressing, and continence), or as requiring substantial supervision to protect himself from threats to health and safety due to a "severe cognitive impairment" (i.e., a deterioration or loss of intellectual capacity that places the individual in jeopardy of harming self or others).

Tax Treatment. Beneficial tax treatment is afforded to *qualified* long-term care insurance contracts.

(1) **Employers** who pay premiums for a nonowner employees can fully deduct the premium payments. The premiums are not includable in the employee's income, and are subject only to "reasonable compensation" limits.[23]

(2) **Individuals** can deduct premiums as medical expenses, but the deduction is limited to expenses in excess of 7.5% of adjusted gross income. This deduction for premiums paid is further subject in 2003 to the following age-based limits: $250 if age 40 or less; $470 if age 41 through 50; $940 if age 51 through 60; $2,510 if age 61 through 70; and $3,130 if age 71 and over (these limits are indexed for inflation).[24]

(3) **Self-employed individuals** can deduct 100% of premiums, subject to the same age-based limits.[25]

(4) **Benefits Received.** Amounts received from a qualified long-term care contract in 2003 are generally not included in income up to the greater of $220 per day or the actual costs incurred. It is not necessary to prove a need for medical care in order to deduct unreimbursed long-term care expenses for nursing homes, assisted-living facilities, adult homes, and home care. This is very much to the taxpayer's advantage.[26]

[1] See National Association of Health Underwriters, "Issues: Managed Care," www.nahu.org/ government/issues/managed_care/index.htm (May 23, 2003).

[2] See generally, *All About Medicare* (Cincinnati: The National Underwriter Company, 2003, revised annually).

[3] See also, *Social Security Manual* (Cincinnati: The National Underwriter Company, 2003, revised annually), paragraph I-27, p. 193.

[4] This is an abbreviated chart, for a more complete description of services and conditions of payment, see *All About Medicare,* paragraphs B-1 to B-38 and paragraphs C-1 to C-49.

[5] In 1997, Congress added two more high deductible plans to the list of 10 standard plans. See *All About Medicare*, paragraph E-6, pp. 101-102.

[6] Obtained from *All About Medicare*, paragraph E-11, pp. 106-109.

[7] See *All About Medicare*, paragraph D-2, p. 83.

[8] See *All About Medicare*, paragraph G-1, p. 121.

[9] See Stephan R. Leimberg & John J. McFadden, *The Tools & Techniques of Employee Benefit and Retirement Planning*, 7th ed. (Cincinnati: The National Underwriter Company, 2001), p. 333.

[10] See Leimberg & McFadden, p. 336.

[11] See *Tax Facts 1* (Cincinnati: The National Underwriter Company, 2003, revised annually), **Question 203** – May an employer deduct the cost of premiums paid for accident and health insurance for employees as a business expense?

[12] See *Tax Facts 1*, **Question 195** – Is the value of employer-provided coverage under accident or health insurance taxable income to the employee? **Question 196** – Are payments received by employees under employer-provided accident or health insurance taxable income?

[13] See *Tax Facts 1*, **Question 202** – How is health insurance coverage for partners, sole proprietors, and S corporation shareholders taxed?

[14] See *Tax Facts 1*, **Question 190** – Are premiums paid for personal health insurance deductible as medical expenses? **Question 191** – Are the benefits received under a personal health insurance policy taxable income?

[15] See *Tax Facts 1*, **Question 283** – What are the limits on amounts contributed to an Archer MSA?

[16] See *Tax Facts 1*, **Question 287** – How are amounts distributed from an Archer MSA taxed?

[17] Life expectancy statistics are from *Aging Into The 21st Century*, National Aging Information Center, prepared in 1996 under contract with the Administration on Aging, U.S. Dept. of Health and Human Services.

[18] This study was conducted in January and February of 2002 and involved a total of 482 nursing homes and 521 home care agencies by the MetLife Mature Market Institute, Westport, CT (released on April 26, 2002).

[19] This projection was made by the General Accounting Office in June of 1991 and was substantiated by the July/August 1999 issue of "Health Affairs" from the Center for Medicare and Medicaid Services.

[20] See *Tax Facts 1*, **Question 276** – How is a long-term care insurance policy that is not a "qualified long-term care insurance contract" taxed?

[21] For an excellent discussion of the issues surrounding qualified versus nonqualified contracts, see Jeff Sadler, *The Long Term Care Handbook*, 2nd ed. (Cincinnati: The National Underwriter Company, 1998), pp. 221-241.

[22] Qualified long-term care insurance is covered in Code section 213(d)(1), as passed by the Health Insurance Portability and Accountability Act of 1996, and clarified by the Taxpayer Relief Act of 1997. See *Tax Facts 1*, **Question 273** – What is a qualified long-term care insurance contract?

[23] See *Tax Facts 1*, **Question 271** – Are long-term care insurance premiums paid by an employer includable in income to the employees? **Question 272** – May an employer deduct as a business expense the premiums paid for a qualified long-term care insurance contract for employees?

[24] See *Tax Facts 1*, **Question 269** – Are premiums paid for a qualified long-term care insurance contract deductible as medical expenses?

[25] See *Tax Facts 1*, **Question 270** – May a self-employed individual deduct premiums paid for a qualified long-term care insurance contract?

[26] See *Tax Facts 1*, **Question 277** – Are benefits received under a qualified long-term care insurance contract taxable income?

THE VALUE OF AN EDUCATION

Having an education will often determine the economic opportunities available over a lifetime. Persons with a bachelor's degree or higher on the average earn about 3 times more than those who have completed less than 9th grade, and about 2 times more than those who have completed only high school.

	Median Annual Income[1]		
	Less than 9th grade	High school graduate	Bachelor's degree or more
Men	$24,692	$36,770	$77,963
Women	$17,131	$24,970	$47,224

THE COST OF AN EDUCATION

The costs of a four-year college education can easily equal the value of a modest three-bedroom family home, but with the payments due and payable over a period of only four years. This makes advanced planning absolutely essential. According to the College Board the average college costs for the academic years 2002-2003 are:[2]

www.collegeboard.com

- Four-year private college $18,273 – up 5.8% from prior year.

- Four-year public college $4,081 – up 9.6% from prior year.

The following table provides a representative sampling of yearly tuition, fees, supplies, room and board at 42 public and private colleges and universities for the 2002-2003 year. Costs (i.e., tuition) for public schools assume that the student is a resident of the state. (Costs for out-of-state students are generally substantially more then shown.) Although projections are based upon cost increases of 5% per year, in recent years actual college costs have increased more than 5%. Since over the past decade college costs have more than kept pace with the rate of inflation, it seems highly likely that these costs will continue to escalate in the years to come.[3]

College Costs Projected Yearly Tuition, Fees, Supplies, Room & Board					
			Assuming Increases of 5% Per Year		
NAME OF INSTITUTION	LOCATION	2003	2008	2013	2018
Auburn University	Auburn, Ala.	9.184	11,721	14,960	19,093
Bowdoin College	Brunswick, Maine	35,990	45,933	58,624	74,821
Brigham Young University	Provo, Utah	9,260	11,818	15,084	19,251
Bucknell University	Lewisburg, Pa.	35,262	45,004	57,438	73,307
The Citadel	Charleston, S.C.	14,301	18,252	23,295	29,731
Colorado State University	Ft. Collins, Colo.	12,415	15,845	20,223	25,810
Columbia College	New York, N.Y.	36,752	46,906	59,865	76,405
Dartmouth College	Hanover, N.H.	35,988	45,931	58,621	74,816
De Paul University	Chicago, Ill.	27,400	34,970	44,632	56,963
Drake University	Des Moines, Iowa	24,000	30,631	39,093	49,894
Duke University	Durham, N.C.	38,229	48,791	62,271	79,475
Emory University	Atlanta, Ga.	36,130	46,112	58,852	75,112
Florida State University	Tallahassee, Fla.	9,012	11,502	14,680	18,735
George Washington Univ.	Washington, D.C.	38,030	48,537	61,947	79,062
Hamline University	St. Paul, Minn.	26,326	33,599	42,882	54,730
Harvard College	Cambridge, Mass.	37,750	48,180	61,491	78,480
Jackson State University	Jackson, Miss.	8,138	10,386	13,256	16,918
Kansas State University	Manhattan, Kans.	8,224	10,496	13,396	17,097
Loyola College in Maryland	Baltimore, Md.	33,055	42,187	53,843	68,719
Marquette University	Milwaukee, Wis.	28,525	36,406	46,464	59,301
Michigan State University	E. Lansing, Mich.	13,572	17,322	22,107	28,215
Middlebury College	Middlebury, Vt.	36,850	47,031	60,025	76,609
Ohio State University	Columbus, Ohio	11,955	15,258	19,473	24,854
Oral Roberts University	Tulsa, Okla.	18,550	23,675	30,216	38,564
Purdue University	W. Lafayette, Ind.	12,750	16,273	20,768	26,506
Rutgers College	New Brunswick, N.J.	14,508	18,516	23,632	30,161
St. Lawrence University	Canton, N.Y.	34,235	43,693	55,765	71,172
Salem International Univ.	Salem, W.Va.	18,402	23,486	29,975	38,256
Seattle University	Seattle, Washington	27,137	34,634	44,203	56,416
Southern Methodist Univ.	Dallas, Tex.	29,896	38,156	48,697	62,152
Stanford University	Stanford, Calif.	39,106	49,910	63,700	81,299
Texas A & M University	College Sta., Tex.	13,326	17,008	21,707	27,704
Tulane University	New Orleans, La.	36,502	46,587	59,458	75,885
University of Arkansas	Fayetteville, Ark.	9,906	12,643	16,136	20,594
University of California	Berkley, Calif.	15,055	19,214	24,523	31,298
University of Louisville	Louisville, Ky.	8,654	11,045	14,096	17,991
University of New Mexico	Albuquerque, N.Mex.	10,728	13,693	17,476	22,304
University of Rhode Island	Kingston, R.I.	13,254	16,916	21,589	27,554
University of Virginia	Charlottesville, Va.	11,000	14,039	17,918	22,868
Vanderbilt University	Nashville, Tenn.	38,847	49,580	63,278	80,760
Yale University	New Haven, Conn.	37,920	48,397	61,768	78,833
Yeshiva University	New York, N.Y.	27,530	35,136	44,843	57,233
Average Cost		23,420	29,891	38,149	48,689

Explanation of Table. Costs for public schools assume the student is a resident of the state. Costs (i.e., tuition) for out-of-state students are generally substantially more then shown. Costs for supplies are included when available. Costs for transportation are not included. Source of 2002-2003 college education costs: author's research of college internet sites during the month of February, 2003, supplemented by direct inquiry when required.

PAYING FOR COLLEGE – HOW IT IS DONE

Essentially, a college education can be provided for in one of four ways:[4]

(1) **Savings** can be obtained from a variety of sources, placed in a variety of names, and accumulated in a variety of savings and investment vehicles with varying degrees of risk (with or without tax advantages).

(2) **Pay-as-you-go** from current income earned by both parents and student.

(3) **Borrowing** from government and private sources.

(4) **Financial aid** from a variety of sources, the majority of which are *needs-based* financial aid given when a family does not have the financial resources to pay the full costs, and *merit-based* financial aid provided through academic and athletic scholarships awarded on the basis of a student's special talents. The specific form of financial aid can vary widely, to include grants, scholarships, loans, and jobs.

SAVINGS

When establishing a college savings program it is essential to initially determine whether the savings will be placed in the parent's name or the child's name.

Questions To Be Considered. Before shifting assets to a child, or a trust for the benefit of a child, the following should be considered:

- **Control** – Will potential loss of control of the funds be unacceptable to the parents or other donors?

- **Taxation of earnings** – How important is it to take advantage of favorable tax treatment during both the accumulation and distribution phases?

- **Impact upon financial aid** – What effect will this have upon qualification for needs-based financial aid?

Some commentators have reasoned that using a child's savings to pay for a child's education could present some difficulties if state law places an obligation on parents to provide for a child's education. The reasoning goes as follows: (1) parent transfers funds to the child's name under the Uniform Transfers to Minors Act; (2) under state law the parent's obligation of support extends to providing the child with a college education; and (3) using the child's money to discharge the parent's support obligation constitutes a breach of a fiduciary obligation by the account custodian. While it is hard to believe that any reasonable court would require a conscientious parent to "double pay" for a child's education, it is not difficult to imagine that the position might be successfully maintained by an estranged spouse in a divorce proceeding. Of course, this issue does not exist unless state law extends a parent's obligation of support to providing for a child's college education.

GIFTS TO MINORS

Gifts can be made to a minor using either a trust or a custodian. Gifts made by parents, grandparents, or others, enjoy many gift and estate tax advantages, and limited income tax advantages.

Annual Gifts. Under the federal gift tax provisions, an individual may give – under most circumstances – up to $11,000 per person, as indexed in 2003 for inflation, annually free of gift tax.[5] This per-donee exclusion is allowed each and every year, but it is not cumulative (i.e., an exclusion unused in any year may not be "carried over" to the following year). With split-gifts a spouse can join in making the gift, and this allows a married couple to increase their gifts to $22,000 per year to each donee (see Present Interest Gifts, page 425). (Under some circumstances it may be advisable to consider using some of the available unified credit – see Larger Gifts, page 426.)

Transfers To Trusts. In order for a gift to qualify for the annual exclusion, the donee must have the right to the immediate use and enjoyment of the property. As a matter of principle, many donors will object to placing title to property in the name of a minor, and it can create problems in dealing with the property. Fortunately, for those who intend to make substantial gifts over a number of years, the Code authorizes two types of trusts that can be used to obtain the annual exclusion:

(1) **Section 2503(c) Trust.** Under this trust, both income and principal may be expended by or on behalf of the beneficiary prior to age 21, and the unexpended income and principal must be paid to the beneficiary upon attaining age 21 or sooner. If the minor beneficiary dies before age 21, the trust corpus passes to the minor's estate or is subject to a general power of appointment by the minor. It is permissible for the trustee to purchase life insurance on the minor's life and pay premiums from trust income (however, if the trust authorizes purchase of insurance on the grantor's life, or on the life of the grantor's spouse, there will be a violation of the grantor trust rules, and all income will be taxable to the grantor). Distributed income is taxable to the minor, and accumulated income is taxable to the trust. The donor should not be named trustee because that will cause the trust assets to be included in his estate if the donor dies prior to the minor's reaching age 21.

(2) **Section 2503(b) Trust**. This trust should be considered by the donor who does not want trust corpus and unexpended income to be distributed at age 21 or sooner. The principal can be paid to the beneficiary at whatever dates are established by the donor, and need not ever be paid to the beneficiary, but rather paid to another person specified by the donor or the trust beneficiary. However, such a trust must provide for a mandatory distribution of income to the beneficiary at least annually, or more frequently (but could be deposited to a custodial account). Making the gift requires a calculation that involves dividing the gift into an income portion (which qualifies for the annual exclusion) and a principal or remainder portion (which is considered a gift of a future interest).

Because establishing either of these trusts can be expensive and time consuming, many donors may find it more convenient to make gifts by transfers to custodians under the Uniform Transfers to Minors Act or the Uniform Gifts to Minors Act.

Transfers To Custodian. Gifts can be made to a minor by transferring property to a custodian under the Uniform Transfers to Minors Act (UTMA) or the Uniform Gifts to Minors Act (UGMA). Because the UGMA places restrictions on the types of property that can be the subject of a custodial gift, most states have now adopted the UTMA. Gifts made under either act can qualify for the annual exclusion. All income from the gift will be taxable to the minor (unless it is used to discharge the legal obligation of another person, in which case the income would be taxable to that person). Unlike a minor's trust, the custodian does not file a separate tax return and the minor reports all income on his own tax return. The minor has the right to receive possession of the property upon attaining the age specified in the relevant state's statute (age varies from state to state, and may depend upon the instructions of the donor or the nature of the transaction that created the custodianship). There can be only one beneficiary per custodial account, and therefore separate accounts must be established for multiple beneficiaries. Likewise, each account can have only one custodian and successor custodians are usually the minor's guardians. If the donor appoints himself as custodian, the property will be included in his taxable estate if he dies while serving as custodian.

Direct Transfers To Educational Institutions. Tuition costs paid directly to an educational organization are considered "qualified transfers" and are free of gift taxes. Apparently, this also includes tuition payments for future years provided the payments are nonrefundable.

Negative Impact On Financial Aid. Whether placed in trust, or held by a custodian, these assets are considered to be available to the child, and the college aid formula expects 35% of the children's assets to be used for college (versus approximately 6% of the parent's assets). See Calculation Process, page 302.

INCOME TAX CONSIDERATIONS

Taxation Of Children. There are some limited advantages to placing income-producing assets in a child's name, particularly if the child is age 14 and over.

(1) **Unearned income** of a child:

    (a) Under age 14 is generally taxed in 2003 as follows:[6]

- First $750 – not taxed (the reduced standard deduction, see item (3)a below).

- Next $750 – taxed to the child at the child's tax rate.

- Above $1,500 – taxed to the child at the *parent's* maximum rate (known as the "kiddie tax").

    (b) Age 14 and over is taxed to the child at the child's tax rate. In 2003 the tax rate for single individuals is:

- 10% on taxable income up to $7,000.

- 15% on taxable income over $7,000 up to $28,400.

(2) **Earned income** of a child is taxed to the child at the child's tax rate (see paragraph (1)(b) above).

(3) **Standard deduction** in 2003 for an individual who may be claimed as a dependent by another taxpayer is *the greater of*:

    (a) $750, or

    (b) The sum of $250 and the dependent's earned income – but it cannot exceed the regular standard deduction (i.e., $4,750 for a single individual in 2003).

(4) **Capital gains** are taxed at the rate of 5% for taxpayers in the 15% or lower marginal income tax bracket, whereas they are generally taxed at the rate of 15% for taxpayers in higher marginal income tax brackets. This offers an opportunity to give appreciated assets to a child age 14 or over, have the child sell the assets, and save substantial income taxes (the parent's holding period and basis carry over to the child). For example, assume parents who are in a 25% tax bracket have stock worth $30,000 that was purchased for $16,000 in 1996. Sale of the stock would result in $2,100 of income taxes $((30,000 - 16,000) \times .15 = 2,100)$. However, if

their child sold the stock it would be subject to only $700 of income taxes $((30,000 - 16,000) \times .05 = 700)$.[7]

Taxation Of Trusts. Although trusts can be very effective in helping to accomplish many financial and estate planning goals, due to the following factors they are generally *ineffective* in reducing income taxes.

- The compressed tax rate schedule applicable to trusts subjects retained trust income to very high rates of tax (e.g., in 2003 trust taxable income in excess of $4,500 is taxed at 28% or more). See income tax table on page 451.

- When taxable income is distributed to children, the "kiddie tax" results in the children being taxed on distributed trust income at the parent's rate.[8]

EDUCATIONAL TAX INCENTIVES

There is a bewildering array of tax-related education incentives available. Some require advance planning in order to establish the savings mechanism providing the tax incentive. Others require no advanced planning — it is merely a matter of determining which should be claimed at the time education expenses are incurred (assuming they are still available when a child goes to college). However, it is very important to prioritize these incentives, since many of them are mutually exclusive. In this regard, see the table on page 289.

No advanced planning is required for the following (just hope the law does not change):

(1) **Hope Scholarship Credit** offers a $1,500 income tax credit for the first two years of post-secondary education — page 290.

(2) **Lifetime Learning Credit** offers a $1,000 income tax credit for post-secondary education and is not limited to the first two years — page 290.

(3) **Education expense deduction** provides an above-the-line $3,000 deduction for qualified educational expenses — page 290.

(4) **Student loan interest deduction** provides an above-the-line $2,500 deduction — page 291.

Advanced planning is generally required to take advantage of:

(1) **Coverdell Education Savings Accounts** allow income tax-free distribution of earnings to pay a beneficiary's qualified education expenses — page

291. (However, contributions are not deductible and are limited to $2,000 per year.)

(2) **Section 529 plans** provide an opportunity for tax-free distributions for qualified higher education expenses – page 292.

(3) **Educational savings bonds** interest is tax-free if used for tuition and fees – page 293.

Employment related incentives depend upon the student's employment at the time of the education expense:

(1) **Employer tuition reimbursement** is excludable from income up to $5,250 per year – page 294.

(2) **Trade or business expense** is a below-the-line deduction for employee educational expenses for maintaining or improving skills – page 294.

Educational Tax Incentives – Phaseouts & Offsets

Incentive	Limit	Tax Nature	Covers	AGI Phaseout	Offsets
Hope Scholarship Credit (§25A)	1,500	Credit against taxes.	First two years of post-secondary education.	S: 41,000-51,000 J: 83,000-103,000	ABCD
Lifetime Learning Credit (§25A)	2,000	Credit against taxes.	Unlimited number of years.		
Education Expenses (§222)	3,000	Above-line deduction (need not itemize).	Qualified educational expenses.	S: 65,000 J: 130,000	A
Student Loans (§221)	2,500	Above-line deduction for interest (need not itemize).	Student loan interest.	S: 50,000-65,000 J: 100,000-130,000	n/a
Coverdell Education Savings Account (§530)	2,000	Contributions not deductible, but earnings are tax-free.	Qualified education expense.[9]	S: 95,000-110,000 J: 190,000-220,000	B
Section 529 Plans	Varies.	Contributions not deductible, but distributions are tax-free.[10]	Tuition, fees, special-needs services, room, board, books, supplies and equipment.	None.	C
Educational Savings Bonds (§135)	Varies.	Interest tax-free.	Qualified educational expenses.	S: 58,500-73,500 J: 87,750-117,750	n/a
Employer Tuition Reimbursement (§127)	5,250	Not included in income.	Covers both undergraduate and graduate programs.	None.	D
Trade or Business Expense (§162)	None.	Below-line deduction (must itemize).	Employee expenses in maintaining or improving skills.	S: 69,750 J: 139,500	n/a

Under column "AGI Phaseout," "S" indicates single taxpayer and "J" married filing joint return.

A – Hope Scholarship and Lifetime Learning Credits are not available if Education Expense (§222) deduction is taken.

B – Earnings on Coverdell Education Savings Account are not tax-free if used for same expenses as Hope Scholarship and Lifetime Learning Credits.

C – Section 529 qualifying expenses are reduced to the extent they are used in determining Hope Scholarship and Lifetime Learning Credits.

D – Hope Scholarship and Lifetime Learning Credits are not available for the same expense excluded as an Employer Tuition Reimbursement.

Hope Scholarship Credit. The Hope Scholarship Credit provides an income tax credit of up to $1,500 per year for each of the first two years of college, calculated as 100% of the first $1,000 of "qualified tuition and related expenses" and 50% of the next $1,000 (the credit is indexed for inflation). Qualified tuition and related expenses *do not* include nonacademic fees such as room and board, medical expenses, transportation, student activity fees, athletic fees, insurance expenses, personal, living, family or other unrelated expenses. The student must be enrolled at least half-time in a qualifying educational institution. However, the credit may not be taken if the student has ever been convicted of a state or federal charge of felony drug possession or distribution. The student may be the taxpayer, his spouse or any dependent. However, an individual who is eligible to be claimed as a dependent on another taxpayer's return may not take the credit. There is no limit in any given year as to the number of Hope Scholarship credits a taxpayer may claim as to his dependents (i.e., the limit is on a *per-student* basis, and multiple Hope Scholarship credits may be claimed in the same year). In 2003 the credit is phased out ratably between modified adjusted gross income of $41,000 to $51,000 for unmarried taxpayers and $83,000 to $103,000 for married taxpayers filing joint returns.

Lifetime Learning Credit. The Lifetime Learning Credit is 20% of the first $10,000 of qualified tuition and related expenses, for a maximum credit of $2,000 per year ($.20 \times 10,000 = 2,000$). "Qualified tuition and related expenses" are the same as under the Hope Scholarship Credit. However, in contrast to the Hope Scholarship Credit, which is on a per-student basis, the Lifetime Learning Credit limit is on a *per-taxpayer* basis, meaning that only $10,000 of educational expenses qualifies per year. In 2003 the credit is phased out ratably between modified adjusted gross income of $41,000 to $51,000 for unmarried taxpayers and $83,000 to $103,000 for married taxpayers filing joint returns. Also, unlike the Hope Scholarship Credit, the Lifetime Learning Credit can be taken for any year of postsecondary education (except a year in which the Hope Scholarship Credit is claimed for the same student), does not require at least half-time enrollment, and study may be intended to improve the student's job skills and need not lead to a degree.

Education Expense Deduction. This provides an above-the-line $3,000 deduction for qualified educational expenses for taxpayers in certain income ranges. The expenses must be for tuition and fees at an eligible post-secondary educational institution (qualified tuition and related expenses are defined in the same manner as for the Hope Scholarship Credit). The deduction is not available to married individuals filing separate returns.

(1) For expenses paid in 2003 a maximum deduction of $3,000 is available for employees who file a single return with adjusted gross income of $65,000 or less and for those who file jointly with adjusted gross income of $130,000 or less.

(2) For expenses paid in 2004 and 2005 the maximum deduction:

    (a) Increases to $4,000 for employees who file a single return with adjusted gross income of $65,000 or less and for those who file jointly with adjusted gross income of $130,000 or less.

    (b) Decreases to $2,000 for employees who file a single return with adjusted gross income that is greater than $65,000 but less than or equal to $80,000 and for those who file jointly with adjusted gross income that is greater than $130,000 but less than or equal to $160,000.

(3) The deduction is scheduled to expire for taxable years beginning after 2005.

Student Loan Interest Deduction. This maximum $2,500 deduction is an "above the line" deduction, meaning that the taxpayer does not have to itemize in order to claim the deduction. In 2003 the deduction is phased out ratably for unmarried taxpayers with modified adjusted gross income of $50,000 to $65,000, and $100,000 to $130,000 for married taxpayers filing joint returns (these threshold limits are adjusted for inflation).

Coverdell Education Savings Account. A Coverdell Education Savings Account (originally called an "Education IRA"), may be created for the purpose of paying the qualified education expenses of a designated beneficiary.

(1) **Contributions.** Annual contributions are limited to $2,000 per beneficiary per year, and the beneficiary must be under age 18 (except in the case of a special needs beneficiary). This $2,000 annual contribution limit is phased out ratably for individual taxpayers with modified AGI between $95,000 and $110,000, and for married taxpayers filing jointly with modified AGI between $190,000 and $220,000. Contributors with modified AGI above these phase-out ranges are not allowed to make contributions. This contribution limit is per beneficiary, meaning that multiple contributors cannot exceed the $2,000 *per beneficiary per year* limit (e.g., if grandfather contributes $1,800 for grandson then grandmother is limited to contributing an additional $200 for grandson).

(2) **Taxation.** Contributions to an Education Savings Account are not income tax deductible, but earnings grow income tax-free. Contributions are treated as completed present interest gifts from the contributor to the beneficiary at the time of the contribution.

(3) **Distributions.** When the funds are distributed to pay the beneficiary's qualified education expenses, neither the principal nor the earnings will

be included in the beneficiary's income. Qualified education expenses include elementary and secondary school tuition, expenses of special needs beneficiaries, post-secondary tuition, fees, books, supplies, uniforms, equipment, and certain room and board expenses. Distributions that are not used to pay for qualified education expenses are taxed to the beneficiary.

(4) **Other Credits.** A taxpayer may claim a Hope Scholarship Credit or Lifetime Learning Credit for the same taxable year there are distributions from an Education Savings Account, provided the distributions are used to pay for different education costs.

(5) **Balance Not Distributed.** Any balance remaining in an Education Savings Account at the time a beneficiary becomes 30 years old (except in the case of a special needs beneficiary) or dies, if earlier, must be distributed. The earnings portion of such a distribution will be includable in gross income of the beneficiary and subject to an additional 10% penalty tax because the distribution was not for educational purposes. However, it is possible to avoid taxation by rolling the account balance over to another Education Savings Account benefiting a different beneficiary, who is a member of the family of the original beneficiary and who has not attained age 30 as of such date (the under-age-30 requirement does not apply to a special needs beneficiary).

Section 529 Plans. Also called qualified tuition programs (QTPs), these are state-sponsored or privately sponsored programs that are authorized by federal law.

(1) **Prepaid educational arrangements** (PEAs) allow the taxpayer to purchase tuition credits or certificates on behalf of a designated beneficiary. These have also been known as "prepaid tuition plans." Private colleges and universities may establish PEAs.

(2) **Educational savings accounts** (ESAs) allow the taxpayer to make contributions funding the "qualified higher education expenses" (QHEEs) of a designated beneficiary. QHEEs include tuition, fees, special-needs services, room and board, and the costs of books, supplies, and equipment, required by a designated beneficiary at an eligible educational institution (post secondary education to include graduate school). Private colleges and universities *may not* establish ESAs.

There is a large difference among individual programs, many of which are more restrictive than required by Section 529. Before selecting a plan, the investor would be well advised to carefully review the individual account agreement.

Federal law generally does not place any limits on who may participate as an account owner, contributor, or designated beneficiary (except that the beneficiary must be an individual). In order to avoid excess contributions, they are typically limited to the amount necessary to provide five years of education at more expensive schools (e.g., some programs allow for contributions of up to $250,000). Contributions must be in cash, are not tax deductible, and are treated as completed gifts eligible for the gift tax annual exclusion ($11,000 in 2003). This gift tax treatment is unusual, given the owner's power to withdraw funds from the account – subject to penalties and taxes – or to designate a new beneficiary. Gifts in excess of the annual exclusion may be "front-loaded," meaning that a donor may avoid using his available unified credit by treating the gift as made over a period of 5 years (for a maximum of $55,000 per spouse, or $110,000 per couple, to each designated beneficiary). However, if the donor front loads an ESA and dies during the 5-year period, any front-loaded gifts allocable to the years after death are included in the donor's estate.

Digging Deeper

For additional information, educational materials, and calculators relating to 529 plans see: www.savingforcollege.com.

State-sponsored ESAs may permit the owner to choose among different investment strategies offered by the plan (1) when the account is opened, (2) once every 12 months, and (3) whenever the beneficiary designation is changed. Certain age-based plans automatically move to more conservative investments as the beneficiary ages. Separate accounting must be maintained for each designated beneficiary, with no pledging of the account assets by either the owner or the beneficiary. However, the account can be attached by the creditors of the owner, but not by the creditors of the beneficiary. In contrast, the value of the account is included in the estate of the designated beneficiary.

All account earnings are tax deferred. Distributions from state-sponsored QTPs used to pay QHEEs are excluded from gross income (prior to 2002 the earnings portions of distributions were taxable to the beneficiary). Beginning in 2004, this exclusion will be extended to "private" PEAs. Distributions not used for QHEEs are subject to a 10% penalty tax on the taxable portion of the distribution.[11]

Education Savings Bonds. The purchase of Series EE or Series I bonds can provide tax-free interest if the proceeds are used for the tuition and fees of a dependent (but not for room, board, books, or other expenses). The bond must be purchased by the owner (after attaining age 24), who must be either the sole or joint owner with a spouse. All interest on the bonds is potentially excludable from income provided the total amount redeemed (i.e., principal plus interest) does not exceed the amount of the student's qualified educational expenses. For example, assume the redemption amount is $15,000 ($7,500 of principal and $7,500 of interest), and qualified educational expenses are $20,000. The entire $7,500 of interest is excluded from income (but subject to a threshold phaseout based upon modified adjusted gross income). However, if the aggregate proceeds of the bond exceed the amount of expenses paid, the amount of excludable interest is reduced pro rata, based on the proportion of educational expenses to redemption amounts. For example, assume the redemption amount is again $15,000 ($7,500 of principal and $7,500 of interest), but qualified educational expenses are only $12,000. The ratio of expenses to the amount redeemed is 80% (12,000 ÷ 15,000 = .80). The excludable interest is limited to $6,000 (.80 × 7,500 = 6,000). There is a phase-out of this interest exclusion once modified adjusted gross income exceeds a designated amount (for joint tax return filers in 2003, the phase-out is between $87,750 and $117,750). See also, the discussion of Series EE and I bonds on page 116.

Employer Tuition Reimbursement. Also known as "educational assistance plans" or "Section 127 plans," under these nondiscriminatory programs an employee may exclude up to $5,250 of employer-provided educational assistance each calendar year. Amounts over $5,250 are included in income and subject to employment and income tax withholding (but expenses related to the employee's current job may be deductible; see below). The educational expenses need not be job related or lead to a degree. Covered expenses include tuition, fees, books, and supplies. Expenses for both undergraduate and graduate level courses are covered.

Trade Or Business Expense. Reimbursements to an employee outside of an educational assistance plan are included in the employee's income and are:

(1) **Deductible** if the education expense was incurred for maintaining or improving skills required in employment – but this is a below-the-line deduction, meaning that employee must itemize and the deduction is subject to a "2% floor" (i.e., is only useful to the extent that miscellaneous itemized deductions exceed 2% of adjusted gross income).

(2) **Not deductible** if the education expense was incurred for meeting minimum requirements for employment or qualifying for a new trade or business.

IRA Withdrawals. Using a traditional IRA or a Roth IRA for education expenses offers varied tax advantages.

(1) **Penalty Tax.** There is no 10% penalty tax on a withdrawal from either a traditional IRA or a Roth IRA when the withdrawal is for the qualified higher education expenses of a taxpayer

(2) **Regular Tax.** The traditional IRA and Roth IRA are both subject to regular income taxes on withdrawals used for education expenses. However, the Roth IRA owner can:

   (a) At any time (and for any reason) withdraw his original nondeductible plan contributions free of income taxes, and

   (b) Withdraw earnings free of income taxes provided the withdrawal occurs after age 59½ and the account has been open for at least five years.

INVESTMENT VEHICLES

As with virtually every investment decision, choosing between various investment vehicles for college savings involves balancing risk and return (see Risk Tolerance And Assessment, page 40). Clearly, a conservative approach to investing is called for as a child approaches college. However, adopting an early-stage conservative investment strategy may not provide the growth necessary for paying ever-increasing college costs (see College Costs Projected, page 282). Since it is generally known when the funds will be needed, it may be helpful to segment savings into four periods according to the child's age. Allocations between stocks, bonds, and cash or near cash should be adjusted according to the risk tolerances of each individual investor (sample allocations are shown in the following table).[12]

| | Stocks | | | Cash & |
Periods	Aggressive Growth	Growth & Income	Bonds	Near Cash
Early Accumulation (ages 0-7)	40%	40%	20%	0%
Late Accumulation (ages 8-14)	30%	40%	30%	10%
Conservation (ages 15-18)	0%	30%	35%	35%
Distribution (ages 19-22)	0%	0%	25%	75%

Stocks. Stocks offer attractive opportunities for substantial investment returns, but can also result in substantial investment losses. Rather than individual stocks, most investors are better advised to purchase mutual funds providing both diversification and professional management (see Popularity & Advantages Of Mutual Funds, page 170).

Bonds. The purchase of bonds with maturity dates that coincide with a child's college attendance offers an effective way of timing cash flow needs with investments. Laddering of bonds should also be considered (see page 26). The following bonds appear most appropriate for college savings:

(1) **Education savings bonds** offer tax advantages, but they must be purchased early in the investment process since they are not marketable securities and, therefore, are not available on secondary markets – page 293.

(2) **Zero coupon bonds** offer guaranteed investment returns on reinvested interest payments – page 105.

(3) **Stripped bonds** are similar to zero coupon bonds but can also offer call protection – page 111.

(4) **Treasury Inflation-Protection Securities (TIPS)** offer protection from inflation – page 110.

(5) **Treasury securities** offer safe and secure investments, particularly during the conservation and distribution phases – page 109.

Certificates Of Deposit. CDs are an obvious short-term investment choice during the distribution phase (see page 84). However, one type of CD that might be considered earlier in the investment process is the CollegeSure® CD issued by the College Savings Bank. This is a certificate of deposit indexed to college costs and, therefore, it is guaranteed to meet future tuition, fees, and room and board. In effect it is a college cost prepayment product that pays an annual percentage yield tied to the rise in college costs each year with a floor rate for added protection. It's backed by the full faith and credit of the United States up to $100,000 _____ *www.collegesure.com* per depositor.

Life Insurance And Annuities. Life insurance and annuities deserve consideration in the investment portfolio, particularly as regards the self-completing nature of the life insurance contract.

(1) **Permanent life insurance.** Life insurance offers tax-deferred cash value accumulations, favorable loan provisions and a preferred status under the financial aid laws. However, there should be a real need for the insurance; otherwise, funds might better be invested where there would be no charges for a death benefit. Since a parent is most likely to be paying for college, it makes sense that a parent be the insured (with the parent or a trust the owner). Provided the parents are adequately insured, life insurance on the child might also be considered (see Life Insurance Products, page 440).

(2) **Annuities.** Fixed annuities, variable annuities and indexed annuities all offer a tax-deferred buildup of account values, but with varying degrees of

risk and return (see page 377). Annuities are subject to additional management fees beyond those applied to mutual funds. Also, if the owner of an annuity is under age 59½, there is a 10% penalty tax upon surrender.

(3) **Ownership.** A minor child should not be the owner of a life insurance contract or annuity (see Minors & Life Insurance, page 443).

(4) **Impact On Financial Aid.** One advantage of life insurance cash values and annuities is that they are not included in the Federal Methodology formula used by the government in determining eligibility for financial aid. However, annuities values are considered in the Institutional Methodology (see page 302).

FINANCIAL AID PROGRAMS

Federal Work-Study Program. This program provides jobs for undergraduate and graduate students with financial need, allowing them to earn money to help pay education expenses. The amount of the Federal Work-Study award depends on the level of need and the funding level of each participating school. Wages will be at least the current federal minimum wage, but they may be higher depending on the type of work done and the skills required. The school pays the student at least monthly. The program encourages community service work and work related to the student's course of study. Jobs are located both on and off campus for a private nonprofit organization or a public agency. Some schools might have agreements with private for-profit employers for Federal Work-Study jobs, which must generally be relevant to the student's course of study.

Digging Deeper

For additional information regarding federal financial aid programs see: http://student aid.ed.gov/students/ publications/student_ guide/index.html.

Federal Pell Grants. These grants for the 2002-2003 school year range from $400 to $4,000. A Federal Pell Grant, unlike a loan, does not have to be repaid. Generally, Pell Grants are awarded only to undergraduate students who have not earned a bachelor's or professional degree. (In some cases, a Pell Grant may be given for attending a post-baccalaureate teacher certificate program.) To determine financial eligibility, the Department of Education uses a standard formula to evaluate the information reported by the student. This formula produces an EFC number that determines both eligibility and amount of the grant (see page 301). The amount of the yearly grant depends not only on the EFC, but also on the cost of attendance, whether the student is full-time or part-time, and whether school is attended for a full academic year or less. The school must make payments to the student at least once per term (semester, trimester, or quarter).

Federal Supplemental Educational Opportunity Grant (FSEOG). These grants range from $100 to $4,000 per year. The amount of the award depends the student's need, the funding level of the school, and the policies of the school's financial aid office. They are limited to undergraduates with exceptional financial need – that is, students with the lowest EFCs who are receiving Federal Pell Grants. An FSEOG, unlike a loan, does not have to be repaid. Although the Department of Education guarantees that each participating school will receive enough money to pay the Federal Pell Grants of its eligible students, there is no such guarantee every eligible student will be able to receive an FSEOG. Students at each school are awarded an FSEOG based on the availability of funds at that school. The school must make payments to the student at least once per term (semester, trimester, or quarter).

Stafford Loans. These loans are considered to be a major form of self-help aid for students.

(1) **Two basic forms** of these loans are available:

  (a) *Subsidized* loans are awarded on the basis of financial need. No interest is charged until the repayment period (i.e., the federal government "subsidizes" the interest).

  (b) *Unsubsidized* loans are not awarded on the basis of need. Interest is charged from the time the loan is disbursed until it is paid in full. Interest can be paid currently or added to the principal loan amount, with interest then based upon the higher total loan (i.e., compounded interest).

(2) **Maximum Loan Amounts.** Following are the maximum amounts that can be borrowed annually by a student enrolled in a program of study for at least a full academic year. For periods of study that are less than an academic year, the amounts are less. Also, these yearly maximum amounts may be reduced if other financial aid is received.

  (a) Dependent undergraduate student:

    1. $2,625 as a first-year student.

    2. $3,500 as a second-year student.

    3. $5,500 thereafter.

4. Total outstanding from all Stafford Loans is limited to $23,000.

(b) *Independent undergraduate student* (or a dependent student whose parents are unable to get a PLUS Loan):

   1. $6,625 as a first-year student, of which $2,625 may be subsidized.

   2. $7,500 as a second-year student, of which $3,500 may be subsidized.

   3. $10,500 thereafter, of which $5,500 may be subsidized.

   4. Total outstanding from all Stafford Loans is limited to $46,000, of which $23,000 may be subsidized.

(c) Graduate student:

   1. $18,500 each academic year, of which $8,500 may be subsidized.

   2. Total outstanding from all Stafford Loans is limited to $138,500, of which $65,500 may be subsidized. This graduate debt limit includes any Stafford Loans received for undergraduate study.

(3) **Interest.** The interest rate charged is variable, but capped at 8.25%. For example, the interest rate for loans in repayment from July 1, 2001 to June 30, 2002 was calculated at 5.99%. With a *subsidized* loan, interest is not charged while the student is enrolled in school at least halftime, during a grace period, or during authorized periods of deferment. Interest begins to accrue once repayment begins. With an *unsubsidized* loan, interest is charged from the day the loan is disbursed until it is paid in full, including in-school, grace, and deferment periods (it can either be currently paid or capitalized).

(4) **Fees.** There is a loan origination fee of up to 4% of the loan. If loan payments are not made when scheduled, collection costs and late fees may be charged. Failure to make payments may have a negative effect the borrower's credit rating.

Perkins Loans. These low-interest loans are provided to students with demonstrated financial need while undertaking either undergraduate or graduate studies. The individual school makes determination of eligibility. Repayment is made to the school.

(1) **Maximum loan amounts** depend upon the level of need and the school's funding level, but the overall limit is:

a. $4,000 for each year of undergraduate study (limited to $20,000 total as an undergraduate).

b. $6,000 for each year of graduate or professional study (limited to $40,000 total as both an undergraduate and graduate / professional student).

(2) **Interest** is charged at a low 5%.

(3) **Fees** are not charged to take out the loan, but fees are charged if payments are not made as scheduled.

(4) **Repayment** must begin within nine months after graduation, leaving school, or dropping below half-time status; and the repayment period can be up to 10 years. Various provisions provide for deferment, forbearance, or cancellation, based upon service as a full-time teacher, nurse, law enforcement official, and other similar vocations.

Parent Loans (PLUS). These are loans made to the parents of dependent undergraduate students who are enrolled at least half-time. To qualify for the loan, the parents must generally subject themselves to a credit check and the student must meet the general eligibility requirements for federal student aid.

(1) **Maximum loan amounts** are equal to the student's cost of attendance minus any other financial aid received.

(2) **Interest** is subject to change during each year of repayment, but is limited to a maximum of 9%. For example, the interest rate for PLUS Loans in repayment from July 1, 2001 to June 30, 2002, was calculated at 6.79%. Interest is charged on the loan from the date that the first disbursement is made until the loan is repaid in full.

(3) **Fees** of up to 4% are charged. If loan payments are not made as scheduled, collection costs and late fees may also be charged.

(4) **Repayment** must generally begin within 60 days after the final loan disbursement for the specific period of enrollment (i.e., there is no grace period, and the parents must begin repaying both principal and interest while the student is still in school). Generally, the various provisions for deferment, forbearance, or cancellation are the same as those that apply to Stafford Loans. However, since PLUS Loans are unsubsidized, the parents are charged interest during any periods of deferment or forbearance.

QUALIFYING FOR FINANCIAL AID

In order to determine who qualifies for financial aid, a formula provided by the federal government subtracts the Expected Family Contribution from the cost of attendance. Among other factors, this formula takes into consideration the assets and income of the parents and the child. Because the formula gives substantially greater weight to the child's income and assets, large gifts should not be made to a child if financial aid is likely to be sought. The process begins with a student filing out a form entitled the Free Application for Federal Student Aid (FAFSA).

www.fafsa.ed.gov/

Expected Family Contribution (EFC).[13] The EFC is the amount of money a family is expected to contribute toward a student's college costs and is used to determine eligibility for federal and nonfederal financial aid programs. The EFC includes both the parent's contribution and the student's contribution, and depends on the student's dependency status, family size, number of family members in school, and taxable and nontaxable income and assets. By comparing the EFC to the student's cost of attendance (COA), a school's financial aid administrator determines the student's financial need for federal student aid from the U.S. Department of Education and other sources. The difference between the COA and the EFC is the student's financial need, and is used in determining the student's eligibility for need-based financial aid.

http://ifap.ed.gov/IFAP
WebApp/currentEFC
InformationPag.jsp

Cost of Attendance – Expected Family Contribution = Financial Need

Since there are three different EFC formulas used depending upon the status of the student, the first step in calculating the EFC is to determine the student's dependency status:

(1) *Dependent student* – this formula for a dependent student uses parental data while the following two formulas for independent students do not.

(2) *Independent student without dependents* other than a spouse.

(3) *Independent student with dependents* other than a spouse.

Two Different Formulas. There are also different formulas used depending upon whether the student is applying for federally sponsored aid or institutionally-based private aid:

(1) The *Federal Methodology* is a formula established by the federal government that takes into account both taxable and nontaxable family income,

assets, family size, and the number of family members currently attending college. It is used to determine eligibility for federally sponsored financial aid such as Pell Grants, Perkins and Stafford Loans, and Federal Work-Study Programs.

(2) The *Institutional Methodology* is used by institutions and organizations to determine a student's eligibility for institutionally based, private aid programs, and may vary from college to college. Additional factors in a family's financial situation are often considered. For example, unlike the Federal Methodology, the Institutional methodology considers the net value of the family residence.

Calculation Process. The calculation process is quite complicated and the following is provided as a guide only.[14] The "simplified" worksheet used in 2003-2004 for a dependent student actually contains 51 separate lines, plus additional schedules. Some terminology has been modified in order to simplify the explanations.

		Notes	
1.	Parent's Adjusted Gross Income	$_____	
2.	Plus: Other Untaxed/Nontaxable Income	$_____	A
3.	Less: Allowable Offsets	$_____	B
4.	Equals: **Parent's Income Contribution**	$_____	
5.	Parent's Investments	$_____	C
6.	Plus: Business/Farm Interests	$_____	D
7.	Plus: Cash, Savings and Checking	$_____	
8.	Equals: Parent's Net Worth	$_____	
9.	Less: Asset Protection Allowance	$_____	E
10.	Equals: Discretionary Net Worth	$_____	
11.	Times: Asset Conversion Rate	12%	
12.	Equals: **Parent's Asset Contribution**	$_____	F
13.	Plus: Available Income (line 4, above)	$_____	
14.	Equals: Adjusted Available Income	$_____	
15.	**Parent's Total Contribution**	$_____	G
16.	Student's Total Income	$_____	H
17.	Less: Allowable Offsets	$_____	I
18.	Equals: Student's Available Income	$_____	
19.	Times: Assessment Rate	50%	
20.	Equals: **Student's Income Contribution**	$_____	
21.	Student's Net Worth	$_____	J
22.	Times: Assessment Rate	35%	K
23.	Equals: **Student's Asset Contribution**	$_____	
24.	Plus: Income Contribution (line 19, above)	$_____	
25.	Equals: **Student's Total Contribution**	$_____	
26.	Plus: Parent's Contribution (line 15, above)	$_____	
27.	Equals: **Expected Family Contribution**	$_____	

NOTES

A – Includes Social Security benefits, child support, workers' compensation benefits, disability income payments, tax-exempt interest, military housing, food and allowance benefits.

B – Allowable parental offsets include: federal income taxes paid; Social Security taxes; state and local income taxes; real estate and sales taxes; employment allowance; and income protection allowance. For example, during the 2003-2004 school year the income protection allowance for a family of four with one child in college is $20,710 ($20,320 for the 2002-2003 school year). This adjustment allows for other children in college (but not for a parent in college).

C – Investments are included net of outstanding investment debt. It does not include the family home, but does include retirement account values. Although home equity is not counted for federal purposes, colleges are likely to consider it when allocating their own funds using the Institutional Methodology.

D – Net of business and farm debt.

E – The education savings and asset protection allowance is very modest and it is based upon the older parent's age. For example, during the 2003-2004 school year for a two-parent family, with the older parent being 45 years old, the allowance is $42,200 ($38,600 for the 2002-2003 school year); if the older parent is 55 years old the allowance increases to $54,500 ($50,300 for the 2002-2003 school year). Different tables are used for independent students (e.g., during the 2003-2004 school year the allowance for a 30-year-old *unmarried* independent student is $6,200, whereas the allowance for a 30-year-old *married* independent student is $12,400).

F – The Parent's Asset Contribution represents the amount of net worth that is expected to be used for the student's education.

G – The Parent's Total Contribution is calculated by reference to a progressive "tax table" that ranges from 22% to 47% depending upon the parent's Adjusted Available Income (line 14).

H – Includes adjusted gross income plus untaxed and nontaxable income and benefits.

I – Allowable student offsets include federal income taxes paid, Social Security taxes, state and local income taxes, and an income protection allowance. For example, during the 2003-2004 school year the income protection allowance for a dependent student is $2,380 (was $2,330 during the 2002-2003 school year). Colleges do not allow the income protection allowance when allocating their own funds using the Institutional Methodology.

J – Student's Net Worth is calculated similarly to the Parent's Net Worth on line 8.

K – Since the student is expected to use up most assets by the end of postgraduate education, 35% of the remaining assets are expected to be used in the second year and each year thereafter.

[1] Income figures are obtained from *Statistical Abstracts of the United States*, 2002, Table 666, p. 440.

[2] As reported in *Trends in College Pricing 2002* (New York: The College Board) and based on data collected in the College Board's Annual Survey of Colleges, 2002-2003. (see www.collegeboard.com/press/cost02/html/cost02a.html).

[3] Annual costs of a college education are based upon the author's research of college internet sites during the month of February, 2003, supplemented by direct inquiry when required.

[4] An excellent resource to financial planning for college is Raymond D. Loewe, *A Professional's Guide To College Planning*, (Cincinnati: The National Underwriter Company, 1998).

[5] See *Tax Facts 2* (Cincinnati: The National Underwriter Company, 2003, revised annually), **Question 530** – What gift tax exclusions are available to a donor?

[6] See *Tax Facts 2*, **Question 410** – How is unearned income of a child treated for federal income tax purposes?

[7] See *Tax Facts 2*, **Question 419** – How is an individual taxed on capital gains and losses?

[8] See *Tax Facts 2*, **Question 410** – How is unearned income of a child treated for federal income tax purposes?

[9] This includes elementary and secondary education (K-12) at private, public, or religious institutions, and postsecondary education at accredited public, nonprofit, and proprietary institutions (college and graduate programs).

[10] Applies to state-sponsored programs. Earnings portion of distributions from private prepaid educational arrangements will be taxable until 2004.

[11] See *Tax Facts 2*, **Question 413** – How are distributions from a qualified tuition program taxed?

[12] See also, the table in Raymond D. Loewe, p. 178.

[13] EFC is used to determine need for assistance from the following types of student financial assistance: Federal Pell Grants; subsidized Federal Direct Stafford/Loans (made under the Direct Loan Program); subsidized Federal Stafford Loans (made under the Federal Family Education Loan [FFEL] Program); and assistance from the "campus-based" programs—Federal Supplemental Educational Opportunity Grants (FSEOG), Federal Perkins Loans, and Federal Work-Study (FWS).

[14] For an excellent explanation of the workings of these financial aids tests see Raymond D. Loewe, p. 35.

DISABILITY – THE LIVING DEATH

No financial plan can be considered complete unless there has been an evaluation of the risks of disability. *Planning to live* is as important as *planning to die*, and the risk is greater. For example, for a male age 40, long-term disability is 2.9 times more likely than death. And for a female age 40, long-term disability is 5.9 times more likely than death. See the table Risk Of Disability vs. Rick Of Death, page 306.

Before disability, most people are able to acquire savings to the extent income exceeds expenses. However, **after disability** caused by a sickness or injury, income will *fall* and expenses will *rise*.

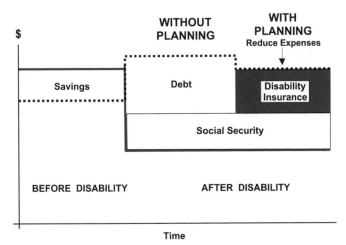

The expenses associated with a long-term disability can be devastating. With death, the funds required are those needed to support a surviving family. With disability, which is often referred to as "the living death," not only is there a need to provide for the family, but the living and medical expenses of the disabled person must also be provided. The advances of modern medicine and equipment, which have enabled many more people to survive crippling accidents and illnesses, have further added to the expenses of long-term care.

Without planning, the expenses of a disability can quickly exhaust the family's savings and create substantial debt. This is true despite the availability of Social Security after six months of continuous and total disability. For most people these payments will rarely fill the gap created between falling income and increasing expenses. When available, Social Security disability payments to a disabled wage earner with children will be substantially more than those to a disabled wage earner without children. The fact that a disabled wage earner is married – and often responsible for the financial needs of a spouse – does not result in an increase in

Social Security payments. Attempting to reduce expenses by selling personal possessions, a car, or even the family home, is unlikely to eliminate the substantial debt that is created by a long-term disability, the living death.

With planning, one of the cornerstones of any disability plan is disability insurance. Just as life insurance protects a family in case of the insured's death, disability income insurance protects *both* the insured and his family in case of the insured's disability. In addition, before disability strikes, the purchase of a comprehensive major medical expense plan offers one of the most effective ways of paying the major expenses of many disabilities. A waiver of premium rider on existing or new life insurance policies will provide for payment of premiums after a stated period of disability.

SOURCES OF INCOME PROTECTION

The main sources of disability income protection include:

- Individual disability income policy – page 308.

- Group coverage – page 313.

- Social Security disability benefits – page 314.

- Workers' compensation – page 315.

THE DISABILITY RISK

The risks of disability are real! For example, for a male age 40, the risk of a long-term disability is 2.9 times more likely than the risk of death. And for a female age 50, the risk of a long-term disability is 3.8 times more likely than the risk of death.

Risk Of Disability vs. Risk Of Death		
Age	Male	Female
25	4.0	7.5
30	4.0	7.6
35	3.3	7.1
40	2.9	5.9
45	2.3	4.7
50	2.3	3.8
55	1.9	2.9
60	1.8	2.6

Note: Disability is defined as lasting 90 days or more. The odds of disability versus the odds of death have been calculated using the 1985 CIDA actuarial update of the 1964 Commissioners Disability Table and the Commissioners 1980 Standard Ordinary Mortality Table.

Disability Statistics[1]

Odds This Year For Different Risks Covered By Insurance

1 out of 5 that your auto will be damaged in an accident (National Safety Council).

1 out of 21 that you will have a disabling accident (National Safety Council).

1 out of 96 that you will have a fire (National Safety Council).

1 out of 114 that you will die (World Almanac).

Income Lost Through Disability Is

2 times as great as *auto* accident losses.

3 times as great as *fire* losses.

Risk Of Disability Within Groups Of People

The following chart indicates the odds of at least one long-term (90-day) disability occurring before age 65 to any one person out of one, two, or three persons.

Chances out of 1,000 of Disability Occurring Prior to Age 65

Age of Each Person	To Any One Person	To Any One Person out of Any Two People	To Any One Person out of Any Three People
30	467	716	849
35	451	699	835
40	430	675	815
45	401	641	785
50	360	590	738

From the chart we can conclude, for example, that 43% of all people age 40 will have a long-term disability prior to age 65.

Long-Term Disabilities

If a long-term (90-day) disability has lasted two years, it will probably continue longer – even for life.

Age When Disabled For 90 Days	Percentage Of People Still Disabled At End Of 2 Years And 90 Days	Percentage Of People Still Disabled At End Of 5 Years And 90 Days
25	63.5%	44.2%
35	69.7	52.6
45	73.6	58.0
55	77.6	59.6

THE INDIVIDUAL DISABILITY INCOME POLICY

Unlike life insurance, disability insurance contracts can differ widely in defining when and how benefits are paid. For example, with few exceptions the insured's *death* will trigger payment of a fixed lump-sum life insurance death benefit to a designated beneficiary, with little more than presentation of a death certificate. In contrast, the insured's *disability* payment of benefits will depend upon determining the degree of disability suffered, the expiration of a waiting period, and possibly disability benefits received from other sources. Disability insurers are far more concerned than life insurers with protecting themselves against adverse claims experience and will carefully scrutinize claims received. Under these circumstances it is extremely important to carefully review and evaluate the terms of each disability income contract.

Who Can Get Coverage. Disability income insurance is generally not available to wealthy individuals, or those who have substantial unearned income. Because *women* experience substantially higher rates of disability, their premiums are typically much higher then those paid by *men* of the same age and in the same occupation. Applications for disability income insurance are carefully underwritten in order to accurately determine occupational classification and evaluate the applicant's medical history. Pre-existing medical conditions, that might be ignored when issuing life insurance, can serve as a basis for denying coverage or be excluded by policy rider. Financial underwriting is essential to determining both insurability and the appropriate amount of coverage according to the applicant's income. In summary, the underwriting process is generally very rigorous and the applicant would be well advised to assure that any application for disability income insurance is carefully and accurately completed.

Definition Of Disability. Generally, benefits are paid either upon the insured's total disability or the insured's residual (partial) disability.[2]

(1) **Total disability** can vary considerably between contracts and may generally be found to fit within one of the four following definitions.

    (a) **Own occupation** – this is the most liberal of definitions, costs the most, and pays if the insured is:

    "unable to perform, due to injury or sickness, the [substantial and material] duties of his regular occupation."[3]

    When applying for this coverage the applicant will be assigned an occupational classification. This is generally limited to professionals.

    (b) **Modified own occupation** – this is the same as "own occupation," but costs less and only pays if the insured remains unemployed:

"unable to perform, due to injury or sickness, the [substantial and material] duties of his regular occupation and must not be working in any gainful [or reasonable] occupation."

(c) **Short-term own occupation** – this offers "own occupation" coverage, but limited to a specified period of time, such as 2 years, 5 years, 10 years, or upon reaching a designated age short of age 65. It pays if the insured is:

"for the first 10 years of disability unable to perform, due to injury or sickness, the [substantial and material] duties of his regular occupation and must not be working in any gainful [or reasonable] occupation. Thereafter, the insured must be unable to work in any gainful [reasonable] occupation for which he is suited by education, training or experience [and with due regard to prior earnings]."

Once the specified period has been reached, further coverage is dependent upon the insured meeting the following "any gainful" test in paragraph (d) below.

(d) **Any gainful work** – also known as any occupation ("any occ") coverage, this is the least liberal of definitions, costs the least, and only pays if the insured is:

"unable to work in any gainful [reasonable] occupation for which he is suited by education, training or experience [and with due regard to prior earnings]."

Note that this definition is considerably less restrictive than that required for total disability under Social Security (page 314).

(2) **Residual disability**, also known as "partial disability," this pays a prorata disability income benefit. Rather than the insured facing an "all or nothing" dilemma, this provision allows the insured to go back to work at a reduced income without losing all disability benefits. It is generally accepted that a residual benefit actually encourages rehabilitation and a return to productive work. For example, it would pay if:

"as a result of injury or sickness the insured's loss of earnings is at least 20% of pre-disability earnings."

(a) **Additional requirements.** In addition to the requisite loss of income, more restrictive policies may also specifically require that the insured be under the care of a physician, and may require that the insured suffer a loss of time on the job, or the ability to perform certain duties.

(b) **When payable.** Most often a residual benefit is payable only after a period of total disability, but it can also be found as a stand-alone benefit (i.e., no prior total disability is required, just a defined percentage reduction of income). When a period of total disability is required before payment of a residual benefit, it is referred to as a *qualification* period. Of course, prior to payment of any benefit the policy's elimination period must be satisfied.

(c) **Amount payable.** The amount of benefits is in direct proportion to the income lost. For example, assume the insured's pre-disability income was $7,000 per month and the policy provided $4,000 per month of disability coverage. Assume also, that after returning to work the insured's earnings are reduced to $4,200 per month, 40% less than earnings before disability $((7,000 - 4,200) \div 7,000 = .40))$. This 40% loss of income produces a residual benefit of $1,600 $(4,000 \times .40 = 1,600)$.

(d) **Minimum benefit.** Most residual disability provisions provide a minimum benefit over a specific period of time (e.g., with loss of earnings between 20% and 50% the benefit paid for the first six months would be 50% of the disability benefit, thereafter the requisite percentage). Also, residual disability provisions typically assume that the insured is totally disabled if the loss of earnings is more than 80% (i.e., full benefits would be paid provided the insured earned less than 20% of pre-disability income).

Benefit Period. This is the length of time that benefits will be paid once the elimination period has been satisfied. Typical benefit periods are 2, 5, and 10 years, or to-age-65. Lifetime and to-age-70 benefit periods are also found. Although most disabilities tend not to last more than one year, a benefit to-age-65 is generally preferred, provided the premium is affordable. The longer benefit protects against the catastrophic losses than can occur with a long-term disability.

Benefit Amount. On average, most insurers will provide an amount of coverage that will allow replacement of approximately 60% of gross earned income before taxes. However, at lower income levels this can be as high as 70-75%, and at higher income levels it can be 30%

Digging Deeper

A handy online calculator can be found at: www.smart money.com/insurance/ disability.

or lower. Included in earned income are salary, commissions, fees, bonuses, and other such forms of compensation for services performed.

Elimination Period. Also called a "waiting period," this is the amount of time, typically 30 days, 60 days, 90 days, 120 days, 180 days, 270 days, or a year or more, that must lapse before benefits are paid. The shorter the waiting period, the higher the premiums. Provided the insured has sufficient resources to self-insure the first three months of a disability, a minimum 90-day elimination period is generally the most cost efficient.

Renewal Provisions. These provisions provide for both the *period* that a contract will remain in force and the *premiums* that will be paid.

(1) **Noncancelable.** Also referred to as a "noncan policy," when a policy is noncancelable the insured individual has a right to continue the policy at a set premium up to a specified age. The insurer does not have a right to either increase the premium or "non-renew" the policy. Typically found with "own occupation" coverage, these policies can be very expensive and have often resulted in adverse claims experience for insurers. Despite this, noncancelable policies are generally available and are attractive for those insureds who can afford the higher premiums.

(2) **Guaranteed renewable.** Under a guaranteed renewable contract, the insurer has a right to increase premiums, but any increase must be done with respect to an underwriting class (i.e., premiums cannot be increased as to a specific insured). Justifications for rate increases must be filed with state insurance departments. Provided the insured pays the premiums as they come due, the contract is guaranteed renewable until the age specified in the policy.

(3) **Conditionally renewable.** This provision is most often found with insureds who are in high-risk occupations and require certain conditions be met for continued coverage (e.g., that the insureds remain in full-time employment). Premiums may also be increased.

Waiver Of Premium. Unlike the typically life insurance policy, a waiver of premium benefit is included in virtually all disability income policies. Premiums are most often waived once the insured has been disabled for 90 days, but some policies waive premiums only after the elimination period has been satisfied. Premiums paid during disability are typically refunded once benefits begin to be paid.

Presumptive Disability. Under this provision, if the insured suffers the loss of two limbs, eyesight, speech, or hearing, he is presumed to be totally disabled, and full benefits are paid without an elimination period being satisfied. This is most often found as part of the basic policy, although it is occasionally available as an optional rider.

Preexisting Conditions. These conditions, both physical and mental, can result in higher premiums being charged, an exclusion from the policy, or a denial of coverage. If an applicant fails to disclose a preexisting condition on the application, the insurer is generally able to deny a claim made within the contestability period (2 years in most states). However, beyond two years, the insurer may still able to deny a claim if it can be shown that the insured had an intention to defraud. To avoid such "post-claims underwriting," it is important for an applicant to make full disclosure of all prior medical conditions. Again, unlike life insurance, with disability income insurance, insurers often engage in post claims investigations in order to determine the validity of claims.

Optional Benefits And Riders. Enhancements to the disability income policy are often available with the use of various optional riders. Although these riders are referred to as the "bells and whistles" of disability coverage, careful attention should be paid to them. Some are very desirable, but can substantially increase the premium (e.g., the guaranteed insurability option and the cost-of-living provision). Others may not be as desirable, yet may be attractive to specific individuals (e.g., the premium refund feature).

Increased Benefits. There are essentially two ways in which additional monthly benefits can be obtained in order to keep up with increasing cost-of-living:

(1) **Pre-disability** purchases of additional benefits without evidence of insurability by either:

   (a) **Automatic increases** in coverage each year that are tied to the consumer price index or other appropriate measure. The insured is required to pay an additional premium but is allowed to refuse the increased coverage (but continued refusals may terminate future automatic increases).

   (b) **Guaranteed insurability** that provides options to purchase substantial additional coverage at specific times without evidence of insurability, subject only to showing that the insured's current income supports the increased coverage.

(2) **Post-disability** increases of benefits through a **cost-of-living** provision under which benefits are periodically increased for inflation based upon either a fixed rate of increase or the consumer price index. Also referred

to as a "cost-of-living-adjustment (COLA)," this provision can be very expensive. Benefit increases can be either in terms of a simple rate (lower benefits) or a compound rate (higher benefits). Benefits may also be subject to a maximum increase or cap.

Social Security Offset Rider. In order to prevent over-insurance, the maximum benefit that insurers will issue generally assumes that the insured will receive some form of government disability benefits. However, many disabled individuals are denied these benefits (page 314). The Social Security offset rider assures an additional specified benefit, but reduced by any benefits from a social benefit program such as Social Security or workers' compensation (i.e., the insured is guaranteed to receive the benefit, either from the rider or the social benefit program, but not from both). Other less satisfactory approaches to a reduction or elimination of the benefits are also used, such as a rider that totally eliminates benefits if any Social Security disability benefits are received (e.g., "all or nothing").[4]

Premium Refund. This rider appears to be designed for those individuals who believe they are unlikely to become disabled, and are willing to pay additional premiums to have a return of premiums. Essentially this rider provides a benefit at stipulated future dates, but reduced by any claims paid under the policy. By providing policy equity the rider is similar to the cash values of a life insurance contract, but unlike cash value life insurance, the equity is contingent upon the amount of claims the insured makes under the policy. Typically the rider will provide a percentage return of premium based upon the insured's age at issue and the years the policy has been in force. For example, assuming an issue age 40, upon surrender of the policy the rider might return 20% of premiums after 8 years, 50% of premiums after 15 years, or 100% of premiums after 25 years, all reduced by any benefits paid.

GROUP COVERAGE

This coverage is available both as an employer-provided benefit to employees and as a benefit plan for affinity groups (e.g., members of professional associations). When employer-provided, the employer owns the contract and pays the premiums, meaning that benefits received by employees are taxable income (page 318). Group disability income insurance is less expensive than individual policies but the benefits amounts are typically lower and shorter in duration (e.g., 6 months to 2 years). Group disability has the advantages of little or no underwriting. Group insurance is generally not guaranteed renewable and is not portable when the insured leaves his employment or the affinity group. Likewise, group disability generally cannot be tailored to the needs of a particular insured.

SOCIAL SECURITY DISABILITY BENEFITS

In 2003, after six months of total and continuous disability, the maximum Social Security disability benefit a typical wage earner could expect ranges from $1,852 per month (age 60) to $1,985 per month (age 25). With a spouse and children this maximum benefit ranges from $2,777 to $2,978 per month. The specific amount of payment depends upon age when disabled and previous contributions to the system.[5] Social Security disability payments are taxed the same as Social Security retirement payments (see Taxation Of Benefits, page 393).

Digging Deeper

Information on the Social Security and Supplemental Security Income disability programs can be obtained at: www.ssa.gov/disability.

In order to qualify for Social Security disability benefits an applicant must meet *all* nine of the following tests:

(1) He is fully insured by: (a) accumulating 40 quarters of coverage (a total of ten years of covered work); or (b) accumulating at least six quarters of coverage provided he has acquired at least as many quarters of coverage as there are years elapsing after 1950 (or, if later, after the year in which he reaches age 21) and before the year in which he becomes disabled.

(2) He has worked under Social Security for at least five of the 10 years (20 out of 40 quarters) just before becoming disabled, or if disability begins before age 31 but after age 23, for at least one-half of the quarters after reaching age 21 and before becoming disabled (but not less than six).

(3) He is unable to engage in "any substantial gainful work that exists in the national economy," whether or not such work exists in the area, a specific vacancy exists, or the applicant would be hired if he or she applied for the work (however, consideration is given to age, education, and work experience).

(4) Such inability results from "a medically determinable physical or mental impairment" which is expected to result in death, or which has lasted (or can be expected to last) for a continuous period of not less than 12 months. A special definition of the term "disability" is provided for individuals age 55 or over who are blind.

(5) He is under 65 years of age.

(6) He has filed an application.

(7) He has furnished the required proof of disability.

(8) He has fulfilled a five-month waiting period.

(9) He accepts state vocational rehabilitation services or has good cause for refusal.

WORKERS' COMPENSATION

These are state administered programs intended to provide medical, rehabilitative, lump-sum, and disability benefits for employees who suffer job-related illnesses and injuries. Both the amount and the length of disability benefits differ from state to state, but benefits will generally replace approximately 70% of income for workers making up to $25,000 or $30,000 per year. Employees with higher incomes have a lower percentage of their income replaced. The biggest disadvantage of workers' compensation is that benefits are only paid for job-related injuries, *off the job disabilities are not covered.*

BUSINESS APPLICATIONS

In addition to disability income insurance, the owners of a business should consider funding their buy/sell agreements with disability buy-out insurance. Also, business overhead expense insurance can provide for payment of specific business expenses during a period of disability.

Disability Buy-Out Insurance. Disability buy-out insurance is designed to provide funds for the purchase of a disabled owner's interest in a corporation or partnership after an extended period of permanent and total disability. The benefits of such insurance include:

(1) Providing funds for the purchase, which funds are not tied to the continued success of the business; and

(2) Assuring that the disabled owner will no longer be a drain on business income and assets. See also, the discussion of business overhead expense insurance on page 316.

A business is usually not eligible for coverage until it has been in existence for two years, although exceptions can be found (e.g., professional corporations). Maximum amounts of coverage typically range from $300,000 to $1,000,000, with specific amounts limited to a percentage of the owner's interest (e.g., 80% of fair market value). As with disability income insurance, definitions of disability vary widely, from inability to engage in one's "own occupation," to inability to perform the duties of "any other occupation" for which one is reasonably suited. It is absolutely essential that the provisions of the purchase agreement be consistent with the definitions and terms of the disability buy-out policy.

Because a disabled individual's chances of recovery are highest in the early months of his disability, the waiting period is extended and typically lasts from 12 months to three years (see The Disability Risk, page 306). This attempts to avoid the forced sale of a business interest while the disabled owner might reasonably expect to return to work. Benefits are paid to the "loss payee," who is that individual or business entity having the contractual obligation to purchase the disabled owner's interest (i.e., entity purchase or cross purchase). Payment of proceeds can vary from lump sum to installment, with lump sum having the advantage of simplicity, but losing the tax advantage of spreading gain over a number of years.

Successive disabilities can cause a problem when the insured returns to work after being disabled for less than the waiting period, and thereafter suffers a second period of disability. Some policies require satisfaction of a new waiting period, while others consider both disabilities to be "continuous," provided the gap between them does not exceed a certain period. If the insured recovers after the end of the waiting period, but prior to the last indemnity payment, some policies will stop all future payments, while others disregard the recovery and make payments as originally scheduled (i.e., a form of "presumptive" disability).

Although the premiums are not tax deductible, the benefits are received tax-free by the loss payee.[6] As with any other lifetime sale of a business interest, the disabled owner is subject to capital gains taxation of any gain on the sale of his business interest.

Business Overhead Expense Insurance. Business overhead expense insurance is designed to provide funds to cover overhead expenses during a business owner's disability. Business overhead expense insurance is intended to help maintain the business; it is not intended to replace disability income insurance or disability buy-out insurance.

(1) *Covered expenses* include those that are tax deductible to the business. Typically, these expenses include employee salaries; utilities; professional fees; rent; mortgage payments; lease payments for furniture and equipment; premiums for health, property, and liability insurance; and fees for laundry, janitorial, and maintenance services. Not included are the insured's salary, salaries of co-workers who perform the same duties as the insured, salaries of family members, and depreciation.

(2) *Monthly benefits* are paid upon the insured's total and continuous disability, and are limited to a maximum amount. Partial disability benefits are also available. During disability, a "carry-forward" provision allows unused benefits to be carried forward from month to month. Extension of the benefit period allows unused benefits to be received beyond the original benefit period.

(3) *Waiting periods* are typically either 30, 60, or 90 days. The cash flow requirements of the business are considered when selecting an appropriate waiting period.

(4) *Benefit periods* are typically limited to 12, 18, or 24 months. Limited benefit periods assume that the insured will dispose of the business interest if disability lasts longer then the benefit period (see Disability Buy-Out Insurance, page 315).

(5) *Optional coverages* are often similar to individual disability income policies (e.g., partial disability riders, guaranteed insurability riders, and lump-sum survivor benefits). Other optional coverages are unique to business overhead expense insurance (e.g., a professional replacement rider covering the cost of hiring someone to perform the insured's duties).

(6) *Eligible businesses* include regular corporations, S corporations, limited liability companies, partnerships, and sole proprietorships. The business must have been in operation for a minimum period of time (e.g., 3 years). The business cannot have more than a specific number of owners (e.g., 5 professionals working in the business). This requirement recognizes that a substantial loss of revenue is less likely if the business has a large number of owner-employees. There are specific issue ages and medical underwriting requirements; and the insured must be actively at work full time (e.g., a minimum of 30 hours per week).

(7) Premiums are deductible as a business expense. Although the proceeds are taxable, they are used for tax-deductible business expenses (i.e., taxable proceeds are offset by deductible business expenses).[7]

TAXATION

As a general rule, when *premiums* are deductible, the *benefits* are taxable; and when premiums come from after-tax income, the benefits are received free of income taxes.[8] Disability income payments under an employer's plan are included in gross income and are fully taxable to the disabled employee, including both pre-retirement and post-retirement payments.[9] However, if the payments have been received under a plan to which the employee has contributed part of the premium, that portion of the benefit attributable to the employee's contributions will be received free of income taxes. The tax treatment is the same, whether such payments are characterized as disability payments, salary continuation, wage continuation, or sick pay.

Taxation Of Premiums & Benefits		
	Premium	**Benefits**
Policy Purchased By Individual Insured.	Not deductible.	Income tax-free.
Employer-Provided Disability Income Plan.[10]	Premium deductible by employer and *not included* in employee's income.	Generally taxable to employee, but limited tax credit may be available (see below).
	Premium deductible by employer and *included* in employee's income.	Income tax-free to employee.
Group DI Coverage Provided By Employer.	Premium deductible by employer and *not included* in employee's income (if self-insured plan the benefit paid is deductible by employer).	Generally taxable to employee, but limited tax credit may be available (see below).
Disability Buy-Out Insurance.	Not deductible.	Income tax-free.
Business Overhead Expense Insurance.	Deductible.	Benefit taxable, but expense paid should be deductible.
Workers' Compensation.	Deductible to employer and not taxable to employee.	Generally income tax-free.
Social Security.	Employer portion of Social Security tax not taxable to employee, employee's portion comes from after-tax income.	Subject to income taxation (page 393).

Tax Credit. Under some circumstances, there is a tax *credit* available to individuals who are: (1) age 65 or older; or (2) under age 65 and retired on permanent and total disability. The credit is equal to 15% of the taxpayer's "Section 22" amount of income for the year: $5,000 for single taxpayers or married taxpayers filing jointly when only one spouse qualifies for the credit (i.e., $750 credit), and $7,500 for married taxpayers when both qualify for the credit (i.e., $1,125 credit). If the taxpayer is under age 65, the base amount is limited to the amount of taxable disability income.

The base amount used to figure the credit must also be reduced: (1) for nontaxable pension or disability benefits received under social security, railroad retirement, and certain other nontax laws; and (2) by one-half of the amount by which adjusted gross income exceeds $7,500 for single taxpayers, and $10,000 for married taxpayers filing jointly. The impact of these rules means that *no credit is available* if a taxpayer receives more than the following amounts of income:

	Nontaxable Social Security, pension, or disability benefits	*or*	Adjusted gross income
Single	$ 5,000		$ 17,500
Married filing jointly with one spouse qualified*	5,000		20,000
Married filing jointly with both spouses qualified*	7,500		25,000

*qualified individual is one who is either age 65 or older, or under age 65 and retired on permanent and total disability.

---

[1] Figures are based upon the Commissioners Disability Table and the Commissioners 1980 Standard Ordinary Mortality Table.

[2] For an excellent discussion of the definitions of disability as used in disability income contracts, see Jeff Sadler, *Disability Income: The Sale, The Product, The Market,* 2nd ed. (Cincinnati: The National Underwriter Company, 1995), pp. 131-143.

[3] The bracketed language in this and the following paragraphs is the alternate language used by some disability insurers, but its use appears to result in the same coverage.

[4] See Jeff Sadler, p. 168.

[5] A more complete description of coverage, benefits, and benefit computations is contained in *Social Security Manual* (Cincinnati: The National Underwriter Company, 2003, revised annually), pp. 75-85 (paragraphs E-12 thru E-28).

[6] See *Tax Facts 1,* (Cincinnati: The National Underwriter Company, 2003, revised annually), **Question 229** – If disability insurance is purchased on the lives of business owners to fund a disability buy-out, what are the tax results?

[7] See *Tax Facts 1,* **Question 228** – Are premiums paid for "overhead expense" insurance deductible as a business expense?

[8] See *Tax Facts 1,* **Question 190** – Are premiums paid for personal health insurance deductible as medical expenses? and **Question 191** – Are the benefits received under a personal health insurance policy taxable income?

[9] See *Tax Facts 1,* **Question 196** – Are payments received by employees under employer-provided accident or health insurance taxable income?

[10] For a detailed description and chart of the disability income plan, see Donald F. Cady, *Field Guide To Estate Planning, Business Planning, & Employee Benefits* (Cincinnati: The National Underwriter Company, 2003, revised annually), p. 252.

OVERVIEW

As a result of individuals *retiring earlier* and *living longer* the average retiree will spend roughly one-third of his or her adult life in retirement. The proverbial "golden years" of retirement have now become the "golden decades." While the clear objective of most individuals is to have financial independence in their retirement years while maintaining their customary pre-retirement standard of living, designing, implementing and monitoring a plan to meet this objective is not easy.

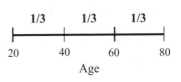

Unfortunately, there are many factors at work that complicate the retirement planning process:

(1) Comprehensive retirement planning is multidimensional; it requires consideration of a diverse array of lifestyle choices involving health care, housing, income, and estate planning issues.

(2) Individuals have enhanced expectations regarding their retirement lifestyle. Today's retirees expect to lead active lives with a full array of medical services and benefits.

(3) The ability of individuals to accumulate sufficient assets to fill the retirement income shortfall has been negatively affected by frequent job changes that reduce retirement benefits; forced early retirements that shorten earnings years; demands for funds to educate children born of late marriages; care-giving of aged parents that reduces income when the caregiver stops working; easily-obtained second mortgages that reduce home equity; and stock market losses that deplete investments.

(4) Upon retirement many individuals lack the investment management skills required to effectively reposition and invest assets for the "long haul."

(5) Financial independence, both before and after retirement, is not merely a matter of earning the most, or even saving the most. It requires a discipline and commitment to live within one's means.

(6) Spending, saving, and investment decisions made years before retirement will directly impact an individual's ability to meet his or her retirement goals. Therefore, in order to realize these goals *planning must begin years before retirement*.

THE RETIREMENT INCOME SHORTFALL

Determining whether there is a retirement income shortfall, or gap, requires first calculating income needs at retirement, then determining likely sources and amounts of income at retirement, and finally comparing income needs with projected income. This process would be relatively straightforward if it were reserved for those clients about to retire in a world of no inflation, on fixed incomes from guaranteed investment returns, and with years in retirement determined precisely by actuarial tables. But in the real world these factors are variables; they are not constants.

Credibility Is Important. Accurately projecting income needs in retirement can be challenging. In the years *immediately before retirement* it is easier to estimate retirement needs but more difficult to do anything about a projected income shortfall (other than reduce the retirement expenses or increase the retirement age). When a client is *years from retirement* it is often difficult to come up with a meaningful estimate of retirement needs. In fact, it is often difficult for the client to accept the calculated current savings that are required in order to fill the retirement income shortfall. For example, a new Volvo sedan that cost approximately $3,000 in 1973 is priced at over $30,000 in 2003 – admittedly with many enhancements, but still with just four wheels. It is doubtful that today's 60-year-old would have believed in 1973 that a car then costing $3,000 would cost $30,000 in 2003. Projecting the same price increases 30 years into the future tell us that a car will cost $300,000 in the year 2033. Likewise, projecting the impact of inflation on retirement income 20, 30 or 40 years in the future can produce figures so large as to cause the process to lose credibility. *A process that lacks credibility will fail to change behavior.*

Periodic Monitoring Is Essential. We do not live in a world of constants, but rather we live in a world of constantly changing variables. Planning for retirement is an ongoing process that must adjust to these changes. Periodic monitoring provides a "reality check" on the client's progress toward a safe and secure retirement. In case of a projected shortfall additional savings may be required. Absent an increase in savings, or a change in investment strategy, the client may have to reduce his or her retirement expectations (e.g., delay retirement, downsize the retirement home, or locate to a less expensive community).

Calculating The Retirement Income Shortfall. There is no perfect method for calculating retirement needs, shortfalls, and savings requirements. It is unlikely that a process requiring twice as much data, or involving twice as many steps, will be twice as accurate. Even if it is conceded that securing more data will result in greater accuracy, this must be balanced against the likelihood that fewer clients will "sit still" for the process. Current savings requirements should be based upon realistic retirement objectives using a process *understood* by the client that produces results *accepted* by the client.

The following seven-step planner attempts to achieve both accuracy and usability while striking a balance between detail and simplicity. Income requirements, sources of income, and required savings are all reduced to monthly amounts (most individuals more easily relate to monthly cash flow). Where simplicity produces less than total mathematical accuracy, the process defaults to the more conservative result (e.g., the accompanying table, Increase-In-Savings Factors on pages 334-335, assumes monthly savings but end-year crediting of interest). Two approaches to determining income requirements are offered, the *replacement ratio method* and the *expense method*.

Remember, these calculations are not an end in themselves, but rather a means of moving a client to action, whether that action is allocating more income to savings, becoming more or less aggressive with respect to investment decisions, or planning for a delayed retirement and scaled down lifestyle.

The Steps. The following seven steps, as set forth on pages 326-333, are designed to determine the required current monthly savings that will meet a future retirement income objective. The tables used do not provide for preservation of capital, therefore they contain built-in conservative assumptions. Likewise, in establishing retirement objectives it would be well to err on the conservative side, by assuming greater longevity, higher income needs, and lower rates of return. The calculations allow for considering the impact of both inflation and taxes.

> **Step 1 – Assumptions & Factors To Be Used.** From current age, retirement age, and assumed age of death two important factors are determined – years *to* retirement and years *in* retirement. Selecting an anticipated rate of inflation allows determination of the inflation factor (line 7), fixed-income factor (line 15), and assets-to-income factor (line 16). Rates of return before and after retirement (lines 8 and 14) allow selection of appropriate accumulation factors (lines 9, 10, and 16). When estimating income required at retirement (line 13) one of two approaches can be taken:
>
> a. **Expense method.** This is the "long-form" approach and is probably more accurate than the replacement ratio method (see below). It is best used when a person is close to retirement age. However, there is no guarantee the results will be any more or less accurate than the replacement ratio method, particularly when projecting retirement costs years into the future. An estimate must be made with regard to those expenses that will either increase or decrease in retirement. *Increased expenses* include medical expenses, health care insurance premiums, care of aging parents, and travel and entertainment expenses. *Decreased expenses* might include education costs, life insurance premiums, and clothing. See the Retirement Needs Worksheet, page 337.

b. **Replacement ratio method.** This is the "short-form" approach. It is generally considered less accurate but is much easier to use with individuals not yet on the verge of retirement. Generally a 70% to 90% replacement ratio of the client's final average salary. See the table of Income Replacement Ratios, page 336.

Step 2 – Inflation Adjusted Income. These are income sources, such as Social Security retirement benefits; whose value today can be estimated and future increases are either keyed to or will likely keep up with inflation (both from today to retirement and after retirement). In step 6 (line 54) these income sources will be subtracted from income needs without inflation adjustments.

Step 3 – Income From Current Assets. These are the value of current assets (and plans) whose value today is either known or can be reasonably estimated, and whose future growth will equal the rate of return before retirement on line 8. These include both tax deferred and currently taxed assets.

Step 4 – Income From Future Savings. In contrast to the current assets reflected in step 4, these are future amounts intended to be saved on a periodic basis. For example, the current value of a retirement plan might be entered in step 3, but intended future contributions would be entered in step 4.

Step 5 – Fixed Income & Amounts Payable At Retirement. These assets or resources are not expected to be available until retirement but their value, either income stream or lump sum amount, is known or can be estimated today.

Step 6 – Retirement Cash Flow. This step is where everything is brought together in order to determine whether there is a retirement income shortfall. The inflation-adjusted income from step 2 is first subtracted from the income requirement at retirement (in today's dollars). Assuming there is an income requirement, the results are multiplied by an inflation factor in order to determine the income need in retirement age dollars. From this amount is subtracted the income streams available from current assets (step 3), future savings (step 4), and fixed amounts payable at retirement (step 5). Allowance is also made for subtracting other potential sources of income (line 58d). The balance equals the retirement income shortfall.

Step 7 – Required Savings. Assuming there is a retirement income shortfall, this step first determines the additional capital required at retirement to meet this shortfall (line 62). The annual and monthly savings required to provide this additional capital are then calculated (lines 64 and 66). However, it may be unrealistic to expect many individuals to commitment to a high-level savings program to meet retirement needs many years in the future. If that is the case, then the final calculation in step 7 produces a lower initial monthly savings, assuming savings are increased each year thereafter by 5%, 6% or 7% (line 69). Note that in the example on page 333 this has reduced the monthly savings from $1,042 to $631 per month. However, in this regard "the earlier the better," as can be seen from the Early Saver vs. Late Saver table on page 398.

Real World Considerations. In Step 1, assumed "composite" rates of return were entered on line 8 (before retirement) and line 14 (after retirement). Although necessary for purposes of illustration, it is important to recognize that over the years investors rarely, if ever, receive a composite rate of return (one exception being the investor who purchases and holds to maturity a 30-year Treasury bond). In some years rates of return will be higher, in some years rates of return will be lower, and in some years rates of return will be negative (i.e., much, much lower). See the discussion titled "Surviving A Bear Market," page 143. See also, the discussion of standard deviation at page 36.

On lines 33-35 of Step 4 it is assumed that the investor's current savings will be continued at the same amount until retirement. On line 66 of Step 7 the monthly savings required is assumed to be constant from today until retirement. On line 69 of Step 7 the monthly savings are assumed to increase each year at a rate of 5%, 6%, or 7% (from line 11). Although necessary for purposes of illustration, it is important to again recognize that rarely, if ever, do investors save at a constant rate of return over the years. Despite their best intentions, most investors tend to do the bulk of their retirement savings later in life, generally due to rising income and decreasing expenses. Unfortunately, the reality of college costs (page 281) often overcomes the advantages of saving early for retirement (page 398).

In attempting to overcome the retirement income gap, investors may be tempted to make high-risk investments in hopes of gaining higher returns. In this regard it is absolutely essential to recognize the types of risks an investor faces (page 16) and the need to balance these risks (see Modern Portfolio Theory, page 21).

Calculating The Retirement Income Shortfall

Step 1 - Assumptions & Factors To Be Used

line		Example	Notes
1	Current Age:	45	
2	Retirement Age:	67	A
3	Years To Retirement (line 2 - line 1):	22	
4	Assumed Age At Death:	90	
5	Years In Retirement (line 4 - line 2):	23	B
6	Inflation Rate:	5%	C
7	Inflation Factor:	2.9253	D

Before Retirement

line		Example	Notes
8	Rate Of Return:	8%	E
9	Growth Factor:	5.4365	F
10	Accumulation Factor:	55.4568	G

A – In addition to determining Years To Retirement the projected Retirement Age is relevant in determining Social Security retirement benefits (see page 341).

B – The tables assume that assets are depleted in retirement. Be conservative in assessing the number of years in retirement (i.e., project more rather then less years).

C – Enter 3%, 4%, or 5%. Used on lines 7, 15 and 16.

D – Obtain from **Future Value Table - One Dollar Principal** on page 456 using years to retirement (line 3) and inflation rate (line 6). Used on line 56.

E – This should be a composite rate of return. If using table on pages 456-457 to determine growth factor on line 9 this entry must be an even rate from 3% to 15%. Used on lines 9, 10 and 12.

F – Obtain from **Future Value Table - One Dollar Principal** on page 456 using years to retirement (line 3) and rate of return (line 8). Used on line 24.

G – Obtain from **Future Value Table - One Dollar Per Annum (End Of Year)** on page 460 using years to retirement (line 3) and rate of return (line 8). Used on lines 36 and 63.

Calculating The Retirement Income Shortfall

Step 1 - Assumptions & Factors To Be Used (cont'd)

Before Retirement (cont'd)

line			Example	Notes
11	Percent Increase In Savings (Per Year):	_____	6%	H
12	Increase In Savings Factor:	_____	.00091	I

Upon & After Retirement

13	Income Required At Retirement:	_____	4,500	J
14	Rate Of Return:	_____	6%	K
15	Fixed Income Factor:	_____	.61578	L
16	Assets-To-Income Factor:	_____	.00401	M
17	Percent Retained After-Tax:	_____	80%	N

H – Enter 5%, 6%, or 7%. If there is a retirement income shortfall, this is the amount that savings could be increased each year to provide for retirement. Used on line 12.

I – Obtain from **Increase-In-Savings Factors** table on pages 334-335 using years to retirement (line 3), rate of return (line 8) and percent increase in savings (line 11). Used on line 68.

J – Obtain from either **Income Replacement Ratios** table on page 336 or **Retirement Needs Worksheet - Expense Method** on page 337. Used on line 53.

K – Enter composite rate of return of 4%, 5%, 6%, 7%, 8%, or 9%. Used on line 16.

L – Obtain from **Fixed Income Factors** table on page 338 using years in retirement (line 5) and inflation rate (line 6). Used on line 44.

M – Obtain from **Assets-To-Income Factors** on pages 339-340 using years in retirement (line 5), inflation rate (line 6), and rate of return (line 14). This factor is needed to calculate monthly withdrawals from a given asset accumulation. In order to keep pace with inflation after the first year the table assumes withdrawals are increased at a rate equal to the rate of inflation (i.e., at 3%, 4%, or 5%). Used on lines 28, 38, 48 and 61.

N – This is the 1 minus the anticipated effective rate of tax in retirement. For example, if the effective rate of tax were assumed to be 20%, then enter 80% (1 - .20 = .80). The *effective* rate of tax is generally less than the *maximum* tax rate; see **Federal Income Tax Rates** on page 451. Used on lines 20, 30, 40 and 51.

Calculating The Retirement Income Shortfall

Step 2 – Inflation Adjusted Income

line		Example	Notes
18a	Social Security Retirement Benefit	1,650	O
18b	Employer Retirement Plan	1,000	P
18c			P
18d			P
18e			P
19	Total: Inflation Adjusted Income – Before-Tax (sum lines 18a -18e)	2,650	Q
20	Times: Percent Retained After-Tax (line 17)	.80	R
21	Equals: Inflation Adjusted Income – After-Tax	2,120	

O – Obtain figure from **Social Security Retirement Benefits** table on page 341. A Benefit Estimate Statement can also be obtained from the Social Security Administration by calling 1-800-772-1213 or visiting www.ssa.gov. Remember, you don't have to project growth of benefit to retirement age since the benefit amount will subtracted from today's dollar need.

P – Enter here only if the plan provides a post-retirement annual inflation adjustment (if plan provides a fixed income enter it on line 42). Obtain from employer. Should be in today's dollars since at line 54 this will be subtracted from today's dollar need. Future merit and promotional salary increases are not considered since it is likely these increases will be offset by an increased standard of living, both before and after retirement.

Q – The underlying assumption is that items entered here will increase at a rate that keeps pace with both pre-retirement and post-retirement inflation. By subtracting out here, any retirement age shortage will already have accounted for inflation-adjusted income.

R – This should be adjusted for income not taxed. For example, if the effective rate is 20% and the only entry is a Social Security Retirement Benefit, only one-half of which is taxed, then this figure should be 90% (1.00 - (.20 x .50) = .90). See discussion of taxation of Social Security on page 393.

Calculating The Retirement Income Shortfall

Step 3 – Income From Current Assets

line			Example	Notes
22a	401(k) Plan		35,000	S
22b	Investment Property		145,000	S
22c				S
22d				S
22e				S
22f				S
22g				S
23	Total: Current Assets (sum lines 22a – 22g)		180,000	
24	Times: Growth Factor (line 9)		5.4365	
25	Equals: Retirement Value Before Conversion Costs		978,570	
26	Less: Conversion Costs		(25,000)	T
27	Equals: Retirement Value Of Current Assets		953,570	
28	Times: Assets-To-Income Factor (line 16)		.00401	U
29	Equals: Income From Current Assets – Before-Tax		3,824	
30	Times: Percent Retained After-Tax (line 17)		.80	V
31	Equals: Income From Current Assets – After-Tax		3,059	

S – Enter current value of assets to be used for retirement income. Do not consider future contributions, this will be calculated in Step 4.

T – This includes items such as real estate fees, fix-up expenses, and other such expenses to covert property to cash. Do not include income taxes, unless they exceed the amount considered in line 30, in which case some additional tax cost might be included on line 26.

U – This is inflation adjusted (i.e., more income is received each year). See the expanded explanation at the bottom of page 339.

V – This should be adjusted upward if line 29 contains after-tax funds (i.e., any after-tax income will not again be taxed and should not be reduced by line 30).

Calculating The Retirement Income Shortfall

Step 4 – Income From Future Savings

line			Example	Notes
32a	401(k) Plan		150	W
32b	Mutual Funds		175	W
32c				W
32d				W
32e				W
32f				W
32g				W
33	Total: Future Monthly Savings			
	(sum lines 32a – 32g)		325	
34	Times: Months In Year	12	12	
35	Equals: Future Annual Savings		3,900	
36	Times: Accumulation Factor (line 10)		55.4568	X
37	Equals: Retirement Value Of Future Savings		216,282	
38	Times: Assets-To-Income Factor (line 16)		.00401	Y
39	Equals: Income From Future Savings – Before-Tax		867	
40	Times: Percent Retained After-Tax (line 17)		.80	Z
41	Equals: Income From Future Savings – After-Tax		694	

W – Enter currently scheduled (planned) contributions. This would also include employer matching contributions.

X – The accumulation factor assumes that the amount on line 35 is saved at the end of the year.

Y – This is inflation adjusted (i.e., more income is received each year).

Z – This should be adjusted upward if line 39 contains after-tax funds (i.e., any after-tax income will not again be taxed and should not be reduced by line 40).

Calculating The Retirement Income Shortfall

Step 5 – Fixed Income & Amounts Payable At Retirement

line		Example	Notes
	Fixed Income		
42a	Fixed Annuity	567	AA
42b			AA
42c			AA
42d			AA
42e			AA
43	Total: Fixed Income (sum lines 42a - 42e)	567	
44	Times: Fixed Income Factor (line 15)	.61578	
45	Equals: Inflation Adjusted Fixed Income – Before-Tax	349	
	Fixed Amount		
46a	Payment Of Note	15,000	BB
46b			
46c			
47	Total Fixed Amount: (sum lines 46a - 46c)	15,000	
48	Times: Assets-To-Income Factor (line 16)	.00401	CC
49	Equals: Inflation Adjusted Income From Fixed Amount – Before-Tax	60	
50	Total Inflation Adjusted Income – Before-Tax (line 45 plus line 49)	409	
51	Times: Percent Retained After-Tax (line 17)	.80	DD
52	Equals: Inflation Adjusted Income – After-Tax	327	

AA – Before tax. Other examples include income from a private annuity or installment sale.

BB – These amounts were not entered on line 22 since they are fixed amounts payable at retirement. Examples might be: (1) expected inheritance, (2) proceeds from sale of a business, (3) severance payment, and (4) repayment of note.

CC – This is inflation adjusted (i.e., take out more each year).

DD – This should be adjusted upward if line 50 contains after-tax funds (i.e., any after-tax income will not again be taxed and should not be reduced by line 51).

Calculating The Retirement Income Shortfall

Step 6 – Retirement Cash Flow

line			Example	Notes
53	Income Required At Retirement (line 13)	_____	4,500	EE
54	Less: Inflation Adjusted Income – After-Tax (line 21)	_____	(2,120)	
55	Equals: Income Required in Today's Dollars	_____	2,380	EE
56	Times: Inflation Factor (line 7)	_____	2.9253	FF
57	Equals: Income Required In Retirement Age Dollars	_____	6,962	
58a	Less: Income From Current Assets (line 31)	_____	(3,059)	GG
58b	Less: Income From Future Savings (line 41)	_____	(694)	HH
58c	Less: Inflation Adjusted Income (line 52)	_____	(327)	II
58d	Less: Other Income	_____	(100)	JJ
59	Equals: Retirement Income Shortfall	_____	2,782	KK

EE – In today's dollars after-tax. Stop at line 55 if no income is required.

FF – This adjusts the need from today's dollars to retirement age dollars.

GG – In retirement age before-tax dollars. This was inflation-adjusted on line 29.

HH – In retirement age before-tax dollars. This was inflation-adjusted on line 39.

II – In retirement age before-tax dollars. This was inflation-adjusted on lines 45 and 49.

JJ – For example, the retiree intends to work during retirement or will receive some other form of retirement income. This should be after-tax. If the amount will not increase during retirement then it should be inflation adjusted by multiplying the anticipated income by a factor obtained from the **Fixed Income Factors** table on page 338.

KK – In retirement age after-tax dollars.

Calculating The Retirement Income Shortfall

Step 7 – Retirement Savings

line			Example	Notes
60	Retirement Income Shortfall (line 59)	_____	2,782	LL
61	Divided By: Assets-To-Income Factor (line 16)	_____	.00401	
62	Equals: Additional Capital Required At Retirement	_____	693,766	
63	Divided By: Accumulation Factor (line 10)	_____	55.4568	
64	Equals: Annual Savings Required To Provide For Retirement	_____	12,510	
65	Divided By: Months In Year	12	12	
66	Equals: Monthly Savings Required		1,042	MM
67	Additional Capital Needed At Retirement (line 62)	_____	693,766	
68	Times: Increase In Savings Factor (line 12)	_____	.00091	
69	Equals: Monthly Savings Required (increased each year)		631	NN

LL – If line 59 shows a shortfall, enter it here.

MM – This is the level monthly savings required to accumulate the additional capital required at retirement. This is conservative (i.e., accumulation is likely to be more than required on line 62) since the Accumulation Factor on line 63 assumes contributions will be made at the end of the year.

NN – This is the initial monthly savings required during the first year assuming savings are increased each year by the percentage shown on line 11.

Increase-In-Savings Factors

Savings Required Per Month Per $1.00 Accumulation - Increase Each Year

	6% Rate Of Return			7% Rate Of Return			8% Rate Of Return		
Years To	Increase Each Year			Increase Each Year			Increase Each Year		
Retirement	5%	6%	7%	5%	6%	7%	5%	6%	7%
1	.08333	.08333	.08333	.08333	.08333	.08333	.08333	.08333	.08333
2	.03950	.03931	.03912	.03931	.03912	.03894	.03912	.03894	.03876
3	.02496	.02472	.02449	.02472	.02449	.02426	.02449	.02426	.02404
4	.01774	.01749	.01725	.01749	.01725	.01701	.01724	.01701	.01677
5	.01345	.01320	.01296	.01320	.01296	.01272	.01295	.01271	.01248
6	.01063	.01038	.01014	.01038	.01014	.00990	.01013	.00990	.00967
7	.00863	.00839	.00816	.00839	.00816	.00793	.00815	.00793	.00771
8	.00716	.00693	.00670	.00692	.00670	.00649	.00669	.00648	.00628
9	.00603	.00581	.00559	.00581	.00559	.00539	.00559	.00539	.00519
10	.00515	.00493	.00473	.00493	.00473	.00453	.00472	.00453	.00435
11	.00443	.00423	.00404	.00423	.00404	.00385	.00402	.00385	.00368
12	.00385	.00366	.00347	.00365	.00347	.00330	.00346	.00329	.00313
13	.00337	.00319	.00301	.00318	.00301	.00285	.00300	.00284	.00269
14	.00297	.00279	.00262	.00279	.00262	.00247	.00261	.00247	.00232
15	.00262	.00246	.00230	.00245	.00230	.00216	.00229	.00215	.00202
16	.00233	.00217	.00202	.00217	.00202	.00189	.00201	.00188	.00176
17	.00208	.00193	.00179	.00192	.00179	.00166	.00178	.00166	.00154
18	.00186	.00172	.00159	.00171	.00159	.00147	.00157	.00146	.00135
19	.00167	.00154	.00141	.00153	.00141	.00130	.00140	.00129	.00119
20	.00151	.00138	.00126	.00137	.00126	.00115	.00125	.00115	.00105
21	.00136	.00124	.00113	.00123	.00113	.00103	.00111	.00102	.00093
22	.00123	.00112	.00101	.00111	.00101	.00092	.00100	.00091	.00083
23	.00111	.00101	.00091	.00100	.00091	.00082	.00089	.00081	.00074
24	.00101	.00091	.00082	.00090	.00082	.00073	.00080	.00073	.00066
25	.00092	.00082	.00073	.00082	.00073	.00066	.00072	.00065	.00059
26	.00084	.00075	.00066	.00074	.00066	.00059	.00065	.00059	.00053
27	.00077	.00068	.00060	.00067	.00060	.00053	.00059	.00053	.00047
28	.00070	.00062	.00054	.00061	.00054	.00048	.00053	.00047	.00042
29	.00064	.00056	.00049	.00056	.00049	.00043	.00048	.00043	.00038
30	.00059	.00051	.00045	.00051	.00045	.00039	.00044	.00039	.00034
31	.00054	.00047	.00041	.00046	.00041	.00035	.00040	.00035	.00031
32	.00049	.00043	.00037	.00042	.00037	.00032	.00036	.00032	.00028
33	.00045	.00039	.00034	.00039	.00034	.00029	.00033	.00029	.00025
34	.00042	.00036	.00031	.00035	.00031	.00026	.00030	.00026	.00023
35	.00038	.00033	.00028	.00032	.00028	.00024	.00027	.00024	.00020

Explanation. These factors provide the initial monthly savings needed to accumulate a targeted amount in 1-35 years, assuming rates of return of 6%, 7% and 8%; and further assuming that the monthly savings will be increased each year by 5%, 6% or 7%. For example, assuming an 8% rate of return and planned 6% increases each year in the amount saved for 22 years, the factor is .00091. Therefore, to accumulate $692,084 of additional capital in 22 years would require saving $630 per month the first year (.00091 × 692,084 = 630). In the second year the required monthly savings would be $668 (1.06 × 630 = 668).

Increase-In-Savings Factors

Savings Required Per Month Per $1.00 Accumulation - Increase Each Year

	9% Rate Of Return			10% Rate Of Return			12% Rate Of Return		
Years To	Increase Each Year			Increase Each Year			Increase Each Year		
Retirement	5%	6%	7%	5%	6%	7%	5%	6%	7%
1	.08333	.08333	.08333	.08333	.08333	.08333	.08333	.08333	.08333
2	.03894	.03876	.03858	.03876	.03858	.03840	.03840	.03823	.03805
3	.02426	.02404	.02382	.02403	.02381	.02360	.02359	.02337	.02316
4	.01700	.01677	.01654	.01676	.01653	.01631	.01629	.01608	.01586
5	.01271	.01248	.01225	.01247	.01224	.01202	.01200	.01179	.01158
6	.00989	.00967	.00945	.00966	.00944	.00923	.00921	.00900	.00881
7	.00792	.00771	.00750	.00769	.00749	.00729	.00726	.00707	.00689
8	.00647	.00627	.00608	.00626	.00606	.00588	.00584	.00567	.00550
9	.00537	.00518	.00500	.00517	.00499	.00481	.00478	.00462	.00446
10	.00451	.00434	.00417	.00432	.00415	.00399	.00395	.00380	.00366
11	.00383	.00367	.00351	.00365	.00349	.00334	.00330	.00316	.00303
12	.00328	.00312	.00297	.00310	.00296	.00282	.00278	.00266	.00254
13	.00283	.00268	.00254	.00266	.00253	.00240	.00236	.00224	.00213
14	.00245	.00231	.00218	.00229	.00217	.00205	.00201	.00190	.00181
15	.00213	.00201	.00189	.00199	.00187	.00176	.00172	.00163	.00154
16	.00187	.00175	.00164	.00173	.00162	.00152	.00148	.00139	.00131
17	.00164	.00153	.00143	.00151	.00141	.00132	.00128	.00120	.00112
18	.00144	.00134	.00125	.00132	.00123	.00115	.00110	.00103	.00097
19	.00128	.00118	.00109	.00116	.00108	.00100	.00096	.00090	.00083
20	.00113	.00104	.00096	.00102	.00095	.00088	.00084	.00078	.00072
21	.00100	.00092	.00085	.00090	.00083	.00077	.00073	.00068	.00063
22	.00089	.00082	.00075	.00080	.00074	.00067	.00064	.00059	.00054
23	.00080	.00073	.00066	.00071	.00065	.00059	.00056	.00051	.00047
24	.00071	.00065	.00059	.00063	.00058	.00052	.00049	.00045	.00041
25	.00064	.00058	.00052	.00056	.00051	.00046	.00043	.00039	.00036
26	.00057	.00052	.00046	.00050	.00045	.00041	.00038	.00035	.00032
27	.00051	.00046	.00041	.00045	.00040	.00036	.00033	.00030	.00028
28	.00046	.00041	.00037	.00040	.00036	.00032	.00029	.00027	.00024
29	.00041	.00037	.00033	.00036	.00032	.00029	.00026	.00024	.00021
30	.00037	.00033	.00030	.00032	.00029	.00025	.00023	.00021	.00019
31	.00034	.00030	.00026	.00029	.00026	.00023	.00020	.00018	.00016
32	.00030	.00027	.00024	.00026	.00023	.00020	.00018	.00016	.00015
33	.00027	.00024	.00021	.00023	.00020	.00018	.00016	.00014	.00013
34	.00025	.00022	.00019	.00021	.00018	.00016	.00014	.00013	.00011
35	.00022	.00020	.00017	.00019	.00016	.00014	.00012	.00011	.00010

Explanation. These factors provide the initial monthly savings needed to accumulate a targeted amount in 1-35 years, assuming rates of return of 9%, 10% and 12%, and further assuming that the monthly savings will be increased each year by 5%, 6% or 7%. For example, assuming a 10% rate of return and planned 5% increases each year in the amount saved for 15 years, the factor is .00199. Therefore, to accumulate $500,000 of additional capital in 15 years would require saving $995 per month the first year (.00199 × 500,000 = 995). In the second year the required monthly savings would be $1,045 (1.05 × 995 = 1,045).

Income Replacement Ratios

Percentages Needed In Retirement

Income Before Retirement	Replacement	
	Amount	Percentage
10,000	8,500	85.0%
15,000	12,800	85.3
20,000	17,000	85.0
25,000	21,300	85.2
30,000	25,000	83.3
35,000	28,500	81.4
40,000	32,000	80.0
45,000	35,500	78.9
50,000	39,000	78.0
55,000	42,500	77.3
60,000	46,000	76.7
65,000	49,500	76.2
70,000	53,000	75.7
75,000	56,500	75.3
80,000	60,000	75.0
85,000	63,500	74.7
90,000	67,000	74.4
95,000	70,500	74.2
100,000	74,000	74.0
125,000	91,500	73.2
150,000	109,000	72.7
175,000	126,500	72.3
200,000	144,000	72.0
250,000	179,000	71.6
500,000	354,000	70.8

Explanation. This table is based upon an algorithm developed in a 1993 study by the American Society of Pension Actuaries. The replacement percentage produces a replacement amount targeted at 85% of final pay not exceeding three times the poverty level, plus 70% of any additional final pay in excess of three times the poverty level (i.e., 70% of final pay in excess of $26,580). The table assumes a poverty level of $8,860, therefore 3 × $8,860 = $26,580 (weighted average poverty thresholds published by the U.S. Census Bureau can be accessed at: www.census.gov/hhes/poverty/threshld). Replacement amounts are further rounded up to the nearest $100. For additional approaches to determining replacement ratios, see Stephan R. Leimberg & John J. McFadden, *The Tools & Techniques Of Employee Benefit and Retirement Planning,* 7th ed. (Cincinnati: The National Underwriter Company, 2001), p. 16.

Retirement Needs Worksheet – Expense Method

	Monthly	Annually
FOOD:		
HOUSING:		
Mortgage/Rent		
Insurance		
Real Estate Taxes		
Utilities		
Maintenance/Repairs		
Furnishings		
Condominium Fees		
CLOTHING/PERSONAL ITEMS:		
Husband		
Wife		
Others		
TRANSPORTATION:		
Payments/Rental Fees		
Gas		
Auto Insurance		
License Fees/Taxes		
Maintenance/Repair		
Other Transportation Expenses		
MEDICAL:		
Doctor		
Dentist		
Prescriptions		
Insurance		
OTHER INSURANCE PREMIUMS:		
Life Insurance		
Long-Term Care Insurance		
OTHER EXPENSES:		
Income Taxes		
Contributions		
Entertainment		
Travel		
Dues		
Miscellaneous		
TOTAL		
Adjustment for inflation factor*	×	×
INFLATION-ADJUSTED TOTAL		

* The adjustment for inflation is made multiplying total expenses by an inflation factor obtained from the Future Value Table - One Dollar Principal, on pages 456-457.

Fixed Income Factors

Average Purchasing Power Of $1.00/Year Over Years Of Retirement

Years In Retirement	Inflation Rate		
	3%	4%	5%
1	1.0000	1.0000	1.0000
2	.98544	.98077	.97619
3	.97116	.96203	.95314
4	.95715	.94377	.93081
5	.94342	.92598	.90919
6	.92995	.90864	.88825
7	.91674	.89173	.86796
8	.90379	.87526	.84830
9	.89108	.85919	.82925
10	.87861	.84353	.81078
11	.86638	.82826	.79288
12	.85439	.81337	.77553
13	.84262	.79885	.75871
14	.83107	.78469	.74240
15	.81974	.77087	.72658
16	.80862	.75740	.71123
17	.79771	.74425	.69634
18	.78701	.73143	.68189
19	.77650	.71891	.66787
20	.76619	.70670	.65427
21	.75607	.69478	.64106
22	.74614	.68314	.62823
23	.73639	.67179	.61578
24	.72682	.66070	.60369
25	.71742	.64988	.59195
26	.70820	.63931	.58054
27	.69914	.62899	.56945
28	.69025	.61891	.55868
29	.68152	.60907	.54821
30	.67295	.59946	.53804
31	.66453	.59007	.52814
32	.65626	.58089	.51853
33	.64814	.57193	.50917
34	.64017	.56317	.50007
35	.63235	.55461	.49123

Explanation. This table provides factors for determining reduced amounts that can be consumed in order to maintain from a fixed income source level purchasing power over a specific period (i.e., portions of early payments are set aside for later consumption). For example, assuming 5% inflation a fixed income of $567 per month over 23 years would provide constant purchasing power of $349 per month (567 × .61578 = 349). Consumption of $349 per month in year 1 is increased to $366 (1.05 × 349) per month in year 2, then to $384 (1.05 × 366) per month in year 3, etc.

Assets-To-Income Factors

Income Per Month Per $1.00 Accumulation - Income Increases At Inflation Rate

	4% Rate Of Return			5% Rate Of Return			6% Rate Of Return		
Years To	Inflation Rate			Inflation Rate			Inflation Rate		
Retirement	3%	4%	5%	3%	4%	5%	3%	4%	5%
1	.08333	.08333	.08333	.08333	.08333	.08333	.08333	.08333	.08333
2	.04186	.04166	.04146	.04206	.04186	.04166	.04226	.04206	.04186
3	.02804	.02777	.02751	.02831	.02804	.02777	.02857	.02830	.02804
4	.02113	.02083	.02053	.02143	.02113	.02083	.02173	.02143	.02113
5	.01699	.01666	.01634	.01731	.01698	.01666	.01763	.01730	.01698
6	.01422	.01388	.01355	.01456	.01422	.01388	.01490	.01455	.01422
7	.01225	.01190	.01156	.01260	.01224	.01190	.01295	.01259	.01224
8	.01077	.01041	.01007	.01113	.01076	.01041	.01149	.01112	.01076
9	.00962	.00925	.00890	.00998	.00961	.00925	.01035	.00998	.00961
10	.00870	.00833	.00797	.00907	.00869	.00833	.00945	.00906	.00869
11	.00794	.00757	.00721	.00832	.00794	.00757	.00870	.00831	.00793
12	.00731	.00694	.00658	.00770	.00731	.00694	.00809	.00769	.00731
13	.00678	.00641	.00604	.00717	.00678	.00641	.00757	.00716	.00678
14	.00633	.00595	.00558	.00672	.00632	.00595	.00712	.00671	.00632
15	.00593	.00555	.00519	.00633	.00593	.00555	.00674	.00632	.00593
16	.00559	.00520	.00484	.00599	.00559	.00520	.00640	.00598	.00558
17	.00528	.00490	.00453	.00569	.00528	.00490	.00610	.00568	.00528
18	.00501	.00462	.00426	.00542	.00501	.00462	.00584	.00541	.00501
19	.00477	.00438	.00401	.00518	.00477	.00438	.00560	.00517	.00477
20	.00456	.00416	.00379	.00497	.00455	.00416	.00539	.00496	.00455
21	.00436	.00396	.00360	.00477	.00435	.00396	.00520	.00476	.00435
22	.00418	.00378	.00341	.00460	.00418	.00378	.00503	.00459	.00417
23	.00402	.00362	.00325	.00444	.00401	.00362	.00487	.00443	.00401
24	.00387	.00347	.00310	.00429	.00386	.00347	.00473	.00428	.00386
25	.00373	.00333	.00296	.00415	.00373	.00333	.00460	.00415	.00372
26	.00360	.00320	.00283	.00403	.00360	.00320	.00448	.00402	.00359
27	.00348	.00308	.00271	.00391	.00348	.00308	.00437	.00391	.00348
28	.00338	.00297	.00260	.00381	.00337	.00297	.00426	.00380	.00337
29	.00327	.00287	.00250	.00371	.00327	.00287	.00417	.00370	.00327
30	.00318	.00277	.00240	.00362	.00318	.00277	.00408	.00361	.00317
31	.00309	.00268	.00232	.00353	.00309	.00268	.00400	.00352	.00308
32	.00301	.00260	.00223	.00345	.00300	.00260	.00392	.00344	.00300
33	.00293	.00252	.00215	.00337	.00293	.00252	.00385	.00336	.00292
34	.00286	.00245	.00208	.00330	.00285	.00245	.00378	.00329	.00285
35	.00279	.00238	.00201	.00324	.00278	.00238	.00372	.00323	.00278

Explanation. This table is used as follows. Assume an accumulation at retirement of $953,660, retirement is expected to last 23 years, 6% interest will be earned after retirement, and inflation will be 5% per year. Multiplying $953,660 by the factor of .00401 produces an initial monthly income of $3,824 (953,660 × .00401 = 3,824). Thereafter, income is increased each year by an additional 5%, or to $4,015 per month in the second year (3,824 × 1.05 = 4,015). To simplify calculation of the table it is assumed that 12 months of income is withdrawn at the beginning of each year. For example, at the beginning of the first year $45,888 is withdrawn to provide $3,824 per month of income (3,824 × 12 = 45,888). At the beginning of the second year $48,180 is withdrawn to provide $4,015 per month of income (4,015 × 12 = 48,180).

Assets-To-Income Factors

Income Per Month Per $1.00 Accumulation - Income Increases At Inflation Rate

	7% Rate Of Return			8% Rate Of Return			9% Rate Of Return		
Years To	Inflation Rate			Inflation Rate			Inflation Rate		
Retirement	3%	4%	5%	3%	4%	5%	3%	4%	5%
1	.08333	.08333	.08333	.08333	.08333	.08333	.08333	.08333	.08333
2	.04246	.04225	.04205	.04265	.04245	.04225	.04284	.04264	.04244
3	.02884	.02857	.02830	.02910	.02883	.02856	.02936	.02909	.02882
4	.02203	.02173	.02142	.02233	.02202	.02172	.02263	.02232	.02201
5	.01796	.01762	.01730	.01828	.01794	.01761	.01860	.01826	.01793
6	.01524	.01489	.01455	.01558	.01523	.01488	.01592	.01556	.01521
7	.01330	.01294	.01258	.01366	.01329	.01293	.01401	.01364	.01328
8	.01185	.01148	.01111	.01222	.01184	.01147	.01259	.01220	.01182
9	.01073	.01034	.00997	.01110	.01071	.01033	.01148	.01109	.01070
10	.00983	.00943	.00905	.01021	.00981	.00942	.01061	.01020	.00980
11	.00909	.00869	.00831	.00949	.00908	.00868	.00989	.00947	.00906
12	.00848	.00808	.00768	.00889	.00847	.00807	.00930	.00887	.00845
13	.00797	.00756	.00716	.00838	.00795	.00754	.00880	.00836	.00794
14	.00753	.00711	.00670	.00795	.00751	.00710	.00838	.00793	.00750
15	.00715	.00672	.00631	.00758	.00714	.00671	.00801	.00756	.00712
16	.00682	.00639	.00597	.00725	.00680	.00637	.00769	.00723	.00679
17	.00653	.00609	.00567	.00697	.00651	.00608	.00742	.00695	.00650
18	.00627	.00583	.00540	.00672	.00625	.00581	.00717	.00670	.00624
19	.00604	.00559	.00517	.00649	.00603	.00558	.00696	.00647	.00601
20	.00584	.00538	.00495	.00629	.00582	.00537	.00676	.00627	.00580
21	.00565	.00519	.00476	.00611	.00563	.00518	.00659	.00609	.00562
22	.00548	.00502	.00458	.00595	.00547	.00501	.00644	.00593	.00545
23	.00533	.00486	.00442	.00581	.00531	.00485	.00630	.00578	.00530
24	.00519	.00472	.00427	.00567	.00518	.00471	.00617	.00565	.00516
25	.00507	.00459	.00414	.00555	.00505	.00457	.00605	.00553	.00503
26	.00495	.00447	.00401	.00544	.00493	.00445	.00595	.00542	.00491
27	.00484	.00435	.00390	.00534	.00482	.00434	.00585	.00531	.00481
28	.00474	.00425	.00379	.00525	.00473	.00424	.00576	.00522	.00471
29	.00465	.00416	.00369	.00516	.00463	.00414	.00568	.00513	.00462
30	.00457	.00407	.00360	.00508	.00455	.00405	.00561	.00505	.00453
31	.00449	.00398	.00351	.00501	.00447	.00397	.00554	.00498	.00445
32	.00442	.00391	.00343	.00494	.00440	.00389	.00548	.00491	.00438
33	.00435	.00383	.00336	.00487	.00433	.00382	.00542	.00485	.00431
34	.00428	.00377	.00328	.00481	.00426	.00375	.00537	.00479	.00425
35	.00423	.00370	.00322	.00476	.00421	.00369	.00532	.00473	.00419

Explanation. This table is used as follows. Assume an accumulation at retirement of $500,000, retirement is expected to last 15 years, 8% interest will be earned after retirement, and inflation will be 3% per year. Multiplying $500,000 by the factor of .00758 produces an initial monthly income of $3,790 (500,000 × .00758 = 3,790). Thereafter, income is increased each year by an additional 3%, or to $3,904 per month in the second year (3,790 × 1.03 = 3,904). To simplify calculation of the table it is assumed that 12 months of income is withdrawn at the beginning of each year. For example, at the beginning of the first year $45,480 is withdrawn to provide $3,790 per month of income (3,790 × 12 = 45,480). At the beginning of the second year $46,848 is withdrawn to provide $3,904 per month of income (3,904 × 12 = 46,848).

Social Security Retirement Benefits

Monthly Projected Benefit - Based Upon 2003 Calculations

Current Annual Earnings	Year Of Birth			
	1941	1942-46	1947-51	1952-56
4,000 - 10,000	425	437	454	472
11,000 - 17,000	654	662	674	687
18,000 - 24,000	805	817	835	854
25,000 - 31,000	956	972	996	1,022
32,000 - 38,000	1,107	1,127	1,158	1,190
39,000 - 45,000	1,258	1,282	1,319	1,357
46,000 - 49,000	1,406	1,438	1,480	1,522
50,000 - 59,000	1,533	1,551	1,575	1,601
60,000 - 66,000	1,594	1,616	1,649	1,680
67,000 - 73,000	1,658	1,683	1,724	1,758
74,000 - 80,000	1,719	1,750	1,794	1,835
81,000 - 87,000	1,775	1,812	1,864	1,913

	Year Of Birth			
	1957-61	1962-66	1967-71	1972-76
4,000 - 10,000	496	511	523	525
11,000 - 17,000	704	715	723	725
18,000 - 24,000	880	897	909	911
25,000 - 31,000	1,056	1,079	1,095	1,098
32,000 - 38,000	1,233	1,261	1,280	1,285
39,000 - 45,000	1,409	1,442	1,466	1,471
46,000 - 49,000	1,551	1,569	1,582	1,585
50,000 - 59,000	1,634	1,654	1,669	1,673
60,000 - 66,000	1,716	1,740	1,756	1,760
67,000 - 73,000	1,799	1,825	1,843	1,847
74,000 - 80,000	1,881	1,910	1,930	1,935
81,000 - 87,000	1,964	1,995	2,018	2,022

Explanation. The indicated retirement benefits are at the worker's Normal Retirement Age (gradually increasing to age 67 by 2022, see page 394). Calculations reflect the midpoint of the indicated range. For example, the $1,357 monthly retirement benefit is based upon $42,000 of Current Annual Earnings (midpoint of 39,000 - 45,000) and a 1954 Year Of Birth (midpoint of 1952-56). The underlying AIME assumptions used to calculate these retirement benefits (the PIAs) are based upon the AIMEs set forth in the 2003 National Underwriter Social Security Slide-O-Scope & Planner. These AIME amounts are approximate and are based upon the assumption that the worker has had 6% pay raises each year through 2003.

Social Security Early Retirement Reduction Factors

Months Before Normal Retirement	Percent Reduction	Reduction Factor	Months Before Normal Retirement	Percent Reduction	Reduction Factor
1	0.56	.9944	25	13.89	.8611
2	1.11	.9889	26	14.44	.8556
3	1.67	.9833	27	15.00	.8500
4	2.22	.9778	28	15.56	.8444
5	2.78	.9722	29	16.11	.8389
6	3.33	.9667	30	16.67	.8333
7	3.89	.9611	31	17.22	.8278
8	4.44	.9556	32	17.78	.8222
9	5.00	.9500	33	18.33	.8167
10	5.56	.9444	34	18.89	.8111
11	6.11	.9389	35	19.44	.8056
12	6.67	.9333	36	20.00	.8000
13	7.22	.9278	37	20.42	.7958
14	7.78	.9222	38	20.83	.7917
15	8.33	.9167	39	21.25	.7875
16	8.89	.9111	40	21.67	.7833
17	9.44	.9056	41	22.08	.7792
18	10.00	.9000	42	22.50	.7750
19	10.56	.8944	43	22.92	.7708
20	11.11	.8889	44	23.33	.7667
21	11.67	.8833	45	23.75	.7625
22	12.22	.8778	46	24.17	.7583
23	12.78	.8722	47	24.58	.7542
24	13.33	.8667	48	25.00	.7500

Explanation. To determine the reduced retirement benefit, multiply the estimated benefits payable upon normal retirement by the reduction factor (the percent reduction represents 5/9 of 1% per month for the first 36 months, plus 5/12 of 1% per month for any additional months). For example, assume a worker was born in 1939 and desires to take early retirement benefits at age 64. This worker's normal retirement age is 65 years and 2 months (see table Normal Retirement Age Determined By Year Of Birth, page 394); therefore this involves taking retirement benefits 14 months before normal retirement age (i.e., the number of months from age 64 to age 65 and 2 months). The reduction factor is .9222. If the worker's benefit at normal retirement age is $1,430 then the reduced benefit for early retirement is $1,319 (1,430 × .9222 = 1,319). To calculate a spouse's early retirement benefit multiply the reduction factor times the spouse's benefit (not the worker's benefit). For example, assuming a worker's normal retirement benefit of $1,430, the spouse's benefit would be $715 (1,430 × .5 = 715). See discussion of Spouse's Benefit, page 393. If the spouse was born in 1940 and wanted to take an early retirement benefit at age 63, this would involve taking retirement benefits 30 months before normal retirement age of 65 years and 6 months. The reduction factor from the above table is .8333 and the spouse's early retirement benefit is $596 (715 × .8333 = 596).

SOURCES OF RETIREMENT INCOME

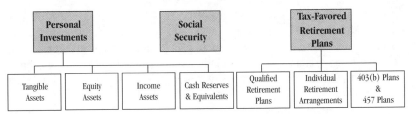

Personal investments, Social Security, and tax-favored retirement plans are considered the proverbial "three-legged stool" of resources for retirement income and security.[1]

Personal Investments include tangible assets (page 203), equity assets (pages 129 and 167), income assets (page 89), and cash reserves and equivalents (page 81). Another important source of retirement income is the nonqualified fixed or variable annuity (page 377).

Social Security provides retirement benefits for the worker, his spouse, and even a divorced spouse (pages 390 and 393).

Tax-Favored Retirement Plans can be established in a variety of ways:

(1) *Qualified retirement plans* such as defined benefit pension plans, money-purchase pension plans, and 401(k) plans, can be installed in a corporation, a partnership, or a sole proprietorship (page 345).

(2) *Individual retirement arrangements (IRAs)*, including both individual retirement accounts and individual retirement annuities, can be established by many taxpayers. With a simplified employee pension plan (SEP) or a SIMPLE IRA, employer contributions can also be made to individual retirement accounts (page 360).

(3) *Section 403(b) plans* are available to employees of public schools and colleges, and certain non-profit hospitals, charitable, religious, scientific and educational organizations (page 370).

(4) *Section 457 plans* are available to employees of state and local governments and tax-exempt organizations (page 371).

TAX LEVERAGE

To better appreciate the advantages of tax-favored retirement plans, we can compare the growth of a tax-favored account to the results obtained when after-tax funds are invested outside a tax-favored plan . . . for example, in certificates of deposit, savings accounts, or treasury bills. Assume that there is $1,000 of before-tax funds available for investment per year over the next 20 years.

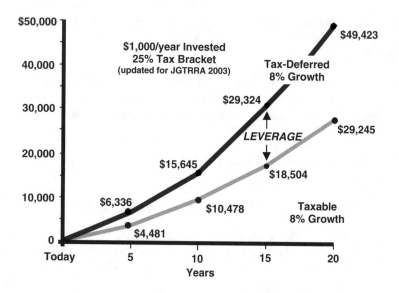

Taxable Growth. If after-tax dollars were invested outside of a tax-favored plan, assuming a 25% tax bracket, of the original $1,000 only $750 per year would remain after-taxes for investment. The earnings will also be taxed, which means that although the investment might pay 8% interest, it would yield only 6% after-taxes. The reduced after-tax funds available for investment, combined with the reduced after-tax yield, means that in 10 years $10,479 will have accumulated, and in 20 years $29,245.

Tax-Deferred Growth. The tax leverage provided by a tax-favored plan offers the opportunity for substantially increased accumulations, because there are no current taxes on contributions, and no current taxes on investment earnings. This means that each year $1,000 will actually be invested, and a full 8% rate of interest will actually be credited, neither being subject to current income taxation. A tax-deferred growth of 8% will accumulate $15,645 in 10 years, and $49,423 in 20 years. Although payments received during retirement will be taxable, after-tax income will usually far exceed that available with investments that are not tax-favored.

QUALIFIED RETIREMENT PLANS

A qualified retirement plan is a tax-favored retirement arrangement established by an employer that is designed to satisfy the requirements of Section 401 of the Internal Revenue Code. The employer may be a corporation, a partnership or a sole proprietorship. The "plan" is the document that sets forth in writing the rules by which employees become participants and the method of calculating the benefits to which they become entitled. Contributions to the plan are transferred to a trustee or insurance company that holds and invests them until they are distributed upon the participant's termination of employment, retirement, or death. Assuming the necessary requirements are met, contributions are deductible to the employer (within limits) and are not currently taxable to the employee/participant. Earnings on plan investments grow tax-deferred and are not taxable to the employee until withdrawn or distributed.[2]

Types Of Qualified Retirement Plans			
	Defined Contribution		**Defined Benefit**
Pension	Money Purchase Pension Plan	<u>page</u> 346	<u>page</u> Defined Benefit Pension Plan 348
	Target Benefit Plan	346	Cash Balance Pension Plan 349
Profit Sharing	Profit Sharing Plan	<u>page</u> 350	<u>page</u>
	401(k) Plan	351	
	Stock Bonus Plan	353	n/a
	ESOP	353	
	Age-Weighted Profit Sharing Plan	355	
	Saving/Thrift Plan	356	

Qualified retirement plans can be categorized in a number of ways. One method involves distinguishing between plans according to the nature of the employer's obligation. Under a **defined contribution** plan the employer makes specific contributions to the plan, after which the participant's retirement benefits are determined by the account value at retirement (i.e., the employee bears the investment risk). In contrast, under a **defined benefit** plan the employer is obligated to provide a specific retirement benefit to the participant (i.e., the employer bears the investment risk).

Another way of categorizing plans involves distinguishing between them according to whether employer contributions can be tied to employer profits. Under a **pension** plan the employer is obligated to provide a "definitely determinable benefit."[3] However, under a **profit sharing** plan employer contributions can be completely discretionary and based on employer profits.

Money Purchase Pension Plan

Under the money purchase pension plan each employee/participant has an individual account into which the employer makes annual contributions pursuant to the plan's contribution formula. These employer contributions are required and the employer is subject to a minimum funding penalty if they are not made. The formula used to determine contribution amounts must be nondiscriminatory and typically sets employer contributions at a specific percentage of the employee's annual compensation. Only the first $200,000 (as indexed in 2003) of each employee's compensation can be taken into consideration. The maximum annual addition that can be contributed to a money purchase plan is the lesser of 100% of the participant's compensation, or $40,000 (as indexed in 2003). In determining the level of employer contributions integration with Social Security is allowed.

The maximum amount an employer may deduct for money purchase plan contributions is 25% of compensation (i.e., generally payroll). Prior to 2002 this 25% limit provided money purchase pension plans with an advantage over profit sharing plans, since the deduction for profit sharing contributions was limited to 15% of payroll. Without this advantage it is likely that employers will increasingly choose to establish the more flexible profit-sharing plan rather than a money purchase pension plan that *requires* annual employer contributions.

Unlike the defined benefit pension plan, under a money purchase pension plan the employee bears the investment risk of the plan (i.e., the employer is obligated only to make the initial contribution, after that the risk of poor investment performance is born by the participant). The employee also bears the risk that the amounts accumulated at retirement might be insufficient to fund retirement needs (e.g., the inflation risk). Upon retirement the participant's account balance can be paid in a lump sum, paid in installments for a number of years, or used to purchase an annuity providing an income for life (this is the origin of the term "money-purchase"). Of all qualified plans the money-purchase pension plan is generally considered the simplest to design, explain, install and administer.

Target Benefit Plan

Under the target benefit plan, calculation of the employer's contribution takes into consideration not only the participant's *compensation* but also the participant's *age* when first entering the plan. By allowing employers to use age as a factor in allocating contributions employers are able to allocate more of their contributions towards older employees.

The target benefit plan is also referred to as a "hybrid plan." Although the target benefit plan is a type of money purchase plan, it initially uses a defined benefit approach to determine a theoretical or "targeted" benefit that is expressed as a defined benefit formula (e.g., 50% of average compensation payable at a normal retirement age of 65). Actuarial assumptions involving investment rates of return and mortality are used to develop a table of contribution percentages (called a target benefit table) that is incorporated into the plan. A defined contribution approach is then used and the employer is required to make fixed annual contributions to the separate account of each participant according to the percentages contained in the target benefit table. An increase in employee compensation will produce an additional benefit under this table (i.e., the increase in compensation produces a separate benefit that is funded with an additional annual contribution). However, the employer *does not guarantee* the ultimate retirement benefit.

The employee/participant bears the entire investment risk. If the earnings are lower than assumed, the actual benefit will be lower than the targeted benefit. Conversely, if the fund's earnings are greater than the actuary has assumed, the participant's actual benefit will be higher than the targeted benefit.

Because the target benefit plan is a defined contribution plan, for plan years beginning after December 31, 2001, the annual additions are limited per participant to the lesser of 100% of compensation, or $40,000 (in 2003).

For example, assume a target plan is adopted with the intention of providing 50% of compensation at a normal retirement age of 65. Assume also that the target benefit table (which sets the annual employer contribution as a percentage of compensation) is calculated by an actuary assuming a straight life annuity at age 65, investment returns of 8% preretirement and 6% postretirement, postretirement mortality based upon the UP 84 unisex table, and with contributions made on the last day of the year. Under such a table the annual contribution percentage is 2.8% for an employee age 30 with 35 years to retirement, whereas the annual contribution percentage is 17.7% for an employee age 50 with 15 years to retirement. The following table illustrates how a target benefit plan, when compared to a money purchase plan, can substantially increase the annual contributions (from $6,150 to $10,620) for an older employee (age 50) who has a higher level of compensation ($60,000). The **Target Benefit** plan results in a total annual contribution of $18,450, with $10,620 of that amount going to Employee D (Percentage Of *Compensation* is 17.7%). In contrast, if the same $18,450 were contributed to a **Money Purchase** plan Employee D would receive only $6,150. The "Percentage of *Contribution*" column shows the employee's compensation as a percentage of total compensation, or 33.0% for Employee D (60,000 ÷ 180,000 = .330). The "Annual Contribution" column assumes that the employer contributes the same $18,450 to a money purchase plan, or 10.25% of total payroll (18,450 ÷ 180,000 = .1025). The annual contribution allocated to Employee D is now only $6,150 (18,450 × .330 = 6,150).[4]

Target Benefit Plan Compared To Money Purchase Pension Plan						
			Target Benefit		Money Purchase	
Employee	Entry Age	Annual Compensation	Percentage of Compensation	Annual Contribution	Percentage of Contribution	Annual Contribution
A	30	30,000	2.8	840	17.0	3,075
B	50	30,000	17.7	5,310	17.0	3,075
C	30	60,000	2.8	1,680	33.0	6,150
D	50	60,000	17.7	10,620	33.0	6,150
Totals		180,000		18,450	100	18,450

Defined Benefit Pension Plan

Under the defined benefit pension plan the employer guarantees a specified benefit at "normal retirement age." Based upon actuarial calculations the employer is required to maintain a level of "minimum funding" such as will assure that funds will be available to pay this guaranteed retirement benefit. Unlike the money-purchase pension plan there are no individual accounts.

The maximum amount of the projected annual benefit at age 65 (paid as a life annuity or as a joint and survivor benefit) is limited to the lesser of $160,000 (as indexed in 2003), or 100% of compensation averaged over the three highest-earning consecutive years (if normal retirement age is earlier than age 62 these maximum limits are reduced). In contrast to the money-purchase pension plan, a defined benefit pension plan has maximum *benefit* limits but not maximum *contribution* limits (i.e., the regulatory concern is directed toward assuring that minimum funding standards are met in order to provide the promised benefit). However, plan contributions must be suspended if the plan is found to be overfunded (i.e., the actuarial assumptions and calculations reveal that there will be more funds than required to fund the promised benefits). In determining the specified benefit integration with Social Security is allowed.

Unlike the money purchase pension plan, under a defined benefit pension plan the employer bears the investment risk of the plan (i.e., the employer is obligated to pay a specified benefit upon the employee's retirement). Up to specific limits the benefits of a defined benefit pension plan are guaranteed by the Pension   *www.pbgc.com* Benefit Guaranty Corporation.

Various formulas are used to determine the employee's benefit.

(1) Under a *flat amount formula* all employees receive the same stated dollar monthly benefit without regard to the employee's level of compensation (e.g., $600 per month for life beginning at age 65). However, some minimum years of employment might be required for the maximum monthly benefit, with reduced benefits for lesser years of employment.

(2) Under a *flat percentage formula* each employee receives a benefit that is based upon a percentage of his average earnings (e.g., 50% of average earnings for life beginning at age 65). However, some minimum years of employment might be required for the maximum monthly benefit, with reduced percentages for lesser years of employment.

(3) Under a *unit credit formula* each employee receives a benefit that is based upon his years of employment (e.g., assuming 1¼% credit for each year of service, an employee with 20 years of service and $100,000 of average earnings would receive a benefit of $25,000, calculated as $1.25 \times 20 \times 100,000 = 25,000$).

The "average earnings" that are used in the above flat percentage and unit credit formulas are often calculated using one of two methods.

(1) The *career average method* takes into consideration all earnings over the employee's years of employment.

(2) The *final average method* considers only a limited number of years just prior to retirement.

Defined benefit pension plans entail high installation and administration costs, are complex to design, and are often difficult to understand. Despite these disadvantages they generally offer the older and more highly compensated employee a higher level of tax-deferred retirement savings and income.[5]

Cash Balance Pension Plan

A cash balance plan is a defined benefit plan that calculates benefits in a manner similar to defined contribution plans. Each employee has a hypothetical account or "cash balance" to which contributions and interest payments are credited. Under the typical plan a fixed percentage of each employee's salary is contributed each year, and both the level of contribution and a minimum rate of return are *guaranteed* by the employer (i.e., the employer bears the investment risk). Contributions may be weighted for age or years of service. Unlike a true defined contribution plan, individual accounts are not maintained and participants may not direct the investments in their accounts. As with the defined benefit pension plan the plan benefits are guaranteed by the Pension Benefit Guaranty Corporation (PBGC).

Compared with traditional defined benefit plans cash balance plans generally provide greater benefits to younger employees and those with shorter service (but at a higher cost), and lower benefits to older, longer service employees (at lower cost).

In an effort to reduce the costs of employee retirement plans, and offer more attractive plans to younger workers with few years of service, employers can convert their traditional defined benefit plans into cash balance plans. This conversation benefits younger workers, who not only can accrue benefits more rapidly, but will also enjoy the added advantages of portability (i.e., if the employee leaves prior to normal retirement age vested account values can be taken in a lump sum, rolled over into an IRA, or otherwise invested). However, these conversations are generally detrimental to older employees, since they occur just as these workers are reaching the age where the defined benefit formulas began to sharply raise the value of their future pension payouts. In effect, the rate of future-benefit accrual for older employees is reduced when a defined benefit plan is converted to a cash balance plan. Controversy over cash-balance conversions has resulted in many employers giving employees the option of staying with the old defined benefit plan, or providing other incentives in order to mitigate loss of anticipated benefits.[6]

Profit Sharing Plan

Employer contributions to a profit sharing plan can be entirely discretionary, made according to a formula provision, or a combination of both. If on a *discretionary* basis, then the employer determines each year whether or not to make contributions to the plan (but a failure to make "recurring and substantial" contributions could result in disqualification of the plan). It is not necessary that the employer actually have current or accumulated profits. If on a *formula* basis, then contributions are made under a formula typically tied to employer profits (e.g., 5% of net profits after taxes, 10% of gross profits in excess of $100,000, or some other profit-driven formula). In either case, for plan years beginning after December 31, 2001, the employer can deduct up to 25% of total payroll of plan participants (the limit was 15% for plan years beginning prior to January 1, 2002).

Once the amount of contribution is determined, it is then allocated among the participants' individual accounts under a nondiscriminatory formula that must be definite and predetermined. For example, each participant might receive an allocation of a percentage determined by comparing his compensation to the total compensation of all plan participants. If the employer's total contribution to the plan was $100,000, and the participant's $150,000 of compensation represented 15% of the $1,000,000 total payroll, then the allocation to his account would be $15,000 (100,000 × .15 = 15,000). For 2003, the maximum compensation base for any participant is limited to $200,000, but subject to an overall "annual additions" limit for any one participant of the lesser of $40,000 or 100% of compensation. In determining this allocation formula integration with Social Security is allowed under most plans.

Upon the participant's termination or retirement, benefits under the plan consist of the participant's account value. This account value reflects total employer contributions, forfeitures from other plan participants, and returns on plan investments (i.e., interest, dividends and capital gains). As with a money purchase pension plan, the employee/participant bears the risks associated with investment performance. In addition, because employer contributions and profits are not assured, unlike the defined benefit plan, the employee is unable to project with any certainty his account values at retirement. In contrast to pension plans, certain profit sharing plans can offer participants the opportunity to take "in-service distributions" prior to retirement (subject to a 10% early withdrawal tax penalty prior to age 59½). In order to avoid this penalty, profit sharing plans sometimes allow participants access to account funds through plan loans at reasonable rates of interest and within specified limits.[7]

401(k) Plan

Known as a cash or deferred arrangement (CODA), a 401(k) plan allows eligible employees to defer current taxes on compensation or bonuses and contribute the funds to an employer-sponsored profit sharing plan. These salary reductions are referred to as "elective deferrals." In addition to meeting the requirements necessary to qualify as a profit sharing or stock bonus plan, a 401(k) plan must: (1) limit the forfeitability and distribution of employee elective deferrals; (2) permit participation by the later of age 21 or one year of service; (3) limit elective deferrals; and (4) meet an annual nondiscrimination requirement (the ADP test), either by comparing ratios of elective deferrals for highly compensated and non-highly compensated employees, by meeting the requirements for a SIMPLE 401(k) plan, or by meeting the requirements for a 401(k) safe harbor plan. In contrast, see SIMPLE IRA Plan, page 364.

Although 401(k) plans are typically funded entirely or in part through employee elective deferrals, it is helpful to remember that 401(k) plans can contain all of the following:

(1) **Employee elective deferrals (salary reductions)** – which the employee elects to have the employer contribute instead of receiving cash (the source might be existing salary, salary increases, or bonuses). The employee elective deferral is limited to $12,000 in 2003 and is not taxable to the employee until withdrawn. (Although most states allow an employee to exclude 401(k) contributions from taxable income, it would be advisable to check with individual state authorities.) Amounts deferred in excess of these limits are not excludable from income, and, if not timely corrected by distribution, will be taxed a second time when distributed from the plan. Employee elective deferrals are subject to Social Security (FICA) and federal unemployment (FUTA) payroll taxes.

(2) **Employer matching contributions** – made by the employer in some ratio to employee elective deferrals (if immediately 100% vested and subject to certain withdrawal restrictions, they are known as "qualified matching contributions").

(3) **Employer nonelective contributions** – made by the employer on behalf of employees and not conditioned upon employee elective deferrals (if immediately 100% vested and subject to certain withdrawal restrictions, they are known as "qualified nonelective contributions").

(4) **Catch-up contributions** – made by employees who are age 50 or over during the plan year can increase the elective deferral by an additional $2,000 in 2003 (increasing to $3,000 in 2004, $4,000 in 2005, and $5,000 in 2006 and thereafter).

Provided it is an "incidental benefit," life insurance can be purchased within a 401(k) plan. Up to 49.9% of accumulated contributions can be used to purchase whole life insurance (24.9% if used to purchase universal life). The participant must include in gross income the "cost" of the insurance coverage (measured by multiplying the difference between the face amount and the cash surrender value by either the Table 2001 rates (previously the P.S. 58 rates) or the insurance companies rates for individual 1-year term life insurance). If the employee dies prior to retirement, death proceeds in excess of cash surrender values are received free of income taxes.[8]

Stock Bonus Plan

A qualified stock bonus plan is similar to a profit sharing plan. However, in contrast to a profit sharing plan, the account values are often fully invested in the employer's stock. (In contrast, a profit sharing plan may not invest more than 10% of its holdings in employer stock, unless it meets the requirements for an "individual account plan.") Separate accounts are established for each participant and allocation of contributions and distributions of benefits are generally subject to the same requirements as a profit sharing plan.[9]

Contributions are made either in cash (which is then used to purchase the stock of the employer) or in the stock of the employer. If made in stock, the amount of the employer's deduction for the contribution is determined by the fair market value of the stock when it is contributed. Unless the stock is publicly traded, some or all of the voting rights must be passed through to participants. Employer contributions are not fixed or required, may vary from year to year, and may or may not come from employer profits.

Distributions are generally in the form of employer stock, but a stock bonus plan may provide for payment of benefits in cash if certain conditions are met. (If employer securities are not readily tradable on an established market, the participant has a right to require the employer (not the plan) to repurchase employer securities under a fair valuation formula. This is referred to as a "put option.") When stock is received in a lump sum distribution any net unrealized appreciation of the stock while held in the plan is not taxed until it is subsequently sold (i.e., taxation of gain is deferred). For example, assume a stock bonus plan purchased stock for $1,000 and it subsequently appreciated in value to $5,000. The stock is then distributed to a participant in a lump sum distribution, at which time the participant pays taxes on $1,000, but would not be currently taxed on the $4,000 of unrealized appreciation.

Employee Stock Ownership Plan (ESOP)

An employee stock ownership plan, or ESOP, is a stock bonus plan, or a stock bonus plan combined with a money purchase plan, which is designed to invest primarily in the common stock of the employer. However, unlike a pure stock bonus plan, the ESOP is typically used as a device for implementing the business continuation and estate planning objectives of its stockholders. The benefits provided by an ESOP are similar to those provided by a profit sharing plan, but they are distributable in stock of the employer, and contributions are not dependent upon employer profits.

An ESOP must meet specific requirements pertaining to coverage, nondiscrimination in contributions, limits on contributions, diversification of investments, and nonforfeiture of rights upon termination of employment.[10] If these requirements are met, then the plan can be useful in:

(1) Motivating employees toward increased productivity (the value of corporate stock held by the trust is dependent upon the corporate profitability).

(2) Providing retirement income as a supplement to Social Security and other retirement benefits.

(3) Generating liquidity for principal stockholders through the sale of stock to the ESOP during lifetime or after death.

(4) Securing funds for corporate growth and expansion with untaxed dollars.

(5) Avoiding taxation of accumulated earnings.

(6) Securing income tax deductions for an employer with little or no cash outlay.

(7) Paying for life insurance on key employees with before-tax dollars.

Leveraged ESOP. A "leveraged" ESOP can be used to borrow money from a financial institution based on the credit (and guarantee) of the employer. (Normally, loans or extensions of credit between an employer and its plans are "prohibited transactions," but the ESOP is exempt from these restrictions.) The borrowed funds are then used by the ESOP trustee to purchase stock from the employer. In turn, the employer typically uses these funds to finance expansion and capital purchases.

Subsequent employer *contributions* to the ESOP are used by the ESOP trustee to repay the debt. In effect, provided employer contributions to the ESOP are within the annual additions limitations, this technique has enabled to employer to: (1) obtain funds for expansion by selling shares to the ESOP; and (2) repay the ESOP's bank loan with fully tax deductible dollars (i.e., in the form of deductible contributions to the ESOP).[11] Had the employer borrowed the funds directly the interest payments would have been deductible, but repayment of principal would not have been deductible.

Distributions to employees may be made entirely in cash or partly in cash and partly in employer securities. Participants must be given the right to demand the entire distribution in the form of employer stock. If the stock is not readily tradable on an established market the participants must also be given the right to require the *employer* to purchase any distributions of employer stock made to them (a "put option").

It has been suggested that the complexity of establishing a leveraged ESOP is usually not necessary since the same tax benefit can be accomplished if the employer borrows funds directly from a financial institution and contributes an amount of its stock to a stock bonus plan each year equal in value to the amount of its loan repayment.[12]

Non-Leveraged ESOP. ESOPs are also used to purchase an owner's stock interest on death (sometimes referred to as a "non-leveraged ESOP"). These arrangements entail giving the ESOP an *option* to purchase stock upon the stock-holder's death. To fund the purchase the trustee of the ESOP acquires life insurance on the life of the stockholder. However, requiring the ESOP to purchase the stock under a formal stock purchase plan should be avoided, since it is likely that this purchase would be treated as a fully taxable stock dividend paid by the corporation to the estate. In contrast, if treated as a sale the transaction would likely produce little or no taxable gain due to the estate's stepped-up basis in the stock (page 440).

Age-Weighted Profit Sharing Plan

Pension plans, both defined contribution (money purchase and target benefit) and defined benefit, require that the employer make recurring annual contributions. These annual obligations can be avoided with profit sharing plans. Under a traditional profit sharing plan employer contributions are generally allocated each year to employees in proportion to relative compensation, either with or without Social Security integration. However, with an age-weighted profit sharing plan the participant's age is taken into account when making these allocations. The results are similar to those produced in target plans, with significantly larger allocations (as a percentage of compensation) to older employees, but with the added flexibility of a profit sharing plan (e.g., fixed annual contributions are required under a target plan, but there is no such requirement under an age-weighted profit sharing plan).

Age-weighted profit sharing plans are also referred to as "cross tested" or "new comparability plans." The name is derived from the *cross testing* that is used in order to satisfy the nondiscrimination regulations.[13] An age-weighted plan that discriminates as to contributions is permissible provided it does not discriminate when compared to benefits that could be provided using the benefits testing. With respect to defined contribution plans cross testing is an "end justifies the means" or "benefit justifies the contribution" test. (With respect to defined benefit plans cross testing is a "means justifies the ends" or "contribution justifies the benefits" test.) It is permissible for a profit sharing plan to fail the nondiscrimination tests for defined contribution plans, provided it actually produces nondiscriminatory benefits using the nondiscrimination tests applicable to defined benefit plans.

The following comparison shows the results obtained from an age-weighted plan as compared to both a *regular* profit sharing plan and an *integrated* profit sharing plan.[14]

Employee	Compensation	Regular	Integrated	Age-Weighted
Sally	$160,000	$24,000	$24,000	$24,000
John	30,000	4,500	3,510	900
% for Sally		84.2%	87.2%	96.4%

To summarize, compared to defined benefit plans and defined contributions plans (both money purchase and target benefit) profit sharing plans offer the flexibility of not having to make annual contributions, but age-weighted profit sharing plans offer the additional advantage of providing significantly larger allocations to older employees.

Saving/Thrift Plan

Savings and thrift plans are defined contribution plans in which *nondeductible* (after-tax) employee contributions made through payroll deduction generally make up a large portion of total contributions. They can be established on either an informal or formal basis. Informal plans do not enjoy the same tax benefits as formal plans, also referred to as "qualified savings/thrift plans." The following describes formal or qualified savings/thrift plans.

To encourage employee savings, the employer will typically match a portion or all of the employees' contributions. Although employee contributions are not deductible, employer-matching contributions are typically excludable from the employee's taxable income. Earnings on employee and employer contributions are not taxed to the employee until withdrawn.

Convenient payroll deduction of employee contributions, together with income tax deferral on employer contributions and tax deferred growth of both employee and employer contributions made these plans an attractive way to save money. At one time they enjoyed widespread use, but have now been largely replaced by Section 401(k) plans offering the opportunity for *deductible* (before-tax) employee contributions (page 351).

Keogh Plans (HR-10)

These are qualified retirement plans for the self-employed. Although such individuals (sole proprietors or partners operating a trade, business, or profession) are not employees in the commonly accepted sense of the term, they are treated as "employees" for the purpose of allowing them to participate in qualified plans ("employees" include any individuals who have net earnings from self-employment in a trade or business). Virtually no distinction is made between pension, profit sharing, and other retirement plans established by the self-employed and those established by corporations.[15]

Qualified Plans Checklist	
Element	**Limitations**
Eligibility to participate.	Also referred to as "participation requirements," these are the minimum waiting periods and age requirements that are frequently used in plans to assure that plans do not discriminate in favor of highly compensated employees. Exclusions are permitted for age and years of service (maximum of age 21 and 1 year service).
Coverage.	A qualified plan must generally satisfy at least one of the following coverage tests: (1) **Percentage Test.** The plan covers at least 70% of the employees who are not highly compensated. (2) **Ratio/Percentage Test.**[16] The plan covers a percentage of non-highly compensated employees that is at least 70% of the percentage of highly compensated employees who are covered *and* the average benefit percentage for non-highly compensated employees is at least 70% of the average benefit percentage for highly compensated employees.
Maximum limits on benefits.	**401(k) Plans.** During calendar year 2003, the allowable employee deferral is $12,000 (during 2003, participants who are age 50 or over may be permitted to make additional catch-up contributions of $2,000). The following dollar amounts are indexed to the CPI and new limits are announced by the IRS in October of each year: **Defined Benefit Plans.** For plan years ending after 12/31/02, benefits are limited to the lesser of 100% of pay, or $160,000. **Defined Contribution Plans.** For 2003, the annual additions limit is the lesser of 100% of salary, or $40,000 (in a profit-sharing plan the total annual employer deduction is increased to 25% of total compensation of plan participants). The types of plans that fall within this category are listed in the table Types Of Qualified Retirement Plans, page 345.

Qualified Plans Checklist (cont'd)	
Element	**Limitations**
Integration.	A plan integrated with Social Security will often permit significantly higher benefits for higher paid employees within certain limits.
	(1) **Defined benefit plans.** May provide additional monthly benefits of up to the lesser of .75% of earnings, or the base benefit percentage for the plan year.
	(2) **Defined contribution plans.** May provide additional contributions of up to 5.7% of pay in excess of current Social Security wage base ($87,000 in 2003).
	In either type of plan the percentage of total contributions/benefits for those above the "integration level" may not be more than two times the percentage of contributions/benefits below that level. In addition, the disparity between the two percentages must be uniform with respect to all participants. If additional requirements are met, the "integration level" may be lower than the Social Security wage base.
Vesting.	Employer contributions need not become immediately and irrevocably vested, but may be contingent upon continued employment. Thus, costs to the employer may be reduced or benefits increased for employees who continue their employment. "Top-heavy" plans, and certain employer matching contributions, are subject to special rapid vesting rules.
Definition of a "top-heavy" plan.	A plan is top heavy if for "key employees" the present value of accrued benefits in a defined benefit plan or account balances in a defined contribution plan exceeds 60% of accrued benefits or account balances for all employees. Key employees include:
	(1) Officers earning more than $130,000 (as indexed for 2003),
	(2) Any 5% owner of the employer, and
	(3) Any 1% owner who earns more than $150,000 per year.

Qualified Plans Checklist (cont'd)

Element	Limitations
For top-heavy plan purposes, definition of the term "officer."	The term "officer" has a very special meaning. Officers of any employer include no more than either: (1) 50 employees; or, if less, (2) the greater of 3 employees or 10% of the employee group. In other words, the maximum number of employees considered officers is 10% of the employee group, up to 50.
Compensation Limit	A plan will not be qualified unless (for the purpose of any of the qualification rules) not more than $200,000 (in 2003) of annual compensation is taken into account.
Fund investment flexibility.	Trustee may direct the investments into nearly any type of investment media, but strict fiduciary standards apply.
Distributions.	Distributions from qualified plans May be subject to either of the following requirements: (1) **Premature distributions** prior to age 59½ are subject to a 10-percent-penalty tax unless distribution is due to death, disability, separation from service after age 55, or in the event of certain specified hardships. The penalty tax may also be waived if the distribution is annuitized, or to the extent needed to pay family medical expenses in excess of 7½% of adjusted gross income. (2) **Required distributions**, also referred to as "minimum distributions," must begin shortly after a participant has reached age 70½. Generally, distributions to a non-5%-owner must be started by April 1 of the year following the year the individual attains age 70½ or retires, whichever is later. Distributions to a 5%-owner cannot be delayed until retirement. A penalty of 50% applies if this requirement is not met.
Federal estate tax status of death benefits.	Fully included in estate.

INDIVIDUAL RETIREMENT ARRANGEMENTS (IRAs)

There are two types of regular individual retirement arrangements, individual retirement accounts and individual retirement annuities. Each is often referred to as an "IRA," or a "traditional IRA." Generally, an individual retirement *account* is set up as a trust or custodial account with a bank, a federally insured credit union, or a savings and loan association; whereas an individual retirement *annuity* is established by purchasing an annuity contract from a life insurance company.[17] The IRA may not hold life insurance.

Contributions may be made up to the time when the individual's tax return is due (excluding extensions). In order to deduct contributions an individual must: (1) have compensation (including earned income as an employee or self-employed person, or alimony); and (2) not have attained age 70½ during the taxable year for which the contribution is made.

In 2003, a deduction may be taken for amounts contributed up to the lesser of $3,000 or 100% of compensation includable in gross income. An additional "catch-up" contribution of $500 is allowed for individuals who attain age 50 before the close of the taxable year. Deductions may be reduced or eliminated if the individual is an "active participant" in a qualified plan. The phase-out range for a *married couple filing jointly* is between $150,000 and $160,000 for a spouse who is not an active participant, and between $60,000 and $70,000 for a spouse who is an active participant. The phase-out range for a *single individual* who is an active participant is between $40,000 and $50,000. Similar deductions may be taken for contributions to the IRA of a lesser-compensated spouse.

Generally, funds accumulated in a plan are not taxable until they are actually distributed. However, amounts distributed prior to age 59½ are considered premature distributions and are subject to a 10-percent penalty tax. Exceptions to the penalty tax include distributions: (1) made on or after death; (2) attributable to disability; (3) that are part of a series of substantially equal periodic payments made (at least annually) for the life or life expectancy of the individual or the joint lives or joint life expectancy of the individual and a designated beneficiary (e.g., an annuity payout); (4) for medical expenses in excess of 7.5% of adjusted gross income; (5) for health insurance premiums for those receiving unemployment compensation; (6) to pay for a first home; or (7) to pay for qualified higher education expenses. Distributions from a plan must usually begin by April 1 of the year after the year in which the individual reaches age 70½. In order to prevent current taxation, IRAs are frequently used for "rollovers" of distributions from qualified plans, 403(b) plans, or eligible 457 government plans. An IRA that meets certain requirements may accept an expanded rate of contribution as a simplified employee pension (SEP) – see page 365.

ROTH IRA

In 2003, the Roth IRA permits individuals to make *nondeductible* contributions to an IRA of up to the lesser of 100% of compensation or $3,000 per year.[18] An additional "catch-up" contribution of $500 is allowed for individuals who attain age 50 before the close of the taxable year. Unlike traditional IRAs, contributions may be made after age 70½, and husband and wife may contribute amounts without regard to whether either of them is a participant in another qualified plan as long as there is sufficient compensation. The annual contribution limit is reduced (dollar-for-dollar) by all contributions to a traditional IRA. Also, the maximum yearly contribution is subject to a pro rata phaseout for *taxpayers filing jointly* with modified adjusted gross incomes between $150,000 and $160,000 (for *single taxpayers* with modified adjusted gross incomes between $95,000 and $110,000). In contrast, with a traditional IRA if the participant is an active participant in a qualified plan the deductible phaseout limits in 2003 are $60,000 to $70,000 for taxpayers filing jointly and $40,000 to $50,000 for single taxpayers.

As with the traditional IRA, the Roth IRA accumulates tax-deferred. Provided the account has been held for at least five years, *distributions are not subject to income taxes* if: (1) the owner is at least age 59½; (2) the distribution is made after the owner's death; (3) the distribution is attributable to the owner being disabled; or (4) the distribution is for qualified first-time home buyer expenses (limited to $10,000 for both the owner and specified family members). A 10-percent penalty tax applies to the taxable portion of withdrawals that are not qualified. Unlike traditional IRAs, there are no requirements that distributions be started or completed by any particular date, unless the owner dies.

Provided modified adjusted gross income does not exceed $100,000, a Roth IRA may generally accept a conversion from a traditional IRA. However, distributions in excess of basis from the traditional IRA are included in gross income (but not for purposes of determining modified adjusted gross income).

The following factors might be considered when determining whether for a particular taxpayer the Roth IRA is better than a traditional IRA, or whether to make a taxable rollover to a Roth IRA: (1) the current age of the taxpayer; (2) the taxpayer's current and anticipated future marginal income tax brackets; (3) the taxpayer's need for a current income tax deduction; (4) the availability of other funds to pay the taxes on Roth IRA contributions or rollovers; and (5) anticipated reduction of taxes on Social Security income caused by receiving untaxed IRA income.

WHICH IRA – ROTH OR TRADITIONAL?

A Roth IRA offers the following potential advantages: (1) if used for higher education expenses, withdrawals can be made prior to age 59½ without penalty; (2) distributions are not required at age 70½; (3) contributions may continue after reaching age 70½; (4) phaseout limits are higher than those for deductible contributions to a Traditional IRA; and (5) tax-free retirement distributions will not push modified adjusted gross income above the threshold that triggers taxation of Social Security benefits (page 393). This analysis focuses on after-tax accumulations and requires assumptions regarding tax rates prior to and after retirement (the above chart may help).

Assuming the **same** tax rate prior to and after retirement: (1) there is no difference between the after-tax distributions from a Roth IRA and a Traditional IRA if all funds can be deposited in a Traditional IRA, or other tax deductible fund (Table A, page 363); (2) the Roth IRA offers the advantage of larger after-tax distributions if before-tax funds exceed the $3,000 limit that can be deposited in a Traditional IRA and the excess must be placed in a nondeductible side fund (Table B, page 364). Further, the Roth IRA advantage increases if the side fund earnings are currently taxed.

Assuming a **lower** tax rate after retirement (e.g., 25% prior to retirement and 15% after retirement), the Traditional IRA generally provides larger after-tax distributions. For active participants, no comparison need be made assuming a tax rate higher than 25% since deductible contributions to a Traditional IRA are phased out before reaching the 28% tax rate (i.e., no deduction is allowed in 2003 for "married filing jointly" once modified adjusted gross income exceeds $70,000 or for a "single individual" once modified adjusted gross income exceeds $50,000). Note that marginal tax rates in the above chart vary according to *taxable income*, whereas IRA contributions are phased out according to *modified adjusted gross income*. Taxable income is equal to adjusted gross income less deductions and personal exemptions.

Assuming a **higher** tax rate after retirement (e.g., 25% prior to retirement and 28% after retirement), the Roth IRA provides larger after-tax distributions.

Table A – This table assumes an 8% interest rate and 25% tax rate. The nondeductible Roth IRA deposit requires $1,333 before taxes $(1,000 \div (1 - .25) = 1,333)$. This is the same as making a deductible deposit of $1,333 to a Traditional IRA. There is no Roth IRA advantage.

	Roth IRA			Traditional IRA		
Year	Deposit	Plus Interest	Value	Deposit	Plus Interest	Value
1	1,000	80	1,080	1,333	107	1,440
2	1,000	166	2,246	1,333	222	2,995
3	1,000	260	3,506	1,333	346	4,675
4	1,000	360	4,867	1,333	481	6,489
5	1,000	469	6,336	1,333	626	8,448
6	1,000	587	7,923	1,333	782	10,564
7	1,000	714	9,637	1,333	952	12,849
8	1,000	851	11,488	1,333	1,135	15,317
9	1,000	999	13,487	1,333	1,332	17,982
10	1,000	1,159	15,645	1,333	1,545	20,861
11	1,000	1,332	17,977	1,333	1,776	23,970
12	1,000	1,518	20,495	1,333	2,024	27,327
13	1,000	1,720	23,215	1,333	2,293	30,953
14	1,000	1,937	26,152	1,333	2,583	34,869
15	1,000	2,172	29,324	1,333	2,896	39,099
16	1,000	2,426	32,750	1,333	3,235	43,667
17	1,000	2,700	36,450	1,333	3,600	48,600
18	1,000	2,996	40,446	1,333	3,995	53,928
19	1,000	3,316	44,762	1,333	4,421	59,683
20	1,000	3,661	49,423	1,333	4,881	65,897
Less Taxes			0			16,474
Net Distribution			49,423			49,423

Table B – This table assumes an 8% interest rate and 25% tax rate. The nondeductible Roth IRA deposit requires $4,000 before taxes (3,000 ÷ (1 - .25) = 4,000). This is the same as making a deductible deposit of $3,000 to a Traditional IRA *plus* a nondeductible deposit of $750 to a Side Fund (3,000 + 750 ÷ (1 - .25) = 4,000). The Roth IRA advantage is $7,823 when compared to a currently taxed side fund (148,269 - 111,202 - 29,245 = 7,822) and $5,517 when compared to a tax deferred side fund (148,269 - 111,202 - 31,550 = 5,517).

	Roth IRA		Traditional IRA		Side Fund		
Year	Deposit	Value	Deposit	Value	Deposit	Currently Taxed	Tax Deferred
1	3,000	3,240	3,000	3,240	750	795	810
2	3,000	6,739	3,000	6,739	750	1,638	1,685
3	3,000	10,518	3,000	10,518	750	2,531	2,630
4	3,000	14,600	3,000	14,600	750	3,478	3,650
5	3,000	19,008	3,000	19,008	750	4,481	4,752
6	3,000	23,768	3,000	23,768	750	5,545	5,942
7	3,000	28,910	3,000	28,910	750	6,673	7,227
8	3,000	34,463	3,000	34,463	750	7,868	8,616
9	3,000	40,460	3,000	40,460	750	9,136	10,115
10	3,000	46,936	3,000	46,936	750	10,479	11,734
11	3,000	53,931	3,000	53,931	750	11,902	13,483
12	3,000	61,486	3,000	61,486	750	13,412	15,371
13	3,000	69,645	3,000	69,645	750	15,011	17,411
14	3,000	78,456	3,000	78,456	750	16,707	19,614
15	3,000	87,973	3,000	87,973	750	18,504	21,993
16	3,000	98,251	3,000	98,251	750	20,410	24,563
17	3,000	109,351	3,000	109,351	750	22,429	27,338
18	3,000	121,339	3,000	121,339	750	24,570	30,335
19	3,000	134,286	3,000	134,286	750	26,839	33,571
20	3,000	148,269	3,000	148,269	750	29,245	37,067
Less Taxes		0		37,067		0	5,517
Net Distribution		148,269		111,202		29,245	31,550

SIMPLE IRA PLAN

A SIMPLE IRA plan ("SIMPLE" stands for Savings Incentive Match Plan for Employees) is easier to install and administer than a qualified plan. It is considered a replacement for the SARSEP and must be established by an employer for employees using either Form 5304-SIMPLE or Form 5305-SIMPLE.[19]

In order to set up a SIMPLE IRA plan the employer must not maintain another employer-sponsored retirement plan (including qualified plans, tax-sheltered annuities, and SEPs) and in the preceding year must have employed 100 or fewer employees earning at least $5,000. The plan must cover any employee who has earned at least $5,000 in any two preceding years and is reasonably expected to earn at least $5,000 in the current year. However, the employer may establish less restrictive eligibility requirements. Self-employed individuals may establish and participate in a SIMPLE IRA plan.

The employee is allowed to contribute up to $8,000 per year (in 2003). Although the deferral amount is expressed as a percentage of compensation there is no limit on this percentage (e.g., in order to defer the maximum $8,000 per year, an employee earning $10,000 could elect to defer 80% of compensation). The $3,000 limit for traditional IRAs does not apply to a SIMPLE IRA. In addition, if the plan so provides, an individual age 50 or over may make catch-up contributions of up to $1,000 in 2003.

The employer is required to either contribute 2% of the entire payroll (under a *nonelective contributions* formula) or match contributions of up to 3% of each employee's salary (under a *matching* formula). However, a special rule permits the employer to elect a lower percentage under the matching formula, but not less than 1%, and it cannot be used for more than two out of any five years.

A SIMPLE IRA plan is not subject to nondiscrimination testing or top-heavy rules, and the reporting requirements are simplified. All contributions are excludable from the employee's income and must be fully vested. The penalty for early withdrawal prior to age 59½ is 25% during the first two years of participation and 10% thereafter (unless one of the exceptions applies).

A SIMPLE 401(k) plan is a 401(k) plan that satisfies the non-discrimination requirement by adopting certain SIMPLE 401(k) provisions that are similar to the above requirements. Such a plan is not subject to nondiscrimination tests and the top-heavy rules, but it will be subject to other qualified plan requirements.

SIMPLIFIED EMPLOYEE PENSION (SEP)

A simplified employee pension (SEP) is an employee's individual retirement account that may accept an expanded rate of contribution from his employer. Because payments are made into an IRA established for each employee they are also referred to as SEP-IRAs. SEPs can be established with sole proprietorships, partnerships or corporations, and are particularly attractive for the self-employed individual who has no other employees or the individual who has additional income from outside employment. Generally, all employees must be included in a SEP except for: (1) employees who have not worked for the employer three out of the last five years; (2) employees who earn less than $450 (as indexed in 2003 for inflation); (3) employees who have not reached age 21; (4) employees covered by a collective bargaining agreement; and (5) non-resident aliens. They are generally easy to set up and require little administration.

SEPs can be established and funded as late as the due date (plus extensions) of the employer's (or self-employed's) tax return. Pre-tax contributions are limited to the lesser of 25% of the first $200,000 (in 2003) of net earned income or $40,000 (with sole proprietorships and partnerships the owners are effectively limited to 20%). No minimum funding standards are imposed. Contributions are not subject to income tax withholding, FICA, or FUTA. Typically these plans are self-directed, in that the individual participant decides how funds will be invested. All earnings within the plan accumulate on a tax-deferred basis. The employer may not prohibit withdrawals from the plan, although they are subject to a penalty tax if made before age 59½. Essentially, there are four types of SEP plans with varying degrees of complexity:

5305-SEP is very easy to implement, requiring only the completion of five questions on IRS Form 5305-SEP. However, this may not be used by employers who maintain other qualified retirement plans, use leased employees, or have had a defined benefit plan.

SEP prototype plans are provided by financial institutions (with or without a fee). Prototype plans are particularly useful if the employer wants to integrate the SEP contributions with Social Security (i.e., provide increased contributions for highly paid employees).

Individually designed plans are typically drafted by an attorney. They tend to be more expensive and complicated, therefore less often used.

SARSEP plans are salary reduction SEPs that allow employees to make pretax contributions to their IRAs.[20] The provisions permitting the establishment of these plans were terminated at the end of 1996. SARSEPs already in existence prior to 1997 may continue to operate under preexisting law, receive contributions, and add new employees, but new SARSEPs may not be established. In their place individuals may wish to consider the SIMPLE IRA (page 364).

IRA DISTRIBUTION PLANNING

New rules for IRA required minimum distributions were finalized in 2002, replacing earlier regulations proposed in 2001 and more complex regulations first issued in 1987. The final rules are simpler and generally result in lower distribution amounts. IRA distributions for years after 2002 must be calculated under the final regulations.

For most individuals, the calculation of required minimum distributions during life is very simple: the account balance as of December 31 of the preceding year is divided by a uniform life expectancy based on the account owner's age in that year, using the Lifetime Required Minimum Distributions table, page 454. This method is used regardless of the age of the beneficiary, except that if the beneficiary is a spouse more than 10 years younger than the owner, a different table is used.

Designated beneficiary (DB) – The individual (or certain trusts) designated to receive the IRA proceeds, either by the terms of the IRA document or by an affirmative election by the IRA owner. Generally, the designated beneficiary will be determined as of September 30 of the calendar year following the calendar year of the owner's death.

Required beginning date (RBD) – This is April 1st of the year following the owner's attaining age 70½.

Required minimum distribution (RMD) – The minimum required payments from an IRA (a penalty tax of 50% is imposed on any RMD not made).

Stretch IRA – Uses a combination of beneficiary designations and life expectancy elections to delay receipt of distributions (also referred to as "multi-generation IRAs"). Typically assumes IRA owner and spouse will not need the funds for retirement or for estate taxes. Use of disclaimers may allow post-mortem planning.

If an individual owns more than one IRA, the required minimum distribution must be calculated separately for each IRA, but the total RMD may then be taken from any one or more of the IRAs. Failure to take a minimum distribution will result in a penalty tax of 50%.

If an IRA owner dies before his required beginning date, distributions must be made under one of two methods: (1) five year rule – the entire interest must be distributed within five years after the death of the IRA owner (regardless of who or what entity receives the distribution); or (2) life expectancy rule – if any portion of the interest is payable to a designated beneficiary, that portion must be distributed over the life (or life expectancy) of the beneficiary, beginning within one year of the owner's death.

If the IRA owner dies on or after his required beginning date, but before his entire interest in the IRA has been distributed, the entire remaining balance must generally be distributed at least as rapidly as under the method of distribution in effect as of the owner's date of death.

Estate taxes on the IRA will be due at the death of the owner or his spouse, depending upon the beneficiary designation. Incorrectly changing the name on an inherited IRA account can result in the IRA becoming subject to income taxes within a year. When dealing with an inherited IRA the following should be determined: (1) whether distributions have started; (2) whether the required beginning date (RBD) has been reached; (3) whether a beneficiary has been named; and (4) who the beneficiary is. The answers will determine which of the following options are available:

IRA inherited by spouse before RBD – A surviving spouse beneficiary may: (1) withdraw the assets within five years; or (2) elect to treat the IRA as her own (or transfer assets to her own IRA), name a new beneficiary, and take distributions over her lifetime (beginning either at end of the year following husband's death or by end of the year he would have turned age 70½). Option (2) allows for naming a new designated beneficiary and deferral of distributions until spouse's age 70½.

IRA inherited by spouse after RBD – A surviving spouse beneficiary may: (1) continue receiving distributions under the method in effect before her husband's death; (2) take distributions over her lifetime, beginning no later than the end of the year following her husband's death; or (3) transfer assets into her own IRA (unless they have been annuitized). In order to treat the IRA as her own she must be the sole primary beneficiary.

IRA inherited by non-spouse before RBD – A non-spouse beneficiary may: (1) withdraw the assets within five years; or (2) take distributions over his or her lifetime, beginning no later than the end of the year following the owner's death (if multiple non-spouse beneficiaries must use life expectancy of oldest beneficiary).

IRA inherited by non-spouse after RBD – A designated beneficiary must withdraw assets over his or her life (or life expectancy), beginning no later than the end of the year following the owner's death.

THE IRA SPECTRUM

Type	Eligibility For Plan	Limits On Contribution
Traditional deductible (page 360)	Not active participant in employer-sponsored retirement plan, or Individual: In 2003, AGI less than $50,000 (phase-out $40,000-$50,000). Married filing jointly: In 2003, AGI less than $70,000 (phase-out $60,000-$70,000).	*Individual*: $3,000. *Married filing jointly*: $6,000. (Combined annual contributions to both Traditional and Roth IRA are limited to $3,000 or $6,000.) Contributions *not* allowed after age 70½. Catch-up for individuals who have reached age 50 is $500.
Traditional nondeductible	No specific requirements.	Same as deductible.
Roth (page 361)	Individual: AGI less than $110,000 (phase-out $95,000 - $110,000) Married filing jointly: AGI less than $160,000 (phase-out $150,000 - $160,000)	*Individual*: $3,000. *Married filing jointly*: $6,000. Contributions allowed after age 70½. Catch-up for individuals who have reached age 50 is $500.
SIMPLE (page 364)	Self-employed or employed by company with 100 employees or less.	*Employer*: 3% matching or 2% non-elective. *Employee*: $8,000 in 2003. Catch-up for individuals who have reached age 50 is $1,000 in 2003.
SEP (page 365)	Self-employed or employed by company with 25 employees or less.	Up to 25% of employees salary or $40,000 maximum. Catch-up for individuals who have reached age is $2,000 in 2003.

Type	Deductible	Tax Advantages	Withdrawals/Distributions
Traditional deductible	Yes.	Tax-deferred earnings, but taxable upon distribution.	Penalty-free if after age 59½, for first home, higher education, or upon death. Withdrawal required at age 70½.
Traditional nondeductible	No.	Same as deductible, but nondeductible contributions create basis.	Same as deductible, but amounts received treated partly tax-free and partly taxable.
Roth	No.	Tax-free earnings. Early withdrawals of contributions tax-free and penalty-free.	Tax-free if after 5 years, after age 59½, for first home, disability, or upon death. Distributions *not* required at age 70½.
SIMPLE	Contributions	Tax-deferred earnings are before taxes.	Required at age 70½. but withdrawals taxable.
SEP	Contributions	Tax-deferred are before taxes.	Required at age 70½. earnings, but withdrawals taxable.

Note: AGI stands for adjusted gross income.

SECTION 403(b) PLAN

A 403(b) plan is also referred to as a "tax sheltered annuity," or "TSA." Rather than "tax sheltered annuity," the Securities and Exchange Commission prefers the term "tax deferred annuity." Many companies now use the terms "tax deferred annuity" and "TDA," particularly when marketing variable annuities. Section 403(b) plans are also referred to as "qualified annuity plans" or "501(c)(3) pensions."[21]

These plans are available to employees of public schools and colleges, and certain non-profit hospitals, charitable, religious, scientific, and educational organizations. The employee may supply the funds by agreeing to a salary reduction, or by foregoing a salary increase, or the employer may make contributions as additional compensation to the employee. Nondiscrimination rules may apply to both salary reduction and employer contributions.

Contributions. Contributions are *before taxes*, meaning that a participant is able to exclude the contributions from current taxable income.[22] Where a reduction in salary is taken to provide the premium payments for a 403(b) plan, Social Security taxes and benefits are based upon the *unreduced* salary (i.e., although income taxes are reduced, there is no reduction in Social Security taxes).

Generally, with a salary reduction plan the lower of these *two* limits may be excluded from income each year:

(1) A limit of $12,000 in 2003, which also includes total salary reduction contributions to Section 401(k) plans, Simplified Employee Pension plans and SIMPLE IRAs. "Catch up" provisions allow: (a) employees who have attained age 50 to increase this amount by an additional $2,000 in 2003; and (b) certain employees with 15 years of service to increase this amount by an additional $3,000.

(2) The lesser of $40,000 or 100% of compensation, made to all 403(b) plans and, under some circumstances, retirement plans.

The compounding effect of before tax contributions and tax-deferred growth may result in substantially increased accumulations. Since the annuity is generally portable to another qualified employer, contributions may be continued when changing employment.

Distributions. Distributions from tax deferred annuities are subject to *ordinary income taxes*, unless rolled over into a traditional Individual Retirement Arrangement (IRA), another 403(b) plan, a 401(k) plan, a 457 government plan, or a 401(a) qualified retirement plan. However, the employee is allowed a tax-free recovery of any investment in the contract.

In addition, withdrawals may be subject to a *10-percent-penalty tax*. However, penalty-free withdrawals are allowed once the participant has attained age 59½, separated from service after attaining age 55, or under other specific circumstances (e.g., death, disability, distributions taken as part of substantially equal periodic payments beginning after separation from service, or distributions used for medical expenses exceeding 7.5% of adjusted gross income).

With some restrictions, *tax-free loans* are also available (the maximum tax-free loan is generally one-half the contract value, or $50,000, whichever is less).

Required distributions of amounts accruing after 1986 generally must begin by April 1st of the year following the year in which the employee retires or attains age 70½, whichever is later. Payments made under an annuity contract may be for the life of the employee (or lives of the employee and his beneficiary), or a period certain not longer than the life expectancy of the employee (or joint and last survivor life expectancy of the employee and his beneficiary).

SECTION 457 PLAN

Section 457 plans are nonqualified deferred compensation plans available to employees of state and local governments and tax-exempt organizations. *State and local governments* include a state, a political subdivision of a state, or any agency or instrumentality of either of them (e.g., a school district or sewage authority). *Tax-exempt organizations* include those types of nongovernmental organizations exempt from tax under Code Section 501 (i.e., most nonprofit organizations that serve their members or some public or charitable purpose, but not a church or synagogue). Section 457 plans can also be made available to independent contractors, but under somewhat different rules. By deferring income, employees are able to reduce current income taxes while saving more for retirement than they would with the typical after-tax savings plan.[23]

Eligible Plans. The term "eligible plans" is used to describe the deferred compensation plans of state and local governments and tax-exempt organizations that comply with the provisions of Section 457. In 2003, *deferrals are limited* to the lesser of $12,000, or 100% of includable compensation ("catch-up" provisions may permit larger deferrals). Benefits usually are not subject to forfeiture. These plans are most often used for the "rank and file" employees of *state and local governments*, who desire to defer limited amounts of compensation on an

attractive tax deferred
basis. Employees are
not taxed until the
benefits are actually
paid or otherwise
made available to
them. *Tax-exempt*
organizations can
only make these
plans available to a
select group of man-
agement or highly

EMPLOYEES
of
State and Local Governments
Tax-Exempt Organizations

ELIGIBLE PLANS	INELIGIBLE PLANS
• Deferrals limited	• Deferrals unlimited
• Benefits not subject to forfeiture	• Benefits subject to forfeiture
• State and local government have no specific coverage requirements	• Tax-exempt organizations must limit coverage to "top hat" group
• Employees taxed when benefits are received	• Employees taxed when there is no substantial risk of forfeiture
• Distribution requirements	• No distribution requirements

compensated employees. The *earliest* plan distributions can be made is at severance of employment, death, an "unforeseeable emergency," or in the calendar
year in which the participant reaches age 70½. Distributions from Section 457
plans are subject to ordinary income taxes. Rollovers are permitted to and from
an eligible Section 457 plan of a state or local government, a qualified plan, a
Section 403(b) tax sheltered annuity, or an IRA.

Ineligible Plans. Also referred to as "Section 457(f) plans," under ineligible
plans employees may make *unlimited deferrals* of compensation, provided the
benefits are subject to a "substantial risk of forfeiture" (this exists if a participant's
right to the compensation is conditioned upon the future performance of substantial services). These plans are most often used by *tax-exempt organizations*
to provide substantial deferrals for a select group of management or highly compensated employees. Use of ineligible plans by *state and local governments* is
generally limited to highly paid employees who can accept a risk of forfeiture,
since such a risk is often unacceptable to the "rank and file" employee. Ineligible
plans are not required to comply with any specific distribution requirements.

Funding. Both eligible and ineligible plans may *not* be formally funded, except
for eligible governmental plans. However, it is customary and desirable for
employers to "informally" fund their obligations through the purchase of annuities
or investment products. Any deferrals, and assets purchased with the deferrals,
must remain the property of the employer and are subject to the employer's general creditors. If life insurance is purchased with amounts deferred, the premiums
are not taxed to the participant as long as the employer remains the owner and
beneficiary of the contract. However, upon the employee's death, payment of the
proceeds to the employee's beneficiary would be taxed under the normal annuity
rules and would not be treated as tax-free death proceeds.

CAFETERIA PLANS

Cafeteria plans, also described as "flexible benefit" plans or Section 125 plans, allow participating employees to choose between a number of non-taxable qualified benefits or taxable cash. Plans typically offer participants a "cafeteria menu" of items, including group term life insurance, medical expense insurance, dependent group term life insurance, child care, and dental expense coverage.[24]

Among the advantages to an *employer* that establishes such a plan are reductions in FICA (Federal Insurance Contributions Act) and FUTA (Federal Unemployment Tax Act) taxes, expansion of employee benefits, and enhanced employee appreciation of the benefit package. *Employee* advantages include the opportunity to select benefits most suited to individual needs; to pay for these benefits with before-tax, rather than after-tax dollars; to obtain benefits that may not be available for individual purchase; and to pay less FICA taxes by reducing taxable income.

The design of cafeteria plans can range from simple "premium only" plans to full-blown flexible benefit plans including flexible spending accounts. Premium-only plans, which are also referred to as "premium-conversion" plans, merely allow employees to use their before-tax, rather than after-tax, dollars for plan contributions. In contrast, flexible spending accounts allow employees to defer before-tax dollars to pay for dependent care expenses and unreimbursed medical expenses (such as deductibles and coinsurance payments, glasses, and eye exams).

The election to defer dollars must be made in advance of the plan year and can be changed only under limited circumstances. With flexible spending accounts, employees forfeit fund balances that are not used up by the end of the plan year, although typically an additional period is allowed after the close of the plan year for submission of claims incurred during the plan year. Forfeitures may be used to offset the employer's cost of administering the plan, reallocated proportionately to other employees, or given to charity.

Former employees may participate, but self-employed individuals may not. All plans are subject to special nondiscrimination rules. Proper administration of cafeteria plans requires preparing plan documents, conducting annual enrollments, tracking claims and benefit payments, and filing yearly 5500 reports.

ANNUITIES

An annuity is a periodic payment intended to begin at either a specific or to-be-designated date and lasting for either a fixed period or for a period measured by a designated life or lives. Upon retirement the retiree faces the challenge of determining how much money can be safely spent each month. Withdrawing funds *too rapidly* will exhaust retirement savings and could lead to impoverishment. Withdrawing funds *too slowly* will lower the retiree's standard of living and could produce an unintended windfall for heirs. By pooling the resources of many individuals the life annuity provides a stream of income that cannot be outlived. For the definition of a *life* annuity, see paragraph (4)(c), page 380.

Compared To Life Insurance. Annuities and life insurance both provide protection against a loss of income. By *creating* an estate life insurance provides protection against dying too soon (i.e., a premature death). In contrast, by systematically *liquidating* an existing sum of money the annuity provides protection against living too long.

Qualified Annuity vs. Nonqualified Annuity. A "qualified" annuity is one that is used as part of a qualified retirement plan that complies with the provisions of Code section 401(a). In contrast, a "nonqualified" annuity is not associated with an employer-provided qualified retirement plan and may be purchased by any individual or entity. Despite its name a "nonqualified" annuity offers unique tax advantages. The following discussion of annuities relates to nonqualified annuities.

Parties To An Annuity. As with a life insurance contract, there are a number of parties to an annuity who acquire different rights and obligations under the annuity contract.

(1) **Owner.** Every annuity contract must have an owner, who is also referred to as an "annuity holder." The owner does not have to be an individual person, but can be a trust or other legal entity. The internal cash value buildup of an annuity is not currently taxable, unless the contract is owned by a corporation or other entity that is not considered under the tax law to be a natural person.[25] (The annuity contract owner has essentially the same ownership rights as the owner of a life insurance contract.) Under the annuity contract the owner names the individual who will serve as the annuitant, names the individual or entity, who will be the beneficiary under the contract, determines when the contract will be annuitized, and has the power to make partial withdrawals from the contract or fully surrender the contract for its cash value.

(2) **Annuitant.** The annuitant is that individual named in the annuity contract whose life serves as the *measuring life* for purposes of determining benefits to be paid under the annuity contract. (In this sense, the *annuitant* under an annuity contract is comparable to the *insured* under a life insurance contract.) Unlike the owner and the beneficiary, the annuitant must be an individual. Annuity contracts can have more than one annuitant (e.g., a contract providing a joint and survivor benefit to husband and wife has two annuitants). While it is most common for the owner and annuitant to be the same person, they can be different (e.g., a father purchases an annuity and makes his 45-year-old son the annuitant in order to use his son's life in calculating benefit payments).

(3) **Payee.** This is the person who receives the annuity payments. Most often the payee is also the owner and annuitant, but the payee can be merely the owner, with another individual as the annuitant.

(4) **Beneficiary.** Should the owner, or under some circumstances the annuitant, die after premiums are paid but before the contract is annuitized (i.e., begins paying out benefits) a death benefit allows for recovery of the amount invested in the contract. The beneficiary is that individual or entity who is named to receive this death benefit. However, the beneficiary typically has no other rights under the contract.

(5) **Insurance Company.** An insurance company issues *commercial* annuities to the annuity owner, whereas *private* annuities are contracts between individuals (page 384). In the annuity contract the company undertakes certain financial obligations to the owner, the annuitant, and the beneficiary.

The Annuity Matrix

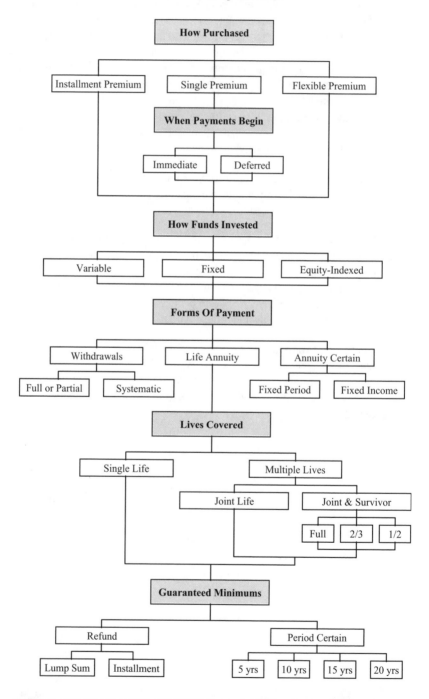

The Annuity Matrix, on page 376, will provide a better understanding of the basic features of the nonqualified annuity.

(1) **How Purchased.** Annuities can generally be purchased by paying installment premiums that are typically level periodic payments, by a *single premium*, or by *flexible premiums*, which allow premiums to be made at varying intervals and in varying amounts.

(2) **When Payments Begin.** When payment is made with a single premium the purchaser has the choice of beginning payments immediately (an *immediate* annuity) or deferring payments until a later date (a *deferred* annuity).

(3) **How Funds Invested.** The individual purchasing an annuity can choose between annuities offering a variety of guarantees and investment options.

   (a) **Fixed Annuity.** The term "fixed annuity" refers to the interest rate paid by the issuing company on the annuity contract. Despite its name, this rate does change. During the accumulation phase a fixed annuity provide a *current* rate that is subject to change after an initial guarantee period typically ranging from 1 to 5 years. A minimum *guaranteed* rate is also provided. Fixed annuity contracts containing a *bailout provision* allow the contract holder to withdraw funds without a surrender charge if the credited interest rate falls below a specific bailout rate (e.g., from 1% to 3% below the initial credited rate). (However, taking advantage of a bailout provision to avoid a withdrawal penalty imposed by the insurance company does not avoid ordinary income taxes and possible penalty taxes imposed by the IRS – see Premature Distribution Penalty Tax, page 386.) The premiums paid for a fixed annuity become part of the insurers general account and the purchaser has no say as to how they are invested. Once annuitized the contract pays a periodic fixed dollar amount under the form of payment that is selected (see Forms Of Payment, page 379).

   (b) **Variable Annuity.** A *variable* annuity allows the owner to select among a number of investment options, to include various mutual funds, bond funds, money market accounts, and a guaranteed account (also referred to as a "fixed" account). Under federal law the variable annuity is consider a "security" and therefore subject to a much higher degree of regulation than the fixed annuity. Anyone selling a variable annuity must have the required securities licenses and a prospectus must be delivered with or preceding a proposal to a prospect or client.

i. **Accumulation Phase.** During the accumulation phase variable
annuity premiums are placed in *separate accounts* that are held
and invested apart from the insurance company's assets held the
general account. (While not precisely the same the separate variable accounts are also referred to as subaccounts, variable subaccounts, flexible accounts, and flexible subaccounts.) As an investment option, most variable annuities offer a *guaranteed account*,
also referred to as a fixed account, which functions much like a
fixed annuity. Subject to both timing and dollar limitations, the
holder of a variable annuity is allowed to periodically transfer
funds between separate accounts, and between separate accounts
and the guaranteed account. This investment flexibility allows the
account holder to reposition investments in response to market
conditions or due to a desire to either increase or decrease risk
(e.g., as retirement age approaches amounts might be transferred
out of stock mutual funds and into the guaranteed account). An
accumulation unit, also referred to as a *unit of credit*, is the
measure used to track the value of a variable annuity during the
accumulation phase. As additional premiums are paid, the annuity
holder is credited with additional accumulation units. The values
of these units fluctuate according to the values of the underlying
investment accounts.

ii. **Distribution Phase.** When a variable annuity is annuitized the
contract's *accumulation units* are exchanged for *annuity units*.
The number of annuity units received depends not only upon the
existing accumulation units, but also upon the insurance company's assumptions regarding mortality, dividend rates, and expenses. In calculating the number of annuity units, the insurance company uses an assumed interest rate (AIR) that, if earned, will produce a level benefit payment. Some annuity contracts allow the
contract holder to select an AIR within a narrow range of rates. By
opting for a lower AIR the conservative contract holder accepts
fewer annuity units, and lower initial dollar payments, in exchange
for an increased likelihood of increasing benefit payments (in an
up market) and a decreased likelihood of decreasing benefit payments (in a down market).[26]

Once annuitized, the number of annuity units remains constant but the dollar amount of the annuity payments will fluctuate depending upon the investment results of the underlying assets. Thus, the annuity holder who elects payments under a variable option is subject to the risk that monthly benefit payments may *decrease* as well as increase. To lessen this risk of loss of income, at the time of annuitization most variable annuity contracts allow the annuity holder to divide the accumulation value and receive both variable and fixed monthly payments. For example, it is common for an individual to purchase a variable annuity during the accumulation period to elect to receive a portion of the benefit payments in the form of a fixed annuity with guaranteed monthly payments.

(c) **Equity-Indexed Annuity.** The equity-indexed annuity (EIA) is a hybrid of the fixed and variable annuities (see discussion, page 383). By linking the interest rate to an equity index the EIA allows the contract holder to benefit from the returns associated with a rising stock market. A minimum guaranteed interest rate provides protection from a falling stock market. A securities license is not needed to sell EIAs.

(4) **Forms Of Payment.** Under the *settlement options*, also referred to as *payout options*, the annuity owner has a contractual right to take payment of the annuity proceeds in a number of ways.

(a) *Withdrawals* from an annuity can be either *partial* or *full*, or made under a *systematic* program providing for periodic income. Although partial or full surrenders may be subject to contract fees or surrender charges, particularly in the early years of a contract, under most annuity contracts systematic withdrawals are made without these charges. Systematic withdrawals typically take one of three forms; interest only, flat dollar amount, or an amount based upon a calculated life expectancy. Because they avoid annuitization of the contract, systematic withdrawals provide the contract owner with a great deal of flexibility to withdraw more or less funds as needed. Withdrawals are subject to ordinary income taxes and possible penalty taxes imposed by the IRS.

(b) An *annuity certain* involves payment of a fixed amount or sum without regard to the life-expectancy of the annuitant or annuitants.

i. Payments for a *fixed period* allow the payee to receive the annuity's accumulated value over a set number of years. This is similar to the fixed payments that are received under an installment sale.

A variation of the fixed period, known as a *temporary life annuity,* provides for the payments to terminate should the annuitant die before the end of the fixed period.

    ii. Payments for a *fixed amount* allow the annuitant to receive set benefit payments for as long as the annuity's accumulated value lasts.

(c) A *life annuity* involves payment of a periodic income for a period of time measured by the life of the annuitant or annuitants.

(5) **Lives Covered.** One or more individuals may be named as the annuitants under a settlement option.

(a) A settlement option involving a *single life* annuity is the simplest and purest form of assuring a stream of income that cannot be outlived. Benefits are paid for the life of a single annuitant, with all payments ceasing upon the annuitant's death.

(b) A settlement option can also involve *multiple lives.* Virtually all multiple life annuities involve two individuals, but in theory it is possible for annuities to cover any number of lives (the following discussion assumes two lives).

    i. A *joint life* annuity provides for payments so long as all both annuitants are alive. However, all payments terminate upon the death of either of the annuitants. There is limited demand for this type of annuity settlement option.

    ii. A *joint and survivor annuity*, also referred to as a "joint and last survivor annuity," provides for benefit payments during the joint lives of two individuals. This is clearly the most popular form of annuity settlement option, particularly when the annuity is issued to provide a retirement income to a husband and wife.

        a. Under a *full* joint and survivor annuity the surviving annuitant continues to receive the same amount as was paid before the first death. This amount continues to be paid until the deaths of both annuitants, at which time all payments cease.

        b. Under a joint and *two-thirds* survivor annuity the surviving annuitant receives payments equal to two-thirds of the full amount that had been received by both annuitants. This reduced amount continues to be paid until the death of the surviving annuitant, at which time all payments cease. The *traditional* form of this annuity distinguishes between the individual designated as the principal annuitant and the individual designated as the secondary annuitant. Payments to the secondary annuitant are reduced by one-third if the principal annuitant dies first, but there is no reduction in payments to the principal annuitant if the secondary annuitant dies first. The more popular *contemporary form* of this annuity reduces payments to the survivor no matter which annuitant dies first.

c. Under a joint and *one-half* survivor annuity the surviving annuitant receives payments equal to one-half of the full amount that had been received by both annuitants. This reduced amount continues to be paid until the death of the surviving annuitant, at which time all payments cease. A reduction in payments to the surviving annuitant may depend upon which annuitant dies first (see the discussion of *traditional* and *contemporary* forms in the paragraph above).

(6) **Guaranteed Minimums.** Contract holders are often reluctant to accept a contract that could result in a loss of all values upon the untimely death of an annuitant or annuitants. Because of this insurance companies offer settlement options that provide for minimum returns.

(a) *Refund* guarantees assure that if the annuitant (or annuitants) dies before receiving cumulative monthly payments equal to the annuity's purchase price the beneficiary will receive the difference between the annuity's purchase price and the cumulative payments received by the annuitant (i.e., the unrecovered portion of the purchase price). Most often these refunds guarantee repayment of the entire purchase price, but some variations provide for lesser amounts (e.g., a fifty percent refund annuity). (Refund guarantees are offered with contracts covering a single life and joint life annuities that terminate on the first death, but refund guarantees are not likely to be found with joint and survivor annuities.)

i. *Lump sum* refunds, also referred to as *cash refunds*, make one single payment to the beneficiary.

ii. *Installment* refunds continue periodic payments to the beneficiary in the same amount as paid to the annuitant, until such time as the cumulative payments equal the purchase price.

(b) *Period certain* guarantees, also referred to as a "life annuity certain" and "life annuity with installments certain," assure that if the annuitant (or annuitants) dies before receiving a stipulated number of payments the remaining guaranteed payments will be made to the beneficiary. Under this option the insurance company is promising to pay the annuity benefit for the longer of the annuitant's lifetime or a certain number of years. Most contracts offer guarantee periods of 5, 10, 15, and 20 years, but other durations are found.

Accumulation Phase vs. Distribution Phase. It is important to recognize that single premium annuities and flexible annuities have two distinct phases. The *accumulation phase* is that period of time from the purchase of the annuity until the annuity holder decides to begin receiving benefit payments under the annuity. The *distribution phase,* also referred to as the liquidation or annuitization phase, is that period of time beginning with the first periodic benefit

Annuity Timeline

payment under the annuity (i.e., when the contract is "annuitized"). Contract holders will often elect different forms of annuities between the accumulation and distribution phases (i.e., a single premium deferred *variable* annuity is initially purchased, but is later annuitized after the accumulation period as a *fixed* annuity providing a guaranteed monthly income).

Fees And Charges. When comparing annuities it is most important to determine the impact of fees and charges, particularly with regard to the projected returns on variable annuities. These fees and charges can include:

(1) *Investment management fees* ranging from 0.25% to 1% or more.

(2) *Administration expense and mortality risk charges* ranging from a low of maybe 0.5% to as high of 1.0% or more.

(3) *Annual maintenance charges* are often not assessed, but can range up to $100.

(4) *Fund exchange charges* by variable annuities are generally waived on a limited number of exchanges per year, but can range up to $10 per transaction.

(5) *Surrender charges* vary between companies and policies but are typically phase-out over a period of 5 to 10 years, with lower charges phased out over longer periods of time.

EQUITY-INDEXED ANNUITY

This is an annuity that guarantees minimum interest earnings but links excess earnings to increases in an identified equity index. Because of the guarantees, it is generally not considered a security and therefore can be sold by agents who are not equity licensed. However, the workings of an equity-indexed annuity (EIA) can be quite complicated and it is important for the agent to fully understand the product. Market conduct and disclosure are important issues with respect to EIAs. Because they can have so many "moving parts," the following discussion provides, at best, only a general outline of EIAs. Individual contracts can vary greatly. Second generation products are being introduced with new features and new complexities.

The EIA is particularly attractive to individuals who are concerned about the safety of principal but who want the opportunity to experience market-related gains. Ideally, they should have available an easily understood product that provides the benefits of market appreciation without the risk of losing principal. In reality, they are likely to be faced with an array of products that are not easy to understand.

The minimum purchase amount is typically $5,000, but this can vary widely and is less for products sold in qualified markets. Both single premium and flexible premium contracts have been introduced. There are usually no sales charges (front-end loads), management fees, or mortality costs. However, there are often large penalties for early withdrawals. Both level and declining surrender charges are used.

Contracts are linked to the growth of an index over a period that can range from one to ten years, although four to seven years appear most popular. This is referred to as the "term" of the contract or the policy period. While growth can be linked to the performance of virtually any equity index, the large majority of EIAs use Standard & Poor's 500 stock index (the S&P 500 Index). Virtually all EIAs that use the S&P 500 Index refer to the price-level version that excludes dividends. The other is the total-return version and it is determined using dividend reinvestment.

Central to the indexed annuity is a guarantee of principal at the end of the term. This is done by taking a set percentage of the purchase amount and accruing interest at a given percent for the contract term (e.g., 90% of a $100,000 deposit plus 3% over seven years provides a $111,000 end-of-term guarantee; $.90 \times 100,000 = 90,000$; $.03 \times 100,000 = 3,000 \times 7 = 21,000$; $90,000 + 21,000 = 111,000$). The reason that most contracts use 90% of deposit and 3% for earnings is due to state law minimum guarantee requirements for fixed annuities.

Most contracts use one of three different methods to determine gain in the contract. For example, assume that upon issue of a contract with a six-year term the S&P Index was 700. Thereafter the index stood as follows:

End Of Year	1	2	3	4	5	6
S&P Index	781	834	823	871	904	880
Point-To-Point	-	-	-	-	-	25.71%
High-Water Mark	-	-	-	-	29.14%	-
Ratchet (27.98%)	11.57%	6.79%	0%	5.83%	3.79%	0%

Using the point-to-point method the gain is calculated using the beginning point of 700 and ending point of 880 (880 - 700 = 180 ÷ 700 = .2571). In contrast, the high-water mark method, also known as the discrete look-back method, uses the highest point of 904 (904 - 700 = 204 ÷ 700 = .2914). The ratchet method, also known as the annual reset method, calculates gain by adding up the sum of annual gains (11.57 + 6.79 + 5.83 + 3.79 = 27.98). A drop in the index is counted as zero. Unlike the other methods, this has the effect of locking in gains and annually resetting the starting point of the index. Earnings are typically not credited until the end of the term, thus there is no compounding of interest earned. Averaging can be done daily, monthly or annually. The usual effect of averaging is to increase the rate in a decreasing market and reduce the rate in a rising market (e.g., averaging the monthly gains the first year would likely result in less than 11.57% gain).

A cap (maximum rate) may be set on annual gains in the contract. The participation rate is the percentage of the index movement that will be credited (this can vary widely from 60% to over 100%). Some contracts guarantee the participation rate for the term of the contract, while other contracts reserve the right to change the participation rate or even lower the cap.

Liquidity features can include nursing home/hospitalization/terminal illness waivers, partial surrenders, and penalty-free withdrawals (e.g., 10% per year). However, loans are not usually allowed. At the end of the contract term the owner can: (1) renew for another term; (2) make a tax-free exchange for another fixed or variable annuity; (3) surrender the contract without penalty; or (4) annuitize the contract.

PRIVATE ANNUITY

The private annuity has been most effectively used in family situations where it is desired to make a transfer of a business interest, or other asset, from one generation to the next free of estate taxes. Under a typical private annuity transaction, a parent will sell part or all of a business interest, or other asset, to his child or children. In return, the children promise to pay the parent an income for life (called a "straight life" annuity). While the annuity obligation cannot be secured, it does represent a contractual obligation that is legally enforceable. Since payments terminate at the parent's death, the annuity has generally been considered to have no value and to escape taxation in the parent's estate.

The amount of the annual payments is determined by using annuity valuation factors. The payments are made up of gain, interest income, and a nontaxable recovery of basis.[27] If it is desired to provide an ongoing income to *both* surviving parents, a reduced income can be paid for as long as either parent is alive (called a "joint and survivor" annuity). Although the value of the survivorship benefit is includable in the estate of the first parent to die, it should escape taxation because of the unlimited marital deduction. At the time the annuity is established, the child receives a "temporary basis" equal to the value used in calculating the annuity. After the parent's death, this temporary basis is adjusted to reflect the amount actually paid.

It would be best to avoid stipulating lower annual payments than those calculated under the annuity tables. Such annuity payments result in a gift from the parent to the child (i.e., the child is not paying full value from his separate funds). If there is a gift element, then its value is the difference between the fair market value of the asset and the present value of the annuity payments.

Furthermore, if the child does not pay full value, the property transferred for the private annuity could be included in the parent's estate as a gift with a retained life estate.

TAXATION OF ANNUITIES

Premiums. Generally, premiums paid into an annuity are not deductible from the annuity holder's income.

Cash Value Build-Up. Provided the annuity contract meets the requirements of Internal Revenue Code Section 72 and a "natural person" owns the annuity, the interest or other earnings on the funds inside the annuity contract will not be currently taxed. However, if the owner is a corporation, or other entity that is not a natural person, the earnings on contributions made after February 28, 1986, are subject to current taxation. One broad exception to this rule is when an annuity is held by a trust, corporation, or other "nonnatural" person *as an agent for* a natural person, in which case the annuity is not subject to current taxation. There are additional exceptions to this nonnatural person rule with other types of annuities.

Withdrawals. The taxation of withdrawals from or partial surrenders of an annuity depends upon the date that the annuity contract was first entered into:

(1) *Entered into after August 13, 1982.* Amounts received are taxed under the "interest first rule," meaning that they are taxable to the extent that the cash value of the contract exceeds the investment in the contract (i.e., treated as distributions of interest first and thereafter as recovery of cost).

(2) *Entered into on or before August 13, 1982.* Amounts received are taxed under the "cost recover rule," meaning that they are not taxable to the extent of the annuity owner's investment in the contract made on or before August 13, 1982 (i.e., treated as recovery of pre-August 14, 1982 cost and thereafter as distributions of taxable interest).

Different rules apply to amounts received under qualified retirement plans, Section 403(b) annuities, and Individual Retirement Arrangements.

Premature Distribution Penalty Tax. Subject to certain exceptions, any distribution of an annuity prior to the taxpayer (payee) having reached age 59½ is subject to a 10-percent-penalty tax on the taxable portion of the annuity payment.[28] For example, assume that the annuity holder purchased an annuity for $25,000 and thereafter surrendered it at age 55 for $32,000. The amount subject to both ordinary income taxes and the 10-percent-penalty tax is the gain of $7,000 (32,000 − 25,000 = 7,000). One exception commonly used to avoid this 10-percent-penalty tax allows for penalty-free payments to a taxpayer of any age, provided they are part of a "series of substantially equal periodic payments" that are made at least annually for the life of the taxpayer, or for the joint lives or joint life expectancies of the taxpayer and a designated beneficiary (e.g., a joint and survivor annuity). However, payments not subject to the 10% penalty by reason of this exception may be subject to recapture if the series of payments is modified (other than by reason of death or disability).

Benefit Payments. The basic rule governing the income taxation of payments received from an annuity contract is designed to return the purchaser's investment in *equal tax-free amounts* over the annuity's payment period. The balance of each payment must be included in income. Therefore, each payment is generally part nontaxable return of cost and part taxable income.[29]

(1) **Expected Return.** To calculate the annuity's exclusion ratio the expected return is divided into the investment in the contract. If payments are for a *fixed period* or *fixed amount* with no life expectancy involved, the expected return is equal to the sum of the guaranteed payments. If payments are to *continue for one life or multiple lives*, the expected return is determined by multiplying the sum of one year's annuity payments by the life expectancy of the measuring life or lives. The life expectancy multiple or multiples are obtained from a series of Annuity Tables provided by the IRS. *Gender-based* tables (I, II, IIA, and III) are generally used if the

investment in the contract does not include a post-June 30, 1986, investment. *Unisex* tables (V, VI, VIA and VII) are generally used if the investment in the contract includes a post-June 30, 1986, investment in the contract.[30] The following summarizes these tables.

Expected Return Multiples		
	Gender Based	
Table I	Ordinary Life Annuities	One Life
Table II	Ordinary Joint Life and Last Survivor Annuities	Two Lives
Table IIA	Annuities for Joint Life Only	Two Lives
	Unisex	
Table V	Ordinary Life Annuities	One Life
Table VI	Ordinary Joint Life and Last Survivor Annuities	Two Lives
Table VIA	Annuities for Joint Life Only	Two Lives
Percent Value of Refund Feature		
Table III	*Gender Based*	
Table VII	*Unisex*	

These tables can be found in Appendix A of *Tax Facts 1*, published annually by The National Underwriter Company.

(2) **Exclusion Ratio With Fixed Return.** This ratio identifies the portion of the annuity payment that is not taxed (i.e., that portion representing the purchaser's basis in the contract). It is expressed as a fraction, or as a percentage, and is determined by dividing the investment in the contract by the expected return. For example, assume that a contract holder purchases an annuity for $100,000 and elects an *annuity certain* paying $1,200 per month for 10 years. The expected return for a fixed period or fixed amount with no life expectancy involved is the sum of the guaranteed payments, or $144,000 ($1,200 \times 12 \times 10 = 144,000$). The exclusion ratio is 69.4%. (It is rounded to the nearest tenth of a percent.)

$$\text{Exclusion Ratio} = \frac{\text{Investment In Contract}}{\text{Expected Return}}$$

$$\text{Exclusion Ratio} = \frac{100,000}{144,000} = 69.4\%$$

This means that 69.4%, or $833, of every monthly payment may be excluded from income ($1,200 \times .694 = 833$). The balance of $367 is included in income ($1,200 - 833 = 367$).

(3) **Exclusion Ratio With Life Expectancy.** Now assume that the contract holder is age 58, purchases an annuity for $100,000, and elects to receive a *life annuity* paying $700 per month for life (i.e., a single life "pure"

annuity). The expected return is determined by multiplying the $700 monthly payment by 12 to arrive at the yearly payment of $8,400, and then multiplying this amount by the contract holder's life expectancy (25.9 years) obtained from the unisex Table V (Ordinary Life Annuities – One Life – Expected Return Multiples). The expected return is $217,560 (700 × 12 × 25.9 = 217,560). The exclusion ratio is 46.0%.

$$\text{Exclusion Ratio} \quad = \quad \frac{\text{Investment In Contract}}{\text{Expected Return}}$$

$$\text{Exclusion Ratio} \quad = \quad \frac{100,000}{217,560} \quad = \quad 46.0\%$$

This means that 46.0% ($322) of every monthly payment may be excluded from income (700 × .460 = 322). The balance of $378 is included in income (700 – 322 = 378). The yearly amount of taxable income is $4,536 (378 × 12 = 4,536). However, if the annuity starting date is after December 31, 1986, this exclusion ratio applies to payments received *until* the investment in the contract is fully recovered. Once the cost has been recovered, all payments are fully includable in income (i.e., the exclusion ratio no longer applies once the annuitant reaches his life expectancy). In this example, the contract holder is fully taxed on the monthly payment of $700 after 311 months of payments are received (100,000 ÷ 322 = 311).

(4) **Exclusion Ratio With Guaranteed Payments.** Assume that the contract holder is age 58, and purchases an annuity for $100,000, electing to receive a *life annuity* paying $550 per month for life *with payments guaranteed for 20 years* (i.e., a single life 20-year-period-certain annuity). The expected return is determined by multiplying the $550 monthly payment by 12 to arrive at the yearly payment of $6,600, and then multiplying this amount by the contract holder's life expectancy (25.9 years) obtained from the unisex Table V (Ordinary Life Annuities – One Life – Expected Return Multiples). The expected return is $170,940 (550 × 12 × 25.9 = 170,940).

Before calculating the exclusion ratio the investment in the contract ($100,000) must be *reduced* to account for the value of the guarantee. The percent value of the guaranteed refund is 9% (from Table VII for age 58 and 20 years). This is multiplied by the unadjusted investment in the contract ($100,000) to determine the value of the refund feature ($9,000). The value of the refund feature is then subtracted from unadjusted investment in the contract to determine the adjusted investment in the contract ($91,000). The exclusion ratio is 53.2%.

$$\text{Exclusion Ratio} \quad = \quad \frac{\text{Investment In Contract}}{\text{Expected Return}}$$

$$\text{Exclusion Ratio} \quad = \quad \frac{91,000}{170,940} \quad = \quad 53.2\%$$

This means that 53.2% ($293) of every monthly payment may be excluded from income ($550 \times .532 = 293$). The balance of $257 is included in income ($550 - 293 = 257$). The yearly amount of taxable income is $3,084 ($257 \times 12 = 3,084$). As in the example in paragraph (3) above, if the annuity starting date is after December 31, 1986, once the investment in the contract has been recovered all payments are fully includable in income.

Estate Taxation Of Annuities. The estate taxation of an annuity will typically differ depending upon whether the annuity is in the accumulation phase or distribution phase (page 382).[31]

(1) **Accumulation Phase.** The value of an annuity must generally be included in the annuity owner's gross estate. (If the decedent furnished only part of the annuity's purchase price, the decedent's gross estate includes only a proportional share of the annuity's value.)

(a) **Owner is also the annuitant.** The value of the annuity death benefit is included in the owner's estate.

(b) **Owner is not the annuitant** If the *owner dies first*, then the value included in the owner's estate is apparently the amount that it would cost to purchase a comparable annuity contract. If the *annuitant dies first*, the annuity death benefit is generally not included in the gross estate of the annuitant, but it is a taxable gift from the surviving annuity owner to the beneficiary.

(2) **Distribution Phase.** The following assumes that the "annuity holder" is both the owner and the annuitant. If payments were made under a straight life annuity, payments cease upon the annuity holder's death; there is no remaining property interest, nothing is passed to survivors, and nothing is included in the annuity holder's estate. However, the value of any survivor benefits is included in the annuity holder's estate (e.g., benefits passing under a refund annuity, a joint and survivor annuity, a fixed period annuity, and a fixed amount annuity). Benefits passing to a surviving spouse generally qualify for the marital deduction, and therefore are not subject to estate taxes.

Gift Taxation Of Annuities. If an individual purchases an annuity, names himself as the annuitant, and immediately gives the annuity contract to another person, the value of the gift is considered to be the amount of premium paid for the annuity. However, if the contract is held for a period of time after it is purchased, then the gift tax value is the single premium that the life insurance company would charge for an annuity providing the same benefits on the life of a person who is the same age as the annuitant when the gift is made. These gifts will not be subject to gift taxes if they are less than the annual exclusion amount of $11,000 in 2003 (see Present Interest Gifts, page 425). Future premiums paid on the annuity will also qualify for the annual exclusion. Likewise, an individual who pays premiums on an annuity contract owned by another individual is considered to make a gift of the premium amounts.[32]

SOCIAL SECURITY

On January 31, 1940, the first monthly Social Security retirement check was issued to a retired legal secretary, Ida May Fuller, of Ludlow, Vermont, in the amount of $22.54. From this humble beginning the Social Security system has grown to represent one leg of a three-legged retirement stool, the other two legs being benefits paid from tax-favored retirement plans and income received from the retirees' personal savings and investments. In 2001 the Social Security system paid average monthly benefits of $874 to 28,837,000 retired workers (payments totalled $269,000,000,000).[33]

Digging Deeper

The Social Security Administration maintains a very informative website at: www.ssa.gov.

Eligibility. A worker's eligibility for Social Security retirement benefits is based upon acquiring 40 quarters of coverage. In 2003 one quarter of coverage is received for each $890 of earnings (up to a maximum of four quarters in one calendar year). Therefore, a worker who earns as little as $3,560 in 2003 and pays $272.34 in Social Security taxes would receive four quarters of coverage (4×890 = 3,560; $3,560 \times .0765 = 272.34$). See Social Security Tax, page 396.

Calculation Of Benefits. The amount of retirement benefits are based on the worker's *primary insurance amount* (PIA), which in turn is a function of the worker's *average indexed monthly earnings* (AIME). In general, calculating Social Security benefits is a three-step process:

The Social Security Administration, using Social Security tax records, reconstructs the retiree's wage history. Wages in prior years are indexed by national wage growth to reflect current value. The highest 35 years are selected, averaged, and then divided by 12 to obtain the worker's AIME.

(1) Once AIME has been determined, it is plugged into a PIA formula. The following amounts are for an individual whose first eligibility begins in 2003 (the dollar amounts differ depending upon the year eligibility begins, are indexed, and are adjusted annually based on the growth in nationwide average annual wages):[34]

   (a) Add 90% of the first $606 or less of AIME;

   (b) Add 32% of AIME in excess of $606 through $3,653; and

   (c) Add 15% of AIME in excess of $3,653.

(2) The benefit is adjusted for the age at which the worker is first to receive the benefit (there also are other categories of benefit adjustments and recalculations).

The AIME is based on the worker's earnings record after wages have been indexed. This indexing creates an earnings history that more accurately reflects the value of the worker's actual earnings in comparison to the national average wage level at the time of eligibility (i.e., it is a form of inflation adjustment). The following steps are involved in determining a worker's maximum retirement benefits (the process is referred to as the "wage indexing" method):

(1) Determine the year the worker becomes age 62. For example, assume 2003.

(2) Determine the **indexing year**, which is the second year before the worker reaches age 62. For example, the indexing year would be 2001 (2003 − 2 = 2001).

(3) Determine the **indexing average wage** for the second year before the year of the worker's eligibility for retirement benefits. The indexing average wage for the year 2001 is $32,921.92 (as published by the Social Security Administration).

(4) Count the number of calendar years after the worker reached age 21 and up to, but not including, the year of attaining age 62. For example, 40 years (from the year of reaching age 22 through the year of reaching age 61). These are called the **computation elapsed years**.

(5) Subtract five from the number of computation elapsed years. The number remaining (if less than two, use two) is the number of years to be used in

computing the AIME. For example, 35 years ($40 - 5 = 35$). These are called the **computation base years**.

(6) List the worker's **Social Security earnings** for each of the computation base years (limited to the Social Security maximum wage base for that year – see Social Security Tax, page 396).

(7) Using the following formula determine the worker's "indexed earnings" **for each computation base year** up to but not including the "indexing year."

<table>
<tr><td>Worker's Actual Earnings
(up to the Social Security
maximum) for year to be
indexed</td><td>×</td><td>Average Earnings of All
Workers in Indexing Year
<u>(second year before age 62)</u>
Average Earnings of All
Workers for Year being Indexed</td></tr>
</table>

For example, assume that in 1980 the worker earned the maximum Social Security wage base income of $25,900. The average earnings of all workers for the year 1980 are $12,513.46 (as published by the Social Security Administration). The calculated worker's indexed earnings for 1980 are $68,140.84 (based on the average earnings in 2001).[35]

$$\$25,900 \ \times \ \frac{\$32,921.92}{\$12,513.46} \ = \ \$68,140.84$$

(8) From the list of indexed earnings (and nonindexed earnings for and after the "indexing year"), select the years of highest earnings (the number of years selected is the computation base years as determined in Step 5). Selected years need not be in consecutive order.

(9) Total the indexed and nonindexed earnings for the selected years and divide the result by the number of months in the number of selected years. This is the worker's **Average Indexed Monthly Earnings (AIME)**. If the worker's income in each of the selected highest years (from Step 8) equaled or exceed the Social Security maximum for that year the worker would have the maximum AIME.

(10) This indexing creates an earnings history that more accurately reflects the value of the individual's actual earnings in comparison to the national average wage level at the time of eligibility.

(11) Determine PIA. For example, assume a worker's first eligibility begins in 2003 (born May 18, 1941), and his AIME is $4,000; his PIA would be $1,572.40, calculated as follows:

90% × $606	=	$545.40
32% × $3,047	=	975.04
15% × $347	=	52.05
Total		$1,572.40

Spouse's Benefit. A spouse age 62 or over is entitled to a spouse's benefit based upon a worker's Social Security record (provided the spouse is not entitled to a retirement benefit based on his or her own PIA equal to or larger than one-half of the worker's PIA). This monthly benefit, starting at normal retirement age, is equal to one-half of the worker's PIA; but the benefit is reduced if the spouse chooses to start receiving benefits before normal retirement age. A divorced spouse who has not remarried is also entitled to a spouse's benefit if married to the worker for at least 10 years before the date the divorce became final. The amount of a divorced spouse's benefit is the same as a spouse's benefit amount. Although the spouse's benefit ends when the worker dies, the spouse will then be entitled to widow(er)'s benefit.[36]

Taxation Of Benefits. Under a two-tier system, up to 85% of Social Security benefits may be subject to income taxation. Under the **first tier**, if modified adjusted gross income (adjusted gross income plus tax-exempt income, or MAGI) plus one-half of Social Security income exceeds a base amount, an individual must include in gross income the *lesser* of: (1) one-half the benefit; or (2) one-half of such excess over the base amount ($32,000 for married couples filing joint returns, zero for married couples filing separately who lived together during any portion of the year, and $25,000 for all other taxpayers). Under the **second tier**, if a taxpayer's MAGI plus one-half his Social Security benefit exceeds an "adjusted" base amount, he must include the *lesser* of: (1) 85% of the Social Security benefit, or (2) the sum of (a) 85% of such excess over the adjusted base amount, plus (b) the smaller of the amount includable under the first tier of taxation (see above), or $4,500 (single taxpayers) or $6,000 (married taxpayers filing jointly). The "adjusted" base amount is $44,000 for married couples filing joint returns, zero for married couples filing separately that lived together during any portion of the year, and $34,000 for all other taxpayers. For example, the taxable benefit would equal $8,550 for a married couple filing jointly who had Social Security benefits of $14,000, adjusted gross income of $37,000 and tax-exempt interest of $3,000:

	The Lesser Of
85% of Social Security benefit (85% × 14,000)	$11,900
	or

Modified adjusted gross income	$40,000
One-half the Social Security benefit	+ 7,000
Total	47,000
Adjusted base amount	(44,000)
The excess multiplied by 85%	2,550
Lesser of amount includable under first tier ($7,000) or $6,000	+ 6,000
Sum of 85% of excess plus smaller of amount includable under first tier, or $6,000	$8,550

There is no longer any reduction in benefits once an individual reaches normal retirement age. However, there can be a reduction of benefits in the year the individual reaches normal retirement age. In 2003 earnings earned during the calendar year before the month the individual reaches normal retirement age will reduce benefits in 2003 by $1.00 for each $3.00 of earnings over $30,720. Earnings earned during and after the month the individual reaches normal retirement age will not reduce benefits.

When To Take Social Security Retirement Benefits. Social Security retirement benefits are based upon the worker's primary insurance amount (PIA). The PIA is the monthly amount that would be paid to a worker who receives benefits at normal retirement age. The normal retirement age differs, depending upon the worker's year of birth.

Normal Retirement Age Determined By Year Of Birth			
Year of birth	Normal Retirement Age	Year of birth	Normal Retirement Age
Before 1938	65 years	1955	66 years, 4 months
1939	65 years, 2 months	1956	66 years, 4 months
1940	65 years, 6 months	1957	66 years, 6 months
1941	65 years, 8 months	1958	66 years, 8 months
1942	65 years, 10 months	1959	66 years, 10 months
1943-1954	66 years	1960 and after	67 years

A worker can take retirement benefits as early as age 62, but the amount received is calculated by *reducing* the PIA by 5/9 of 1% per month for the first 36 months, plus 5/12 of 1% for any additional months. For example, a worker taking payments three years prior to normal retirement age will receive only 80% of his PIA (i.e., 100 - (5/9 × 36) = 80). In addition, a worker who no longer pays Social Security taxes fails to *increase* his PIA.

Many authorities agree that, for the average worker, it is best to wait until normal retirement age in order to take full (unreduced) retirement benefits. Despite this, Social Security records indicate that well over 50% of retiring workers take early (reduced) benefits. Clearly, if life expectancy is less than average, then taking an early benefit is indicated. However, if an individual is in good health, and does not require the money to provide for retirement, the following table may assist in making the decision.

Cross-Over Point*			
Discount Rate	When Reached	Discount Rate	When Reached
0%	13 yr, 3 mo	6%	19 yr, 12 mo
2%	14 yr, 9 mo	8%	26 yr, 7 mo
4%	16 yr, 9 mo	10%	Never

* Assumes payments begin 36 months prior to normal retirement age, and Social Security benefit increases of 2.4% per year (the average increase during the 10-year period 1994-2003).

The above table compares the present values of the income streams produced by reduced (early) and unreduced (normal) retirement benefits. For example, using a discount rate of 4%, for the first 16 years and 8 months the present value of reduced retirement payments are greater than the present value of unreduced retirement payments (assuming retirement three years prior to normal retirement age, and 2.4% annual increases in retirement benefits); when the cross over point is reached at 16 years and 9 months, the present value of the unreduced benefits will finally exceed the present value of the reduced benefits. Absent other considerations, a person who views the time value of money at 4% should consider early retirement if he expects to live less than 16 years and 9 months. On the other hand, if he expects to live at least 16 years and 9 months, he should wait until normal retirement. See also, Compound Interest & Present Value of Money, page 71.

Supplemental Security Income (SSI). This is a Federal income supplement program funded by general tax revenues (*not* Social Security taxes) that is designed to help aged, blind, and disabled people, who have little or no income. It provides cash to meet basic needs for food, clothing, and shelter. In 2000 average monthly benefits of $378 were paid to 6,602,000 recipients (payments totaled $31,564,000,000).[37]

www.ssa.gov/notices/supplemental-security-income

EMPLOYMENT TAXES

Social Security Tax. In 2003 the Social Security Tax (FICA) is 7.65% on the first $87,000 of earned income, and it is paid by both the employer and employee. For example an employee who is paid wages of $87,000 in 2003, pays $6,655.50 in Social Security Taxes (7.65% of $87,000). The employer must also pay $6,655.50. (This tax consists of two taxes: (1) the OASDI tax (old-age, survivors, and disability inusrance); and (2) the Hospital Insurance (HI) tax (for Medicare Part A)). Although $87,000 is the maximum amount of wages on which the 6.20% OASDI tax is paid by both the employer and the employee, there is no maximum amount for the 1.45% hospital insurance tax; all wages are subject to that tax. The following chart shows the historical increases of this tax over the past 50 years.

Historical Increases Of Social Security Taxes

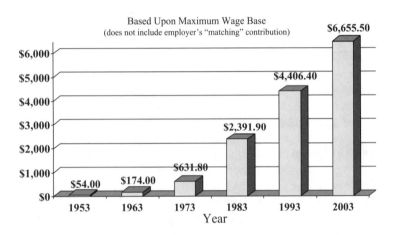

Self-Employment Tax. An individual who is self-employed must pay a Self-Employment Tax on net earnings from self-employment when these earnings are $400 or more. The tax is equal to the combined employer-employee Social Security tax and is 12.40% OASDI tax on the first $87,000 of self-employment income in 2003, or a maximum tax of $10,788.00, plus 2.90% hospital insurance tax on all self-employment income in 2003. Self-employed individuals may deduct one-half of their self-employment taxes for income tax purposes as a trade or business expense. This is the "Social Security Tax" for people who work for themselves.

Federal Unemployment Tax. In addition to these Social Security Taxes, Unemployment Taxes may have to be paid. In 2003, the Federal Unemployment Tax (FUTA) is 6.2% of the first $7,000 of wages paid to each employee, or $434 (credit is given to employers for contributions to state unemployment funds).

PROJECTED EARNINGS

5% Annual Increase In Earnings

Present	Yearly Earnings In				Total Earnings Over Next	
Earnings	5 Years	10 Years	15Years	20Years	10 Years	20 Years
10,000	12,763	16,289	20,789	26,533	125,779	330,660
12,000	15,315	19,547	24,947	31,840	150,935	396,791
14,000	17,868	22,805	29,105	37,146	176,090	462,923
16,000	20,421	26,062	33,263	42,453	201,246	529,055
18,000	22,973	29,320	37,421	47,759	226,402	595,187
20,000	25,526	32,578	41,579	53,066	251,558	661,319
25,000	31,907	40,722	51,973	66,332	314,447	826,649
30,000	38,288	48,867	62,368	79,599	377,337	991,979
35,000	44,670	57,011	72,762	92,865	440,226	1,157,308
40,000	51,051	65,156	83,157	106,132	503,116	1,322,638
45,000	57,433	73,300	93,552	119,398	566,005	1,487,968
50,000	63,814	81,445	103,946	132,665	628,895	1,653,298
60,000	76,577	97,734	124,736	159,198	754,674	1,983,957
70,000	89,340	114,023	145,525	185,731	880,452	2,314,617
80,000	102,103	130,312	166,314	212,264	1,006,231	2,645,276
90,000	114,865	146,601	187,104	238,797	1,132,010	2,975,936
100,000	127,628	162,889	207,893	265,330	1,257,789	3,306,595

8% Annual Increase In Earnings

Present	Yearly Earnings In				Total Earnings Over Next	
Earnings	5 Years	10 Years	15 Years	20 Years	10 Years	20 Years
10,000	14,693	21,589	31,722	46,610	144,866	457,620
12,000	17,632	25,907	38,066	55,931	173,839	549,144
14,000	20,571	30,225	44,410	65,253	202,812	640,667
16,000	23,509	34,543	50,755	74,575	231,785	732,191
18,000	26,448	38,861	57,099	83,897	260,758	823,715
20,000	29,387	43,178	63,443	93,219	289,731	915,239
25,000	36,733	53,973	79,304	116,524	362,164	1,144,049
30,000	44,080	64,768	95,165	139,829	434,597	1,372,859
35,000	51,426	75,562	111,026	163,133	507,030	1,601,669
40,000	58,773	86,357	126,887	186,438	579,462	1,830,479
45,000	66,120	97,152	142,748	209,743	651,895	2,059,288
50,000	73,466	107,946	158,608	233,048	724,328	2,288,098
60,000	88,160	129,535	190,330	279,657	869,194	2,745,718
70,000	102,853	151,125	222,052	326,267	1,014,059	3,203,337
80,000	117,546	172,714	253,774	372,877	1,158,925	3,660,957
90,000	132,240	194,303	285,495	419,486	1,303,791	4,118,577
100,000	146,933	215,892	317,217	466,096	1,448,656	4,576,196

Explanation of Tables. These tables assume that earnings increase at an annual rate of either 5% or 8%. For example, at annual increases of 5% an individual earning $50,000 today would be earning $81,445 in 10 years, and total earnings over 10 years would be $628,895.

EARLY SAVER VS. LATE SAVER

The Advantage Of Saving Early For Retirement
Assuming 8% Interest

Age	Early Saver	Late Saver	Age	Early Saver	Late Saver	Age	Early Saver	Late Saver
30	$2,000	0						
31	2,000	0						
32	2,000	0						
33	2,000	0						
34	2,000	0						
35	2,000	0						
36	2,000	0						
37	2,000	0						
38	2,000	0						
39	2,000	0						
40	0	$2,000	40	$2,000	0			
41	0	2,000	41	2,000	0			
42	0	2,000	42	2,000	0			
43	0	2,000	43	2,000	0			
44	0	2,000	44	2,000	0			
45	0	2,000	45	2,000	0			
46	0	2,000	46	2,000	0			
47	0	2,000	47	2,000	0			
48	0	2,000	48	0	$2,000			
49	0	2,000	49	0	2,000			
50	0	2,000	50	0	2,000	50	$2,000	0
51	0	2,000	51	0	2,000	51	2,000	0
52	0	2,000	52	0	2,000	52	2,000	0
53	0	2,000	53	0	2,000	53	2,000	0
54	0	2,000	54	0	2,000	54	2,000	0
55	0	2,000	55	0	2,000	55	2,000	0
56	0	2,000	56	0	2,000	56	0	$2,000
57	0	2,000	57	0	2,000	57	0	2,000
58	0	2,000	58	0	2,000	58	0	2,000
59	0	2,000	59	0	2,000	59	0	2,000
60	0	2,000	60	0	2,000	60	0	2,000
61	0	2,000	61	0	2,000	61	0	2,000
62	0	2,000	62	0	2,000	62	0	2,000
63	0	2,000	63	0	2,000	63	0	2,000
64	0	2,000	64	0	2,000	64	0	2,000
Total Invested	$20,000	$50,000		$16,000	$34,000		$12,000	$18,000
Amount At Age 65	$214,296	$157,909		$85,008	$72,900		$31,676	$26,973

Explanation of Table: This table demonstrates the advantage of beginning to save early for retirement. For example, a 40-year-old Early Saver who saves $2,000 per year for eight years, and earns 8% per year on his savings, will accumulate $85,008 by age 65. In comparison, a 48-year-old Late Saver who saves $2,000 per year until age 65 will accumulate only $72,900. Whereas the Late Saver has invested $18,000 more than the Early Saver, he has accumulated $12,108 less than the Early Saver (34,000 - 16,000 = 18,000; 85,008 - 72,900 = 12,108). If savings had been placed in a tax-deferred investment, then the Amount At Age 65 will likely be reduced by income taxes.

PENALTY OF WAITING

What It Takes To Save $100,000 By Age 65
Assuming 6% Interest

Current Age	Monthly Deposit	Total Deposits	Penalty Of Waiting 1 Year	Penalty Of Waiting 5 Years
21	40.42	21,342	877	4,707
22	43.06	22,219	905	4,867
23	45.88	23,124	945	5,043
24	48.92	24,069	973	5,208
25	52.17	25,042	1,007	5,387
26	55.66	26,049	1,037	5,567
27	59.40	27,086	1,081	5,758
28	63.44	28,167	1,110	5,944
29	67.77	29,277	1,152	6,137
30	72.45	30,429	1,187	6,334
31	77.49	31,616	1,228	6,535
32	82.94	32,844	1,267	6,740
33	88.83	34,111	1,303	6,950
34	95.20	35,414	1,349	7,168
35	102.12	36,763	1,388	7,382
36	109.63	38,151	1,433	7,604
37	117.81	39,584	1,477	7,830
38	126.73	41,061	1,521	8,059
39	136.48	42,582	1,563	8,289
40	147.15	44,145	1,610	8,528
41	158.87	45,755	1,659	8,769
42	171.79	47,414	1,706	9,010
43	186.06	49,120	1,751	9,257
44	201.87	50,871	1,802	9,507
45	219.47	52,673	1,851	9,760
46	239.14	54,524	1,900	10,017
47	261.22	56,424	1,953	10,277
48	286.16	58,377	2,001	10,536
49	314.47	60,378	2,055	10,800
50	346.85	62,433	2,108	11,067
51	384.17	64,541	2,160	11,338
52	427.57	66,701	2,212	11,610
53	478.56	68,913	2,265	11,878
54	539.23	71,178	2,322	12,160
55	612.50	73,500	2,379	12,433
56	702.58	75,879	2,432	12,697
57	815.74	78,311	2,480	12,971
58	961.80	80,791	2,547	13,268
59	1,157.47	83,338	2,595	13,542
60	1,432.21	85,933	2,643	14,067

Explanation of Table: This table shows the amount of money that must be deposited at the beginning of each month in order to accumulate $100,000 by age 65. Interest is credited at a 6% net annual rate and is compounded monthly (i.e., it is credited at the end of each month assuming a 6% annual after tax or untaxed growth). The penalty of waiting 1 year is calculated by subtracting total deposits at the current age from total deposits one year later (e.g., at age 45 the penalty of waiting one year is 54,524 - 52,673, or 1,851). The penalty of waiting 5 years is calculated by subtracting total deposits at the current age from total deposits five years later (e.g., at age 45 the penalty of waiting five years is 62,433 - 52,673, or 9,760).

HOW MONEY GROWS

How Much Monthly Savings Will Accumulate To

Save Per Month	Accumulated At 5%		
	5 Years	10 Years	20 Years
50	3,414	7,796	20,637
100	6,829	15,593	41,275
250	17,072	38,982	103,187
500	34,145	77,965	206,373
1,000	68,289	155,929	412,746

Save Per Month	Accumulated At 8%		
	5 Years	10 Years	20 Years
50	3,698	9,208	29,647
100	7,397	18,417	59,295
250	18,492	46,041	148,237
500	36,983	92,083	296,474
1,000	73,967	184,166	592,947

Save Per Month	Accumulated At 10%		
	5 Years	10 Years	20 Years
50	3,904	10,328	38,285
100	7,808	20,655	76,570
250	19,521	51,638	191,424
500	39,041	103,276	382,848
1,000	78,082	206,552	765,697

Explanation of Table. All accumulations assume monthly contributions are made on the first day of the month with interest compounded monthly. All results are rounded to the nearest whole dollar. Accumulated amounts assume the funds are invested at a rate of 5%, 8% or 10% *before taxes* (i.e., during the accumulation phase appreciation is not subject to current income taxation). For example, if an individual invested $100 per month and earned 8% compounded monthly, at the end of 10 years the funds would accumulate to $18,417. Referring to the table How Money Goes on page 401, if this $18,417 were invested at 5% per year compounded monthly, it would provide $195 per month for 10 years or $121 per month for 20 years. Withdrawing interest only without invading principal would provide $77 per month. All withdrawal amounts are before taxes.

HOW MONEY GOES

How Much Can Be Withdrawn Monthly From A Given Accumulation

Amount Accumulated	At 5% Interest			At 8% Interest		
	10 Years	20 Years	Forever	10 Years	20 Years	Forever
3,414	36	22	14	41	28	23
3,698	39	24	15	45	31	25
3,904	41	26	16	47	32	26
6,829	72	45	28	82	57	46
7,397	78	49	31	89	61	49
7,796	82	51	32	94	65	52
7,808	82	51	33	94	65	52
9,208	97	61	38	111	77	61
10,328	109	68	43	124	86	69
15,593	165	102	65	188	130	104
17,072	180	112	71	206	142	114
18,417	195	121	77	222	153	123
18,492	195	122	77	223	154	123
19,521	206	128	81	235	162	130
20,637	218	136	86	249	171	138
20,655	218	136	86	249	172	138
29,647	313	195	124	357	246	198
34,145	361	224	142	412	284	228
36,983	391	243	154	446	307	247
38,285	404	252	160	461	318	255
38,982	412	256	162	470	324	260
39,041	412	257	163	471	324	260
41,275	436	271	172	497	343	275
46,041	486	303	192	555	383	307
51,638	545	339	215	622	429	344
59,295	626	390	247	715	493	395
68,289	721	449	285	823	567	455
73,967	781	486	308	891	615	493
76,570	809	503	319	923	636	510
77,965	824	512	325	940	648	520
78,082	825	513	325	941	649	521
92,083	973	605	384	1,110	765	614
103,187	1,090	678	430	1,244	857	688
103,276	1,091	679	430	1,245	858	689
148,237	1,566	974	618	1,787	1,232	988
155,929	1,647	1,025	650	1,879	1,296	1,040
184,166	1,945	1,210	767	2,220	1,530	1,228
191,424	2,022	1,258	798	2,307	1,591	1,276
206,373	2,180	1,356	860	2,487	1,715	1,376
206,552	2,182	1,357	861	2,489	1,716	1,377
296,474	3,132	1,948	1,235	3,573	2,463	1,976
382,848	4,044	2,516	1,595	4,614	3,181	2,552
412,746	4,360	2,713	1,720	4,975	3,430	2,752
592,947	6,263	3,897	2,471	7,146	4,927	3,953
765,697	8,088	5,032	3,190	9,228	6,362	5,105

Explanation of Table. Withdrawals are assumed to be made at the beginning of each month with interest compounded monthly on the remaining funds invested at either 5% or 8% interest. Results are rounded to the nearest whole dollar. All calculations and amounts are before taxes. It is intended that this table be used with the table How Money Grows on page 400 (i.e., first obtain the amount accumulated from How Money Grows then enter this table). See explanation at the bottom of page 400.

CONSUMER PRICE INDEX

(annual average)

Year	Yearly Increase	Cumulative Increase	Purchasing Power of the Dollar
1981	10.3	90.9	1.10
1982	6.2	96.5	1.04
1983	3.2	99.6	1.00
1984	4.3	103.9	.96
1985	3.6	107.6	.93
1986	1.9	109.6	.91
1987	3.6	113.6	.88
1988	4.1	118.3	.85
1989	4.8	124.0	.81
1990	5.4	130.7	.77
1991	4.2	136.2	.73
1992	3.0	140.3	.71
1993	3.0	144.5	.69
1994	2.6	148.2	.68
1995	2.8	152.4	.66
1996	3.0	156.9	.64
1997	2.3	160.5	.62
1998	1.6	163.0	.61
1999	2.2	166.6	.60
2000	3.4	172.2	.58
2001	2.8	177.1	.56
2002	1.6	179.9	.56

Source: Bureau of Labor Statistics, Washington, D.C., and Statistical *Abstract of the United States*, 2002, Table 680 on page 449 and Table 681 on page 451. The Consumer Price Index (CPI) is a measure of the average change in prices over time in a fixed "market basket" of goods and services purchased by urban consumers. The items include food, clothing, shelter, fuels, transportation, fares, charges for doctors' and dental services, drugs, etc. purchased for day-to-living. The reference base year is the 1982-84 period (i.e., 1982-84 = 100).

[1] See *The 21st Century Retirement Security Plan*, (Center for Strategic and International Studies: 1999), at www.csis.org/retire/retireplan.html.

[2] See *Tax Facts 1*, (Cincinnati: The National Underwriter Company, 2003, revised annually), **Question 296** – What are the primary tax advantages of a qualified pension, annuity, profit sharing, or stock bonus plan?

[3] See *Tax Facts 1*, **Question 297** – What is a pension plan?

[4] This example is a simplified version of a more complete explanation contained in: Stephan R. Leimberg & John J. McFadden, *The Tools & Techniques of Employee Benefit and Retirement Planning*, 7th ed. (Cincinnati: The National Underwriter Company, 2001), pp. 201-202. The annual employer contribution percentages are based upon a target benefit table contained on page 201 of this publication.

[5] See *Tax Facts 1*, **Question 352** – What special qualification requirements apply to defined benefit pension plans?

[6] See *Tax Facts 1*, **Question 303** – What is a cash balance plan?

[7] See *Tax Facts 1*, **Question 299** – What is a profit sharing plan?

[8] See *Tax Facts 1*, **Question 302** – What is a 401(k) plan?

[9] See *Tax Facts 1*, **Question 300** – What is a stock bonus plan?

[10] See *Tax Facts 1*, **Question 304** – What is an employee stock ownership plan?

[11] See Leimberg & McFadden, p. 62.

[12] See *Advanced Sales Reference Service* (Cincinnati: The National Underwriter Company), Section 59, Pension And Profit Sharing, ¶ 270.1.

[13] See *Tax Facts 1*, **Question 313** – What are the requirements for cross tested plans?

[14] This example is taken from Leimberg & McFadden, p. 204.

[15] See *Tax Facts 1*, **Question 355** – What special qualification rules apply to Keogh plans?

[16] These are actually two Code requirements combined into one test by the regulations.

[17] See *Tax Facts 1*, **Question 230** – What is an individual retirement plan?

[18] See *Tax Facts 1*, **Question 236** – How much may an individual contribute to a Roth IRA?

[19] See *Tax Facts 1*, **Question 259** – What is a SIMPLE IRA plan?

[20] See *Tax Facts 1*, **Question 258** – What is a SAR-SEP? What requirements must be met if a simplified employee pension is offered on a cash or deferred basis?

[21] Section 501(c)(3) describes certain tax-exempt organizations.

[22] See *Tax Facts 1*, **Question 430** – What are the tax benefits of a tax sheltered annuity?

[23] See *Tax Facts 1*, **Question 149** – What requirements must an IRC Section 457 plan meet?

[24] See *Tax Facts 1*, **Question 96** – What is a cafeteria plan?

[25] See *Tax Facts 1*, **Question 2** – How are annuity contracts held by corporations and other non-natural persons taxed?

[26] See Leimberg et al., *The Tools & Techniques of Financial Planning*, 6th ed., (Cincinnati: The National Underwriter Company, 2002), p. 317.0

[27] See *Tax Facts 1*, **Question 41** – How are payments received under a private annuity taxed?

[28] For a listing of other exceptions to the 10% premature distribution penalty tax see *Tax Facts 1*, **Question 5** – What penalties apply to "premature" distributions under annuity contracts?

[29] See *Tax Facts 1*, **Question 1** – What general rules govern the income taxation of payments received under annuity contracts and living proceeds from life insurance policies and endowment contracts?

[30] Other elections may be used, see *Tax Facts 1*, Appendix A.

[31] See *Tax Facts 1*, **Question 500** – What, in general, are the estate tax results when decedent has been receiving payments under an annuity contract, or under an optional settlement of endowment maturity proceeds or life insurance cash surrender values?

[32] See *Tax Facts 1*, **Question 600** – What constitutes a gift of a life insurance policy or annuity contract? What constitutes a gift of a premium?

[33] *Statistical Abstract of the United States,* 2002, Table 519, page 346.

[34] These dollar amounts differ depending upon the year eligibility begins, are indexed, and are adjusted annually based on the growth in nationwide average annual wages. See *Social Security Manual*, (Cincinnati: The National Underwriter Company, 2003, revised annually), Section F-10.

[35] For a more complete example of the steps involved, see *Social Security Manual*, Section F-8.

[36] For additional information regarding the spouse's benefit, see *Social Security Manual*, Sections E-29 thru E-37.

[37] *Statistical Abstract of the United States,* 2002, Table 534, page 353.

THE ESTATE PLANNING PROCESS

In a broader sense estate planning involves not just planning for the orderly and efficient accumulation, conservation and distribution of an estate. A comprehensive and organized estate plan will also involve planning for retirement, gift and income taxes, creditor protection, liquidity, disability, long-term care, and special situations such as continuation of a family business, management of estate assets, and support of a handicapped child or aged parents. Given such a diverse array of objectives it is no wonder that an effective estate plan will involve the coordinated efforts of the financial advisor, life underwriter, trust officer, and attorney. The estate planning process begins when the client moves past procrastination and is willing to begin the process of gathering facts, establishing goals, and identifying problems.

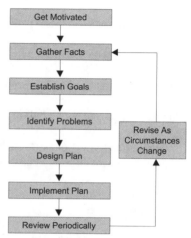

Get Motivated. Estate planning is about people and their desire to provide for themselves and their loved ones. For some people the motivation will be found in their desire to develop and adopt an effective estate plan providing for the support of their surviving family and the orderly distribution of their estate. Others will be motivated to assure the survival of a business, to provide for their church or a charity, or to avoid being best remembered for their generosity to the federal government. Despite these lofty goals, for a variety of reasons many people resist planning their estates. In fact, it has been observed that the greatest enemy of estate planning is procrastination.[1] However, with persistence from their advisors, sooner or later most individuals can be motivated to devote the time and energy necessary to engage in the process of planning their estate.

Gather Facts. This process takes time and much detail needs to be obtained. The planner can be most effective in helping the client gather all of the data needed. Facts relating to people, property, and existing legal instruments must be gathered.

Establish Goals. Estate planning is a goal oriented process. This is the most difficult yet most important part of the process. Again, the planner can be effective in getting the client thinking about what is to be accomplished and priorities. goals and objectives At each step there are specific things to consider and decisions to be made.

Identify Problems. In the course of determining the facts and comparing them to the client's stated goals, some of the more commonly identified problems include:

(1) No will, outdated will or inappropriate will.

(2) Lack of sufficient estate liquidity to pay estate settlement costs.

(3) Lack of sufficient income for surviving family.

(4) Life insurance owned by wrong individual or payable to wrong beneficiary.

(5) Assets pass to wrong individuals.

(6) Improper titling of assets such as jointly-held property that conflicts with other estate disposition instruments.

(7) Failure to name a guardian of minor children and provide for management of their assets.

(8) "Special needs" situations involving disabled children and dependant parents.

(9) Failure to establish the estate tax value of estate assets, particularly closely-held business interests.

Design Plan. The estate plan is designed to meet the client's objectives. This involves not only changes to, or adoption of, various estate planning tools such as wills, trusts, and powers of attorney; but it will also likely require "fine tuning" of existing beneficiary designations of life insurance and employee benefits, the retitling of specific assets, and the purchase of various life insurance and investment products.

Implement Plan. While only an attorney should draft legal documents and oversee their execution, many of the client's other advisors are involved in implementation of the plan. For example, the life insurance agent will assist in obtaining needed life insurance coverage and the financial advisor will assist in selecting appropriate financial instruments. At this stage, it is most important for the client to keep others informed.

Review Periodically. It has been said that the only constant is change, and this is certainly true when it comes to an individual's personal and financial circumstances. Generally, each estate plan should be reviewed at least once every 2-3 years, but the following events indicate a need for a more immediate review:

(1) Marriage or divorce.

(2) Birth of a child.

(3) Movement to another state.

(4) Promotion or job change.

(5) Retirement.

(6) Receiving of a large inheritance.

(7) Changes in health.

(8) Disability of a family member or acceptance of a caregiver role.

(9) Death of a family member.

(10) Acquisition or sale of a business.

(11) Changes in the relative ownership interests in a business.

(12) Changes in the estate or inheritance tax laws.

COMMON ESTATE PLANNING TOOLS

Many and varied tools, techniques, and instruments are available to help meet the client's estate planning objectives. Some of the more commonly used include:

THE ESTATE FUNNEL

The estate funnel helps to explain the types of property found in most estates, the problems often encountered in settling an estate, and the objectives of estate planning. All property is created in one of two ways, either people at work or capital at work. Wages are the product of people at work, while interest, dividends, and capital appreciation are the products of capital at work. The property found in most estates generally falls into one of five categories:

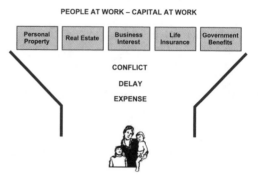

PEOPLE AT WORK – CAPITAL AT WORK

| Personal Property | Real Estate | Business Interest | Life Insurance | Government Benefits |

CONFLICT

DELAY

EXPENSE

Personal property, such as furniture, cars, jewelry, cash, bonds, savings, and other personal effects.

Real estate, such as a home, a vacation house, land, and rental property such as apartments or office buildings.

Business interests, in the form of closely held corporations, partnerships, or sole proprietorships.

Life insurance, either group insurance or individual policies.

Government benefits, such as social security, disability, retirement and survivor income benefits.

Conflict. Unfortunately, at death there is often a great deal of conflict. This occurs due to the differing and conflicting ways in which many of these assets pass to the family or other heirs. For example, personal property can pass by will, by state law if there is no will, by title, or by trust. Real estate and business interests may also pass by all of these means, as well as by agreement. Generally life insurance passes by beneficiary designation, and government benefits by federal statute.

Delay. These conflicts, together with the generally slow probate process, can easily result in a delay of *1 to 2 years or more.*

Expense. Considerable expense may also be incurred during the estate settlement process. For example, existing debts must be paid. There are also medical expenses, funeral expenses, attorney fees, income taxes and estate taxes. The final result can be *shrinkage of 30% or more* by the time an estate is passed to the surviving family.

The basic objectives of estate planning are to provide for the orderly and efficient accumulation, conservation and distribution of an estate, while avoiding conflict, shortening delays and reducing expenses.

EVALUATING THE RISK OF DEATH

One Individual. The following tables provide the odds of death within the next 10 and 20 years for an individual according to age and sex. For example, a male age 38 has a 3.7% chance of dying within the next 10 years and an 11.8% chance of dying within the next 20 years; whereas a female age 38 has a 3.0% chance of dying within the next 10 years and an 8.7% chance of dying within the next 20 years.

Odds Of Death Within 10 Years								
Age	Male	Female	Age	Male	Female	Age	Male	Female
21	1.8	1.2	36	3.2	2.6	51	10.7	7.1
22	1.8	1.2	37	3.5	2.8	52	11.6	7.5
23	1.8	1.3	38	3.7	3.0	53	12.6	8.0
24	1.8	1.3	39	4.1	3.2	54	13.7	8.6
25	1.8	1.3	40	4.4	3.4	55	14.9	9.2
26	1.8	1.4	41	4.7	3.7	56	16.2	9.9
27	1.9	1.4	42	5.1	3.9	57	17.6	10.6
28	1.9	1.5	43	5.5	4.2	58	19.1	11.5
29	2.0	1.6	44	6.0	4.5	59	20.7	12.4
30	2.1	1.7	45	6.5	4.8	60	22.4	13.4
31	2.2	1.8	46	7.1	5.1	61	24.2	14.5
32	2.4	1.9	47	7.7	5.5	62	26.2	15.7
33	2.6	2.0	48	8.3	5.9	63	28.4	17.1
34	2.8	2.2	49	9.1	6.3	64	30.7	18.6
35	3.0	2.4	50	9.8	6.7	65	33.2	20.3

Odds Of Death Within 20 Years								
Age	Male	Female	Age	Male	Female	Age	Male	Female
21	4.0	2.9	36	10.0	7.6	51	32.3	20.6
22	4.1	3.1	37	10.9	8.1	52	34.8	22.1
23	4.3	3.3	38	11.8	8.7	53	37.4	23.8
24	4.5	3.5	39	12.7	9.3	54	40.2	25.6
25	4.7	3.7	40	13.8	9.9	55	43.1	27.6
26	5.0	3.9	41	14.9	10.5	56	46.2	29.9
27	5.3	4.1	42	16.1	11.2	57	49.4	32.4
28	5.6	4.4	43	17.5	11.9	58	52.7	35.1
29	6.0	4.7	44	18.9	12.7	59	56.1	38.1
30	6.4	5.0	45	20.4	13.6	60	59.5	41.2
31	6.9	5.4	46	22.1	14.5	61	62.9	44.6
32	7.4	5.7	47	23.9	15.6	62	66.3	48.1
33	8.0	6.1	48	25.8	16.7	63	69.7	51.9
34	8.6	6.6	49	27.9	17.9	64	73.0	55.8
35	9.3	7.1	50	30.0	19.2	65	76.2	59.9

Source: Calculations are based upon the Commissioners 1980 Standard Ordinary Mortality Table.

Two Individuals. The risk of *at least one of two individuals* dying is substantially greater than the risk of one individual dying. For example, within the next 10 years the risk of a male age 50 dying is 9.8% and the risk of a female age 45 dying is 4.8% (see Evaluating The Risk Of Death - One Individual, page 409); but the risk of at least one of them dying within the next 10 years is 14.2%. And this risk increases considerably with time (i.e., for a male age 50 and a female age 45 the risk of at least one of them dying within the next 20 years increases to 39.5%).

Odds Of At Least One Death Within 10 Years – Male & Female

		Male Age									
		20	**25**	**30**	**35**	**40**	**45**	**50**	**55**	**60**	**65**
Female Age	**20**	2.9	2.9	3.2	4.1	5.5	7.6	10.9	15.9	23.3	33.9
	25	3.1	3.1	3.4	4.3	5.7	7.7	11.0	16.0	23.4	34.1
	30	3.4	3.4	3.8	4.6	6.0	8.1	11.3	16.3	23.7	34.3
	35	4.1	4.1	4.4	5.3	6.6	8.7	12.0	16.9	24.2	34.7
	40	5.1	5.1	5.5	6.3	7.6	9.7	12.9	17.8	25.0	35.4
	45	6.5	6.5	6.8	7.6	9.0	11.0	14.2	19.0	26.1	36.4
	50	8.3	8.3	8.6	9.4	10.8	12.7	15.9	20.6	27.6	37.6
	55	10.8	10.8	11.1	11.9	13.2	15.1	18.1	22.7	29.5	39.3
	60	15.0	15.0	15.3	16.0	17.2	19.1	21.9	26.3	32.8	42.1
	65	21.7	21.7	22.0	22.7	23.8	25.5	28.2	32.2	38.2	46.7

Odds Of At Least One Death Within 20 Years – Male & Female

		Male Age									
		20	**25**	**30**	**35**	**40**	**45**	**50**	**55**	**60**	**65**
Female Age	**20**	6.6	7.4	9.0	11.8	16.2	22.7	32.0	44.7	60.6	76.9
	25	7.4	8.2	9.8	12.6	16.9	23.3	32.6	45.2	61.0	77.1
	30	8.7	9.5	11.1	13.8	18.1	24.4	33.5	46.0	61.5	77.4
	35	10.6	11.4	13.0	15.7	19.9	26.0	35.0	47.1	62.4	77.9
	40	13.3	14.1	15.6	18.2	22.3	28.3	36.9	48.7	63.5	78.6
	45	16.9	17.6	19.1	21.6	25.5	31.2	39.5	50.8	65.0	79.4
	50	22.3	23.0	24.4	26.7	30.3	35.7	43.5	54.0	67.3	80.8
	55	30.4	31.0	32.3	34.4	37.6	42.4	49.4	58.8	70.7	82.8
	60	43.5	44.0	45.0	46.7	49.3	53.2	58.9	66.6	76.2	86.0
	65	61.4	61.7	62.4	63.6	65.4	68.1	71.9	77.2	83.7	90.5

Source: Calculations are based upon the Commissioners 1980 Standard Ordinary Mortality Table.

Facts About Parents. The odds of a parent not seeing a child graduate from college are surprisingly high. For example, if a *father* is age 35 when his child is born there is a 1 in 13 change that he will not be alive to see his child begin college, and a 1 in 9 change that he will not be alive to attend his child's graduation. If a *mother* is age 35 when her child is born there is a 1 in 17 change that she will not be alive to see her child begin college, and a 1 in 12 change that she will not be alive to attend her child's graduation. When a child is dependent upon his or her parent to provide for their college education it makes sense to obtain life insurance on the parent's life. With life insurance the parent can assure that his or her child will have the funds to go to college. See page 281 regarding the value of a college education.

Odds Of A Father Seeing His Child Graduate From College		
Father's Age When Child Is Born	Fathers Who Will Die Before Child	
	Enters College	Graduates
25	1 in 26	1 in 18
30	1 in 19	1 in 13
35	1 in 13	1 in 9
40	1 in 9	1 in 6

Odds Of A Mother Seeing Her Child Graduate From College		
Mother's Age When Child Is Born	Mothers Who Will Die Before Child	
	Enters College	Graduates
25	1 in 33	1 in 23
30	1 in 24	1 in 17
35	1 in 17	1 in 12
40	1 in 12	1 in 9

Source: Calculations are based upon the Commissioners 1980 Standard Ordinary Mortality Table.

OWNERSHIP OF PROPERTY

Where more than one person owns real estate or certain types of personal property, the form of ownership determines how the property is passed upon death. The form of ownership also determines the extent to which the property is includable in the gross estate for federal estate tax purposes.

Tenancy In Common. Where the property is owned in a tenancy in common, each tenant – or co-owner – has a fractional, divisible interest in the property. Upon the death of a co-owner, his fractional interest is probate property and passes by will or by state intestacy laws. Each surviving co-tenant retains his proportionate interest in the property. The fair market value of the decedent's fractional interest is includable in the federal gross estate.

Joint Tenancy With Right Of Survivorship. Where the property is owned in joint tenancy with right of survivorship, each joint tenant has an undivided interest in the entire property. The survivorship right is the key characteristic: upon the death of a joint tenant, the decedent's interest passes by operation of law to the surviving tenant or tenants. The decedent's interest is not a probate asset and therefore cannot be disposed of by will or intestacy law. For federal estate tax purposes, joint tenancy with right of survivorship does not necessarily prevent all or any of the property from inclusion in the federal gross estate upon the death of a joint owner. However, a joint-and-survivorship property interest created between spouses after 1976 is considered to be a "qualified joint interest." As such, only one-half of the value is included in the gross estate for federal tax purposes. All other joint-and-survivorship property is fully includable in the gross estate of the first owner to die, except to the extent that the decedent's estate can demonstrate that the survivor contributed to the purchase price. However, jointly owned property obtained through gift or inheritance is included in proportion to the decedent's ownership interest.

Tenancy By The Entirety. Some states recognize a tenancy by the entirety. Generally, this form of ownership parallels joint-and-survivorship property except that only a husband and wife may create it.

Community Property. In community property states each spouse is considered to own an undivided one-half interest in such property during the marriage, and each spouse is free to dispose of his or her share of community property upon death. One-half of the fair market value of community property is includable in the decedent spouse's estate.

POWERS OF ATTORNEY

A power of attorney is a written document executed by one individual, the "principal," authorizing another person, the "attorney-in-fact," to act on his behalf.

General. Under a general power of attorney the powers are very broad and authorize the attorney-in-fact to enter into and discharge virtually all legal obligations on behalf of his principal.

Special. Under a special power of attorney the powers are very limited and authorize the attorney-in-fact to perform only specific functions on behalf of the principal. Typically, either power of attorney is limited to acts being performed at a time when the principal himself has legal capacity (e.g., is not disabled, mentally incompetent or under some other incapacity).

Durable. A durable power of attorney authorizes the attorney-in-fact to act even if the principal is incapacitated. This is particularly useful in estate planning situations where it may be desired to make gifts, file tax returns, or provide for the lifetime management of assets. The durable power of attorney has been recognized in some form in all states. Such powers of attorney may be either *immediate*, giving the attorney-in-fact power to act prior to an incapacity, or *contingent*, giving the attorney-in-fact power to act only when the principal has become incapacitated.

Health Care Power of Attorney. This document authorizes the power-holder to make medical treatment decisions for the principal if he cannot make them for himself.

Health Care Advance Directive. This document combines and expands the Health Care Power of Attorney and the traditional Living Will (page 413) into a single, comprehensive document. Unlike most living wills, the health care advance directive is not limited to cases of terminal illness, but rather can be used when the individual cannot make or communicate decisions because of a temporary or permanent illness or injury; thereby affording some degree of control over important health care decisions.

www.ama-assn.org/
public/booklets/livgwill.htm

LIVING WILL

The traditional living will, also referred to as a "health care proxy," states the individual's wishes about life-sustaining medical treatments in case of a terminal illness. It is a legal document that allows an individual to state in advance his unwillingness to be subjected to life-sustaining medical measures once there is no chance of recovery. Such a document relieves others of the legal and emotional burden of making such decisions. For example, it can ease a doctor's fears of civil or criminal liability, since he is abiding by his patient's wishes in withholding or withdrawing life-prolonging treatment. It can ease the stress and emotional pain for the family, which might otherwise be faced with having to make a most difficult decision as to what their loved one would have wanted. Further, it offers some hope of avoiding the legal battles that have occurred when a medical facility is unsure of its responsibility to the patient, and thus provides the family some protection from the financial devastation that a protracted death can cause. Almost all of the states have some form of legislation governing living wills. Generally such a document must be in writing, dated, and witnessed by two persons who are not family members or possible heirs. The document must usually be notarized if a durable power of attorney is included giving another person the power to make medical treatment decisions. In addition, language can be included providing for organ donation. Copies of the living will should be given to close relatives, the family doctor and the family attorney. Both the living will and the durable power of attorney can be revoked at any time by either destroying all copies or by executing a signed and notarized statement revoking the prior document.

INTESTATE SUCCESSION

When someone dies without a will, state law effectively provides a "one-size-fits-all" will through intestate succession statutes.[2] It is important to remember, though, that just as a will may not control all of a decedent's property, state intestate succession statutes may not determine how all of a decedent's property is distributed at death. Determining how the law will divide the property of a decedent who dies without a will can be complex. Property may pass by title (e.g., joint ownership with rights of survivorship), by contract (e.g., a life insurance beneficiary designation), or by some state statute other than the intestate succession statute (e.g., homestead statutes, right of election statutes, family allowance and support statutes, and statutes in common law states preserving the community property nature of property previously acquired by a married couple in a community property state).

ANATOMY OF A WILL

A will is used to dispose of property at death. However, it is important to recognize that not all property passes by will. For example, a will does not determine who receives property held in joint tenancy with rights of survivorship (page 411). That property passes automatically to the surviving joint tenant. Likewise, a will does not control who receives life insurance proceeds paid to a named beneficiary other than the insured's estate. The following extracts from a sample "simple" will are provided in order to illustrate some of the very basic language found in most wills.[3] Will provisions tend to be rather lengthy, particularly those relating to executor powers; therefore the ellipses (. . .) indicate text that has not been included. Common clauses that are not shown include provisions establishing trusts, providing for disposition when a beneficiary predeceases the testator, replacement of executors, appointment of a guardian for minor children, common disaster or simultaneous death clauses, and tax savings trusts (often referred to as an "exemption trust will," see page 428). Only an attorney should be relied upon to draft and prepare a will.

Introduction is where the testator (the maker of the will) declares his or her residency, intention to make a will and intention to revoke all prior wills. The term "testatrix" is sometimes used in referring to a woman who makes a will.

Debts and expenses are to be paid from estate assets. This clause has little practical impact since most states would otherwise require payment.

Taxes can be allocated to specific beneficiaries, but the wording "without any apportionment" means that taxes will not be allocated (i.e., they will be born proportionately by all beneficiaries).

LAST WILL AND TESTAMENT

I, Jimmy Jones, a resident of the city of Marietta, Cobb County, Georgia, do hereby declare this to be my last will and testament and do hereby revoke all prior wills and codicils made prior to this will.

I direct that all my legally enforceable debts, funeral expenses, expenses of my last illness and administrative expenses, be paid by my Personal Representative from the assets of my estate as soon as practicable after my death.

I direct that all inheritance, transfer, succession and other death taxes, which may be payable with respect to any property includible as a part of my gross estate, shall be paid from my residuary estate, without any apportionment thereof.

Personal property when it is passed by will is "bequeathed." It can be given to whomever desired and is often passed outside a will under a letter of instructions.

I give and bequeath to my daughter, Janice Jones, all of my clothing, household furnishings, jewelry, automobiles, books, pictures, and all other articles of tangible personal property owned by me at the date of my death.

Real property when it is passed by will is "devised."

I give and devise to my son, Kenneth Jones, my interest in my summer home located at 1331 Seaview Lane, Block Island, Rhode Island.

Specific bequests are used when the testator wishes to pass particular items of property to certain individuals.

I give and bequeath 1,000 shares of IBM Stock to my nephew, Lance Dobson. I give and bequeath the sum of Ten Thousand ($10,000) dollars to my sister, Sara Black, if she survives me.

Residuary estate clause transfers all assets not previously disposed of.

All the rest, residue, and remainder of the property which I own at the date of my death, real and personal, tangible or intangible, regardless of where it is situated, I give, devise and bequeath to my wife, Betty Jones.

Executor powers are often listed in order to supplement, clarify, or expand upon those provided to executors under state law.

In the management, care and disposition of my estate I confer upon the Executor of this Will, and any successors in office, the power to do all things and execute such instruments as may be deemed necessary or proper, including the following powers, all of which may be exercised without order of or report to any court.
(1) To sell, exchange or otherwise dispose . . .
(2) To invest all monies in such stocks, bonds, securities . . .
(3) To retain for investment any property or . . .
(4) To vote in person or by proxy any corporate stock or other . . .

(5) To employ real estate brokers, accountants and . . .
(6) To compromise, settle or adjust any claim or demand by . . .
(7) To renew any indebtedness, as well as to borrow . . .
(8) To retain and carry on any business in which I may . . .
(9) To register any stock, bond or other security in the name of . . .

Appointment of executor, who is also referred to as a personal representative or a fiduciary. The term "executrix" is sometimes used when referring to a woman.

I appoint my brother, William Jones, as the executor under this will. If for any reason he fails to qualify or ceases to act, I appoint the Trust Company Bank Of Cobb County as my executor. I confer upon my executor . . .

Attestation clause, also referred to as the **execution clause**, states that the document is intended to be the testator's will and the date that it is signed. The testator then signs in the presence of witnesses.

IN WITNESS WHEREOF, I have hereunto set my hand and affixed by seal to this my Will, this _____ day of _____, 20__.

_____
TESTATOR

Witness clause, contains the signatures of those individuals who witnessed the testator's signing of his will. Although most states require only two witnesses, having three witnesses will meet the most stringent of state requirements. Adding the witness's addresses will make it easier to locate them if necessary. Some state laws provide for a **self-proving will** by including a notarized affidavit. This allows a will to be admitted to probate without locating the witnesses for the purpose of attesting to the will.

This will was signed by Jimmy Jones, the testator, and declared to be his last will in our presence. We, at his request and in his presence and in the presence of each other, state that we witnessed his signing and declaration and at his request we have signed our names as witnesses tthis _____ day of _____, 20__.

_____
WITNESS   Address

_____
WITNESS   Address

_____
WITNESS   Address

LETTER OF INSTRUCTIONS

A letter of instructions is intended to provide written assistance and guidance to the surviving family regarding items not covered in the will. Typically, it is addressed to the deceased's spouse, but it may also be addressed to children, particularly if they will be called upon to assist the spouse in the settlement of the estate and business interests. It will not have any effect on the provisions of the will. Items that might be covered in the instructions include:

(1) Funeral and burial arrangements: Where, by whom, what kind, and at what cost?

(2) Anatomical gifts: Identify the nature and location of any anatomical gift declarations you have made.

(3) Memorials and contributions: Identify what organizations or institutions might be appropriate recipients of memorials or charitable donations made in your memory.

(4) Preparation of obituary: Should your obituary be prepared in advance and be updated periodically? To which newspaper should it be sent?

(5) Notifications of friends, relatives, business associates, and colleagues in charitable or civic groups. Identify those persons to be contracted upon your death, noting any particular requests or messages to be given, and listing their current addresses and phone numbers.

(6) Location of your safe-deposit box and its key.

(7) Location of your will and estate planning documents: Include any trusts, buy sell agreements, or extraneous writings incorporated in your will.

(8) Medical and hospital coverages and location of the policies.

(9) Social Security and Veterans Administration benefits: Identify current or potential benefits.

(10) Life insurance: Indicate where policies are located and what steps should be taken to collect policy proceeds.

(11) Location and explanation of title documents and other records relating to your assets. Include deeds, stocks, bonds, bank accounts and deposits, retirement plans, and vehicle titles.

(12) Identify obligations involving periodic payments, such as your home mortgage, car loans, and other debts, including amount and to whom payable.

(13) Identify your attorney and professional advisers (including your accountant, broker, trust officer, and insurance agent) who you currently use or recommend.

(14) Key employees and business friends to keep business operating until sale. The value of an ongoing business is much greater than a closed one!

Source: Kenneth Vercammen, Attorney At Law, 2053 Woodbridge Ave., Edison, NJ.

PROBATE

Although the term is now used in referring to the entire estate settlement process, "probate" originally referred to the act of proving a will before a court or other authorized person. Courts having jurisdiction over probate matters are called probate courts, surrogates courts or orphans courts. The first step in settling an estate is to offer the will for probate. If the will is not likely to be contested, informal proceedings, usually called probate in *common form*, establish that the document offered is the valid last will of the decedent. However, if there is any doubt regarding validity, formal probate proceedings, usually known as probate in *solemn form*, are required.

After admission of the will to probate, the court appoints an **executor** (male) or **executrix** (female) and provides them with letters testamentary as evidence of their appointment. If there is no will the court appoints an administrator (male) or administratrix (female) and provides them with letters of administration. The **personal representative** (a term including an executor, executrix, administrator and administratrix) is then qualified to carry out his duties. Typically the personal representative will hire an attorney to advise and assist in settling the estate. The personal representative then collects, safeguards and manages estate assets, has assets appraised, prepares lists of assets, converts personal property into cash, distributes assets as directed by the decedent (pursuant to specific bequests in the will), disposes of business interests, publishes notices giving creditors of the estate an opportunity to file their claims, and pays death taxes, income taxes, property taxes, court costs, appraisal fees, and fees and reimbursement expenses of the personal representative and the attorney. After a court accounting (called a judicial settlement of the account) is made and accepted by the court, the personal representative makes a distribution of the net estate to the heirs as required by either the will or the statute of intestate succession.

In recent years much has been written about the benefits of "avoiding probate." The advantages cited include avoiding fees associated with the probate process, maintaining confidentiality, better control of assets, reduction in delays and avoiding ancillary probate of property located in another state. However, there are some distinct advantages to having an estate go through probate. For example, protection is provided beneficiaries by having a court oversee the collection and distribution of assets. By giving creditors notice and the opportunity to make claims against the estate, beneficiaries are provided with clear title to estate assets. In addition, the Uniform Probate Code, as enacted by many states, simplifies and streamlines the probate process by providing for self-proved wills, proof of a will by affidavit of witnesses, waiver of bond and unsupervised administration.

THE FEDERAL ESTATE TAX

One of the potential expenses of settling an estate is the federal estate tax. Proper planning involves anticipating and reducing the estate tax liability wherever possible as well as providing for payment of the tax. Unlike other expenses of settling an estate, it can be particularly burdensome in that it is generally due and payable in cash 9 months after death, at which time a federal estate tax return (Form 706) must be filed and the tax paid. If certain strict conditions are met, payment of the federal estate tax can be deferred.[4] However, this does not mean that payment of applicable *state* inheritance and estate taxes can be similarly postponed. The penalty for failure to file a timely federal return is 5% of the tax for each month the return is past due, up to a maximum of 25%.

The estate tax computation is not difficult, and in many ways resembles the calculations involved in determining income tax (see Estate Tax Calculation Steps, page 421). When we file our income tax return each year, the calculations involve terms such as gross income, taxable income, deductions, and credits. When an estate tax return is filed, we are likewise dealing with terms such as gross estate, adjusted gross estate, taxable estate, deductions, and credits.

Gross Estate. Generally, the gross estate includes all property of any description and wherever located, to the extent the decedent had any interest in the property at the time of death.[5] It may even include property previously given away or over which the decedent had no control at the time of his death. For example, assume that in 2003 the estate totals $2,700,000.

Adjusted Gross Estate. In determining the adjusted gross estate, we can subtract the decedent's debts, such as loans, notes, and mortgages, plus the debts of the estate, such as funeral and administrative expenses.[6] If these debts totalled $200,000, then the adjusted gross estate would be $2,500,000.

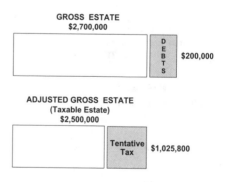

Also assumed there is no surviving spouse and that the adjusted gross estate is equal to the taxable estate. In the usual calculation sequence, debts (including funeral expenses), administrative expenses, and losses during administration are subtracted from the gross estate (as reduced by exclusions) to arrive at the adjusted gross estate. Charitable and marital deductions are then subtracted from the adjusted gross estate to determine the taxable estate.[7] The principal deduction in this latter step is the marital deduction. Since it has been assumed that there is no surviving spouse, there can be no marital deduction, and therefore the adjusted gross estate is equal to the taxable estate. (In community property states, the assumption of "no surviving spouse" means that all property is assumed to be separately owned.)

Tentative Tax. With a taxable estate of $2,500,000 the tentative tax would be $1,025,800.

Unified Credit. However, in 2003 there is a unified credit available that can offset up to $345,800 of the tentative tax.[8] Generally, the unified credit allows an individual to pass $1,000,000 of property free of federal gift and estate taxes during lifetime or at death. After taking advantage of the credit, the estate will still owe a tax of $680,000, which means that the amount of the original estate remaining for the children or other heirs has been reduced to $1,820,000. This represents a shrinkage of 27%.

BENEFIT OF UNIFIED CREDIT
($345,800)

| | C R E D I T | TAX | $680,000 |

REMAINING

| $1,820,000 |

Under EGTRRA 2001, the unified credit is scheduled to increase during the years 2004 to 2009.[9] These increases are: $555,800 in 2004 and 2005, $780,800 in 2006 thru 2008, and $1,455,800 in 2009. The corresponding unified credit equivalents, also called "applicable exclusions" or "applicable exclusion amounts," are: $1,500,000 in 2004 and 2005, $2,000,000 in 2006 thru 2008, and $3,500,000 in 2009.

Because of the "unified" gift and estate tax rates, prior taxable gifts made during lifetime would, in effect, reduce the amount of credit available at death. Upon death all adjusted taxable gifts made since 1976 are added to the estate when calculating the estate tax. However, this is not as bad as it might first appear, since the estate is, in effect, given a credit for prior gift taxes actually paid, or payable. The impact of this system is to push later transfers made during lifetime or at death into higher and higher tax brackets (due to the progressive estate and gift tax rates).

ESTATE TAX CALCULATION STEPS[10]

Gross Estate	$_____
Less: Debts of Decedent	(_____)
Administration Expenses	(_____)
Losses during Administration	(_____)
Adjusted Gross Estate	$_____
Less: Marital Deduction	(_____)
Charitable Deduction	(_____)
Taxable Estate	$_____
Plus: Adjusted Taxable Gifts	_____
Computation Base	$_____
Tentative Tax	$_____
Less: Post-1976 Gift Taxes Payable	(_____)
Unified Credit	(_____)
State Death Tax Credit	(_____)
Pre-1977 Gift Tax Credit	(_____)
Foreign Death Tax Credit	(_____)
Credit for Tax on Prior Transfers	(_____)
Estate Tax Payable	$_____

Full value of property passed to spouse (the marital deduction) or charity (the charitable deduction) may be taken as a deduction. Transfer taxes payable at death may also include the generation-skipping transfer tax.[11] See pages 452-453 for estate and gift tax rates.

STATE DEATH TAXES

In addition to the federal estate taxes it is important to plan for payment of state death taxes. Historically states have imposed one of three forms of death taxes:

(1) A **regular estate tax** similar to the federal estate tax, but with state specific rates and modifications to federal provisions.

(2) Some states impose an **inheritance tax**, differing from an estate tax in that it is a tax on the right to *inherit* property; while an estate tax is imposed on the right to *transmit* property. An inheritance tax, therefore, is levied on each beneficiary's share and not on the estate as a whole.

(3) The trend in recent years has been for states to replace their regular estate taxes and inheritance taxes with a **credit estate tax** that merely absorbs the maximum allowable state death tax credit under the federal estate tax.

Where the amount of regular state inheritance or estate tax is less than the maximum federal credit amount, the state will collect an amount equal to the maximum federal credit. Under EGTRRA 2001, the credits allowed were reduced by 25% in 2002, 50% in 2003, and will be reduced by 75% in 2004 (e.g., for a $2,000,000 estate passing to an adult child the maximum credit of $99,600 in 2001 was reduced to $74,700 in 2002, $49,800 in 2003, and will be further reduced to $24,900 in 2004; for a $1,000,000 estate the maximum credit is $0 for 2003-2004). From 2005 to 2009 the credit is replaced with a deduction. In states maintaining an independent state death tax system, a deduction is likely to be of less benefit to the taxpayer than a credit. These changes will not increase or decrease overall estate taxes paid by an estate if a state imposes only a death tax equal to the federal credit (i.e., a "pick-up" state). However, the reduction and repeal of the state death tax credit will result in significant revenue losses in many states, and has lead to enactment of new state death tax laws designed to recoup the lost revenue (e.g., a state law imposing a state death tax, "equal to the federal credit as it existed prior to EGTRRA 2001").

THE TAX LINE

The tax line will help in understanding and explaining the basic concepts underlying those estate planning techniques that are designed to minimize or avoid gift and estate taxes. Within the family unit, the tax line can be thought of as a horizontal dotted line existing between generations – although technically it exists between individuals who are not married to each other. Above the line are husband and wife. Below the line are the children. By taking advantage of the marital deduction, above the line both husband and wife can pass 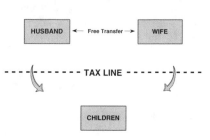 unlimited amounts of property between themselves – by gift during lifetime, or by will at death (page 423). But husband and wife are limited as to the amount of property they can pass to their children, free of gift and estate taxes. As long as property remains above the tax line, it will continue to appreciate. Effective estate tax planning must be designed to: (1) use "present interest" gifts and the unified credit to pass property down through the line; (2) avoid unnecessary future appreciation above the line; and (3) use life insurance and the life insurance trust to create untaxed property below the line. The concepts on pages 425, 426, 428, and 434 demonstrate techniques that can be used in dealing with the tax line.

MARITAL DEDUCTION

By taking advantage of the marital deduction unlimited amounts of property can be passed between spouses, during lifetime or at death, and free of gift taxes and estate taxes.[12] However, the marital deduction is generally not allowed if the property represents a terminable interest (i.e., an ownership right that will come to an end after a period of time or upon the occurrence of some specified event in the future). Generally, in order to qualify for the marital deduction, property must pass in a manner that would cause it to be included in the surviving spouse's estate. In theory, this affords a delay in estate taxation, but not an escape from estate taxation, because property passed to the surviving spouse in excess of the unified credit equivalent ($1,000,000 in 2003) will be eventually subject to estate taxes (at least to the extent that it is not consumed by the surviving spouse). The marital deduction can be obtained through the use of any of the following techniques:

(1) **Outright transfer** – passes property directly to the surviving spouse. This can be accomplished in a variety of ways, to include: joint ownership with rights of survivorship; beneficiary designation; bequest or devise; inheritance; and dower or curtesy (or under state intestate succession laws).

(2) **Power of appointment trust** – gives the surviving spouse a right to all income for life and general power of appointment over the trust assets (i.e., the unlimited right to withdraw property during lifetime or appoint property at death). In the Exemption Trust Will on page 428 the "A" trust represents a power of appointment trust, which is also referred to as a "marital deduction trust."

(3) **QTIP trust** – gives the surviving spouse a right to all income for life, with principal to children, or others, upon death of the surviving spouse (the executor or executrix must make this election, it cannot be mandated in will). See page 436.

(4) **Estate trust** – can accumulate income without payments to the surviving spouse, but must be paid to the estate of the surviving spouse (i.e., surviving spouse determines who eventually receives property placed in this trust, plus any accumulated income).

(5) **Qualified domestic trust** – assures collection of the federal estate tax when the surviving spouse is a non-citizen.

TRANSFERRING APPRECIATION

Estate planning techniques have traditionally focused on preparing for the eventual disposition of estate assets upon death, disability, or retirement. However, with the impact of inflation and the rapid growth of many estate assets, particularly business interests, effective planning should also include consideration of a lifetime transfer of these interests to children or other heirs. When adopting one or more of these estate freezing techniques, the objective is to create a freeze line beyond which future appreciation is transferred to another. By this means substantial value can sometimes be transferred to the next generation without being subject to estate taxes. However, complex tax rules restricting the transfer of appreciation must also be considered (i.e., the Chapter 14 special valuation rules).[13]

The most popular of these estate freezing techniques includes:

(1) **Installment sales** where an asset is sold today in return for payments made over a specified number of years;

(2) **Private annuities** where property is sold in return for a promise to make periodic payments for life;

(3) **Intentionally defective trusts** followed by gifts and installment sales;

(4) **Family partnerships** which allow children to share in the partnership's growth and profits;

(5) **Recapitalizations** followed by a gift of common stock;

(6) **Family holding companies** which are similar to partnerships;

(7) **Grantor retained income, annuity and unitrusts**, where a grantor places property in trust but retains rights to payments; and

(8) **Remainder interest transactions** which involve the current sale of a future interest in property.

To take advantage of any of these techniques the transfers must take place prior to the appreciation. This often means that it is up to the client's advisors to motivate him to take actions that will not produce tax savings until many years in the future. However, it would be well to remember that when an estate freezing technique culminates in the sale of a business interest, or other estate asset, the value represented by that interest is replaced in the estate by either the proceeds of the sale, or the obligation of the purchaser, both of which are estate assets subject to taxation. Likewise, if there is a giving of a substantial interest, use of the available unified credit means that it effectively cannot again be used at death. In either case, the sale or giving of an asset generally shifts only future appreciation out of an estate. Exceptions to this general rule are valuation discounts, private annuities and "present interest" gifts (see Present Interest Gifts, below).

PRESENT INTEREST GIFTS

Making gifts on a regular basis is an estate planning tool which can reduce estate taxes while avoiding gift tax liability. For example, assume that a donor has money that is not needed for his own support. Under the federal gift tax provisions, an individual may give – under most circumstances – up to $11,000 per person, as indexed in 2003 for inflation, annually free of gift tax.[14] Thus, with three children the donor could give each of them $11,000 per year. (With split-gifts the spouse joins in making the gift, and this allows a married couple to increase their gifts to $22,000 per year to each donee.)

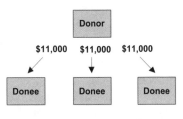

This per-donee exclusion is allowed each and every year, but it is not cumulative (i.e., an exclusion unused in any year may not be "carried over" to the following year). In order for the gift to be one that qualifies for the annual exclusion, it must be a present interest gift: the donee must be entitled to its immediate use and enjoyment. If within the year the donor makes only present-interest gifts, and gifts do not exceed a total of $11,000 per donee, the donor will not be required to file a gift tax return for that year and – under most circumstances – have no further income, gift or estate tax consequences from the gift. Likewise, the gift is not included in the donee's taxable income.

Although the donee is not liable for income taxes upon receiving the gift, if the property is subsequently sold the donee would be liable for reporting and paying taxes on any gain realized from the sale. For the purpose of calculating gain the donee's income tax basis is generally the same as the donor's basis in the property, often referred to as a "substituted" basis.

Present interest gifts that qualify for the annual exclusion are particularly attractive in reducing the donor's estate, since they will: (1) avoid the gift tax; and (2) likely be excluded from his estate for federal estate tax purposes no matter how soon death occurs after making the gift (e.g., the day after or even the moment after the gift is made). (One important exception is that proceeds of a life insurance policy transferred from the insured within three years of the insured's death are brought back into the insured's estate.) Assuming an estate of $1,500,000, estate growth of 8%, and gifts of $11,000 per year over 10 years, there is a potential tax savings of $94,655.

While gifts are generally discussed in a family setting, anyone can make gifts under these rules, whether the donor is a father, mother, child, distant relative, or even a benevolent stranger. In most states a gift to a minor under either the Uniform Transfers to Minors Act or the Uniform Gift to Minors Act will qualify as a present interest gift, even though the minor does not have legal capacity to make demands upon the custodian. The irrevocable life insurance trust offers an excellent means of taking advantage of the yearly opportunity to make present interest gifts through annual gifts to the trust for premium payments (see Life Insurance Trust, page 434).

LARGER GIFTS

The unified credit of $345,800 allows an individual to give away $1,000,000 of property in 2003, without paying a gift tax.[15] (Assuming the individual had not used any of his unified credit in prior years). In larger estates this can result in substantial savings by removing future appreciation on the gift from the estate. For example, assuming 8% appreciation, a $5,000,000 estate will grow to $6,298,560 in 2006, resulting in estate taxes of $1,977,338, and leaving $4,321,222 for the heirs. In contrast, a gift of $1,000,000 reduces the estate to $4,000,000. This reduced estate will grow to $5,038,848 in 2006, resulting in estate taxes of $1,857,870 and $4,440,690 for the heirs ($3,180,978 estate after taxes + $1,259,712 appreciated gift).

		Value At 8% Appreciation			
	Year 2003	Year 2006	Year 2009	Year 2010	Year 2011
NO GIFT					
Estate Size	5,000,000	6,298,560	7,934,372	8,569,121	9,254,651
Less: Estate Tax	1,905,000	1,977,338	1,995,467	0	4,385,058
Total To Heirs	3,095,000	4,321,222	5,938,905	8,569,121	4,869,593
GIFT OF $1,000,000					
Original Estate Size	5,000,000				
Less: Gift	1,000,000				
Remaining Estate	4,000,000	5,038,848	6,347,497	6,855,297	7,403,721
Less: Estate Tax		1,857,870	1,731,374	0	3,917,047
Estate To Heirs		3,180,978	4,616,123	6,855,297	3,486,674
Plus: Value Of Gift	1,000,000	1,259,712	1,586,874	1,713,824	1,850,930
Total To Heirs		4,440,690	6,202,997	8,569,121	5,337,604
Advantage Over NO GIFT		119,468	264,092	0	468,011

SIMPLE WILL

A will is the single most basic and necessary tool in estate planning. By having a will, we can be sure that property goes to whom we want, and in the amounts we want, rather than as provided under a state's intestacy laws. Although there are various types of wills, the most common is often called the simple will. The majority of simple wills provide for: (1) payment of just debts and expenses; (2) appointment of an executor or executrix; (3) specific bequests; (4) transfer of the entire estate to the surviving spouse; (5) if there is no surviving spouse, then transfer of the estate to children or other heirs; and (6) appointment of a guardian or guardians for minor children and their property.

This example illustrates an estate having a value of $2,500,000 in 2003.

ESTATE

$2,500,000

Upon The First Death, the simple will generally passes all property to the surviving spouse. Note that no taxes will be paid on this transfer. This is possible because of the unlimited marital deduction. Although the simple will defers taxes by taking maximum advantage of the unlimited marital deduction, it fails to use the unified tax credit available at the first death.

UPON THE FIRST DEATH

All Property To Spouse

No Taxes $2,500,000

UPON THE SECOND DEATH

To Children

Upon The Second Death, the estate will be heavily taxed in the amount of $680,000, and this tax

$680,000   T A X $1,820,000

must generally be paid before the balance of the estate can be passed to the children. After payment of these taxes the estate remaining to be passed to the children is $1,820,000. This estate has now been reduced to only 73% of its original size.

For the individual who has a relatively small estate, the simple will is usually adequate. However, as an estate grows, this most basic of wills has failed to take advantage of the unified credit that is available at the first death and resulted in unnecessarily high taxes which are payable upon the surviving spouse's subsequent death. This failure to provide any tax savings means that federal estate taxes will consume 27% of the estate in our example.

Note that in order to simplify this explanation it has been assumed that the surviving spouse had no separate property and the estate of $2,500,000 is the same as the adjusted gross estate (page 419). Had there been separate property, the taxes at the second death would be greater than shown. It is also assumed that death occurs in 2003, there has been no prior use of the unified credit through lifetime gifts, and the surviving spouse is a U.S. citizen. Under EGTRRA 2001, a taxable estate of $2,500,000 will no longer be subject to estate taxes in the years 2009 and 2010.

EXEMPTION TRUST WILL

A will creating an exemption trust can result in substantial savings by taking full advantage of the unified credit, which allows an individual in 2003 to pass $1,000,000 of property free of federal gift and estate taxes during lifetime or at death. The trust can also provide for the continued management of part or all of an estate. As in the Simple Will chart on page 427, our example in 2003 uses an estate of $2,500,000 (equivalent to the adjusted gross estate) and assumes there were no prior lifetime taxable gifts that required use of the unified credit.

Upon The First Death, with the typical exemption trust will, the estate is divided into two parts, with one part equal to $1,000,000 placed in a family or non-marital trust ("B" trust in the chart). No taxes are paid on this amount since the trust takes full advantage of the $345,800 unified credit available in 2003 (i.e., the amount that each individual can pass tax-free to the next generation). Unless there is a disclaimer, the remaining $1,500,000 of the estate is passed to the surviving spouse. This qualifies for the unlimited marital deduction and can be passed free of federal estate taxes. Although it is

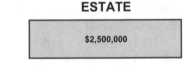

ESTATE

$2,500,000

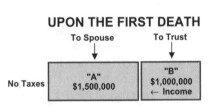

UPON THE FIRST DEATH

To Spouse   To Trust

No Taxes   "A" $1,500,000   "B" $1,000,000 ← Income

sometimes given outright, this portion of the estate is often placed in trust, which is referred to as either the "A" trust or the "marital deduction" trust. If the property is placed in trust, the spouse should be given a life estate with a power of appointment or a QTIP interest. The surviving spouse can also be given a right to all income from the "B" trust, as well as the right to demand, each year, either $5,000 or 5% of the trust corpus, whichever amount is larger. Property subject to a $5,000 or 5% demand right held at death is subject to taxation in the surviving spouse's estate only to the extent of the demand right.

Of course, there may be circumstances in which the testator will not wish to take advantage of the unlimited marital deduction (page 423). For example, by taking full advantage of the marital deduction, a business asset will continue to appreciate in the estate of the surviving spouse. This potential appreciation would be eliminated by passing the business to the children or other heirs upon the first death. However, the cost to do this is the early payment of estate taxes on any business value in excess of $1,000,000. Generally, the marital deduction is unavailable when the surviving spouse is not a United States citizen unless the transfer is to a qualified domestic trust that assures collection of the federal estate tax when the surviving spouse is a non-citizen.

Upon The Second Death, the estate subject to taxation will generally be limited to $1,500,000. After paying taxes of $210,000, there remains $1,290,000 to be passed to the children, or other heirs, along with the $1,000,000 from the "B" trust (assuming that the surviving spouse had no separate property). The amount previously placed in the "B" trust passes tax-free to the children under the terms previously established in that trust. Since the surviving spouse has no power to control the disposition of property placed in this trust, it is not subject to taxation in her estate.

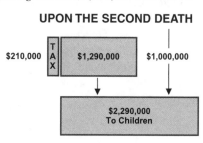

To simplify the above example, the tax is calculated assuming there are no debts, expenses, deductions, or prior taxable gifts. This means the computation base is equal to the gross estate (see Estate Tax Calculation Steps on page 421). The tentative tax of $555,800 is calculated from the tax table on page 452. Subtracting the unified credit of $345,800 produces a tax of $210,000 (555,800 - 345,800 = 210,000).

The exemption trust will is often referred to as a "limited trust will," in that the amount placed in the "B" trust is limited to the unified credit equivalent, $1,000,000 in 2003 – if no lifetime taxable gifts were made. (This trust is also referred to as a bypass, unified credit, credit shelter, credit amount, or credit equivalent bypass trust.)

When a large amount of property is held by a husband and wife in joint title with right of survivorship, the "A" trust could be overqualified and there may not be $1,000,000 of other property available to place in the "B" trust. In contrast, when a tax-driven formula is used to determine the amount going to the "B" trust, it may become overfunded (e.g., when a will directs that the amount to the "B" trust shall be the maximum amount that can be passed without paying an estate tax). Under such formulas, the substantial increases in the unified credit equivalent under EGTRRA 2001 could place unanticipated large amounts in the "B" trust, leaving little or nothing to go to the "A" trust.

COMPARISON OF WILLS

With the Simple Will leaving all property outright to the surviving spouse in 2003, the children would receive $1,820,000 (chart, page 427). On the other hand, with the Exemption Trust Will, they would receive $2,290,000 (chart, page 428). By using this estate planning tool, it is possible for a husband and wife to take full advantage of the unified credit remaining at each of their deaths.

SIMPLE WILL

ESTATE

$1,820,000
To Children

EXEMPTION TRUST WILL

ESTATE

$2,290,000
To Children

Another way of viewing this is to compare the amount of money being left to the federal government in the form of federal estate taxes. With the simple will the government receives $680,000, whereas with the exemption trust will the government gets only $210,000. That is a saving of $470,000!

SIMPLE WILL   EXEMPTION TRUST WILL

T
A
X

$680,000
To Government

27% Shrinkage

T
A
X

$210,000
To Government

8% Shrinkage

A SAVINGS OF $470,000

Trust Characteristics & Tax Implications

Type	Characteristics	Tax Implications		
		Income	Gift	Estate
Revocable	Created during grantor's life. If unfunded, acts as a will substitute. If funded, can manage property for benefit of grantor, spouse and other beneficiaries (see page 433).	Trust income taxable to grantor.	None, grantor retains control of property and there is no gift.	No estate tax advantages, but payment of insurance proceeds to trust can provide greater flexibility than settlement options.
Irrevocable	Created during grantor's life. Grantor gives up all control over assets in order to gain estate tax advantages (see page 434).	Trust pays tax if income accumulated in trust. Beneficiaries pay taxes if income distributed. Income taxed to grantor if certain strings attached.	When property placed in trust there is a gift. With "Crummey powers," gifts are considered present interest gifts that qualify for the annual exclusion.	Generally not included in estate, except proceeds of life insurance given to trust within 3 years of death, or if grantor retains interest in trust.
Testamentary	Created upon death pursuant to a will.	None, trust created at death.	None, trust created at death.	Taxable in testator's estate.
Minor's Trust (Section 2503(c))	Created during grantor's life. Trust's accumulated income and principal must be paid to beneficiary upon attaining age 21.	Trust pays taxes if income accumulated in trust. Beneficiaries pay taxes if income is distributed.	When property placed in trust there is a gift that qualifies for the annual exclusion.	Not included in grantor's estate, except life insurance given within 3 years of death.
Income Trust (Section 2503(b))	Created during grantor's life. Trust must distribute income annually, but principal need not be paid to beneficiary.	Beneficiaries pay taxes when income is distributed.	When property placed in trust there is a gift that qualifies for the annual exclusion.	Not included in grantor's estate, except life insurance given within 3 years of death.

TRUSTEE DUTIES & SELECTION

The trustee is named in the trust document and has the duty of administering and managing trust assets in accordance with the intentions of the trust grantor; and solely for the benefit of the trust beneficiaries. As a fiduciary, the trustee occupies a position of special trust and confidence and is prohibited from acting in any manner that is adverse or contrary to the interests of the trust beneficiaries (e.g., self-dealing is absolutely prohibited). It has been suggested that some of the desirable characteristics of a trustee include:[16]

(1) **Sensitivity** to the needs and circumstances of the trust beneficiaries.

(2) **Availability** over an extended time period (i.e., permanence) and geographically near the trust beneficiaries.

(3) **Competent** as to legal ability, intellectual and emotional capacity.

(4) **Expertise** in accounting, tax planning and record keeping.

(5) **Experience** with a proven "track record" in trust administration.

(6) **Knowledgeable** as to the nature, value, and extent of the trust assets (e.g., of a particular business interest).

(7) **Financially secure**, so beneficiaries could successfully seek compensation if the trust is mishandled.

(8) **Impartiality** with no conflicts of interest and with unquestioned integrity.

Essentially, there are three choices when selecting a trustee: (1) family member; (2) outside individual; or (3) corporate trustee such as a bank trust department or trust company. Selection of an *individual* trustee (family member or outside individual) often has the advantage of securing a trustee whose knowledge of the family situation enables him to make good decisions that are sensitive to the beneficiaries needs and individual situations. However, individual trustees may not necessarily be competent to administer trusts containing substantial assets, may not have the time or expertise required to do a competent job, may become incapacitated, and are subject to charges of self-dealing, particularly when the trustee is also a trust beneficiary. In contrast, *corporate* trustees are typically more objective when making decisions, have experience in trust administration, maintain a staff whose primary responsibility is to carry out the duties of a trustee, and are not subject to either disability or death. Given the obvious advantages and disadvantages of individual and corporate trustees, many trusts appoint individual and corporate co-trustees.

REVOCABLE LIVING TRUST

The revocable living trust (RLT) is a *will substitute* that can accomplish many estate planning objectives. It is an agreement that is established during lifetime and it may be amended or revoked at any time prior to the grantor's disability or death. The primary advantages of the RLT allow a grantor to: (1) provide for the management of assets upon his mental or physical disability and avoid conservatorship proceeding; (2) reduce costs and time delays by avoiding probate; (3) lessen the chances of a successful challenge or election against a will; (4) maintain confidentiality by not having to file a public will; and (5) avoid ancillary administration of out-of-state assets.

During Lifetime. The grantor establishes the RLT and typically names himself as the sole trustee. This is accompanied by a retitling and transfer of property to the trust. Because the grantor maintains full control over trust assets there are no income, gift, or estate tax consequences (e.g., the assets are *not* removed from the grantor's estate).[17] Two additional documents are typically executed together with the RLT:

- The **durable power of attorney** authorizes the power-holder to act for the grantor when the grantor is disabled.

- The **pour-over will** functions as a "fail safe" device to transfer at death any remaining assets into the RLT, to undergo minimal probate as a means of clearing the estate of creditor claims, and to appoint guardians of any minor children.

Upon Disability. If the grantor becomes disabled due to legal incompetency or physical incapacity, a designated successor trustee steps in to manage the grantor's financial affairs. Disability is determined under trust provisions providing a standard of incapacity

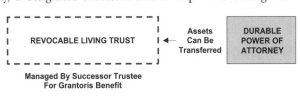

(e.g., certification by two physicians that the grantor is unable to manage his financial affairs). Also, during the grantor's disability, the holder of the durable power of attorney is authorized to transfer additional grantor-owned assets to the trust.

Upon Death. The RLT becomes irrevocable when the grantor dies. Assets held in trust are then disposed of according to the terms of the trust. This can include an outright distribution to the trust beneficiaries, or the trust may contain provisions establishing separate tax-savings subtrusts similar to the marital and family trusts under the exemption trust will. Although the RLT is not a panacea, it clearly offers substantial benefits for many individuals. The utility of a funded revocable trust increases with the grantor's age, when there is an increased likelihood of incompetency or incapacity and the need for asset management.

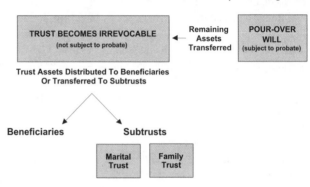

LIFE INSURANCE TRUST

The trust is one of the most basic tools of estate planning. When made *irrevocable* and funded with life insurance, it accomplishes multiple objectives. For example, it can:

- Provide Income for a Family

- Provide Funds for Estate Settlement Costs

- Avoid Increasing Estate Taxes

- Avoid Probate Costs

- Provide for Management of Assets

- Maintain Confidentiality

- Take Advantage of Gift Tax Laws

- Help Create a Minimal Drain on Present Funds

During Lifetime, it is possible for a grantor to establish a trust that will eventually accomplish all of these objectives. The beneficiaries of such a trust are normally members of the grantor's family and likely to be estate beneficiaries. Just as the surviving spouse is often made a beneficiary of the family trust under the exemption trust will (as in the "B" trust on page 428), the surviving spouse can also be made a beneficiary and given "present interest" demand powers under the irrevocable life insurance trust. Once the trust is created, policies on the life of the grantor can be given to the trust. If no such policies were available, then the trustee would obtain the needed life insurance. In either case, funds are given to the trust, which, in turn, pays the premiums to the insurance company. In order to take full advantage of the gift tax laws, the beneficiaries must have a limited right to demand the value of any gifts made to the trust each year. However, in order not to defeat the purpose of the trust, the beneficiaries should not exercise this right to demand. In this way, each year up to $10,000 per beneficiary, as indexed for inflation, can be given tax-free to the trust. The *right* to demand qualifies gifts for the annual exclusion as "present interest" gifts (page 425). Where there is more than one trust beneficiary this power is often limited to the greater of $5,000 or 5% of the trust corpus (often referred to as a "5-or-5" power).

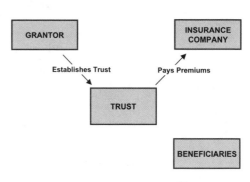

Upon Death, the grantor's property passes to his estate. At the same time, the insurance company also pays a death benefit to the trust. If the policies have been purchased by the trustee, or if the grantor has lived for over 3 years after having given the insurance to the trust, the death benefit will be received free of federal estate taxes.[18] There are basically two ways the trustee can make these funds available for payment of estate settlement costs. The trust either **makes loans** to the estate, or the estate **sells assets** to the trust. In any event, guided by specific will and trust provisions the beneficiaries can receive distributions of **income** and **property**. There may also be provisions in both the

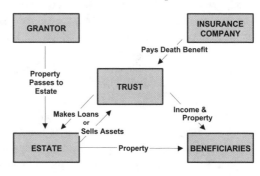

trust and the grantor's will that provide for a merging of the trust and estate assets, with subsequent management of the combined assets for the beneficiaries. These are often referred to as "pourover" provisions.

The Trustee. During the insured's lifetime the trustee is typically an individual other than the grantor who:

(1) Takes possession of the life insurance policies;

(2) Applies for a taxpayer identification number using IRS form SS-4, Application for Employer Identification Number;

(3) Opens a checking account;

(4) Receives funds placed in the trust;

(5) Notifies beneficiaries of their right to make demands of these funds; and

(6) Pays premiums as they come due.

It is usually advisable for a corporate trustee to be named at the insured's death. The new trustee then administers the life insurance proceeds according to the trust provisions.

QTIP TRUST

QTIP stands for "qualified terminable interest property." The QTIP trust provides a way to defer estate taxes by taking advantage of the marital deduction, yet "control from the grave" by directing who will eventually receive the property upon the death of the surviving spouse. Under such a trust all income must be paid at least annually to the surviving spouse. (Property placed in a QTIP trust must be income producing and the surviving spouse is typically given the power to force the trustee to make trust property productive.) The trust can be invaded only for the benefit of the surviving spouse, and no conditions can be placed upon the surviving spouse's right to the income (e.g., it is not permitted to terminate payments of income should the spouse remarry). However, in order to qualify the executor must make an irrevocable election to have the marital deduction apply to property placed in the trust.[19] This requirement not only gives the executor the power to determine how much, if any, of the estate will be taxed at the first death, it also provides great flexibility for post death planning based upon changing circumstances. This election by the executor cannot be mandated by the deceased prior to his death. It must be done on the estate tax return and cannot be revoked after the date for filing the return.

Our example assumes that in 2003 we have an estate of $3,000,000. (To simplify the example, the taxes are calculated assuming no debts, expenses, deductions, or prior taxable gifts, and no prior use of the unified credit.)

Upon The First Death, the estate is divided into *two* parts, with one part equal to $1,000,000 placed in a family or nonmarital trust ("B" trust in the chart). No taxes are paid on this amount since the trust takes full advantage of the $345,800 unified credit (i.e., the amount of credit in 2003 that allows each individual to pass $1,000,000 tax-free to the next generation). The remaining $2,000,000 is placed in the QTIP trust. The executor may elect to have all, some or none of this property treated as marital deduction property. Assume that in order to equalize the estates and save overall estate taxes the executor decides to make a partial election of $1,500,000 (i.e., of the $2,000,000 placed in the QTIP trust only $1,500,000

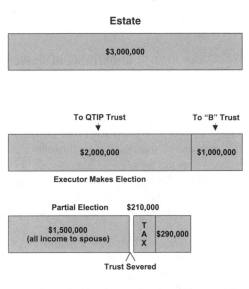

will be sheltered from estate taxes at the first death). This means that $500,000, the "nonelected" property, will be taxed at the first death. Although $210,000 of estate taxes must be paid, the remaining $290,000 will now be excluded from the taxable estate of the surviving spouse (any appreciation of this property after the first death will also be excluded). If authorized under the trust document or by state law, the executor can sever the QTIP trust into separate trusts.

Upon The Second Death, the estate subject to taxation is limited to $1,500,000 (the amount remaining in the trust for which estate taxes were deferred). After paying taxes of $210,000, there remains $1,290,000. This amount, together with the $290,000 from the severed trust and the $1,000,000 from the "B" trust, are passed to the beneficiaries under the terms previously established in these trusts.

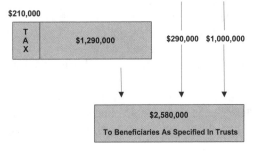

Potential tax savings come from two sources. The appreciation of assets removed from the surviving spouse's estate will not be taxed. Also, in large estates, equalizing the estate between spouses can move assets from higher to lower tax rates.

This example shows the QTIP trust being used only with the "B" trust (family trust). When the "A" trust (marital trust) is also used, it provides the executor even greater flexibility in allocating assets between the QTIP trust and "A" trust (see an example using the "A" trust with an Exemption Trust Will on page 428).

CHARITABLE REMAINDER TRUST

The charitable remainder trust enables an individual to make a substantial deferred gift to a favored charity while retaining a right to payments from the trust. Under the right circumstances use of such a trust offers multiple tax and nontax advantages, particularly to the individual who owns substantially appreciated property. These advantages include a charitable deduction resulting in reduced taxes, an increase in current cash flow, avoidance of capital gains upon a sale of the appreciated property, the eventual reduction or elimination of estate taxes, and the satisfaction of knowing that property placed in the trust will eventually pass to charity.

After establishing a charitable remainder trust, the grantor gives property to the trust while retaining a right to payments from the trust. (The term "grantor" is used to describe a person who establishes a trust, whereas the term "donor" is used to describe a person who makes a gift. For simplicity, only the term "grantor" has been used in describing the charitable remainder trust.)

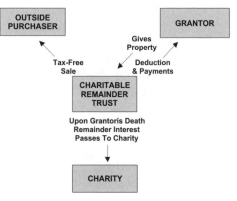

At the time the property is given to the trust, the grantor can claim a current income tax deduction equal to the present value of the charity's remainder interest.[20] Upon receipt of the gift, the trustee will often sell the appreciated property and reinvest the proceeds in order to better provide the cash flow required to make the payments to the grantor. This sale by the trust is usually free of any capital gains tax to the trust, but may be taxable to a beneficiary upon distribution.[21] Upon the grantor's death the property placed in the charitable remainder trust passes to the designated charity.

A **unitrust** would provide for the grantor to receive annually a fixed *percentage* of the trust value (valued annually), whereas an **annuity trust** would provide for the grantor to receive annually a fixed *amount*.[22] Either type of trust could require that payments be made for the joint lives of the grantor and another person, such as the grantor's spouse. Characteristics common to both unitrusts and annuity trusts are: (1) payments must be made at least annually and may not be less than 5%, nor more than 50%, of the net fair market value of the trust assets (determined when trust is created with an annuity; determined annually with a unitrust); (2) value of charity's remainder must be at least 10% of trust assets; (3) the trustee cannot be required to invest in specific assets (e.g., stock in a corporation or life insurance); and (4) payments may be for a term not greater than 20 years, or for the life or lives of the beneficiary(ies). Any individual beneficiary must be living when the trust is created.

INCOME IN RESPECT OF A DECEDENT

The term "income in respect of a decedent" (IRD) refers to those amounts which a decedent was entitled to as gross income, but which were not includable in his taxable income for the year of his death.[23] For example, the following are considered IRD: (1) payments to a surviving spouse under an individual deferred compensation agreement; (2) compensation for services rendered before death; (3) renewal commissions of a life insurance agent; (4) dividends declared but unpaid to a stockholder prior to his death; (5) interest owed the decedent at the time of his death; (6) the decedent's distributive share of partnership income; (7) amounts paid for unrealized receivables upon the sale or liquidation of a partnership interest; (8) distributions from a 403(b) tax deferred annuity; (9) distributions from a decedent's individual retirement account; and (10) proceeds from sales on the installment method.

It is important to recognize that, unlike other property included in an estate, the recipient of IRD does not receive a stepped-up basis for the purpose of computing gain or loss (see the discussion of Stepped-Up Basis below). Thus, the estate or beneficiary who receives IRD will pay tax on that income in the same manner as the decedent. If the income would have been ordinary income to the decedent, then it is ordinary income to the estate or beneficiary. Likewise, if the income would have been treated as capital gains to the decedent, then it is treated as capital gains to the estate or beneficiary. However, an income tax deduction is available which somewhat alleviates this "double" taxation (i.e., subjecting the IRD to both estate taxation and income taxation). The recipient of IRD generally may take an income tax deduction for any estate taxes paid by the estate on the IRD. This is a *deduction* to be used in determining the income taxes of the estate or beneficiary receiving the IRD; it is not a *credit* against the income tax due.

STEPPED-UP BASIS

In Years 2001-2009, 2011 And Later. At death, the income tax basis of appreciated property in an estate is increased, or "stepped-up," to its fair market value as of the date of death.[24] For this reason, when property is subsequently sold there is no taxable gain if the sales price, or amount realized, is the same as the value on the date of death. However, when property has decreased in value the basis will be "stepped-down" under the same rules as govern the determination of a step-up in basis. The step-up in basis applies only to property that is included in the decedent's estate for federal estate tax purposes. This value can sometimes be influenced by the personal representative of the estate by filing an election to have the gross estate, including stock in a closely held corporation, valued on an **alternate valuation date**, usually six months after death. If this is done, the stepped-up basis equals the fair market value as of the alternate valuation date. With property owned jointly between husband and wife, the stepped-up basis applies to only one-half of the property, since only one-half the value of such property is included in the estate of the first to die. There is no step-up in basis when property is acquired by a decedent (the donee) within one year of death and this same property is then at death passed back to the original donor or the donor's spouse.

In Year 2010. Under EGTRRA 2001, in 2010 the step-up in basis is replaced by a modified carryover basis.[25] This is essentially a carryover basis, but modified to allow: (1) an aggregate step-up of $1,300,000; plus (2) a spousal step-up of $3,000,000 for assets passed to a surviving spouse; plus (3) the decedent's unused losses. The $1.3 million and $3 million are indexed for inflation after 2010 (assuming that the sunset provision of EGTRRA 2001 does not take affect). To be entitled to the $3 million spousal step-up, the property must be "qualified spousal property" (i.e., the interest cannot be a terminable interest). Not eligible for a step-up in basis will be items considered to be income in respect of a decedent (IRD) and property received by the decedent within three years of death (except for certain gifts from the decedent's spouse). In order to comply with this modified carryover basis system, detailed and onerous record keeping will have to be maintained for virtually all assets.

LIFE INSURANCE PRODUCTS

Estate plans are only as good as the financial arrangements that support them. The cash for estate settlement costs must come from somewhere. The family must have the cash sooner or later, since everyone is going to die. The only question is when. There are three ways to pay these estate settlement costs:

(1) *From Estate Resources – the 100% method.* But in many cases the estate will not have sufficient liquid assets. Even when the costs can be paid by

selling estate assets, the family pays 100-cent dollars from the decedent's hard-earned and hard-taxed estate. Under the Insurance Plan, the family pays the costs with discounted dollars – discounted to the extent that the cumulative premiums paid will likely be far less than the insurance proceeds received by the family.

(2) *By Borrowing the Money – the 100%+ method.* But the credit standing of the family could be affected by the decedent's death. Changing economic trends also influence a lender's decisions about making loans. By borrowing, the family is obligated to pay interest as well as to pay back the principal. Under the Insurance Plan, the borrower pays the equivalent of 1% to 5% interest during his life and his family never has to worry about paying back the principal.

(3) *The Insurance Plan – the discounted dollars method.* This is the only funding device that will guarantee a definite sum of money to be available at an indefinite time in the future. The cost of that money will be only a few cents on the dollar when death occurs in the early years of the contract, and may involve a substantial discount even when death does not come for many years. Furthermore, this money will be income tax-free to the family, since the death proceeds of life insurance are received free of federal income tax.

Term Insurance. Term insurance provides protection for a limited period of time. However, the premium for this protection will usually increase each and every year, until it becomes prohibitively expensive for most people to maintain. While term insurance can provide a lot of protection for a lesser cost, it builds no cash values and has no permanent values. In this sense it has been described as "rented" but not "owned." Term insurance is available in many forms, the most common being annual renewable, five-year renewable (and/or convertible), 10-year renewable and convertible (R&C), 15-year R&C, 20-year R&C, and term to a specific age, such as age 65. A specialized form of term insurance, decreasing term, is also available, and usually purchased to cover a decreasing loan or mortgage obligation. Term insurance can be tailored to fit almost any temporary insurance need – level, decreasing, or even increasing.

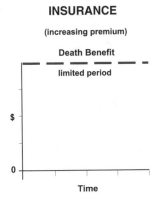

INSURANCE

(increasing premium)

Permanent Insurance. In contrast to term insurance, permanent insurance provides for a tax-deferred build-up of cash values over the life of the contract. This cash value element, combined with level or limited premium increases, means that the death benefit will be available for an unlimited period. While the outlay for permanent insurance is usually greater than term insurance in the early years, most plans provide for payment of a level premium. Even if the plan requires an increasing premium, these increases are usually limited in both amount and duration. Typically, both the cash values and the death benefits are guaranteed, unless they are dependent upon payment of projected dividends.

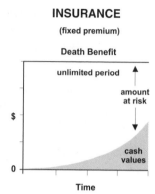

Universal Life Insurance. This product offers flexible premium payments, an adjustable death benefit, and cash values that are sensitive to current interest rates. Most contracts pay a current interest rate which is highly competitive with that available in the money market. However, these rates are subject to change and are not guaranteed over the life of the contract. The guaranteed interest rate is usually very modest and will likely result in a lapse of the policy if additional premiums are not paid. Likewise, most universal life policies offer lower current (nonguaranteed) mortality charges, but provided for higher guaranteed mortality charges. Taken together, the lower guaranteed interest rate and higher guaranteed mortality charges represent the "down-side risk" of a universal life contract. The policyholder is asked to accept this risk in return for the opportunity to receive the benefits of higher current interest rates and lower charges for the amount-at-risk element in the contract.

Variable Life Insurance. In many respects variable life insurance is similar to universal life insurance, except that the underlying cash values can be invested in an equity portfolio, typically a mutual fund or bonds. While these investments can provide a hedge against inflation, and the possibility for growth in both cash reserves and death benefits, there is also the risk that investment performance will be poor and that the cash reserves will decrease or be lost. The policyowner is usual-

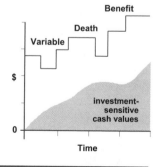

ly given the opportunity to redirect his investment to another portfolio although some limitations and restrictions may be imposed. Since variable life insurance is a security, the agent must hold a valid federal securities license (and state license where required) in order to sell the product. In addition, a prospectus must be delivered with or preceding a specific proposal to a prospect or client.

Survivorship Life Insurance. Also known as last-to-die insurance or second-to-die insurance, survivorship life insurance insures two lives and pays a death benefit after the death of both insureds. Generally, the premium required is less than that for comparable insurance on either individual life, since the odds of two individuals dying during any given year are substantially less than of one individual dying. While the many potential uses of survivorship life include charitable gifts, family income for surviving children, key person insurance, and funding installment sales within a family; survivorship life is most often used to fund the payment of estate taxes, when the marital deduction defers taxes until the death of both spouses (page 423). Survivorship life offers the advantage of simplicity by paying a death benefit exactly when taxes are due – upon the second death. With a rated or uninsurable client, coverage can usually be obtained, provided the spouse is insurable at standard rates. However, there are some disadvantages to relying solely upon survivorship life insurance to fund the payment of estate taxes. For example, when the marital deduction is used to defer all estate taxes until the second death, appreciation of assets in the surviving spouse's estate can substantially increase total estate taxes. After divorce the unlimited marital deduction is no longer available, unless the bulk of the estate is left to a new spouse.

First-To-Die Life Insurance. Also known as "joint life insurance," first-to-die life insurance, insures two or more lives, and pays a benefit upon the first death. Generally, the premium required for a permanent product is substantially less than those for individual policies on each insured. Uses for first-to-die life insurance include: (1) income replacement in two wage-earner families (e.g., to pay off mortgage); (2) social security replacement for retirees; (3) estate tax payment to facilitate early transfer of appreciating assets to heirs; (4) key person insurance; and (5) funding business purchase agreements.

MINORS & LIFE INSURANCE

Minor As Owner Or Beneficiary. Insurance companies will not knowingly accept a minor as the direct owner or beneficiary of a life insurance contract. Although trusts provide the most flexible way of managing policies and proceeds, establishing and administering them involves both time and expense. Ownership and beneficiary arrangements involving minors are governed by either the Uniform Transfers to Minors Act (UTMA) or the Uniform Gifts to Minors Act (UGMA). At the beginning of 2003, 48 states had statutes based upon the UTMA.

The older and more restrictive UGMA was still in effect in the states of South Carolina and Vermont. It is important to consult individual state laws, since states typically alter the text of the uniform versions.

If the beneficiary designation includes a custodial nomination, the proceeds can be transferred to a custodian without appointing a guardian. Any trust company or adult other than the insured can be nominated custodian (an adult under state UTMAs is usually age 21). A designation paying a death benefit to a child of the insured might read: "to [name of child], child of the insured; provided that if any proceeds become payable when [name of child] is a minor as defined in the [state] Uniform Transfers to Minors Act, such proceeds shall be paid to [name of adult] as custodian for [name of child] under the [state] Uniform Transfers to Minors Act." Note that this language covers the possibility that the child might become an adult by the time a death benefit is paid. A substitute custodian should be named in case the primary custodian cannot serve.

Without a custodial nomination, it is likely that the insurance company will require appointment of a guardian of the minor's property prior to making payment of death proceeds. The only exception allows for payment of small amounts, usually $10,000, to either a trust company or an adult member of the minor's family (a no-nomination transfer).

To give an *existing* policy to a minor, the owner merely signs a change of ownership form. To give a *new* policy, the custodian is designated as owner on the application. In either situation the ownership designation might read: "to [name of adult] as custodian for [name of child] under the [state] Uniform Transfers to Minors Act." In contrast, the purchase of a policy using custodial funds is a reinvestment of funds. If the minor is the insured then the minor's estate should be named beneficiary. If someone else is the insured then the beneficiary must be the minor, the minor's estate, or a custodian, and the designation must be irrevocable so long as the custodianship remains in effect. In this situation the beneficiary designation might read: "to [name of child], child of the insured, if living, otherwise to the estate of [name of child]; provided that the proceeds shall be paid to [name of adult] as custodian for [name of child] under the [state] Uniform Transfers to Minors Act if the proceeds become payable while such custodianship remains in effect; without the right to change while such custodianship remains in effect."

Minors As Insured. Children's insurance is also referred to as "juvenile insurance." Despite some advantages, placing insurance on a child's life is not without controversy. Opponents maintain that the lack of an underlying economic risk makes the purchase inappropriate and, further, that the wrong person is being insured. Clearly, if family resources are limited they should first be used to obtain adequate amounts of insurance on a child's parents (upon whom the child is economically dependent). Opponents also contend that if cash accumulations are desired it is better to save outside of a life insurance contract, thereby avoiding charges for the death benefit. Obviously, insuring a child can raise different issues than those encountered when insuring a spouse, parent, estate owner, employee or stockholder.

However, there are some advantages to placing insurance on a child's life. The death proceeds can be used to pay medical bills and funeral expenses, provide a financial cushion for a grieving family or establish a lasting memorial (e.g., a scholarship fund in the child's name). Virtually any form of permanent life insurance policy can be used. Single premium or limited payment plans are often used, or additional funds can be placed in a prepaid premium account (also referred to as a "premium deposit fund"). Loans or withdrawals from policy cash values can be used for educational expenses, as a down payment on the purchase of a home, to start a business, or for emergency expenses. Adding a guaranteed purchase option will assure that in future years the child can purchase additional death benefits without evidence of insurability.

Since a minor cannot directly own a policy on his own life, it is important that the individual applying for the insurance have an insurable interest in the child's life (see below). Initially the contract will typically be owned by a parent, grandparent, trust, or obtained as a custodial gift under the Uniform Transfers to Minors Act or Uniform Gifts to Minors Act. The amount of death benefit that can be purchased may be limited by state law and will be limited by insurance company underwriting standards.

INSURABLE INTEREST

The issuance of an insurance contract to someone who does not have an insurable interest in the life of the insured is void as a matter of public policy. Generally stated, an insurable interest arises from the relation of the party obtaining the insurance to the insured, provided there is a reasonable expectation of advantage or benefit from the continuance of the insured's life. An insurable interest is based upon relationships which involve: (1) pecuniary or economic advantage through the continued life of the insured or loss by reason of his death; or (2) love and affection in case of individuals closely related by blood or marriage.

The following are generally considered to have insurable interests:

(1) A person on his own life;

(2) A wife in her husband's life and a husband in his wife's life;

(3) A fiancée in her fiancé's life and a fiancée in his fiancée's life;

(4) A parent on a minor child's life (but not necessarily on an adult child's life);

(5) A creditor in the life of his debtor;

(6) An employer in the life of a key employee (but not a rank and file employee);

(7) Each of the partners, and the partnership itself, in the life of a partner whose death would result in a substantial loss;

(8) Each of the partners to a buy/sell agreement in the life of another partner, provided the beneficiaries do not stand to gain upon the death of the insured; and

(9) Among stockholders in a closely held corporation to the extent, and on the same basis, that an insurable interest exists among partners.

If the applicant has no insurable interest at the time a policy is taken out, the proceeds will be taxed as gain from a wagering contract.[26] If a policy is found to be void for lack of an insurable interest, the insurance company is generally required to refund premiums paid plus interest. Since the existence of an insurable interest is governed by the case and statutory law of each state, it is essential to refer to these specific state laws for answers to questions regarding an insurable interest.

TRANSFER FOR VALUE

The transfer for value of a life insurance contract jeopardizes the income tax-free payment of its proceeds.[27] Under the transfer for value rule, if a policy is transferred for a valuable consideration, the death proceeds will be taxable as ordinary income, except to the extent of the consideration, the net premiums and certain other amounts paid by the transferee. The transfer for value rules extend far beyond outright sales of policies. The naming of a beneficiary in exchange for any kind of valuable consideration would constitute a transfer for value. Consideration does not have to be in money, but could be an exchange of policies or a promise to perform some act or service. However, the mere pledging or assignment of a policy as collateral security is not a transfer for value. A bona fide gift is not considered to be a transfer for value and subsequent payment of the proceeds to the grantee (donee) will be income tax-free. Also, specific exceptions to this rule allow a transfer for consideration to be made to the following, without jeopardizing the income tax-free nature of the death benefit:

(1) Transfers to the insured.

(2) Transfers to a partner of the insured.

(3) Transfers to a partnership in which the insured is a partner.

(4) Transfers to a corporation in which the insured is a stockholder or officer.

(5) Transfers between corporations in a tax-free reorganization if certain conditions exist.

COST OF LIFE INSURANCE

Net Cost Method. Prior to introduction of the interest adjusted net cost method, the cost of life insurance was frequently determined by the "net cost" method, which consisted of simply adding up the net premiums (premiums less dividends), subtracting out any cash values, dividing by the number of years, and then dividing by the number of thousands of insurance. For example, assume a $150,000 nonparticipating contract with premiums of $900 per year yields $6,000 of cash values in the 10th year:

Premiums per year	900
Number of years	× 10
Total premiums paid	9,000
Less cash values	(6,000)
	3,000
Number of years	÷ 10
Cost per year	300
Number of thousands	÷ 150
Cost per year per thousand	2.00

Interest Adjusted Net Cost Method. But the above calculation fails to account for the time value of money. The interest adjusted net cost (IANC) method has been adopted by most states in order to provide some index for comparing one life insurance contract with another, and is particularly useful where there is a difference in amount and timing of premiums, availability of dividends and amounts of cash values. The IANC method assumes that the purchaser would be helped by comparing the results of his purchase to those that he could obtain by investing his money in a 5% savings account, with interest compounded annually. The basic question involves determining what amount of annual deposit would be required to end up with the same cash accumulation. Assuming the same $150,000 nonparticipating contract:

Life Insurance Contract		
Premiums per year		900.00
Cash values in 10 years	6,000	
5% Savings Account		
Cash value objective	6,000	
Interest factor (table, page 17.0)	÷ 13.207	
Annual deposit required		(454.30)
Cost per year for insurance		445.70
Number of thousands of coverage		÷ 150
Cost per year per thousand		2.97

OWNERSHIP & BENEFICIARY ARRANGEMENTS

	Advantages	Disadvantages
POLICY OWNER		
Insured	Insured retains control of policy and owns cash values.	Proceeds subject to estate tax. Policy transferred within 3 years also included in estate.
Spouse of Insured	Simple to arrange. Insured retains indirect control of policy (provided marriage stable).	If spouse predeceases insured policy ownership could return to insured (by will, intestacy laws or policy provisions). Proceeds not given away or consumed included in spouse's estate.
Children of Insured	Simple to arrange. Not taxed in estate. No costs to establish.	Insured loses control of policy (or never had control if children were applicants). If children minors, must have legal guardian appointed before proceeds paid (time consuming and costly).
Irrevocable Trust	Proceeds not subject to estate tax. Continued maintenance of policy if insured becomes incompetent. See page 434.	Insured does not control policy and cannot change or revoke trust. Costs to establish and trustee fees after death.
POLICY BENEFICIARY		
Individual - paid as lump sum	Simple to arrange. No costs to establish or collect proceeds. No delay in payment of death benefit.	Control of proceeds by beneficiary may lead to loss of funds or refusal to make proceeds available to pay settlement costs and taxes. With minor beneficiary guardian must be appointed.

	Advantages	Disadvantages
POLICY BENEFICIARY (cont'd)		
Individual – paid under settlement option	Simple to arrange. No costs to establish or collect proceeds. Funds remaining with carrier are secure.	Not flexible, insurance company must pay under original option despite beneficiaries changing circumstances. Proceeds not available to pay estate settlement costs and taxes.
Estate of Insured	Simple to arrange. No costs to establish or collect proceeds. Provides liquidity to estate.	Proceeds subject to estate tax and claims of creditors, as well as increasing probate costs.
Irrevocable Trust	Flexible, trust can give trustee broad authority to pay or withhold benefits, provide for successor beneficiaries, and make proceeds available for settlement costs. Provides professional management and investment advice. Not subject to claims of creditors.	Time consuming to establish. Initial costs for drafting of trust and trustee fees after funded by death benefit. Must coordinate with remainder of estate plan.

[1] See Robert A. Esperti & Renno L. Paterson, *21st Century Wealth* (Denver: Quantum Press, 2000), p. 129.

[2] For a listing of the various state laws on intestacy, see Donald F. Cady, *Field Guide To Estate Planning, Business Planning, & Employee Benefits* (Cincinnati: The National Underwriter Company, 2003, revised annually), p. 111.

[3] For a more in-depth discussion of how to review a will, see Stephan R. Leimberg et al., *The Tools & Techniques Of Estate Planning*, 12th ed. (Cincinnati: The National Underwriter Company, 2001), p. 519.

[4] See *Tax Facts 1*, (Cincinnati: The National Underwriter Company, 2003, revised annually), **Question 751** – Who needs to file a return and pay the tax, and when are they due?

[5] See *Tax Facts 1*, **Question 753** – What items are includable in a decedent's gross estate?

[6] See *Tax Facts 1*, **Question 763** – What deductions are allowed in computing the taxable estate of a decedent?

[7] See *Tax Facts 1*, **Question 764** – What is the estate tax marital deduction and what is the limitation on the deductible amount?

[8] See *Tax Facts 1*, **Question 767** – What is the unified credit, and how is it applied against the estate tax?

[9] EGTRRA 2001 stands for the Economic Growth and Tax Relief Reconciliation Act of 2001.

[10] See *Tax Facts 1*, **Question 752** – How is the federal estate tax computed?

[11] See *Tax Facts 1*, **Question 850** – What is a generation-skipping transfer (GST) on which a generation-skipping transfer tax (GST tax) is imposed?

[12] See *Tax Facts 1*, **Question 764** – What is the estate tax marital deduction and what is the limitation on the deductible amount?

[13] Code sections 2701-2704 are together referred to as "Chapter 14," and contain special valuation rules that maximize the gift tax value of many intra-family transfers by assigning zero value to specific retained interests (unless the retained interest is entitled to "qualified payments"). Affected by Chapter 14 are buy/sell agreements, family holding companies, family limited partnerships, grantor retained income trusts, personal holding companies, recapitalizations, and remainder interest transactions. See *Tax Facts 1*, **Question 812** – What are the Chapter 14 special valuation rules?

[14] See *Tax Facts 1*, **Question 817** – What gift tax exclusions are available to a donor?

[15] See *Tax Facts 1*, **Question 802** – How is the gift tax computed? and **Question 822** – What is the unified credit, and how is it applied against the gift tax?

[16] See Leimberg et al., p. 506.

[17] See *Tax Facts 1*, **Question 744** – What is a grantor trust? How is a grantor trust taxed?

[18] See *Tax Facts 1*, **Question 551** – If policies on insured's life are placed in an irrevocable life insurance trust, are the proceeds includable in his estate?

[19] See *Tax Facts 1*, **Question 764** – What is the estate tax marital deduction and what is the limitation on the deductible amount?

[20] See *Tax Facts 2*, (Cincinnati: The National Underwriter Company, 2003, revised annually), **Question 327** – Can a deduction be taken for a contribution to a charitable remainder trust or a pooled income fund?

[21] See William J. Wagner, *The Ultimate Trust Resource*, 2nd ed. (Cincinnati: The National Underwriter Company, 2002), p.105.

[22] See *Tax Facts 2*, **Question 328** – What is a charitable remainder annuity trust? and **Question 329** – What is a charitable remainder unitrust?

[23] See *Tax Facts 2*, **Question 428** – What is income in respect of a decedent and how is it taxed? Is the recipient entitled to an income tax deduction for estate and generation-skipping transfer taxes paid on this income?

[24] See *Tax Facts 2*, **Question 414** – What is "tax basis"?

[25] Ibid.

[26] See *Tax Facts 1*, **Question 130** – If an existing life insurance policy is sold or otherwise transferred for a valuable consideration, are the death proceeds wholly tax-exempt?

[27] See *Tax Facts 1*, **Question 63** – Will the sale or other transfer for value of an existing policy or any interest in a policy cause loss of income tax exemption for the death proceeds? and **Question 64** – What constitutes a "transfer for value" of a life insurance policy or an interest in a policy?

FEDERAL INCOME TAX RATES

(Updated for JGTRRA 2003)

MARRIED FILING JOINTLY

Taxable Income		Tax	Plus	Of Excess
Over	To	Equals	%	Over
0	14,000	0	10	0
14,000	56,800	1,400.00	15	14,000
56,800	114,650	7,820.00	25	56,800
114,650	174,700	22,282.50	28	114,650
174,700	311,950	39,096.50	33	174,700
311,950		84,389.00	35	311,950

MARRIED FILING SEPARATELY

Taxable Income		Tax	Plus	Of Excess
Over	To	Equals	%	Over
0	7,000	0	10	0
7,000	28,400	700.00	15	7,000
28,400	57,325	3,910.00	25	28,400
57,325	87,350	11,141.25	28	57,325
87,350	155,975	19,548.25	33	87,350
155,975		42,194.50	35	155,975

SINGLE

Taxable Income		Tax	Plus	Of Excess
Over	To	Equals	%	Over
0	7,000	0	10	0
7,000	28,400	700.00	15	7,000
28,400	68,800	3,910.00	25	28,400
68,800	143,500	14,010.00	28	68,800
143,500	311,950	34,926.00	33	143,500
311,950		90,514.50	35	311,950

HEAD OF HOUSEHOLD

Taxable Income		Tax	Plus	Of Excess
Over	To	Equals	%	Over
0	10,000	0	10	0
10,000	38,050	1,000.00	15	10,000
38,050	98,250	5,207.50	25	38,050
98,250	159,100	20,257.50	28	98,250
159,100	311,950	37,295.50	33	159,100
311,950		87,736.00	35	311,950

ESTATES AND TRUSTS

Taxable Income		Tax	Plus	Of Excess
Over	To	Equals	%	Over
0	1,900	0	15	0
1,900	4,500	285.00	25	1,900
4,500	6,850	935.00	28	4,500
6,850	9,350	1,593.00	33	6,850
9,350		2,418.00	35	9,350

FEDERAL ESTATE & GIFT TAX RATES
(Unified Rate Schedule)

TAXABLE ESTATE/GIFT OVER	TO	TAX EQUALS*	PLUS %	OF EXCESS OVER
0	10,000	0	18	0
10,000	20,000	1,800	20	10,000
20,000	40,000	3,800	22	20,000
40,000	60,000	8,200	24	40,000
60,000	80,000	13,000	26	60,000
80,000	100,000	18,200	28	80,000
100,000	150,000	23,800	30	100,000
150,000	250,000	38,800	32	150,000
250,000	500,000	70,800	34	250,000
500,000	750,000	155,800	37	500,000
750,000	1,000,000	248,300	39	750,000
1,000,000	1,250,000	345,800	41	1,000,000
1,250,000	1,500,000	448,300	43	1,250,000

Upper Brackets: 2003

| 1,500,000 | 2,000,000 | 555,800 | 45 | 1,500,000 |
| 2,000,000 | | 780,800 | 49 | 2,000,000 |

Upper Brackets: 2004

| 1,500,000 | 2,000,000 | 555,800 | 45 | 1,500,000 |
| 2,000,000 | | 780,800 | 48 | 2,000,000 |

Upper Brackets: 2005

| 1,500,000 | 2,000,000 | 555,800 | 45 | 1,500,000 |
| 2,000,000 | | 780,800 | 47 | 2,000,000 |

Upper Brackets: 2006

| 1,500,000 | 2,000,000 | 555,800 | 45 | 1,500,000 |
| 2,000,000 | | 780,800 | 46 | 2,000,000 |

Upper Brackets: 2007-2009

| 1,500,000 | | 555,800 | 45 | 1,500,000 |

* Less unified credit of $345,800 in 2003. Under EGTRRA 2001, the estate tax unified credit is scheduled to increase during the years 2004 to 2009. These increases are: $555,800 in 2004 and 2005, $780,800 in 2006 thru 2008, and $1,455,800 in 2009. In 2010 the estate tax is repealed, but will return in 2011 under the sunset provisions of EGTRRA 2001. In 2011 and thereafter, the estate tax unified credit is $345,800. The gift tax unified credit remains level at $345,800, except for 2010 when it decreases to $330,800. If any part of the prior $30,000 gift tax exemption was used for gifts made after 9/8/76, the unified credit must be reduced by 20% of the amount of the exemption used. Included in the table for the year 2011 and later is a 5% "add on" tax on amounts between $10,000,000 and $17,184,000.

(continued on next page)

FEDERAL ESTATE & GIFT TAX RATES (continued)

TAXABLE ESTATE/GIFT				OF EXCESS
OVER	TO	TAX EQUALS*	PLUS %	OVER

Upper Brackets: 2011 and later

1,500,000	2,000,000	555,800	45	1,500,000
2,000,000	2,500,000	780,800	49	2,000,000
2,500,000	3,000,000	1,025,800	53	2,500,000
3,000,000	10,000,000	1,290,800	55	3,000,000
10,000,000	17,184,000	5,140,800	60	10,000,000
17,184,000		9,451,200	55	17,184,000

Gift Tax: 2010

TAXABLE GIFT				OF EXCESS
OVER	TO	TAX EQUALS**	PLUS %	OVER
0	10,000	0	18	0
10,000	20,000	1,800	20	10,000
20,000	40,000	3,800	22	20,000
40,000	60,000	8,200	24	40,000
60,000	80,000	13,000	26	60,000
80,000	100,000	18,200	28	80,000
100,000	150,000	23,800	30	100,000
150,000	250,000	38,800	32	150,000
250,000	500,000	70,800	34	250,000
500,000		155,800	35	500,000

*Less unified credit of $345,800 in 2003. Under EGTRRA 2001, the estate tax unified credit is scheduled to increase during the years 2004 to 2009. These increases are: $555,800 in 2004 and 2005, $780,800 in 2006 thru 2008, and $1,455,800 in 2009. In 2010 the estate tax is repealed, but will return in 2011 under the sunset provisions of EGTRRA 2001. In 2011 and thereafter, the estate tax unified credit is $345,800. The gift tax unified credit remains level at $345,800, except for 2010 when it decreases to $330,800. If any part of the prior $30,000 gift tax exemption was used for gifts made after 9/8/76, the unified credit must be reduced by 20% of the amount of the exemption used. Included in the table for the year 2011 and later is a 5% "add on" tax on amounts between $10,000,000 and $17,184,000.

**Less credit of $330,800 in 2010.

See page 421 for calculation steps.

TABLE 2001 RATES

One Year Term Premiums For $1,000 Of Life Insurance Protection

Age	Table 2001	Age	Table 2001	Age	Table 2001	Age	Table 2001	Age	Table 2001
15	.38	29	.83	43	1.29	56	4.68	69	18.70
16	.52	30	.87	44	1.40	67	5.20	70	20.62
17	.57	31	.90	45	1.53	68	5.66	71	22.72
18	.59	32	.93	46	1.67	69	6.06	72	25.07
19	.61	33	.96	47	1.83	60	6.51	73	27.57
20	.62	34	.98	48	1.98	61	7.11	74	30.18
21	.62	35	.99	49	2.13	62	7.96	75	33.05
22	.64	36	1.01	50	2.30	63	9.08	76	36.33
23	.66	37	1.04	51	2.52	64	10.41	77	40.17
24	.68	38	1.06	52	2.81	65	11.90	78	44.33
25	.71	39	1.07	53	3.20	66	13.51	79	49.23
26	.73	40	1.10	54	3.65	67	15.20	80	54.56
27	.76	41	1.13	55	4.15	68	16.92	81	60.51
28	.80	42	1.20						

Application: As a measure of the value of insurance protection provided under: (1) split-dollar plans; (2) qualified pension and profit sharing plans; and (3) tax sheltered annuities.

Source: Notice 2002-8, 2002-4 IRB 398; Revenue Ruling 55-747, 1955-2 CB 228; and Revenue Ruling 66-110, 1966-1 CB 12. Notice 2002-8 provides Table 2001 rates for below age 15 and above age 81 (Appendix C, *Tax Facts 1 (2003)* contains the full table).

LIFETIME REQUIRED MINIMUM DISTRIBUTIONS

Age	Distribution Period	Age	Distribution Period	Age	Distribution Period	Age	Distribution Period	Age	Distribution Period
70	27.4	80	18.7	90	11.4	100	6.3	110	3.1
71	26.5	81	17.9	91	10.8	101	5.9	111	2.9
72	25.6	82	17.1	92	10.2	102	5.5	112	2.6
73	24.7	83	16.3	93	9.6	103	5.2	113	2.4
74	23.8	84	15.5	94	9.1	104	4.9	114	2.1
75	22.9	85	14.8	95	8.6	105	4.5	115 &	
76	22.0	86	14.1	96	8.1	106	4.2	Over	1.9
77	21.2	87	13.4	97	7.6	107	3.9		
78	20.3	88	12.7	98	7.1	108	3.7		
79	19.5	89	12.0	99	6.7	109	3.4		

Application: Used in calculating lifetime required minimum distributions from IRAs, qualified plans, and TSAs. For example, assume an individual turned age 74 in 2003, and on the previous December 31, 2002, his account balance was $325,000. Using this table, his life expectancy is 23.8 years. He must receive a distribution of $13,655 (325,000 ÷ 23.8 = 13,655) for the 2003 year, no later than December 31, 2003. Use of this table is required for 2003 and later.

Source: Reg. §1.40(a)(9)-9, A-2

COMMISSIONERS
1980 STANDARD ORDINARY MORTALITY TABLE

Age	Male deaths per 1,000	Male average future lifetime	Female deaths per 1,000	Female average future lifetime	Age	Male deaths per 1,000	Male average future lifetime	Female deaths per 1,000	Female average future lifetime
0	4.18	70.83	2.89	75.83	50	6.71	25.36	4.96	29.53
1	1.07	70.13	.87	75.04	51	7.30	24.52	5.31	28.67
2	.99	69.20	.81	74.11	52	7.96	23.70	5.70	27.82
3	.98	68.27	.79	73.17	53	8.71	22.89	6.15	26.98
4	.95	67.34	.77	72.23	54	9.56	22.08	6.61	26.14
5	.90	66.40	.76	71.28	55	10.47	21.29	7.09	25.31
6	.85	65.46	.73	70.34	56	11.46	20.51	7.57	24.49
7	.80	64.52	.72	69.39	57	12.49	19.74	8.03	23.67
8	.76	63.57	.70	68.44	58	13.59	18.99	8.47	22.86
9	.74	62.62	.69	67.48	59	14.77	18.24	8.94	22.05
10	.73	61.66	.68	66.53	60	16.08	17.51	9.47	21.25
11	.77	60.71	.69	65.58	61	17.54	16.79	10.13	20.44
12	.85	59.75	.72	64.62	62	19.19	16.08	10.96	19.65
13	.99	58.80	.75	63.67	63	21.06	15.38	12.02	18.86
14	1.15	57.86	.80	62.71	64	23.14	14.70	13.25	18.08
15	1.33	56.93	.85	61.76	65	25.42	14.04	14.59	17.32
16	1.51	56.00	.90	60.82	66	27.85	13.39	16.00	16.57
17	1.67	55.09	.95	59.87	67	30.44	12.76	17.43	15.83
18	1.78	54.18	.98	58.93	68	33.19	12.14	18.84	15.10
19	1.86	53.27	1.02	57.98	69	36.17	11.54	20.36	14.38
20	1.90	52.37	1.05	57.04	70	39.51	10.96	22.11	13.67
21	1.91	51.47	1.07	56.10	71	43.30	10.39	24.23	12.97
22	1.89	50.57	1.09	55.16	72	47.65	9.84	26.87	12.28
23	1.86	49.66	1.11	54.22	73	52.64	9.30	30.11	11.60
24	1.82	48.75	1.14	53.28	74	58.19	8.79	33.93	10.95
25	1.77	47.84	1.16	52.34	75	64.19	8.31	38.24	10.32
26	1.73	46.93	1.19	51.40	76	70.53	7.84	42.97	9.71
27	1.71	46.01	1.22	50.46	77	77.12	7.40	48.04	9.12
28	1.70	45.09	1.26	49.52	78	83.90	6.97	53.45	8.55
29	1.71	44.16	1.30	48.59	79	91.05	6.57	59.35	8.01
30	1.73	43.24	1.35	47.65	80	98.84	6.18	65.99	7.48
31	1.78	42.31	1.40	46.71	81	107.48	5.80	73.60	6.98
32	1.83	41.38	1.45	45.78	82	117.25	5.44	82.40	6.49
33	1.91	40.46	1.50	44.84	83	128.26	5.09	92.53	6.03
34	2.00	39.54	1.58	43.91	84	140.25	4.77	103.81	5.59
35	2.11	38.61	1.65	42.98	85	152.95	4.46	116.10	5.18
36	2.24	37.69	1.76	42.05	86	166.09	4.18	129.29	4.80
37	2.40	36.78	1.89	41.12	87	179.55	3.91	143.32	4.43
38	2.58	35.87	2.04	40.20	88	193.27	3.66	158.18	4.09
39	2.79	34.96	2.22	39.28	89	207.29	3.41	173.94	3.77
40	3.02	34.05	2.42	38.36	90	221.77	3.18	190.75	3.45
41	3.29	33.16	2.64	37.46	91	236.98	2.94	208.87	3.15
42	3.56	32.26	2.87	36.55	92	253.45	2.70	228.81	2.85
43	3.87	31.38	3.09	35.66	93	272.11	2.44	251.51	2.55
44	4.19	30.50	3.32	34.77	94	295.90	2.17	279.31	2.24
45	4.55	29.62	3.56	33.88	95	329.96	1.87	317.32	1.91
46	4.92	28.76	3.80	33.00	96	384.55	1.54	375.74	1.56
47	5.32	27.90	4.05	32.12	97	480.20	1.20	474.97	1.21
48	5.74	27.04	4.33	31.25	98	657.98	.84	655.85	.84
49	6.21	26.20	4.63	30.39	99	1000.00	.50	1000.00	.50

Source: Selected figures from published table. Age is given as nearest birthday.

FUTURE VALUE TABLE

The Sum To Which One Dollar Principal Will Increase

Years	3%	4%	5%	6%	7%	8%	9%
1	1.0300	1.0400	1.0500	1.0600	1.0700	1.0800	1.0900
2	1.0609	1.0816	1.1025	1.1236	1.1449	1.1664	1.1881
3	1.0927	1.1249	1.1576	1.1910	1.2250	1.2597	1.2950
4	1.1255	1.1699	1.2155	1.2625	1.3108	1.3605	1.4116
5	1.1593	1.2167	1.2763	1.3382	1.4026	1.4693	1.5386
6	1.1941	1.2653	1.3401	1.4185	1.5007	1.5869	1.6771
7	1.2299	1.3159	1.4071	1.5036	1.6058	1.7138	1.8280
8	1.2668	1.3686	1.4775	1.5938	1.7182	1.8509	1.9926
9	1.3048	1.4233	1.5513	1.6895	1.8385	1.9990	2.1719
10	1.3439	1.4802	1.6289	1.7908	1.9672	2.1589	2.3674
11	1.3842	1.5395	1.7103	1.8983	2.1049	2.3316	2.5804
12	1.4258	1.6010	1.7959	2.0122	2.2522	2.5182	2.8127
13	1.4685	1.6651	1.8856	2.1329	2.4098	2.7196	3.0658
14	1.5126	1.7317	1.9799	2.2609	2.5785	2.9372	3.3417
15	1.5580	1.8009	2.0789	2.3966	2.7590	3.1722	3.6425
16	1.6047	1.8730	2.1829	2.5404	2.9522	3.4259	3.9703
17	1.6528	1.9479	2.2920	2.6928	3.1588	3.7000	4.3276
18	1.7024	2.0258	2.4066	2.8543	3.3799	3.9960	4.7171
19	1.7535	2.1068	2.5270	3.0256	3.6165	4.3157	5.1417
20	1.8061	2.1911	2.6533	3.2071	3.8697	4.6610	5.6044
21	1.8603	2.2788	2.7860	3.3996	4.1406	5.0338	6.1088
22	1.9161	2.3699	2.9253	3.6035	4.4304	5.4365	6.6586
23	1.9736	2.4647	3.0715	3.8197	4.7405	5.8715	7.2579
24	2.0328	2.5633	3.2251	4.0489	5.0724	6.3412	7.9111
25	2.0938	2.6658	3.3864	4.2919	5.4274	6.8485	8.6231
26	2.1566	2.7725	3.5557	4.5494	5.8074	7.3964	9.3992
27	2.2213	2.8834	3.7335	4.8223	6.2139	7.9881	10.2451
28	2.2879	2.9987	3.9201	5.1117	6.6488	8.6271	11.1671
29	2.3566	3.1187	4.1161	5.4184	7.1143	9.3173	12.1722
30	2.4273	3.2434	4.3219	5.7435	7.6123	10.0627	13.2677
31	2.5001	3.3731	4.5380	6.0881	8.1451	10.8677	14.4618
32	2.5751	3.5081	4.7649	6.4534	8.7153	11.7371	15.7633
33	2.6523	3.6484	5.0032	6.8406	9.3253	12.6760	17.1820
34	2.7319	3.7943	5.2533	7.2510	9.9781	13.6901	18.7284
35	2.8139	3.9461	5.5160	7.6861	10.6766	14.7853	20.4140
36	2.8983	4.1039	5.7918	8.1473	11.4239	15.9682	22.2512
37	2.9852	4.2681	6.0814	8.6361	12.2236	17.2456	24.2538
38	3.0748	4.4388	6.3855	9.1543	13.0793	18.6253	26.4367
39	3.1670	4.6164	6.7048	9.7035	13.9948	20.1153	28.8160
40	3.2620	4.8010	7.0400	10.2857	14.9745	21.7245	31.4094

FUTURE VALUE TABLE

The Sum To Which One Dollar Principal Will Increase

Years	Rate					
	10%	11%	12%	13%	14%	15%
1	1.1000	1.1100	1.1200	1.1300	1.1400	1.1500
2	1.2100	1.2321	1.2544	1.2769	1.2996	1.3225
3	1.3310	1.3676	1.4049	1.4429	1.4815	1.5209
4	1.4641	1.5181	1.5735	1.6305	1.6890	1.7490
5	1.6105	1.6851	1.7623	1.8424	1.9254	2.0114
6	1.7716	1.8704	1.9738	2.0820	2.1950	2.3131
7	1.9487	2.0762	2.2107	2.3526	2.5023	2.6600
8	2.1436	2.3045	2.4760	2.6584	2.8526	3.0590
9	2.3579	2.5580	2.7731	3.0040	3.2519	3.5179
10	2.5937	2.8394	3.1058	3.3946	3.7072	4.0456
11	2.8531	3.1518	3.4785	3.8359	4.2262	4.6524
12	3.1384	3.4985	3.8960	4.3345	4.8179	5.3503
13	3.4523	3.8833	4.3635	4.8980	5.4924	6.1528
14	3.7975	4.3104	4.8871	5.5348	6.2613	7.0757
15	4.1772	4.7846	5.4736	6.2543	7.1379	8.1371
16	4.5950	5.3109	6.1304	7.0673	8.1372	9.3576
17	5.0545	5.8951	6.8660	7.9861	9.2765	10.7613
18	5.5599	6.5436	7.6900	9.0243	10.5752	12.3755
19	6.1159	7.2633	8.6128	10.1974	12.0557	14.2318
20	6.7275	8.0623	9.6463	11.5231	13.7435	16.3665
21	7.4003	8.9492	10.8038	13.0211	15.6676	18.8215
22	8.1403	9.9336	12.1003	14.7138	17.8610	21.6447
23	8.9543	11.0263	13.5523	16.6266	20.3616	24.8915
24	9.8497	12.2392	15.1786	18.7881	23.2122	28.6252
25	10.8347	13.5855	17.0001	21.2305	26.4619	32.9190
26	11.9182	15.0799	19.0401	23.9905	30.1666	37.8568
27	13.1100	16.7386	21.3249	27.1093	34.3899	43.5353
28	14.4210	18.5799	23.8839	30.6335	39.2045	50.0656
29	15.8631	20.6237	26.7499	34.6158	44.6931	57.5755
30	17.4494	22.8923	29.9599	39.1159	50.9502	66.2118
31	19.1943	25.4104	33.5551	44.2010	58.0832	76.1435
32	21.1138	28.2056	37.5817	49.9471	66.2148	87.5651
33	23.2252	31.3082	42.0915	56.4402	75.4849	100.6998
34	25.5477	34.7521	47.1425	63.7774	86.0528	115.8048
35	28.1024	38.5749	52.7996	72.0685	98.1002	133.1755
36	30.9127	42.8181	59.1356	81.4374	111.8342	153.1519
37	34.0040	47.5281	66.2318	92.0243	127.4910	176.1247
38	37.4043	52.7562	74.1797	103.9874	145.3397	202.5434
39	41.1448	58.5593	83.0812	117.5058	165.6873	232.9249
40	45.2593	65.0009	93.0510	132.7815	188.8835	267.8636

FUTURE VALUE TABLE

The Sum To Which One Dollar Per Annum Will Increase
Paid At The *Beginning* Of Each Year

Years	3%	4%	5%	6%	7%	8%	9%
1	1.0300	1.0400	1.0500	1.0600	1.0700	1.0800	1.0900
2	2.0909	2.1216	2.1525	2.1836	2.2149	2.2464	2.2781
3	3.1836	3.2465	3.3101	3.3746	3.4399	3.5061	3.5731
4	4.3091	4.4163	4.5256	4.6371	4.7507	4.8666	4.9847
5	5.4684	5.6330	5.8019	5.9753	6.1533	6.3359	6.5233
6	6.6625	6.8983	7.1420	7.3938	7.6540	7.9228	8.2004
7	7.8923	8.2142	8.5491	8.8975	9.2598	9.6366	10.0285
8	9.1591	9.5828	10.0266	10.4913	10.9780	11.4876	12.0210
9	10.4639	11.0061	11.5779	12.1808	12.8164	13.4866	14.1929
10	11.8078	12.4864	13.2068	13.9716	14.7836	15.6455	16.5603
11	13.1920	14.0258	14.9171	15.8699	16.8885	17.9771	19.1407
12	14.6178	15.6268	16.7130	17.8821	19.1406	20.4953	21.9534
13	16.0863	17.2919	18.5986	20.0151	21.5505	23.2149	25.0192
14	17.5989	19.0236	20.5786	22.2760	24.1290	26.1521	28.3609
15	19.1569	20.8245	22.6575	24.6725	26.8881	29.3243	32.0034
16	20.7616	22.6975	24.8404	27.2129	29.8402	32.7502	35.9737
17	22.4144	24.6454	27.1324	29.9057	32.9990	36.4502	40.3013
18	24.1169	26.6712	29.5390	32.7600	36.3790	40.4463	45.0185
19	25.8704	28.7781	32.0660	35.7856	39.9955	44.7620	50.1601
20	27.6765	30.9692	34.7193	38.9927	43.8652	49.4229	55.7645
21	29.5368	33.2480	37.5052	42.3923	48.0057	54.4568	61.8733
22	31.4529	35.6179	40.4305	45.9958	52.4361	59.8933	68.5319
23	33.4265	38.0826	43.5020	49.8156	57.1767	65.7648	75.7898
24	35.4593	40.6459	46.7271	53.8645	62.2490	72.1059	83.7009
25	37.5530	43.3117	50.1135	58.1564	67.6765	78.9544	92.3240
26	39.7096	46.0842	53.6691	62.7058	73.4838	86.3508	101.7231
27	41.9309	48.9676	57.4026	67.5281	79.6977	94.3388	111.9682
28	44.2188	51.9663	61.3227	72.6398	86.3465	102.9659	123.1354
29	46.5754	55.0849	65.4388	78.0582	93.4608	112.2832	135.3075
30	49.0027	58.3283	69.7608	83.8017	101.0730	122.3459	148.5752
31	51.5028	61.7015	74.2988	89.8898	109.2182	133.2135	163.0370
32	54.0778	65.2095	79.0638	96.3432	117.9334	144.9506	178.8003
33	56.7302	68.8579	84.0670	103.1838	127.2588	157.6267	195.9824
34	59.4621	72.6522	89.3203	110.4348	137.2369	171.3168	214.7108
35	62.2759	76.5983	94.8363	118.1209	147.9135	186.1021	235.1247
36	65.1742	80.7022	100.6281	126.2681	159.3374	202.0703	257.3760
37	68.1594	84.9703	106.7095	134.9042	171.5610	219.3159	281.6298
38	71.2342	89.4091	113.0950	144.0585	184.6403	237.9412	308.0665
39	74.4013	94.0255	119.7998	153.7620	198.6351	258.0565	336.8825
40	77.6633	98.8265	126.8398	164.0477	213.6096	279.7810	368.2919

FUTURE VALUE TABLE

The Sum To Which One Dollar Per Annum Will Increase
Paid At The *Beginning* Of Each Year

Years	Rate					
	10%	11%	12%	13%	14%	15%
1	1.1000	1.1100	1.1200	1.1300	1.1400	1.1500
2	2.3100	2.3421	2.3744	2.4069	2.4396	2.4725
3	3.6410	3.7097	3.7793	3.8498	3.9211	3.9934
4	5.1051	5.2278	5.3528	5.4803	5.6101	5.7424
5	6.7156	6.9129	7.1152	7.3227	7.5355	7.7537
6	8.4872	8.7833	9.0890	9.4047	9.7305	10.0668
7	10.4359	10.8594	11.2997	11.7573	12.2328	12.7268
8	12.5795	13.1640	13.7757	14.4157	15.0853	15.7858
9	14.9374	15.7220	16.5487	17.4197	18.3373	19.3037
10	17.5312	18.5614	19.6546	20.8143	22.0445	23.3493
11	20.3843	21.7132	23.1331	24.6502	26.2707	28.0017
12	23.5227	25.2116	27.0291	28.9847	31.0887	33.3519
13	26.9750	29.0949	31.3926	33.8827	36.5811	39.5047
14	30.7725	33.4054	36.2797	39.4175	42.8424	46.5804
15	34.9497	38.1899	41.7533	45.6717	49.9804	54.7175
16	39.5447	43.5008	47.8837	52.7391	58.1176	64.0751
17	44.5992	49.3959	54.7497	60.7251	67.3941	74.8364
18	50.1591	55.9395	62.4397	69.7494	77.9692	87.2118
19	56.2750	63.2028	71.0524	79.9468	90.0249	101.4436
20	63.0025	71.2651	80.6987	91.4699	103.7684	117.8101
21	70.4028	80.2143	91.5026	104.4910	119.4360	136.6316
22	78.5430	90.1479	103.6029	119.2048	137.2970	158.2764
23	87.4973	101.1741	117.1552	135.8315	157.6586	183.1679
24	97.3471	113.4133	132.3339	154.6195	180.8708	211.7930
25	108.1818	126.9988	149.3339	175.8501	207.3327	244.7120
26	120.0999	142.0786	168.3740	199.8406	237.4993	282.5688
27	133.2099	158.8173	189.6989	226.9499	271.8892	326.1041
28	147.6309	177.3972	213.5827	257.5834	311.0937	376.1697
29	163.4940	198.0209	240.3327	292.1992	355.7869	433.7452
30	180.9434	220.9132	270.2926	331.3151	406.7370	499.9570
31	200.1378	246.3236	303.8477	375.5160	464.8202	576.1005
32	221.2516	274.5292	341.4294	425.4631	531.0350	663.6656
33	244.4767	305.8374	383.5210	481.9033	606.5199	764.3655
34	270.0244	340.5896	430.6635	545.6808	692.5727	880.1703
35	298.1268	379.1644	483.4631	617.7493	790.6729	1013.3458
36	329.0395	421.9825	542.5987	699.1867	902.5071	1166.4977
37	363.0434	469.5106	608.8305	791.2109	1029.9981	1342.6224
38	400.4478	522.2667	683.0101	895.1983	1175.3378	1545.1657
39	441.5926	580.8261	766.0914	1012.7041	1341.0251	1778.0906
40	486.8518	645.8269	859.1423	1145.4856	1529.9086	2045.9542

FUTURE VALUE TABLE

The Sum To Which One Dollar Per Annum Will Increase
Paid At The *End* Of Each Year

Years	3%	4%	5%	6%	7%	8%	9%
				Rate			
1	1.0000	1.0000	1.0000	1.0000	1.0000	1.0000	1.0000
2	2.0300	2.0400	2.0500	2.0600	2.0700	2.0800	2.0900
3	3.0909	3.1216	3.1525	3.1836	3.2149	3.2464	3.2781
4	4.1836	4.2465	4.3101	4.3746	4.4399	4.5061	4.5731
5	5.3091	5.4163	5.5256	5.6371	5.7507	5.8666	5.9847
6	6.4684	6.6330	6.8019	6.9753	7.1533	7.3359	7.5233
7	7.6625	7.8983	8.1420	8.3938	8.6540	8.9228	9.2004
8	8.8923	9.2142	9.5491	9.8975	10.2598	10.6366	11.0285
9	10.1591	10.5828	11.0266	11.4913	11.9780	12.4876	13.0210
10	11.4639	12.0061	12.5779	13.1808	13.8164	14.4866	15.1929
11	12.8078	13.4864	14.2068	14.9716	15.7836	16.6455	17.5603
12	14.1920	15.0258	15.9171	16.8699	17.8885	18.9771	20.1407
13	15.6178	16.6268	17.7130	18.8821	20.1406	21.4953	22.9534
14	17.0863	18.2919	19.5986	21.0151	22.5505	24.2149	26.0192
15	18.5989	20.0236	21.5786	23.2760	25.1290	27.1521	29.3609
16	20.1569	21.8245	23.6575	25.6725	27.8881	30.3243	33.0034
17	21.7616	23.6975	25.8404	28.2129	30.8402	33.7502	36.9737
18	23.4144	25.6454	28.1324	30.9057	33.9990	37.4502	41.3013
19	25.1169	27.6712	30.5390	33.7600	37.3790	41.4463	46.0185
20	26.8704	29.7781	33.0660	36.7856	40.9955	45.7620	51.1601
21	28.6765	31.9692	35.7193	39.9927	44.8652	50.4229	56.7645
22	30.5368	34.2480	38.5052	43.3923	49.0057	55.4568	62.8733
23	32.4529	36.6179	41.4305	46.9958	53.4361	60.8933	69.5319
24	34.4265	39.0826	44.5020	50.8156	58.1767	66.7648	76.7898
25	36.4593	41.6459	47.7271	54.8645	63.2490	73.1059	84.7009
26	38.5530	44.3117	51.1135	59.1564	68.6765	79.9544	93.3240
27	40.7096	47.0842	54.6691	63.7058	74.4838	87.3508	102.7231
28	42.9309	49.9676	58.4026	68.5281	80.6977	95.3388	112.9682
29	45.2188	52.9663	62.3227	73.6398	87.3465	103.9659	124.1354
30	47.5754	56.0849	66.4388	79.0582	94.4608	113.2832	136.3075
31	50.0027	59.3283	70.7608	84.8017	102.0730	123.3459	149.5752
32	52.5028	62.7015	75.2988	90.8898	110.2182	134.2135	164.0370
33	55.0778	66.2095	80.0638	97.3432	118.9334	145.9506	179.8003
34	57.7302	69.8579	85.0670	104.1838	128.2588	158.6267	196.9824
35	60.4621	73.6522	90.3203	111.4348	138.2369	172.3168	215.7108
36	63.2759	77.5983	95.8363	119.1209	148.9135	187.1021	236.1247
37	66.1742	81.7022	101.6281	127.2681	160.3374	203.0703	258.3760
38	69.1594	85.9703	107.7095	135.9042	172.5610	220.3159	282.6298
39	72.2342	90.4091	114.0950	145.0585	185.6403	238.9412	309.0665
40	75.4013	95.0255	120.7998	154.7620	199.6351	259.0565	337.8825

FUTURE VALUE TABLE

The Sum To Which One Dollar Per Annum Will Increase
Paid At The *End* Of Each Year

			Rate			
Years	10%	11%	12%	13%	14%	15%
1	1.0000	1.0000	1.0000	1.0000	1.0000	1.0000
2	2.1000	2.1100	2.1200	2.1300	2.1400	2.1500
3	3.3100	3.3421	3.3744	3.4069	3.4396	3.4725
4	4.6410	4.7097	4.7793	4.8498	4.9211	4.9934
5	6.1051	6.2278	6.3528	6.4803	6.6101	6.7424
6	7.7156	7.9129	8.1152	8.3227	8.5355	8.7537
7	9.4872	9.7833	10.0890	10.4047	10.7305	11.0668
8	11.4359	11.8594	12.2997	12.7573	13.2328	13.7268
9	13.5795	14.1640	14.7757	15.4157	16.0853	16.7858
10	15.9374	16.7220	17.5487	18.4197	19.3373	20.3037
11	18.5312	19.5614	20.6546	21.8143	23.0445	24.3493
12	21.3843	22.7132	24.1331	25.6502	27.2707	29.0017
13	24.5227	26.2116	28.0291	29.9847	32.0887	34.3519
14	27.9750	30.0949	32.3926	34.8827	37.5811	40.5047
15	31.7725	34.4054	37.2797	40.4175	43.8424	47.5804
16	35.9497	39.1899	42.7533	46.6717	50.9804	55.7175
17	40.5447	44.5008	48.8837	53.7391	59.1176	65.0751
18	45.5992	50.3959	55.7497	61.7251	68.3941	75.8364
19	51.1591	56.9395	63.4397	70.7494	78.9692	88.2118
20	57.2750	64.2028	72.0524	80.9468	91.0249	102.4436
21	64.0025	72.2651	81.6987	92.4699	104.7684	118.8101
22	71.4028	81.2143	92.5026	105.4910	120.4360	137.6316
23	79.5430	91.1479	104.6029	120.2048	138.2970	159.2764
24	88.4973	102.1741	118.1552	136.8315	158.6586	184.1679
25	98.3471	114.4133	133.3339	155.6195	181.8708	212.7930
26	109.1818	127.9988	150.3339	176.8501	208.3327	245.7120
27	121.0999	143.0786	169.3740	200.8406	238.4993	283.5688
28	134.2099	159.8173	190.6989	227.9499	272.8892	327.1041
29	148.6309	178.3972	214.5827	258.5834	312.0937	377.1697
30	164.4940	199.0209	241.3327	293.1992	356.7869	434.7452
31	181.9434	221.9132	271.2926	332.3151	407.7370	500.9570
32	201.1378	247.3236	304.8477	376.5160	465.8202	577.1005
33	222.2516	275.5292	342.4294	426.4631	532.0350	664.6656
34	245.4767	306.8374	384.5210	482.9033	607.5199	765.3655
35	271.0244	341.5896	431.6635	546.6808	693.5727	881.1703
36	299.1268	380.1644	484.4631	618.7493	791.6729	1014.3458
37	330.0395	422.9825	543.5987	700.1867	903.5071	1167.4977
38	364.0434	470.5106	609.8305	792.2109	1030.9981	1343.6224
39	401.4478	523.2667	684.0101	896.1983	1176.3378	1546.1657
40	442.5926	581.8261	767.0914	1013.7041	1342.0251	1779.0906

PRESENT VALUE TABLE

The Worth Today of One Dollar Due In The Future

Years	3%	4%	5%	6%	7%	8%	9%
				Rate			
1	.9709	.9615	.9524	.9434	.9346	.9259	.9174
2	.9426	.9246	.9070	.8900	.8734	.8573	.8417
3	.9151	.8890	.8638	.8396	.8163	.7938	.7722
4	.8885	.8548	.8227	.7921	.7629	.7350	.7084
5	.8626	.8219	.7835	.7473	.7130	.6806	.6499
6	.8375	.7903	.7462	.7050	.6663	.6302	.5963
7	.8131	.7599	.7107	.6651	.6227	.5835	.5470
8	.7894	.7307	.6768	.6274	.5820	.5403	.5019
9	.7664	.7026	.6446	.5919	.5439	.5002	.4604
10	.7441	.6756	.6139	.5584	.5083	.4632	.4224
11	.7224	.6496	.5847	.5268	.4751	.4289	.3875
12	.7014	.6246	.5568	.4970	.4440	.3971	.3555
13	.6810	.6006	.5303	.4688	.4150	.3677	.3262
14	.6611	.5775	.5051	.4423	.3878	.3405	.2992
15	.6419	.5553	.4810	.4173	.3624	.3152	.2745
16	.6232	.5339	.4581	.3936	.3387	.2919	.2519
17	.6050	.5134	.4363	.3714	.3166	.2703	.2311
18	.5874	.4936	.4155	.3503	.2959	.2502	.2120
19	.5703	.4746	.3957	.3305	.2765	.2317	.1945
20	.5537	.4564	.3769	.3118	.2584	.2145	.1784
21	.5375	.4388	.3589	.2942	.2415	.1987	.1637
22	.5219	.4220	.3418	.2775	.2257	.1839	.1502
23	.5067	.4057	.3256	.2618	.2109	.1703	.1378
24	.4919	.3901	.3101	.2470	.1971	.1577	.1264
25	.4776	.3751	.2953	.2330	.1842	.1460	.1160
26	.4637	.3607	.2812	.2198	.1722	.1352	.1064
27	.4502	.3468	.2678	.2074	.1609	.1252	.0976
28	.4371	.3335	.2551	.1956	.1504	.1159	.0895
29	.4243	.3207	.2429	.1846	.1406	.1073	.0822
30	.4120	.3083	.2314	.1741	.1314	.0994	.0754
31	.4000	.2965	.2204	.1643	.1228	.0920	.0691
32	.3883	.2851	.2099	.1550	.1147	.0852	.0634
33	.3770	.2741	.1999	.1462	.1072	.0789	.0582
34	.3660	.2636	.1904	.1379	.1002	.0730	.0534
35	.3554	.2534	.1813	.1301	.0937	.0676	.0490
36	.3450	.2437	.1727	.1227	.0875	.0626	.0449
37	.3350	.2343	.1644	.1158	.0818	.0580	.0412
38	.3252	.2253	.1566	.1092	.0765	.0537	.0378
39	.3158	.2166	.1491	.1031	.0715	.0497	.0347
40	.3066	.2083	.1420	.0972	.0668	.0460	.0318

PRESENT VALUE TABLE

The Worth Today of One Dollar Due In The Future

Years	Rate						
	10%	11%	12%	13%	14%	15%	18%
1	.9091	.9009	.8929	.8850	.8772	.8696	.8475
2	.8264	.8116	.7972	.7831	.7695	.7561	.7182
3	.7513	.7312	.7118	.6931	.6750	.6575	.6086
4	.6830	.6587	.6355	.6133	.5921	.5718	.5158
5	.6209	.5935	.5674	.5428	.5194	.4972	.4371
6	.5645	.5346	.5066	.4803	.4556	.4323	.3704
7	.5132	.4817	.4523	.4251	.3996	.3759	.3139
8	.4665	.4339	.4039	.3762	.3506	.3269	.2660
9	.4241	.3909	.3606	.3329	.3075	.2843	.2255
10	.3855	.3522	.3220	.2946	.2697	.2472	.1911
11	.3505	.3173	.2875	.2607	.2366	.2149	.1619
12	.3186	.2858	.2567	.2307	.2076	.1869	.1372
13	.2897	.2575	.2292	.2042	.1821	.1625	.1163
14	.2633	.2320	.2046	.1807	.1597	.1413	.0985
15	.2394	.2090	.1827	.1599	.1401	.1229	.0835
16	.2176	.1883	.1631	.1415	.1229	.1069	.0708
17	.1978	.1696	.1456	.1252	.1078	.0929	.0600
18	.1799	.1528	.1300	.1108	.0946	.0808	.0508
19	.1635	.1377	.1161	.0981	.0829	.0703	.0431
20	.1486	.1240	.1037	.0868	.0728	.0611	.0365
21	.1351	.1117	.0926	.0768	.0638	.0531	.0309
22	.1228	.1007	.0826	.0680	.0560	.0462	.0262
23	.1117	.0907	.0738	.0601	.0491	.0402	.0222
24	.1015	.0817	.0659	.0532	.0431	.0349	.0188
25	.0923	.0736	.0588	.0471	.0378	.0304	.0160
26	.0839	.0663	.0525	.0417	.0331	.0264	.0135
27	.0763	.0597	.0469	.0369	.0291	.0230	.0115
28	.0693	.0538	.0419	.0326	.0255	.0200	.0097
29	.0630	.0485	.0374	.0289	.0224	.0174	.0082
30	.0573	.0437	.0334	.0256	.0196	.0151	.0070
31	.0521	.0394	.0298	.0226	.0172	.0131	.0059
32	.0474	.0355	.0266	.0200	.0151	.0114	.0050
33	.0431	.0319	.0238	.0177	.0132	.0099	.0042
34	.0391	.0288	.0212	.0157	.0116	.0086	.0036
35	.0356	.0259	.0189	.0139	.0102	.0075	.0030
36	.0323	.0234	.0169	.0123	.0089	.0065	.0026
37	.0294	.0210	.0151	.0109	.0078	.0057	.0022
38	.0267	.0190	.0135	.0096	.0069	.0049	.0019
39	.0243	.0171	.0120	.0085	.0060	.0043	.0016
40	.0221	.0154	.0107	.0075	.0053	.0037	.0013

PRESENT VALUE TABLE

The Worth Today of One Dollar Per Annum
Paid At The *Beginning* Of Each Year

				Rate			
Years	3%	4%	5%	6%	7%	8%	9%
1	1.0000	1.0000	1.0000	1.0000	1.0000	1.0000	1.0000
2	1.9709	1.9615	1.9524	1.9434	1.9346	1.9259	1.9174
3	2.9135	2.8861	2.8594	2.8334	2.8080	2.7833	2.7591
4	3.8286	3.7751	3.7232	3.6730	3.6243	3.5771	3.5313
5	4.7171	4.6299	4.5459	4.4651	4.3872	4.3121	4.2397
6	5.5797	5.4518	5.3295	5.2124	5.1002	4.9927	4.8897
7	6.4172	6.2421	6.0757	5.9173	5.7665	5.6229	5.4859
8	7.2303	7.0021	6.7864	6.5824	6.3893	6.2064	6.0330
9	8.0197	7.7327	7.4632	7.2098	6.9713	6.7466	6.5348
10	8.7861	8.4353	8.1078	7.8017	7.5152	7.2469	6.9952
11	9.5302	9.1109	8.7217	8.3601	8.0236	7.7101	7.4177
12	10.2526	9.7605	9.3064	8.8869	8.4987	8.1390	7.8052
13	10.9540	10.3851	9.8633	9.3838	8.9427	8.5361	8.1607
14	11.6350	10.9856	10.3936	9.8527	9.3577	8.9038	8.4869
15	12.2961	11.5631	10.8986	10.2950	9.7455	9.2442	8.7861
16	12.9379	12.1184	11.3797	10.7122	10.1079	9.5595	9.0607
17	13.5611	12.6523	11.8378	11.1059	10.4466	9.8514	9.3126
18	14.1661	13.1657	12.2741	11.4773	10.7632	10.1216	9.5436
19	14.7535	13.6593	12.6896	11.8276	11.0591	10.3719	9.7556
20	15.3238	14.1339	13.0853	12.1581	11.3356	10.6036	9.9501
21	15.8775	14.5903	13.4622	12.4699	11.5940	10.8181	10.1285
22	16.4150	15.0292	13.8212	12.7641	11.8355	11.0168	10.2922
23	16.9369	15.4511	14.1630	13.0416	12.0612	11.2007	10.4424
24	17.4436	15.8568	14.4886	13.3034	12.2722	11.3711	10.5802
25	17.9355	16.2470	14.7986	13.5504	12.4693	11.5288	10.7066
26	18.4131	16.6221	15.0939	13.7834	12.6536	11.6748	10.8226
27	18.8768	16.9828	15.3752	14.0032	12.8258	11.8100	10.9290
28	19.3270	17.3296	15.6430	14.2105	12.9867	11.9352	11.0266
29	19.7641	17.6631	15.8981	14.4062	13.1371	12.0511	11.1161
30	20.1885	17.9837	16.1411	14.5907	13.2777	12.1584	11.1983
31	20.6004	18.2920	16.3724	14.7648	13.4090	12.2578	11.2737
32	21.0004	18.5885	16.5928	14.9291	13.5318	12.3498	11.3428
33	21.3888	18.8735	16.8027	15.0840	13.6466	12.4350	11.4062
34	21.7658	19.1476	17.0025	15.2302	13.7538	12.5139	11.4644
35	22.1318	19.4112	17.1929	15.3681	13.8540	12.5869	11.5178
36	22.4872	19.6646	17.3742	15.4982	13.9477	12.6546	11.5668
37	22.8323	19.9083	17.5469	15.6210	14.0352	12.7172	11.6118
38	23.1672	20.1426	17.7113	15.7368	14.1170	12.7752	11.6530
39	23.4925	20.3679	17.8679	15.8460	14.1935	12.8289	11.6908
40	23.8082	20.5845	18.0170	15.9491	14.2649	12.8786	11.7255

PRESENT VALUE TABLE

The Worth Today of One Dollar Per Annum
Paid At The *Beginning* Of Each Year

				Rate			
Years	10%	11%	12%	13%	14%	15%	18%
1	1.0000	1.0000	1.0000	1.0000	1.0000	1.0000	1.0000
2	1.9091	1.9009	1.8929	1.8850	1.8772	1.8696	1.8475
3	2.7355	2.7125	2.6901	2.6681	2.6467	2.6257	2.5656
4	3.4869	3.4437	3.4018	3.3612	3.3216	3.2832	3.1743
5	4.1699	4.1024	4.0373	3.9745	3.9137	3.8550	3.6901
6	4.7908	4.6959	4.6048	4.5172	4.4331	4.3522	4.1272
7	5.3553	5.2305	5.1114	4.9976	4.8887	4.7845	4.4976
8	5.8684	5.7122	5.5638	5.4226	5.2883	5.1604	4.8115
9	6.3349	6.1461	5.9676	5.7988	5.6389	5.4873	5.0776
10	6.7590	6.5370	6.3282	6.1317	5.9464	5.7716	5.3030
11	7.1446	6.8892	6.6502	6.4262	6.2161	6.0188	5.4941
12	7.4951	7.2065	6.9377	6.6869	6.4527	6.2337	5.6560
13	7.8137	7.4924	7.1944	6.9176	6.6603	6.4206	5.7932
14	8.1034	7.7499	7.4235	7.1218	6.8424	6.5831	5.9095
15	8.3667	7.9819	7.6282	7.3025	7.0021	6.7245	6.0081
16	8.6061	8.1909	7.8109	7.4624	7.1422	6.8474	6.0916
17	8.8237	8.3792	7.9740	7.6039	7.2651	6.9542	6.1624
18	9.0216	8.5488	8.1196	7.7291	7.3729	7.0472	6.2223
19	9.2014	8.7016	8.2497	7.8399	7.4674	7.1280	6.2732
20	9.3649	8.8393	8.3658	7.9380	7.5504	7.1982	6.3162
21	9.5136	8.9633	8.4694	8.0248	7.6231	7.2593	6.3527
22	9.6487	9.0751	8.5620	8.1016	7.6870	7.3125	6.3837
23	9.7715	9.1757	8.6446	8.1695	7.7429	7.3587	6.4099
24	9.8832	9.2664	8.7184	8.2297	7.7921	7.3988	6.4321
25	9.9847	9.3481	8.7843	8.2829	7.8351	7.4338	6.4509
26	10.0770	9.4217	8.8431	8.3300	7.8729	7.4641	6.4669
27	10.1609	9.4881	8.8957	8.3717	7.9061	7.4906	6.4804
28	10.2372	9.5478	8.9426	8.4086	7.9352	7.5135	6.4919
29	10.3066	9.6016	8.9844	8.4412	7.9607	7.5335	6.5016
30	10.3696	9.6501	9.0218	8.4701	7.9830	7.5509	6.5098
31	10.4269	9.6938	9.0552	8.4957	8.0027	7.5660	6.5168
32	10.4790	9.7331	9.0850	8.5183	8.0199	7.5791	6.5227
33	10.5264	9.7686	9.1116	8.5383	8.0350	7.5905	6.5277
34	10.5694	9.8005	9.1354	8.5560	8.0482	7.6005	6.5320
35	10.6086	9.8293	9.1566	8.5717	8.0599	7.6091	6.5356
36	10.6442	9.8552	9.1755	8.5856	8.0700	7.6166	6.5386
37	10.6765	9.8786	9.1924	8.5979	8.0790	7.6231	6.5412
38	10.7059	9.8996	9.2075	8.6087	8.0868	7.6288	6.5434
39	10.7327	9.9186	9.2210	8.6183	8.0937	7.6338	6.5452
40	10.7570	9.9357	9.2330	8.6268	8.0997	7.6380	6.5468

PRESENT VALUE TABLE

The Worth Today of One Dollar Per Annum
Paid At The *End* Of Each Year

				Rate			
Years	3%	4%	5%	6%	7%	8%	9%
1	.9709	.9615	.9524	.9434	.9346	.9259	.9174
2	1.9135	1.8861	1.8594	1.8334	1.8080	1.7833	1.7591
3	2.8286	2.7751	2.7232	2.6730	2.6243	2.5771	2.5313
4	3.7171	3.6299	3.5460	3.4651	3.3872	3.3121	3.2397
5	4.5797	4.4518	4.3295	4.2124	4.1002	3.9927	3.8897
6	5.4172	5.2421	5.0757	4.9173	4.7665	4.6229	4.4859
7	6.2303	6.0021	5.7864	5.5824	5.3893	5.2064	5.0330
8	7.0197	6.7327	6.4632	6.2098	5.9713	5.7466	5.5348
9	7.7861	7.4353	7.1078	6.8017	6.5152	6.2469	5.9952
10	8.5302	8.1109	7.7217	7.3601	7.0236	6.7101	6.4177
11	9.2526	8.7605	8.3064	7.8869	7.4987	7.1390	6.8052
12	9.9540	9.3851	8.8633	8.3838	7.9427	7.5361	7.1607
13	10.6350	9.9856	9.3936	8.8527	8.3577	7.9038	7.4869
14	11.2961	10.5631	9.8986	9.2950	8.7455	8.2442	7.7862
15	11.9379	11.1184	10.3797	9.7122	9.1079	8.5595	8.0607
16	12.5611	11.6523	10.8378	10.1059	9.4466	8.8514	8.3126
17	13.1661	12.1657	11.2741	10.4773	9.7632	9.1216	8.5436
18	13.7535	12.6593	11.6896	10.8276	10.0591	9.3719	8.7556
19	14.3238	13.1339	12.0853	11.1581	10.3356	9.6036	8.9501
20	14.8775	13.5903	12.4622	11.4699	10.5940	9.8181	9.1285
21	15.4150	14.0292	12.8212	11.7641	10.8355	10.0168	9.2922
22	15.9369	14.4511	13.1630	12.0416	11.0612	10.2007	9.4424
23	16.4436	14.8568	13.4886	12.3034	11.2722	10.3711	9.5802
24	16.9355	15.2470	13.7986	12.5504	11.4693	10.5288	9.7066
25	17.4131	15.6221	14.0939	12.7834	11.6536	10.6748	9.8226
26	17.8768	15.9828	14.3752	13.0032	11.8258	10.8100	9.9290
27	18.3270	16.3296	14.6430	13.2105	11.9867	10.9352	10.0266
28	18.7641	16.6631	14.8981	13.4062	12.1371	11.0511	10.1161
29	19.1885	16.9837	15.1411	13.5907	12.2777	11.1584	10.1983
30	19.6004	17.2920	15.3725	13.7648	12.4090	11.2578	10.2737
31	20.0004	17.5885	15.5928	13.9291	12.5318	11.3498	10.3428
32	20.3888	17.8736	15.8027	14.0840	12.6466	11.4350	10.4062
33	20.7658	18.1476	16.0025	14.2302	12.7538	11.5139	10.4644
34	21.1318	18.4112	16.1929	14.3681	12.8540	11.5869	10.5178
35	21.4872	18.6646	16.3742	14.4982	12.9477	11.6546	10.5668
36	21.8323	18.9083	16.5469	14.6210	13.0352	11.7172	10.6118
37	22.1672	19.1426	16.7113	14.7368	13.1170	11.7752	10.6530
38	22.4925	19.3679	16.8679	14.8460	13.1935	11.8289	10.6908
39	22.8082	19.5845	17.0170	14.9491	13.2649	11.8786	10.7255
40	23.1148	19.7928	17.1591	15.0463	13.3317	11.9246	10.7574

PRESENT VALUE TABLE

The Worth Today of One Dollar Per Annum
Paid At The *End* Of Each Year

Years	10%	11%	12%	13%	14%	15%	18%
				Rate			
1	.9091	.9009	.8929	.8850	.8772	.8696	.8475
2	1.7355	1.7125	1.6901	1.6681	1.6467	1.6257	1.5656
3	2.4869	2.4437	2.4018	2.3612	2.3216	2.2832	2.1743
4	3.1699	3.1024	3.0373	2.9745	2.9137	2.8550	2.6901
5	3.7908	3.6959	3.6048	3.5172	3.4331	3.3522	3.1272
6	4.3553	4.2305	4.1114	3.9975	3.8887	3.7845	3.4976
7	4.8684	4.7122	4.5638	4.4226	4.2883	4.1604	3.8115
8	5.3349	5.1461	4.9676	4.7988	4.6389	4.4873	4.0776
9	5.7590	5.5370	5.3282	5.1317	4.9464	4.7716	4.3030
10	6.1446	5.8892	5.6502	5.4262	5.2161	5.0188	4.4941
11	6.4951	6.2065	5.9377	5.6869	5.4527	5.2337	4.6560
12	6.8137	6.4924	6.1944	5.9176	5.6603	5.4206	4.7932
13	7.1034	6.7499	6.4235	6.1218	5.8424	5.5831	4.9095
14	7.3667	6.9819	6.6282	6.3025	6.0021	5.7245	5.0081
15	7.6061	7.1909	6.8109	6.4624	6.1422	5.8474	5.0916
16	7.8237	7.3792	6.9740	6.6039	6.2651	5.9542	5.1624
17	8.0216	7.5488	7.1196	6.7291	6.3729	6.0472	5.2223
18	8.2014	7.7016	7.2497	6.8399	6.4674	6.1280	5.2732
19	8.3649	7.8393	7.3658	6.9380	6.5504	6.1982	5.3162
20	8.5136	7.9633	7.4694	7.0248	6.6231	6.2593	5.3527
21	8.6487	8.0751	7.5620	7.1016	6.6870	6.3125	5.3837
22	8.7715	8.1757	7.6446	7.1695	6.7429	6.3587	5.4099
23	8.8832	8.2664	7.7184	7.2297	6.7921	6.3988	5.4321
24	8.9847	8.3481	7.7843	7.2829	6.8351	6.4338	5.4509
25	9.0770	8.4217	7.8431	7.3300	6.8729	6.4641	5.4669
26	9.1609	8.4881	7.8957	7.3717	6.9061	6.4906	5.4804
27	9.2372	8.5478	7.9426	7.4086	6.9352	6.5135	5.4919
28	9.3066	8.6016	7.9844	7.4412	6.9607	6.5335	5.5016
29	9.3696	8.6501	8.0218	7.4701	6.9830	6.5509	5.5098
30	9.4269	8.6938	8.0552	7.4957	7.0027	6.5660	5.5168
31	9.4790	8.7331	8.0850	7.5183	7.0199	6.5791	5.5227
32	9.5264	8.7686	8.1116	7.5383	7.0350	6.5905	5.5277
33	9.5694	8.8005	8.1354	7.5560	7.0482	6.6005	5.5320
34	9.6086	8.8293	8.1566	7.5717	7.0599	6.6091	5.5356
35	9.6442	8.8552	8.1755	7.5856	7.0700	6.6166	5.5386
36	9.6765	8.8786	8.1924	7.5979	7.0790	6.6231	5.5412
37	9.7059	8.8996	8.2075	7.6087	7.0868	6.6288	5.5434
38	9.7327	8.9186	8.2210	7.6183	7.0937	6.6338	5.5452
39	9.7570	8.9357	8.2330	7.6268	7.0997	6.6380	5.5468
40	9.7791	8.9511	8.2438	7.6344	7.1050	6.6418	5.5482

AMORTIZATION TABLE

Annual Payment Necessary To Amortize A Loan Of $1,000

Years	5%	6%	7%	8%	9%	10%	12%	15%
					Rate			
2	537.80	545.44	553.10	560.77	568.47	576.20	591.70	615.12
3	367.21	374.11	381.06	388.04	395.06	402.12	416.35	437.98
4	282.01	288.60	295.23	301.93	308.67	315.48	329.24	350.27
5	230.97	237.40	243.90	250.46	257.10	263.80	277.41	298.32
6	197.02	203.37	209.80	216.32	222.92	229.61	243.23	264.24
7	172.82	179.14	185.56	192.08	198.70	205.41	219.12	240.37
8	154.72	161.04	167.47	174.02	180.68	187.45	201.31	222.86
9	140.69	147.03	153.49	160.08	166.80	173.65	187.68	209.58
10	129.50	135.87	142.38	149.03	155.83	162.75	176.99	199.26
11	120.39	126.80	133.36	140.08	146.95	153.97	168.42	191.07
12	112.83	119.28	125.91	132.70	139.66	146.77	161.44	184.49
13	106.46	112.97	119.66	126.53	133.57	140.78	155.68	179.12
14	101.02	107.59	114.35	121.30	128.44	135.75	150.88	174.69
15	96.34	102.97	109.80	116.83	124.06	131.48	146.83	171.02
16	92.27	98.96	105.86	112.98	120.30	127.82	143.40	167.95
17	88.70	95.45	102.43	109.63	117.05	124.67	140.46	165.37
18	85.55	92.36	99.42	106.71	114.22	121.94	137.94	163.19
19	82.75	89.63	96.76	104.13	111.74	119.55	135.77	161.34
20	80.24	87.19	94.40	101.86	109.55	117.46	133.88	159.77
21	78.00	85.01	92.29	99.84	107.62	115.63	132.25	158.42
22	75.97	83.05	90.41	98.04	105.91	114.01	130.82	157.27
23	74.14	81.28	88.72	96.43	104.39	112.58	129.56	156.28
24	72.47	79.68	87.19	94.98	103.03	111.30	128.47	155.43
25	70.95	78.23	85.82	93.68	101.81	110.17	127.50	154.70
26	69.56	76.91	84.57	92.51	100.72	109.16	126.66	154.07
27	68.29	75.70	83.43	91.45	99.74	108.26	125.91	153.53
28	67.12	74.60	82.40	90.49	98.86	107.46	125.25	153.06
29	66.05	73.58	81.45	89.62	98.06	106.73	124.67	152.66
30	65.05	72.65	80.59	88.83	97.34	106.08	124.15	152.31
35	61.07	68.98	77.24	85.81	94.64	103.69	122.32	151.14
40	58.28	66.47	75.01	83.87	92.96	102.26	121.31	150.57

INDEX